TUBULAR FLOWER

IRIS FAMILY

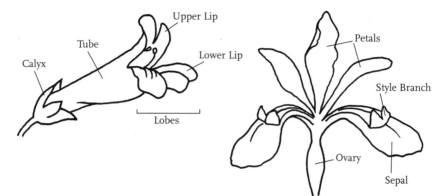

Upper Lip

Tube

Calyx

Lower Lip

Lobes

Petals

Style Branch

Ovary

Sepal

ASTER FAMILY COMPOSITE FLOWER

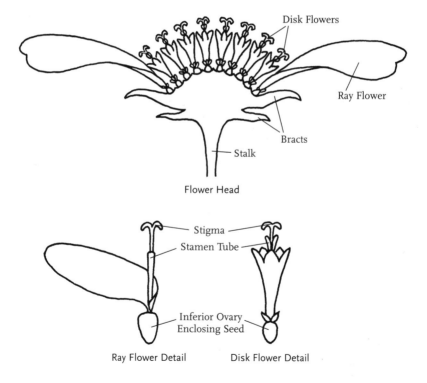

Disk Flowers

Ray Flower

Bracts

Stalk

Flower Head

Stigma

Stamen Tube

Inferior Ovary
Enclosing Seed

Ray Flower Detail

Disk Flower Detail

WILDFLOWERS
of the PACIFIC NORTHWEST

Mark Turner & Phyllis Gustafson

TIMBER PRESS FIELD GUIDE

Dedicated to
My father, Byron Turner, and my
father-in-law, John McClendon, who
inspired me to learn about wildflowers.
　　　　　　　　　　　　　—Mark

My grandmother, Arcliss Taylor,
my father, Charles Taylor, and my
mother-in-law, Eleanor Gustafson,
for sharing their love of native plants.
　　　　　　　　　　　　　—Phyllis

Page 1: *Eriogonum compositum*, *Castilleja hispida*, and *Ipomopsis aggregata*, Willamette
National Forest, Oregon. Pages 2–3: Yellow Island Preserve, Washington. Page 5: *Epilobium
luteum*, Mount Rainier National Park, Washington. Page 8: *Penstemon fruticosus*, Malheur
National Forest, Oregon. Page 57: *Leucanthemum vulgare*, Del Norte County, California.
Page 185: *Balsamorhiza sagittata* and *Phlox speciosa*, Kittitas County, Washington. Page 297:
Lilium columbianum, Mount Baker–Snoqualmie National Forest, Washington. Page 305:
Phyllodoce empetriformis, Olympic National Park, Washington. Page 399: *Lupinus arcticus*
subsp. *subalpinus*, Mount Rainier National Park. Page 457: *Boschniakia strobilacea*, Grants
Pass, Oregon. Page 473: Lithosol plant community, Quilomene Wildlife Area, Washington.

Published in 2006 by
Timber Press, Inc.
The Haseltine Building
133 S.W. Second Avenue, Suite 450
Portland, Oregon 97204-3527, U.S.A.
www.timberpress.com
For contact information regarding editorial, marketing, sales, and distribution
in the United Kingdom, see www.timberpress.co.uk

Designed by Susan Applegate
Printed in China

Reprinted 2006

Library of Congress Cataloging-in-Publication Data

Turner, Mark, 1954 Apr. 8–
Wildflowers of the Pacific Northwest/Mark Turner and Phyllis Gustafson; photography by Mark Turner.
　　p. cm.— (Timber Press field guide)
Includes bibliographical references and index.
ISBN-13: 978-0-88192-745-0
ISBN-10: 0-88192-745-7
1. Wild flowers—Northwest, Pacific—Identification. 2. Wild flowers—Northwest, Pacific—Pictorial
works. I. Gustafson, Phyllis, 1940– II. Title. III. Series.

QK144.T87 2006
582.13'09795—dc22

2005016921

A catalog record for this book is also available from the British Library.

Contents

Preface

Avid plant enthusiasts find the Pacific Northwest of North America one of the most fascinating and richest places in the world to study temperate plants. Until now there has been no up-to-date field guide for the entire region, and we have often found the need for such a guide in our individual travels to the far-flung corners of our respective states. Phyllis has spent her life living among the flowers of southern Oregon and northern California. She has a true love of plants that grow in that area, especially the Klamath Mountains. Mark grew up on the opposite coast with a whole different array of native plants but some years ago moved to northwestern Washington and became fascinated by the plants of his new home. He now spends many weeks a year out looking for new plants to photograph.

The great beauty that surrounds us in the mountains, on the prairies, in bogs, and along seashores has drawn both of us into this project. We want to share the awe we have for these places and their specialized plants. Nothing excites us more than sharing with folks who are just becoming aware of the diversity of the plants of this region.

When this book was first conceived, the need for it was evident, and we were both anxious to work on a photographic field guide to flowers for the whole region. You will find in this book many nonnative plants. We think it is important to know that even pretty flowers are sometimes in the wrong place. The disturbance of soils for urbanization, or the removal of plant and mineral resources for human use, creates huge areas where pioneering plants can take hold. These plants, which can reproduce easily and quickly, are called weeds.

We hope that with this book more people become knowledgeable about native plants and their habitats, and that this knowledge leads to a desire to see native plants reintroduced to disturbed places and to see undisturbed areas protected.

While working on this project we were humbled by the accumulated knowledge available to us at the turn of a page or stroke of a key. The work started with early botanists, first from France, then Spain, the Austro-Hungarian empire, and Russia. Next many English explorers came to the West to study the richness of this flora. In this book you will find plants named for Archibald Menzies, John Scouler, Thomas Coulter, William Tolmie, and, among the most intrepid plant collectors of all, David Douglas, along with many others.

We are also indebted to the botanical gardens, large nurseries, horticultural societies, and private enthusiasts who sponsored many of these expeditions. Our heroes are not only the plant collectors but also the botanists at the many institutions who received the seeds and specimens, studied them, assigned them to families, and gave each plant a name. These names sometimes even commemorate the collec-

9

tor, such as Beckwith, Nuttall, Howell, Suksdorf, Newberry, and Henderson. All of these individuals demonstrated great courage, often braving difficult travel conditions, in their tireless drive to find and identify undiscovered plants.

Today we are able to study the knowledge assimilated from the work of these and many other field botanists in the floras of the region. Charles Piper's *Flora of the State of Washington* was published in 1906. *Illustrated Flora of the Pacific States* by LeRoy Abrams, printed in four volumes starting in 1923, was the first to assemble all known plants from Washington, Oregon, and California, and was further enhanced with a botanical drawing of each plant. We are also indebted to Morton Peck, author of *A Manual of the Higher Plants of Oregon*, published in 1941 and still the only complete flora of the state of Oregon. Each of these and many smaller regional floras are still in use and have contributed to the knowledge contained in the newer floras.

Our objective for this book was not to record every plant but rather to produce an easy-to-carry guide to encourage and promote the study of the flora of the region. Botany is an ever-changing science, and we have tried to use the most up-to-date plant names. Some names will last, while others will be lost as more knowledge is gained about the anatomy and reproductive systems of flowering and fruiting plants. The name changes may at times seem confusing, but we consider these changes a chance to learn about the relationships between plants and plant families, knowledge gained through the efforts of our present-day pioneers: the leaders and students of botanical science. We hope this field guide will be a stepping-stone from the fascinating lives of the many explorers of the 16th century to the present and into the future, where new scientific studies are sure to further change the face of botany.

Most of all, we hope you will use this book to enjoy the flowers.

Acknowledgments

Wildflowers of the Pacific Northwest would not have been possible without the help of the many people who generously lent their time, expertise, and patience.

Our families put up with long absences during the field work and photography. When we were home we spent nearly every waking hour holed up in our offices with our reference books and computers. Thank you, Dick, for your gung ho enthusiasm, encouragement, and hours of assistance. Thank you, Natalie, Zach, and Ian: without your support and encouragement we wouldn't have made it. Zach learned Geographic Information System (GIS) software to merge several source maps into the ecoregions map and the base map for all the distribution maps. Ian helped with manipulating the distribution data to reformat it from one record per specimen from the herbaria to one record per species. Natalie helped proofread, gave advice on language and opinions on photo selection, and provided endless support. Thanks to Mary Taylor, and to Daniel and Eric Gustafson and Karen Lisa Devita, for their understanding and constant interest in this project.

Special thanks from Mark to Betty and John McClendon for their support, encouragement, and companionship, and for the great meals and many nights spent in a comfortable bed at their southern Oregon home. John introduced Mark to the flora of the Siskiyous, taught him to use a technical key, and shared his love for the plants up until the night he died. In-laws don't come any better.

Finding and photographing most of the plants in this guide in two growing seasons would have been impossible without the help of the many individuals who shared their local knowledge. Most led field trips for native plant societies in Washington (WNPS) and Oregon (NPSO), and some spent many additional days helping Mark find and identify plants. Among these very generous plant lovers were Jennifer and Lance Barker, who made Grant County, Oregon, a destination every three weeks; Bruce Barnes, who shared his knowledge of the Blue Mountains south of Pendleton, Oregon; Chuck Easton, who made sure Mark found the elusive *Synthyris pinnatifida* subsp. *lanuginosa* and other alpine gems in the Olympics; Tanya Harvey, who shared native plants growing in her garden and woodland and led Mark to sites in Lane and Linn counties, Oregon; Don Heinze, who led Mark to several sites in Josephine County, Oregon; Marie Hitchman, who shared an enjoyable rainy day in the Olympic Mountains alpine zone; Norm Jensen, who pointed out rare endemics on the Agate Desert near Medford, Oregon, and was on several southern Oregon NPSO field trips; Don Knoke, who encouraged many visits to Kittitas County, Washington, and identified many plants there; Frank Lang, who shared his years of experience on the Cascade-Siskiyou National Monument; Steve Link, who led a great trip on the Arid Lands Ecology Reserve adjacent to the Hanford Nuclear Reservation in Washington; Walt Lockwood, who joined Mark on the trail in the North Cascades and Olympics; Ginny Maffitt, who shared her love of penstemons and took Mark to locations near Portland and in the Columbia Gorge; Barbara Robinson, eastern Columbia Gorge expert; Loren Russell, who led a fast-paced swing through the Wallowa Mountains; Paul Slichter, who scouted many locations with a GPS and shared nearly a week at Steens Mountain; Veva Stansell, who took us to special places on the southern coast of Oregon; Thayne Tuason, who shared a day around Leavenworth, Washington; and Jean Zach, who scouted locations and called to say, "You need to come to the Tri-Cities," or some other Columbia Basin site, when plants started blooming.

Many native plant society field trip participants led Mark to nice specimens along the trail, offered suggestions and feedback about what plants should be included and how they should be treated, and were patient with a photographer who just can't spend less than 15 minutes on a plant. Thanks go also to the organizers of the field trips at both WNPS and NPSO annual meetings and study weekends, as well as to those responsible for Botany Washington.

Almost every trip Mark made into the

mountains since moving to Washington in 1990 became an opportunity to photograph flowers. Many of these were hikes or climbs with friends in the Bellingham branch of The Mountaineers or as a leader of Bellingham Troop 3 Boy Scout outings. All remained patient and understanding even while in a hurry to move on down the trail.

Thank you to the individuals who provided photos for the plants Mark failed to locate in the field. They are listed separately at the back of the book on page 475.

Thanks to Margaret Rambo and Pat Parent for their suggestions and help with the drawings. Josef Halda encouraged the continued study of local plants and the completion of our book. Boyd Kline helped with numerous plant locations and identifications over the years. To our many friends in the North American Rock Garden Society, we thank you for your constant interest.

We are deeply grateful for the assistance of the following individuals, who reviewed portions of the manuscript, pointed out errors and inconsistencies, and suggested numerous improvements: Ed Alverson, Barbara L. Benner, Elizabeth Binney, Paula Brooks, Frank Callahan, Florence Caplow, Scott Clay-Poole, Tom Cottrell, Rex Crawford, George Douglas, Lana D'Souza, Mark Egger, Sharon Eversman, Rod Gilbert, Melanie and Steve Gisler, Ed Guerrant, Richard Halse, Harvey Janszen, Kevin Kane, Don Knoke, Laurie Kurth, Frank Lang, Penny Latham, Matt Lavin, Ben Legler, Steve Link, Rhoda Love, Andrew MacDougall, Penn Martin, Carrina Maslovat, Kathleen Moran, David Morgan, Bill Null, Therese H. Ohlson, Richard Olds, Jenifer Parsons, Jenifer Penny, Kathy Pyle, Brigitte Ranne, Douglas Reynolds, Jim Riley, Ann M. Risvold, Hans Roemer, Charlene Simpson, Veva Stansell, Fred Weinmann, and David Wilderman. Please note that any errors that may have slipped through are the responsibility of the authors, not our reviewers.

Finally, this book would not be in your hands without the encouragement and talented support of the people at Timber Press. Neal Maillet, acquisitions editor at the inception of the project, encouraged us to propose the book in the first place. Little did we know how much work Neal was getting us into. Jane Connor, publisher, shared our vision for a comprehensive, attractive, and user-friendly guide to the Northwest's great flowers. She was gracious and patient as we missed deadlines to finish checking details. Susan Applegate created the page design, building elegantly on our rough original concept and accepting our input, a collaboration that is rare in publishing. Eve Goodman provided initial editorial guidance, especially in matters of style and organization.

This book has been our lives for two and a half years. Thank you to each and every one of you who touched upon it during that time. Thank you, too, dear reader, for choosing to carry our book on your journey in search of Northwest flowers.

How to Use This Book

Wildflowers of the Pacific Northwest is designed for ease of use in the field to help you identify the flowers you find. It includes color photographs, clear and concise descriptions, and range maps for 1220 flowering plants found from southern British Columbia to northern California. Additional related species are mentioned in the text.

Most common native species are here, as are a goodly number of weeds and many rare and endemic plants. Our goal in selecting plants was to include as many as possible that are likely to be found while exploring this large territory. We put particular emphasis on central and eastern Washington and Oregon and on the Klamath-Siskiyou region in southern Oregon and northern California because most other field guides have glossed over these areas. While 1220 plants is a wide selection, many species and varieties had to be omitted. We chose the showier species at the expense of plants with small and nearly insignificant flowers.

Although grasses, sedges, rushes, and trees all have flowers, most people don't think of them as wildflowers, and you won't find them here. Many woody shrubs are included, however, because a lot of them have showy flowers and are likely to be encountered along the trail or roadside.

As you look up the flowers you find, be sure to use all of the information provided. The text and photographs complement each other. The range maps present the county (in the United States) or forest district (in British Columbia) where documentation shows the plant to have been found. Keep in mind that habitat, not shown on the individual maps, is also critically important.

How to Identify a Plant

It is very easy to miss a critical detail about a plant you want to identify if you don't adopt a systematic way of looking. While we're usually attracted first to the flowers and their shape and color, the rest of the plant is also important.

Start by getting an overall impression of the plant. Is it woody like a tree or shrub? How big is it? Does it grow like a vine, form a mat on the ground, make a clump of stems, or have a single stem that stands by itself? Are the stems stiff and strong or are they weak? Are there any spines, prickles, or hairs?

Examine the leaves. Are they mostly right at the ground (basal) or do they grow along the stem? Some plants have both basal and stem leaves. What shape are the leaves? Stem leaves can be opposite each other or arranged alternately. Leaves can be attached to the stem with a long petiole, clasp the stem, have little appendages at the attachment point (stipules), or appear to have the stem growing through the leaf. Many plants have compound leaves with several leaflets. You may need to count the leaflets and note how they're arranged. Leaf texture is another clue. Are they soft, leathery, hairy on one or both sides, or spiny?

Study the flowers. Identification usually requires a close look at the color, arrangement, and number of the flowering parts. Color is obvious but may change as the flowers age or among individuals of the same species. Sometimes petals have spots or blotches of a second color. Count the petals. Some flowers don't have petals, or the petals are very small and inconspicuous. Count the sepals, located at the base of the flower. For many plants, this will be enough to make an identification. However, you may also need to look closely to count the stamens. Sometimes you need to see whether these sex parts are longer or shorter than the petals. The position of the ovary can also be important. For a few flowers, such as penstemons, you have to look closely to see how thick the hairs are inside and outside the flower. A hand lens with a magnification of 10× is useful for this close level of examination, can add a lot to your enjoyment of wildflowers, and doesn't weigh much in your pack. If you need help with technical terms, see the glossary at the back of the book and the illustrations on the endpapers.

Observe the habitat. Does the plant grow in the forest or out in the open? What is the soil like? What else is growing around the plant? Are you at the seashore, in the mountains, or somewhere in between? All of these clues will help you learn about new plants.

Organization

The flowers in this book are organized first by color and then by number of petals, family, genus, and species. The fastest way to look up an unknown flower is to turn to the appropriate color section and leaf through the pages until you come to flowers with the same shape or number of petals. Then examine the photographs and read the descriptions until you find a match. Use the maps to tentatively eliminate plants that don't grow where you are; this should help narrow your search, although you could be lucky enough to discover a range extension or find a plant not included in this book. Once you have a preliminary identification you may want to reread the description as you study the plant carefully a second time.

Some plants are easier to recognize than others. Large families like the asters and genera such as *Penstemon* are especially challenging and may require consulting a technical manual for additional information.

Flower colors can vary, so you may need to look in more than one section. Cross-references to other flowers in the same genus with different blossom colors are provided. Each plant has been included only once to make room for the largest number of species. Creamy whites are included with white flowers, but pale yellows are with darker yellow flowers. Sometimes the distinction isn't very clear. Reddish purple flowers are with reds, bluish purples with blues. Keep in mind that flower colors often vary within a species. Occasionally the variation is dramatic, as in sulphur lupines, which come in both yellow (where we've included it) and blue forms. Baby blue-eyes also come in white with black spots.

If you recognize which family your plant belongs to, it may be faster to begin at the families section (page 50) and go to the descriptions from there. Each family is described briefly, with page references given for the family members in each color.

The index includes both common and

Latin plant names. If you know a plant's name but aren't sure what it looks like, turn to the index to find it quickly.

Photographs

In most cases there is one photograph for each plant. These were selected to show as many important identifying characteristics as possible. Flowers receive more emphasis than foliage, which may appear somewhat soft-focus or in the background. Use the photographs to get a general feel for what the plant looks like, and then read the description. Unfortunately, it is often impossible to show all of the characteristics of a flowering plant in a single photograph.

Plant Names

Each plant has a unique Latin name composed of at least two parts: genus and species. In some cases there are also subspecies and varieties, but for the purposes of this book these are mostly lumped together under the main species. Because plant names can change over time, generally due to botanical research, we've listed Latin synonyms where needed (in parentheses). The first name listed is the accepted name at the time of publication. For the most part these follow the names in the USDA Plants Database (plants.usda.gov) or the Oregon Flora Project (oregonflora.org). The names given in the standard technical keys are listed as synonyms if they are different from the currently accepted name.

Each plant also has one or more common names. The same plant may be called by different names in different places, or the same name may refer to different plants in different places. Some plants have so many common names that we weren't able to list them all.

Descriptions

Each description is written in a similar way so that you can quickly scan for individual characteristics. The descriptions start with a general overview of the plant habit, such as erect, spreading, cushion, or shrub. Stems and leaves are next, followed by details about the flowers. Finally you'll find information about where the plant grows, such as soil preferences and elevation range.

Each plant entry also includes the plant's height, whether it is native or introduced, its growth cycle (annual, biennial, or perennial), rarity, bloom time, habitat, presence in the region's four national parks, and whether it was collected during the Lewis and Clark expedition. Many fruits and berries are described; unless otherwise noted, these should be considered inedible.

Height. Plant heights are given in inches or feet and are for typical specimens under normal growing conditions. You may find individuals that are taller or shorter than the figures given, but if you're looking at a plant that is only 4 inches tall and the height in the book is given as 18–24 inches, there's a good chance you need to reconsider your identification. When measurements are given in the descriptions without specifying length or width, they refer to length or height. For help converting units, see the ruler on the edge of the back cover.

Growth cycle. Plants have one of three growth cycles. Annuals come up from seed, flower, produce seeds, and die in one growing season. Biennials take two years to produce seeds. In the first year the seed germinates and the plant only puts down roots and grows leaves. The second year it blooms, produces seeds, and dies. You'll find both the flowering and nonflowering individuals of biennials every year. Perennials live for a long time, and most flower every year although some may only bloom occasionally or lie dormant for many years between blooms. In challenging environments such as subalpine and alpine areas with short growing seasons, perennials may reproduce vegetatively rather than by seed even though they bloom. You can often identify a perennial by looking for the previous year's dried leaves, flower stalks, or seed heads.

Abundance. The abundance of a plant is another clue you can use to identify it. Botanists speak of a population of plants, which simply means a group of individual specimens of a species growing in close proximity to one another. A population can have very few individuals, be a dense stand covering the ground, or anything in between. We've used *endemic, rare, uncommon, locally common,* and *common* to describe plant populations. The terms refer to how likely you are to find the plant in our region. Some plants that are uncommon or rare here are prolific in other parts of the continent.

The term *endemic,* as used in this book, indicates a very limited geographic range. Within that range you may find many populations with lots of individual plants, as with the beautiful Olympic harebell, which thrives on rocky sites at high elevations in the Olympic Mountains. Another easily found endemic is the Steens Mountain thistle, which blooms all along the Steens loop road above about 7000 feet in midsummer. On the other hand, Ashland lupine is found only in a very small area within a few hundred feet of the summit of Mount Ashland in the Siskiyous. The areas covered by this book that have the largest number of endemic species are the Olympic, Siskiyou, Steens, Wallowa, and Wenatchee mountains and the Columbia Gorge.

A *rare* plant has few individuals in each population, and they may be far apart. Bolander's lily is found only on widely scattered sites in southern Oregon and northern California, with few individuals in each population. Some rare plants are also endemic, and many are threatened or endangered. Be especially respectful of any rare species you are lucky enough to find.

Uncommon plants are just that. There may be large numbers of plants in just a few places, or there could be only a few plants in each of many places. Washington lily is found throughout the Oregon Cascades, but most populations have few individuals.

Locally common plants have a wide range, and in some places you'll find large numbers of individuals. Glacier lilies are abundant in alpine meadows throughout the North Cascades and Cascades but are almost never found at low elevations.

Common plants are found in large numbers in many habitats and locations. Yarrow, camas, and field mint are all found in abundant quantities throughout most of our region.

Many of the Northwest's most common plants, especially those growing around built-up areas and along roadsides and trails, were brought here from other parts of the world. Some are plants that escaped from cultivation, while others were accidentally introduced from Europe or Asia decades ago. Some are seriously invasive and will quickly and easily crowd out native species. Almost everyone would call these alien plants weeds. Avoid spreading seeds or other parts of invasive plants that could take root.

Bloom time. Most wildflowers only bloom for a fairly short period each year. The exceptions are often weedy species. We've subdivided spring and summer into early, mid, and late. Few of our flowers bloom in autumn and even fewer in winter or year-round. The bloom times given are related more to weather conditions than to calendar dates and should be used with caution. For high-elevation plants that bloom following snowmelt, there's really only one season: summer.

In general, early spring begins in mid March at low elevations, although you may find flowers as early as February in warm, exposed locations such as the Washington side of the Columbia Gorge and the sun-baked sites along Puget Sound. Midspring comes with the leafing out of the big-leaf maples. Late spring arrives as the Oregon white oak leaves reach full size.

Early summer runs through the solstice, or immediately after the snow melts at high elevations. In midsummer the alpine meadows are at their lush maximum growth. By late summer the soil has mostly dried out and blooms are slowing down; asters and gentians are replacing lupines and paintbrushes. Autumn is short as seeds mature and foliage dies back.

Habitat. In real estate it's location, location, location. For plants it's habitat, habitat, habitat. The subject is so important we've given it a chapter all its own. See "Climate, Geography, and Plant Habitats."

Elevation. We've used *low*, *mid*, and *high*, as well as *subalpine* and *alpine*, to describe the elevation range where a plant is most likely to grow. Because the Northwest is so diverse, these terms are necessarily vague. In general a plant will be found at lower elevations in the northern or coastal parts of its range than in the south or hundreds of miles inland. Low elevations range from sea level to about 2000 feet but can also include valley floors in mountainous regions. Mid elevations range from about 2000 to 5000 feet and include the high plains of eastern Washington and Oregon as well as montane forests below the subalpine zone, which begins around timberline. High elevations include everything above about 5000 feet, including the treeless alpine and transitional subalpine zones.

National parks. The Northwest is blessed with four outstanding scenic and natural areas in Olympic, Mount Rainier, North Cascades, and Crater Lake national parks. Each is a popular tourist destination and has its own unique flora. In this book we've called attention to the plants found in these parks, abbreviating park names as follows: OLYM for Olympic, MORA for Mount Rainier, NOCA for North Cascades, and CRLA for Crater Lake.

Lists of these plants were taken from *Flora of Mount Rainier National Park* by David Biek, *Flora of the Olympic Peninsula* by Nelsa Buckingham et al., *NOCA Vascular Plants* by North Cascades National Park, and *A Crater Lake National Park Vascular Plant Checklist* by Peter Zika.

The Northwest has many other public lands administered by several different federal, state, provincial, or local governmental agencies. Plant lists for many of these areas are available from the appropriate agency or native plant society.

Lewis and Clark. The Northwest's most famous explorers, Meriwether Lewis and William Clark, were the first to bring many of the region's native plants—long used and valued by Native Americans—to the attention of the scientific community. Throughout this book, plants "discovered" by Lewis and Clark are marked **L&C**.

Maps

Each plant entry includes a map showing the counties (United States) or forest districts (Canada) in which the plant has been found. This information should give you a general idea about where a plant grows, though you also need to take habitat and geographic distribution into consideration.

The maps are based on herbarium specimen records from sources in Canada, Washington, Oregon, and California. An herbarium specimen is a plant that has been collected by an individual, pressed, dried, and placed in a library of specimens. These plants are usually first identified by the collector. Sometimes, but not always, they are reviewed and checked by another botanist. In some cases specimens may have been identified incorrectly, or the location may have been written down wrong. Plant names can also change over the years.

The herbarium specimens used to produce our maps span more than 100 years of plant collecting in the Northwest. In a few cases a plant was collected once many decades ago and hasn't been seen since. Some areas have been more popular for plant collecting than others. The west side of the Cascades, the national parks, other well-traveled areas, and places where an individual was particularly interested in the plants are better represented than some of the eastern counties, with fewer people and more agricultural land.

In short, the maps should be used as a guide, not absolute gospel.

The distribution data for the maps was provided by CalFlora, the Oregon Flora Project, the University of Washington Herbarium, the Washington State University Herbarium, the University of British Columbia Herbarium, the National Herbarium of Canada, the Canadian Museum of Nature, and the British Columbia Conservation Data Centre.

Serendipity

For the most part, plants don't grow in isolation. Often when you stop along the trail to study a plant that catches your eye you'll discover several other interesting flowers lurking nearby. Take the time to look around and explore. You may also find interesting plants growing in unexpected places. Even areas that look trashed at first glance can be home to beautiful flowers. One of our favorite flower sites in central Washington is littered with old appliances and ATV tracks.

The Northwest is home to an incredible diversity of wildflowers. Keep your eyes open for the flowers that pop up in almost any location—from sidewalk cracks to roadside ditches to pristine mountain meadows—each spring and summer. With this book in your pack, pocket, or glove box, you'll be prepared to identify them, and in time, many flowers will become like old friends you want to visit again and again.

Climate, Geography, and Plant Habitats

Washington, Oregon, northern California, and southern British Columbia—the area encompassed by this field guide—share major climatic and physical features that affect vegetation. Within the region there is also great habitat diversity, each habitat creating the conditions for different plant communities to thrive. Weather, landforms, soils, elevation, and disturbance all affect our diverse environments. As a result, the Northwest is privileged to have thousands of vascular plant species, from the wildflowers that are the focus of this book to some of the largest and oldest trees in the world.

The Pacific Ocean is the chief determinant of the weather patterns throughout the region. It is the source of the precipitation for which the Northwest is famous, and it moderates temperatures year-round, although its influence diminishes east of the mountains. West of the Coast Range, and to a large extent in the broad valleys immediately to the east, winters are cool and rainy with little snowfall. As the jet stream swings north in the summer, generally moderate and dry conditions prevail. Summer temperatures are warmer in the southern and interior parts of the region than in the north or along the coast.

Rainfall is greatest along the north coast, diminishing to the south and east. Along the southern Oregon and northern California coastline, summer fog contributes to the moisture required by giant redwoods and the plants that grow in the understory beneath them. To the north the coastal forest is dominated by Sitka spruce, transitioning inland to Douglas-fir, western hemlock, and western red cedar. This temperate coniferous rain forest along the coast from southeastern Alaska to northern California is unique, with the greatest biomass per acre of any place on earth.

The second important influence, the mountains, modifies the weather coming in off the ocean. Two major mountain ranges form north–south ridges parallel to the coast. The Coast Range, broadly defined to include the spine of Vancouver Island, the Olympic Mountains, and extending south into northern California's Klamath Mountains, catches massive amounts of precipitation during the winter months. Along the mountain crest, deep moisture-laden snow typically doesn't melt out until mid July in the Olympics, a little earlier in the Klamaths. East of the Coast Range, a "rain shadow" dramatically reduces the precipitation on the east side of Vancouver Island, the Sunshine Coast, the Puget Sound lowlands, the Willamette Valley, and the intermountain valleys of southern Oregon and northern California. Rainfall rises rapidly again as the clouds push up against the Cascades.

The larger Cascade Mountain Range, the backbone of our region, is characterized by high peaks and deep valleys. Studded by a string of volcanoes that rise above the rest of the summits, the Cascades catch nearly all of the rest of the moisture blowing in from the coast. Dense snow piles up from November to April, taking months to melt in spring and summer. The major volcanic peaks can even make their own weather as winds are pushed up and around them. The northern Cascades are home to the largest number of glaciers in the lower 48 states, a testament to record-setting snowfall. Even where the glaciers have melted away, their former presence is obvious from the U-shaped valleys left in their wake.

In the basin east of the Cascades, conditions are generally dry year-round, with what little precipitation that falls coming in the winter months. This vast area, hundreds of miles east of the ocean, is also characterized by cold winters and hot summers. While Forks, on Washington's coast, averages almost 120 inches of rainfall annually, the area around Kennewick, 280 miles to the east in central Washington, receives fewer than 8 inches in an average year.

This intermountain area includes the east slopes of the Cascades, the Okanagan Valley, Columbia Plateau, and the basin and range province of southeastern Oregon. Forested mid elevations are dominated by ponderosa pine, Douglas-fir, and lodgepole pine. Valleys, including the immense channeled scablands of the Columbia Plateau in central Washington, have sagebrush and grasses as their major vegetation. Most wildflowers bloom in early spring before the soil dries out from summer's blistering heat.

The northern Rocky Mountains extend into northeastern Washington and southeastern British Columbia, rising from the Columbia Plateau. Precipitation increases with elevation, but this far inland there is less of it; the air is also colder and the winter snow lighter and drier. Even so, the climate is marine-influenced, and many of the same species found in the Cascades also grow in the Northern Rockies.

The Blue Mountains stretch across north-central and eastern Oregon into southeastern Washington and include the Strawberry, Greenhorn, Elkhorn, Aldrich, and Maury ranges, and the Ochoco, Blue, and Wallowa mountains. This region is also dominated by coniferous forests, grading into shrub-steppe habitats in the lower elevations.

In addition to the influence the mountains have on precipitation and temperature, the rocks from which they are built determine the composition of the soils on their slopes and in the valleys between them. Volcanic peaks and the Columbia River basalt flow are the best-known and most common source of rock in the Northwest, but they are not uniform throughout the region. In fact, Northwest geology is quite complex. Besides the widespread basalt, there are areas of sandstone, limestone, granite, and serpentine.

Serpentine-derived soils, which have high concentrations of magnesium and nickel and generally reduced fertility, are most common regionally in the Klamath-Siskiyou Range in northwestern California and southwestern Oregon. A high number of endemic plants grow on serpentine, which is also found in central Washington's Wenatchee Mountains and the Twin Sisters near Mount Baker.

Plants are sensitive to the depth of soil as well as to its mineral composition and moisture content. Thin ridgetop soils support plants that have adapted to harsh conditions while excluding species that need to sink their roots deeper or have greater water requirements. Where the living is easier, the slow-growing specialists are crowded out by faster-growing species. It's not so much that the plants that live in harsh conditions can't also grow in better conditions as that they can't compete. Challenging environments are often home to the greatest diversity of plant species, while less demanding habitats tend toward large numbers of a smaller group of plants.

Ecoregions

The relationships of precipitation, geology, physiography, vegetation, climate, soils, land use, wildlife, and hydrology within a geographical area can be used to paint a broad picture of the ecology of that area. Within each area of ecological similarity, called ecoregions or biogeoclimatic zones, a visitor can expect to find comparable populations of plants and animals. The first part of this chapter introduced the major influences that define the ecoregions of the Northwest. This section will explore each of these ecoregions. A basic understanding of ecoregions helps to explain the relationships between habitats and the plants that grow there.

Ecoregion definitions vary somewhat depending on which agency and researcher developed them. Each system starts with a very broad grouping and progresses to ever finer distinctions and smaller geographical areas. The USDA Forest Service definitions, first presented by Robert G. Bailey in 1978, differ from the U.S. Environmental Protection Agency (EPA) definitions, based on the work of James M. Omernik. In British Columbia a similar classification system was developed by Dennis A. Demarchi. The important concept they have in common is describing the interrelationships among the ecological elements and providing a framework for predicting the flora and fauna to be found within the ecoregion. The descriptions here follow EPA Level III Ecoregions and Ministry of Sustainable Resource Management Ecoregions of British Columbia. They are described from north to south and west to east. Some British Columbia ecoregions have been combined for the sake of clarity and to draw a more cohesive cross-border picture. Although the map shows hard boundary lines, in reality ecoregion boundaries are wide and diffuse.

Coast Range. Running the length of the region, the Coast Range is characterized by high rainfall and productive coniferous forests dominated by Sitka spruce with a mixture of western hemlock, western red cedar, yellow cedar, and Douglas-fir in inland areas. Redwoods dominate near the coast in the southern portion of the range. Much of the area has been heavily logged and the original forest mosaic replaced with intensively managed Douglas-fir plantations. The hills and mountains are relatively low. Wetlands are common. Western Vancouver Island is the northern extension of the Coast Range.

Pacific Ranges. These high and rugged mountains, the southernmost part of the Coast Mountains in British Columbia, rise abruptly from deep fjords and numerous islands in the Strait of Georgia. Canada's largest trees grow in this maritime climate. The forest makeup is similar to the Cascade ranges to the south. Western hemlock dominates at lower elevations, mountain hemlock higher up, and western cedar, yellow cedar, and Douglas-fir on drier sites. Subalpine fir is dominant at higher elevations just below treeline.

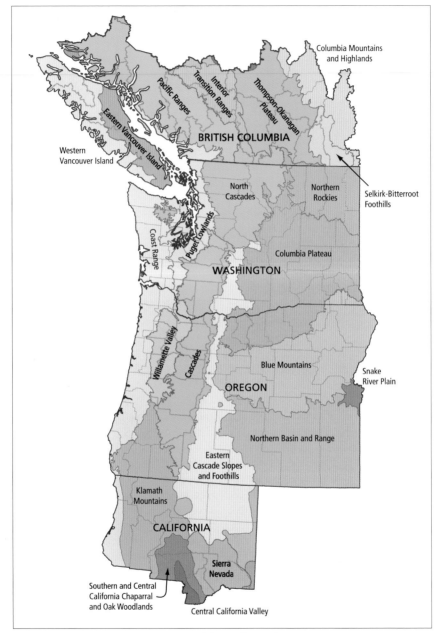

Columbia Mountains
and Highlands

Transition Ranges
Interior
Pacific Ranges
Thompson-Okanagan
Plateau

Eastern Vancouver Island

BRITISH COLUMBIA

Western
Vancouver Island

North
Cascades

Northern
Rockies

Selkirk-Bitterroot
Foothills

Coast Range

Puget Lowlands

Columbia Plateau

WASHINGTON

Willamette Valley

Cascades

Blue Mountains

Snake
River Plain

OREGON

Northern Basin and Range

Eastern
Cascade Slopes
and Foothills

Klamath
Mountains

CALIFORNIA

Sierra
Nevada

Southern and Central
California Chaparral
and Oak Woodlands

Central California Valley

Ecoregions of the Pacific Northwest

COAST RANGE Pacific rhododendron, *Rhododendron macrophyllum,* blooming under coast redwoods, *Sequoia sempervirens.* Del Norte Coast Redwoods State Park, California.

Puget Lowlands. Much of this ecoregion lies in the rain shadow of the Olympic Mountains and Vancouver Island, with rainfall varying accordingly. It includes the many islands, peninsulas, and bays around Puget Sound and the Strait of Georgia as well as glacial outwash plains and river floodplains. The climate is mild year-round due to the maritime influence. Originally covered by dense coniferous forests, the region is now predominately urbanized or agricultural, and many nonnative species can be found here. The Eastern Vancouver Island, Georgia-Puget Basin, and Lower Mainland ecoregions are included here. They experience the most annual sunshine and mildest average annual temperature in British Columbia.

Willamette Valley. Like the Puget Lowlands, much of the Willamette Valley has been converted to agriculture and urban environments. Prior to conversion, the area was home to rolling prairies, mixed deciduous and coniferous forests, and extensive wetlands of which only remnants remain. Situated between the Coast Range and the Cascades, the Willamette Valley receives less precipitation, has less dramatic terrain, and supports a different mosaic of vegetation. Rolling hills, terraces, and floodplains make up most of the landforms.

Klamath Mountains. In southern Oregon and northern California the Coast Range transitions into the physically and biologically diverse Klamath Mountains, a predominately east–west range in a region oriented north–south. The Klamaths, which include the Siskiyous, are highly dissected and folded with a mix of igneous, sedimentary, and some metamorphic rock. This

PACIFIC RANGES Glaciated Mount Garibaldi rises above Garibaldi Lake as viewed from a subalpine meadow on the shoulder of Black Tusk. Garibaldi Provincial Park, British Columbia.

PUGET LOWLANDS Salt marsh at low tide near the mouth of the Duckabush River on Hood Canal. Kitsap County, Washington.

WILLAMETTE VALLEY Farmland along the Coast Fork of the Willamette River, spring. Photographed from Mount Pisgah Arboretum east of Eugene, Oregon.

KLAMATH MOUNTAINS Common madia, *Madia elegans*, and sea blush, *Plectritis congesta*, on a hillside with Oregon white oaks, *Quercus garryana*, in the foothills of the Klamath Mountains. Waters Creek Trail, Josephine County, Oregon.

ecoregion is considerably drier than the adjacent Coast Range and experiences a lengthy summer drought. It is a transition zone with a blend of northern California and Pacific Northwest conifers and a high number of endemic wildflowers. The Klamaths have the largest number of cone-bearing tree species of any like-sized area in the world. The Cascade-Siskiyou National Monument, set aside for its biological diversity, is along the Oregon-California border at the eastern edge of the Klamath Mountains.

North Cascades. This is the most rugged and least disturbed ecoregion in the Northwest south of British Columbia. High mountains contrast with deep valleys, and the underlying rocks are more sedimentary and metamorphic than in the adjacent

Cascades to the south. The North Cascades region has a wide range of elevation zones, from lowland forests to high alpine summits, and an equally wide range of climate zones, from maritime rain forest in the west to a dry continental climate in the east. It is home to the largest number of glaciers in the conterminous United States, which have left deep valleys in their wake as they retreated from their maximum extent some 10,000 years ago. There is extensive subalpine and alpine habitat beginning at about 4000 feet elevation. North Cascades National Park and the mountainous portion of Olympic National Park are both in this ecoregion. In British Columbia the Cascade Ranges and Okanagan Range, including Manning Provincial Park, share most of the characteristics of the North Cascades.

NORTH CASCADES Mount Hagan ridge above a moist subalpine meadow with snowpatch buttercup, *Ranunculus eschscholtzii*, and pink mountain-heather, *Phyllodoce empetriformis*. North Cascades National Park, Washington.

Cascades. Running from approximately Snoqualmie Pass south to northern California, the Cascades are predominately volcanic in origin and are home to numerous volcanoes, both active and dormant. Like the North Cascades, the Cascade Mountains have experienced significant alpine glaciation. Alpine and subalpine habitats are less extensive here, especially in the southern part of the ecoregion, where a high-elevation montane forest is more common. The climate is moist and temperate, supporting an extensive and productive fir and hemlock coniferous forest. The east slopes are characterized by a high plateau, while the west slopes have steep ridges and deep river valleys. Mount Rainier and Crater Lake national parks are located in the Cascades ecoregion, as is Mount St. Helens National Volcanic Monument.

Interior Transition Ranges. This mountainous region lies on the east side of the Pacific Ranges as they slope down toward the Thompson-Okanagan Plateau. Rainfall is higher in the north and west, with the southern and eastern portions of the region experiencing more of a rain shadow effect. Subalpine forests at higher elevations are predominately Engelmann spruce, alpine fir, and lodgepole pine. Downslope to the east is a montane forest with white spruce, quaking aspen, lodgepole pine, and Douglas-fir. Lowest elevations include an open mix of scattered ponderosa pines, bunchgrasses, and sagebrush grasslands. The Fraser and lower Thompson river valleys have significant agriculture.

Eastern Cascade Slopes and Foothills. The rain shadow of the Cascades is a dominant

CASCADES Mount Rainier seen from Paradise Meadow, with lupines and paintbrush. Mount Rainier National Park, Washington.

influence on the Eastern Cascade Slopes and Foothills. Like the Interior Transition Ranges to the north, this region experiences greater temperature extremes and receives less precipitation than the mountainous regions to the west. Ponderosa pine dominates the open forests, with some lodgepole pine also found in this relatively high-elevation ecoregion. These forests are highly susceptible to wildfire. In southern Oregon this ecoregion includes the Klamath River Basin and the mountains and high plateaus that surround it.

Sierra Nevada. This region of rugged mountains and deep valleys has the greatest biological diversity in California, with a large number of endemic species. Much of the range is built of granite and has been heavily glaciated, in contrast to the mostly sedimentary Klamath Mountains to the west and Cascades to the north. Ponderosa pine on the west side and lodgepole pine on the east side dominate lower elevations, with fir and spruce found higher on the mountains below the alpine zone. The great majority of the Sierra Nevada lies south of the range of this book. Two other California ecoregions—Southern and Central California Chaparral and Oak Woodlands, and Central California Valley—just touch our area between the Klamath and Sierra Nevada mountains.

Thompson-Okanagan Plateau. One of the driest and warmest ecoregions in Canada, this rain shadow ecoregion ranges from open Ponderosa pine forests, grasslands, and sagebrush in the river valleys to moist subalpine forests of Engelmann spruce, subalpine fir, and lodgepole pine. Precipitation generally rises with elevation, falling as snow in the winter and short thunder-storms in the summer. Temperatures are more extreme in this continental region, with colder winters and warmer summers than the more marine-influenced areas to the west. The Okanagan and Thompson rivers have cut into the gently rolling glacial deposits that cover much of this region.

Columbia Plateau. This vast and relatively flat ecoregion dominates central and eastern Washington and extends into northern Oregon and the Okanagan Highland in British Columbia. The Columbia Plateau is the result of millennia of basalt flows, which produced the nearly 2-mile-thick layer of basalt that underlays it. The driest part of the Northwest, the Columbia Plateau receives as little as 8 inches of precipitation annually. Vegetation is predominately sagebrush and bunchgrasses, highlighted most springs by immense displays of wildflowers. Extensive grazing, the introduction of cheatgrass, and agricultural use through irrigation and dry-land wheat farming in the somewhat moister eastern portion have altered significant areas of this ecoregion. The least disturbed area is the buffer zone around the Hanford Nuclear Reservation, as public access is restricted.

Blue Mountains. Cutting a wide swath across central and northeastern Oregon, the Blues are a complex of mountains that are generally lower and more open than either the Cascades or the Northern Rockies. Except for the higher peaks in the Wallowa and Elkhorn ranges, the Blue Mountains are volcanic in origin. Within this ecoregion are many subregions reflecting a diversity of habitats, from the broad valleys of the Grand Ronde, Wallowa, and Baker rivers to the high peaks of the Wallowas. This ecoregion also includes the John Day

COLUMBIA PLATEAU Arrowleaf balsamroot dominates this view of the Columbia River between Hood River and The Dalles. The Nature Conservancy's Tom McCall Preserve, Oregon.

BLUE MOUNTAINS View of Hurricane Creek valley with Matterhorn and Sacajawea peaks in the Eagle Cap Wilderness on the skyline. Wallowa-Whitman National Forest, Oregon.

area, with low precipitation and wide temperature swings both daily and annually. The wettest part of the region receives precipitation coming up the Columbia River Gorge and lies east and south of Pendleton, Oregon, and Walla Walla, Washington.

Northern Basin and Range. A large portion of southeastern Oregon, northern Nevada, and far northeastern California are within the Northern Basin and Range ecoregion. This arid land contains tablelands, scattered mountains, intermontane basins, and dissected lava plains. Sagebrush-steppe vegetation is common in the areas without mountains but is impacted by grazing in many places. The semiarid uplands and partially forested Steens Mountain are included in this region, as are the extensive wetlands of the Malheur and Warner lakes areas.

Snake River Plain. This ecoregion, bordering the upper Snake River primarily in Idaho, touches eastern Oregon. It is a dry intermontane basin and range area that is considerably lower and more gently sloping than surrounding ecoregions. The natural vegetation is primarily sagebrush and bunchgrasses, but much of the region has been altered by grazing and irrigated agriculture.

Selkirk-Bitterroot Foothills. This is a transition zone between the relatively dry areas to the west and the higher and wetter Columbia Mountains and Canadian Rockies to the east. Vegetation of this ecoregion is similar to the Northern Rockies across the border to the south.

Northern Rockies. Despite being hundreds of miles inland, the Northern Rockies have

NORTHERN BASIN AND RANGE Orange sneezeweed, *Hymenoxys hoopesii*, and paintbrush, *Castilleja* species, above Wildhorse Lake on Steens Mountain. Harney County, Oregon.

SNAKE RIVER PLAIN Creamy eriogonum, *Eriogonum heracleoides*, spur lupines, *Lupinus arbustus* var. *calcaratus*, northern mule's ears, *Wyethia amplexicaulis*, and bitterbrush, *Purshia tridentata*, in a meadow above Pine Creek. Pine Valley Ranch near Halfway, Oregon.

a climate and vegetation that are marine-influenced. Like the Cascades, Douglas-fir, subalpine fir, Engelmann spruce, western red cedar, western hemlock, and grand fir grow here, as does ponderosa pine. The range is neither as high nor as snow-covered as the Canadian Rockies to the north and east, although the highest elevations are alpine, and glacial lakes abound. Lewis and Clark traversed this rugged range more than 200 years ago as they crossed from the Missouri River to the Columbia. Unlike the other ecoregions crossed by Lewis and Clark, the Northern Rockies is still home to all the species that were present during the expedition, even though there has been substantial logging, mining, and development in the intervening years.

Habitats and Local Environments

Ecoregions describe the conditions for numerous plant communities in broad terms, but as useful as ecoregions are for picturing the overall ecology of large areas, individual and sometimes very local habitats or environments determine the actual mix of species to be found. All plants need soil, nutrients, water, and sunlight to grow and bloom. Environments deficient in one or more of these won't have many flowers.

Different species have a range of requirements for soil, which anchors plants in place as well as providing a nutrient source. Some need deep, rich soil, while others eke out an existence in thin, rocky habitats.

The largest number of Northwest wildflowers bloom early in the season while there is still significant moisture in the soil. You'll find many more flowers in April and May than in September. In the mountains the peak bloom follows the snowmelt, usually mid July through mid August.

You'll find few flowers in the deep westside forests because not enough light reaches the ground under the thick canopy. Those that do bloom there are usually at least semiparasitic, relying on a complex relationship with fungi and living on decaying trees to make their food. Forest edges and openings are better habitats for flowers. Meadows, areas above treeline, and the vast arid sage-steppe areas of eastern Washington and Oregon are all home to large numbers of wildflowers.

Each plant entry in this field guide includes notes on where to look for the plant and in what growing conditions.

Coastal. The coastal environment encompasses several smaller and more specific habitats, including sandy beaches and dunes, salt marshes, and rocky shores. The dense coastal forest often grows right down to kiss the high tide line. Coastal habitats are found both on the outer Pacific Ocean coast and along the hundreds of miles of Puget Sound, Hood Canal, Strait of Juan de Fuca, and Strait of Georgia shoreline.

Coastal habitats occupy a very narrow strip where land meets salt water. Plants that grow here may have to develop tolerance to salt, drifting sand, or thin and rocky soils. Sandy beaches and rocky shores are both coastal habitats that support very little terrestrial plant life due to the constant and vigorous action of the tides. Just shoreward, out of reach of all but the largest waves, sand gives way to soil, and wildflowers such as sand verbena, beach pea,

and gumweed begin to appear. Huckleberries, elderberries, and salal grow right down to the edge of the beach, forming a dense understory beneath the forest canopy. Rocky headlands and sea stacks are often home to nearly impenetrable shrub communities.

Sand dunes are found along the coast between central Washington and southern Oregon but are most common between Coos Bay and Florence. They support very few flowers and are often dominated by the invasive European beach grass.

Salt marshes, found along inland shores with little surf, are productive habitats where you'll often find acres of American glasswort splashed with pockets of fleshy jaumea and brass buttons.

West-side forest. The dense forests on the west slopes of the Coast Range, Cascades, and Northern Rockies are a mosaic of mostly coniferous trees with numerous streams and rivers. Dominant tree species, depending on moisture and elevation, include Sitka spruce, redwood, western hemlock, western red cedar, Douglas-fir, and mountain hemlock. Where undisturbed at lower elevations, trees often grow to massive size. Unfortunately, most of this old growth has been cut for timber, and much of the forest is now second or third growth.

Mosses, ferns, and lichens abound in the understory, as do huckleberries, ocean spray, and devil's club. Look for calypso orchids and coralroots in deep shade with rich humusy soil. Forest edges and openings often have large stands of cow parsnip, fireweed, and pearly everlasting. Some of the arnicas and monkeyflowers grow along streams. From about Snoqualmie Pass south, bear grass can be found both in the forest and in open areas.

COASTAL Douglas's iris, *Iris douglasiana*, on a bluff above the coastline at Cape Blanco. Cape Blanco State Park, Oregon.

WEST-SIDE FOREST Western trilliums, *Trillium ovatum*, in an opening in mixed coniferous forest near Mount Baker. Ridley Creek Trail, Mount Baker–Snoqualmie National Forest, Washington.

Rocky outcrops are home to some of the saxifrages and paintbrushes. The ground is sometimes carpeted with redwood sorrel or miner's lettuce. Elevation makes a big difference in the forest plant communities, as do local variations in soils and precipitation. Even within this generally moist habitat you'll find both wet and dry pockets. Boggy depressions are fairly common at all elevations.

East-side forest. Much drier and more open than the west-side forest, the east-side forest is dominated by ponderosa and lodgepole pine, although you'll also find some Douglas-fir here. Grasses are more common in the understory than ferns and mosses. Mature east-side trees never reach the immense size of the largest west-side trees, though on a good site ponderosa pines can reach 130 feet tall and more than 3 feet in diameter. The east-side forest encompasses all of the forested regions east of the Cascades except for the Northern Rockies in northeastern Washington and portions of the Blue and Wallowa mountains where increased precipitation allows west-slope species to grow.

The open understory supports a wide range of species, although usually not in large quantities at any one site. Heartleaf arnica, silvercrown, asters, daisies, milkvetches, clovers, lupines, bluebells, gentians, and geraniums all find a home under the pines. Wet and boggy areas are less frequently encountered than on the west side. Look for buckbean, wapato, and water lilies in shallow ponds.

Microclimates and variations in soils affect vegetation in the east-side forests as much as they do elsewhere in the Northwest. Latitude and elevation also play a

EAST-SIDE FOREST Tailcup lupines, *Lupinus caudatus*, under ponderosa pines, *Pinus ponderosa*, south of John Day. Morning Hill Farm, Grant County, Oregon.

role. Similar species grow at higher elevations in northern California than in southern British Columbia.

Subalpine. A short growing season and ample precipitation, mostly in the form of winter snow, characterize this habitat found at the upper limits of tree growth. The forest here is dominated by subalpine fir, Engelmann spruce, and mountain hemlock, with deciduous larches also found near and east of the Cascade crest. Open meadows, both wet and dry, are interspersed with rocky outcrops and pockets of forest. The subalpine is a transition zone between the forests at lower elevations and the treeless alpine zone above.

Hurricane Ridge in the Olympics, Heather Meadows in the North Cascades, Paradise and Sunrise at Mount Rainier, and the rim drive at Crater Lake are all easily accessible subalpine areas. The shrub layer includes mountain-ash, heathers, and huckleberries. Wildflowers explode into bloom during the short summer season. Red paintbrushes, white valerian and bistort, and blue lupines contrast with golden arnica. Glacier and avalanche lilies, subalpine buttercups, and marsh-marigolds bloom right next to the melting snow.

Alpine. Some of the harshest growing conditions in the Northwest are found in the true alpine zone, which rises above timberline on the mountain crests. Snow lingers deep and late, and soils are usually thin and rocky. Wind howls across the ridges, and flowering plants often seek protection in the microclimates behind larger rocks or krummholz trees. Most plants are perennial and take a cushion form so that the wind flows over them. Because the condi-

SUBALPINE Lupines, *Lupinus latifolius*, and Sitka valerian, *Valeriana sitchensis*, dominate a ridgetop meadow, with mountain hemlocks, *Tsuga mertensiana*, near Mount Baker. Cougar Divide, Mount Baker Wilderness, Washington.

ALPINE Pink mountain-heather, *Phyllodoce empetriformis*, carpets the rocky ridge at Maple Pass, with Corteo and Black peaks in the background. North Cascades National Park, Washington.

tions are so tough, large colonies of wildflowers are much less common here than in the subalpine zone a little lower on the mountain.

Moss campion, catchfly, alpine goldenrod, sedum, heather, pussytoes, draba, smelowskia, spreading phlox, and several members of the aster family all make their home among the rocks of the alpine zone.

Shrub-steppe. Spanning vast tracts of the Columbia Basin in central Washington and the high plains of central and southeastern Oregon, the shrub-steppe can be underwhelming at first glance. Trees are practically nonexistent in this arid region. Big sagebrush, bitterbrush, and rabbitbrush dominate the shrub layer, covering 10–60% of the ground. In between grow a variety of bunchgrasses as well as many mosses and lichens. Undisturbed shrub-steppe has very little bare ground and a larger proportion of grasses than shrubs. With disturbance, particularly grazing, sagebrush coverage increases and highly flammable and invasive annual cheatgrass often replaces native perennial bunchgrasses. As with other Northwest habitats, differences in moisture, soils, and exposure create microclimates that favor different flowering plants. Most shrub-steppe wildflowers bloom in the spring.

Several balsamroots and lupines can blanket large areas of shrub-steppe in April. Milkvetches and penstemons follow later. Look for mariposa lilies in late spring.

Dry rocky sites. Some of the more interesting wildflowers grow on rocky hilltops in thin soils called lithosols. They tend to be among the earliest bloomers and include Douglas's bladderpod, bitterroot, sage-

SHRUB-STEPPE Round-headed desert buckwheat, *Eriogonum sphaerocephalum*, and big sagebrush, *Artemisia tridentata*. Benton County, Washington.

DRY ROCKY SITES Gairdner's penstemon, *Penstemon gairdneri*, and desert yellow daisies, *Erigeron linearis*, on a lithosol slope. Kittitas County, Washington.

brush violet, Hood's phlox, desert yellow daisy, desert parsleys, and buckwheats. These plants are able to push their roots down into the cracks in the rocks, where they can stay cool and moist, while everything above ground looks completely dry.

In addition to the thin-soil ridges, dry rocky sites can include talus slopes and basalt cliffs. Hot rock penstemon, thickleaf thelypody, Richardson's penstemon, and several sedums make their home in these tough conditions.

Vernal-wet. Winter rains accumulate in shallow pools where relatively thin soils lie directly over a layer of impervious rock, usually basalt. Successive rings of flowers bloom around the edges as the pools dry up in spring and early summer. Examples of this vernal-wet habitat may be found throughout the Columbia Plateau and on top of Table Rocks in the Rogue River valley of southern Oregon. Sometimes the vernal pools are interspersed with hummocks that have entirely different vegetation. Some species of popcorn flower, downingia, bog deervetch, miniature lupine, hesperochiron, poverty and tomcat clovers, meadowfoam, and camas thrive in vernal-wet habitats.

Defined a bit more broadly, vernal-wet habitats can be any place that is wet early in the season and dry by late spring or early summer. Even drying roadside ditches can be considered vernal-wet.

Bog/fen/wetland. Year-round water creates several habitats, depending on how much water is flowing through. These range from bogs, with almost no water flow, to streamside riparian communities.

Bogs are generally acidic, with a pH of 3–4, and low in essential nutrients. They often support a thick layer of sphagnum mosses, with flowering plants, small shrubs, and trees growing on slightly higher hummocks. Many coastal bogs that originally supported native cranberries have been converted to commercial cranberry production. Other bog plants are Labrador tea, bog rosemary (barely coming south of the Canadian border), western bog laurel, and the diminutive, carnivorous roundleaf sundew.

Fens differ from bogs in that they always have water flowing through them, may be found on hillsides, and may be either slightly acidic, neutral, or basic with a pH up to about 8. Southwestern Oregon and northwestern California are home to particularly interesting fens that support large populations of California pitcher-plants, an endemic insectivorous species. Particularly accessible sites are just off Highway 101 north of Florence, Oregon, and off Highway 199 in Del Norte County, California. Fens are also home to California lady's-slippers, California bog asphodel, Vollmer's tiger lily, Wiggins' lily, and other rare and uncommon species. Fens are very sensitive environments that should be observed only from the solid ground around their edges.

Flowing streams, from tiny mountain trickles to the shores of the mighty Columbia River, are home to many flowering plants. We've lumped all of these wet habitats together because they share the common characteristic of year-round water.

Lake/pond. The shallow edges of freshwater lakes and ponds are home to a great many aquatic species not covered in this book. Many are rushes and sedges; others grow primarily submerged and are not particularly showy. However, a few semi-

VERNAL-WET Vernal pools with sea blush, *Plectritis congesta*, and slender goldfields, *Lasthenia californica*, on an overcast April day. By June this area is completely dry and brown. Lower Table Rock near Central Point, Oregon.

BOG/FEN/WETLAND California pitcher-plants, *Darlingtonia californica*, dominate a fen. Del Norte County, California.

LAKE/POND Mount Baker reflected in a small pond. Schreiber's Meadows, Mount Baker National Recreation Area, Washington.

aquatic species stand out, including cattails, water lilies, and wapato.

Moist streambanks. Moist cool soils adjacent to streams large and small, often in the shade of the forest canopy but sometimes out in full sun, provide a productive habitat for many plants with a long growing season or late bloom period. Plants that grow here like plenty of water but don't want their roots as wet as those that thrive in the water itself. While some of these streambanks may technically be defined as wetlands, you're not as likely to get your feet soggy hiking here, particularly after the spring rains have passed. Moist streambanks are found at all elevations from the coast to alpine areas.

Look for some of the bog orchids, bittercress, corydalis, American licorice, fringed grass of parnassus, saxifrages, currants, gooseberries, buttercups, Lewis's monkeyflower, and arrowleaf groundsel, among the many other plants found along streams.

Meadow. Any area devoid of significant tree or shrub cover can be considered a meadow. What grows within a meadow is very dependent upon the elevation, soils, and precipitation. In this book *meadow* is used to differentiate plants that grow out in the open from those that live under the forest canopy.

Disturbed. Roadsides, vacant lots, cropland, grazing areas, gardens, and clearcuts are all examples of disturbed sites. Many of the plants growing in these areas are commonly thought of as weeds, and a large proportion are originally from Europe or

MOIST STREAMBANKS This moist subalpine streambank wildflower community includes Lewis's monkeyflower, *Mimulus lewisii*, green corn lily, *Veratrum viride*, and arrowleaf groundsel, *Senecio triangularis*. Mount Rainier National Park, Washington.

MEADOW Ponderosa pines, *Pinus ponderosa*, in an open grass and wildflower meadow on Hyatt Prairie. Jackson County, Oregon.

DISTURBED Common sunflowers, *Helianthus annuus*, border a Methow River valley pasture grazed by cows. Okanagan National Forest near Winthrop, Washington.

Asia. Some are particularly noxious and invasive, such as Scotch broom, Canada thistle, knapweed, and herb Robert.

Putting It Together

Pacific Northwest plant habitats are affected by large factors such as the weather coming off the Pacific Ocean and the rise of the major mountain ranges. They're also impacted by soil and the rocks from which the soil is derived. Elevation, exposure to the sun, moisture level available to plant roots, and relationships with surrounding plants also play a role in defining habitat. Within similar environments you can expect to find the same or similar species, whether you're looking across broad ecoregions or among localized microhabitats.

Exploring for Wildflowers

Wildflowers are all around us—along city sidewalks, beside the highway, and in more pristine environments from coastal bluffs to subalpine meadows. In this book we've defined wildflowers broadly to include native and nonnative, common and rare, diminutive and giant species. From early spring until autumn you're likely to find something in bloom almost anywhere you look in the Pacific Northwest.

Searching for plants you've never seen before can be a good excuse to take a trip to the mountains, beach, or sagebrush plains. So can going to visit old friends in the flower community. Some people return to a few nearby haunts throughout the year to watch the progression of blooms.

Although wildflowers are found almost everywhere, some locations have a higher concentration of species than others. It's not our goal to lead you to specific sites, a subject that has filled several books already. Rather, we'll give you some hints about the kinds of places that will be most productive to look. The previous chapter details plant environments.

Access, Fees, and Permits
Wildflowers have no need to respect property boundaries. They grow wherever the conditions are right, regardless of whether their roots are sunk into public or private land. Many landowners are justifiably concerned about strangers traipsing across their property even if it's just to look at flowers. Ask permission before going onto private land. Remember to leave gates the way you found them, and walk softly.

Public lands are generally open to wildflower explorers, but entrance or parking fees may be required. These charges can change from year to year and are not consistent from one state or province to another. Before venturing out, it's worth checking with the appropriate land management agency to find out whether you'll be charged. The fees help maintain the parking areas and may also help with trail construction.

Private preserves, such as those owned by The Nature Conservancy or local conservation groups, also vary in their access restrictions. Usually there is no fee, but donations are gratefully accepted.

Learning about Flowers
This guide is packed with information about most of the wildflowers you're likely to encounter in the Northwest. No book can cover every detail, however, so we have included information about additional resources.

Technical books. Serious botanists rely on technical keys to positively identify the plants they find. These books can be intimidating to a first-time user but go into much greater detail than is possible in a book like this one. Technical floras are thick and heavy and may call for you to use a hand lens and take flowers apart to see distinguishing characteristics. You'll find yourself turning to the glossary frequently, and even then being baffled on occasion. Visit your library to look up plants in these books before you invest in a copy.

There are three major floras for the region covered by this book. In British Columbia, consult *Illustrated Flora of British Columbia* by George Douglas et al., an eight-volume set. Washington and Oregon as far south as Roseburg are covered in *Flora of the Pacific Northwest* by C. Leo Hitchcock and Arthur Cronquist, which is abbreviated from the five-volume *Vascular Plants of the Pacific Northwest*. Southern Oregon flora is more related to northern California, for which you need *The Jepson Manual: Higher Plants of California* by James Hickman. See the bibliography for full publication information.

Like-minded flower explorers. It's more fun to go looking for flowers with others who share your interest. There are native plant societies in each state and province. Local chapters sponsor field trips to prime wildflower locations throughout the season and welcome nonmembers who want to learn more about their flora. Sometimes you'll find announcements of these field trips in your newspaper. Each state or provincial group also has a Web site with links to local chapters and field trips.

Some other groups that lead plant hikes and field trips include parks and recreation departments, Sierra Club, and Audubon Society groups. Check your newspaper or the organization's newsletter for information.

Web sites. It isn't practical to take the Internet with you in the field, but many Web sites have a wealth of information about native plants. Use your favorite search engine to find a plant by typing in the plant's

Two friends study spring wildflowers on a Puget Sound prairie remnant on a Nature Conservancy island preserve.

Latin name. Like all Web searches, there will be some irrelevant results, and you'll need to evaluate the source of the page before deciding how reliable it is likely to be.

Grow by the Inch, Die by the Foot

Sometimes we get so carried away with the excitement of finding new and interesting plants that we forget to pay attention to the impact we're making on their environment. You've heard the adage, "Take nothing but pictures and leave nothing but footprints." Often even our lightest footprints do significant damage. National park rangers like to remind us that plants "grow by the inch and die by the foot." Our footsteps easily break delicate woody stems that take years to grow back, particularly in subalpine and alpine environments with short growing seasons. They compact the soil, reducing the air and water reaching roots, and they form social trails that other hikers follow.

We can minimize our impact by following Leave No Trace (LNT) principles. Though designed to protect wild lands, these principles apply equally well in heavily traveled areas: 1) plan ahead and prepare, 2) travel and camp on durable surfaces, 3) dispose of waste properly (pack it in, pack it out), 4) leave what you find, 5) minimize campfire impacts, 6) respect wildlife, and 7) be considerate of other visitors. Much information on LNT techniques is available at www.lnt.org.

Perhaps most important for the wildflower hunter is to travel on durable surfaces. You don't want to be responsible for destroying the very plants you've come to enjoy. If there is an established trail, stay on it. In some cases, as in heavily visited national parks, you absolutely must stay on established trails, and rangers will remind

you of the policy if they find you have strayed. You'll often find more examples of a plant that's a bit too far off the trail to examine just by hiking a little further up the trail.

In areas where there are no trails, you don't want to create a new trail that will encourage others to follow in your footsteps. Think about where you're walking and consider the consequences of your actions. Perhaps you can step from rock to rock. If not, grasses and sedges handle footsteps better than woody plants like heathers and huckleberries. When hiking with a group, practice "meadow walking," which means spreading out and hiking side by side rather than following the leader in a single-file line.

When you come to an interesting plant you would like to study, be aware of what you're trampling as you move around your

"Don't hike here" sign from a revegetation project in North Cascades National Park.

subject. Be careful where you set your pack. And when it's time for lunch, choose a rock, log, or grassy area to sit down.

With rare exceptions, you don't need to pick a flower to identify it. Leave the plant collecting to the professionals who have learned techniques for preserving specimens and have received permission to collect from land managers.

Safety

Searching for wildflowers is generally a low-risk activity, but there are hazards you should be aware of.

Weather. What starts as a beautiful, warm, sunny day can quickly turn cold, windy, and rainy. Dress appropriately and be prepared for unexpected changes, especially at high elevations.

Lightly dressed hikers pass through a field of subalpine lupines, *Lupinus arcticus* subsp. *subalpinus,* high in Paradise Meadow at Mount Rainier as clouds form behind them.

Poisonous plants. In some areas poison-oak (page 224) is thick. Learn to recognize its distinctive three leaves and woody stems. Some people are particularly sensitive to the rash-inducing chemicals in the leaves and stems. Poison-ivy is similar, though much less common in our region. Stinging nettle (page 472) is another irritant to watch out for, although the effects don't last as long.

Rattlesnakes. Rattlesnakes aren't particularly common, and you're unlikely to see one of these generally shy reptiles, but be cautious when you're in their territory. Watch where you step and where you place your hands throughout the area east of the Cascades. Rattlesnakes usually sound their distinctive warning rattle before you get too close, but avoid surprising or cornering one.

Ticks. Ticks are common in parts of our region, especially in tall grasses and weeds. They usually take several hours to attach themselves, so you should have time to do a thorough tick check when you return to your car or home.

Traffic. Many wildflowers grow at the side of roads. Find a safe place to pull over and park, making sure you're out of the travel lane. Walk on the left, facing traffic. Stay well out of the road when examining flowers. Even on lightly traveled forest roads you should expect vehicles to come by while you're stopped.

Rockfall. You don't want to be either the cause or the victim of falling rock. Many areas with interesting flowers are on or near cliffs. Volcanic rock, our most common geologic formation, is often fractured and loose. Even on trails it is easy to kick rocks down on the people hiking the switchbacks below.

Rising tide. There aren't a lot of wildflowers right on the beach, but several species do like to grow just above the high tide line or on top of coastal sea stacks. If you climb around these areas, make sure you don't get trapped by a rising tide. Consult a tide table just as you would before exploring tide pools.

Know your limits. As you approach or exceed your own limits, you're more likely to have an accident. Know how far you can hike in a day, and at what elevation.

Have Fun

Searching for and learning about wildflowers is a lot of fun, whether you're a beginner or a certified Hitchcock-carrying plant nut. There's always a new place to go or a new plant to find. You can go out intentionally searching for plants or just casually enjoy learning about them while backpacking, kayaking, or visiting historic sites. There are enough flowers in the Northwest to keep you busy for years if you choose to try to find them all. Explore the trails through your neighborhood or travel to an exotic corner of the state. The choice is yours. Wherever you go, you're likely to find something in bloom if the season is right.

Dwarf monkeyflower, *Mimulus nanus*, pushes up through a crack in the asphalt at Crater Lake National Park.

Plant Families

Botanists classify plants in increasing levels of detail starting with two classes: angiosperms (flowering plants) and gymnosperms (nonflowering plants). The angiosperms are divided into two subclasses, monocots (having one seed leaf) and dicots (having two seed leaves). The next levels, superorders and orders, are not often used and are followed by plant families.

The family is the highest botanical classification level in common usage. Plants in the same family share many characteristics that are usually easily distinguished by the layperson. For instance, it is easy to recognize a member of the iris family, Iridaceae, by the flower parts coming in threes and by the flat stems and leaves. Some families are further divided into subfamilies, tribes, and subtribes, but these divisions are usually of interest only to serious botanists.

Below the family is the genus, the part of the plant name you are likely to become most familiar with. It is usually easy to identify the features common to plants in the same genus. The genus is the first part of the binomial, or two-part Latin plant name, and is always written with an initial capital letter, as in *Eriogonum*. The species is the second part of the binomial name and is the level that identifies an individual plant. The species name follows the genus and is always written in lowercase, as in *Eriogonum umbellatum*. Some species are further divided into subspecies (subsp.) and varieties (var.), which have smaller differences that may or may not be distinguishable by the layperson.

Learning about plant families and their major characteristics is one tool you can use to help you understand the relationships among the various plants you find. Some families are large, with many genera and species, while others have only a few members. Each family treated in this field guide is described here in the same order in which it appears in the book, but these descriptions should not be considered a technical key.

3 or 6 Petals

ALISMATACEAE—WATER-PLANTAIN FAMILY. Freshwater plants floating or growing on mud. Leaves palmately veined, submersed, generally linear to oval, blades above water linear to arrow-shaped. Flowers 3 green sepals and 3 large white or pink petals, many stamens. White, page 58.

ARISTOLOCHIACEAE—PIPEVINE FAMILY. Leaves heart-shaped. Flowers solitary, 3 sepals partly fused into bowl shape with 3 long thin "tails" and 12 stamens, no petals. Seed with fleshy appendage. Ovary inferior or partly inferior. Green/brown, page 458.

BERBERIDACEAE—BARBERRY FAMILY. Spreading to erect shrubs or herbs from rhizomes. Leaves are simple or pinnately compound. Sepals and petals 6 or 9, in whorls of 3. Berry usually purple-black. White, page 58; yellow, page 186.

IRIDACEAE—IRIS FAMILY. Leaves usually strap-like, with parallel veins, arranged in fans. Flower parts, in threes, are the same on each side. Ovary inferior. Yellow, page 187; red, page 306; blue, page 400.

LILIACEAE—LILY FAMILY. Leaves with parallel veins. Flowers with 3 petals and sepels, and 3 or 6 stamens. Ovary superior. White, page 59; yellow, page 188; orange, page 298; red, page 306; blue, page 401; green/brown, page 459.

LYTHRACEAE—LOOSESTRIFE FAMILY. Stems sometimes 4-angled. Leaves entire. Flowers radially symmetrical, sepals and petals 4–6 alternating. Ovary superior but inside fused sepals. Red, page 314.

ORCHIDACEAE—ORCHID FAMILY. Leaves with parallel veins. Flowers irregularly shaped, ovary inferior. Sepals 3 petal-like, petals 3, lowest usually different, often enlarged. Stamen 1 fused with stigma. White, page 71; red, page 315; green/brown, page 461.

PAPAVERACEAE—POPPY FAMILY. Annuals to trees. Yellowish sap. Leaves basal and on stem, toothed or dissected. Flowers radially symmetrical. Ovary superior. Sepals 2 or 3, fall as flower bud opens. Petals 4–6, free, many stamens. White, page 74; yellow, page 190; orange, page 299.

POLYGONACEAE—BUCKWHEAT FAMILY. Leaves alternate, with a paper sheath around the node where the petiole attaches, each a different shape. Flowers small with colored sepals and no true petals. Stamens 2–9, often in whorls. White, page 75; yellow, page 191; red, page 316; green/brown, page 463.

SPARGANIACEAE—BUR-REED FAMILY. Growing in or at edge of ponds. Stems are slender, cylindric, and solid with upper part floating or erect. Leaves narrow and flat, sometimes triangular, floating. Flowers in ball-like sphere, sessile, without petals, female at base, male on upper section. Flower parts 1–6, very showy. White, page 80.

4 Petals

BRASSICACEAE—MUSTARD FAMILY. Leaves alternate. Flowers with 4 sepals shorter than the 4 petals, held in a double cross shape. Seedpods unique, with outer covering over a single row of seeds on each side of a papery division. White, page 80; yellow, page 193; red, page 320; blue, page 405.

CAPPARIDACEAE—CAPER FAMILY. Annuals (ours), shrubs, or trees. Leaves palmately dissected into 3–7 leaflets. Flowers solitary or in clusters at stem top. Sepals 3–4, fused or free, persistent. Petals 4, free, becoming narrow toward base. Seedpods spreading or hanging capsules. Plants have musty odor when rubbed. Yellow, page 200.

CORNACEAE—DOGWOOD FAMILY. Leaves with parallel veins, opposite or whorled, deciduous. Tiny flowers white, green, or pale yellow, surrounded by large white petal-like bracts. Ovary inferior. Fruit red, white, or blue, soft on outside, 1–2 hard stones inside. White, page 86.

FUMARIACEAE—FUMITORY FAMILY. Leaves are many times divided. Sepals 2, fall as flower opens. Petals 4 in 2 pairs, 1 or both of outer pair spurred or pouched, inner pair united and sometimes crested. Ovary superior. White, page 87; yellow, page 201; red, page 323.

GENTIANACEAE—GENTIAN FAMILY. Flowers large, with 4–5 petals fused, forming flattened to narrow bell shape with spreading lobes. Stamens 4–5, fused to wall, alternate with lobes. Sinuses between lobes often with various uniquely shaped appendages. Ovary superior on stalk. Red, page 324; blue, page 405; green/brown, page 464.

NYCTAGINACEAE—FOUR-O'CLOCK FAMILY. Leaves opposite, entire, not usually same size. Bracts free or fused into calyx-like unit with solitary flower or cluster of flowers. Petal-like sepals fused into trumpet shape with 4 or 5 lobes and the tube constricted at base. No true petals present. Ovary superior. White, page 88; yellow, page 201; red, page 325.

ONAGRACEAE—EVENING PRIMROSE FAMILY. Flowers in spikes, clusters, or solitary, often open at dusk or dawn, darkening in color with age. Flowers in parts of 4, free. Pollen on interconnected threads. Ovary inferior. White, page 89; yellow, page 202; red, page 325.

PLANTAGINACEAE—PLANTAIN FAMILY. Leaves in basal rosette. Flowers in dense spike at top of long leafless stem. A single bract is just under each tiny flower, 4 sepals form calyx holding bell-shaped tube with 4 spreading to erect colorless lobes. Dries brown and papery. Ovary superior. Green/brown, page 465.

RUBIACEAE—MADDER FAMILY. Stems rough, with 4 sides. Leaves in pairs or whorls. Flowers in clusters or solitary. Calyx 4-lobed or missing. Flower petals small, with 4 lobes fused at base forming cross. Ovary inferior, forming 2 rounded seeds. White, page 90; yellow, page 204.

5 Irregular Petals

FABACEAE—PEA FAMILY. Shrubs, herbs, or trees. Leaves compound. Flower shape unique to this family, with 5 petals, 1 large at top, 2 lower joined to form crescent-shaped keel. Ovary superior. Fruit is a pod, often inflated, with 1 or 2 rows of seeds attached along 1 edge. White, page 92; yellow, page 205; red, page 330; blue, page 407; green/brown, page 466.

POLYGALACEAE—MILKWORT FAMILY. Leaves simple, pinnately veined, entire. Flowers in cluster are pea-like; sepals and petals free or fused together. Red, page 337.

VIOLACEAE—VIOLET FAMILY. Leaves basal or on stem, sometimes both. Flowers usually solitary in parts of 5. Irregular shape. Larger petal at bottom, with spur or pouch at base; pair of side petals and another pair of petals at top. Lower 2 stamens with nectaries project into spur. Pistil with unique

peak; ovary superior. White, page 98; yellow, page 210; blue, page 416.

5 Symmetrical Petals (Ovary Superior)

CARYOPHYLLACEAE—PINK FAMILY. Leaves usually opposite, not divided. Flowers few to many in open cluster or solitary in leaf axil. Sepals 4–5, free or fused, tube with lobes. Petals 4–5, very small or larger than sepals, usually notched or divided. Stamens 10 or fewer. White, page 99; red, page 337; green/brown, page 467.

CLUSIACEAE—ST. JOHN'S WORT FAMILY. Annuals, perennials, or shrubs. Leaves on stems simple, often with black dots or clear glands. Flowers in clusters or solitary. Sepals 5, persistent, often fused at base, overlapping. Stamens many, free or fused into clusters. Yellow, page 213.

CRASSULACEAE—STONECROP FAMILY. Fleshy. Leaves basal and on stem, not compound. Flowers in clusters, usually with bracts. Flower sepals 3–5, free; petals 3–5, free or fused. Stamens same number as sepals. Seedpods with 3–5 chambers, many seeds. Yellow, page 214; red, page 340.

DROSERACEAE—SUNDEW FAMILY. Bog dwellers. Carnivorous. Leaves in flattened rosette with insect-catching hairs on upper surface. Flowers in parts of 5, single to few on long leafless stem. Red, page 340.

ERICACEAE—HEATH FAMILY. Bark peeling. Leaves simple, evergreen or deciduous. Flowers in cluster or solitary, usually with bracts. Petals 4–5, usually free or fused. Stamens 8–10. Fruit is a capsule or berry. White, page 108; yellow, page 217; red, page 341; green/brown, page 467.

GERANIACEAE—GERANIUM FAMILY. Leaves palmately lobed or divided. Flowers in loose clusters in parts of 5, with 10 stamens. Mature seed clings to elongated style and coils, driving seed into soil. White, page 112; red, page 347.

LIMNANTHACEAE—MEADOWFOAM FAMILY. Growing in moist places. Plants small.

Leaves divided pinnately, segments narrow. Flower sepals and petals 4–5; petals generally longer than sepals, tips toothed. Stamens 8–10, pistils 4–5. Blooms in early spring. Seeds nutlets. White, page 113.

LINACEAE—FLAX FAMILY. Long thin stems. Leaves on stem, usually linear. Flower cluster open to dense, nodding in bud, petals short-lived. Stamens 4–5, alternate, with 4–5 petals. Blue, page 418.

MALVACEAE—MALLOW FAMILY. Leaves lobed, somewhat maple-like. Juice sticky. Flower sepals form 5-lobed calyx; petals 5, free, wide. Stamens fused at base, forming column around long pistil with style tips extending above. Orange, page 299; red, page 349.

PAEONIACEAE—PEONY FAMILY. Perennials. Stems several, clustered. Leaves large, deeply dissected or compound. Flowers solitary or few in cluster. Sepals 5, persistent after flowering. Petals 5–10. Pistils 2–5, large, coarse. Seeds large, black. Red, page 351.

PORTULACACEAE—PURSLANE FAMILY. Plants usually fleshy. Stems hairless. Leaves opposite, not compound. Flower with 2 sepals, free or fused at base; petals 5–18, free or fused. Many stamens. White, page 113; orange, page 299; red, page 352.

RANUNCULACEAE—BUTTERCUP FAMILY. Leaves basal and alternate on stem; petioles usually flat at base. Flowers radially symmetrical or irregular with spurs, as in *Delphinium*. Sepals and petals usually 5 to many; sepals green, withering early or petal-like when no petals are present. Stamens 10 to many. Fruit is a cluster of many hard seeds, a berry, or many seeds in a dry pod. White, page 116; yellow, page 218; red, page 355; blue, page 419.

SARRACENIACEAE—PITCHER-PLANT FAMILY. Bog dwellers. Carnivorous, with leaves modified to tubes with hood. Flowers solitary on leafless stem, nodding; sepals and petals free. Stamens many. Yellow, page 223.

ZYGOPHYLLACEAE—CALTROP FAMILY. The single species in our area forms large mats with pinnately divided leaves. Flowers single in axils. Seed nutlet with stout spines. Yellow, page 223.

5 Symmetrical Petals (Ovary Inferior)

ANACARDIACEAE—SUMAC FAMILY. Shrubs or trees. Leaves simple, compound, deciduous or evergreen. Flowers with 5 sepals fused at base, 5 petals free. Fruit with a single seed. Plants in Pacific Northwest toxic, may produce contact dermatitis. Yellow, page 223.

APIACEAE—PARSLEY FAMILY. Hollow stems with ribs, arising from ground. Leaves basal and on stem, usually compound. Small flowers in umbels, 5 petals. White, page 120; yellow, page 224; red, page 356; green/brown, page 467.

ARALIACEAE—GINSENG FAMILY. Shrubs or woody vines. Stems branched. Leaves simple or compound, alternate. Tiny flowers in umbels. Flowers with 5 petals alternating with 5 stamens. Fruit is a berry. White, page 127.

HYDRANGEACEAE—HYDRANGEA FAMILY. Trees, shrubs, or vines. Leaves opposite, simple, entire, lobed or toothed, deciduous or evergreen. Flowers in clusters or solitary at tip or on upper stem. Sepals and petals 4–7, free. Stamens at least twice the number of petals. Seeds many, small. White, page 127.

LOASACEAE—BLAZING-STAR FAMILY. Rough or stinging hairs. Leaves alternate, pinnately lobed. Flowers with 5 sepals persistent in seed; 5 free petals. Many stamens with thread-like filaments. Many seeds in capsules. Yellow, page 229.

ROSACEAE—ROSE FAMILY. Leaves usually pinnately or palmately compound, alternate with stipules. Flowers in groups or solitary. Sepals 5, often alternate with bractlets; petals 5, free; stamens 5 to many; pistils 1 to many. Fruit can vary in form: pome (apple), raspberry-like, achene (group of single seeds), or follicle. White, page 128; yellow, page 230; red, page 357.

SAXIFRAGACEAE—SAXIFRAGE FAMILY. Plant hairy, usually glandular. Leaves oblong to round, entire to maple-like. Flowers 1 to many. Petals sometimes spotted, 10 stamens, filaments generally flat. White, page 138; yellow, page 236; red, page 361; green/brown, page 468.

5 Irregular Petals Forming a Tube

LAMIACEAE—MINT FAMILY. Stems erect, 4-sided. Leaves entire to deeply lobed, opposite. Flowers usually clustered around stem or at top, subtended by leaves or bracts. Flowers 1- or 2-lipped; upper lip entire or lobed, flat to hood-shaped but occasionally none; lower lip 3-lobed. Fruit is a nutlet. Plants often though not always have a mint smell. White, page 145; red, page 362; blue, page 423.

LENTIBULARIACEAE—BLADDERWORT FAMILY. Carnivorous. Growing in wet places or in water. Leaves none or in basal rosette, entire. Flowers in cluster or single, on long leafless stem. Sepals united, flower united, 2 lips, upper lip with 2 lobes, lower lip with 3 lobes and spur at base. Small seed in capsule. Yellow, page 237; blue, page 425.

OROBANCHACEAE—BROOMRAPE FAMILY. Erect, fleshy, nongreen parasites. No leaves. Flowers in spike, cluster, or solitary. Calyx tubular or cup-shaped, lobes 0–5. Corolla 2-lipped, 5-lobed, with 4 stamens. Capsules with many small seeds. Red, page 364; blue, page 425; green/brown, page 469.

SCROPHULARIACEAE—FIGWORT FAMILY. Generally glandular. Leaves alternate. Flowers in spike or cluster with bracts, or in axils. Petals 4–5, united, 2-lipped. Stamens usually 4 in 2 pairs, sometimes sterile staminode. Flower shapes include: wide tube with 2 flaring lips; narrow tube with upper lip arching to pointed spout; radially symmetrical. White, page 146;

yellow, page 237; orange, page 300; red, page 364; blue, page 426.

VERBENACEAE—VERVAIN FAMILY. Leaves opposite, toothed. Flowers in spike or head, slightly 2-lipped. Ovary not lobed, later separating as 4 nutlets. Without mint-like odor. White, page 148.

5 Symmetrical Petals Forming a Tube

APOCYNACEAE—DOGBANE FAMILY. Milky sap. Erect. Leaves not compound, entire. Flower clusters of 1 to many, axillary or terminal blossoms. Sepals fused at base, petals fused in bell shape. White, page 148; red, page 377.

ASCLEPIADACEAE—MILKWEED FAMILY. Milky sap. Leaves simple, opposite or whorled. Flowers solitary or in cluster. Sepals 5, reflexed; petals 5, forming cuplike structures with horn-like appendages on central filament column. Red, page 377.

BORAGINACEAE—BORAGE FAMILY. Prostrate to erect. Leaves usually simple, entire. Flowers in clusters or 1-sided coil, uncoiling in seed; each flower a 5-lobed tube usually with 5 appendages at top, alternating with 5 stamens and sometimes arching over tube. White, page 148; yellow, page 248; orange, page 300; red, page 378; blue, page 438.

CONVOLVULACEAE—MORNING-GLORY FAMILY. Twining or trailing. Flowers single or in cluster, with 5 free sepals overlapping; petals fused, bell-shaped, pleated, twisted in bud. White, page 153; red, page 378.

HYDROPHYLLACEAE—WATERLEAF FAMILY. Prostrate to erect. Leaves simple to pinnately compound. Flowers in coil or solitary. Fused bell-shaped calyx persists after flowering. Petals 5, bell-shaped or flattened. Stamens 5. White, page 154; blue, page 441.

MENYANTHACEAE—BUCKBEAN FAMILY. Aquatic. Leaves simple or 3 sessile leaflets. Flowers with 5-lobed calyx; corolla 5-lobed, flat to funnel-shaped; stamens 5; pistil 1.

Ovary superior or partially inferior. Few to many seeds in capsule. White, page 158.

OXALIDACEAE—WOOD SORREL FAMILY. No stems or very short. Leaves with petiole, 3 lobes, clover-like. Petals with thin stalk-like base; stamens 10. Flat seed is in explosive cylinder or round capsule. White, page 158; yellow, page 249.

PLUMBAGINACEAE—LEADWORT FAMILY. Leaves simple, entire or lobed. Flowers in cluster; sepals fused to form folded tube, often papery, persistent. Petals 5, united at base. Red, page 379.

POLEMONIACEAE—PHLOX FAMILY. Simple or compound leaves on stem or in basal rosette. Flowers in clusters, heads, or solitary. Flowers bell-shaped or a short tube with flattened lobes and open throat. White, page 159; yellow, page 250; orange, page 301; red, page 379; blue, page 443.

PRIMULACEAE—PRIMROSE FAMILY. Annuals or perennials, hairless or with glands. Leaves simple. Flowers sometimes on long leafless stems. Flower parts 4 or 5. Calyx deeply lobed; petals spreading to reflexed; ovary usually superior. Seed a capsule with few to many small seeds. White, page 161; red, page 383.

RHAMNACEAE—BUCKTHORN FAMILY. Shrubs, vines, or trees. Plants sometimes thorny. Simple leaves with petioles, clustered on short shoots. Flowers in small to large clusters atop stems or solitary in axils. Sepals 4–5; petals none or 4–5, often narrowing toward the base. Seed in stone in 2–5 fused fleshy cells. White, page 162; blue, page 446.

SANTALACEAE—SANDALWOOD FAMILY. Herbs, shrubs, or trees. Parasites on roots of other plants. Leaves stemless, entire. Flowers small clusters in axils on upper plant. Calyx tubular to bell-shaped, with 4–5 lobes. No petals. Ovary inferior or superior. Single-seeded fruit in persistent calyx. White, page 163.

SOLANACEAE—NIGHTSHADE FAMILY. Simple leaves with petiole, entire or deeply lobed. Flower calyx with 5 lobes. Petals 5, fused, trumpet-shaped or flattened. Fruit is a tomato-like berry or capsule. White, page 164; blue, page 447.

5 Petals Joined into a Bell

BALSAMINACEAE—TOUCH-ME-NOT FAMILY. Annuals with juicy sap. Leaves simple, alternate. Flowers showy, of irregular shape. Sepals 3: 2 small, green; 1 large, colored, forming a spur. Petals 5, fused into unequal lobes. Pods explode when ripe. Orange, page 301.

CAMPANULACEAE—BELLFLOWER FAMILY. Leaves on stems, simple. Flowers in clusters, spikes, or solitary. Flowers either bell-shaped or 2-lipped, petals fused at base or almost entirely. Stamens 5, free or fused. Red, page 386; blue, page 447.

CAPRIFOLIACEAE—HONEYSUCKLE FAMILY. Shrubs or vines. Leaves simple or compound, opposite. Narrow tubular flowers with 5 lobes held in pairs. White, page 164; yellow, page 250; orange, page 301; red, page 386.

CUCURBITACEAE—CUCUMBER FAMILY. Trailing or climbing, with many tendrils. Male flowers in clusters, single female flower in axil. Fruit is similar to a gourd or melon. White, page 165.

DIPSACACEAE—TEASEL FAMILY. Erect stem often with thorns. Leaves simple. Flowers in dense, cylindrical, persistent head. Calyx 4-lobed, with sharp tips, persists after flowering. Petals 4–5, form narrow tube, extending lobes unequal. Blue, page 449.

GROSSULARIACEAE—GOOSEBERRY FAMILY. Shrubs with erect stems, without or with many spines. Simple, deciduous leaves clustered on tips of twigs, palmately 3- to 5-lobed. Flowers usually in hanging clusters. Sepals usually 5 and spreading, 5 petals fused at base, alternating with 5 stamens. Berries of many colors. White, page 165; yellow, page 251; orange, page 302; red, page 388.

VALERIANACEAE—VALERIAN FAMILY. Often with a strong unpleasant odor. Leaves simple or pinnately lobed or compound. Flowers in dense clusters, irregularly shaped, often 2-lipped, 5-lobed tubes with spurs or swollen base. White, page 167; red, page 390; blue, page 449.

Composite Flowers

ASTERACEAE—ASTER FAMILY. Largest family on earth. Mostly herbs. Leaves various. What appears to be a single flower is a tightly crowded compound head of numerous small flowers of 2 types: ray flowers, with a ligule, often on outer edge of head; and disk flowers, with complete tubes and no ligule. All combinations of ray and disk flowers occur. White, page 167; yellow, page 251; orange, page 302; red, page 391; blue, page 449; green/brown, page 469.

Many Petals

CACTACEAE—CACTUS FAMILY. Thick, fleshy, round to flat structures with spines. Flowers solitary, with many petals. Yellow, page 295; red, page 397.

CYPERACEAE—SEDGE FAMILY. Grass-like. Stems slender, solid, erect. Flowers perfect, in tight clusters of 6 to many fine, soft bristles. White, page 183.

NYMPHAEACEAE—WATER LILY FAMILY. Aquatic. Floating or submersed leaves arising from roots on long petioles. Flowers solitary, large, showy. White, page 183; yellow, page 296.

No Obvious Petals

ARACEAE—ARUM FAMILY. Many small flowers crowded on a spadix and partially surrounded by a spathe, as in skunk cabbage, the only member of this family in our area. Yellow, page 296.

CELASTRACEAE—STAFF-TREE FAMILY. Erect shrubs (ours), vines, or trees. Leaves simple, evergreen (ours), or deciduous. Flowers in clusters at leaf axils, cup-like with 4–5 sepals and 4–5 tiny petals. Fruit is a capsule. Red, page 397.

CHENOPODIACEAE—GOOSEFOOT FAMILY. Herbs or erect shrubs with simple, usually alternate leaves sometimes covered with a white scaly coating. Tiny flowers in dense spikes or cymes. Includes edibles such as spinach and beets. Red, page 398; green/brown, page 470.

CUSCUTACEAE—DODDER FAMILY. Twining yellow or orange vine, parasitic on many flowering plants and sometimes causing considerable damage. Leaves reduced to tiny scales. Flowers tiny. Orange, page 303.

EMPETRACEAE—CROWBERRY FAMILY. Low evergreen shrubs. Leaves alternate, linear, stiff, heath-like. Flowers solitary or few in clusters, both male and female. Fruit is berry-like, with 2–9 stones. Crowberry is our only species in this family. Red, page 398.

EUPHORBIACEAE—SPURGE FAMILY. Milky sap. Petals absent. Petal-like bracts often brightly colored; stamens and glands in a central cluster or a 3-lobed ovary hanging to 1 side of the stamens. White, page 183; green/brown, page 471.

TYPHACEAE—CATTAIL FAMILY. Wetland plants. Stems round, stiff. Leaves flat, stiff, with parallel veins. Flowers in thick cylindrical spike, male flowers separate above female flowers. Green/brown, page 472.

URTICACEAE—NETTLE FAMILY. Most plants in our area are covered with stinging hairs. Flowers tiny, green, without petals, in small clusters of hanging stems. Leaves opposite. Green/brown, page 472.

Sagittaria cuneata ALISMATACEAE

Arum-leaf arrowhead, wapato, duck potato
Locally common, late spring, perennial,
6–18 in. Bog/fen/wetland, lake/pond

Aquatic with emersed, floating, or submersed leaves, long flower stems emerging from water. Emersed leaves 2–6 in. long, the 2 lower lobes shorter than the upper lobe. Bracts beneath inflorescence ⅓–1¼ in. long. Flowers up to 1 in. across and in whorls of 3. White petals are rounded. Female flowers with cluster of pistils are in bottom whorl, with shorter stalks than male flowers above with 15–25 stamens. Flower stalk elongates in seed. Grows in ponds, slow-moving water, at low to mid elevations. Native

OLYM, NOCA

Sagittaria latifolia ALISMATACEAE

Broadleaf arrowhead, wapato
Locally common, late summer, perennial,
1–4 ft. Bog/fen/wetland, lake/pond

Aquatic with emersed, floating, or submersed leaves. Each leaf arises on long stem from base. Emersed leaves arrow-shaped, 2–15 in., nearly as long as they are broad, with lower lobes about as long as upper lobe. Bracts beneath inflorescence ⅕–½ in. long. Flowers up to 1½ in. across and in whorls of 3 in a tall spike at top of leafless stem. White petals fall soon after opening. Female flowers in bottom whorl below male flowers with 25–40 stamens. Grows in freshwater ponds, ditches, marshes, at low elevations. Native

OLYM, **L&C**

Achlys triphylla BERBERIDACEAE

Vanilla leaf, deer foot, sweet after death
Common, early spring–midsummer,
perennial, 8–16 in. Coastal, west-side forest

Spreading by underground roots, 3 fan-shaped, coarsely toothed leaflets at top of 4–15 in. stems. Central leaflet divided into 3 lobes. Leaves horizontal. Stem single, longer than leaf, holds spike of small white flowers with long stamens giving a starry look. Berries reddish purple. Similar *A. californica*, deer foot, has 6–8 lobes on central leaflet, and brown berries. Called vanilla leaf for the sweet smell of the dried leaves. Native OLYM, MORA, NOCA, CRLA

Vancouveria hexandra BERBERIDACEAE
Northern inside-out flower
Locally common, early summer, perennial,
8–16 in. Coastal, west-side forest

Spreading from underground stems. Long
basal stems hold pinnately compound deciduous leaves, with 3 leaflets in each of 2–3 divisions. Leaflets square to heart-shaped, top surface hairless, slightly hairy underneath, stem
turning light in color with age. Flower stalk hairless, above
leaves, bearing whorls of long-stalked, small, white, nodding
flowers. Flowers in parts of 6, petals bent backward, flared out,
looking inside out. Grows in deep shade in conifer forests at
low to mid elevations. The taller redwood ivy, *V. planipetala*,
with hairy flower stalks, grows in California, southern Oregon.
Siskiyou inside-out flower, *V. chrysantha*, in the
Siskiyou Mountains, has yellow flowers. Native
OLYM, MORA, NOCA, CRLA

Iris chrysophylla IRIDACEAE
Yellowleaf iris
Uncommon, late spring, perennial, 2–8 in.
Meadow, west-side forest

Stems erect or stemless, leaves pointing upward. Rhizomes creeping to 12 in. Leaves evergreen, light yellowish green, about ¼ in. wide, pink or red at
base. Flower stem to 8 in., holds 2 flowers. Flowers white sometimes tinged blue, or cream to pale yellow with darker veining,
perianth tube 1½–4 in. long and slender, narrow petals held
horizontal to the ground. Grows in open forests, woodlands, at
low elevations. Native CRLA

Allium amplectens LILIACEAE
Slimleaf onion, paper onion
Locally common, late spring, perennial, 6–12
in. Vernal-wet, west-side forest, shrub-steppe

Erect flower stem with withering leaves. Leaves
2–4, narrow, somewhat rounded in cross section, attached along stem. Cluster of 10–50
white to light pink, papery flowers tops stem;
tips of petals do not turn up; ovary distinctly 6-
crested. Petals cup up and over ovary as they wither. Grows in
vernal-wet clay and serpentine soils that become hot and dry,
below 7000 ft. Native NOCA, CRLA

See other *Iris*: yellow, page 187; blue, page 400
See other *Allium*: red, page 306

Allium brandegeei (*Allium tribractea-tum* var. *diehii*) LILIACEAE

Brandegee's onion, three-bracted onion
Rare, midsummer, perennial, 1–3 in.
Meadow, alpine, subalpine

Erect stem, white flowers. Two leaves very narrow, slightly concave, longer than flower stem, staying green through flowering. Flower stem 1–4 in. tall, slender, slightly flattened, not winged. Few to many flowers in cluster above 2–3 egg-shaped bracts with pointed tips, 3–7 prominent veins. White flower petals with greenish to reddish midrib become papery with age, stamens shorter than petals, anthers oblong, yellowish. Grows in gravelly places in meadows, volcanic slopes into alpine areas. Native

Allium fibrillum LILIACEAE

Blue Mountain onion, Jones' onion
Locally common, late spring–early summer, perennial, 2–8 in. East-side forest, alpine, subalpine

Erect single flowering stem. Leaves paired, equal to or taller than flowering stem, green at flowering. Flowers short, widely bell-shaped, white or pink with green midrib, with 6 low, curving, smooth-edged appendages on ovary. Grows in moist, heavy soils at high elevations. More common and smaller than *A. brandegeei*, which looks similar. Native

Allium madidum LILIACEAE

Mountain swamp onion
Rare, late spring, perennial, to 12 in.
Bog/fen/wetland, alpine, subalpine

Stem erect, equal to or longer than the leaves. Leaves 2, stiff, with deeply grooved midvein, staying green through flowering. Umbel contains 25–35 white flowers, petals with green or pale pink midvein, pollen dark purple to dull yellow. Often found in large stands in swampy to wet places at mid to high elevations, including Eagle Cap in Wallowa Mountains. Native

Calochortus bruneaunis LILIACEAE
Bruneau mariposa lily
Rare, late spring–early summer, perennial, 4–15 in. East-side forest, shrub-steppe

Stem upright. Leaves 4–8 in. long, linear, basal, withered by flowering; upper leaves on stem rolled inward. Inflorescence consists of 1–4 erect pure white or slightly lavender flowers. Sepals with dark spots near base. Petals with very pale greenish stripe on outside from pointed tip to base, inside a dark red or purple arch just above a yellow blotch and a red stripe running from below blotch to base. Grows among dry grass or sagebrush in juniper or pine woodlands. Native

Calochortus elegans LILIACEAE
Elegant cat's ear
Uncommon, late spring–early summer, perennial, 3–6 in. West-side forest, alpine, subalpine

Stem ascending, slender, often weak or bent. Basal leaves 1–2, green through flowering, 4–8 in. long. Flowers 2–6, facing upward. Petals greenish white to pale lavender-white, purple crescent near base, hairy with long straight hairs along edges except for hairless pointed tips. Grows in open, rocky soils at edges of forests at mid to high elevations. Native CRLA, **L&C**

Calochortus eurycarpus LILIACEAE
Wing-fruited mariposa lily, big-pod mariposa lily
Locally common, early summer, perennial, 4–18 in. Meadow, east-side forest

Stem erect, stiff. Leaves consist of 1 flat basal and 1 bract-like stem leaf. Flowers 2 in. across, white, lavender, or reddish, with red blotch in center of petal; at petal base, nectary glands have few long hairs around shorter yellow hairs covering nectary. Grows in sunny open meadows, edges of wooded slopes, at mid to high elevations. Native

See other *Calochortus*: red, page 310; blue, page 402

Calochortus howellii LILIACEAE
Howell's mariposa
Rare, early summer, perennial, 12–16 in.
West-side forest

Stem erect. Single leaf from base slightly longer than stem, pair of linear bract-like leaves at base of flower stalks. Flower white, petals widely rounded at outer end, hairless on outside, inside covered with white hairs turning dark brown over green and deep brown flower center. Three narrow sepals white, slightly shorter than petals. Endemic to Siskiyou Mountains in dry open forests on rocky serpentine at 1300–3700 ft. Similar *C. umpquaensis*, endemic to Douglas County, Oregon, is 8–12 in. tall with deep purple or reddish blotches inside petals near center of flower. Native

Calochortus subalpinus LILIACEAE
Subalpine mariposa lily
Uncommon, midsummer, perennial, to 8 in.
Meadow, west-side forest, east-side forest,
alpine, subalpine

Stem upright, unbranched, with basal grass-like leaf. Leaf flat, about as long as stem. Flowers 1–5, clustered at top, creamy white, with long hairs inside, often with purple crescent near base of petal. Sepals about same length as petals; each sepal with a single purple dot. Grows in forests, dry meadows, at mid to high elevations. Native NOCA

Chlorogalum pomeridianum LILIACEAE
Wavyleaf soap plant, amole
Locally common, early summer, perennial,
2–8 ft. Meadow, west-side forest

Stem upright, slender, bearing many branches. Basal leaves linear, 8–24 in. long, with wavy edges; stem leaves bract-like. Inflorescence consists of many branches with slender flower stalks about same length as width of flower. Flowers open in evening, close early next morning. Flower petals linear, recurving, white with green or purple midvein, stamens purple or yellow with yellow or cream pollen. Grows on bluffs, in grasslands, chaparral, dry woods, below 5000 ft. Similar *C. angustifolium*, narrow-leaf soap plant, grows in same areas but is smaller, with straight leaf edges, and flower petals do not recurve. Native

Clintonia uniflora LILIACEAE
Queen-cup, bead lily
Common, midsummer, perennial, 2–6 in.
Coastal, west-side forest, east-side forest

Rosette of 2–3 leaves, from roots running in deep soils forming ground cover of plants. Leaves 4–6 in. long, 1–2 in. wide, oblong, with pointed tip, more or less hairy especially along edges. Stem erect, hairy, topped with 1 white flower 1–2 in. across, slightly cup-shaped at base, petals opening wide and flat to face upward. Seeds in very bright blue berries. Grows in shaded, moist forests from coastline to timberline. Native OLYM, MORA, NOCA, CRLA

Disporum hookeri (*Prosartes hookeri*) LILIACEAE
Hooker's fairybell
Common, late spring, perennial, 1–3 ft.
Coastal, west-side forest

Upright. Stems with few horizontally spreading branches, the upper stems somewhat hairy. Leaves clasping, arranged parallel to the ground enabling them to catch light, slightly hairy along veins on underside; short hairs on edges point forward; sharp points at tips. Flowers 1–3 at tips of stems, consisting of greenish or creamy white hanging bells with spreading lobes, with stamens extending outward. Berry dark yellow to bright red. Grows in shaded woods, deep forests to 5000 ft. Rainwater runs down parallel-veined leaves, drips off sharply pointed tips, protecting flower. Native OLYM, MORA, NOCA, CRLA

Disporum smithii LILIACEAE
Smith's fairybell, fairy lantern
Uncommon, early summer, perennial, 1–3 ft.
Coastal, west-side forest

Upright. Stems with branches that spread widely. Roots creeping, in time making loose thicket. Stems, leaves hairless. Leaves dark, shiny green, alternate, clasping stems. Flower clusters of 1–7 hang from underside of stems. Flowers are ½ in. long, creamy white, narrow bells flaring only slightly at tip. Berries longer than wide, orange to red. Grows in deep moist woods, redwood forests, at low to mid elevations. Similar *D. trachycarpum*, roughfruit fairybells, which grows on Steens Mountain, has hairy stems and fleshy round berries covered with soft bumps—the most evident characteristic. *Trachycarpum* means "rough-fruited." Native OLYM, MORA, NOCA

See other *Clintonia*: red, page 311

Erythronium citrinum LILIACEAE
Lemon fawn lily
Locally common, midspring, perennial, 6–8 in.
Meadow, west-side forest

Erect flower stem with 1–3 slightly nodding flowers. Stems 6–8 in. tall. Leaves 2, lance-shaped to oval, usually with wavy edges, mottled with white or brown. Flowers white with light green or greenish yellow patch, fading to pinkish, with very small sac-like appendages at base of the 3 petals, stigma shallowly 3-lobed. Grows in mixed light woods below 4000 ft. Very similar *E. howellii* does not have sac-like appendages. The most common of all, *E. oregonum*, shares the same habitat, with longer stigma lobes, flattened filaments, and central patch of deeper yellow. Native

Erythronium klamathense LILIACEAE
Klamath fawn lily
Uncommon, midspring, perennial, 2–8 in.
West-side forest, alpine, subalpine

Erect flower stem, plain green leaves. Leaves 2–7 in. long, lance-shaped, bright green, folded along main vein, somewhat wavy-edged, lie on ground. Stem carries 1–3 flowers. Flowers white with yellow base, aging to light pink. Petals with folded appendages at base. Grows in meadows, openings in forests, at 3600–5400 ft. Blooms at snowmelt. Can be confused with *E. montanum*. Native CRLA

Erythronium montanum LILIACEAE
Avalanche lily
Locally common, midspring, perennial, 6–8 in.
Alpine, subalpine

Erect flowering stem from pair of plain green leaves. Leaves shiny, 4–8 in. long, ½ as wide, with undulating edges and sharply pointed tips. Raceme of 1–4 flowers tops stem. Flowers glistening white, yellow to orange-yellow at base, sometimes turning pink with age. Grows in damp meadows at upper mid to high elevations. Blooms just after snowmelt, sometimes in spectacular large patches. Native

OLYM, MORA, NOCA

See other *Erythronium*: yellow, page 188; red, page 312

Erythronium oregonum LILIACEAE
Oregon fawn lily
Common, midspring, perennial, 6–16 in.
Coastal, meadow, west-side forest

Erect flower stem, pair of leaves mottled with large patches of white, light green, brown, or greenish black, 4–9 in. long, about ½ as wide, wavy-edged. Flowers in raceme of 1–3 flowers. Flowers creamy white to white, with or without 1 or more bands of reddish to brown markings surrounding darker yellow area at base; anthers cream to yellow; filaments flattened. Three true petals have sac-like folded appendages at base. Grows in light woods, open meadows, at low elevations. Subsp. *leucandrum* has white anthers. Native
OLYM, NOCA

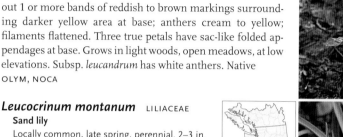

Leucocrinum montanum LILIACEAE
Sand lily
Locally common, late spring, perennial, 2–3 in.
East-side forest

Basal rosette of leaves, no stem. Leaves 6–15, 4–8 in. long, linear, flat, base surrounded by thin dry bracts. Flowers with pleasant scent, 4–8, each with short stalk, white, with 2–3 in. slender tube, 6 lance-shaped 1 in. petals, stamens and styles about ½ the length of petals. Grows on moist low ground in sandy flats, scrub, or forests, at mid elevations. Native

Lilium washingtonianum LILIACEAE
Washington lily
Uncommon, midsummer, perennial, 2–8 ft.
West-side forest

Stem sturdy, erect, unbranched, with large white flowers. Leaves in 1–9 whorls, nearly clasping stem, widely oval, with pointed tip, 2–5 in. long, more or less wavy. Inflorescence very fragrant, consists of few to 25 trumpet-shaped flowers nodding or facing outward, atop stem. Flowers white, sometimes pale lavender on outside, with tiny purple spots on inside, trumpet-shaped, tips slightly curved back. Flowers sometimes fade to pink with age. Grows in dry woods, often through shrubs, at mid to high elevations. Named for Martha Washington, not the state of Washington. Native CRLA

See other *Lilium*: orange, page 298; red, page 313

Lloydia serotina LILIACEAE
Alpine lily
Uncommon, midsummer, perennial, 4–8 in.
Alpine, subalpine

Short ascending plant with more or less upward-facing flowers. Leaves grass-like from base and alternating on stem, somewhat fleshy. Flowers single or few atop stems, open cups about ¾ in. wide, white with rose to purple or green pencil markings. Grows among grasses and sedges in wet meadows and rock ledges in subalpine and alpine areas. Circumboreal. Native OLYM, MORA, NOCA

Maianthemum dilatatum LILIACEAE
False lily of the valley, May lily
Locally common, late spring, perennial, 6–15 in. Moist streambanks, west-side forest

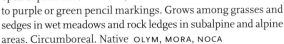

Stems erect, often in clumps from creeping roots. Leaves heart-shaped, to about 8 in. long by 4 in. wide, shiny, with 2–6 in. petioles, blades held more or less horizontally. Flowers fragrant, white, many in cone-shaped cluster topping stem above leaves, unique with parts in fours, not threes or sixes as with rest of lily family. Berries in autumn light green with brown mottling, turning bright red. Grows in moist shady places at low elevations. Native OLYM, MORA, NOCA

Maianthemum racemosum (*Smilacina racemosa*)
LILIACEAE
Large false Solomon's seal
Common, midspring, perennial, 12–37 in.
Coastal, west-side forest

Stem upright, unbranched, usually arched with cluster of flowers at end, showy in flower and berry. Leaves alternate, sessile or clasping stem, oblong, with pointed tips, 3–8 in. long, hairless above. Flowers 20 or more, small, white, in tight panicle 2–5 in. long. Berries green with brown mottling when young, turning bright red with age. Grows in moist places in forests at low to mid elevations. Similar but smaller *M. stellatum* has flowers held in small raceme with 10 or fewer flowers, berries dark blue to reddish black. Native OLYM, MORA, NOCA, CRLA

Maianthemum stellatum (*Smilacina stellata*) LILIACEAE
Star Solomon's seal
Common, late spring, perennial, 1–2 ft.
Coastal, west-side forest, east-side forest

Stem upright, unbranched, arching above middle. Stem straight or may zigzag between leaves. Leaves alternate, sessile or clasping stem, widely oval, with pointed tip. Flowers 12 or fewer, starry-looking, with individual stalks at top. Berries greenish yellow turning blue or black with age. Grows in moist woods, along streams, throughout western North America below 6500 ft. This and large false Solomon's seal, *M. racemosum*, have very similar leaf structure. Native

OLYM, MORA, NOCA, CRLA

Tofieldia glutinosa (*Triantha glutinosa*)
LILIACEAE
Western false asphodel, sticky false asphodel
Locally common, midsummer, perennial,
12–40 in. Bog/fen/wetland, meadow

Stem erect from clump of basal leaves. Stems smooth on bottom, covered with red sticky glands on hairs above. Leaves iris-like, ½ as long as flower stem. Flowers in small dense cluster at top, buds are pinkish or red, open to white flowers with stamens extending beyond petals. Seed in erect, red, fleshy, 3-lobed capsule. Grows in bogs, fens, small streams, wet meadows from valleys to subalpine areas. Subsp. *occidentalis* has fleshy white capsule. Native OLYM, MORA, NOCA, CRLA

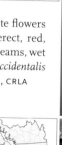
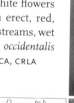

Trillium albidum LILIACEAE
Giant white wakerobin
Locally common, early spring, perennial, 8–28 in. Coastal, meadow, west-side forest

Stem erect, single to large clumps, lower stems bare, sessile leaves at top. Leaves 5–6 in. across, 3–8 in. long, usually lightly mottled with brown. Flowers often rose- or spicy-scented, sessile above leaves. Green sepals, 3 held horizontally, 1–3 in. long. Petals 3, erect to spreading, white to creamy white, sometimes purplish at base, oval, widest just above middle, 2–4 in. long. Grows in moist mixed woods, coniferous forests, in deep loam to 6000 ft. Native

See other *Trillium*: red, page 314

Trillium ovatum LILIACEAE
Western trillium
Common, early spring, perennial, 4–18 in.
Coastal, west-side forest, east-side forest

Stem erect, lower stem bare. Leaves 2–8 in.
long, linear to widely egg-shaped, with
pointed tip. Flowers on 1–2½ in., erect to
weak stalk above leaves. Sepals green, lance-
shaped. Petals ½–3 in. long, oval, with
pointed tip, white fading to pink or deep rose-red. Seed capsule
is a green or white berry. Grows in cool moist mixed woods,
coniferous forests, redwoods, to 6000 ft. Subsp. *oettinger* has
small nodding flowers, linear to lance-shaped leaves with very
short stalks; grows in mixed forests in California's Marble
Mountains. Subsp. *ovatum* has wide sessile leaves, upright
flowers with petals ½–2¾ in. long; grows
from coast to 5000 ft. Native
OLYM, MORA, NOCA, CRLA, **L&C**

Trillium rivale LILIACEAE
Brook wakerobin
Locally common, early spring, perennial,
1½–6 in. Coastal, west-side forest

Stem erect. Leaves on short petioles, plain
or usually marked with silver along veins,
oval, with pointed tips. Flower on stalk above leaves, nodding to
outward-facing, white or pale pink, often with darker markings
or spots. Stem bends with age until white berry-like pod is
touching the ground. Grows in moist areas at edge of mixed
woods, under shrubs, often in rocky serpentine. Native

Triteleia grandiflora var. *howellii*
(*Brodiaea howellii*) LILIACEAE
Bicolor triteleia, Howell's triteleia
Common, late spring, perennial, 1–2 ft.
Coastal, shrub-steppe

Stem erect. Leaves 2–3, narrow, 4–16 in.
long, with ridge down back side. Flowers
5–20 in loose head. Flower is a tube about 1
in. long, 6 lobes with flat edges, white with
blue midveins or blue with darker-colored
midveins that show on back of buds. Anthers broad on flat
filaments all attached at the same level. Grows in grasslands,
open shrublands. Native

See other *Triteleia*: yellow, page 190; blue, page 404

Triteleia hyacinthina (*Brodiaea hyacinthina*) LILIACEAE
White hyacinth, fool's onion
Common, late spring–early summer, perennial,
8–24 in. Coastal, vernal-wet, meadow

Stem erect, topped with white flowers. Leaves few, 8–16 in. long, narrow, with ridge down back. Flower head dense, flowers white sometimes tinted purple outside, tubes bowl-shaped, lobes widely ascending with green midveins, anthers extended, yellow to whitish. Grows in spring-wet grasslands from coast to mid elevations. Native OLYM, MORA, NOCA, CRLA

Veratrum californicum LILIACEAE
California corn lily, California false hellebore
Common, midsummer, perennial, 3–6 ft.
Vernal-wet, meadow, alpine, subalpine

Large erect plant with many large leaves. Emerging plant large with tight clasping point. Leaves alternate, mature to 8–15 in. long, oval, parallel veins with few curly hairs on lower surface. Inflorescence is a dense panicle, flowers on spreading to upward-pointing branches at top. Flowers are small white or greenish white open stars without teeth. Grows in streambanks, moist meadows, sometimes in large patches, at 3200–11,000 ft. Can be confused with *V. viride*, green corn lily, with greenish flowers in a loose panicle with drooping side branches. All *Veratrum* are poisonous to humans and cattle. Native OLYM, MORA, **L&C**

Xerophyllum tenax LILIACEAE
Bear grass
Common, late spring–midsummer, perennial,
1–5 ft. Coastal, meadow, west-side forest,
alpine, subalpine

Erect sturdy flower stems from base of grasslike evergreen leaves. Plant large at bloom, nonflowering leaf clumps for many years. Leaves 1–2 ft. long, narrow, minutely toothed, tough, strong, smaller on stem. Inflorescence tops stout elongating stem somewhat wider in middle, ending with noticeable nipple. Flowers each with separate stalk, white, small, saucer-shaped, with 6 oblong petals opening wide, stamens extending outward. Found in dry openings, on ridges in open conifer forests. Leaves used by Native Americans both historically and currently for basket making, also sold as florist greens. Native OLYM, MORA, CRLA, **L&C**

See other *Veratrum*: green/brown, page 460

69

Zigadenus elegans (Zygadenus elegans)

LILIACEAE

Alpine death camas, glaucous zigadene
Locally common, midsummer, perennial,
1–3 ft. Meadow, alpine, subalpine

Stem erect from basal clump of grass-like leaves. Leaves coated with blue powder, 4–20 in. long, narrow, flat or folded, few along stem reducing in size upward. Inflorescence is open cluster 2–6 in. long at stem top. Flowers cream, with a green V-shaped gland near base of each petal forming circle inside flower, petals about ½ in. long, stamens same length. Grows in wet meadows, bogs, lakeshores, at high elevations. Poisonous. Native OLYM, **L&C**

Zigadenus paniculatus (Zygadenus paniculatus) LILIACEAE

Panicled zigadene, foothill death camas
Uncommon, early spring, perennial, 12–30 in.
East-side forest, shrub-steppe

Stem erect. Leaves mostly basal, 8–20 in. long, less than ½ in. wide, short, edged with stiff hairs. Inflorescence is a branched cluster at top; flowers on main stem bisexual; petals white, unequal, with 3 outer petals shorter than 3 inner, all oval with pointed tips; stamens longer than petals. Flowers on side branches usually male, with stamens only. Grows in dry forests, sagebrush, at mid to high elevations. Poisonous. Native

Zigadenus venenosus (Zygadenus venenosus) LILIACEAE

Meadow death camas
Common, perennial, 6–18 in. Vernal-wet,
meadow

Stem erect, shiny. Basal leaves 4–15 in. long, narrow, edged with stiff hairs. Cream flowers in spike on ascending stalks; petals with narrow base, rounded tip, marked by yellowish rounded gland; stamens longer than petals. Grows in spring-wet meadows, hillsides, at low to high elevations. Poisonous. Var. *gramineus* has stem leaves wrapping around stem. Var. *venenosus* has stem leaves that do not wrap around stem. Some members of the Lewis and Clark expedition became ill from eating this bulb. Native OLYM, MORA, NOCA

Cephalanthera austiniae *(Eburophyton austiniae)* ORCHIDACEAE
Phantom orchid
Rare, early summer, perennial, 8–22 in.
West-side forest

Erect, all white. Stem bare at bottom with white leaf-like bracts 1–2 in. long on petioles along upper stem. Flowers white, 10–20 in leaf axils, petals longer than lip, small yellow patch on lip. Grows in rich forest soils in deep shade only in Pacific Northwest, where it grows in relationship with a single family of fungus that in turn forms association with several species of trees. Able to lie dormant for years between flowerings. Take photographs but don't disturb this rare, endangered plant. Native OLYM, MORA, NOCA

Cypripedium californicum ORCHIDACEAE
California lady's-slipper
Rare, early summer, perennial, 7–45 in.
Coastal, bog/fen/wetland

Stem erect, slippers on upper stem. Stem and lance-shaped alternate leaves hairy. Basal leaves 2–6 in. long, somewhat ribbed, bracts along stem similar, reducing in size upward. Flowers 3–12. Flower with upper erect sepal ½–1 in. long, yellowish green to yellow, 2 lower petals smaller, similar. Pouch white, sometimes lightly spotted with brown or pink. Grows only at edges of streams and rivers, in fens, and on very moist slopes, at low to mid elevations. Native

Cypripedium montanum ORCHIDACEAE
Mountain lady's-slipper
Rare, early summer, perennial, 10–30 in.
West-side forest, east-side forest

Stem erect, with clasping leaves. Leaves alternate, lance-shaped. Flowers 1–3, depending on age of plant, attached above leaf. Flower pouch large, white, with purple veins; petals purple, elongated, twisted; upper and lower purple sepals wider than petals and wavy. Grows in mixed conifer forests in deep humus, sometimes along roads, at low to mid and into high elevations. This and all lady's-slippers need the association of soil fungi and should never be disturbed. Native L&C

See other *Cypripedium*: green/brown, page 461

Goodyera oblongifolia ORCHIDACEAE
Rattlesnake-plantain, rattlesnake orchid
Common, midsummer, perennial, 7–14 in.
West-side forest, east-side forest

Basal rosette of thick leaves, erect flower stem. Leaves sessile, oblong tapering to base, entire, deep green usually with prominent white midvein and smaller white side veins, often white patches, but occasionally entirely plain green. Flower stem with few bracts, flowers held densely at top. Flowers white, tubular, with upper petals and sepals forming hood over lower. Grows in dry conifer forests in leaf compost at low to mid elevations. Leaf rosettes often found without flowers. Native OLYM, MORA, NOCA, CRLA

Piperia elegans (*Habenaria greenei, Platanthera greenei*) ORCHIDACEAE
Elegant rein orchid, Greene's coastal habenaria
Uncommon, early summer, perennial, 12–15 in. Meadow, west-side forest

Basal leaves 2–5, oblong, 2–12 in. long. Flowering stem erect, bare below, with white or pale green flowers on top section. Flowers musky-smelling, not clove-like; long spur on back of flower is parallel to stem. Spur is strap-shaped, to ½ in. long, curved slightly upward at tip. Grows in dry open places in mixed and conifer forests below 1600 ft. Called rein orchid for the strap-shaped spur. *Piperia transversa*, royal rein orchid, also whitish, has straight spur pointing back and across stem, is sweetly clove-scented. Native OLYM, MORA, NOCA

Platanthera dilatata var. *dilatata*
(*Habenaria dilatata*) ORCHIDACEAE
White bog orchid, bog candle
Locally common, midsummer, perennial, 12–45 in. Bog/fen/wetland, meadow, subalpine

Stems stout, erect. Basal and stem leaves lance-shaped, gradually smaller upward. Inflorescence consists of waxy white flowers loosely spaced to crowded with leaves on stem. Flowers spicy-fragrant, to 1 in. across, lower petal very slender at tip and abruptly expanded near base. Spur on back of flower can be longer or shorter than lower petal and straight to slightly curved. Grows in bogs, fens, spongy places, seepages in high mountains. Called bog candle because it is so noticeably sturdy and white. Native OLYM, MORA, NOCA, CRLA

See other *Piperia*: green/brown, page 462
See other *Platanthera*: green/brown, page 462

Platanthera leucostachys (*Habenaria dilatata* var. *leucostachys*) ORCHIDACEAE
Sierra bog orchid
Uncommon, early summer, perennial, 4–40 in.
Coastal, bog/fen/wetland, moist streambanks, west-side forest, east-side forest, alpine, subalpine

Erect plant, leaves along stem. Leaves 2–8 in., larger at base of stem, small leaves among flowers on upper stem. Flowers small, white to cream, crowded along stem, spicy-smelling; lower petal abruptly wider below middle, then narrowing toward tip. Very long spur is elegantly curved at back of flower and pointing downward. Grows in wet places, meadows, along streams, at mid to subalpine elevations. Native OLYM, MORA, NOCA, CRLA

Platanthera orbiculata (*Habenaria orbiculata*, *Lysias orbiculata*) ORCHIDACEAE
Round-leaved bog orchid
Uncommon, midsummer, perennial, 1–2 ft.
Coastal, moist streambanks, meadow, west-side forest, east-side forest

Erect flower stem from 2 large basal leaves. The 2 nearly round leaves are flat on ground, 2–3 in. across, shiny above, silver beneath.
Flowers numerous but not crowded on stem, white to greenish; upper sepal short, rounded; side petals spreading, egg-shaped; lower petal linear to ½ in. long; spur longer than lower petal, often more than 1 in., curved. Grows in moist meadows, forests, along streams. Native NOCA

Spiranthes porrifolia (*Spiranthes romanzoffiana* var. *porrifolia*) ORCHIDACEAE
Western ladies' tresses
Uncommon, early summer, perennial, 6–24 in.
Coastal, bog/fen/wetland, meadow, west-side forest

Stem erect, with dense spike of flowers. Basal leaves several to 6 in., becoming smaller upward. Flowers in dense spiral spike, cream to yellowish; upper sepal and 2 petals fused together forming a cylinder with tips spreading; 2 lower sepals not fused; lower petal bending down, with fine hair on tip; sepals and petals all about the same length. Grows in freshwater marshes, wet meadows, seeps, at low to mid elevations. *Spiranthes* is Greek for "coiled flowers," as all *Spiranthes* blossoms are held in a spiral spike. Differences between this species and *S. romanzoffiana* are subtle; notice the hair on tip of lower petal. Native

Spiranthes romanzoffiana

ORCHIDACEAE
Hooded ladies' tresses
Uncommon, midsummer, perennial, 8–24 in.
Bog/fen/wetland, meadow, west-side forest,
subalpine

Stem erect, with dense spike of flowers. Basal leaves to 5 in. long; stem leaves reduced to bracts. Flowers pure white, in 3 precise rows, twisting as they spiral upward. Flower with upper petals and sepals fused into inflated hood; lower petal violin-shaped, extending down and back toward stem, tip hairless. Grows in wet places, along streams, bogs, marshes, in prairies and meadows, in all elevations to timberline. Native

OLYM, MORA, NOCA, CRLA

Argemone munita   PAPAVERACEAE

Prickly poppy
Locally common, all summer, annual or
perennial, 20–34 in. Shrub-steppe

Stems stout and upright, branched, with long yellow spines. Sap yellow to orange, milky. Leaves sessile, covered with spines on both sides, oblong, 2–6 in. long, irregularly and often deeply divided, lobes with spiny teeth. Flowers at stem tips above bracts covered with upright spines. Flower sepals with appendages have long spines forming horns that are shed before flowering; petals 6, silky, white, 1–2 in. long. Seedpod cylindrical, densely spiny. Grows on sandy and gravelly soils, dry washes. Note that the sap contains several poisonous alkaloids. Rare in Oregon. Native

Meconella oregana (Platystigma oreganum, Platystemon oreganus)

PAPAVERACEAE
White meconella, Oregon meconella
Uncommon, early spring, annual, 1–4 in.
Vernal-wet

Spreading branches, several flowering stems. Plants slender, without hairs. Leaves egg-shaped. Basal leaves with short petioles; stem leaves smaller, sessile. Flowers with very thin stalks, 4–6 petals, white, 4–6 stamens. Seedpod ½–¾ in., linear, often twisted. Grows in open vernal-moist areas with sandy or gravelly soils, often hidden among grasses, at low elevations. Plants complete growth cycle as the vernal seepages dry. Native

Eriogonum compositum
POLYGONACEAE
Heartleaf buckwheat, northern desert buckwheat
Locally common, late spring–early summer, perennial, 8–30 in. Dry rocky sites, shrub-steppe

Clump of large basal leaves, large flat flower head. Leaves to 10 in. long, heart-shaped, on petioles longer than leaves, green above, with dense, white, fuzzy hairs underneath. Flower heads cream or yellow on sturdy 8–20 in. stems, leaf-like bract at joint of stem and flower stalks. Grows in sandy loam, gravelly soils, talus, on cliffs and open rocky slopes, at low to high elevations. Size of leaves and inflorescence can vary greatly with local conditions. Native
MORA, CRLA

Eriogonum elatum   POLYGONACEAE
Tall buckwheat
Locally common, all summer, perennial, 15–45 in. Dry rocky sites, shrub-steppe

Erect clump with upward-pointing basal leaves. Stems branched. Leaves large, lance-shaped, often square at base, with long peti-oles; lower surface slightly hairy; upper surface smooth, sometimes shiny. Inflorescence tops tall stem, small leaf-like bracts at base of long stalk holding small cluster of white to partly red flowers with hairy base. Grows on dry hill-sides, open sagebrush flats in sandy to gravelly soils, at low to high elevations. Native

Eriogonum nudum   POLYGONACEAE
Naked eriogonum, barestem buckwheat
Common, all summer, perennial, 1–5 ft. Dry rocky sites, subalpine

Erect leafless stems, basal leaves. Stems can be very tall, smooth or with few leaves on lower section. Leaves small with long hairy petioles, egg-shaped, widest at tip end, felted with white hairs on underside, sometimes with wavy edges. Inflorescence on long stalks, consisting of widely spaced heads of flowers. Flowers white, yellow, or pink. Often grows in abundant stands in dry open places from near sea level to high elevations. Native

See other *Eriogonum*: yellow, page 191; red, page 316

Eriogonum ovalifolium var. nivale
POLYGONACEAE
Cushion buckwheat
Locally common, midsummer, perennial,
½–2 in. Dry rocky sites, alpine, subalpine

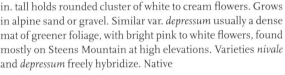

Mats with short flower stems. Tiny round leaves entire, coated with dense white-woolly hairs, in tight round clusters forming crowded mats. Flower stalk less than 2 in. tall holds rounded cluster of white to cream flowers. Grows in alpine sand or gravel. Similar var. *depressum* usually a dense mat of greener foliage, with bright pink to white flowers, found mostly on Steens Mountain at high elevations. Varieties *nivale* and *depressum* freely hybridize. Native
OLYM, MORA, NOCA, CRLA

Eriogonum ovalifolium var. purpureum (*Eriogonum ovalifolium* var. *celsum*) POLYGONACEAE
Cushion buckwheat
Locally common, all summer, perennial, 2–8 in. Dry rocky sites, alpine, subalpine

Dense mats of oval leaves, erect flower stems. Leaves egg-shaped, coated with hairs, entire. Flower stalks upright, 2–8 in. long, topped with head-like clusters of white, creamy yellow, or purplish flowers. Grows on sandy or gravelly soils, usually on east-facing slopes, at mid to high elevations. The name var. *ovalifolium* has been misapplied to this plant. Var. *ovalifolium* is a common plant with similar but usually larger leaves and yellow flowers. Native

Eriogonum pyrolifolium
POLYGONACEAE
Dirty socks, pyrola-leaved eriogonum, alpine buckwheat
Locally common, all summer, perennial, 2–5 in. Dry rocky sites, alpine, subalpine

Tuft of old and new leaves and erect flower stem, single root. Basal leaves greenish yellow, oval to egg-shaped, smooth or hairy above, white-haired below, with brown to green hairy petiole. Flowers in small crowded cluster with 2 linear bracts at base. Petals white or greenish white, aging to red or pink, hairy on outside, with purple anthers, unpleasant-smelling. Grows on sandy or pumice soils in high-elevation subalpine and alpine areas. Var. *pyrolifolium* has hairless foliage and is found on upper slopes of Mount Scott on Crater Lake rim. Native MORA, NOCA, CRLA

Eriogonum strictum POLYGONACEAE
Strict desert buckwheat
Locally common, all summer, perennial, 6–18 in.
Dry rocky sites, shrub-steppe, alpine, subalpine

Mat 4–14 in. across with erect oval leaves. Basal leaves woolly on underside, stalks slender. Flower stem to 16 in., leafless, small leaf-like bract at axils of few flower stalks in wide cluster. Flowers creamy white, yellow, or tinted rose. Grows in rocky places in shrublands, mountains, at low to high elevations. Subsp. *proliferum* (pictured) has white flowers and pointed leaves ½–1½ in. long, white-woolly on both sides, with brownish top surface. Subsp. *strictum* has shorter leaves, more open inflorescence; found in Blue and Wallowa mountains. Native

Polygonum bistortoides POLYGONACEAE
Western bistort, American bistort
Common, all summer, perennial, 1–2 ft.
Meadow, alpine, subalpine

Stem long, erect, unbranched. Leaves mostly basal with long petioles, few small leaves along stem. Flowers white or pinkish in dense thick spike. Flowers with 5 lobes fused only at base, 8 stamens sticking out beyond, giving the plant a rather fuzzy look. Grows in wet meadows, edges of streams, at high elevations and on subalpine slopes where it can form large stands, usually mixed with other wildflowers. Native
OLYM, MORA, NOCA, CRLA, **L&C**

Polygonum cuspidatum POLYGONACEAE
Japanese knotweed
Common, all summer, perennial, 3–8 ft.
Bog/fen/wetland, disturbed

Dense mat with freely branched stems from spreading rhizomes. Male, female flowers on separate plants. Leaves on stem, 4–8 in. long, with shorter petioles, egg-shaped to round, often wider than long, sharply pointed tip. Inflorescence widely branched, 6 in. Flower stalks among leaves on upper stem, lengthening with age. Flowers white, 5-lobed. Grows on wet ground, disturbed places, at low to mid elevations. *Polygonum bohemicum* (pictured) is a newly identified hybrid between *P. cuspidatum* and *P. sachalinense*, giant knotweed, which is erect and 6–9 ft. tall. Differences among the 3 are primarily the size and shape of leaves. All are considered noxious weeds and will crowd out native vegetation. Nonnative OLYM, MORA, NOCA

See other *Polygonum*: yellow, page 193; red, page 317

Polygonum douglasii POLYGONACEAE
Douglas's knotweed
Common, all summer, annual, 8–16 in.
Meadow, shrub-steppe, alpine, subalpine

Erect hairless annual, long upright branches
angled just below joints. Stem covering at
joints raggedly torn at tip. Leaves long and
narrow to oval, never round. Flowers 1–4
per node, with short stalks; petals reflexed
in fruit, small, green or pink, with red or white edges. Some
flowers never open; others open wide. Plants on serpentine
lose leaves before flowering, others just after flowering. Grows
in open dry meadows, slopes, at mid to high elevations. Subsp.
majus (pictured) flowers open wider than those of the species.
Subsp. *spergulariiforme* is erect, with leaves that fall before flowering, and grows in rocky places such as ser-
pentine. Subsp. *johnstonii* is erect, with
leaves that persist through flowering, and
grows into subalpine areas. Native
OLYM, MORA, NOCA, CRLA

Polygonum lapathifolium (*Persicaria*
incarnata) POLYGONACEAE

Willow smartweed, dockleaf smartweed
Locally common, all summer, annual, 8–32 in.
Bog/fen/wetland, moist streambanks, disturbed, meadow
More or less upright, branched, willowy-looking. Leaves lance-
shaped, petiole with plain brown shiny appendage at base.
Inflorescence on gland-coated stalks, drooping spikes of white,
pink, most often greenish flowers that remain closed. Grows in
moist soils, meadows, swamps, roadsides, at low to mid elevations. Native OLYM, MORA

Polygonum minimum
POLYGONACEAE
Broadleaf knotweed
Common, all summer, annual, to 12 in.
West-side forest, east-side forest, alpine,
subalpine

Stems ascending, red, branched to 12 in.
long, more or less angled at the joints in
zigzag fashion. Leaves broadly oval to round, with very short
or no stalks. Most leaves congested near ends of stems, few
evenly spaced below, persisting throughout season. Flowers
white, pink, solitary on short stalks at joints on stems. Grows in
meadows, open rocky places, at low to high elevations. Native
OLYM, MORA, NOCA, CRLA

Polygonum paronychia POLYGONACEAE
Beach knotweed
Locally common, all spring and summer,
perennial, 1–3 ft. Coastal

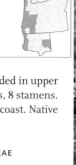

Prostrate to upright, low, shrub-like perennial
with woody base. Sessile leaves dense at stem
tips with noticeable joint to frayed stem covering. Leaves narrow, oblong, with edges rolled
under, ½–1½ in. long. Underside of leaf mid-
vein is finely toothed. White to pink flowers crowded in upper
leaf axils consist of 5 lance-shaped petal-like lobes, 8 stamens.
Grows on dunes and in other sandy places along coast. Native
OLYM

Polygonum phytolaccifolium POLYGONACEAE
Alpine knotweed
Locally common, all summer, perennial, 20–40
in. Meadow, alpine, subalpine

Stems erect, stout. Leaves hairless, 4–10 in.
long, with wide bases or heart-shaped tapering
to a sharp tip. Flowers in loose, nearly leafless,
branched inflorescence, white to greenish
white. Grows in seasonally moist meadows,
near subalpine or alpine springs, rocky places,
at high elevations. Native NOCA

Polygonum shastense POLYGONACEAE
Shasta knotweed
Uncommon, midsummer, perennial, 6–12 in.
Alpine, subalpine

Prostrate to upright from woody stems with many branches.
Leaves flat, becoming twisted when older, oblong to widely oblong, with pointed to rounded
tip, hairless on both sides. Flowers consist of
2–3 in. clusters with leaves along upper
branches. Calyx red with darker midvein, 8 stamens, style with 3 lobes. Grows in rocky
slopes, gravelly places in mountains. Native
CRLA

Sparganium natans (*Sparganium minimum*) SPARGANIACEAE

Small bur-reed

Locally common, all spring and summer, perennial, floating. Lake/pond

Rooted in sediment. Leaves dark green, long, narrow, limp, with ends often floating across water surface. Flowers above water on stem, 2–3 female flower heads, each about ⅓ in. across when mature, topped by 1 male round flower head. Female flowers bur-like in fruit. Grows in shallow water to 2 ft. deep at low to high elevations. Other common bur-reeds are *S. emersum*, with single male flower head separated from others, and *S. eurycarpum*, with stiff leaves and flower stems arising from water. Native MORA, NOCA, CRLA

Arabidopsis thaliana BRASSICACEAE

Thale cress, mouse-ear cress

Common, all spring, annual, 4–16 in. Disturbed

Stem erect, branched. Leaves mostly basal, few on stems, lance-shaped, with few teeth or entire, few branched hairs. Flowers small, on expanding stem top, 4 white petals. Seedpods linear, erect, ⅓–½ in. long, slightly rounded to flat. Many seeds in single row inside pod. Common in disturbed areas and around universities where it is used for genetic research. This has become a model plant for genetic research because of its 6-week life cycle and large quantity of seed. The studies are providing information about all plants, how they develop, reproduce, and respond to stress and disease. Nonnative OLYM, NOCA

Arabis drummondii BRASSICACEAE

Drummond's rockcress

Locally common, all spring, biennial or perennial, 4–35 in. Alpine, subalpine

Stems erect, branched or unbranched. Leaves mostly basal, 1–3 in. with petioles, lance-shaped, with sharp tip, sparsely toothed to entire; upper leaves clasping stem, ½–2 in. long. Flowers white or pink. Seedpods erect, with rounded tip, crowded, 2–4 in. long, hairless. Grows in open areas on gravel or talus at mid to alpine elevations. The few interesting hairs on basal leaves are U-shaped and attached at center. Similar *A. furcata*, with no petioles on lower leaves, has smaller sessile upper leaves, similar white flowers; grows in rocky places at low elevations. Native OLYM, MORA, NOCA

See other *Arabis*: red, page 320

Arabis holboellii BRASSICACEAE
Holboell's rockcress
Common, all summer, biennial or perennial,
6–36 in. Dry rocky sites

Stems erect, stout. Basal leaves ½–2 in. long,
linear to spoon-shaped, toothed, with pointed
tip, dense with hairs; stem leaves linear, entire,
hairy on underside, clasping. Flower petals
white to purplish pink. Seedpods straight or
curved, pointing downward from curved stalk, close to or
pressed against stem. Grows in rocky soils on open sites at mid
to alpine elevations. Var. *retrofracta* has straight seedpods on
reflexed stalks and very small leaf hairs. Var. *pinetorum* has
curved seedpods on arched stalks and dense leaf hairs. Similar
A. *puberula* has gray stems with fine dense hairs; gray, often
toothed or lobed leaves, basal leaves up to 1¼
in. and oblong, stem leaves crowded and clasping; seedpods hanging but not pressed against
stem, 1–1½ in. long, with rounded tips; grows
in rocky places among sagebrush and juniper
at mid to high elevations. Native
OLYM, MORA, NOCA

Capsella bursa-pastoris BRASSICACEAE
Shepherd's purse
Common, all spring and summer, annual, 4–20 in. Coastal,
disturbed, meadow, alpine, subalpine
Rosette of leaves with straight erect stems. Stems unbranched
or branched. Leaves with 1–2 in. petioles, lance-shaped, slightly
toothed to pinnately lobed. Flowers small, white, with green or
reddish calyx, clustered at top of elongating stems. Seedpods
present with flowers, on stalks spreading outward from stem, heart-shaped to triangular,
flat. Grows on disturbed soils from coastline to
alpine. Widespread in North America. Nonnative OLYM, MORA, NOCA

Cardamine angulata BRASSICACEAE
Angled bittercress
Locally common, late spring, perennial, 1–2 ft.
Moist streambanks, west-side forest
Erect unbranched stems, hairless or with few hairs. Leaves
mostly on stems with long petioles, palmately divided, 3 egg- to
lance-shaped leaflets to 3 in. long, widely toothed or lobed.
Flowers clustered at stem top, petals ⅓–½ in. long, white or
pale pink. Seedpods flat, linear, ½–1½ in. long, erect on ascending stalks. Grows in shady, shrubby, or deep forests, along
streams to high elevations. Native OLYM, MORA

See other *Cardamine*: red, page 322

Cardamine breweri   BRASSICACEAE
Brewer's bittercress
Common, all spring and summer, perennial,
6–24 in. Bog/fen/wetland, moist
streambanks, meadow, west-side forest

One to few decumbent or erect stems.
Leaves somewhat fleshy, divided, 3–5 heart-
shaped leaflets with wavy to shallowly lobed
edges, terminal leaflet larger than others.
Small flowers at tips of stalks. Seedpods long, upward-pointing. Grows in wet sites, along forest streams, springs. Native
OLYM, MORA

Cardamine cordifolia   BRASSICACEAE
Large mountain bittercress
Locally common, late spring, perennial,
8–24 in. Moist streambanks, meadow,
alpine

Upright. Stem leaves from base to inflorescence, few basal. Leaves nearly round, 1–4
in., fleshy, with shallow rounded teeth.
Lower leaves with short petioles. Inflorescence without bracts. Flower petals white,
¼–½ in., egg-shaped or oval, narrowing to
long and thin near base. Seedpods erect,
straight, ¾–1½ in. long. Grows in streambanks, alpine meadows. Var. *lyallii* has smaller flowers, petals about ½ in. long,
and grows throughout the range. Native NOCA

Cardamine hirsuta   BRASSICACEAE
Hairy bittercress
Locally common, early spring–midsummer,
annual, 5–12 in. Vernal-wet, disturbed

Erect succulent stem with many branches.
Stem hairless, leafy below inflorescence.
Basal leaves few to none; stem leaves many,
with 3–11 pairs of oblong leaflets, the top
leaflet larger, entire or toothed. Flowers
white, with 4 stamens. Seedpods pointing
upward, slender, hairless. Common weed
often in bloom from January to May in
lawns, roads, ditches. *Cardamine occidentalis* is similar but no
basal rosette and several leaves on stems. Flower petals large, to
¼ in. *Cardamine pensylvanica* also has no basal rosette; stem
leaves have 5–11 widely elliptic leaflets. Native look-alike *C.
oligosperma* has 6 stamens and is now less common, particularly in urban areas. Nonnative

Cardaria draba (Lepidium draba)
BRASSICACEAE
Whitetop, hoary cress, heart-podded hoarycress
Locally common, all spring and summer,
perennial, 1–2 ft. Disturbed, meadow

Erect stem with clasping leaves. Roots from
spreading rhizomes, forming dense patches.
Stems hairy below, hairless above, divided in
inflorescence. Leaves 1–2 in. long, widely
lance- to egg-shaped. Basal leaves with short petioles, entire or
toothed; upper leaves clasping stem, with base lobes wrapped
somewhat around stem. Flowers on expanding upper stems, 4
petals white. Seedpods heart-shaped, hairless, on short stalks.
Grows on disturbed, often salty soils. Native to Eurasia, a noxious weed here, particularly on agricultural land. Nonnative
OLYM, NOCA

Draba verna BRASSICACEAE
Spring draba, common draba, spring whitlowgrass
Common, early spring, annual, 2–6 in.
Disturbed, meadow

Rosette of leaves with upright, leafless, hairless
stems. Leaves widely lance- to spoon-shaped,
1–1½ in., hairy. Flowers in clusters at end of
branched elongating stems, petals white, each deeply divided
into 2 lobes. Seedpods egg-shaped, to 1/3 in. long, hairless.
Grows in disturbed soils, open areas throughout Pacific Northwest, at mid elevations. A tiny plant most often seen in large
patches. Nonnative OLYM, MORA, NOCA

Idahoa scapigera BRASSICACEAE
Scale pod
Uncommon, early spring, annual, 2–4 in.
Vernal-wet, meadow

Rosette with long, leafless, shiny stems. Leaves
numerous with petioles, egg-shaped, entire or
with few lobes, ½–2 in. Flower stems 1–5 in.
tall, numerous, each with single tiny flower.
Flowers with reddish or purplish calyx, white
petals. Seedpods nearly flat and distinctively
round to egg-shaped, entire. Grows in moist meadows,
foothills, at low to mid elevations. Found from California to
British Columbia and east to Montana. Noticed for its most distinctive pod and named for the state of Idaho. Native

See other *Draba*: yellow, page 195

83

4 petals

Lepidium campestre BRASSICACEAE
Field peppergrass, poorman's peppergrass
Common, late spring–early summer, annual
or biennial, 8–16 in. Disturbed, meadow

Erect, with basal rosette, densely hairy. Stem branched at top, leafy. Leaves in rosette with stalks 2–3 in. long, blade widely oval, entire or with toothed lobes on outer section of leaf. Stem leaves sessile or clasping, with lobes wrapped partway around stem. Flowers small, with narrow white petals, yellow anthers. Seedpod oval, concave on flattened side, notched with pointed style at top, flattened outer edge. Grows in disturbed places, fields, roadsides, at mid elevations. Similar *L. perfoliatum* has upper leaves oval to round, with tiny teeth, completely surrounding stem; flowers yellowish, with tiny petals; seedpods on short stalks, tips notched, forming below as flowering continues. Nonnative OLYM, MORA

Rorippa nasturtium-aquaticum
BRASSICACEAE
White watercress
Common, all year long, perennial, floating
Bog/fen/wetland, lake/pond

Floating or prostrate in mud. Stems succulent, 1 to many, 4–25 in. long, rooting at nodes. Leaves pinnately divided; leaflets 3–7, oval to egg-shaped, entire to wavy-edged. Flowers small in terminal clusters, white. Seedpods ½ in. thin cylinder, straight to curving upward. Grows in slow-moving fresh water, marshes, edges of lakes, at elevations below treeline worldwide. Grown commercially for salad greens. Native OLYM

Smelowskia calycina var. americana
(*Hutchinsia calycina* var. *americana*)
BRASSICACEAE
Alpine smelowskia, American false candytuft
Rare, all summer, perennial, 2–8 in. Alpine

Cushion of leaves with few erect flower stems. Plant covered with white hairs. Leaves soft and pliable, oval, pinnately divided, mostly basal with petioles, also few sessile leaves scattered on stems. Inflorescence is dense at stem top. Flowers small, sepals pinkish or purplish pink, petals spoon-shaped, white or tinted purple. Seedpods egg-shaped, to ½ in., held pointing upward. Grows on ridges and slopes high in the alpine at 6000–10,000 ft. Very similar *S. ovalis* has smaller petals and seedpods, lacks hairs on petioles. Native OLYM, MORA

84

See other *Rorippa*: yellow, page 198

Smelowskia ovalis BRASSICACEAE
Alpine false candytuft, small-fruit Smelowskia, Lassen Peak smelowskia
Rare, midsummer, perennial, less than 6 in.
Alpine

Cushion small, leaves and stems densely coated with white hairs. Basal leaves divided pinnately, segments entire or toothed, petioles hairless. Stems with few leaves topped with flowers. Flowers composed of 4 small spoon-shaped petals held in a cup of 4 shorter hairy sepals. Seedpod egg-shaped, less than 1/5 in. long. Grows in rocky places in alpine. Highest-growing plant on Mount Rainier. Very similar to *S. calycina* var. *americana*, which is larger, with hairs on the petioles. Native
MORA, NOCA

Thelypodium laciniatum BRASSICACEAE
Thick-leaf thelypody
Uncommon, early summer, biennial, 1–6 ft.
Dry rocky sites, shrub-steppe

Stems erect, thick, with many erect branches. Leaves in basal rosette and lower stem leaves are short-petioled, thickish, divided pinnately, and drop by flowering. Upper leaves toothed to entire, pointed at tip. Flowers are dense on upper branches, petals linear, white or purplish, wrinkled. Seedpods flat, spreading outward from stem on straight stalks, 1–4 in. long, narrowed between seeds. Grows in basalt cliffs, rocky hills, at low to mid elevations. Native

Thlaspi arvense BRASSICACEAE
Field pennycress
Common, all summer, annual, 6–24 in.
Disturbed, meadow

Erect stems with numerous branches or unbranched. Few basal leaves with short petioles, narrowly oval, shedding before bloom time; stem leaves clasping, toothed or wavy-edged. Flowers small and white atop stems. Seedpods ascending, round to widely oval, less than 3/4 in. across, flat, with papery edges and notched tip. Grows in disturbed soils along roads, fields, at low to mid elevations. Nonnative OLYM, MORA, **L&C**

Thlaspi montanum var. *montanum*
(*Thlaspi fendleri*) BRASSICACEAE
Fendler's pennycress, mountain pennycress
Uncommon, late spring–early summer,
perennial, 4–12 in. West-side forest, alpine,
subalpine

Cushion. Stems upright, hairless, rarely
branched. Leaves oblong, green or purplish.
Basal leaves many, 1/3–1 in. long, entire,
with petioles; stem leaves becoming smaller upward, shallowly
toothed, clasping stem. Flowers numerous in 1–3 in. head, with
white to pinkish purple, spoon-shaped petals. Seedpods flat,
circular, with tip notched; stalk 1–2 times longer than seedpod.
Grows on talus, alluvial slopes, grassy spots, below 7000 ft. Native OLYM, MORA

Thysanocarpus curvipes
BRASSICACEAE
Fringe pod, lace pod
Common, all spring, annual, 6–18 in.
Vernal-wet, meadow

Erect, with slender stem. Stem may be
branched, hairs on lower section. Leaves
lance-shaped. Basal and lower stem leaves
1/2–2 in. long, toothed or shallowly lobed;
upper leaves sessile or clasping stem, often arrow-shaped,
toothed or entire. Flowers small, petals white to purplish, narrow. Seedpods with single seed in center, more or less round, to
1/3 in. across, hanging from curved stalks, margins around flattened seed with thick radiating spokes. Grows in meadows and
washes below 6000 ft. Native OLYM

Cornus nuttallii CORNACEAE
Pacific dogwood
Common, late spring–early summer, perennial, 10–50 ft. Coastal, west-side forest
Deciduous shrub or tree with dark brownish black or reddish slightly hairy bark.
Small branches are gray to green. Leaves opposite, deep green, 1 1/2–4 in., with curving
parallel veins, oval, pointed on tip, underside slightly hairy and lighter in color. Inflorescence consists
of 4–7 petal-like bracts, pointed at the tip, white or pinkish, 2–3
in. long; center of small flowers greenish to white. Fruit is a
bright red, round cluster of oval fleshy berries, each with 1
smooth seed. Grows in shaded moist places in Puget Lowlands
and forests. Often seen reblooming in early fall when leaves
turn red. Provincial flower of British Columbia. Native
OLYM, MORA, NOCA, CRLA, **L&C**

Cornus sericea (Cornus stolonifera)
CORNACEAE
Red-osier dogwood
Common, late spring–early summer, perennial, 6–18 ft. Coastal, bog/fen/wetland, west-side forest, alpine, subalpine

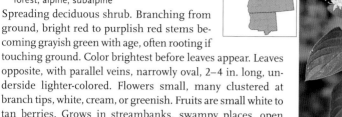

Spreading deciduous shrub. Branching from ground, bright red to purplish red stems becoming grayish green with age, often rooting if touching ground. Color brightest before leaves appear. Leaves opposite, with parallel veins, narrowly oval, 2–4 in. long, underside lighter-colored. Flowers small, many clustered at branch tips, white, cream, or greenish. Fruits are small white to tan berries. Grows in streambanks, swampy places, open meadows, at low to subalpine elevations. Subsp. *occidentalis* is rough, hairy. Subsp. *sericea* is hairless or has few long hairs but is not rough. Flower petals very small. Native OLYM, MORA, NOCA, CRLA

Cornus unalaschkensis (Cornus canadensis, Chamaepericlymenum unalaschkense)
CORNACEAE
Bunchberry, dwarf dogwood, western cordilleran bunchberry
Common, late spring–early summer, perennial, 4–8 in. Bog/fen/wetland, west-side forest

Trailing or ascending stems from rhizomes, less than 8 in. tall, evergreen leaves turning red in winter or sometimes deciduous. Leaves 4–6 in whorl with short petioles. Above leaves is a single head of 4 whitish petal-like bracts with small flowers in center. Fruit is a tight bunch of red berries, each with 1 pit. Most common of dwarf dogwoods, bunchberry grows in deep duff of moist forests or bogs throughout western mountains. *Cornus canadensis* is a very similar eastern species; the name has been frequently misapplied in the Northwest. Native OLYM, MORA, NOCA, CRLA, **L&C**

Corydalis caseana FUMARIACEAE
Sierra corydalis
Uncommon, midsummer, perennial, 2–3 ft.
Moist streambanks, east-side forest

Upright, with blue-green waxy powder on leaves and stems. Leaves pinnately divided into many short oval lobes. Flower spikes crowded with many flowers. Flowers white or pink with purple tip; spur ½–⅔ in. long from point of stalk attachment. Grows in damp, shady places, mostly along streams, at mid elevations. Native

See other *Corydalis*: yellow, page 201; red, page 323

4 petals

Dicentra cucullaria FUMARIACEAE
Dutchman's breeches
Uncommon, late spring, perennial, 6–18 in.
West-side forest, east-side forest

Upright. Flower stems without leaves. Leaves arise from ground with long slender petioles, pinnately divided into 3 lobes, divided 2 more times into long thin segments. Flowers pendulous, with 2 large spurs pointing upward, white to pale pink, hanging from 1 side of stems, which are taller than leaves. Grows in moist shaded places in woods and on gravelly banks, including Columbia River. Native

Dicentra formosa subsp. *oregona* FUMARIACEAE
Oregon bleeding heart
Endemic, midspring, perennial, 6–12 in.
West-side forest

Spreading and upright stems and leaves from large, reddish, fleshy roots. Plant is bluish or tinted reddish with bluish waxy powder on both sides. Leaves 8–20 in. long with long petioles, divided into odd number of oblong segments. Inflorescence on long stalk, cluster of nodding flowers just above the foliage. Flowers cream with rose inner petal tips. Grows in sunny to shaded rocky places, usually on serpentine. Native

Abronia mellifera NYCTAGINACEAE
White sand verbena
Locally common, all summer, perennial, 6–16 in.
Shrub-steppe

Mat. Stems sprawling to erect, hairless or with stemmed glands. Leaves 2–4 in. with petioles, oval to round, entire. Flowers clustered in head atop 3–6 in. stalk. Flowers many, fragrant, white to greenish; ¾ in. long tube of 5 fused petals opens flat, each flower ¼–½ in. across. Grows in sandy soils at 200–5000 ft. Native

See other *Dicentra*: red, page 323
See other *Abronia*: yellow, page 201; red, page 325

Circaea alpina ONAGRACEAE
Enchanter's nightshade
Locally common, late spring–early summer,
perennial, 5–14 in. Moist streambanks, west-
side forest

Stems erect, with numerous leaves. Leaves opposite, with winged petioles, 1–2½ in. long,
heart-shaped, with pointed tips, slightly
toothed, with short hairs on underside. Flower
stalk erect, leafless, densely coated with glands and hairs, cluster of 8–12 flowers at top. Flowers tiny, white, with 2 reflexed
sepals, 2 upright deeply notched petals. Grows in damp soils
along streams, in forests and other cool places, at low to mid elevations. Although the species name is *alpina* this plant is not
found in alpine habitat. Native OLYM, MORA, NOCA

Epilobium ciliatum subsp. ciliatum
(*Epilobium adenocaulon*) ONAGRACEAE
Common willowherb
Common, all spring and summer, perennial,
1–6 ft. Bog/fen/wetland, moist streambanks,
disturbed, meadow

Erect stems in loose clump from basal rosette
of leaves. Lance-shaped toothed leaves with
conspicuous veins on short petioles. Inflorescence glandular, consisting of many branches with small opposite leaves, leafy bracts at base of flower stalks. Flowers pale
pink to white, petals up to ⅓ in. long. Abundant in moist
meadows, streambanks, roadsides, disturbed sites, at low to
mid elevations. A widely variable species, the taxonomy of this
and very similar subsp. *watsonii* and subsp. *glandulosum* is
difficult and confusing. Native

Gayophytum diffusum (*Gayophytum nuttallii, Gayophytum humile*)
ONAGRACEAE
Spreading groundsmoke
Common, midsummer, annual, 4–20 in.
Disturbed, east-side forest, shrub-steppe

Erect stem often has many branches. Leaves
narrow, to 2 in. long, becoming much smaller
toward top. Flower petals small, white with yellow or greenish
spot at base with long stamens, fading to reddish. Seed capsule
constricted between seeds. Grows in open mountain forests,
sagebrush-steppe. Several other species of *Gayophytum* are in
our area, all small and difficult to distinguish. Native
NOCA, CRLA

See other *Epilobium*: yellow, page 203; red, page 328

Oenothera caespitosa ONAGRACEAE
Stemless evening primrose, fragrant evening primrose, tufted evening primrose
Uncommon, late spring–early summer, perennial, 3–9 in. Disturbed, east-side forest, shrub-steppe

Flat rosette of leaves, spreading flower stems. Leaves linear to narrowly oval, irregularly toothed or lobed, central vein and short petiole often tinted red. Flowers showy, white, petals to 2 in. long and wide, deeply divided at tip giving petal the appearance of a heart. Flowers open after sunset, stay open until bright morning sun, turn red with age. Flowers lack stalks, ovary attached directly to roots. Seed capsules persist many years at base under leaves. Grows in sagebrush-steppe, talus slopes, pine forests, at low to high elevations. Rare in Washington. Native **L&C**

Oenothera pallida ONAGRACEAE
Pale-stemmed evening primrose
Uncommon, all summer, biennial or perennial, 6–24 in. Shrub-steppe

Stem erect, whitish, branched, with reddish cast toward base. Leaves with short stalks, linear to narrow, lance-shaped, less than 2 in. long. Leaves near base are smaller than those further up stem. Flowers fragrant, white, opening in evening among leaves on upper part of stems, turning pink the second day as they wither. Seedpods somewhat contorted. Grows on sand dunes and sandy soils, generally at low elevations. Native

Galium aparine RUBIACEAE
Cleavers, goose grass
Locally common, all spring and summer, annual, 8–40 in. Meadow, west-side forest, east-side forest

Climbing to erect or sprawling. Stems 4-angled when young, brittle. Leaves in whorls of 6–8, round to oval, ½–1¼ in. long, with tiny, long, sharp point at rounded tip. Leaves have hooked bristles pointing back toward the plant. Flowers white to greenish on spreading stalks clustered in most leaf axils. Seed 2 sessile nutlets covered with hooked bristles. Grows in dry to moist forests, partly shaded areas along beaches, in fields, as a weed in gardens. The name *cleavers* means "to cling," in this case by hooked hairs on both leaves and seeds. Native OLYM, MORA, NOCA, CRLA

See other *Oenothera*: yellow, page 203
See other *Galium*: yellow, page 204

Galium boreale RUBIACEAE
Northern bedstraw
Common, late spring–early summer, perennial,
8–16 in. Coastal, bog/fen/wetland, meadow,
west-side forest, east-side forest

Upright stem with whorls of 4 leaves, plant
sticky to touch. Leaves somewhat leathery,
½–1½ in. long, narrow to lance-shaped, blunt
tips. Inflorescence dense with many clusters
of numerous cream flowers. Flower bisexual, with 4 petals,
later 2 nutlets side by side, covered with unhooked but curved
hairs or hairless. Grows in wet places to moist meadows, forest
edges, rocky slopes, from coastline to mid elevations. Native
OLYM, NOCA

Galium oreganum RUBIACEAE
Oregon bedstraw
Locally common, all summer, perennial, 8–12 in.
Coastal, west-side forest

Erect stem with whorls of 4 broadly egg-shaped
leaves. Leaf 1–2 in. long, smooth, with 3 main
veins. Inflorescence atop stem in loose cluster
of few greenish or yellowish white flowers.
Flower has 4 lobes. Each flower produces 2
nutlets covered with long hooked hairs. Grows
in open conifer forests into mid elevations. All bedstraws that
have hooked hairs on nutlets are spread by passing animals;
nutlets often stick to clothing, so humans also help with prop-
agation. Native OLYM, MORA, NOCA, CRLA

Galium serpenticum RUBIACEAE
**Many-flowered bedstraw, intermountain
bedstraw**
Locally common, all summer, perennial, 6–15 in.
Meadow, west-side forest, east-side forest

Cluster of branching hairless stems from
woody base. Leaves lance-shaped in whorls of
4. Small clusters of greenish yellow to whitish
flowers at ends of branches and stems. Fruit is
a nutlet with long, straight hairs. Grows in dry
slopes, meadows, open pine forests, rocky
banks, at mid to high elevations. Native

Galium trifidum RUBIACEAE
Small bedstraw
Locally common, all summer, perennial,
4–20 in. Coastal, bog/fen/wetland, moist
streambanks, west-side forest

Sprawling or tangled, weak-stemmed.
Stems 4–25 in. long. Stems and leaves covered with sandpaper-like bristles. Leaves narrow, in whorls of 4–6. Flower clusters of 1–3 flowers are held on ends of short side stems with whorls of leaves. Flowers 3-lobed, white or pink. Seed nutlets smooth. Grows to high elevations in bogs, ditches, edges of streams, on both fresh- and saltwater beaches. Similar *G. bifolium* has a single 3-lobed flower per stalk, stalks in pairs in elongating cluster. Leaves 2–4 in whorl. There are many other galiums in our region not included here. Most are sprawling and hard to tell apart without a technical manual. Native OLYM, MORA, NOCA, CRLA

Astragalus canadensis var. mortonii
FABACEAE
Morton's locoweed
Uncommon, all summer, perennial, 12–32
in. East-side forest, shrub-steppe

Numerous erect to decumbent stems. Leaves 3–5 in. long, with pinnately separated leaflets 13–21, oblong, rounded tips, slightly hairy on underside. Flower stalks stout, 1–8 in. long, calyx bears straight black and white hairs. Flowers to 150 in dense 2–6 in. raceme, creamy white, keel usually purplish-tipped. Seedpod sessile, erect, oblong, 1/3–3/4 in. long. Grows in open forests. Similar var. *brevidens* has calyx densely covered with short soft hairs. Native

Astragalus cottonii (Astragalus australis
var. *olympicus*) FABACEAE
Olympic Mountain milkvetch
Endemic, all summer, perennial, 4–20 in.
Alpine, subalpine

Upright to scrambling. Stems gray, hairy, spreading from taproot. Leaves divided, 11–17 oblong leaflets, each to ½ in. long, densely coated with long soft hairs on both sides. Flower stalk 1–2 in. long, with 8–15 flowers, mixed black and white hairs on calyx, greenish white- and purple-veined petals. Seedpods (pictured) shiny, fat, nearly 1 in. long with pointed tip, not mottled with color. Endemic to Olympic Mountains on talus slopes. Native OLYM

See other *Astragalus*: yellow, page 205; blue, page 407

Astragalus hoodianus FABACEAE
Hood River milkvetch
Locally common, late spring–early summer,
perennial, 1–2 ft. Meadows, shrub-steppe

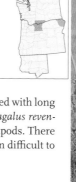

Erect stem 1–2 ft. tall, entire plant luminous
with shiny stiff hairs. Leaves upright from near
base with 11–15 leaflets. Flower stalk sturdy,
8–12 in., flower head 2–3 in. long, with many
creamy white to white flowers. Calyx coated
with white hairs. Seedpods leathery, oblong, covered with long
fine hair. Grows in dry hillsides, savannas. *Astragalus reven-
tiformis* differs, with black calyx hair, hairless seedpods. There
are many *Astragalus* species east of Cascades, often difficult to
tell apart even with a technical manual. Native

Astragalus lentiginosus FABACEAE
Freckled milkvetch, mottled locoweed
Common, all summer, perennial, 4–16 in.
East-side forest, shrub-steppe

Stems prostrate to ascending, hairless or coated
with silver hairs. Leaves linear to widely oval,
divided into 19 oval leaflets. Flowers 3–50 clustered on upright stalk. Flower petals white to
cream or tinted purplish, the colors sometimes
mixed. Seedpods straight, papery to leathery,
hairless or covered with short hairs, strongly inflated, with flattened tip curved upward. Grows in dry open places at low to
mid elevations. This widespread species is variable, with 4 subspecies in Oregon and Washington. Native

Astragalus reventiformis FABACEAE
Yakima milkvetch
Locally common, late spring–early summer,
perennial, 8–15 in. Shrub-steppe

Spreading, with numerous stems 8–15 in.
Leaves erect to spreading, with many oblong to
linear leaflets. Leaflets to ½ in. long, covered
with ash-colored rigid hairs beneath or on both
sides. Flower stalks erect, about 8 in. tall, with
a loose head 2–3 in. long, cream to white flowers. Calyx has black hairs. Seedpod oblong,
without hairs. Grows in dry areas, sagebrush deserts, grassy
hills, stony hilltops. Much like *A. hoodianus*, which has white
hair on calyx and seedpods with long hairs. *Astragalus sclero-
carpus* is somewhat more sprawling, has black hairs on seedpods, which are curved like a crescent moon when dry; grows
on sand along both sides of Columbia River upstream from
The Dalles. Native

Astragalus speirocarpus FABACEAE
Medick milkvetch, spiral-pod rattle-weed, curvepod milkvetch
Uncommon, early spring, perennial, 8–12 in. Shrub-steppe

Spreading from root with many branches, coated with gray, stiff, straight, sharp hairs pressed to surface. Leaves 2–3 in. long, divided into 9–17 linear to oblong leaflets with indented or rounded tips. Flower stems shorter than leaves, flowers on upper stem spreading outward and upward, petals cream to lavender or tinted bluish. Seedpods spirally coiled, pointed at both top and stout tip. Grows in dry plains, sagebrush deserts. Native

Astragalus succumbens FABACEAE
Columbia milkvetch, sprawling rattle-weed, crouching locoweed
Locally common, late spring–early summer, perennial, 4–10 in. Shrub-steppe

Spreading perennial of lax stems. Plant covered with very short, weak hairs. Stems lie out from erect central stem or point downward. Leaves 1–3 in. long. Leaflets egg-shaped to almost round, to ½ in. long. Flower head large, crowded with cream flowers often tinted rose toward base. Wing petals longer than top petal. Grows in rocky or sandy soils in dry areas. Native

Astragalus umbraticus FABACEAE
Bald Mountain milkvetch
Uncommon, midspring, perennial, 8–20 in. West-side forest

Ascending perennial with spreading branches, more or less hairless. Leaves 2–5 in. long, divided into 11–23 oblong leaflets with rounded, notched tips. Flowers 10–25, spreading outward from stem; petals greenish white. Seedpod curved, papery firm but not bladder-like, hairless bean on very short stalk turning black with age. Grows in dry woodlands at low to mid elevations in northwestern California and western Oregon. Native

Astragalus whitneyi FABACEAE
Whitney's locoweed
Uncommon, all summer, perennial, 2–10 in.
Alpine, subalpine

Tuft with spreading branches. Stems point upward with lower leaf stalks fused around stem. Leaflets 13–19, oblong. Flowers well separated, cream; upper petal in some varieties pink or purple. Seedpods are large, inflated, egg-shaped bladders, somewhat transparent, green to tan blotched with red. Grows in rocky soils at mid to high elevations. When dry you can hear the seed rattle inside large inflated chamber. There are 3 varieties in Oregon and Washington. Native

Glycyrrhiza lepidota FABACEAE
American licorice, licorice root
Common, midsummer, perennial, 1–4 ft.
Moist streambanks, disturbed

Upright to spreading, without hairs or covered with glandular hairs. Leaves pinnately divided; leaflets 9–19, lance- to egg-shaped. Flowers greenish white or yellow, pea-like in dense upright cluster. Seedpods covered with hooked thorns. Grows on moist soil in open or disturbed places, along riverbanks, and roadsides. *Glycyrrhiza* is Greek, meaning "sweet root." Native

Lathyrus lanszwertii FABACEAE
Mountain pea
Locally common, late spring–early summer, perennial, 1–3 ft. Meadow, west-side forest, east-side forest

Stems ascending or climbing, angled but without wings. Midvein extends beyond leaf tip to form a short stubby tendril (var. *aridus*) or long winding tendril (var. *lanszwertii*). Leaf bears 6–10 leaflets opposite one another, or alternate and scattered. Flowers 2–10, white, cream, purple, or lavender, on stalk above leaves. Grows in open meadows, dry woodlands, forests, at low to mid elevations. Similar *L. torreyi*, Torrey's pea, has leaves shorter and wider, lightly coated with hairs, tendril reduced to bristles; grows mostly at low elevations but found to 5200 ft. Native

See other *Lathyrus*: red, page 331; blue, page 408

Lotus micranthus FABACEAE
Small-flowered lotus, desert deervetch
Locally common, late spring, annual, 4–10 in.
Coastal, disturbed, west-side forest

Stems thin, sprawling to erect. Leaves with 3 or 5 stalkless oval leaflets often covered with white waxy powder. Flower stalk long, with 3 leaf-like bracts near top; single pea flower very pale yellow, salmon, or pink, does not always fully open. Flower fades quickly; long bean-like seedpod follows. Abundant along coast, continues into open and disturbed sites in oak and fir woodlands at low to mid elevations. Native OLYM, MORA, NOCA

Lotus unifoliolatus var. *unifoliolatus* (*Lotus purshianus*)
FABACEAE
Spanish lotus, American bird's-foot trefoil, Spanish clover
Common, all summer–autumn, annual, 8–18 in. Coastal, west-side forest, alpine, subalpine

Prostrate to erect. Single stem sometimes branched, hairy. Leaf palmately divided into 3 lance-shaped leaflets, held on main stem with long stalk above it. Flower stalk holds a single leaf, divided 3 times, and a single white to pale pink flower. Grows on roadsides, edges of moist places, from coast to mountain forests and alpine. Native OLYM, NOCA

Lupinus albicaulis (*Lupinus andersonii*) FABACEAE
Sickle-keeled lupine
Locally common, midsummer, perennial, 1–2 ft. West-side forest

Erect plant, flowers on upright stem above leaves. Silky hairs cover the foliage. Leaves palmately divided into 5–10 leaflets. Flower spike 4–15 in. long, loosely arranged, dull white, purple, or yellow, keel strongly upward-curving, tip pointing up through petals. Grows on open dry slopes in foothills and mountains. Native OLYM, CRLA

See other *Lotus*: yellow, page 206; red, page 332
See other *Lupinus*: yellow, page 207; blue, page 409

Lupinus leucophyllus FABACEAE
Velvet lupine, white-leaved lupine
Uncommon, early summer, perennial, 1–2 ft.
East-side forest, shrub-steppe, subalpine

Erect, branched just above soil line. Plant covered with white-woolly stiff hairs. Leaves with 2–3 in. long petioles, blade divided palmately, 7–11 leaflets. Flower heads dense on stalk 4–8 in. long and stout. Flowers white or lavender, often turning brown with age; patch on front of banner petal yellow to brown; back of banner densely hairy. Grows in rocky open hillsides, in flats with sagebrush, at low to high elevations. Native

Trifolium eriocephalum FABACEAE
Woolly-head clover
Common, early summer, perennial, 6–24 in.
Meadow, alpine, subalpine

Stem erect, unbranched. Plant obviously hairy. Basal and stem leaves palmately divided, 3 leaflets very narrow. Flower head roundish, often pointed to 1 side or down. Flowers white, tinged light yellowish or red, soon reflexing. Grows in moist meadows, bogs, drier rocky areas, at high elevations. *Trifolium latifolium* intergrades with both this species and *T. longipes*. Native

Trifolium howellii FABACEAE
Canyon clover
Uncommon, early spring, perennial, 4–24 in.
Bog/fen/wetland, meadow

Erect robust perennial, usually hairless. Stem to 2 ft. long. Leaves on stems, stipules green, ½–1 in., entire. Leaves with 3 egg-shaped leaflets, each 1–4 in. long. Flower head upright, elongated, with upper flowers spreading, lower flowers reflexed, greenish white or pinkish. Similar rounder flower head of *T. eriocephalum* holds its head up, while *T. howellii* turns downward in flower. Grows in wet meadows, swamps, shady places, at low to mid elevations. Native

See other *Trifolium*: yellow, page 209; red, page 333; blue, page 415; green/brown, page 466

Trifolium longipes FABACEAE
Long-stalked clover
Locally common, all summer, perennial, 2–15 in. Moist streambanks, meadow, east-side forest

Stems erect to lax. Basal and stem leaves. Leaves divided palmately; leaflets 3, narrow to oval, toothed. Flower heads usually more than 1 per plant, rounded, dense, on long stalk often curved or bent near top. Flowers white, purple-pink, or 2-colored. Grows in damp meadows, streambanks, open slopes, at mid to high elevations. Most often found in higher mountains. *Trifolium latifolium* intergrades with both this species and *T. eriocephalum*. Native OLYM, CRLA

Trifolium repens FABACEAE
White lawn clover
Common, perennial, 2–4 in.
Disturbed, meadow

Mats to 2 ft. across. Stems root at the nodes as they creep along the ground. Leaves from ground level, palmately divided into 3 egg-shaped leaflets, larger at the tip end. Flower head with no bract at base, tight and round, at end of long leafless stem arising from creeping stem. Flowers at bottom of head reflex, hanging down as they mature. Flowers white to cream, sometimes tinted pink. Introduced in lawns, fields, and meadows throughout the west. A parent of *T. hybridum*, alsike clover, which has leaves arising from sprawling to erect stems, and pink flowers. Nonnative OLYM, MORA, NOCA

Viola canadensis VIOLACEAE
Canada violet
Locally common, early summer, perennial, 8–15 in. Coastal, west-side forest

Stem prostrate to upright, to 15 in. long. Leaf blades toothed, heart-shaped to broadly oval, with sharply pointed tips and short hairs. Petioles long at base, becoming shorter along flower stems. Flower petals mostly white with yellow patches. The 2 side petals have white beard at the base. The 3 lower petals have maroon veins, and the 2 upper petals have lavender backs. Grows in openings in mixed forests. Native NOCA

98

See other *Viola*: yellow, page 210; blue, page 416

Viola macloskeyi VIOLACEAE
Macloskey violet
Common, midspring, perennial, ½–5 in.
Bog/fen/wetland, meadow, west-side forest,
east-side forest, alpine, subalpine

Upright plants forming patches from running
roots. Leaves round to kidney-shaped, very
thin, entire or slightly toothed. Flowers white,
with upper 2 petals often curving back so the
tips almost touch. The 2 side petals sometimes bearded. Lower
3 petals purple-veined, turning creamy white toward base. Spur
white. Grows near seeps and slow-moving water at mid to high
elevations. Native OLYM, MORA, NOCA, CRLA

Viola primulifolia subsp. occidentalis (Viola lanceolata
subsp. *occidentalis*) VIOLACEAE
Western bog violet
Rare, early summer, perennial, 3–8 in.
Bog/fen/wetland

Tuft. Leaves from base with petiole 1–4 in.
long, blade narrow to widely egg-shaped,
slightly scalloped to entire, with pointed or narrowly rounded tip. Flower stems usually
shorter than leaves. Flowers white, lower petal
veined purple, more or less ⅓ in. long, side
petals hairy near center, spur short. Grows in areas of serpentine rock, on wet hillsides, in creeks, or in fens with *Darlingtonia californica*. Rare and endemic in Siskiyou Mountains at
300–1600 ft. Native

Arenaria aculeata (Arenaria congesta var. aculeata)
CARYOPHYLLACEAE
Prickly sandwort
Locally common, late spring–early summer,
perennial, 2–8 in. Dry rocky sites, alpine,
subalpine

Mat-forming. Stems 2–8 in., upright, with
leaves at right angles. Leaves ⅓–1⅓ in., stiff,
narrow, with sharp point and blue waxy coating, hairless. Mat of leaves feels prickly to the
touch. Flowers few, contained in loose clusters
at stem top on stalks up to 1 in. long. Flower petals rounded.
Seedpods oblong, yellow-tan. Grows on rocky ridges, outcrops,
volcanic soils, at high elevations. *Arenaria capillaris* is similar
but leaves are often taller than the flowers and thread-like but
not sharply pointed. Native

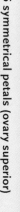

Arenaria capillaris CARYOPHYLLACEAE
Mountain sandwort, thread-leaved sandwort
Uncommon, early summer, perennial, 4–8 in.
Shrub-steppe, alpine, subalpine

Mat from spreading woody base. Leaves from base linear, thread-like, erect or often curved, not rigid, 1–3 in., green. Mat of leaves feels soft to the touch. Flower stems 2–6 in. high with 2–3 pairs of leaves. Few flowers on stalks ½–¾ in. long at stem top. Flowers about ½ in. across with 5 short, nearly round sepals often tinted purple, 5 white petals twice as long as sepals, 10 stamens. Grows on sands in steppe, subalpine, and alpine to 8000 ft. Native
OLYM, MORA, NOCA

Arenaria congesta CARYOPHYLLACEAE
Ballhead sandwort
Uncommon, all summer, perennial, 4–12 in.
Dry rocky sites, east-side forest, alpine, subalpine

Cushion, small and green. Stems with 2–3 pairs of small leaves. Leaves linear, needle-like, with sharp point, ½–3 in. long. Flowers head-like, may be dense or open. Flower sepals with papery edges, often sharply pointed; petals white, longer than sepals. Grows in dry rocky or sandy soils, rock crevices, into high elevations. Native

Arenaria franklinii CARYOPHYLLACEAE
Franklin's sandwort
Uncommon, late spring–early summer, perennial, 2–4 in. Shrub-steppe

Mound of many short upright stems. Branches slender, brittle. Leaves sessile pairs on stems, lance-shaped, ⅓–¾ in. long, sharply pointed at tips. Flower stems un-branched, leafy, few white flowers in dense cluster. Flower petals shorter than long, narrow, pointed sepals. Grows in dry sandy or rocky soils. Var. *franklinii* has long, tapered, narrow sepals much longer than petals. Var. *thompsonii* has sepals about same length as petals. Native

Arenaria pumicola CARYOPHYLLACEAE
Pumice sandwort
Endemic, midsummer, perennial, 4–8 in. Alpine

Stems upright from branched woody base. Leaves 1–2 in. long, upward-pointing, narrow, bearing straight hairs along edges, blunt-tipped. Flower stems 3–8 in. long, hairless on lower sections, glands near top, with 2–3 pairs of leaves. Open clusters of few to many flowers, each carried on a ⅓–1 in. stalk. Flowers small, white. Grows on granite or pumice sand. Endemic to southern Cascades, found at Crater Lake National Park. Native CRLA

Arenaria serpyllifolia CARYOPHYLLACEAE
Thyme-leaf sandwort
Locally common, midspring, annual, 1–10 in. Disturbed

Tuft or sometimes prostrate. Stems with fine hairs. Leaves opposite on stems, sessile, egg-shaped, with sharply pointed tips, 3–5 veins. Flowers few to many, with short stalks, atop stems. Grows in disturbed sandy soils, gravel bars, dry woods, at 500–6000 ft. *Serpyllifolia* refers to the leaves being similar to the linear or slightly oval leaves of *Thymus serpyllifolia*, mother of thyme. Nonnative OLYM, MORA, NOCA

Cerastium arvense CARYOPHYLLACEAE
Field chickweed
Common, early spring–early summer, perennial, 4–10 in. Meadow, west-side forest, east-side forest, alpine, subalpine

Mat with erect flowering stems. Plant does not flower first year. Leaves linear to widely lance-shaped, ⅓–1½ in. long, with pointed tips, with little hair or hairless. Clusters of small leaves in axils of larger leaves on lower portion of flower stem. Single to few flowers atop stems. Flower white, ⅓ in. across, deeply lobed petals 3 times longer than sepals. Grows in moist shady places, meadows, bald rocky places, outcrops with thin vernal-wet soils, subalpine. Similar *C. beeringianum* does not have clusters of small leaves in axils of larger leaves. Native OLYM, MORA, NOCA, CRLA, **L&C**

Cerastium beeringianum

CARYOPHYLLACEAE
Alpine chickweed
Locally common, midsummer, perennial,
½–4 in. Alpine, subalpine

Prostrate stems with leaves, erect flower stalks. Leaves opposite on stems, none at base, small, lance-shaped, without clusters of smaller leaves in leaf axils. Open clusters of flowers. Flowers each in a cup bearing hairs topped with glands; 5 white flower petals lobed, longer than sepals. Grows with grass in alpine rocky soils at high elevations. Native NOCA

Cerastium fontanum subsp. vulgare (Cerastium

vulgatum) CARYOPHYLLACEAE
Large mouse ear, common chickweed
Common, early spring–autumn, biennial or perennial. Disturbed, meadow

Prostrate mat, hairy but not glandular. Stems without flowers are mat-forming; flowering stems upright. Leaves to 1 in. long, lance-shaped to oblong. Flower bracts have colorless edges. Calyx without glands, tip edges tan or colorless, petals about same size as or smaller than calyx lobes. Grows in disturbed places, marshy or grassy places, lawns, below 7000 ft. Nonnative OLYM, MORA, NOCA

Holosteum umbellatum CARYOPHYLLACEAE

Jagged chickweed
Locally common, all spring and summer, annual, 2–10 in. Disturbed, meadow

Stems erect, unbranched, with glands mid-stem. Leaves clustered on lower stem, 1–4 pairs, opposite, widely egg-shaped, to 1 in. long, hairless or with few glands on hairs on edges. Inflorescence tops stem with long stalks in shape of umbrella, flowers at tips. Flowers white, 5 narrow petals with uneven edges. Grows in meadows, disturbed soils to 4500 ft. Called jagged chickweed for the uneven tips of the flower petals. Nonnative OLYM

Honckenya peploides CARYOPHYLLACEAE
Sea purslane, seabeach sandwort
Common, late spring–early summer, perennial, 2–12 in. Coastal

Mat 4–30 in. across. Stems many-branched, leafy, with tips pointed upward. Leaves egg-shaped, fleshy, sessile, in 3–10 pairs. Flowers single or clustered at tops of short stalks from leaf axils. Sepals form calyx, with lobes often longer than 5 white petals, 10 stamens, 3 styles. Grows on sandy or rocky ocean beaches. Native OLYM

Minuartia nuttallii subsp. fragilis (Arenaria nuttallii subsp. fragilis) CARYOPHYLLACEAE
Brittle sandwort
Uncommon, midsummer, perennial, 4 in.
Alpine, subalpine

Mat-forming, yellowish green, dense with gland-tipped hairs. Stems topped by flowers are ascending, very easily broken. Leaves numerous, narrow, with sharply pointed tip recurving back toward stem. Flower sepals forming calyx have 3 noticeable veins and hairs along edges, petals about twice as large as sepals. Grows in limestone talus, basins, at 5300–7800 ft. Native NOCA

Minuartia obtusiloba (Arenaria obtusiloba) CARYOPHYLLACEAE
Alpine sandwort
Uncommon, midsummer, perennial, 1–3 in.
Alpine, subalpine

Mat green with glands on stems and leaves. Leaves tiny, needle-shaped, flexible. Flowers on erect stems, small, sepals with narrowly rounded tips and edges rolled inward, petals 1½ times larger than sepals. Grows with dwarf willows or on steep rocky slopes at high elevations. Native OLYM, MORA, NOCA

Minuartia tenella (*Arenaria stricta* var. *puberulenta*) CARYOPHYLLACEAE
Slender sandwort
Locally common, late spring–early summer, annual or perennial, 4–12 in. Coastal, meadow

Stems slender, erect, with few branches above, glandular. Leaves lance-shaped to oval to ½ in. long; upper leaves smaller. Flowers at tips of branches; 5 sepals lance-shaped, with pointed tips, each containing 3 noticeable veins; 5 oblong petals same length or longer than sepals. Grows in dry soils, open grassy areas, coastal bluffs. Native

Moehringia macrophylla (*Arenaria macrophylla*)
CARYOPHYLLACEAE
Big-leaf sandwort
Locally common, late spring–early summer, perennial, 3–8 in. Coastal, west-side forest, east-side forest

Single stem to cushion, descending to upright. Stem square or grooved to round, leafy, often branched. Leaves opposite, lance-shaped, with pointed tips, 1–2½ in. long, more or less evenly spaced, reducing in size upward. Flowers 2–5 in open cluster on short stalks near stem tops. Flowers small, with 5 sharply pointed sepals, 5 white rounded petals about same size as sepals. Grows in moist, shaded to dry forests and open rocky slopes, including serpentine, at low to high elevations. Native OLYM, MORA, NOCA

Sagina saginoides CARYOPHYLLACEAE
Alpine pearlwort
Locally common, midsummer, biennial or perennial, ½–5 in. West-side forest, east-side forest, alpine, subalpine

Cushion of slender ascending stems. Flowerless leaf rosettes often present. Leaves narrowly linear in basal tufts ½ in. or less long. Flower stalks thread-like, hairless, ⅓–1 in. long. Flowers consist of 4–5 hairless sepals slightly longer or shorter than the 4–5 white petals. Grows in moist areas, along streams, at mid to high elevations. Superficially moss-like. Common in most mountains of Pacific Northwest. Similar *S. procumbens*, arctic pearlwort, with stout stems and petals less than ½ as long as sepals, is found in gravelly or sandy soils, sidewalk cracks, disturbed places. Native OLYM, MORA, NOCA

Silene campanulata CARYOPHYLLACEAE
Bell catchfly
Locally common, all summer, perennial, 4–15
in. West-side forest

Erect stems with nodding flowers. Plant may
or may not be hairy or have sticky glands.
Leaves lance-shaped to round, sessile, becoming somewhat smaller near top. Flowers along
stem and at top, white to greenish or pink,
calyx enlarged and bell-shaped, petals divided into 4–6 lobes,
each lobe divided into 6–8 linear sections. Grows in light
forests, thickets, at low to mid elevations. Native CRLA

Silene douglasii CARYOPHYLLACEAE
Douglas's catchfly, Douglas's campion
Common, all spring and summer, perennial,
4–15 in. Meadow, west-side forest, east-side
forest, shrub-steppe

Mound, flower stems lax becoming upright.
Stems and leaves coated with fine hairs. Leaves
lance-shaped, opposite, becoming smaller up
stem, lower leaves 1–2½ in. long. White to
greenish or pinkish flowers, each a cup ½ in.
deep with fine hairs but no glands, petals
longer and barely notched at tip, 2 appendages
topping each petal at flower center. Grows in dry open slopes,
grassy areas, shrublands, forests, at mid to high elevations.
Native OLYM, MORA, NOCA, CRLA

Silene latifolia subsp. *alba* (*Lychnis alba*)
CARYOPHYLLACEAE
White campion, evening lychnis
Common, all summer, biennial or perennial,
12–40 in. Disturbed, meadow

Erect, with branched root. Stems with hairs on
lower section, glandular near top. Leaves egg-
shaped, lower leaves 2–4 in., reducing in size
upward. Flowers erect on short stalks or sessile, open in afternoon. Calyx ½–¾ in., inflated, petals white, tips wide, deeply notched
into 2 lobes, 2 appendages above each petal in
center of flower dividing into 2 lobes. Male flowers with 10 stamens and female flowers with 5 styles are on separate plants.
Grows in fields, along roads, at low elevations. Widespread.
Nonnative OLYM, MORA

See other *Silene*: red, page 338

Silene menziesii CARYOPHYLLACEAE
Menzies' campion, Menzies' catchfly
Locally common, all summer, perennial,
4–12 in. Meadow, west-side forest, east-side
forest

Mat to erect, with many stems. Stems short-haired below, glandular above. Leaves 1–2½ in. long, lance-shaped, hairless. Flowers ascending; calyx glandular; petals 5, small, white, each divided into 4 lobes rounded at tips; at center 2 very small appendages with 2–4 teeth top each petal. Similar male, female flowers on separate plants. Grows in moist forests, woodlands, streambanks, moist meadows, at mid to high elevations. Native OLYM, MORA, NOCA, CRLA

Silene oregana CARYOPHYLLACEAE
Oregon campion, Oregon catchfly
Locally common, all summer, perennial,
6–10 in. East-side forest, alpine, subalpine

Few erect stems. Stems hairy throughout, with glands on upper portion. Leaves egg-shaped; lower leaves 2–3 in. long; upper leaves ½–2 in. long. Flowers on short stalks or sessile. Calyx ⅓–½ in. high, covered with glands, 5 petals, white fading to pink, each divided into 4 lobes, inner lobes longer and forked, 4 inner appendages pointed. Grows in open forests at high elevations. Native MORA

Silene parryi (Silene douglasii var. macounii)
CARYOPHYLLACEAE
Parry's catchfly, white catchfly
Locally common, midsummer, perennial,
8–20 in. Meadow, alpine, subalpine

Upright tuft, leaves mostly basal. Stems with short hairs on lower section, glandular above. Basal leaves narrowly egg-shaped, 1–3 in. long, becoming smaller upward. Flowers 2–4 in loose clusters near top. Flower calyx with glands along ribs, 5 white or greenish petals. Petals divided into 4 rounded lobes, center lobes larger, 2 small rounded appendages at center of each petal. Grows on rocky slopes, in dry meadows, open forests of subalpine, at high elevations. Native OLYM, MORA, NOCA

Stellaria graminea CARYOPHYLLACEAE
Grass-leaf starwort
Common, all spring and summer, perennial,
4–24 in. Disturbed

Sprawling to 20 in. Stems slender. Stems and
leaves with few hairs. Leaves opposite, evenly
spaced, linear to lance-shaped, ⅓–1⅓ in. long,
flat, entire. Flowers numerous in clusters at

stem tips. Flowers have 5 short sepals with tips
pointed, may be densely hairy on edges, 5 white petals slightly
longer than sepals. Grows in lawns, gardens, disturbed soils.
From Europe. *Stellaria humifusa*, a native in the salt marshes,
has fleshy leaves on stems to 15 in. long, forming mats. Nonnative OLYM, MORA, NOCA

Stellaria longipes CARYOPHYLLACEAE
Long-stalked starwort
Uncommon, all summer, perennial, 4–12 in.
Meadow, alpine, subalpine

Ascending to erect, hairless. Stems with evenly
spaced leaves. Leaves sessile, stiff, narrowly
lance-shaped, ½–1 in. long, smooth, shiny.
Flowers white, 1–7 at stem tips on long erect
stalks. Sepals 5, small, with pointed tips, 5
slightly longer petals divided into 2 lobes.

Grows along streams, in seeps, moist to wet meadows, at high
elevations. Circumboreal. Native OLYM, MORA, NOCA, CRLA

Stellaria media CARYOPHYLLACEAE
Common chickweed
Common, all spring and summer, annual or
perennial, 6–18 in. Disturbed, meadow

Erect to prostrate annual, often overwintering.
Stems have single row of wavy hairs running
along 1 side. Leaves ⅓–1¾ in. long, egg-
shaped, flat, shiny, entire. Flowers 1 to many
in clusters near stem tips, bracts around
flowers leaf-like. Flower petals white, 2-lobed,
slightly shorter than sepals or missing. Grows

in oak woods, meadows, disturbed soils. Often
a weed in gardens and lawns. Native of south-
western Europe. *Stellaria crispa*, a hairless common native, is
prostrate to spreading, often to 20 in. The white flowers are
small, with very small or no petals. Nonnative
OLYM, MORA, NOCA

Allotropa virgata ERICACEAE
Sugarstick, candystick
Locally common, midsummer, perennial,
5–15 in. West-side forest

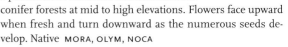

Erect, nongreen, hairless. A thick white
stalk with deep red stripes that arises from
the ground and persists long after seed dispersal. Flowers are bowl-shaped, white, with
5 petals and 10 stamens. Grows in mixed or
conifer forests at mid to high elevations. Flowers face upward
when fresh and turn downward as the numerous seeds develop. Native MORA, OLYM, NOCA

Arctostaphylos canescens ERICACEAE
Hoary manzanita
Locally common, midspring, perennial, 1–6
ft. West-side forest

Upright shrub without burl. Twigs and fruit
densely covered with short soft hairs and
often glands. Leaves erect, on petioles about
1/3 in. long, blade round to egg-shaped, tip
sharp or softly pointed, both sides with same
surface, with short hairs or white powdery
wax. Inflorescence single-stemmed or 1- to
4-branched, bracts leaf-like, lance-shaped.
Flower bell-shaped, white to pale pink. Fruit with white hairs.
Grows on hills, ridges, slopes, with chaparral or in forests, at
low to mid elevations. Manzanita without burls do not resprout
after fire, while those with burls do. Native

Arctostaphylos columbiana ERICACEAE
Hairy manzanita
Locally common, all spring, perennial, 3–10
ft. West-side forest

Tall upright shrub without burl at base.
Twigs have matted to stiff white hairs, often
glandular. Widely oval, dull green leaves,
alike on both sides with stiff white hairs,
sometimes with glands. Large leaf-like
bracts frame base of inflorescence. Flowers
white to pink, bell-shaped, in ample clusters
near tips of twigs. Somewhat flattened berries, brownish red
to bright red. Grows in dry rocky or clay soils at low elevations,
mostly on western side of Coast Range but also found further
inland. Native OLYM, MORA

See other *Arctostaphylos*: red, page 341

Arctostaphylos nevadensis ERICACEAE
Pinemat manzanita
Locally common, all spring, perennial, 6–20 in.
West-side forest, alpine, subalpine

Mounding or prostrate shrub, usually less than 1 ft. tall, branches reaching outward more than 3 ft. No burl at base. Stems covered with short fine hairs. Leaves bright green, shiny on both sides, widely oval, with pointed tips. Flowers bell-shaped, white, in short clusters. Berries round, brown, shiny. Grows in all soils, often on rocky slopes, at mid to high elevations. Similar to *A. uva-ursi* but generally larger and with pointed leaf tips, berry more brownish red than bright red. Native MORA, NOCA, CRLA

Cassiope mertensiana ERICACEAE
White heather, Mertens' mountain-heather
Locally common, early summer, perennial, 4–12 in. Alpine, subalpine

Low-growing shrub, densely matted from creeping roots. Stems reclining with erect tips. Leaves opposite, evergreen, concave but not rolled under. Flowers hang from near top of branch on reddish stalks, sepals reddish or green, flowers pure white, bell-shaped, with 5 lobes. Grows in subalpine and alpine areas, around rocks and in late snowmelt areas. Native OLYM, MORA, NOCA

Chimaphila menziesii ERICACEAE
Menzies' pipsissewa, little prince's pine
Uncommon, all spring, perennial, 2–6 in.
West-side forest, east-side forest

Small, upright, evergreen plant with few leaves near ground. Lance-shaped to narrowly oval leaves are dull green, often with white central vein and pointed tips, usually toothed. Flowers 1–3, on nodding stems, waxy, fragrant. Petals white, cream, or light pink, reflexed back from large green ovary surrounded by yellow to brown stamens with hairy filaments. Grows in well-drained places in dense forests, rotting wood, leaf mold. Uncommon but found at low to high elevations. Pipsissewa is a Cree name meaning "it breaks into small pieces" in reference to the leaves, which are thought to help dissolve kidney stones. Native OLYM, MORA, NOCA

See other *Chimaphila*: red, page 342   **109**

Gaultheria shallon ERICACEAE
Salal
Common, late spring–early summer,
perennial, 1–3 ft. Coastal, west-side forest

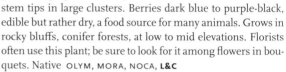

Vigorous erect shrub to 4 ft. tall, forming dense impenetrable thickets. Stems hairy. Leaves glossy, evergreen, thick, leathery, alternate. Flowers urn-shaped, white or pale pink, hanging individually from 1 side of stem tips in large clusters. Berries dark blue to purple-black, edible but rather dry, a food source for many animals. Grows in rocky bluffs, conifer forests, at low to mid elevations. Florists often use this plant; be sure to look for it among flowers in bouquets. Native OLYM, MORA, NOCA, **L&C**

Ledum glandulosum (Rhododendron
glandulosum) ERICACEAE
Trapper's tea
Common, early summer, perennial, 35–60 in.
Bog/fen/wetland, alpine, subalpine

Erect evergreen shrub with smooth bark, fine hairs on new growth. Leaves ½–2 in. long, leathery, oblong, occasionally with rolled entire edges, hanging down when mature; underside white with dense hairs. Flowers cream to white, 5 spreading petals, 8–10 stamens slightly longer than petals. Common in bogs. Native NOCA

Ledum groenlandicum (Rhododendron groenlandicum)
ERICACEAE
Labrador tea
Locally common, early summer, perennial,
2–5 ft. Coastal, bog/fen/wetland

Evergreen shrub with spreading branches. Leaves spicy-fragrant, oblong, 1–3 in. long, leather-like, smooth above, with felt-like rusty red hairs beneath, edges rolled under. Leaves hang down when mature. Flowers white, numerous in terminal clusters with stamens extended outward. Grows in bogs, swampy places, at low to mid elevations. Native OLYM, MORA

See other *Gaultheria*: red, page 342

Moneses uniflora (Pyrola uniflora)
ERICACEAE
One-flowered moneses, single delight, wood nymph
Uncommon, late spring–early summer, perennial, 2–6 in. West-side forest

Single upright stem from mostly basal leaves. Leaves oval to round, not leathery, 1–2 in. long, with sharp to rounded teeth, raised veins. Single nodding flower, waxy, fragrant, white or occasionally pale pink, 5 petals and 10 stamens with filaments that are wider at the base. Flower center with large, rounded, green ovary with long style and prominent stigma. Grows in mossy places or on rotting wood in deep coniferous forests from coastline to mid elevations. Out of flower can be confused with *Orthilia secunda*, which has similar leaves. Native

OLYM, MORA, NOCA

Monotropa uniflora ERICACEAE
Indian pipe, ghost plant
Rare, late spring–early summer, perennial, 2–10 in. Coastal, west-side forest

Pure white plant, groups of erect stems. Plant is occasionally pinkish, turning black with age. Stems fleshy, unbranched, with small, oval, colorless scales. Single flower at top is nodding, to 1 in. long, a cylinder-shaped bell formed by 5 overlapping petals. Grows in humus in deep shaded conifer forests at low elevations. Distinguished from phantom orchid, *Cephalanthera austiniae*, another white saprophyte, which has several outward-facing flowers along stem. Native OLYM, MORA, NOCA, CRLA

Orthilia secunda (Pyrola secunda)
ERICACEAE
One-sided wintergreen, one-sided pyrola
Locally common, all summer, perennial, 3–8 in. West-side forest, east-side forest

Erect stems woody at base, unbranched with arching tops. Leaves with short petioles, only on lower stem. Leaf blades evergreen, widely egg-shaped, ½–2 in. long, entire or finely toothed. Flowers hang from 1 side of upper arching stem. Flowers cream to greenish white, closed bells with straight style projecting out. Grows in dry to moist, shady conifer forests at mid to high elevations. Circumboreal. Native

OLYM, MORA, NOCA, CRLA

See other *Monotropa*: yellow, page 217

Pyrola picta ERICACEAE
White-veined pyrola, white-veined wintergreen
Common, all summer, perennial, 4–8 in.
West-side forest, east-side forest

Erect flower stem from basal rosette of white-veined leaves. Plants occasionally leafless. Leaves 2–4 in. long, egg-shaped, upper side dark green, underside often bluish when young. Flowers clustered on upper stem, with short bent stalks and 5 white to greenish petals, sometimes tinted pink. Style protruding, curved downward. Grows in dry forests at low to high elevations. Leafless plants are thought to be saprophytic. *Picta* means "brightly marked," in reference to the white-veined leaves. Native OLYM, MORA, NOCA, CRLA

Rhododendron albiflorum
ERICACEAE
White rhododendron
Locally common, early summer, perennial, 3–7 ft. West-side forest, alpine, subalpine

Deciduous shrub with erect branched stems. Twigs have reddish hairs, peeling bark. Thin crinkled leaves are alternate in clusters, especially at stem tips. Leaves with rusty-colored hairs on upper side, 2–4 in. long, oblong, turning brilliant reddish orange in autumn. Flowers clustered on last year's growth. Petals white, fused at base to form wide shallow bells with 5 lobes. Grows in moist to dry soils in conifer forests and along streams in upper forests and subalpine. Native OLYM, MORA, NOCA

Geranium richardsonii GERANIACEAE
Richardson's geranium
Locally common, all summer, perennial, 8–32 in. Meadow, east-side forest

Upright. Stem hairs with red glands on tips. Basal leaves 2–6 in. wide, with long petioles, palmately divided, 5–7 diamond-shaped lobes sometimes divided again to smaller lobes. Flower stem with small-leaved stalks, 1–3 flowers at top. Petals 5, ⅓–¾ in. long, with soft hairs, white to pale pink with lavender veins. Grows in moist places, often associated with aspen trees in steppe, mostly east of Cascade Mountains in central and southern Oregon. Native

See other *Pyrola*: red, page 344; green/brown, page 467
See other *Rhododendron*: red, page 344
See other *Geranium*: red, page 348

Floerkea proserpinacoides
LIMNANTHACEAE
False mermaid
Common, late spring–early summer, annual,
⅓–2 in. Bog/fen/wetland, west-side forest,
east-side forest

Stems decumbent to erect and sometimes
branched. Leaves few, pinnately divided into
3–5 linear leaflets. Flowers solitary, tiny, with 3
oval white or purplish petals much shorter than the 3 lance-
shaped sepals, 3–6 stamens. Grows in wet, rocky or mossy, partially shaded places in conifer forests or sagebrush at mid elevations. Can form large patches in small streams, ditches.
Native NOCA

Limnanthes floccosa subsp. grandiflora
LIMNANTHACEAE
Woolly meadowfoam
Endemic, midspring, annual, 2–6 in. Vernal-wet

Stems spreading to 6 in. with some hairs.
Leaves divided into linear segments. White
cup-shaped flower has sepals and petals ⅜ in.
long, with green lines inside and white hairs at
base of petals. Calyx covered with long white
hairs on both sides. Grows near vernal pools in
the Rogue River valley in Jackson County, Oregon. Showy. Rare
and endangered. Very similar *L. floccosa* subsp. *pumila* is hairless, smaller, usually less than 4 in. tall, with petals ¼–⅓ in.;
grows only in 2 locations in Rogue River Basin of Jackson
County, Oregon, at edges of vernal pools; very rare and endangered. Native

Claytonia megarhiza var. bellidifolia
PORTULACACEAE
Alpine spring beauty
Rare, midsummer, perennial, spreading, to 3 in.
Alpine

Rosette of basal leaves from a thick carrot-like
root. Basal leaves spoon-shaped, 1–4 in. long,
with wide rounded tips; stem leaves few, narrow. Flowers many, sessile or stalked, with 2
green or reddish sepals and 5 white petals aging to pink. Grows
among loose rocks and on talus in alpine. Native NOCA

See other *Claytonia*: red, page 352

Claytonia perfoliata (*Montia perfoliata*)

PORTULACACEAE
Miner's lettuce
Common, late spring, annual or biennial,
2–12 in. Coastal, vernal-wet, disturbed,
west-side forest, east-side forest

Stems spreading or ascending. Basal leaves few to many, oval or almost round, with stalks to 10 in. long; stem leaves 2, fused together to form a disk beneath flowers. Flowers 5–40, on stalks or sessile, white to pale pink, small. Grows in spring-damp, often shady places in the south, open to shady places in the north, often on disturbed soils, from sea level to mid elevations. *Claytonia parviflora* grows in similar places, has many shiny, bright green, linear, basal leaves, stem leaves fused. *Claytonia rubra*, less than 6 in., is also similar, with many diamond-shaped basal leaves. Native

OLYM, MORA, NOCA, CRLA, **L&C**

Claytonia sibirica (*Montia sibirica*)

PORTULACACEAE
Candy flower, Siberian miner's lettuce
Locally common, midspring, annual or
perennial, 6–14 in. Coastal, vernal-wet,
meadow, west-side forest, east-side forest

Spreading to erect, with stolons that sometimes form new plants. Stems few to several. Foliage color varies from green to bronze. Basal leaves egg-shaped, with long petioles; stem leaves opposite, heart-shaped, sessile but not fused together. Flowers in open clusters of 1–3, each cluster with small elliptical bract at base. Petals ¼–½ in., white with pink pencil markings. Grows in moist places in forests, streambanks, along coast and to mid elevations. At upper elevations, growing in shaded swamps, seeps, and wet meadows, is similar *C. cordifolia*, which has no bracts below the inflorescence and has white flowers without pencil markings. Native

OLYM, MORA, NOCA, **L&C**

Lewisia nevadensis PORTULACACEAE
Nevada lewisia
Uncommon, late spring, perennial, 1–4 in. Vernal-wet, meadow,
west-side forest, east-side forest, alpine, subalpine

Sprawling central rosette of basal leaves 1–5 in. across. Plant without glands. Leaves few, long, strap-like, with rounded tip. Stems each with 1 white or faintly pink flower. Grows in gravel flats, meadows, open spaces, at mid to high elevations. Hybridizes with *L. pygmaea* where the 2 come together. Native

See other *Lewisia*: orange, page 299; red, page 352

Lewisia oppositifolia PORTULACACEAE
Opposite-leaved lewisia
Endemic, late spring, perennial, 2–8 in.
Vernal-wet

Upright plant with central rosette of leaves. Leaves few to many, fleshy, lance-shaped, standing upright from central root. Flower stems 1–3 with 2–5 large, white or palest pink flowers in loose cluster. Flowers held upright, opening wide with sun, petals notched or uneven to squared along top edge. Grows in spring-wet places in sparse pine and cedar woods, often on serpentine, at low to mid elevations. Native

Lewisia triphylla PORTULACACEAE
Three-leaf lewisia
Uncommon, early summer, perennial, 1–4 in.
Vernal-wet, shrub-steppe, alpine, subalpine

Stems weak, sprawling, topped with flowers. Leaves 2–5, thread-like, to 2½ in. long, only on upper part of stem. Flowers small in loose clusters of 1–10. Petals 5–9, with rounded tips, often with pink pencil lines, white or pink, stamens 3–5, stigmas 3–5. Grows in damp sand, wet gravelly slopes, damp meadows where snows are late to melt, at mid to alpine elevations. First found and noted (though not collected) by Meriwether Lewis, this is the only lewisia without a basal rosette. Native
MORA, NOCA, CRLA

Montia chamissoi (*Claytonia chamissoi*) PORTULACACEAE
Chamisso's montia
Locally common, late spring–early summer, perennial, 2–7 in. Vernal-wet, bog/fen/wetland, alpine, subalpine

Stems more or less upright, with runners bearing pink overwintering bulblets. Leaves small, to 2 in. long, fleshy, oval, opposite, about the same size throughout. Flowers pink to white, in few loose clusters at stem tops. Sepals much shorter than petals. Grows floating or on wet sandy to loamy soils at mid to high elevations. Native
OLYM, CRLA

See other *Montia*: red, page 354

Montia linearis PORTULACACEAE
Narrow-leaved montia
Locally common, midspring, annual, 2–8 in.
Vernal-wet, west-side forest, east-side forest,
shrub-steppe

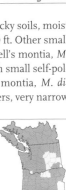

Erect, with many branches from base.
Stems 2–8 in. long. Leaves narrow, ½–2 in.
long, alternate on stem, none basal. Flowers in clusters of 2–15 on side of stem tips,
petals white or pale pink. Grows in sandy to rocky soils, moist
meadows, openings in woodlands, below 8000 ft. Other small
annual montias found in same habitats: Howell's montia, *M.
howellii*, spreading, not erect, ⅓–3 in. tall, with small self-pollinating flowers usually not opening; dwarf montia, *M. dichotoma*, only 1–2 in. tall, with tiny white flowers, very narrow
leaves; branching montia, *M. diffusa*, to 8 in.
tall with distinctive, stalked, diamond-shaped leaves 1–2 in. long, many spreading
stems. Native OLYM, MORA, **L&C**

Actaea rubra RANUNCULACEAE
Red baneberry, western baneberry
Locally common, early summer, perennial,
1–3 ft. West-side forest, east-side forest

Erect to upright. Stems may be branched
near top. Leaves on lower stem 1–4, about 2 ft. long including
long petiole, divided into 3 delicate maple-like sections lobed
again, toothed; upper leaves smaller. Inflorescence at stem end
a bottlebrush head of small white flowers. Flower petals fall
shortly after opening. Berries glossy red, in clusters appearing
in July. Occasional plant with white berries. Grows in deep soil
pockets in conifer or mixed forests, streambanks, below timberline. Berries toxic, not
eaten by any animals. Native

OLYM, MORA, NOCA, CRLA

Anemone deltoidea RANUNCULACEAE
Columbia windflower
Locally common, midsummer, perennial,
4–10 in. West-side forest

Single erect stem. One basal leaf divided
into 3 coarsely toothed leaflets; whorl of 3 sessile stem leaves
below the flower. One flower, 1½–2½ in. wide, with 5 white
petal-like sepals. Grows in moist forests in shaded areas at mid
to high elevations. Native OLYM, MORA, NOCA, CRLA

See other *Anemone*: red, page 355; blue, page 419

Anemone occidentalis (*Pulsatilla occidentalis*) RANUNCULACEAE

Western pasque flower, old man of the mountain, tow-headed baby
Locally common, early summer, perennial, 6–24 in. Alpine, subalpine

Erect stem lengthens to 20 in. or more in seed. Stems stout, 1 to few. Leaves divided 2–3 times into narrow lobes. Basal leaves on long petioles; stem leaves sessile. Flowering begins soon after plant emerges following snowmelt. Flowers single, 1–2 in. wide, creamy white, usually with pale blue stain on underside. Seed heads on very showy cylinder-shaped stalks with long silky feather-like hairs attached to seed. Grows in open rocky slopes, alpine meadows. Native OLYM, MORA, NOCA, CRLA

Caltha leptosepala subsp. *howellii*

(*Caltha biflora*) RANUNCULACEAE
Marsh-marigold, broad-leaved marsh-marigold
Locally common, late spring, perennial, 6–12 in. Vernal-wet, bog/fen/wetland, alpine, subalpine

Stems 1 to few upright. Basal leaves with 2–10 in. petioles, nearly round, often heart-shaped, 1–4 in. across, shiny, entire or slightly toothed. Flower stem 2–12 in. tall with 1–2 flowers. Flower with 5–12 petal-like sepals that are white, with greenish yellow center, often stained blue on underside. Grows in marshes, streambanks, pond edges, at high elevations. Often found at the edge of snowmelt. Native OLYM, MORA, NOCA, CRLA

Caltha leptosepala subsp. *leptosepala* var. *leptosepala* RANUNCULACEAE

Alpine white marsh-marigold, elkslip marsh-marigold
Common, early spring, perennial, 2–12 in. Bog/fen/wetland, alpine, subalpine

Tuft. Stems buried. Leaves arising from soil, longer than broad, to 6 in. long, heart-shaped, thick, shiny, entire, with rounded tip. Flowers 1 per stem, white with blue or greenish on outside. Grows in wet soils, seepages, at edges of snowmelt. A large-leaved variety common in Rocky Mountains and high mountains of Washington. Native OLYM, MORA, NOCA

Cimicifuga elata RANUNCULACEAE
Tall bugbane
Uncommon, early summer, perennial, 3–7
ft. West-side forest

Upright. Stems long, with fine hairs and glands. Leaves large, divided into 3 sections, each shallowly divided, sharply pointed, maple-like. Flower stems 2–3 ft., topped with long thin flower head of white to pale pink flowers. Flowers with small sepals that quickly fall; numerous long white stamens form a conspicuous, long, bottle-brush-looking flower head. Grows in moist shady woods at lower elevations. *Elata* means "tall." Native OLYM

Clematis ligusticifolia RANUNCULACEAE
Western white clematis, virgin's bower
Locally common, midsummer, perennial,
vine, to 50 ft. Moist streambanks, west-side
forest, east-side forest

Woody vine tangled into treetops or usually found growing along ground, clambering through bushes, over fences. Leaves with main stalk carrying 5–15 leaflets, each with 3 lobes, coarsely toothed. Flowers white in loose clusters, male and female flowers on separate vines often twined together. Male flowers have many stamens; female flowers have many pistils, stamens with no pollen. Seed with long feathery tails attached form fluffy sphere. Grows in wet places, along streams, at low to mid elevations. Native OLYM, NOCA

Clematis vitalba RANUNCULACEAE
Traveler's joy
Locally common, all summer, perennial, to
50 ft. Disturbed, west-side forest

Woody vine climbing trees, shrubs, fences, or sprawling on ground if without supports. Leaves divided pinnately, leaflets entire or upper lobed with stalk twining around supports. Flowers, in loose clusters from leaf axils, contain both male and female parts, about ¾ in. across, 5 greenish white petal-like sepals. Seed at center of fluffy head of long twisted tails. Grows in limey soils, sand, waste places in woodlands and open areas. Very similar to the native *C. ligusticifolia*, found in wet places, with coarsely toothed leaves and separate male and female flowers. Nonnative OLYM, NOCA

118

See other *Clematis*: red, page 355

Coptis laciniata RANUNCULACEAE
Cut-leaved goldthread
Uncommon, midspring, perennial, 4–10 in.
West-side forest

Erect. Stems short, stout. Basal leaves evergreen, divided into 3 triangular toothed lobes.
Flower stem 3–10 in., leafless, with 1–2 flowers
at top. Sepals narrow, 5–8, greenish, petal-like.
Petals 5–7, white, club-shaped, fall early leaving many thread-like stamens. Grows in seeps, streambanks,
often among mosses on wet sites in conifer forests, below 3000
ft. Native OLYM

Ranunculus aquatilis RANUNCULACEAE
White water buttercup
Common, all summer, perennial, floating
Bog/fen/wetland, lake/pond

Aquatic in shallow water. Leaves of 2 types:
common submerged leaves are divided into
long thread-like segments; leaves floating on
surface are few, shiny, almost round, divided
into 3 parts, each then shallowly cut again.
Flowers white, 5 petals at end of long stems in
floating mat. Grows in any slow-moving to still
water at low to high elevations. Native

OLYM, MORA, NOCA

Trautvetteria caroliniensis RANUNCULACEAE
False bugbane
Locally common, early summer, perennial,
24–40 in. Moist streambanks, west-side forest,
east-side forest

Erect, forming colonies from spreading underground roots. Stems hairless below, curly
hairs in inflorescence. Leaves mostly basal,
large, more or less round, deeply palmately divided, 5–10 lobes, toothed; medium green on
upper surface, lighter underneath. Inflorescence flat-topped with 5 or more flowers.
Flower sepals 3–7, white, falling off early;
showy fluffy flowers have 50–70 white sta-
mens, 10 or more pistils. Grows in moist shaded forests, along
streams, at mid to high elevations. Foliage very similar to that
of closely related tall bugbane, *Cimicifuga elata*. Native

OLYM, MORA, NOCA

See other *Ranunculus*: yellow, page 218

Trollius laxus RANUNCULACEAE
American globeflower
Locally common, late spring–early summer, perennial, 4–20 in. Alpine, subalpine
Basal leaves with erect sturdy flower stems. Leaves about 2 in. across, round in outline, divided to center into 5 lobes, unevenly toothed. Flowers large, single at stem tops, 5 greenish white to cream petals, many yellow stamens, the outer ones modified into flat structures. Flowering occurs just after snowmelt in high mountains. Native
OLYM, MORA, NOCA

Angelica arguta APIACEAE
Sharptooth angelica
Locally common, late spring, perennial, 2–7 ft. Vernal-wet, bog/fen/wetland, meadow
Erect, mostly hairless, with possible hairs on underside of leaf. Stem hollow, with noticeable sheath surrounding petiole. Leaves divided into 3 egg-shaped to triangular, sharply pointed leaflets, 2–6 in. long and often lobed. Twenty to 60 small clusters of hairless flower heads on 1–4 in. stalks form flat umbel. Petals usually white, occasionally yellow or pink. Widespread, found along waterways and in wet places at low elevations. *Arguta* refers to the sharp teeth on leaves that are often toothed again. Native
OLYM, MORA, NOCA, **L&C**

Angelica genuflexa APIACEAE
Kneeling angelica
Locally common, late spring, perennial, 3–8 ft. Coastal, bog/fen/wetland, meadow
Stout with hairy to hairless foliage. Stem hollow, often purplish, shiny. Leaves pinnately compound. First pair of leaflets bends back sharply at stalk. Both common and species names (the latter meaning "having knee-like joints") refer to the uniquely bent leaf stalk. Egg- to lance-shaped leaflets 1–4 in. long, coarsely toothed. Petioles enlarged at base and sheathing stem. Umbel of 25–50 clusters of hairy flower heads with conspicuous bractlets on 2–7 in. stalks. White or pale pink flowers. Grows in streambanks, wet places, at low elevations. Native OLYM, MORA, NOCA

Angelica lucida APIACEAE
Sea-watch, seacoast angelica
Locally common, late spring, perennial,
2–4½ ft. Coastal, bog/fen/wetland, meadow
Stem single and stout, hairless. Leaves 4–12 in., pinnately divided into 3 leaflets, green, shiny on both sides, petioles sheathed at axis with stem. Leaflets 1–4 in. long, oval, irregularly toothed. Small white flowers without bracts occur in 20–40 tight clusters on 1–3 in. stalks, forming an umbel. Grows on bluffs, beaches, streams near coast, infrequently inland. Native OLYM

Cicuta douglasii APIACEAE
Douglas's water-hemlock, western water-hemlock
Common, early summer, perennial, 2–6 ft.
Coastal, vernal-wet, bog/fen/wetland, meadow, west-side forest, east-side forest
Stems single to few arising from a thickened base with open chambers. Sap turns reddish brown when exposed to air. Leaves 3 times pinnately divided into narrow lance-shaped to oblong leaflets ⅓–4 in. long, coarsely saw-toothed. Secondary veins end at gap between teeth. White to greenish flowers in 15–30 small crowded clusters form a mostly bractless umbel. Widespread in wet places, shallow water, below 3000 ft. Very toxic plant, should be carefully avoided. If you get juice of plant on your hands, wash immediately. Even small amounts can cause death if eaten. Native OLYM, MORA, NOCA

Conium maculatum APIACEAE
Poison-hemlock
Common, early summer, biennial, 6–8 ft.
Coastal, disturbed, meadow
Taproot white. Stems erect, streaked or spotted purple. Petioles enlarged and sheathing at base. Leaf blades 8–12 in. long, pinnately divided, fern-like. Numerous white flowers form compact clusters within umbels. Smells musty when crushed. Introduced from Europe, found mostly below 3000 ft. in marshes, ditches, along beaches, other wet places. So toxic even a tiny amount of sap, leaf, or seed can cause severe sickness if eaten. Always watch children when visiting wet places where this plant is rampant. *Maculatum* means "marked" or "spotted." Nonnative OLYM, MORA, NOCA

Daucus carota APIACEAE
Queen Anne's lace, wild carrot
Common, late summer, biennial, 1–3 ft.
Coastal, disturbed, meadow, west-side
forest

Stem erect, branching. Leaves pinnately divided to form linear leaflets. Lacy heads composed of hundreds of small flowers. As flowers age, outer edge of inflorescence elongates and curls over center, creating effect of a bird's nest, noticeable in late summer and autumn. Umbel often bears 1 central pink, purple, or brown flower, a possible guide for pollinating insects. Grows on roadsides, disturbed soils, from coast to 4000 ft. Parent plant of our cultivated carrot, with similar odor. *Daucus pusillus*, a native annual, is less abundant, smaller, and without the single colored flower in center. Nonnative OLYM, NOCA

Glehnia littoralis subsp. *leiocarpa*
(*Glehnia leiocarpa*) APIACEAE
Beach silvertop, beach carrot, American glehnia
Locally common, early summer, perennial
Coastal

Prostrate, spreading outward from woody base. Leaves fleshy, with 1–4 in. petiole; blade 1–6 in. wide, divided pinnately, and divided again to 3 egg-shaped leaflets with coarse teeth. Leaflets hairless above, white matted hairs beneath. Inflorescence is tight cluster of white flowers on hairy stalks. Grows in sandy beaches and dunes. Native OLYM

Heracleum maximum (*Heracleum lanatum*) APIACEAE
Cow parsnip
Common, late spring–early summer,
perennial, 3–10 ft. Coastal, vernal-wet,
disturbed, meadow, west-side forest, east-
side forest, alpine, subalpine

Erect, stout, strongly scented, covered with long hairs. Stem single, hollow, usually branched. Leaves huge, maple-like, with 4–16 in. long petiole enlarged at base and widely sheathing. Leaf blade divided palmately into 3 parts, each to 12 in. long and coarsely toothed. Umbels of flower heads often more than 10 in. across, flat. Grows in streambanks, open or lightly shaded woods, moist places, from near coastline to high elevations. A large plant appropriately named for Hercules, son of Zeus, a mortal of extraordinary power and size. Native
OLYM, MORA, NOCA, **L&C**

5 symmetrical petals (ovary inferior)

Ligusticum apiifolium APIACEAE
Celery-leaf lovage, parsley-leaf lovage
Locally common, early summer, perennial, 1–5
ft. Coastal, meadow, west-side forest

Erect, lightly coated with short stiff hairs. Stem
branched, leafy. Basal leaves include 4–12 in.
petiole, blade oblong to round to 10 in. across,
pinnately separated into widely triangular segments, each then divided 2 times; leaflets oval,
lobed. Stem leaves same, smaller. Inflorescence stalks 4–14 in.,
topped by 12–23 clusters of white flowers in rounded umbel.
Grows in meadows, shady woods, below 5000 ft. Native OLYM

Ligusticum grayi APIACEAE
Gray's lovage
Common, all summer, perennial, 3–36 in. West-
side forest, east-side forest, alpine, subalpine
Erect, hairless. Stem leafless or with few small
leaves. Basal leaves divided 3 times into leaflets
less than 2 in. long, egg-shaped, with narrowly
pointed lobes. Flowers in 5–14 small compact
clusters in an umbel at stem top without bracts
under the flowers. Grows in bogs, wet to dry
openings in upper forests and subalpine meadows. Native MORA, NOCA

Lomatium canbyi APIACEAE
Canby's desert parsley, chucklusa
Rare, early spring, perennial, 2–6 in.
Vernal-wet, east-side forest, shrub-steppe
Stout, erect. Stems hairless. Basal leaves shiny gray-green, pinnately divided into very short narrow seg-
ments. Flower stalk 2–5 in., light to dark red or
brown. Flowers white with purple anthers,
clustered in tight bunches to form large round
umbel with bractlets as long as flowers. Grows
in barren, rocky sagebrush-steppe at mid elevations. See *L. piperi* and *L. gormanii*, both similar species. Native

See other *Lomatium*: yellow, page 224; red, page 356; green/brown,
page 467

Lomatium gormanii APIACEAE

Gorman's lomatium, salt and pepper
Locally common, all spring, perennial,
4–10 in. East-side forest, shrub-steppe

Stems erect to spreading. Leaves sheath
stem, divided into lobed linear to oblong
segments, hairless or with few hairs. Umbels are beyond leaves, with 4–10 unequal
stalks, each bearing rounded clusters of
white or lavender flowers containing dark purple anthers.
Grows in steppe and on mountain ridges at mid elevations.
Among the first to bloom in spring. See similar *L. piperi*, also
with purple anthers and also called salt and pepper. Native

Lomatium macrocarpum APIACEAE

**Giant-seed lomatium, large-fruited biscuit-
root, large-fruited desert parsley**
Common, early spring, perennial, 4–20 in.
West-side forest, shrub-steppe, alpine,
subalpine

Prostrate, finely haired. Stems very short.
Leaves hairy, divided pinnately 3 times, create fine low-growing net of foliage, gray with
purple underneath. Inflorescence held on
stems beyond foliage. Flowers very small
and white, yellow, or purplish, with turned-down bracts under
only 1 side of cluster. Grows in rocky slopes, woodlands, at low
elevations. Named for the large seeds, *macro* meaning "large"
and *carpum*, "fruit." Native NOCA

Lomatium piperi APIACEAE

Salt and pepper, Piper's desert parsley
Uncommon, early spring, perennial, 2–4 in.
Shrub-steppe

Prostrate, tiny. Leaf blades deep green, twice
pinnately dissected into linear leaflets to 1
in. long. Clusters of white flowers with purple anthers form umbels on unequal stalks.
Grows in rocky slopes with sagebrush, pine
woodlands, arid areas, at low to mid elevations. Called salt and pepper in reference to
the white flowers and dark purple anthers. See *L. gormanii*, a
similar species also known as salt and pepper. Native

Oenanthe sarmentosa APIACEAE
Pacific water parsley
Locally common, all summer, perennial, 1–4 ft.
Coastal, vernal-wet, bog/fen/wetland, meadow

Clump or single stem, plant hairless. Stem ascending to reclining, rooting at nodes. Leaves on 4–12 in. stalks, widely egg-shaped, pinnately divided into toothed, egg-shaped leaflets with veins pointing to tips of teeth. Inflorescence consists of 5–20 flower clusters in flat-topped umbel. Flowers many, white-petaled. Grows in marshes, ditches, pond edges, seasonally wet places, from near coastline to mid elevations. Native OLYM, MORA, NOCA

Osmorhiza berteroi (*Osmorhiza chilensis*) APIACEAE
Common sweet cicely, sweet root, mountain sweet cicely
Common, late spring–early summer, perennial, 1–4 ft. Coastal, vernal-wet, meadow, west-side forest, east-side forest

Stems erect, 1 to few branches above midstem. Leaves hairy, numerous, held horizontally, 2–6 in. long, twice pinnately segmented into threes. Leaflets widely egg-shaped, 1–3 in. long, toothed or lobed. Long leafless flower stalk 2–10 in. Flowers tiny, inconspicuous, greenish white. Black seed is needle-shaped, with tail on end, and bristles that sometimes catch on clothing. Grows in open forests, shaded woodlands, at low to high elevations. *Osmorhiza purpurea* is very similar but leaves not hairy and grows in moister forests. Native OLYM, NOCA

Perideridia bolanderi APIACEAE
Bolander's yampah, olasi, mountain false caraway
Common, early summer, perennial, 6–36 in. Meadow, east-side forest, shrub-steppe

Erect. Stems branched. Basal leaves with 1–6 in. petioles, pinnately dissected to thread-like sections, some longer and wider than others, often lobed and toothed; the few stem leaves are smaller. Umbel consists of numerous clusters of small white flowers sustained by thin tan bractlets. Grows in meadows, scrub pine, woodlands with summer-dry clay soils, at mid to high elevations. Native

See other *Osmorhiza*: yellow, page 227

Perideridia gairdneri APIACEAE
Gairdner's yampah
Common, late summer, perennial, 1–4 ft.
Coastal, vernal-wet, meadow, west-side
forest, east-side forest, alpine, subalpine

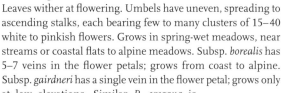

Erect, slender plant smelling like caraway.
Basal leaves with blade divided 1–2 times
pinnately into 3–5 pairs of 1–12 in. long,
narrow segments; stem leaves less divided.
Leaves wither at flowering. Umbels have uneven, spreading to
ascending stalks, each bearing few to many clusters of 15–40
white to pinkish flowers. Grows in spring-wet meadows, near
streams or coastal flats to alpine meadows. Subsp. *borealis* has
5–7 veins in the flower petals; grows from coast to alpine.
Subsp. *gairdneri* has a single vein in the flower petal; grows only
at low elevations. Similar *P. oregana* is
smaller, with broader and better-developed
bractlets. Native OLYM, NOCA, **L&C**

Sium suave APIACEAE
Water parsnip
Locally common, midsummer, perennial,
1–3 ft. Bog/fen/wetland, meadow

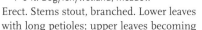

Erect. Stems stout, branched. Lower leaves
with long petioles; upper leaves becoming
sessile. Submerged leaves twice divided into lobed leaflets.
Upper leaves once divided pinnately to linear, minutely saw-
toothed leaflets. Veins of leaflets not in line with teeth or
notches below teeth. Flower petals white, wide, becoming narrow at tip. Bracts at base of 10–20 stems reflexed. Grows in
swamps, marshes, shallow water at edges of waterways, at low
to mid elevations. Native OLYM

Sphenosciadium capitellatum
APIACEAE
**Rangers button, swamp white heads,
woolly-headed parsnip**
Locally common, all summer, perennial, 2–5
ft. Bog/fen/wetland, lake/pond, meadow,
east-side forest

Erect. Stem branched, bearing large leaves.
Petioles 4–15 in. long, forming sheaths noticeably enlarged
around stems. Leaf blade oblong, 4–15 in., divided 3–4 times;
leaflets lance-shaped, ½–5 in. long, irregularly lobed or
toothed. Flower stalks 3–16 in. long, holding round tight clusters of small white or purplish flowers with narrow-tipped
petals. Grows in wet soils near lakes, streams, or meadows, at
mid elevations. Toxic to animals, rarely eaten. Native

Oplopanax horridus ARALIACEAE
Devil's club
Locally common, late spring–early summer,
perennial, 3–10 ft. Bog/fen/wetland, meadow,
west-side forest

Erect or sprawling shrub, densely covered with
long yellow spines. Stems thick, mostly unbranched, often bent, tangling and forming
thickets. Leaves to 14 in. across, deciduous, alternate on stem, maple-like, heavily toothed, with spines on
veins and petiole. Many inflorescences in long spikes or cones
atop stems. Flowers greenish white, small, with stamens exerted beyond petals. Berries scarlet. Grows in streambanks and
moist places within forests. Spines on all parts of plant are ir-
ritating when touched. Native OLYM, MORA, NOCA, CRLA

Philadelphus lewisii HYDRANGEACEAE
Lewis's mock-orange, western syringa
Common, early summer, perennial, 3–9 ft.
West-side forest, east-side forest

Large, woody, erect to spreading shrub with
many stems and branches. Stems red-brown,
turning gray with age. Leaves opposite, deciduous, oval to egg-shaped, 1–4 in. long, entire to
toothed, with 3 veins running from base to tip
of leaf. Flowers fragrant, 6 or more clustered at end of stem,
about 1 in. across, with 4 or occasionally 5 white petals, many
stamens with large amounts of yellow pollen clustered in center. Grows in moist woods, conifer forests, rocky canyons, at
low to mid elevations throughout western North America. State
flower of Idaho. First collected by Lewis and Clark and named
for Meriwether Lewis. Native

OLYM, MORA, **L&C**

Whipplea modesta HYDRANGEACEAE
Whipplevine, yerba de selva
Common, late spring–early summer, perennial,
mat. West-side forest

Mat of trailing stems. Main stem somewhat
woody; bark gray-brown, peeling in narrow
strips. Leaves oval to egg-shaped, shallowly
toothed, on very short petioles, with coarse hairs. Leaves persist
on stems after withering. Inflorescence consists of dense terminal clusters on short erect shoots from main stem. Flowers
small, with 5–6 white egg-shaped petals. Grows in conifer
forests, openings, on banks, below 5000 ft. Native

OLYM, MORA, NOCA

Amelanchier alnifolia ROSACEAE
Western serviceberry, saskatoon
Common, midspring, perennial, 5–20 ft.
Moist streambanks, west-side forest, east-side forest, shrub-steppe

Deciduous shrub. Roots spread out forming colonies of gray to reddish brown branched bushes. Leaves alternate, thin, oval to round, serrate on upper ½. Flowers 3–15, pure white, forming clusters, each blossom about 1¼ in. across with 5 narrow petals, 10–20 stamens. Fruit red, becoming deep purple-black. Grows in open meadows, fencerows, woodlands, streambanks, conifer forests, at low to high elevations. Fruit is good for making jelly. Var. *semiintegrifolia* is common in Pacific Northwest, with petals about ½ in. long and ovary densely grayish with fine hairs on top. Native
MORA, NOCA, **L&C**

Aruncus dioicus (Aruncus sylvester)
ROSACEAE
Goat's beard, spaghetti flower, bride's feathers
Common, early summer, perennial, 2–7 ft.
Moist streambanks, west-side forest

Stems several, erect, from creeping roots, robust, hairless, holding large leaves. Leaves slightly hairy, divided pinnately 3 times to center vein; leaflets widely oval, 1–6 in. long, sharply toothed with pointed tips. Flower stalks in loose groups on stems above leaves. Flowers white, tiny, hanging or drooping in dense long strings; male and female flowers on separate plants. Grows in streambanks, edges of moist conifer forests, roadside ditches, at low elevations. Native OLYM, MORA, NOCA

Crataegus douglasii ROSACEAE
Black hawthorn
Locally common, late spring, perennial, 6–18 ft. Meadow, west-side forest, east-side forest

Deciduous upright shrub or small tree usually with ½–¾ in. thorns. Leaves on short twigs, usually about 2 in. long, wedge-shaped, entire to slightly toothed at narrow base, sides rounded to wide-toothed or with shallowly lobed tip. Flowers clustered at branch tips or in leaf axils, 5 white petals from cup-shaped base, 10 stamens. Fruit plump, purple-black, with 4–5 hard seeds, edible. Grows along streams, in forests, meadows, ditches, fencerows, sagebrush, at low to high elevations. Similar *C. suksdorfii*, with 20 stamens, grows in western Washington, western British Columbia, and from Willamette Valley to southwestern Oregon. Native NOCA

Fragaria chiloensis ROSACEAE
Beach strawberry, coast strawberry
Locally common, all spring and summer,
perennial, mat. Coastal

Mat of short, rooting, prostrate stems. Leaves
large, thick, leathery, divided into 3 leaflets.
Leaflets almost round, round-toothed, densely
hairy on underside. Central tooth on leaf is
shorter than its neighbors. Flowers 5–9 on
leafless stalks. Flower white, large, ¾–1 in. across, with 5 petals.
Strawberry is small. Grows in ocean dunes and beaches, into
adjacent grasslands. One of the parents of cultivated strawber-
ries. Native OLYM

Fragaria vesca ROSACEAE
Greenleaf strawberry, woods strawberry
Common, late spring, perennial, 4–12 in.
West-side forest, east-side forest

Mat of leafless stolons. Leaves thin, slightly
hairy, green on both surfaces, divided into 3
widely oval leaflets with very prominent veins,
deeply toothed. Terminal tooth of leaflet longer
than neighboring teeth. Flowers small, 2–5 on
a stem. Berries small, bright red, edible. Grows
in partly shaded forests at 100–6500 ft. Var.
crinita, woodland strawberry, is silvery on lower surface of
leaves, hairless above; flower stems about same height as
leaves. Var. *bracteata* has flower stems elongating, becoming
much longer than leaves as fruit ripens. Native
OLYM, MORA, NOCA, CRLA

Fragaria virginiana ROSACEAE
Virginia strawberry, mountain strawberry
Common, late spring, perennial, 2–6 in.
Meadow, west-side forest, east-side forest

Mat. Leaves thin, noticeably blue-green, without hairs on upper surface, divided into 3
leaflets on short stalks, each toothed from middle to tip, central tooth shorter than its neighbors. Leaf veins not prominent, as in *F. vesca*.
Flowers often 1 per stem, which does not ex-
ceed height of leaves; petals almost round, white or slightly
pink. Fruit succulent, palatable. Grows in openings in woods,
streambanks, meadows, from near coastline to subalpine zone.
Native OLYM, MORA, NOCA, CRLA

5 symmetrical petals (ovary inferior)

Holodiscus discolor ROSACEAE
Ocean spray, creambush, ironwood
Common, late spring–early summer,
perennial, 4–9 ft. Coastal, meadow, west-
side forest, east-side forest

Shrub with stiff slender stems. Stems somewhat hairy, reddish when young, aging to
gray. Leaves alternate, 1–5 in. long, oval or
somewhat triangular, large rounded teeth
with fine secondary teeth or very small rounded lobes, deeply
veined; petiole round, with no flat edges. Flowers white to
cream on leafless sprays 4–10 in. long, about as wide. Flowers
less than 1/8 in. in size, each a tiny saucer-shaped cup of 5 petals
with hairs on outer surface, inside hairless. Fragrant. Flowers
fade to tan in late summer and remain on the bush through
most of winter. Grows in rocky open places
to moist woods, from sea level to mid elevations. Native OLYM, MORA, NOCA, **L&C**

Horkelia daucifolia ROSACEAE
Carrot-leaved horkelia
Rare, all summer, perennial, 6–12 in. West-
side forest

Rosette grayish, not strong-smelling. Stems
ascending, reddish. Leaves 2–6 in. long, pinnately divided into 10–20 crowded leaflets, each divided ¾ to
base into many linear silky-haired narrow lobes. Inflorescence
clustered at stem top, consisting of 5–25 creamy to white
flowers drying to yellowish brown, with 5 oval petals narrowing
to slender stalk at base; 5 green pointed sepals are slightly
shorter; 10 stamens become wider at base. Grows on serpentine, clay, other soils in dry open places, at
low to mid elevations. Native

Horkelia fusca ROSACEAE
Dusky horkelia, pink pinwheels
Locally common, late spring–early summer,
perennial, 4–20 in. Meadow, east-side
forest, alpine, subalpine

Tufted. Stems upright. Basal leaves 5–12 in.
long, fern-like, pinnately divided, 9–19
bright green leaflets, oval, divided into opposite linear segments or toothed; stem leaves similar, becoming smaller upward. Flowers cluster at stem top. Flowers white or pink, about
½ in. across, with reddish cup-shaped calyx, petals wider at tip
end, very narrow at base, 10 stamens, 10–25 pistils. Grows in
damp meadows, forest openings, rocky slopes, at high elevations. Native CRLA

Horkelia hendersonii ROSACEAE
Henderson's horkelia
Endemic, all summer, perennial, 5–8 in. Alpine, subalpine

Tufted, soft grayish. Leaves cylindrical, 1–4 in., spreading to erect, crowded with 10–20 wedge-shaped densely hairy leaflets, 5-toothed. Inflorescence dense with 5–20 flowers topping reddish stem with few small leaves. Flower base densely hairy; reddish lance-shaped sepals and linear to oblong white petals slightly shorter in length than small narrow bractlets just below sepals. Grows in granitic soils at 6500–7600 ft. Rare in northwestern California and southwestern Oregon. Found on Mount Ashland in Jackson County, Oregon. Native

Ivesia baileyi var. *beneolens* ROSACEAE
Owyhee ivesia
Uncommon, midspring, perennial, 2–8 in. Alpine, subalpine

Low tufted green perennial. Stems growing outward or hanging downward. Basal leaves many, 2–6 in. long, bearing 2–14 pairs of leaflets, each somewhat separated from others; leaflets small, oval, deeply lobed. Stem leaves much smaller or absent. Inflorescence tightly clustered, more than 10 flowers atop stalks over twice the length of leaves. Petals white or pale yellow, 5 stamens, 6 or fewer pistils. Grows in vertical crevices in rimrock, volcanic rocks and cliffs, at mid to high elevations in southeastern Oregon. Native

Luetkea pectinata ROSACEAE
Partridgefoot
Common, all summer, perennial, 4–6 in. Westside forest, alpine, subalpine

Mats with rooting runners creating new plants, thick with evergreen leaves, upright stems. Leaves ½ in., divided into sharply pointed linear segments. Upright stems leafy, tall, straight, with white flowers in dense spikes. Flowers small, 5 white petals, approximately 20 obvious stamens. Grows in moist meadows, conifer forests, subalpine and alpine, often where snow persists. Native
OLYM, MORA, NOCA, CRLA

See other *Ivesia*: yellow, page 231

131

Oemleria cerasiformis (*Osmaronia cerasiformis*) ROSACEAE
Indian plum, osoberry
Common, early spring, perennial, 3–15 ft.
Moist streambanks, west-side forest

Small tree or multistemmed shrub, with male and female flowers on separate plants. Leaves narrowly oval, smooth or with edges somewhat rolled under, with strong odor of cucumber when broken. Flowers bell-shaped, greenish white, with unpleasant odor. All flowers with 15 stamens, female flowers with 5 pistils. Hanging clusters of flowers open in late winter before leaves emerge. Fruit pink turning deep blue when ripe, looks like small plum covered with white waxy powder. Grows in edges of shaded forests, oak savannas, chaparral, at low to mid elevations. Our earliest blooming native shrub. A common roadside plant around Puget Sound. Native
OLYM, MORA, NOCA

Petrophyton hendersonii (*Petrophytum hendersonii*) ROSACEAE
Olympic rockmat
Endemic, midsummer, perennial, 3–6 in.
Alpine

Tight leafy mat with woody base. Rosettes crowded with evergreen leaves, reddish when stressed. Leaves oblong, widest at tip end, to ¾ in. long, sparsely hairy. Flower stalk to 3 in. bearing dense spike of tiny white flowers with many stamens. As spike elongates it often bends with upper ½ turned out or downward. Grows in rock crevices in alpine. In Greek, *petro* means "rock" and *phyton* means "plant." This refers to the habit the plants in this genus have of growing in rock crevices. Rare and known only from Olympic Mountains in Washington. Native OLYM

Physocarpus capitatus ROSACEAE
Pacific ninebark
Locally common, late spring–early summer, perennial, 6–12 ft. Coastal, moist streambanks, west-side forest

Deciduous shrub with thin brown bark shredding into many layers on older wood. Leaves 1–2 in. long, with petioles to ¾ in., 3- to 5-lobed and toothed, shiny green above. Inflorescence is a round snowball-like cluster. Flowers more or less ½ in. across, with 5 white rounded petals, many stamens, hairs divided like a star on the calyx. Grows in moist places such as streambanks, north-facing slopes, edges of forests, at low to mid elevations. Native OLYM, MORA, NOCA

Prunus emarginata   ROSACEAE
Bitter cherry
Common, late spring, perennial, 3–30 ft.
Coastal, meadow, west-side forest, east-side
forest

Shrub to small tree, often produces thickets.
Bark reddish brown to gray, rows of pores
around the trunk. Leaves deciduous, 1–1½ in.
long, widest toward rounded tip, with fine
teeth. Flowers in flat-topped cluster. Flower petals 5, white to
pinkish, more or less 20 stamens. Fruit is a bitter cherry ⅓ in.
in diameter, bright red. Grows in mixed forests, rocky slopes, at
mid to alpine elevations. Var. *mollis* is tree-like, to 50 ft., calyx
and lower leaf surface thickly short-hairy; found west of Cascades. Var. *emarginata* is shrub-like, with many stems to 12 ft.
tall; found east of Cascades. Important food for
birds. Native OLYM, MORA, NOCA, CRLA, **L&C**

Prunus virginiana   ROSACEAE
Chokecherry, common chokecherry
Common, late spring, perennial, 2–12 ft. Moist
streambanks, west-side forest, east-side forest

Shrub or small tree. Leaves 2–3 in., deciduous,
oblong or oval, with round base and pointed
tips, finely toothed. White flowers, many, in
clusters that are much longer than wide. Fruit dark red or purple to black. Grows in wooded, rocky slopes, edges of forests,
along streams, at low to mid elevations. Found throughout
western North America excluding Alaska. Important food for
birds. Native OLYM, NOCA, **L&C**

Rubus discolor (*Rubus procerus*)   ROSACEAE
Himalayan blackberry
Common, early summer, perennial, 3–9 ft.
Coastal, disturbed, meadow

Sprawling to arching bramble, stems often
reaching 30 ft. in length. Stems 5-angled,
armed with many curved thorns with stout
broad base. Leaves often more or less evergreen, divided palmately, 3–5 leaflets widest at
the middle, sharply toothed, white on under-
side. Flowers numerous, clustered white or pink. Fruit shiny,
black, with many small sections forming an oval to round berry.
Invasive in disturbed moist areas along roads, ditches, and
fences at low to mid elevations, this is our common and very
tasty introduced blackberry. Native to Europe and Asia. Compare to *R. laciniatus*, also invasive, with similar growth habit
and fruit but deeply cut leaves. Nonnative OLYM, NOCA

See other *Rubus*: red, page 360

Rubus idaeus ROSACEAE
Western red raspberry
Locally common, late spring–early summer,
perennial, 1–6 ft. Moist streambanks,
meadow, west-side forest, east-side forest

Slender, erect to arching bramble. Stems
purple or yellow, often coated with whitish
powder, armed with thinly spaced straight
thorns. Leaves divided, 3–5 oval leaflets,
petioles and midveins usually thorny and glandular. Leaflets
sharply toothed, shiny on top, densely coated with white hairs
underneath. Flowers clustered, white. Berries yellowish or light
red. Grows in streambanks, open meadows, moist woods,
thickets, at low to mid elevations. Native MORA, NOCA

Rubus laciniatus ROSACEAE
Cut-leaved blackberry, evergreen blackberry
Common, late spring–early summer,
perennial, to 30 ft. Coastal, disturbed,
meadow

Stout, sprawling to arching bramble. Stems
5-angled, with strong recurved thorns.
Leaves evergreen, divided palmately, 3–5
leaflets. Leaflets deeply lobed with each lobe
sharply toothed and pointed, underside
hairy and green. Flowers more than 1 in., often more than 10
per cluster. Petals 5, oval, pink or white. Blackberries oval,
black, shiny, delicious. Weedy and invasive in moist disturbed
places at low to mid elevations. Compare to *R. discolor*, a more
common invasive nonnative blackberry, with undivided
leaflets. Nonnative OLYM, MORA, NOCA

Rubus lasiococcus ROSACEAE
Dwarf bramble, creeping raspberry
Locally common, all summer, perennial, 1–4
in. West-side forest, east-side forest

Creeping on ground, rooting at nodes.
Stems round to 6 ft. long, thornless. Leaves
divided palmately, the 3 leaflets widely oval,
finely toothed, green on top and underside.
Flower small, petals widely oval, white. Fruit
tiny, raspberry-like, red, densely hairy. Grows in open forests at
mid to relatively high elevations. Can be confused with *R. pe-
datus*, which has 3–5 leaflets but narrower petals. Native
OLYM, MORA, NOCA, CRLA

Rubus leucodermis ROSACEAE
Blackcap raspberry, black raspberry, white-stemmed blackcap
Common, late spring, perennial, 3–7 ft.
Meadows, alpine, subalpine

Arching to erect bramble. Stems coated with whitish powder, many recurved thorns with wide, usually curved base. Leaf petiole ½–2 in., blade palmately divided into 3–5 oval leaflets shallowly lobed and toothed, underside white-hairy. Flowers few, small, white to pink, in clusters near tops of branches, 5 reflexed sepals longer than petals. Raspberries hairy, about ⅓ in. across, red turning purple to black. Grows in rocky moist areas from near sea level to alpine. Very tasty. Native

OLYM, MORA, NOCA, CRLA

Rubus parviflorus ROSACEAE
Thimbleberry
Common, all spring and summer, perennial,
2–9 ft. Coastal, west-side forest, east-side forest

Erect shrub often making dense thickets. Stems woody, bark brown and shredding, no thorns. Leaves broad, maple-like, with 3–5 finely toothed lobes pointed at tips, green on upper and lower surfaces. Petioles and flower stems often with stemmed glands. Flowers in clusters of 2–9. Flowers large, white, textured like crumpled paper, each petal to 1 in. across. Fruit red, raspberry-like, slightly hairy. Grows in moist shady woods below alpine. Fruit edible and tasty but seedy. Native OLYM, MORA, NOCA, CRLA, **L&C**

Rubus pedatus ROSACEAE
Strawberry bramble, five-leaved bramble, dwarf bramble
Locally common, late spring–early summer, perennial, 1–4 in. Coastal, moist streambanks, west-side forest, east-side forest, alpine, subalpine

Trailing and rooting at nodes. Stems thornless. Leaves with long erect petioles arising at nodes, divided palmately. Leaflets 3–5, oval, with sharply cut teeth. Flowers solitary on long stalks about same height as leaves, 5 small white petals clearly separated, reflexed when fully open. Fruit bright red and juicy, shiny, 1–6 separate drupelets in cluster. Grows in moist mossy woods, along streams, bog margins, from near coast to subalpine and nearly timberline. Fruit small but tasty. Can be confused with *R. lasiococcus*, with only 3 leaflets and broader petals. Native

OLYM, MORA, NOCA

Rubus ursinus   ROSACEAE
Trailing blackberry, dewberry, Pacific blackberry
Common, late spring–early summer, perennial, low vine. Disturbed, meadow, west-side forest, east-side forest

Trailing tangles on ground. Stems round, vigorous. Thorns recurved, not flattened. Leaves divided into 3 distinct leaflets to 6 in. long, dark green on both sides, toothed, middle leaflet with 3 lobes. Flowers white or pink, more than 1 in. across, borne in clusters. Male, female flowers on separate plants. Blackberries small, longer than wide. Grows at low to mid elevations. Fruit is delicious. Native OLYM, MORA, NOCA, CRLA

Sanguisorba annua (*Sanguisorba occidentalis*)   ROSACEAE
Western burnet
Locally common, late spring–early summer, annual or perennial, 4–25 in.
Bog/fen/wetland, disturbed, meadow, west-side forest, east-side forest

Stem ascending. Basal leaves withered by bloom time; stem leaves 1–5 in. long, divided pinnately. Leaflets 9–17, sessile, oval, deeply lobed, with linear segments. Flower spikes at branch tips barrel-shaped, with greenish white flowers, petals lacking, 4 sepals shorter than the 2 well-exserted stamens. Grows in open areas, especially on disturbed soils. Similar *S. canadensis* is 10–40 in., with toothed rather than lobed leaflets; grows in bogs, wet places. Native NOCA

Sorbus scopulina   ROSACEAE
Cascade mountain-ash
Locally common, late spring–early summer, perennial, 3–12 ft. West-side forest, east-side forest, alpine, subalpine

Erect shrub, sticky, with whitish stemmed glands on new growth. Leaves deciduous, alternate, pinnately divided. Leaflets 9–13, yellow-green, 1–3 in. long, narrow, lance-shaped, with sharply pointed tips, fine-toothed. Inflorescence is a 2–4 in. round-topped cluster. Flowers white, small, petals nearly round. Fruit small, round, orange to red, present after leaves fall in autumn. Grows in meadows, canyons, along streams, open conifer forests, at mid to alpine elevations. Var. *cascadensis* usually grows west of Cascade Range crest, with leaflets seldom more than 11, round petals, red fruit. On east side is var. *scopulina*, usually with 13 leaflets, oval petals, orange-red fruit. Native OLYM, MORA, NOCA, CRLA, **L&C**

Sorbus sitchensis ROSACEAE
Sitka mountain-ash
Locally common, late spring–early summer,
perennial, 3–12 ft. Meadows, alpine, subalpine

Erect shrub, red-brown hairs on young growth.
Leaves long, divided into 7–11 blue-green
leaflets with rounded tips. Leaflets broader
near tip, toothed. Inflorescence is a 2–4 in.
round-topped cluster of small white flowers.
Berries bright red with whitish waxy coating, hanging after
leaves fall in autumn. Grows in rocky open slopes at mid to
alpine but mostly subalpine elevations. Berries very tart, eaten
mostly by migrating birds, although suitable for jelly. Var. *grayi*
leaflets are toothed just above middle. Var. *sitchensis*, found in
western British Columbia and Washington, has leaflets toothed
½–¾ of the way around. Native
OLYM, MORA, NOCA, CRLA, **L&C**

Spiraea betulifolia var. *lucida*
ROSACEAE
White spiraea, birchleaf spiraea
Uncommon, all summer, perennial, 1–2 ft.
Coastal, meadow, west-side forest, east-side
forest

Erect shrub. Stems creeping below ground,
branching, more or less hairless. Leaves dark green above, pale
below, oval, 1–3 in. long, hairless and shiny or with stiff hairs
on edges, toothed mostly on upper edges. Flowers many, in flat-
topped cluster 2–5 in. across. Flower petals dull white, sometimes tinted lavender or pink, with many stamens. Grows in
streambanks, edges of lakes, meadows, rocky areas, from near
sea level to 4000 ft. Native OLYM, MORA, NOCA

Spiraea ×*pyramidata* ROSACEAE
Pyramid spiraea
Locally common, early summer, perennial,
20–40 in. Meadow, west-side forest

Erect to spreading shrub. Leaves on upper section coated with crisp hairs. Leaves oblong, 1–3
in. long, entire or toothed above middle. Inflo-

rescence conical or pyramid-shaped, about 2
times as long as it is wide, crowded with white flowers, buds
may be slightly pink. Flower sepals reflexed, petals small and
round. Grows in bottoms of valleys along streambanks, moist
to dry places in canyons, at low to mid elevations. Native NOCA

See other *Spiraea*: red, page 360

Boykinia major SAXIFRAGACEAE
Mountain boykinia, large boykinia
Locally common, all summer, perennial, 1–3
ft. Moist streambanks, meadow

Erect, stout stem coated with glands. Leaves
with petioles 2–12 in. tall, with conspicuous,
toothed, leaf-like stipules. Leaf blades to 8
in. across, lobed halfway to base, lobes with
straight sides, entire or toothed. Flower
head dense, more or less flat-topped. Flower petals white, about
1/5–1/4 in. across, broadly oval to round. Grows in shaded areas,
moist meadows, banks. Native OLYM, CRLA

Boykinia occidentalis (*Boykinia elata*) SAXIFRAGACEAE
Western boykinia, coastal boykinia
Common, all summer, perennial, 1–2 ft.
Coastal, bog/fen/wetland, moist
streambanks

Tufted plant, mostly basal leaves with reddish hairs often topped with glands. Basal
leaves on long stalks, blades to 4 in. across,
heart-shaped, lobed less than 1/3 of the way
to the base; stem leaves becoming stalkless,
smaller. Flowers small, white, in open clusters on reddish glandular stems. Grows in
shaded areas, moist woods, banks of streams at sea level to mid
elevations. Native OLYM, MORA

Heuchera glabra SAXIFRAGACEAE
Smooth alumroot
Locally common, all summer, perennial,
6–24 in. Coastal, moist streambanks,
west-side forest, east-side forest

Tuft with ascending stems. Basal leaves with
long hairless petioles, widely heart-shaped,
with 5 sharp-toothed lobes, hairless; stem
leaves 1–2, much smaller. Flowers in sprays
topping wiry stems, numerous, small,
white. Grows on moist rocky cliffs, in meadows with mosses, in streambanks and
splash zones of streams and rivers, from sea
level to mid elevations. Native OLYM, MORA, NOCA

See other *Heuchera*: yellow, page 236

Heuchera micrantha   SAXIFRAGACEAE

Small-flowered alumroot, crevice heuchera, crevice alumroot

Locally common, late spring–early summer, perennial, 6–24 in. West-side forest, east-side forest, alpine, subalpine

Tuft of leaves and stiff upright stems. Variable species—some plants smooth, others with densely glandular or hairy surfaces. Basal leaves with long petioles, heart-shaped to oval, with 5–7 shallow lobes, toothed, hairy underneath. Flowers tiny, calyx green or more often red, petals white, in small clusters at tips of stalks. Grows on cool rocky cliffs, banks, from near sea level to subalpine. Var. *micrantha* has rounded leaf lobes, petioles and lower stem slightly hairy or hairless. Var. *diversifolia* has oval leaf blade deeply and sharply lobed, petioles with long soft hairs. Native OLYM, MORA, NOCA

Lithophragma tenellum   SAXIFRAGACEAE

Slender woodland star

Locally common, early spring, perennial, 3–12 in. West-side forest, east-side forest, shrub-steppe

Tuft with sticky, hairy, upright stems, not purplish. Basal leaves deeply divided into 3 lobes, divided again to 3, teeth more or less round, no bulblets in leaf axils. Flowers 12 or fewer in raceme that elongates as flowers open, petals white or pale pink, 3 shallow lobes on each tip and 2 much smaller lobes at base, not as deeply cut as in *L. glabrum* but similar to those of *L. parviflorum*. Grows in sagebrush plains to pine forests, dry places, rocky slopes, at low to high elevations. Native

Mitella stauropetala   SAXIFRAGACEAE

Side-flowered mitrewort, cross-shaped mitella, cross-shaped bishop's cap

Uncommon, late spring–early summer, perennial, 6–20 in. Bog/fen/wetland, moist streambanks, west-side forest, east-side forest, alpine, subalpine

Tuft of leaves, erect stems. Leaves nearly round, lobed, round-toothed, slightly hairy on both sides. Leafless stems to 20 in. hold tiny flowers on 1 side, opening from bottom to top. Flowers whitish, may be tinted purple, narrow petals divided into 3 slender segments. Grows in bogs, wet places in shady woodlands, at high elevations. One-sided flower arrangement in this species is stronger than the otherwise similar *M. trifida*. Native OLYM

See other *Lithophragma*: red, page 361
See other *Mitella*: yellow, page 236; green/brown, page 468

Mitella trifida SAXIFRAGACEAE
Three-toothed mitrewort, three-cornered bishop's cap
Uncommon, late spring–early summer, perennial, 6–15 in. West-side forest, east-side forest

Tuft of leaves, erect flower stem. Leaves widely oval, 1–3 in. wide, divided palmately, 5–7 indistinct shallow lobes, sometimes with rounded teeth. Flowering stem 6–15 in. tall, tiny flowers held mostly but not always on 1 side, blooming from bottom to top. Flowers white or purplish, in narrow cup, petals with 3 oval lobes at tips. Uncommon but grows in shady places in moist woods at low to mid elevations. Native
OLYM, MORA, NOCA, CRLA

Parnassia fimbriata SAXIFRAGACEAE
Fringed grass of parnassus
Locally common, all summer, perennial, 1–2 ft. Bog/fen/wetland, moist streambanks, meadow, west-side forest, east-side forest, alpine, subalpine

Tuft upright to spreading. Leaves round or heart-shaped. Flowers held well above leaves, 5 white oval petals with fringed edges near center. A stamen-like gland on top of each petal has 9 or fewer flat lobes with rounded tips. Grows in wet meadows, rocky seeps, in all elevations. Native OLYM, MORA, NOCA

Saxifraga bronchialis SAXIFRAGACEAE
Spotted saxifrage, yellow-dot saxifrage
Uncommon, late spring–early summer, perennial, 2–6 in. Alpine, subalpine

Matted cushion, somewhat moss-like, upright flower stems. Basal leaves small, evergreen, oblong, with bristles on edges, spine at tip, tightly overlapping to form rosettes; stem leaves well spaced, alternate the length of flower stem. Flowers 3–5 at stem top, white with yellow, orange, purple, or maroon spots on outer ½ of petals. Grows in rocky openings on cliffs, scree, crevices, in subalpine and alpine areas. *Saxifraga tolmiei* grows in similar habitats and is also mat-forming, with stonecrop-like leaves, but has shorter flower stems and no spots on petals. Native OLYM, MORA, NOCA

See other *Saxifraga*: yellow, page 237

Saxifraga caespitosa (*Saxifraga cespitosa*)
SAXIFRAGACEAE
Tufted saxifrage
Locally common, all spring and summer, perennial, 2–12 in. Coastal, alpine, subalpine

Tight mat of leaves crowded into rosettes, flowers on short stems above. Leaves wider at top of rosette, divided into 3–5 lobes. Flower stem has 1 leaf near middle, holds 1 or few flowers well above foliage. Flowers white to cream in a green or purple cup, sepals and petals the same length. Grows in damp rocky slopes, cliffs, from sea level to alpine around the world except for eastern North America. Subsp. *subgemmifera* (pictured), a lowland form with weaker stems, has leaves with long, thin, sometimes cobweb-like hairs. Native OLYM, MORA, NOCA

Saxifraga ferruginea SAXIFRAGACEAE
Rusty saxifrage
Locally common, all summer, perennial, 6–20 in. Coastal, vernal-wet, west-side forest, alpine, subalpine

Rosette of 1–3 in. leaves, tall erect stem. Leaves egg-shaped, fleshy, with coarse sharp teeth near tip. Flower stem rusty-colored, with widely spreading branches, lower bracts with bulblets that make new plantlets. Flower petals oval, 3 upper petals larger, each with 2 yellow to orange spots, 2 lower petals smaller and plain white. Grows in wet banks, rocks, from sea level to subalpine. Some plants have all or most flowers replaced by bulblets. Native OLYM, MORA, NOCA, CRLA

Saxifraga integrifolia SAXIFRAGACEAE
Grassland saxifrage, early saxifrage
Locally common, all spring, perennial, 5–14 in. Coastal, vernal-wet, meadow, west-side forest

Rosette of leaves, erect stem. Leaves 1–3 in., oval, hairy, entire or with very small teeth; petioles short. Flower stems reddish, covered with glands, holding ball-shaped clusters of flowers. Petals widely oval, white, green, or tinted purplish. Grows in spring-moist meadows at low to high elevations. A highly variable species with several named varieties that often intergrade. Native OLYM, NOCA

Saxifraga lyallii SAXIFRAGACEAE
Lyall's saxifrage, red-stemmed saxifrage
Uncommon, midsummer, perennial, 4–16 in. Moist streambanks, meadow, alpine, subalpine

Basal leaf rosette, long red flower stem from center. Leaves glossy, fan-shaped, deeply toothed across wide tip end. Flower stems leafless, hairy or not, reddish to purple, flowers at top, each on a short stalk. Flower petals and sepals same size; petals white with 2 yellow or greenish dots at base. Grows in damp meadows, rocky ledges, at high elevations. Native MORA

Saxifraga mertensiana SAXIFRAGACEAE
Mertens' saxifrage
Uncommon, all spring and summer, perennial, 6–16 in. Moist streambanks, west-side forest, east-side forest, alpine, subalpine

Tuft of round leaves, stem erect. Leaves 1–4 in. across, with heart-shaped base, irregularly toothed, on noticeably hairy petioles. Flower stem has 1–3 leaves near base, widely spreading branches at top. Flowers white, in small few-flowered clusters, petals without spots. Flowers sometimes replaced by bulblets that make new plantlets. Grows in streambanks, on wet mossy rocks, at low to high elevations. Native OLYM, MORA, NOCA, CRLA

Saxifraga nelsoniana subsp. *cascadensis* (*Saxifraga punctata* var. *cascadensis*) SAXIFRAGACEAE
Nelson's brook saxifrage
Uncommon, midsummer, perennial, 5–7 in. Bog/fen/wetland, moist streambanks, west-side forest, east-side forest, alpine, subalpine

Tuft of long-stemmed leaves. Leaves ascending, hairless, round, 1–3 in. across, with even, triangular, gland-tipped teeth. Flower stems longer than leaves, hairless, with some glands on upper branches. Flowers few, with purplish stalks, in long spreading inflorescence. Flower petals nearly round, abruptly narrowing toward base, white, with 2–3 greenish yellow dots near base. Grows along high mountain streams, waterfalls, in crevices. Native OLYM, MORA, NOCA

Saxifraga occidentalis SAXIFRAGACEAE
Western saxifrage
Locally common, all spring and summer,
perennial, 4–10 in. Meadow, west-side forest,
east-side forest, alpine, subalpine

Basal rosette of leaves, erect flower stem.
Leaves oval, 1–3 in. long, leathery, with coarse,
evenly spaced teeth; immature leaves with reddish hairs on underside. Flower stem often
reddish, hairy on lower section, glandular above, many
branches with clusters of numerous flowers. Flowers with oval
to widely oval petals, white or pale pink with no spots; pollen orange. Grows in moist to dry openings with moss or grass from
near sea level to subalpine. A variable species with several
named varieties best separated with a technical manual. Native
MORA, NOCA

Saxifraga odontoloma (*Saxifraga arguta*)
SAXIFRAGACEAE
**Stream saxifrage, mountain meadow saxifrage,
brook saxifrage**
Uncommon, midsummer, perennial, 1–2 ft.
Bog/fen/wetland, moist streambanks, meadow,
alpine, subalpine

Tuft of nearly round leaves, erect flower stalks.
Leaves 1–3 in. across, evenly sharp-toothed, with glands on tips;
petioles hairless, 1½–3 in. long. Inflorescence purplish, to 12
in. long, widely spreading, with flowers on stalk tips. Flower
sepals reflex about equal to petals; petals round, white, with 2
greenish yellow dots; calyx pink to purplish; anthers purple.
Grows in wet meadows, edges of streams and lakes, at low to
subalpine elevations. Native OLYM, MORA, NOCA

Saxifraga oregana SAXIFRAGACEAE
Oregon saxifrage
Locally common, all spring and summer,
perennial, 1–3 ft. Bog/fen/wetland, moist
streambanks, meadow

Rosette of leaves, tall erect stem. Leaves linear
to widely egg-shaped, 3–10 in., base tapering
into petiole, entire to sharply toothed. Flower
stem more than 12 in. tall, leafless. Inflorescence consists of
clusters of small white flowers along stem, dense at top. Flower
sepals reflexed back, petals oval. Grows in bogs, marshes, wet
meadows, streambanks, at low to high elevations. Native
NOCA

Saxifraga rufidula (Saxifraga occiden-
talis var. *rufidula*) SAXIFRAGACEAE
Rusty-haired saxifrage
Uncommon, late spring–early summer,
perennial, 2–8 in. West-side forest, alpine,
subalpine

Rosette of oval leaves, erect flower stem.
Leaves leathery, 3–4 in. long, round-toothed,
with reddish hairs on underside. Flowers
numerous, distributed on ascending branches, becoming
dense toward tip in a flat-topped cluster. Flower sepals spread
outward, oval petals about same length, white with no spots,
ovary superior. Grows in moist, shady, rocky places from near
coast to subalpine zone. Some plants from Mount Olympus
vicinity lack petals. Rare in California. Native OLYM

Saxifraga tolmiei SAXIFRAGACEAE
Tolmie's saxifrage
Uncommon, all summer, perennial, mat
Alpine, subalpine

Mats flat and creeping, erect flower stems.
Plant holds old leaves under new deep
green ones. Leaves fleshy, ½–¾ in., widest
at divided tip, 3 lobes. Flower stems 1–3 in.,
somewhat hairy, glandular above, holding 1
or more flowers. Flowers unspotted, white or cream, held in
shallow purplish red cups. Grows in rocky talus, on outcrops to
alpine slopes, blooming just as snow melts through autumn.
Saxifraga bronchialis grows in similar habitats and also forms
small mats, with stiff, pointed leaves and sharp hairs on edges,
but with longer flower stems and prominent colored dots on
petals. Native OLYM, MORA, NOCA, CRLA

Tellima grandiflora SAXIFRAGACEAE
Fragrant fringecup
Locally common, late spring, perennial,
15–34 in. Moist streambanks, west-side
forest

Tuft of heart-shaped leaves, upright stem.
Plant slightly hairy throughout. Leaves 2–3
in. wide, with shallow lobes, sharp teeth;
stem leaves become smaller and clasp stem. Flower spike 1-
sided, with many flowers. Flower in a deep cup with deeply
fringed petals opened flat, white lightly tinted with green or
sometimes red, very fragrant. Grows in moist forests, along
streams, below treeline. Native OLYM, MORA, NOCA

Tiarella trifoliata SAXIFRAGACEAE
Foamflower, triple sugar scoop
Common, late spring–early summer, perennial,
6–24 in. Moist streambanks, west-side forest,
east-side forest

Mound of leaves, tall stems, slightly hairy
throughout. Basal leaves on long petioles, 1–5
in. across, lobed, sharp-toothed; stem leaves
smaller, undivided but toothed. Flowers small,
held in spreading cluster at top of thin stems, 5 petals, thread-
like, 10 stamens extending upward. Grows in moist shady
woods, edge of streams, rivers, below 4000 ft. Var. *trifoliata* (pictured), with leaves divided into 3 separate leaflets on short
stalks, is shallowly lobed, sharp-toothed, found almost exclu-
sively west of Cascades. Var. *unifoliata* is shallowly lobed, with
3–5 lobes, sharply toothed; grows on both sides
of Cascades and in the Olympics, generally at
higher elevations. Native
OLYM, MORA, NOCA, CRLA

Lycopus uniflorus LAMIACEAE
Northern water horehound, bugleweed
Uncommon, late summer, perennial, 4–20 in.
Bog/fen/wetland, moist streambanks, meadow

Erect, scentless. Stem square, unbranched,
with fine hairs. Leaves lance-shaped, with coarse teeth, opposite, sessile, all about the same size. Flowers white or pale pink,
small, stalkless, numerous in whorls clustered at leaf axils.
Flower 2-lipped; lower lip 3-lobed, hairy inside, 2 stamens,
ovary with 4 lobes. Grows in wet places, lake edges, streambanks, riverbanks, bogs, at low to mid elevations. Flowers
smaller and not as dense as *Mentha arvensis*.
Native OLYM, MORA, NOCA

Marrubium vulgare LAMIACEAE
Horehound
Common, all year long, perennial, 1–3 ft.
Disturbed, meadow

Erect, white-woolly, branched, square stems.
Leaves opposite, with short petioles, egg-
shaped to round, round-toothed. Flowers in
whorls around stem at base of leaves. Flower with 2 lips, the
upper rounded or divided into 2 sharp points, the lower larger.
Grows in roadsides, disturbed dry soils, especially overgrazed
areas. Native of Europe, grows worldwide. Traditionally used
as a cough remedy. Nonnative OLYM

Mentha arvensis LAMIACEAE
Field mint
Common, mid to late summer, perennial,
12–30 in. Coastal, moist streambanks,
meadow

Stems upright, leafy. Plant strongly mint-
scented. Stem branched, square, slightly
hairy. Leaves 1–3 in., opposite, egg-shaped,
with sharp point, saw-toothed, hairy; lower
leaves on short petioles; upper leaves sessile. Flowers in clusters around stem; calyx with 5 lobes; petal tube white, pink, or
violet, with 4 equal lobes. Grows in moist places, along streams,
near lakes or in fields, at low to mid elevations. Plants, both native and European, now circumboreal. Used by Native Americans as a tea. Native OLYM, MORA, NOCA

Castilleja attenuata (*Orthocarpus*
attenuatus) SCROPHULARIACEAE
**Narrowleaf paintbrush, narrowleaf owl's
clover**
Uncommon, midspring, annual, 4–20 in.
Meadow

Upright stem. Leaves thread-like, upper
ones divided into 3 lobes. Bracts divided
into 3 lobes, green with tips white. Flower
slender, white or pale yellow, dotted with pale purple or white;
beak straight. Grows in grasslands at low to mid elevations.
Native

Castilleja tenuis (*Orthocarpus hispidus*)
SCROPHULARIACEAE
Hairy paintbrush, hairy owlclover
Locally common, midsummer, annual, 4–18
in. Meadow

Upright hairy annual. Stems finely hairy.
Leaves long, thin, pointed. Flower bracts
less than 1 in. long, ½–1½ in. wide, with
3–7 thin, lance-shaped lobes, green or
slightly tipped with dull reddish brown, not
showy. Flowers white, occasionally yellow;
flower beak straight, extending just beyond
bracts. Grows in moist open fields, meadows, at low to mid
elevations. Native

See other *Castilleja*: yellow, page 237; red, page 365

Pedicularis contorta

SCROPHULARIACEAE
Coiled-beak lousewort
Uncommon, midsummer, perennial, 6–16 in.
Meadow, west-side forest, east-side forest,
alpine, subalpine

Clump of erect, hairless stems and leaves.
Basal and lower stem leaves, blades oblong,
2–8 in. long, carried on long petioles, deeply
lobed, with 25–41 linear toothed segments. Flower spike 2–11
in. long, bracts shorter than flowers. White or cream flowers
have few dark spots; upper lip curved downward more than
180°, with tip of beak curving upward; lower lip composed of 3
wide, spreading lobes. Grows in open forests and meadows at
mid to high elevations. Native OLYM, MORA, NOCA

Penstemon deustus SCROPHULARIACEAE

Hot rock penstemon
Locally common, early summer, perennial, to
18 in. Dry rocky sites, east-side forest, shrub-
steppe

Erect to ascending, sparsely covered with
glands, slightly to very sticky. Stems stiff, single to several. Leaves 1½ in. long, lance-
shaped, toothed, reducing in size up the stem.
Flowers in loose whorls, small, creamy white to pale tan, beelines in throat red to brown. Grows in dry rocky places, basalt
cliffs, other volcanic soils, mostly at mid elevations. Native
NOCA, CRLA

Veronica peregrina SCROPHULARIACEAE

Purslane speedwell
Common, all summer, annual, 2–12 in.
Bog/fen/wetland, meadow, west-side forest,
east-side forest

Erect stem hairless or with hairs and glands.
Leaves slightly succulent, linear to spoon-
shaped, 3 times longer than wide, entire or
finely toothed. Flower spike at stem top, single;
small white flowers on very short stalk in axil of
small bracts. Grows in moist places. Subsp.
xalapensis stems are covered with small, glistening, stemmed
glands. Native OLYM, MORA, NOCA

See other *Pedicularis*: yellow, page 246; red, page 373
See other *Penstemon*: yellow, page 247; red, page 375; blue, page 427
See other *Veronica*: blue, page 436

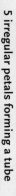

Verbena bracteata   VERBENACEAE
Bigbract verbena, prostrate verbena, creeping vervain
Uncommon, late summer, annual or perennial, 2–10 in. Vernal-wet, moist streambanks, disturbed, meadow, shrub-steppe

Prostrate with sparse hairs. Stems few to numerous, with long spreading branches. Leaves ½–2½ in., oval, with pointed tip, coarsely toothed or lobed, with coarse hairs; petiole flattened. Inflorescence is a spike with bract at base, dense with flowers. Flower small, white, lavender, or blue, almost hidden by bracts. Grows in disturbed places, open drying mud at edges of lakes or ponds. Can be invasive. Native

Apocynum cannabinum
APOCYNACEAE
Indian hemp, hemp dogbane
Locally common, all summer, perennial, 1–3 ft. Coastal, disturbed, meadow, west-side forest, shrub-steppe

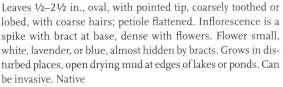

Stems stout, upright, branched at top. Milky sap. Leaves clasping stem or nearly so, 2–3 in. long, yellowish green, ascending, opposite, elliptical to egg-shaped, with pointed tips. Flowers in short-stalked clusters along stem, bell-shaped, greenish or white. Grows in moist places that do not dry out, near streams, springs, among agricultural crops, at low to mid elevations. Used as an important source of fiber by Native Americans. Native

Cryptantha affinis   BORAGINACEAE
Slender cryptantha
Common, late spring, annual, 6–20 in. East-side forest, shrub-steppe

Erect single-stemmed annual covered with coarse white hairs. Leaves very narrow, entire, mostly basal, with some scattered up the stem. Flowers tiny in small coils, partially covered by upward-curving hairs. Seeds usually 4 nutlets. Found throughout Pacific Northwest growing in dry places. Similar *C. flaccida* has only 1 nutlet per flower. Native MORA

See other *Apocynum*: red, page 377

Cryptantha celosioides BORAGINACEAE
Cockscomb cryptantha, northern cryptantha
Locally common, late spring, biennial or
perennial, 8–16 in. East-side forest, shrub-
steppe

Erect short-lived perennial. Stems stout, 1 to
several, densely covered with bristles. Leaves
very narrow, bright green, 1–3 in. long, mostly
crowded near ground; stem leaves reducing in
size upward. Inflorescence is showy head of large white flowers
with 5 petals. This showy plant can be seen in the east Columbia River Gorge and other dry places at low to mid elevations.
Native

Cryptantha circumscissa BORAGINACEAE
Matted cryptantha, opening cryptantha
Uncommon, early spring–midsummer, annual,
1 in. Shrub-steppe

Small cushion, ball-shaped, about 1 in. tall, 4
times as wide. Many branches, bristly throughout. Leaves linear, less than ½ in. long, densely crowded, surrounding the flowers. Flowers
very small, with yellow eyes, occurring singly
on top of cushion in clusters. Calyx splits in a
circle around seeds when mature. Grows in
sandy, dry soils usually at low elevations but including Steens
Mountain. Native

Cryptantha flaccida BORAGINACEAE
Weak-stem cryptantha
Common, late spring, annual, 4–16 in.
East-side forest, shrub-steppe

Upright, with sharp bristly hairs that mostly
stand straight up. Stem branches ascending,
usually divided in the inflorescence. Leaves linear to oblong, to 2 in., mostly near base, a few
scattered on stem. Flowers in coils at top are
small, white, sometimes touching each other,
surrounded by dense calyx bristles that curve to
a hooked tip. Most flowers have single nutlet.
Grows in dry gravelly soils in open sites
throughout our region at low to mid elevations. Native

Cryptantha intermedia
BORAGINACEAE
Large-flowered cryptantha
Common, late spring, annual, 4–20 in.
Meadow, shrub-steppe

Upright branched annual covered with rough sharp hairs. Leaves linear to narrowly lance-shaped, ½–2 in. long, mostly near base and alternate on stem. Flowers well spaced on uncoiling stem top. Flowers to ⅓ in. across, white with bright yellow eye. Grows in dry, sandy or rocky places at low to high elevations. Native OLYM, MORA

Cryptantha interrupta (*Cryptantha spiculifera*)
BORAGINACEAE
Bristly cryptantha
Uncommon, late spring, biennial, 6–16 in.
Vernal-wet, shrub-steppe

Tuft of basal leaves, stems erect, usually numerous. Leaves with bristly gray hairs on both sides. Basal leaves oblong, ¾–2½ in. long, 1/16–½ in. wide; stem leaves not crowded, becoming small upward. Inflorescence is a crowded spike, white flowers held within hairy or bristly bracts, lobes flat, spreading, ¼–⅓ in. wide. Grows in dry to slightly damp sandy soils or silt in low-elevation arid areas. Native

Cryptantha leucophaea BORAGINACEAE
Gray cryptantha
Rare, late spring–early summer, perennial, 8–15 in. Shrub-steppe

Upright, stout perennial. Plant is densely covered with sharp white hairs, giving it a gray appearance. Leaves mostly basal, 1–2½ in., narrowly linear, with sharp tip; stem leaves small, sessile. Flowers pure white. Nutlets smooth and shining. Grows in sandy places among sagebrush. A sensitive plant in Washington, known from only a few sites, with a shrinking range. Native

Cryptantha pterocarya
BORAGINACEAE
Wing-nut cryptantha
Uncommon, all spring, annual, 4–15 in.
Meadow, shrub-steppe

Erect, with some upright branches. Stems with rough hairs pointing upward. Leaves short, narrow, linear to oblong, bristly, mostly basal becoming fewer and smaller upward. Flowers white, in 2 spikes, atop each stem. Lower flowers widely spaced; upper flowers close together, overlapping. Nutlets broadly winged. Grows in sandy, gravelly soils in the basin bottom lands. The common name refers to the wide wings on the seeds. Native

Cryptantha sobolifera BORAGINACEAE
**Crater Lake cryptantha, alpine cryptantha,
Waterton Lakes cryptantha**
Locally common, all summer, perennial, 2–8 in.
Alpine, subalpine

Upright from woody base. Stems, leaves coated with bristly hairs, those on lower leaf surfaces with bulbous bases. Leaves narrow, clustered at base, few upward. Inflorescence narrow to head-like, dense with leaf-like bracts coated with white to yellow bristly hairs under tight coils of flowers. Flower white, the inside of tube yellow. Grows in pumice and sandy soils, ridges, at mid to high elevations. Native CRLA

Hackelia diffusa BORAGINACEAE
Spreading stickseed, diffuse stickseed
Locally common, late spring, perennial, 12–20
in. East-side forest, shrub-steppe

Erect, covered with soft to stiff whitish hairs. Stems several, branching from base. Leaf blades 1/3–1/2 in. wide. Basal leaf blades taper to margined petiole, together are 3–8 in. long; stem leaves smaller, sessile, sometimes clasping. Flowers on spreading branches at top. Flowers white or rarely blue, open wide, almost 1/2 in. across. Seed distinguished from *H. micrantha* by having more prickles on areas between margins. Grows in rocky places in sagebrush-steppe and ponderosa pine forests, on cliffs and talus in the Columbia River Gorge. Native NOCA

See other *Hackelia*: blue, page 438

Plagiobothrys figuratus
BORAGINACEAE
Fragrant popcorn flower
Locally common, late spring–early summer,
annual, 6–15 in. Coastal, vernal-wet,
bog/fen/wetland, meadow

Erect, unbranched or branched from base,
hairy. Leaves linear; lower leaves 2–5 in.
long, occurring in pairs; upper leaves few,
½–2 in. long, alternate. Inflorescence often consisting of paired
spikes of mostly loose coils becoming 2–8 in. at end of season,
calyx coated with long shaggy hairs, sometimes rusty-colored.
Flowers fragrant, showy, white with large yellow center. Grows
in wet grassy areas, edges of water. Can be confused with
Cryptantha intermedia, which rarely has opposite lower leaves
and is generally more hairy. Native OLYM

Plagiobothrys nothofulvus
BORAGINACEAE
Rusty popcorn flower
Common, early spring, annual, 8–16 in.
Coastal, vernal-wet, meadow, west-side
forest, east-side forest

Rosette and many erect stems. Stems and
leaves have rusty-colored to pale yellow,
spreading, slightly sticky hairs; sap purple. Leaves linear, basal,
crowded, 1–4 in. long; stem leaves few, alternate. Flowers ¼ in.
across, white with tiny yellow throat, very tightly coiled at top.
Often seen in early spring in huge waves in grasslands, woodlands. Grows from sea level to low elevations. Native

Plagiobothrys scouleri   BORAGINACEAE
Scouler's popcorn flower
Common, early spring, annual, 1–8 in.
Coastal, vernal-wet

Prostrate sprawling to rarely erect, hairy
throughout. Leaves linear to lance-shaped;
lower leaves in 1–4 opposite pairs; upper
leaves alternate. Flower is a small, short,
white tube with 5 spreading lobes, yellow
eye, on 1 side of coiled stalk. Grows in moist
meadows, edges of vernal pools, at low elevations along the
coast and elsewhere in Oregon, Washington, and British Columbia. Similar *P. mollis* is a sprawling perennial plant that
roots at the nodes, found in sagebrush scrub and grasslands in
Oregon and northern California. There are other similar, annual popcorn flowers in our region. Native OLYM, NOCA

Plagiobothrys tenellus BORAGINACEAE
Pacific popcorn flower
Common, midspring, annual, 2–5 in. Meadow,
shrub-steppe

Annual with several erect stems, shaggy-
haired, basal rosette. Leaves egg-shaped at
base, with few smaller stem leaves alternate.
Flowers more than 10, in a coil that is tight toward the tips. Seed is a thick nutlet in a distinctive cross shape. Grows in grasslands, woodlands, forests,
at low to mid elevations throughout western North America.
Native NOCA, **L&C**

Calystegia atriplicifolia subsp. *atriplicifolia*
(*Convolvulus nyctagineus*) CONVOLVULACEAE
Night-blooming morning glory
Locally common, late spring–midsummer,
perennial, 8–18 in. Meadow, east-side forest

Erect or trailing vine. Stems not twining.
Leaves triangular, about 2 in. at midrib, alternate. Flower stalk shorter than leaf, single
flower creamy white to tinted pink, 1–2 in.
long. Grows in dry rocky slopes in open woods,
grassy slopes. Native

Calystegia occidentalis CONVOLVULACEAE
Western morning glory
Locally common, late spring–early summer,
perennial, twining. West-side forest, east-side
forest, shrub-steppe

Stems prostrate or climbing, twisting around support. Stem
and leaves coated with very fine hairs. Leaf
arrow-shaped, ½–1½ in. at midvein, lobes at

base rounded or double-pointed, with rounded
or squared indentation at top of leaf. Flowers
1–4 on stalk, bractlets at flower base entire or
lobed like leaf, overlapping calyx. Flower cream
to white, 5 petals united into open funnel
shape. Grows in dry soils in pine woodlands,
chaparral, on slopes, at low to subalpine elevations. Native

See other *Calystegia*: red, page 378

153

Calystegia sepium   CONVOLVULACEAE
Hedge morning glory
Common, all summer, perennial, vine, to 50
in. Coastal, west-side forest

Vine, nonwoody, climbing or twisting. Leaf
arrow-shaped, 1–3 in. at midvein, central tip
pointed, lower lobes about ⅓ the length of
central lobe, rounded tips. Flower bracts
longer and covering calyx. Flower single,
widely bell-shaped without division, white or pinkish, 1½–2½
in. long. Found in salt- and freshwater marshes, along rivers,
clambering over other foliage. Two very similar genera are
called morning glory: *Calystegia*, climbing perennials from a
central root, and *Convolvulus*, trailing annuals from a central
root. Native OLYM, NOCA, **L&C**

Hesperochiron californicus
HYDROPHYLLACEAE
California hesperochiron
Locally common, mid to late spring,
perennial, 2–5 in. Vernal-wet, meadow, east-
side forest, shrub-steppe

Rosette of 6–8 leaves, white flowers. Leaves
egg-shaped, about 1 in. wide, densely to
sparsely hairy on both sides. Single flower
on stem about the length of the leaves, white or tinted blue,
bell-shaped, about as long as or longer than it is wide, with 5
spreading oblong lobes, yellow and hairy inside. Grows in wet
pastures, meadows, at mid to high elevations. Native

Hesperochiron pumilus   HYDROPHYLLACEAE
Dwarf hesperochiron
Locally common, late spring–early summer,
perennial, 1–4 in. Vernal-wet, meadow, east-
side forest, shrub-steppe

Basal leaf rosette with erect to spreading
flower stems. Leaves 2–10, from root, short
petioles with leaf blades less than 1 in. wide,
linear, oblong to egg-shaped, usually without hairs. Flowers 2–8, on separate stalks,
flat, saucer-shaped, wider than high, with
egg-shaped petals, opening wide, white or possibly tinted purple, center bright yellow, hairy, with noticeable dark beelines.
Stamens 5, with black to purple pollen. Grows in vernal-wet
meadows, rocky openings, at low to subalpine elevations.
Native NOCA

Hydrophyllum fendleri
HYDROPHYLLACEAE
Fendler's waterleaf
Locally common, late spring–early summer, perennial, 10–36 in. West-side forest, east-side forest, alpine, subalpine

Erect plant. Stems have rigid hairs. Spreading leaves oblong, 2–12 in. long, divided pinnately to 9- to 13-lobed leaflets with stiff hairs on both sides. Inflorescence consists of dense clusters atop stalks. White to purple flowers have long hairs on outside, 5 stamens extending outward. Grows in moist, open or brushy areas, to subalpine. Var. *albifrons* leaflets have long, tapered, pointed tips and 4–8 teeth on each edge. Native OLYM, MORA, NOCA, CRLA

Hydrophyllum tenuipes
HYDROPHYLLACEAE
Pacific waterleaf, slender-stem waterleaf
Locally common, midspring–midsummer, perennial, 12–30 in. Coastal, west-side forest

Erect stem with large leaves. Stem with reflexed bristles. Leaves with soft hairs on 2–12 in. petioles, blades oval to round, 3–8 in. wide, divided pinnately to odd number of deeply cut, toothed lobes with sharp points. Flowers, in compact clusters, consist of cream, greenish, lavender, or blue bells, stamens and pistils extending well beyond petals. Sepals bristly along edges. Grows on rich soils in moist shaded sites, at low to mid elevations. Native OLYM, MORA, NOCA

Nemophila parviflora
HYDROPHYLLACEAE
Small-flowered nemophila, woods nemophila
Locally common, all spring, annual, 6–24 in. Disturbed, meadow, west-side forest, east-side forest

Sprawling, delicate stems to 2 ft., branched, soft-haired or hairless. Leaves pinnately divided, with 5 toothed dissimilar lobes. Flowers small, with white or pale blue petals, solitary from axils of stem and leaf. Grows in meadows, forests, along streams, ridges, below 7000 ft. Var. *parviflora* lower leaves opposite, upper alternate, thin, deeply cut, with 5 lobes, lower pair often to central vein; lobes with very sharp point at tip; grows at low elevations. Var. *austiniae* leaves are all opposite, shallowly lobed or coarsely toothed; grows mostly east of Cascade Mountain Range. Native OLYM, MORA, NOCA, CRLA

See other *Hydrophyllum*: blue, page 441
See other *Nemophila*: blue, page 442

Nemophila pedunculata
HYDROPHYLLACEAE
Meadow nemophila
Common, all spring, annual, 3–10 in.
Coastal, meadow, west-side forest, east-side forest

Prostrate. Leaves oblong to egg-shaped, opposite, with petioles shorter than leaf, divided pinnately, 5–9 lobes. Single flower on stalk same length as nearby leaf. Flower bell- to bowl-shaped, petals white or blue, usually veined or center dotted with darker color or tips spotted purple. Grows on bluffs in grass, sandy places, woods, streambanks along coast and inland to high elevations. Native

Phacelia corymbosa   HYDROPHYLLACEAE
Serpentine scorpionweed, rock phacelia
Uncommon, midspring, perennial, 8–18 in.
Dry rocky sites

Basal leaf rosette and upright flower stems coated with gland-tipped hairs throughout. Leaves greenish gray, lance-shaped, ½–3 in. long; stem leaves smaller. Stems not branched. Flowers many in dense round clusters on upper stem. Calyx with long, ridged, straight hairs, 5 white petals wider and longer than calyx, stamens extending well beyond. Found only on rocky serpentine in dry open places at low to mid elevations. Native

Phacelia hastata   HYDROPHYLLACEAE
Silverleaf phacelia
Locally common, late spring–early summer, perennial, 6–36 in. Disturbed, east-side forest, shrub-steppe, alpine, subalpine

Erect, occasionally decumbent, stems and leaves silver with stiff hairs, glandless. Stems often branched. Leaves mostly basal, ½–5 in. long, narrowly oblong, usually entire; lower leaves may be lobed, becoming smaller up stem. Flowers in dense tightly coiled cluster, petals fused most of the length, bell-shaped, white or lavender; stamens extending beyond petals. Grows in flats, shrublands, forests, talus, pumice, at mid to alpine elevations. Var. *compacta* is 2–8 in. tall, has calyx lobes with sticky glands; grows in upper forests, subalpine, alpine. Var. *hastata* has calyx lobes without glands, few stiff hairs, most pressed to surface; grows at mid elevations. Native NOCA, CRLA

See other *Phacelia*: blue, page 442

Phacelia heterophylla

HYDROPHYLLACEAE
Varied-leaf phacelia
Uncommon, midsummer, biennial or
perennial, 1–3 ft. Disturbed, meadow, east-side
forest, shrub-steppe

Erect, with curved ascending side stems.
Stems weak, with stiff hairs, glandular. Leaves
gray-green, basal, with petiole longer than
lance-shaped to oval, divided leaf blades. Leaflets 1–2 pairs and
1 larger at tip. Inflorescence has short, very bristly hairs, long
and narrow, with flower stalks among leaves. Flower calyx hairy,
often purplish, petals fused, bell-shaped, yellowish or greenish
white to lavender, stamens extending outward. Grows in rocky
slopes, flat open areas, at low to high elevations. Similar *P.
nemoralis* has stinging hairs on the stems,
grows west of Cascade Mountains. Native
NOCA, CRLA, **L&C**

Romanzoffia sitchensis

HYDROPHYLLACEAE
Sitka romanzoffia, Sitka mistmaiden
Rare, early spring, perennial, 4–8 in. Coastal,
west-side forest, alpine, subalpine

Stems spreading to upright, coated with
straight hairs. Leaves mostly basal, fleshy, nearly round, to 1½
in. across, shallowly lobed, on petioles to 3 in. with thickened
and usually hairy base. Flowers few to several on stalks 6 in. or
less, widely bell-shaped, white with yellow center. Grows on
wet rocks, cliffs, and mountain ledges to 7000 ft, at sea level in
British Columbia and Alaska. Similar *R. californica* is up to 12
in. tall, with few smaller leaves alternate along
stem, flowers in loose cluster at stem top, funnel-shaped, white with a yellow band inside;
found west of Cascades from central Oregon
south. Native OLYM, MORA, NOCA

Romanzoffia tracyi   HYDROPHYLLACEAE
Tracy's mistmaiden
Uncommon, all spring, perennial, 1–5 in.
Coastal

Forming round tuft. Grows from cluster of brown tubers. Leaf
petiole ½–3 in., with soft hairs. Leaf nearly round, ½–1½ in.
wide, smooth to soft-hairy, petiole widened at base. Flowers in
compact cluster often shorter than leaves, calyx lobes lance-
shaped, with pointed tip; petals and calyx hairy. Uncommon
on rocky ocean bluffs to 90 ft. Native OLYM

157

Menyanthes trifoliata

MENYANTHACEAE
Buckbean
Locally common, late spring–early summer,
perennial, 6–18 in. Bog/fen/wetland,
lake/pond

Ascending to prostrate stems 2–12 in. long.
Basal leaves divided into 3 oblong entire
leaflets, each sessile or with short petiole.
Foul-smelling flower cluster tops stem. Flowers white tinted
pink, funnel-shaped, with ¼–½ in. spreading lobes with tips
reflexed back, many long hairs on inner surface. Grows in
water at edges of bogs, marshes, along lakes, wet meadows,
seeps, below 10,000 ft. Native OLYM, MORA, NOCA

Nephrophyllidium crista-galli (*Fauria*

crista-galli) MENYANTHACEAE
Deer cabbage
Uncommon, late spring–midsummer,
perennial, 6–24 in. Bog/fen/wetland,
lake/pond

Tuft with erect flower stem. Leaves kidney-
shaped to nearly round, with stout petioles
2–6 in. high, blade with finely scalloped
edges. Flower stalk naked, 6–24 in. tall,
flowers on single stalk or 1- to 2-branched. Calyx lobes spreading out from white flower with 5 flat lobes that extend just beyond calyx tube. Petals with membranous fringed ridges along
midline and edges. Grows in wet places, sphagnum bogs, wet
meadows. Native OLYM

Oxalis oregana OXALIDACEAE

Redwood sorrel, wood sorrel, Oregon oxalis
Common, all spring and summer, perennial,
2–8 in. Coastal, west-side forest

Prostrate, with thick creeping roots. Leaves
clustered at root tips, each on slightly hairy
petiole less than 8 in. long. Leaf divided into
3 heart-shaped leaflets often maroon underneath, plain or marbled above. Flowers
solitary on long stalks, white to pink, petals
lance-shaped, ½–1 in., often with darker pinkish red veins.
Grows on undisturbed floors of redwood or Douglas-fir forests
at low elevations. Native OLYM, MORA, NOCA, **L&C**

See other *Oxalis*: yellow, page 249

Oxalis trilliifolia   OXALIDACEAE
Trillium-leaved sorrel
Locally common, early summer, perennial,
5–10 in. Coastal, west-side forest

Creeping, with clusters of large clover-like
leaves. Leaves carried on 2–8 in. petioles, 3
leaflets, each 1½ in. or less, heart-shaped, with
fold in center. Cluster of 2–9 flowers on stalk
less than 10 in. high arising above leaves. Flowers white to pale pink, 5 petals, each ½ in. long, sometimes
with reddish veins. Grows in dense conifer forests at low to mid
elevations. Native MORA

Ipomopsis congesta   POLEMONIACEAE
Ballhead gilia
Uncommon, midsummer, perennial, 4–12 in.
Meadow, alpine, subalpine

Stem erect to spreading, hairless or densely
coated with fine hairs. Leaf ⅓–1½ in., hairy,
entire or divided, 3–5 lobes. Inflorescence is a
round ball of flowers atop stem. Flower tube is
yellow, longer than calyx with white oblong
lobes, stamens extending beyond lobes. Grows
in dry open places in shrubs, forests, subalpine
and alpine, at mid to high elevations. There are
7 subspecies, including subsp. *viridis*, frilly gilia, which has
weak sprawling stems, stamens and pistil not extending beyond lobes; found at timberline in Wallowa Mountains. Native

Leptodactylon pungens   POLEMONIACEAE
Granite gilia
Locally common, early spring–midsummer,
perennial, 4–24 in. East-side forest, shrub-
steppe, alpine, subalpine

Small shrub. Leaves tiny, needle-like, with very
sharp tips, living leaves clustered at tips of
branches, persisting, turning black on lower
parts of stems after dying. Flowers with funnel-shaped tube, white to salmon pink with
purplish shading, opening in evening, continuing next day only with cloud cover. Grows in
rocky open places, shrub-steppe, open dry forests, subalpine
talus or granite slopes, in high deserts at all elevations. Native
CRLA

See other *Ipomopsis*: red, page 381

159

Linanthus harknessii

POLEMONIACEAE

Harkness' linanthus, Harkness' flaxflower

Locally common, midsummer, annual, 4–16 in. Meadow

Stems erect, thread-like, many branches at top. Leaves divided into thin segments. Flowers single on stalks at stem tops. Flowers small, white or blue, funnel-shaped, the tube shorter than the lobes, stamens extending outward. Not bicolored. Grows in open flat areas at mid elevations. There are similar thread-like, small-flowered *Linanthus* in our region that are difficult to distinguish. Native NOCA

Linanthus nuttallii (*Linanthastrum nuttallii*)

POLEMONIACEAE

Nuttall's linanthus

Common, midspring, perennial, 4–8 in. West-side forest, east-side forest, alpine, subalpine

Spreading mound, bristly, all parts fragrant. Stems many. Leaves divided, usually 5 linear parts. Flowers clustered at stem top, white to cream, tube funnel-shaped, throat yellow. Grows in dry open flats, openings in forests, sometimes in serpentine, at all elevations. Sometimes forms rather large, very showy mounds. Subsp. *nuttallii* is hairless or nearly so, grows east of Cascade Mountain Range. Native MORA, NOCA

Navarretia divaricata POLEMONIACEAE

Mountain navarretia

Common, early summer, annual, 1–4 in. Dry rocky sites, alpine, subalpine

Small mat. Stems brown or purple, spreading and branched in pairs or whorled. Basal leaves narrow, not lobed; stem leaves lobed to sharply pointed thread-like sections. Inflorescence white-haired in center, bracts and calyces with sharp tips. Flower white, small, with 4–5 lobes, stamen and style usually not extended much beyond tube. Grows in gravelly, often volcanic soils at low to high elevations. Subsp. *divaricata* is white with white or pink lobes, grows throughout the range. Subsp. *vividior* has dark violet-blue flowers, grows in northern California and Oregon. Native NOCA

See other *Linanthus*: red, page 381
See other *Navarretia*: yellow, page 250

Navarretia intertexta POLEMONIACEAE
Needle-leaved navarretia, needle navarretia
Locally common, early summer, annual, 2–4 in.
Coastal, vernal-wet, meadow, west-side forest,
east-side forest, shrub-steppe

Stems erect or spreading, branched or unbranched. Stems brown, with sparse, crisp,
white hairs to hairless. Leaves on stems ¼–2
in. long, divided into narrow segments forked
at tip, 3 sharp needle-like segments with shaggy white hair.
Flowers in dense clusters at tips of branches. Flower tube funnel-shaped, less than ½ in., white to pale blue, stamens extending beyond tube. Grows in drying spring pools, open
meadows, below 6000 ft. *Navarretia leucocephala*, in same habitat, has light green stems and pinnately lobed leaves; branched,
generally spreading habit; stamens exserted
beyond white flower tube. Native

Phlox hoodii POLEMONIACEAE
Hood's phlox, cushion phlox
Locally common, late spring–early summer,
perennial, 2–4 in. Dry rocky sites, east-side
forest, shrub-steppe, alpine, subalpine

Mat to ground-hugging, dense mound. Stems
woolly but not glandular. Leaves sharply
pointed at tip, very white-woolly at base. Flowers 1–3, sessile,
among hairy bracts at tips of branchlets. Flower with hairy
calyx, white to lavender. Grows in open dry forests, rocky or
sandy areas, sagebrush or juniper woods, at low to high elevations. Native

Dodecatheon dentatum PRIMULACEAE
White shooting star, dentate shooting star
Uncommon, early summer, perennial, 6–16 in.
Moist streambanks, meadow, west-side forest,
east-side forest, alpine, subalpine

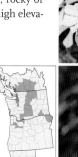

Erect stem, upright to spreading leaves. Plant
hairless. Leaf blades oval to egg-shaped or
sometimes heart-shaped, toothed or wavy-
edged, on slender stalks as long as or longer
than the blades. Flowers 1–6 at top of 5–15 in.
stem, pure white with 1–2 purple dots at base, 5 of all parts.
Grows on wet cliffs, in shady places along streams, wet meadows. Native OLYM, NOCA

See other *Phlox*: red, page 381
See other *Dodecatheon*: red, page 383

Glaux maritima   PRIMULACEAE
Sea milkwort
Locally common, midspring, perennial,
2–10 in. Coastal, bog/fen/wetland

Stem erect, fleshy. Leaves opposite on stem,
sessile, about ¼–½ in., oblong to linear,
with rounded tip. Flowers solitary in axils,
stemless, white or pinkish, small cup-
shaped tube with 5 lobes and 5 stamens.
Grows in coastal marshes, tidal flats, beaches, also in brackish
marshes and alkaline flats inland. Note that the flowers do not
have true petals. Native OLYM

Ceanothus cuneatus   RHAMNACEAE
Buckbrush
Common, late spring, perennial, 6 in.–13 ft.
West-side forest

Rigid upright shrub with evergreen leaves.
Stems freely branching; older branches
silver-gray; young branches may be brown
with fine hairs, often spine-tipped. Leaves
less than 1½ in., opposite, oblong to round,
thick, gray-green; upper surface smooth;
lower surface gray with fine hair. Flower
clusters of 20–60 on branches. Flowers
white, pale blue, or lavender, with short stalks. Flowers very
aromatic. Grows in hot dry sites with poor soils, including serpentine, at low to mid elevations. Native

Ceanothus integerrimus   RHAMNACEAE
Deer brush
Locally common, late spring–early summer,
perennial, 3–12 ft. West-side forest, east-
side forest

Erect deciduous shrub. Stems yellow to pale
green. Leaves alternate, lance-shaped to
widely oblong, 1–3 in. long, thin, upper surface bright green with few or no hairs, lower
side lighter in color, hairy. Inflorescence to 6
in. long, consisting of many stalked clusters
of white to pale blue flowers. Seedpods
sticky. Grows in openings in mixed forests at low to mid elevations. Native

See other *Ceanothus*: blue, page 446

Ceanothus sanguineus   RHAMNACEAE
Redstem ceanothus, Oregon tea tree
Common, late spring–early summer, perennial,
3–10 ft. Coastal, west-side forest

Erect shrub. Stems green when new, becoming red to purple. Leaves deciduous, alternate, petiole less than 1 in., blade thin, widely oval, with pointed tip, tiny teeth. Flowers white on red stalks at tips on stems, cluster less than 5 in. long, very fragrant. Grows in dry open sites, edges of forests, at low to mid elevations. Native OLYM, MORA, NOCA, **L&C**

Ceanothus velutinus   RHAMNACEAE
Snowbrush, tobacco brush, varnish-leaf
Locally common, late spring–early summer, perennial, 3–11 ft.
West-side forest, east-side forest

Erect to spreading shrub. Stems brown, round, smooth. Leaves shiny, evergreen, strongly fragrant, sticky. Leaf widely oval, with round tip, 1–3 in. long, finely toothed. Flowers white in thick rounded clusters less than 6 in. long at stem tops. Grows in open woods, brushy sites, at most elevations. Var. *velutinus* leaf is gray with dense fine hairs on underside. Grows only inland, not near coast, at mid to high elevations. Var. *hookeri* has leaves with underside light green, hairless; grows to small tree only near coast below 2900 ft. Common in disturbed areas along roads, in timber-harvested areas. Native OLYM, MORA, NOCA, **L&C**

Comandra umbellata   SANTALACEAE
Bastard toad-flax
Locally common, early summer, perennial, 4–12 in. Disturbed, meadow, shrub-steppe, alpine, subalpine

Many erect, stout stems from extensive roots can form large patches. Stems with waxy coating, branched, many leaves. Leaves alternate, sessile, thick, and lance-shaped, with sharply pointed tip. Flowers in cluster atop stems, each in cup-shaped calyx above small bract. Flower with 5 petal-like white to dirty white or pinkish sepals, with tuft of hair at base of anthers. Grows in dry rocky places, meadows, along roads, at mid to subalpine elevations. Subsp. *californica* has oval calyx lobes, the prominent form in California and west of Cascades, but extending up Columbia Gorge. Subsp. *pallida* has leaves with heavy waxy coating, calyx lobes lance-shaped; found entirely east of Cascades. The 2 varieties merge where they meet. Native NOCA

163

Solanum nigrum SOLANACEAE
Black nightshade
Locally common, late summer, annual or
perennial, 6–16 in. Coastal, disturbed

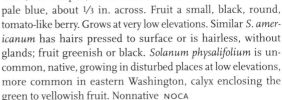

Shrub-like, branching, with spreading hairs
and some glands on surfaces. Leaves egg-
shaped, entire or wavy with few uneven
teeth. Flowers in small open clusters. Calyx
short, bell-shaped, lobed. Flower white to
pale blue, about 1/3 in. across. Fruit a small, black, round,
tomato-like berry. Grows at very low elevations. Similar *S. amer-
icanum* has hairs pressed to surface or is hairless, without
glands; fruit greenish or black. *Solanum physalifolium* is uncommon, native, growing in disturbed places at low elevations,
more common in eastern Washington, calyx enclosing the
green to yellowish fruit. Nonnative NOCA

Sambucus nigra subsp. *cerulea*
CAPRIFOLIACEAE
Blue elderberry
Common, early summer, perennial, 4–20 ft.
West-side forest, east-side forest

Shrub or small tree, erect, usually as wide
as it is tall. Stems hairless. Leaves deciduous, with 3–9 leaflets 3–8 in. long, oval to
lance-shaped, with pointed tip, sharply serrate. Flowers white,
in large flat-topped inflorescence with central stem shorter and
weaker than branches. Flowers small, round, with 5 petals.
Blue-black berries covered with white waxy powder. Grows in
mixed conifer forests, forest-steppe transitions, open talus
slopes, at mid to high elevations. Native OLYM, MORA, **L&C**

Sambucus racemosa CAPRIFOLIACEAE
Red elderberry
Locally common, early summer, perennial,
6–18 ft. Coastal, west-side forest

Shrub or small tree with smooth, dark reddish brown bark. Leaves deciduous, with
5–7 leaflets, each 2–6 in. long, lance-shaped,
with pointed tip, with small sharp teeth,
dark green, hairless on top, lighter on un-
derside with small hairs. Flowers small, dense in a broad oval
cyme, 5 cream petals. Berries red without white wax. Grows in
moist places below alpine. Var. *racemosa* differs, with stiff hairs
on underside of leaf especially along veins; common on moist,
open, logged areas and woods near coast to mid elevations. Var.
melanocarpa is similar but has black fruit and is found more
often east of Cascades. Native OLYM, MORA, NOCA

See other *Solanum*: blue, page 447

Viburnum edule   CAPRIFOLIACEAE
Highbush cranberry, mooseberry
Locally common, early summer, perennial, 3–9
ft. Meadows, moist streambanks, west-side
forest, east-side forest

Spreading to erect, deciduous shrub. Bark
smooth, reddish on young branches. Leaves
opposite, shallowly 3-lobed, with sharp teeth,
hairs on lower surface, turning brilliant red in
autumn. Flowers in small clusters on short stems with single
pair of small leaves. Flower white, 5-lobed. Fruit red to orange,
berry-like, with large flat pits and acid juice. Grows with other
shrubs in moist places at edges of forests and streams. Native
OLYM, MORA, NOCA

Marah oreganus   CUCURBITACEAE
Coast manroot, bigroot
Locally common, all spring, perennial, 3–20 ft.
Coastal, meadow, west-side forest

Vine scrambling over shrubs or small trees.
Stems with dense flexible prickles, tendrils
branched, attached at leaf axil. Leaf 6–8 in.
across, heart-shaped at base, divided palmately
into 5–7 pointed lobes, maple-like. Flowers
white, deeply cup-shaped, with 5 lobes, at stalk
top. Fruit widely oval, tapering to point at tip, streaked dark
green, covered with small prickles. Grows in forest edges,
moist fields, from near coast to 6000 ft. Fruits look like cucum-
bers but are very bitter, not good to eat. Native OLYM, NOCA

Ribes bracteosum   GROSSULARIACEAE
Stink currant
Locally common, late spring–early summer,
perennial, 4–9 ft. Moist streambanks, west-side
forest

Erect shrub with long upright clusters of white
flowers. Stems thornless, sparsely hairy. Leaf
2–7 in. across, palmately divided, with 5–7
lobes; top surface shiny; lower surface with yellow glands. Skunky-smelling. Inflorescence
consists of 20–50 flowers in upright spike 6–12
in. long. Flower saucer-shaped, with green sepals and white
petals. Fruit bluish black with bluish waxy powder. Grows in
moist to wet places along streams, in thickets and woods, below
4500 ft., mostly west of Cascade Mountain crest. Native
OLYM, MORA, NOCA

See other *Ribes*: yellow, page 251; orange, page 302; red, page 388

Ribes cereum GROSSULARIACEAE
Wax currant, squaw currant
Locally common, late spring–early summer, perennial, 2–6 ft. East-side forest, alpine, subalpine

Shrub with more or less upright stems, nasty odor. Leaves gray-green, shiny, round, almost 2 in. across, finely toothed, shallowly, palmately lobed. Flowers hang in clusters at tips of branches. Flower white with greenish to pale pink tint, tube long, 5 sepal lobes curling back, 5 small petals. Berries large, red-orange. Grows at dry edges of forests, often among rocks, at mid to high elevations. Var. *cereum* often has hairy leaves with glands on both sides, bracts at top of flower tube with wide, toothed tips. Var. *colubrinum* has hairless leaves ½–1½ in. wide, grows mostly east of Cascade Mountain crest. Native
CRLA, NOCA, **L&C**

Ribes divaricatum GROSSULARIACEAE
Coast black gooseberry, straggly gooseberry
Locally common, early spring, perennial, 3–9 ft. Coastal, meadow, moist streambanks, west-side forest

Shrub with arching stems. Stems may or may not be bristled, with few to many stout spines at nodes. Leaves deciduous, widely heart-shaped, 1–2 in. across, palmately lobed, toothed, hairy on underside. Flowers 3–5 on stalks hanging under leaves, sepals purplish or greenish purple, more or less reflexed, petals in center shorter, erect, white, pink, or red, stamens extending beyond petals. Berries shiny black. Grows in wet areas, edges of forests, from coastal bluffs to alpine. Var. *divaricatum* has white petals, grows at top of range on Mount Rainier. Native OLYM, MORA, NOCA, **L&C**

Ribes viscosissimum
GROSSULARIACEAE
Sticky currant
Locally common, early summer, perennial, 2–6 ft. Moist streambanks, west-side forest, east-side forest, alpine, subalpine

Upright to spreading shrub covered with glands that secrete a very gummy substance. Stems to 40 in. long, without spines. Leaves gray-green, thick, fragrant, round, palmately divided into 5 toothed lobes. Flowers bell-shaped, whitish green to yellowish white, 4–15 in erect to hanging cluster. Berries black, covered with bluish wax, very gummy. Grows in streambanks, damp to dry woods, at mid to high elevations. Native

MORA, NOCA, **L&C**

Plectritis macrocera VALERIANACEAE
White plectritis, longhorn plectritis
Locally common, midspring, annual, 2–18 in.
Vernal-wet, meadow

Erect stems. Leaf petioles short, blades almost round, opposite. Inflorescence is round head of flowers at stem top. Flower tubes with 5 lobes about equal in size, white, occasionally pale pink; color uniform, without spotting; spur thick, blunt. Grows in seasonally wet areas, open to partly shaded, at low to high elevations. Native NOCA

Valeriana sitchensis VALERIANACEAE
Sitka valerian, mountain heliotrope
Locally common, midsummer, perennial, 1–4 ft.
Meadows, west-side forest, subalpine, alpine

Erect sturdy stems, most leaves along stem. Leaves deeply lobed or coarsely toothed, hairless to slightly hairy. Inflorescence is tight head at stem top. Flowers white or pale pink tubes opening to 5 lobes, stamens and pistil extending beyond lobes. Grows in wet places at mid to alpine elevations. Common species in North Cascades subalpine meadows. Distinguished from *V. scouleri* by coarsely toothed leaf margins, more stem leaves, flowers more often white than pink. Native OLYM, MORA, NOCA, CRLA

Achillea millefolium ASTERACEAE (anthemis tribe)
Common yarrow
Common, all summer, perennial, 1–2 ft. Most habitats

Loose clumps. Aromatic fern-like leaves. Leaves pinnately divided, alternate, hairy; stem leaves clasping, size diminishing at top. Inflorescence is flat-topped cluster of many flower heads. Ray flowers usually 5, disk flowers 10–30, both are same color or contrasting white, pink, purple. Grows in wet to dry soil in meadows, open places, in all elevations. Native
OLYM, MORA, NOCA, CRLA

See other *Plectritis*: red, page 390
See other *Valeriana*: red, page 391

Anthemis cotula
ASTERACEAE (anthemis tribe)
Stinking mayweed, dogfennel
Common, all summer, annual, to 10 in.
Coastal, disturbed, meadow

Spreading mound. Foliage with strong, unpleasant scent. Stems erect, branching, slightly hairy. Stem leaves 2 or 3 times pinnately divided into linear segments. Flower heads single at stem tops, white rays turn downward with age, prominent yellow central disk. A weed abundant in fields, sand dunes, along roads, many other disturbed places, below 6500 ft. Nonnative OLYM, MORA, NOCA

Leucanthemum vulgare (Chrysanthemum leucanthemum)
ASTERACEAE (anthemis tribe)
Oxeye daisy
Common, all summer, perennial, 1–3 ft.
Disturbed, meadow, west-side forest, east-side forest

Erect, smells somewhat like chrysanthemums. Stems many, seldom branched, from creeping root. Basal leaves with petioles, pinnately lobed and toothed; stem leaves becoming smaller and sessile. Flower head 1 per stem, 1–1¼ in. across, with fewer than 22 white ray flowers and many yellow disk flowers. Grows in pastures, meadows, clearings, roadsides, at low to mid elevations. Nonnative OLYM, MORA, NOCA

Aster eatonii (Symphyotrichum eatonii)
ASTERACEAE (aster tribe)
Eaton's aster, Oregon aster
Locally common, late summer, perennial, 2–4 ft. Bog/fen/wetland

Stems erect, hairy in upper parts. Basal leaves fall before blooming; stem leaves sessile, narrow, lance-shaped, 2–6 in. long, entire. Inflorescence long and narrow, with many leafy-bracted flower heads. Flowers with numerous white or pink ray flowers supported in a cup of green bracts of different lengths. Grows in moist to wet soils, often near streams. Native NOCA

See other *Aster*: blue, page 449

Aster oregonensis (*Sericocarpus oregonensis* var. *oregonensis*) ASTERACEAE (aster tribe)
Oregon white-top aster
Uncommon, late summer, perennial, 2–5 ft.
Meadows, west-side forest

Erect. Stems with few or no hairs. Leaves mostly on stem, the lower withering before flowering, 1–3 in. long, lance-shaped, with sharply pointed tips. Flower heads in flat-topped clusters, each with very short stalk; calyx white with green, pointed tips. Ray flowers 5, white; disk flowers with purple anthers. Grows in open places in woods at mid to high elevations. Native

Aster paucicapitatus (*Eucephalus paucicapitatus*)
ASTERACEAE (aster tribe)
Olympic aster, Olympic Mountain aster
Uncommon, late summer, perennial, 8–24 in.
Alpine, subalpine

Compact. Several upright stems. Lowest leaves reduced, scale-like, oblong, 1–2 in. long, covered with gland-tipped hairs. Flower head large, solitary; center of disk flowers ½–1 in. across; ray flowers 9–13, white, about ½ in. long, turning pink with age. Grows on ridges and open slopes in subalpine; occasionally found on Vancouver Island. Native OLYM

Aster radulinus (*Eurybia radulina*) ASTERACEAE (aster tribe)
Rough-leaved aster
Locally common, late summer–autumn, perennial, 8–28 in.
West-side forest, east-side forest

Erect stems with large leaves. Stems, leaves covered with rough hairs. Leaves mostly with petioles, 1–4 in. long, widely oval, firm, sharply toothed. Flower heads held in cyme, each with 10–15 white or light purple ray flowers and yellow disk; cup bracts have purple edges. Grows in dry woods, forests, at low elevations. Native OLYM

Bellis perennis   ASTERACEAE (aster tribe)
English daisy, lawn daisy
Common, all year long, perennial, 1–8 in.
Coastal, disturbed, meadow

Tuft with fibrous roots. Leaves in basal rosette, egg-shaped, with pointed tip, 2–4 in. long, with petioles and blade about equal length. Flower stalk leafless, to 8 in. long. Flower head single, white or slightly pink to purple, with numerous narrow ray flowers, many yellow disk flowers. This pretty little European weed has invaded lawns, meadows, roadsides, at low elevations. Nonnative
OLYM, MORA, NOCA

Conyza canadensis   ASTERACEAE (aster tribe)
Canadian fleabane, horseweed
Common, all summer, annual or biennial, 8–40 in. Disturbed

Single, erect, stiff-haired, leafy stem. Leaves alternate, to 4 in. long, entire or shallowly scalloped. Flower heads in large branched cyme clustered at branch ends. Flowers with very short white petals, cup 1/8 in. in diameter, resinous bracts with brown midvein. Grows in disturbed soils, roadsides, around the world usually in low-elevation sites. Native   OLYM, NOCA

Ericameria resinosa (*Haplopappus resinosus*)
ASTERACEAE (aster tribe)
Columbia goldenweed
Uncommon, late summer, perennial, 8–24 in.
East-side forest

Multibranched pungent shrub with very black old wood, slender young shoots covered with sticky resin. Leaves linear to narrowly oval, usually less than 1/2 in. long, with tip curved downward. Flower heads single or few at stem top, white or very pale yellow. Ray flowers none to 7, disk flowers 10–15. Mostly found in crevices on basalt outcrops, rocky soils. Native

See other *Ericameria*: yellow, page 256

Erigeron annuus   ASTERACEAE (aster tribe)
Annual fleabane
Common, all summer, annual, 3–5 ft.
Disturbed, meadow

Erect, sparsely hairy. Stems with hairs spreading outward. Leaves oval, about 5 in. long, coarsely toothed, smaller on upper stem. Inflorescence branched; multiple leafy stalks with many flower heads. Flower heads have 80–120 rays, each about ½ in. long, white or pale blue, not reflexed, surrounding yellow disks. Grows in moist soils worldwide, often as a weed. Native to eastern United States. Similar *E. strigosus* has stem hairs pressed to the surface and entire leaves. Nonnative OLYM, NOCA

Erigeron compositus
ASTERACEAE (aster tribe)
Cut-leaved daisy, fernleaf fleabane
Locally common, late spring–early summer, perennial, 4–10 in. West-side forest, east-side forest, shrub-steppe, alpine, subalpine

Tuft small. Stems glandular, unbranched, usually leafless. Basal leaves spoon-shaped, always lobed, sometimes divided again, usually covered with hairs, sometimes densely so. Flower head solitary; purple-tipped bracts form a cup holding white, pink, or blue ray flowers, or sometimes, at higher altitudes, rayless. Many yellow disk flowers. Grows in sandy, rocky soils at mostly mid to high elevations. Native
OLYM, MORA, NOCA, CRLA, **L&C**

Erigeron coulteri   ASTERACEAE (aster tribe)
Coulter's daisy, Coulter's fleabane
Locally common, midsummer, perennial, 8–28 in. Vernal-wet, moist streambanks, meadow, east-side forest, alpine, subalpine

Erect straight stems, sometimes branched above midstem, with basal and stem leaves. Leaves widely oblong, 2–5 in., hairy on upper side, smooth below, usually entire or with 2–6 pairs of shallow teeth. Lowest leaves have short petioles, the upper clasping stem. Flower head single (rarely up to 4), less than ½ in. across, atop stem with 45–140 white ray flowers, yellow disk. Found in streambanks, wet meadows, conifer forests, to treeline. Native

See other *Erigeron*: yellow, page 257; red, page 391; blue, page 453

Erigeron divergens

ASTERACEAE (aster tribe)
Diffuse daisy, spreading fleabane
Locally common, early summer, biennial,
6–18 in. Meadow, east-side forest, shrub-
steppe

Upright, branching at midstem. Basal leaves
oblong, about 1 in. long, with short petioles
covered with reflexed to spreading hairs;
upper leaves smaller, very narrow, but not clasping stem.
Flower heads many, about ⅓ in. across, with 100–150 white,
pink, or blue ray flowers; yellow disk flowers become wider at
the throat, glands near and on flower head. Grows in waste
places, dry soils, at low to high elevations in deserts and pine
forests. Native NOCA

Erigeron eatonii ASTERACEAE (aster tribe)

Eaton's fleabane, Eaton's shaggy daisy
Uncommon, all summer, perennial, 2–12 in.
East-side forest, shrub-steppe

Prostrate to upright. Stem with no to few
branches from lower stem, upward-pointing hairs. Leaves narrow, 3-veined, mostly
basal, present at blooming; stem leaves
much smaller. Flower heads usually held
singly on long stalk. Ray flowers white, tinted blue or pink on
underside, slightly twisted. Grows in sandy rocky flats in sagebrush or pine, juniper scrub, open grasslands, at mid to high elevations. Var. *villosus*, Eaton's shaggy daisy, has conspicuous
long white hairs on underside of head, more hairs throughout,
no glands. Native

Erigeron filifolius ASTERACEAE (aster tribe)

Threadleaf fleabane, threadleaf daisy
Locally common, late spring–early summer,
perennial, 8–40 in. Meadow, shrub-steppe

Tall, erect. Stems with multiple branches
often form large clumps. Leaves 1–3 in.,
narrow, mostly basal, few on stems smaller,
covered with white upcurved hairs. Flower
heads solitary to numerous, ⅓ in. wide,
rays 15–125 white, blue, or pink with yellow disk flowers.
Found in many habitats, grassy open sites, rocky or sandy soils,
below 6000 ft. The common var. *filifolius* has thread-like leaves,
numerous flower heads on a stem, each with 15–75 rays. More
sturdy var. *robustior* has solitary flower head topping stem,
widespread east of Cascade Mountains. Native NOCA

Erigeron flettii ASTERACEAE (aster tribe)
Olympic Mountain fleabane

Endemic, midsummer, perennial, 2–6 in. Alpine
Tiny. Leaves mostly basal, oblong to spoon-
shaped, 2 in. long, hairless or somewhat hairy
with sticky glands, finely toothed; few stem
leaves smaller on upper stem. Flower heads
single on short stems, cups green with purple-
tipped bracts; 25–50 white rays ⅓ in. long; yellow disk about ½ in. across. Grows on rocky ridges high in the
Olympic Mountains. Native OLYM

Erigeron peregrinus ASTERACEAE (aster tribe)
Wandering daisy, peregrine fleabane

Uncommon, all summer, perennial, 4–18 in.
Bog/fen/wetland, west-side forest, east-side
forest, alpine, subalpine
Clump. Leaves lance- to spoon-shaped, hairless or sparsely hairy. Lower leaves with petioles; few upper stem leaves smaller, clasping.
Flower head single on unbranched stem. Ray
flowers 30–105, white, purple, or rose. Grows
in bogs, wet meadows, or subalpine, alpine
talus and openings. Grows on mountains at
mid to high elevations. Var. *callianthemus*, peregrine fleabane, has hairless entire leaves, deep rose-purple
flowers in cups very dense with glands. Var. *peregrinus*, wandering daisy, found only at high elevations in Coast Range, has
toothed leaves soft with short hairs, flower cup bracts not glandular. Native OLYM, MORA, NOCA, CRLA

Erigeron philadelphicus ASTERACEAE
(aster tribe)
Philadelphia daisy, pink fleabane

Common, early summer, biennial or perennial,
1–4 ft. Disturbed, meadow, shrub-steppe
Erect. Stems hairless or with long spreading
hairs. Basal leaves oblong to egg-shaped, 3–6
in. long, with few teeth; stem leaves lance`to
egg-shaped and clasping stem, not much
smaller than basal leaves. Flower heads single
to many at stem top. Ray flowers 150 to many, white or pinkish,
somewhat twisting. Disk flowers yellow. Grows in moist places
in forests, along streams, at low elevations. Native
OLYM, MORA, NOCA

Hieracium albiflorum
ASTERACEAE (chicory tribe)
White-flowered hawkweed
Common, all summer, perennial, 1–3 ft.
West-side forest, east-side forest

Erect, with white milky sap, no stolons. Stem single, densely hairy on lower portion. Leaves mostly basal, oblong to lance-shaped, 3–7 in. long, toothed, covered with long coarse hairs; stem leaves few, smaller, alternate on lower stem, with bare stems above. Flower heads in open cymes; disk flowers 15–30, small, white, ray-like; no ray flowers. Grows in dry forests, shady openings in woods, in all elevations. Native OLYM, MORA, NOCA

Prenanthes alata ASTERACEAE (chicory tribe)
Western rattlenake root
Locally common, late summer–autumn, perennial, 6–18 in. Coastal, west-side forest

Erect. Stems with milky sap, often branched upper section. Leaves mostly on stem, arrow-shaped, with irregular pointed teeth; petiole with flat wing. Flowers in wide cluster at stem top, not in elongated spike, often nodding. Flower head about 1 in. across, white to pink or lavender, with 10–15 ray flowers; extended long, stiff, brown bristles occur as seed develops. Grows in moist open forests, streambanks, rocky beaches. *Prenanthes* is Greek and means "drooping flower." *Alata*, which means "protruding ridges wider than thick," refers to the winged leaf stalks. Native OLYM, MORA, NOCA

Anaphalis margaritacea
ASTERACEAE (everlasting tribe)
Pearly everlasting
Common, midsummer, perennial, 8–40 in.
Coastal, disturbed, meadow, west-side forest, east-side forest, alpine, subalpine

Loose clumps. Stems erect, unbranched from spreading root. Leaves alternate along stem, narrow, green on upper side with sparse white hairs, underside thickly covered with white-woolly hairs. Inflorescence consists of crowded clusters at stem tops. Flowers small, yellowish, each surrounded by pearly white bracts. Widespread in forest openings, meadows, roadsides, slopes, at all elevations. Often used as a cut flower in dried bouquets. Native OLYM, MORA, NOCA

See other *Hieracium*: yellow, page 268; orange, page 302

Antennaria dimorpha
ASTERACEAE (everlasting tribe)
Low pussytoes
Uncommon, midspring, perennial, 1–3 in.
Shrub-steppe

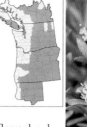

Mat from much-branched base. Single carrot-like root, unlike most pussytoes does not make stolons. Branches prostrate, short. Basal leaves and few stem leaves linear to slightly spoon-shaped, gray with interwoven, matted hairs. Single flower head tops stem with either male flowers in small head or female flowers in head about twice as big. Flowers dull white inside large cup of dirty brown bracts, the papery tips extending beyond flowers. Grows in dry places below 6000 ft. Native

Antennaria flagellaris ASTERACEAE
(everlasting tribe)
Spreading pussytoes, flagellate pussytoes
Uncommon, late spring–early summer,
perennial, ½ in. Vernal-wet, shrub-steppe

Open mat. Obvious, spreading, reddish stolons have leafy tips. Each tip will grow into new plant. Leaves narrow, oval, entire, gray-haired. Flower held singly on short stem, facing upward. Male and female flowers form a whitish fluff. Grows in dry rocky soils, open areas, vernal-wet in sagebrush-steppe. Native

Antennaria howellii ASTERACEAE (everlasting tribe)
Howell's pussytoes
Uncommon, all summer, perennial, 6–16 in. West-side forest,
east-side forest, alpine, subalpine

Stems erect. Basal leaf rosette. Leaves prostrate, spoon-shaped, on ½ in. tapered petioles, with white hairs underneath, green and sparsely hairy above; interspersed with stolons to 8 in. long, with similar but stemless leaves. Inflorescence is a cluster of 5–12 flower heads on hairy stalks. Flowers held in cup of sharply pointed bracts with cobweb-like hairs at base, upper cup light brown to white. Grows in open forests at 4000–7000 ft. Native OLYM, MORA, NOCA, CRLA

See other *Antennaria*: red, page 393

Antennaria lanata
ASTERACEAE (everlasting tribe)
Woolly pussytoes
Locally common, midsummer, perennial,
4–8 in. Alpine, subalpine

Tufted, erect, densely woolly. Basal leaves
1–4 in. long, lance-shaped, wider at tip;
stem leaves lance-shaped, progressively
smaller, often with dark tips. Flower heads
congested in rounded cluster at stem top. Female flower head
cups formed of greenish black bracts; male flower head bracts
with white tips. Grows in alpine or subalpine meadows or rocky
slopes. The Latin word *lanatus* means "woolly." Native
OLYM, MORA, NOCA

Antennaria luzuloides
ASTERACEAE (everlasting tribe)
**Woodrush pussytoes, small-flowered
everlasting**
Locally common, late spring–early summer,
perennial, 3–10 in. East-side forest, shrub-
steppe

Tufts with no stolons. Leaf clumps gray,
prostrate, point upward. Basal leaves ½ in.
or longer, linear to spoon-shaped; stem
leaves alternate on upper stem. Flower stalks 3–10 in., bearing
heads of 8–30 flowers. Male and female flowers occur separately in cups of straw-colored to white, sharply pointed bracts.
Grows in dry open slopes, prairies, at mid elevations. Native
NOCA

Antennaria media (Antennaria alpina
var. *media*)
ASTERACEAE (everlasting tribe)
Alpine pussytoes
Locally common, all summer, perennial, 2–5
in. Alpine, subalpine

Stems erect. Dense mats, with stoloniferous
roots forming many rosettes. Basal leaves
white to gray, densely woolly, less than ½ in.
long, linear to spoon-shaped; stem leaves
sparse, narrow, often brown-tipped. Flowers in 2–7 heads tightly
grouped at stem top. Cup formed by very dark blackish green or
brown bracts, woolly at bottom. Grows on exposed ridges, high
meadows, snow basins, at high elevations. Native
OLYM, MORA, NOCA, CRLA

Antennaria racemosa
ASTERACEAE (everlasting tribe)
Racemose pussytoes
Locally common, all summer, perennial, 5–20 in. West-side forest, east-side forest, shrub-steppe, alpine, subalpine

Basal leaf rosettes and intermingled procumbent stolons. Leaf blades oval, with ½ in. petioles, green above, covered with matted white hairs beneath; leaves progressively smaller toward stolon tips. Inflorescence consists of individual flower heads along the upper part of 5 in. or longer stalks. Female flower head slightly larger than male. Grows in open woods, often near streams, at mid to high elevations. *Racemosa* refers to stalked flowers arranged along a central stem. Native OLYM, MORA, NOCA

Antennaria stenophylla
ASTERACEAE (everlasting tribe)
Narrow-leaved everlasting
Locally common, late spring–early summer, perennial, 1–6 in. Shrub-steppe

Prostrate plant from central root, gray throughout with matted hairs. Leaves erect, 1–2 in. long, very narrow, occurring in tufts from base and along flower stem. Flower stalk erect, with tight cluster of 2–24 cone-shaped flower heads. Cup of dark brown to black bracts with lighter tips, flowers hidden in dull whitish fluff. Grows on dry ridges and hills. Native

Antennaria umbrinella ASTERACEAE (everlasting tribe)
Umber pussytoes, brown everlasting
Uncommon, midsummer, perennial, 3–10 in. Shrub-steppe, alpine, subalpine

Green to gray with matted hairs, woody base. Stolons spread out to 3 in. Basal leaves spoon-shaped to oblong; stem leaves narrower, with sharp dark tip and a small appendage. Flower heads cone-shaped. Cup woolly at base, bracts marked with brown medium spot and brown or white spot at rounded tips, flowers white to tan. Grows in moist to wet subalpine, alpine

meadows of high mountains. Resembles *A. media*, which has pointed bract tips. Native OLYM, MORA, NOCA

Gnaphalium palustre

ASTERACEAE (everlasting tribe)
Lowland cudweed
Common, all summer, annual, 1–12 in.
Vernal-wet, meadow

Clump with hairy white stems and leaves.
Stems branch from base with many leaves.
Alternate, spoon-shaped, entire leaves clasp
stem. Flower heads very small, develop in
leaf clusters atop stems. White pistillate flowers are held in
brown cups. Grows in moist places, usually in lowlands but can
grow into high elevations. Native OLYM, NOCA

Gnaphalium uliginosum   ASTERACEAE (everlasting tribe)

Marsh cudweed
Locally common, all year long, annual, 1–10
in. Vernal-wet, moist streambanks

Erect to spreading, many short branches,
entirely covered with white or gray matted
hairs. Leaves narrow to linear, wider near
top, tips pointed, on stem and flower stalks.
Flower heads cluster at stalk ends, small,
somewhat hidden in wool and longer overlapping leaves. Flower heads bell-shaped,
bearing more than 100 pistillate flowers,
4–5 bisexual; cups pale green at base; bracts tipped dark brown
to black. Grows in moist to wet places. *Uliginosum* means
"growing in swamps or wet places." Nonnative OLYM, NOCA

Pseudognaphalium canescens subsp. *thermale*

ASTERACEAE (everlasting tribe)
Slender cudweed, white everlasting
Uncommon, late summer–autumn, biennial
or perennial, 12–30 in. Disturbed, meadow,
east-side forest

Basal tufts of leaves, erect flower stems,
scented, with gray matted hairs throughout.
Leaves ½–3 in. long, linear; stem leaves upward-pointing, leaves on nonblooming
stems spoon-shaped, upper stem leaves with
wing running down stem. Flower heads
with short stalks, many in tight clusters pointing upward. Calyx
straw-colored with white to straw-colored flowers. Grows in dry
woodlands, roadsides, at mid to high elevations. Native
OLYM, MORA

Adenocaulon bicolor

ASTERACEAE (senecio tribe)
Trail plant, pathfinder
Locally common, all summer, perennial, 3–40
in. Disturbed, west-side forest, east-side forest

Erect, widely branched at stem top. Stem white
with woolly hairs on lower section, upper stem
with glands. Leaves with winged petioles,
mostly basal, thin, triangular to egg-shaped,
shallowly lobed, with soft white hairs beneath, green and
smooth above. Flowers without rays, few in a head, very small,
white, male and female flowers on thin stems. Grows in moist
shaded woods below 6500 ft. White undersides of leaves turn
over on flexible stalks when disturbed, creating a path, thus the
common name. Native OLYM, MORA, NOCA

Dimeresia howellii

ASTERACEAE (senecio tribe)
Dimeresia, doublet
Uncommon, all spring, annual, 1 in. Shrub-
steppe, alpine, subalpine

Cushion less than 2 in. across from single root.
Plant with cobwebby hairs below, glands
above. Stem short. Leaves clustered around
flower head, egg-shaped, ⅓–1½ in. long, en-
tire. Inflorescence consists of sessile clusters of 2(–3) rayless
flowers, each surrounded by many bristles. Flower tubes and
throat pale purplish, lobes 5, open flat, white. Grows in dry volcanic sand, scree or barren ridges, at high elevations. *Dimeresia*
is Greek, meaning "two," for the usually 2-flowered heads. Native

Petasites frigidus ASTERACEAE (senecio tribe)

Coltsfoot, western coltsfoot, alpine coltsfoot
Locally common, early spring, perennial, 1–2 ft.
Coastal, vernal-wet, bog/fen/wetland, west-side
forest, alpine, subalpine

Stout erect stem with tight cluster of whitish
to pink rayless flowers that open before leaves
emerge. Flower stalks continue to lengthen as
large leaves unfold. Leaves palmately divided,
lobes coarsely toothed. Flowers in often purplish bell-shaped
cup; male, female flowers in separate heads. Grows in bogs,
stream edges, roadsides, other wet soils. Var. *palmatus* (pictured) has large leaves to 16 in. across with lobes deeply cut to
base; blooms March, April at low elevations. Var. *nivalis* has
leaves less than 8 in. across, not deeply divided, with short or no
teeth. Blooms July and August at high elevations, often immediately after snowmelt. Native OLYM, NOCA

Blepharipappus scaber

ASTERACEAE (sunflower tribe)
Blepharipappus, rough eyelashweed
Locally common, all summer, annual, 4–12
in. Disturbed, meadow, east-side forest,
shrub-steppe

Slender, upright, branched annual, hairless to covered with short stiff hairs. Leaves alternate, sessile, usually pointed upward, 1–2 in., linear, with rolled edges. Flower heads have 3–8 ray flowers, white with purple undersides, very wide, deeply lobed into 3 parts; 6–25 white disk flowers with purple anthers. Grows in dry soils, pine and juniper woodlands, disturbed places of steppe, at 3000–10,000 ft. Very similar to *Layia glandulosa*, which has yellow disk flowers. *Pappus* is Greek for "eyelash." Native

Chaenactis douglasii

ASTERACEAE (sunflower tribe)
Dusty maidens, hoary false yarrow
Uncommon, early summer, biennial or
perennial, 6–25 in. Shrub-steppe, alpine,
subalpine

Ascending, stout perennial with persistent basal rosette. Stems thinly coated with gray cobweb-like hairs, sticky glands, or both. Leaves thick, less than 6 in. long, largest pinnately divided to midrib into crowded linear lobes, longest near midleaf. Lobes contorted, again divided; tips reflexed so that leaf curls. Flower heads single to many, each on separate stalks. Disk flowers in glandular cup, white to pinkish, anthers extending above head. Grows in rock crevices in dry open areas at low to alpine elevations. Var. *douglasii* is branched below middle. Var. *alpina*, a small mound, grows only in alpine areas. Native

Layia glandulosa

ASTERACEAE (sunflower tribe)
White layia, white daisy tidytips
Locally common, midspring, annual, 6–24
in. Shrub-steppe

Single erect stem, glandular, sometimes spicy-smelling. Leaves linear to oval. Basal leaves lobed; upper leaves entire. Flower heads on stalks to 3 in. long. Ray flowers 3–14, white, 3-lobed on tips. Few to many yellow disk flowers. Grows in open and sandy soils below 4500 ft. Similar *Blepharipappus scaber* has white disk flowers with purple anthers. Native

Wyethia helianthoides

ASTERACEAE (sunflower tribe)
White mule's ears, white-headed wyethia
Uncommon, late spring–early summer,
perennial, 12–30 in. Meadow, shrub-steppe

Clump of upward-pointing leaves, stems bearing single flower. Plant is densely coated with matted hairs, becoming hairless as season progresses. Basal leaves oval, 10–16 in. long; upper leaves smaller. Flower head contains 13–21 white ray flowers, each 1–2 in. long, disk of many yellow flowers. Grows in moist places, open grasslands and shrublands, below 6500 ft. Native

Centaurea diffusa   ASTERACEAE (thistle tribe)

Diffuse knapweed, tumble knapweed
Common, all summer, annual or perennial,
8–32 in. Disturbed, meadow, shrub-steppe

Upright, diffusely branched, with hairy gray coating. Leaves 4–8 in., pinnately cut into deep lobes; upper leaves smaller. Flower heads numerous. Narrow bell-shaped to oval cup of pale yellow-green bracts are fringed like a comb and end with slender sharp spines turned outward. White disk flowers (occasionally lavender or pink), elongate to create petal-like fringe. Grows in many steppe soils. Along with spotted knapweed, *C. biebersteinii*, and yellow starthistle, *C. solstitialis*, this aggressive invasive weed heavily dominates range lands, largely reducing livestock and wildlife forage because of the lack of palpability. Nonnative

OLYM, MORA, NOCA, CRLA

Cirsium canovirens

ASTERACEAE (thistle tribe)
Gray-green thistle
Locally common, all summer, biennial or
perennial, 15–40 in. Shrub-steppe

Gray-green erect plant, usually 1 branched stem. Stem tops covered with gray or white felted hairs. Lowest leaves oval, to 15 in. long, lobed and edged with spines, covered with matted woolly hairs, thicker on underside; stem leaves smaller, very prickly with spines. Flower heads 1–2 in. across in raceme-like clusters at tops of stalks. Flowers dull white or pale lavender in cups lightly covered with cobwebby hairs; outer bracts end in spines. Grows on clay or rocky soils in arid places, including Steens Mountain. Native

See other *Wyethia*: yellow, page 294
See other *Centaurea*: yellow, page 295; red, page 394; blue, page 456
See other *Cirsium*: red, page 394

Cirsium cymosum

ASTERACEAE (thistle tribe)
Peregrine thistle, Greene's thistle
Locally common, all summer, perennial, 2–5
ft. East-side forest, shrub-steppe

Erect, straight stems, usually unbranched
below inflorescence, covered with soft, cobwebby, straight hairs. Leaves attached with
little or no stalk, often clasping stem, nar-
rowly oblong, pinnately divided, with many spines at lobe tips.
Leaves lightly coated with cobwebby straight hairs on upper
side, heavier on underside especially along midrib. Flower
heads few to many, cream to pale brown, in cyme on short or
absent stalks. Bracts of ½–1 in. cups are sticky, with short
prickles. Grows in rocky soils, sometimes serpentine, in shrublands and open woods, including Cascade-
Siskiyou National Monument. Native

Cirsium scariosum

ASTERACEAE (thistle tribe)
Elk thistle
Uncommon, early summer, biennial or
perennial, 5–40 in. Meadow

Erect. Stems often very short, fleshy, ridged,
hairless to hairy with soft or coarse hairs.
Basal leaves oblong, entire or deeply lobed, hairless or with few
matted hairs above, thick white matted hairs below, petioles
often spiny; stem leaves few to none. Flower heads dense, sessile, in basal leaf rosette or clustered at stem tops. Flowers are
white or purple tubes with lobes almost as long. Grows in moist
places, meadows, at mid to high elevations. Dwarf and taller
plants sometimes grow together. Native

Brickellia grandiflora

ASTERACEAE (thoroughwort tribe)
**Large-flowered tasselflower, large-flowered
thoroughwort**
Locally common, late summer–autumn,
perennial, 8–30 in. East-side forest, shrub-
steppe

Stems upright, usually unbranched except
in inflorescence. Leaves opposite, blades lance-shaped to triangular, scalloped to toothed, heart-shaped base with ¼–1 in.
petioles. Flower heads at stem tips in small clusters, erect to
nodding, no ray flowers. Disk flowers whitish. Widespread
among rocks, canyons, on cliffs, at low to mid elevations. Native

Eriophorum chamissonis CYPERACEAE
Russet cotton-grass
Locally common, all summer, perennial, 4–30 in. Bog/fen/wetland

Stems erect from runners, triangular, solid, longer than leaves. Leaves narrow, becoming wider and wrapping around stem at base, ending in a sharp point. Inflorescence is a single spikelet with numerous, large, silky, white to brown bristles held upright, 3–5 times as long as the purplish brown scales holding them. Grows in bogs, wet meadows. *Eriophorum angustifolium* subsp. *scabriusculum*, narrow-leaved cotton-grass, with several spikelets of white bristles in a loose cluster on nodding stalks, is more common in subalpine wet meadows at Mount Rainier. Native OLYM, NOCA

Nymphaea odorata NYMPHAEACEAE
Fragrant water lily
Locally common, mid to late summer, perennial. Lake/pond

Floating. Leaves usually attached by long stalks to extensive root system in sediments, 2–12 in. across, round except for narrow pie-shaped slit where stem is attached. Flower very fragrant, white, pink, or purple, floating on or held just above water, about 5–8 in. across, opening in morning and closing in late afternoon. Grows in ponds or edges of lakes, sometimes clogs waterways. Highly ornamental plant with many horticultural varieties. Native to eastern United States. Invasive in lakes and ponds, on the Washington noxious weed list. Nonnative OLYM

Croton setigerus (*Eremocarpus setigerus*)
EUPHORBIACEAE
Turkey mullein, dove weed
Common, all summer–autumn, annual, 1–8 in. Disturbed, meadow, shrub-steppe

Cushion. Sap clear, not milky. Stem with many branches from base, spreading or upright. Leaves mostly in tight rosettes at tips of stems. Leaf entire, alternate with petiole to 2 in. long, blade gray-green, 1–2½ in. long, egg-shaped, with wide base, dense with soft star-shaped hairs. Male flowers small in cluster above 2–3 female flowers. Grows in open or disturbed places below 3000 ft. Native

Mahonia aquifolium (*Berberis aquifolium*) BERBERIDACEAE
Shining Oregon-grape, tall Oregon-grape
Common, all spring, perennial, 1–4 ft.
Coastal, disturbed, west-side forest, east-side forest

Woody shrub with upright to spreading stems. Stems have yellow inner bark. Leaves alternate on stem, 3–10 in. long, pinnately divided, 5–9 leaflets held along central stalk. Leaflets holly-like, leathery, shiny on upper side, dull underneath, 1–3 in. long, with a single central vein, edged with 12–29 very sharply pointed spines. Flowers bright yellow, in dense clusters at stem ends. Berries edible, dark blue, egg-shaped to round, covered with whitish waxy powder. Grows in oak woodlands, forests to sagebrush slopes, below 7000 ft. State flower of Oregon. Native
OLYM, MORA, NOCA, **L&C**

Mahonia nervosa (*Berberis nervosa*) BERBERIDACEAE
Dwarf Oregon-grape, dull Oregon-grape
Locally common, all spring, perennial, 6–24 in. Coastal, west-side forest

Erect stemmed shrub, yellow bark, yellowish cast to leaves turning reddish in winter. Stems spreading, stiff, holding pairs (one terminal) of 9–19 leaflets horizontally to soil. Leaflets glossy, palmately veined, 1–3 in. long, smooth, lance-shaped, leathery, with even rows of 6–12 sharply pointed teeth. Flower stems in center short with erect heads of yellow flowers. Flowers have all parts in 6. Berries blue, coated with white waxy powder, egg-shaped, edible but sour. Grows in conifer forests to 6500 ft.
Native OLYM, MORA, NOCA, **L&C**

Mahonia repens (*Berberis aquifolium* var. *repens, Mahonia amplectens*) BERBERIDACEAE
Trailing Oregon-grape
Common, late spring–early summer, perennial, 4–8 in. West-side forest, east-side forest

Prostrate or low-growing. Stems woody. Leaves divided into 5–7 egg-shaped, dull-surfaced leaflets 1–3 in. with 15–43 teeth. Flowers yellow, in terminal cluster at top of short stem, followed by egg-shaped, edible, blue berries. Often considered a variety of tall Oregon-grape, *M. aquifolium*, and growing in the same habitats: woodlands, conifer forests, canyons, but can also grow in drier areas at low to mid elevations. Native
NOCA, **L&C**

Iris bracteata   IRIDACEAE
Siskiyou iris
Uncommon, late spring, perennial, 12 in.
West-side forest

Erect stems, broad stiff leaves. Stems enclosed
with short, overlapping bracts, often reddish.
Leaves evergreen, shiny, leathery, dark green
on upper side, pale on underside, reddish at
base. Flower petals yellow to cream with noticeable veins of red-brown or maroon, perianth tube below
petals very short and stout. Grows in shade, on serpentine,
below 2500 ft. An important aid in identification of native iris is
length of perianth tube between flower and enlargement of
ovary where seeds are being formed. Native

Iris innominata   IRIDACEAE
Golden iris, rainbow iris
Uncommon, late spring, perennial, 6–24 in.
West-side forest

Clump of grass-like leaves, upright unbranched stems. Leaves evergreen, ⅛ in. wide,
deep red at base, forming dense clumps that
bend back and out from center. Flowers light
to deep golden yellow, cream, apricot, orchid
pink, or deep blue-purple, with prominent
veins, perianth tube about ¾ in. long and stem below ovary
about same length as tube. Grows on partly shaded, rich, well-
drained slopes below 6000 ft. *Innominata* is Latin for "no
name," for this was the last West Coast iris found (in 1928) and
named. Native

Iris pseudacorus   IRIDACEAE
Yellow flag
Common, early summer, perennial, 1–3 ft.
Bog/fen/wetland, lake/pond

Erect stems and leaves. Leaves 1 in. wide, stiff.
Flowers numerous, bright yellow, with brown
marks outlining crest area, petals narrow near
middle. Grows in waterways and other wet
areas throughout North America at low elevations. A European native used as a symbol for
Louis VII, called fleur de Louis, now a design known as fleur-
de-lis. Invasive weed of wetlands. Nonnative NOCA, OLYM

See other *Iris*: white, page 59; blue, page 400

Sisyrinchium californicum
IRIDACEAE
Golden-eyed grass
Uncommon, early summer, perennial, 6–16
in. Coastal, vernal-wet, meadow, west-side
forest, alpine, subalpine

Clumps of leaves and stems. Stems flat,
with extensions on the sides, taller than
leaves. Leaves to 12 in., dull green, turning
black when dead. Flowers yellow with brown markings, clustered at stem top, opening in first few hours of sunlight, withering later in the day. Grows in moist places near coast, to subalpine. Native OLYM, CRLA

Erythronium grandiflorum   LILIACEAE
Glacier lily
Common, early spring, perennial, 6–12 in.
Alpine, subalpine
Erect flowering stem from a pair of shiny,
unmarbled, midgreen leaves. Leaves 4–8
in. long, less than ½ as wide. Stem 6–12 in.
with 1 or 2 nodding bright yellow flowers.
Flowers lighter-colored at the base, petals
strongly reflexed, anthers cream to yellow
or dark red, longer than pistil. Grows in
alpine or subalpine meadows, forest openings, among sagebrush, at mid to high elevations but also low elevations in Columbia River Gorge. Found blooming just after snowmelt. Similar to white-flowered *E. montanum*, avalanche lily, in same
habitat. Native OLYM, MORA, NOCA, CRLA, **L&C**

Fritillaria glauca   LILIACEAE
Siskiyou fritillary
Endemic, early spring, perennial, 1–6 in.
Dry rocky sites, alpine, subalpine

Erect, unbranched, leafless stem. Leaves
2–4, oblong, covered with bluish white waxy
powder, to 3 in. long, folded, resembling
miniature tulip leaves. Flowers 1 or 2, shallow bells, nodding to outward-facing, yellow
or greenish yellow with red or brown mark-
ings or reversed. Grows on serpentine with many rocks in full
sun at 1100–6700 ft. This rare plant, our shortest fritillary, has
been known to hybridize with small forms of *F. affinis*. Native

See other *Sisyrinchium*: blue, page 401
See other *Erythronium*: white, page 64; red, page 312
See other *Fritillaria*: red, page 312; green/brown, page 459

Fritillaria pudica   LILIACEAE
Yellow bells
Common, early spring, perennial, 3–12 in.
Meadow, east-side forest, shrub-steppe, alpine, subalpine

Stem erect, unbranched. Leaves 2–8, narrow, scattered along stem. Flower usually 1, sometimes 2, at stem top, facing outward to hanging. Flowers are clear yellow aging to orange but can have faint brown markings inside, often turning deep red when withered. Grows in heavy soils that bake in summer, with grass or brush, or in light woods, at low to high elevations. Native **L&C**

Narthecium californicum   LILIACEAE
California bog asphodel
Locally common, all summer, perennial, 8–24 in. Bog/fen/wetland, moist streambanks, meadow

Stem erect above flat basal leaves. Leaves 2 to several, linear, overlapping, 4–12 in. long. Flowers in 3–6 in. cluster atop stem. Flowers with 1/3–3/4 in. stalk, small, yellow, consisting of 6 petals and 6 stamens with wool on the filaments; anthers brick red. Grows in wet meadows, fens, streambanks, at mid to high elevations. Native

Streptopus amplexifolius   LILIACEAE
Clasping twisted stalk
Common, late spring–early summer, perennial, 12–40 in. West-side forest, east-side forest

Stems upright, repeatedly branched. Stems smooth, often bent at nodes and looking zigzagged. Leaves oval, with sharp point, 3–6 in. long, surrounding or clasping stem. Yellow, cream, or white bell-shaped flowers hang under leaves on sharply kinked or twisted stalks, tips flaring out and curving upward. Berries watermelon red. Grows in moist rich soils in forests, woods, along streams, from near coastline to mid elevations. Native
OLYM, MORA, NOCA, CRLA

See other *Streptopus*: red, page 313

189

Triteleia hendersonii   LILIACEAE
Henderson's stars
Rare, early summer, perennial, 4–12 in.
West-side forest

Stem erect, umbel at top. Basal leaves 2–3, narrow, about same length as stem, often withered by flowering. Umbels loose, with 6–15 flowers. Flowers pale to salmon yellow, midveins dark blue to brown, tube funnel-shaped, with 6 segments slightly longer, opening wide, 6 blue anthers. Grows in rocky soils in canyons and on hillsides. The rare *T. crocea*, found in Jackson County, Oregon, has bright yellow lobes; grows in open conifer forests and on dry slopes. Native

Triteleia ixioides (*Brodiaea lutea*)
LILIACEAE
Pretty face
Uncommon, late spring–early summer, perennial, 8–24 in. Coastal, west-side forest

Stem ascending. Leaves 8–15 in., entire, curved upward or horizontal. Flowers in umbel with stalks curved upward. Flower yellow to straw-colored, with dark stripe on each lobe; tube shorter than lobes that open wide or slightly reflex; 3 large straight or inward-curved appendages in center surround blue or sometimes yellow anthers. Grows in sandy, gravelly soils at forest edges from coast to 9000 ft. Native

Platystemon californicus   PAPAVERACEAE
Cream cups
Locally common, late spring–early summer, annual, 4–12 in. Coastal, meadow

Tuft of erect leaves, upright flower stalk. Leaves and stems covered with long shaggy hairs, sap colorless. Basal and stem leaves linear to oblong, entire, opposite. Single flower atop 4–8 in. stalk. Flower sepals 3, hairy; petals 6, oval, pale yellow to white, with deeper yellow spot in center; many stamens with flattened filaments. Grows among open grass in sandy soils and is especially thick after fires at low elevations. (Note: Usually more erect than pictured here.) Native

190   See other *Triteleia*: white, page 68; blue, page 404

Eriogonum caespitosum
POLYGONACEAE
Cushion eriogonum, cushion desert buckwheat
Locally common, early summer, perennial, to 4
in. Shrub-steppe, alpine, subalpine

Mat of white-woolly leaves. Plant with woody
base, much-branched to mats 18 in. in diameter. Leaves covered with white hair on both
sides, oblong to egg-shaped, to 1 in. long, with
edges rolled under. Flowering stem bare, to 4 in. long, with single head of flowers supported by single small cup. Flowers yellow, fading to red, of 2 types: small infertile, larger fertile.
Grows in sandy or rocky soils at high elevations. Native

Eriogonum douglasii POLYGONACEAE
Douglas's eriogonum, Douglas's buckwheat
Locally common, midspring, perennial, 1–12
in. Dry rocky sites, east-side forest, shrub-
steppe, alpine, subalpine

Cushion 2–16 in. across. Stems from woody
base densely branched. Leaves linear to oval,
in clusters along stems and at tips, very white
with tiny fuzzy hairs on both sides. Halfway up
flower stem is small whorl of leaf-like bracts.
Flowers numerous in single round ball on
hairy stalk, sitting in a cup with bracts turned back. Flower
buds blood red opening to creamy yellow. Grows in dry, sandy,
gravelly places, sagebrush or juniper flats, Ponderosa forests,
into high elevations. Native

Eriogonum heracleoides POLYGONACEAE
**Creamy eriogonum, parsley desert buckwheat,
Wyeth's buckwheat**
Common, early spring, perennial, 6–20 in.
Dry rocky sites, shrub-steppe

Mats loose, 2–16 in. across, shrubby at base.
Leaves green, mostly on lower stem and basal,
1–2 in., narrow to oblong, hairy mostly on underside. Inflorescence usually with whorl of
reflexed leaf-like bracts midway on stem and
second whorl where flower stalks branch.
Flowers clustered, cream, with long-stalked base, turning red
with age. Grows in loamy sandy or gravelly slopes at mid to
high elevations. Plants with leaves less than ¼ in. wide are var.
angustifolium; plants with wider leaves are var. *heracleoides*.
Plants without bracts on stems are var. *minus*, most often found
in central Washington and east to Spokane. Native

See other *Eriogonum*: white, page 75; red, page 316

Eriogonum marifolium

POLYGONACEAE

Marum-leaved buckwheat

Locally common, all summer, perennial,
4–10 in. West-side forest, east-side forest,
alpine, subalpine

Sturdy stems from mats up to 30 in. across.
Male and female flowers on separate plants.
Leaf clusters at ends of short stems. Leaves
very small to 1¼ in. long, oval, pointed at tip, with woolly hairs
shed in late summer from olive-green upper surface. Flower
clusters supported by narrow leaf-like bracts. Male flowers dull
yellow, very small; female flowers bright yellow, often turning
red, somewhat larger. Grows in sandy soils at mid and high elevations. The species and common names refer to this plant's
resemblance to *Teucrium marum*, Mediter-
ranean germander, a common garden plant.
Native CRLA

Eriogonum sphaerocephalum

POLYGONACEAE

Round-headed desert buckwheat

Common, early summer, perennial, 6–16 in.
Shrub-steppe

Shrub 1–2 ft. across, erect flower stems.
Leaves small, in whorls at branch tips, undersides densely covered with matted hairs, upper sides less hairy. Flower cluster
rounded, with whorl of leaf-like bracts at branching of flowering stalks or in midstalk. Flowers yellow or cream on 1–4 in.
stalks. Grows in steppe, with sage and other brush, at low and
mid elevations. Var. *sphaerocephalum*, the common variety in
Washington and south to northern Califor-
nia, has bright yellow flowers, is slightly
hairy. Native

Eriogonum umbellatum var. *dichrocephalum* (*Eriogonum umbellatum* var. *aridum*)

POLYGONACEAE

Sulphur-flower buckwheat

Uncommon, midsummer, perennial, 4–8 in.
East-side forest, alpine, subalpine

Low mat of leaf clusters. Leaves narrow to widely rounded,
pointed at tip, with few to dense hairs on upper and lower surfaces. Flower stem to 6 in. tall supports whorl of bracts and hairless flower stalks. Flowers cream to pale yellow, aging to reddish yellow. Grows in sandy or gravel soils, rimrock, at high
elevations in Oregon and California. Similar *E. umbellatum* var.
hausknechtii is more common at high elevations in Washington, parts of Oregon. Native

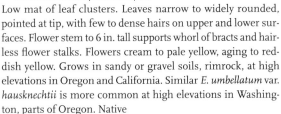

Eriogonum umbellatum var. *polyanthum* POLYGONACEAE
Sulphur flower, sulphur eriogonum
Common, all summer, perennial, 4–15 in.
Dry rocky sites, east-side forest, shrub-steppe,
alpine, subalpine

Mat to small shrub with erect flower stalks.
Stems low, woody. Leaves narrow to widely
oval, ¼–1 in. long, with petioles about same
length, clustered. Lower blade surface white-fuzzy with matted hairs; upper surface green with hairs. Flower stems sturdy,
leafless. Flower cluster with several noticeable leaf-like bracts in
single whorl at base, bract tips usually reflexed downward.
Flowers bractless within clusters, bright yellow or cream, fading to red or orange. Grows in dry soils, often abundant in open
or rocky places, at low to mid or alpine eleva-
tions. Many varieties intergrade, differ in
height, openness of umbels, presence of bracts
on flower stems, so they are difficult to distinguish. Native CRLA

Polygonum davisiae POLYGONACEAE
Davis' knotweed
Locally common, all summer, perennial, less
than 16 in. Alpine, subalpine

Stems in clump or single, decumbent to upright. Leaves sessile
or with short petiole. Leaf yellow-green, often coated with white
waxy powder, lance-shaped to round, less than 2 in. long. Flowers in small clusters of 2–5 at leaf axils. Petals yellow, green, or
purple. Grows in rocky sites or talus above treeline. Similar *P.
newberryi*, with 5–25 flowers in cluster, grows in pumice in
alpine areas, including Crater Lake, Mount
Shasta, and Mount Rainier in Cascades of Oregon and Washington. Native

Alyssum alyssoides BRASSICACEAE
Pale alyssum, pale madwort
Locally common, all spring, annual or biennial,
4–8 in. Disturbed, meadow, shrub-steppe
Annual, few sprawling or ascending stems.
Stems and leaves with hairs divided and
spreading like stars. Leaves oblong to egg-shaped, undivided,
entire. Flowers have linear petals, creamy yellow fading to
white. Seedpod densely hairy, round, with bulge over seed.
Grows in disturbed or rocky places at mid elevations. Very similar to *A. desertorum*, desert madwort, which has hairless pods
and is less common in our region. Nonnative

See other *Polygonum*: white, page 77; red, page 317

Barbarea orthoceras BRASSICACEAE
American winter cress
Common, mid to late spring, biennial or
perennial, 1–2 ft. Vernal-wet, meadow

Stem erect, stiff, branched. Basal leaves pinnately divided, usually into 5(–7) lobes, the
end lobe egg-shaped, toothed or entire;
stem leaves become less lobed, smaller upward, often clasping. Flowers small in clus-
ters at top of expanding stem, with 4 yellow petals. Seedpods,
ascending, consist of 1–2 in. thin cylinders on short stalks.
Grows in wet meadows, rocks, along waterways; found on
beaches to 10,000 ft. Native OLYM, MORA, NOCA

Brassica nigra BRASSICACEAE
Black mustard
Common, all spring and summer, annual,
1–5 ft. Disturbed, meadow

Stems erect, slender, with dense stiff hairs,
widely branched near top. Basal leaves pinnately lobed, with even, small teeth and
rough hairs, green but not shiny; stem
leaves similar but smaller, sessile. Flowers
clustered in stem tops, with 4 yellow petals
to ½ in. long. Seedpods on erect stalks, pods
⅓–½ in. long, pressed close to stem. Abundant in fields, disturbed places, at low and mid elevations. Nonnative MORA

Brassica rapa (*Brassica campestris*) BRASSICACEAE
Field mustard
Common, all spring, annual or biennial, 2–3
ft. Disturbed, meadow

Erect stems, many branches, upper stem
leaves clasping. Plant covered with whitish
powder. Leaves greenish, pinnately divided,
2–4 side lobes with rounded tips, larger lobe
at end. Flowers in many small clusters atop
stems, yellow with 4 petals. Seedpods point
outward or upward; pod to 3 in. long with
narrow beak at top. Grows in orchards,
grain and other fields, at low and mid elevations. Nonnative OLYM, MORA, NOCA

Descurainia pinnata BRASSICACEAE
Short-fruited tansy mustard
Common, late spring–early summer, annual or
biennial or perennial, 6–24 in. East-side forest,
shrub-steppe

Erect, covered with grayish white hairs. Stem
single, may branch only near top. Leaves in
basal rosette ½–4 in. long, lance- to egg-
shaped, pinnately lobed; upper leaves smaller,
entire. Flowers in small clusters near top. Flower yellow, with
small spoon-shaped petals. Seedpods erect, to 1 in. long, linear, straight, both ends sharply pointed with stalks longer than
pod. Grows in open places and meadows, with sagebrush or
aspen, at mid to high elevations. Subsp. *filipes* has erect seedpods. Subsp. *incisa* has seedpods spreading outward from
stem. There are many *Descurainia* species, all
difficult to distinguish. Native OLYM, NOCA

Draba albertina BRASSICACEAE
Alberta draba
Locally common, midsummer, annual or
biennial or perennial, 4–16 in. Meadow, east-
side forest, alpine, subalpine

Several stems from mat. Stems branched at
leaf axils, hairs near bottom coarse and forked.
Basal leaves small to 1½ in., oblong to egg-shaped, sometimes
with tiny teeth; stem leaves few or none. Flowers yellow on
upper stem, not clustered, 35 or fewer. Grows in moist meadows, steam banks, rock crevices or gravelly places, at high elevations. Native OLYM

Draba crassifolia BRASSICACEAE
Thick-leaved draba
Locally common, midsummer, annual or
biennial or perennial, 2–8 in. Alpine, subalpine

Erect stems from mat. Stems leafless. Leaves
spoon-shaped to widely oval, thick like a succulent, ⅓–1 in. long, hairless on upper side,
with a few simple or forked hairs below. Flowers yellow fading to white, in clusters of 3–20
atop stem. Seedpods lance-shaped, to ½ in.
long, hairless, on short stalks. Grows in talus, dry meadows, in
subalpine or alpine, including Malheur National Forest. Native
NOCA

See other *Draba*: white, page 83

Draba cusickii BRASSICACEAE
Steens draba
Uncommon, midsummer, perennial, 3–5 in.
Alpine, subalpine

Prostrate cluster of leaves or leaf rosettes
with erect flower stalks. Bright green leaves
oblong, coated with short hairs, longer hairs
along edges. Flower stalks 3–5 in. tall, flowers loosely held near and at top. Flower pe-
tals 4, bright yellow. Seedpods flattened, ¼–⅓ in. long. Grows
on outcrops in subalpine and alpine on Steens Mountain.
Native

Draba densifolia BRASSICACEAE
Alpine whitlow-grass, denseleaf draba
Uncommon, early summer, perennial, 4–6
in. Alpine, subalpine

Cushion. Leaves many, linear, about 4 times
as long as they are wide; midvein obvious;
long stiff hairs sparsely sited along edges,
otherwise without hairs. Flowers at stem top
above cushion. Petals 4, pale yellow to white,
less than ¼ in. long. Grows in alpine rocky
slopes, barren outcrops. Native

Erysimum arenicola BRASSICACEAE
Cascade wallflower, perennial sand-dwelling wallflower
Locally common, midsummer, perennial, 12–15 in.
Shrub-steppe, alpine, subalpine

Erect stem, rosette of leaves. Leaves bright green, 1–3 in. long,
oblong to spoon-shaped, coarsely toothed; stem leaves smaller.
Large head of bright yellow flowers atop
stem arising from center of rosette. Flower

petals ⅔–¾ in. long, opening widely. Seedpods 2–3 in. long, about same width on all 4
sides, becoming twisted. Grows in rocky
areas, sandy places, at 5000–7500 ft. Native
OLYM, MORA, NOCA

Erysimum capitatum BRASSICACEAE
Western wallflower, rough wallflower
Common, all summer, biennial or perennial,
2–4 ft. Meadows, west-side forest, east-side
forest, shrub-steppe

Erect, 1 or few stems from rosette of many
leaves, few branched forked hairs on herbage.
Leaves linear to spoon-shaped, toothed or entire with sharply pointed tip, to 10 in. Flowers
clustered at top, developing seedpods below. Flowers often fragrant, orange to yellow, occasionally reddish or cream; petals
spoon-shaped, narrowing where attached. Seedpods erect or
spreading, 1–6 in. long, narrow, 4-sided, straight or curved.
Found in many drier habitats in all elevations. Var. *capitatum*
has basal leaves often less than 4 in. long, lance-shaped, with
rounded tips; flower petals deep orange to
bright yellow; found on serpentine. Native
OLYM, **L&C**

Erysimum occidentale BRASSICACEAE
Pale wallflower
Locally common, all summer, biennial or
perennial, 8–20 in. Shrub-steppe
Erect, gray-haired throughout. Stems stout, 1
to several. Leaves many, narrow. Basal leaves
numerous, linear, entire or toothed, 2–4 in. including long petiole; stem leaves similar, becoming sessile above. Flowers pale
yellow in dense clusters at top. Seedpods ascending, 2–4 in.
long, flat with slender point, on stout stalks. Grows in dry
slopes, sandy soils. Native

Lesquerella douglasii BRASSICACEAE
Douglas's bladderpod
Locally common, late spring–early summer,
perennial, 4–8 in. Shrub-steppe
Decumbent to ascending plant with silvery
hairs. Stems 4–18 in. long with flowers at end.
Basal leaves egg-shaped to oval, gradually tapering to short petiole, entire or with few teeth;
stem leaves smaller. Flowers in showy clusters,
with yellow, spoon-shaped petals. Seedpods
ball-shaped, with long beak on end, on spreading stalks. Grows
in open, gravelly or sandy soils. Native NOCA

Lesquerella occidentalis
BRASSICACEAE
Western lesquerella
Locally common, late spring–early summer, biennial or perennial, 2–8 in. Dry rocky sites, alpine, subalpine

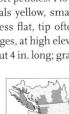

Erect to prostrate, densely coated with hairs. Stems usually unbranched from leafy rosette. Basal leaves ⅓–3 in., oval to round, wavy-edged to toothed, with long petioles; few stem leaves small, oval, entire or with few teeth, with short petioles. Flowers at top of elongating stems. Flower petals yellow, small, nearly round. Seedpods oblong, more or less flat, tip often beaked, hairy. Grows in rocky soils, talus, ridges, at high elevations. Subsp. *occidentalis* has erect stems about 4 in. long; grayish, basal, toothed or lobed leaves; grows in eastern Oregon. Native

Raphanus sativus BRASSICACEAE
Wild radish
Common, all spring and summer, annual or biennial, 1–4 ft. Disturbed, meadow

Erect, rough with sparse, short, stiff hairs. Stems with many branches in upper portion. Basal and lower stem leaves pinnately lobed, the terminal lobe widely oval to round and 4–8 in. long, with short petiole; upper leaves sessile, toothed. Flowers many at stem tops, usually purple, pale yellow, or rarely white. Seedpod 1–2 in. long, rounded at base, tapering to long sharp beak pointing upward. Pod does not break between seeds. Common weed of disturbed soils, fields, roadsides, at low elevations. Nonnative OLYM

Rorippa curvisiliqua BRASSICACEAE
Western yellow cress
Common, all spring and summer, annual or biennial, 4–20 in. Bog/fen/wetland, moist streambanks

Stem with many ascending branches from base. Basal leaves oblong to lance-shaped, entire to deeply pinnately divided, lobes entire or toothed, largest lobe at tip end; upper leaves few, small. Yellow flowers clustered at top of elongating stem, curved seedpods form below. Grows in wet soils at edge of rivers, streams, seeps, below 3000 ft. Native OLYM, MORA, NOCA

See other *Rorippa*: white, page 84

Rorippa palustris BRASSICACEAE
Marsh yellowcress
Common, early summer, annual or biennial or
perennial, 16–40 in. Bog/fen/wetland, meadow
Single erect stem, unbranched or branched
from base. Leaves pointing upward from short
petioles or sessile, toothed or deeply lobed. Yellow flowers atop branches; petals spoon-shaped. Erect seedpods oblong to nearly round
on spreading stalks. Grows in wet spots below 6500 ft. throughout North America. *Palustris*, meaning "wet places," refers to where it grows. Native OLYM

Schoenocrambe linifolia BRASSICACEAE
Plains mustard
Locally common, late spring–early summer,
perennial, 8–18 in. East-side forest, shrub-steppe
Stems erect, many with slender branches.
Stems and leaves hairless. Leaves linear to
lance-shaped; lower leaves pinnately divided;
upper leaves entire. Flowers on short stalks in
elongating racemes at stem tops. Flowers
showy, with yellow petals about 1/3 in. long.
Seedpods ascending, narrow, 1–2 in. long.
Grows on dry rocky hills, cliffs. Native

Sisymbrium altissimum BRASSICACEAE
Tumble mustard, Jim Hill mustard
Common, all spring and summer, annual or
biennial, 2–4 ft. Disturbed, meadow, shrub-steppe
Stems erect, with many branches, few narrow
leaves. Leaves in basal rosette and on lower
stem widely lance-shaped, pinnately divided,
with leaflets or lobes toothed; upper leaves
scattered on stem with linear to thread-like
lobes or leaflets. Flowers small, pale yellow,
few, clustered at tips of most branches. Seedpods rigid, 2–4 in. long on stalks as big around
as the pods, spreading outward from stem.
Widespread weed of disturbed soils, fields,
roadsides, at low to mid elevations. After growth cycle, plant
uproots and blows with the wind as a tumbleweed, dispersing
seeds. Nonnative OLYM, MORA, NOCA

4 petals

Sisymbrium officinale (*Erysimum officinale*) BRASSICACEAE
Hedge mustard
Locally common, all spring and summer, annual, 6–36 in. Coastal, disturbed, meadow

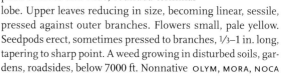

Stem single, stiff, erect, with branches only near top. Stem has spreading or sharp hairs. Leaves pinnately divided; lower leaves 2–3 pairs of lobes and wide, rounded terminal lobe. Upper leaves reducing in size, becoming linear, sessile, pressed against outer branches. Flowers small, pale yellow. Seedpods erect, sometimes pressed to branches, 1/3–1 in. long, tapering to sharp point. A weed growing in disturbed soils, gardens, roadsides, below 7000 ft. Nonnative OLYM, MORA, NOCA

Stanleya pinnata BRASSICACEAE
Prince's plume
Locally common, midspring, perennial, 1–5 ft. Dry rocky sites, shrub-steppe

Clump, few to many erect flower stems from base. Leaves lance-shaped, gray-green, usually coated with white waxy powder. Basal and lower stem leaves 2–6 in. long, deeply lobed; upper leaves with few lobes or entire. Flower spike dense with yellow buds and flowers. Flowers consist of reflexed or spreading sepals, 1/3–3/4 in., petals densely coated at center with long wavy hairs, stamens extending outward. Seedpods 1–3 in. long, hanging down. Grows in open sites in dry sandy sagebrush and talus below 6000 ft. Native

Cleome lutea CAPPARIDACEAE
Yellow bee plant
Common, late spring–early summer, annual, 1–3 ft. Moist streambanks, shrub-steppe

Erect, hairless. Stems leafy. Leaves palmately separated to 5 linear leaflets, each 1/2–2 1/2 in. long. Flowers consist of 4 yellow sepals fused at base with lance-shaped tiny-toothed tips; 4 yellow petals oblong to egg-shaped and 6 yellow stamens extending beyond petals. Seedpods long, rounded, curved, hanging on long curved stalks. Grows in sandy soils in deserts, steppe, often in riparian areas. Native

Cleome platycarpa CAPPARIDACEAE
Golden bee plant, golden spiderflower
Uncommon, late spring–early summer, annual,
6–36 in. Shrub-steppe

Erect, densely branched from base. Stems
green, tinted purple, heavily covered with glistening hairs. Leaves to 2 in. long, divided
palmately into 3 leaflets, petioled. Flowers in
tight clusters, golden yellow with 4 small outer
sepals, 4 petals, 6 stamens extended beyond petals giving
flower a starburst look. Seedpods oblong, flat-hairy, hanging at
base of flower cluster. Grows in alkaline, volcanic soils in dry
steppe areas, at 4000–5000 ft. Found at John Day Fossil Beds
National Monument, coloring folds of Painted Hills after
spring rains. Very similar yellow bee plant, *C. lutea*, grows in
same area, has 5 leaflets and large, round, pea
pod–like fruits. Native

Corydalis aurea FUMARIACEAE
Golden corydalis
Locally common, mid to late spring, annual or
biennial, 4–15 in. East-side forest, shrub-steppe

Upright or prostrate, with many branches, taprooted winter-hardy annual or biennial, hairless. Leaves parsley-like, deeply divided pinnately to many linear segments. Flowers in short spikes atop
stems, yellow with short rounded spur curved downward.
Grows in moist to dry soils, open to lightly shaded areas, at
5000–7500 ft. *Corydalis* means "lark" in Greek, referring to the
spurs, which are similar to those of larks. Native OLYM

Abronia latifolia NYCTAGINACEAE
Yellow sand verbena
Locally common, all spring and summer,
perennial, 1–4 in. Coastal

Prostrate, forming dense mats to 3 ft. across,
fleshy, glistening with glands. Leaves thick,
rounded, 1–2 in. across. Flower clusters bright
yellow on 1–3 in. stalks. Flower ¼–½ in.
across, 5 petals forming a long slender tube
¼–¾ in. long with tips folded wide open.
Grows on coastal sand, in scrub. Native OLYM

See other *Corydalis*: white, page 87; red, page 323
See other *Abronia*: white, page 88; red, page 325

Camissonia andina (*Oenothera andina*)

ONAGRACEAE

Obscure evening primrose, plateau primrose

Uncommon, late spring–early summer, annual, 1–6 in. Shrub-steppe

Erect, slender, with many branches, lower branches nearly leafless. Leaves many, clustered at stem tops, linear to oval, entire. Flowers sessile, above leaves, 4 yellow petals fading to red with age. Grows in sandy soils, where wet in spring, with sagebrush, juniper, at low to high elevations. Native

Camissonia cheiranthifolia ONAGRACEAE

Beach evening primrose

Locally common, all spring and summer, perennial, less than 24 in. Coastal

Densely hairy, prostrate to upright stems from rosette of leaves. Leaves gray, narrowly oval to egg-shaped, with tiny teeth. Flowers solitary along elongating stems in leaf axils. Flowers small, nodding, 4 petals, yellow fading reddish, sometimes with 2 red dots at base. Seedpods with 4 angles, usually coiled halfway to all the way around. Grows on coastal dunes, sandy beaches. Native

Camissonia subacaulis (*Oenothera subacaulis*)

ONAGRACEAE

Northern suncup

Common, early spring, perennial, prostrate Vernal-wet, bog/fen/wetland, east-side forest

Prostrate, with leaf rosette. Leaves lance-shaped, irregularly lobed or entire, with winged petiole somewhat or mostly below soil, up to 5 in. long. Erect flower sessile, with a long tube that looks like a stem, 4 separated sepals supporting 4 longer, notched, yellow petals. Seed capsule oblong to nearly round, forms underground. Grows in vernal-wet meadows, woods with clay soils, bogs, at 1600–8500 ft. *Subacaulis* means "not much stem," referring to the stemless flower. Native **L&C**

Camissonia tanacetifolia (*Oenothera tanacetifolia*) ONAGRACEAE
Tansy-leaved evening primrose
Locally common, midspring, perennial, prostrate. Vernal-wet, disturbed, meadow, shrub-steppe

Rosette or mat, densely covered with spreading to flattened hairs. Leaves 2–12 in. long, pinnately, irregularly, and deeply lobed. Flowers erect, stemless; sepals reflexed back; petals to ¼ in. long, deep yellow, turning red when withered. Seedpods form underground. Grows in clay soils in open moist places. Native

Epilobium luteum ONAGRACEAE
Yellow fireweed, yellow willowherb
Locally common, late summer, perennial, 8–35 in. Bog/fen/wetland, moist streambanks, meadow, west-side forest, alpine, subalpine

Stems erect, usually unbranched, flowers yellow. Stems bear opposite sessile leaves. Leaves 1–3 in. long, serrate, widely lance-shaped. Flowers near stem top nod in bud, then become upright; 4 petals ½–¾ in. long, widely oval, with notched tip. Tube 1½–3 in. long, becomes seedpod. Grows in seeps, edges of lakes, streams, springs, at mid to high elevations. *Epilobium* is Greek and refers to the sepals and petals located on top of the long pod, the ovary tube. Native OLYM, MORA, NOCA

Oenothera biennis ONAGRACEAE
Common evening primrose
Common, all summer, biennial, 12–40 in. Disturbed, moist streambanks

Stem erect, with reddish tint at base. Leaves 2–8 in. long on stem, oval, often toothed, may be lobed at base. Flowers in dense spike; petals 4, more than 1 in. long; buds green or yellowish, opening to yellow flower that turns dull orange with age. Grows in disturbed areas at low elevations. A worldwide weed originating in eastern North America. Nonnative

See other *Epilobium*: white, page 89; red, page 328
See other *Oenothera*: white, page 90

Oenothera villosa (*Oenothera strigosa*)
ONAGRACEAE
Hairy evening primrose
Common, midsummer, biennial or
perennial, 1–4 ft. Meadows, west-side
forest, east-side forest

Rosette with erect hairy stem. Basal leaves
spoon-shaped, 1–4 in. long, with petioles
½–2 in. long; stem leaves 4–12 in., hairy,
lance-shaped to oval, entire or with tiny teeth. Inflorescence is
a few-flowered open spike. Flower sepals often tinted red, petals
⅓–¾ in. long, yellow to orange, open in the evening, not fading to red. Capsules straight. Grows in dry shrublands, roadsides, at mid to high elevations. Native
OLYM

Galium ambiguum subsp.
siskiyouense RUBIACEAE
Yolla bolly bedstraw
Uncommon, midspring, perennial, 2–16 in.
West-side forest

Mat, with male and female flowers on separate plants. Stem with 4 sides when young.
Leaves in whorls of 4, linear, thick, hairless
or with bristly hairs on edges, pointed tips.
Flowers yellowish, male flowers in clusters, female flowers single in leaf axil with very hairy ovary and fruit. Grows in Siskiyou
Mountains in light shade. Var. *ambiguum*, which grows in similar range and habitat, has thin leaves, with female flowers and
fruit only lightly hairy. Native

Galium multiflorum RUBIACEAE
Shrubby bedstraw
Uncommon, late spring, perennial, 6–14 in.
Meadow, shrub-steppe

Erect, woody at base. Stems 4-sided when
young. Leaves in whorls of 4; 2 pairs of unequal size; the larger pair ⅓–⅔ in., broadly
egg-shaped, with rounded base and wide tip
with small point. Flowers in groups of few
clustered at and near stem top. Male and fe-
male flowers on separate plants. Flowers bell-shaped, pale yellow, whitish, or pinkish. Grows in rocky places among sagebrush, on east side of Cascades. Native

See other *Galium*: white, page 90

Galium porrigens RUBIACEAE
Climbing bedstraw
Locally common, late spring–early summer, perennial, 25–60 in. Coastal, west-side forest, shrub-steppe

Climbing, with thin, tangled, woody stem, tiny prickles. Leaves in whorls of 4 with rounded tips, short point at tip end, often falling mid-season. Male and female flowers on separate plants. Male flowers in clusters at ends of stems; female flowers single in leaf axils; both with 4 yellowish or reddish petals. Seed is a single berry. Grows among bushes in shrublands, chaparral or forests, at low to mid elevations. *Galium* means "milk," as some species have been used in curdling milk. Native

Astragalus filipes FABACEAE
Thread-leaved locoweed, slimpod milkvetch
Locally common, late spring, perennial, 12–40 in. East-side forest, shrub-steppe

Clump. Stems slender. Leaves 1–5 in. long, scale-like appendage at base fused around stem into papery sheath; leaflets 5–23, to 1 in. long, well separated, narrow to thread-like, with rounded to notched tip. Flower stalks above leaves. Flowers 4–30, well spaced on stalk, lax to reflexed; petals open dull white, fade to pale yellow. Pods pendulous, about 1 in. long, straight, flat. Grows in dry open areas in sagebrush or pine, mostly in western part of steppe at mid elevations. Native

Cytisus scoparius FABACEAE
Scotch broom
Common, late spring–early summer, perennial, 5–7 ft. Coastal, disturbed, meadow, west-side forest, east-side forest

Erect shrub. Stems not round but angled with 5 edges, not barbed, hairy when young. Leaflets oval, downy hairs pressed close to surface, sessile, divided into 3 parts on older stems. Flowers bright yellow, on upper stems in the union with the simple leaflets. Grows in disturbed places at low elevations, where it becomes invasive. Nonnative OLYM, MORA, NOCA

See other *Astragalus*: white, page 92; blue, page 407

Lotus corniculatus FABACEAE
Bird's-foot trefoil
Common, all summer, perennial, 1–2 ft.
Disturbed, meadow

Stems solid, decumbent or ascending from small root. Stems and leaves hairless or with a few rigid hairs. Leaves divided pinnately to 5 leaflets, lowest 2 are stipules, 3 leaflets at stem tip. Flowers 3–8 in circle on long leafless stalk, bright yellow turning brown with age. Naturalized in disturbed soils below 3500 ft. Often planted as a pasture species. Nonnative

Lotus nevadensis (*Lotus nevadensis* var. *douglasii*)
FABACEAE
Nevada deervetch
Locally common, late spring–early summer, perennial, 2–8 in. Meadow, west-side forest, east-side forest

Mat with upward-pointing stems. Leaves gray or green, widely spaced. Leaflets 3–5, irregularly spaced, oval, with rounded tips, wavy hairs. Flower heads on lower part of plant on long, branched stalks; upper are nearly sessile. Flower heads with 3–12 bright yellow flowers. Grows in open oak, pine, or fir forests, fern-laden meadows, at mid to high elevations. Native OLYM

Lotus pinnatus FABACEAE
Bog deervetch, meadow bird's-foot trefoil
Locally common, late spring–early summer, perennial, 8–18 in. Vernal-wet, west-side forest, east-side forest

Prostrate to sprawling to erect, hairless. Lower stems inflated. Leaves with 5–7 opposite, widely oval leaflets. Flowers 4–10, held in cluster at stem top. Flower with yellow banner sharply bent back, other petals white. Grows in wet soils, slow shallow water, often drying in summer, at mid elevations. Native

  See other *Lotus*: white, page 96; red, page 332

Lupinus arboreus FABACEAE
Tree lupine, yellow bush lupine
Locally common, all spring and summer,
perennial, to 80 in. Coastal

Green to silver-haired shrub. Stems woody, upright. Leaves occur on stems with petioles 1–2
in. long. Leaves palmately divided into 5–12
leaflets. Flower spike 4–12 in. long, with fragrant, sulphur-yellow flowers about ½ in. long.
Grows on coastal bluffs, sand dunes and inland. Native in California, introduced in Oregon, Washington, and Canada to control erosion on sand dunes and steep banks. Plants with purple
or lilac flowers are sometimes found and thought to be hybrids.
Native OLYM

Lupinus arbustus (*Lupinus laxiflorus*)
FABACEAE
Spur lupine
Locally common, midsummer, perennial, 8–25
in. East-side forest, shrub-steppe

Erect, green or gray with silky hairs. Basal
leaves with long petiole, becoming shorter on
stems, with 7–13 leaflets. Flower calyx with
spur pointing back, blossom yellow to cream
fading to blue or pink; upper petal hairy on
back, patch white, cream, or none. Grows in open areas in sagebrush and in mixed forests. Var. *calcaratus* (pictured) has
flowers usually more than ⅓ in.; grows in northeastern Oregon to California and to the east. Other varieties with variation
in size and hairiness with blue-violet flowers also grow east of
Cascade Mountain Range. Native

Lupinus croceus FABACEAE
Mount Eddy lupine
Locally common, all summer, perennial, 15–24
in. West-side forest, alpine, subalpine

Erect, green, hairy. Stems branch from base
bearing numerous leaves. Leaf petioles 1–3 in.
long; blades divided into 5–8 oblong leaflets,
each 1½–3 in. long. Flower stalks 2–12 in.
high, with bright yellow-orange, hairless flow-
ers. Seedpod just more than 1 in. long, ½ in. wide, hairy. Grows
in dry rocky places at mid and high elevations. Native

See other *Lupinus*: white, page 96; blue, page 409

Lupinus sulphureus FABACEAE
Sulphur lupine
Locally common, all summer, perennial,
15–40 in. Shrub-steppe

Erect, green. Stems and leaves covered with
sparse fine hair. Leaves on stems divided
palmately, 9–15 narrow oval leaflets with
pointed tips. Flowers in dense spike, pale
sulfur yellow, occasionally bluish, banner
with few hairs on back. Pods silky. Grows on dry slopes, gravelly
soils. Similar *L. sabinianus* has rounded, lance-shaped, green
leaflets with silky hairs on both sides and deeper yellow flowers.
Both species grow in Blue Mountains. Native

Medicago lupulina FABACEAE
Black medic, yellow trefoil
Locally common, late spring–early summer,
annual or perennial, 4–20 in. Disturbed,
west-side forest, east-side forest

Stems prostrate to upright. Plant bears fine
hairs. Leaves consist of 3 leaflets, each
⅕–⅘ in. long, finely toothed on upper ½.
Flowers tiny, yellow, pea-like, in round to
spiky clusters at top of stalks arising along
stems. Seedpods black, tightly coiled about
5 times, without prickles. Grows in disturbed areas and forests
at low to high elevations. A native of Eurasia. Introduced as a
forage crop, now grows over most of the United States. A common lawn weed. Nonnative OLYM, MORA, NOCA

Melilotus officinalis FABACEAE
Yellow sweetclover
Locally common, all summer, annual or
biennial or perennial, 20–40 in. Meadow

Erect stems. Plant has very sweet fragrance.
Leaves compound with 3 oblong leaflets,
toothed along edges. Tall, open, spike-like
heads of small yellow flowers, often on arching stalks mostly above leaves. Pods small,
egg-shaped, with crisscrossed sculpturing.
Common in hay fields, along roads in most
of the United States, southern Canada. Native of Eurasia. Introduced here as a forage crop. *Melilotus alba*, a white-flowering
sweetclover with flowers slightly smaller and seedpods pen-
ciled with network of veins, is indistinguishable before flowering. Nonnative OLYM, MORA, NOCA

See other *Medicago*: blue, page 414

Oxytropis monticola *(Oxytropis campestris)* FABACEAE
Common false locoweed
Locally common, all summer, perennial, 6–24 in. Alpine, subalpine

Erect, covered with silky silver-gray hairs. Leaf divided into 17–45 oval leaflets, pointed at tip. Flower spike of yellow to yellowish white flowers is well above the leaves. Grows in dry, sandy, relatively rocky soils, crevices of rocky ledges. Usually found high in mountains. Variable, circumboreal. Native OLYM, MORA

Thermopsis montana *(Thermopsis rhombifolia)*
FABACEAE
Mountain goldenbanner, mountain golden-pea
Locally common, late spring–early summer, perennial, 2–4 ft. East-side forest

Erect sturdy stems. Plant hairless, bright green. Leaves on stem compound with 3 oval ½ in. long leaflets up to 6 times longer than wide. Flowers large, bright yellow, held in spike above leaves. Grows in meadows, shrubby places near streams in forests. Similar to lupines but leaves are like clovers with only 3 parts. Inedible by browsing animals. Native OLYM

Trifolium campestre FABACEAE
Field clover, hop clover
Locally common, all summer, annual or biennial
Disturbed, meadow

Stems upright to lax. Leaves with petioles longer than the 3 egg-shaped leaflets, finely toothed. Flowers bright yellow, 15–25 in a nearly round cluster, reflexing downward soon after opening and becoming brown with age. Grows in disturbed soils, along roads, in lawns, at low elevations. European native common in most of United States but rare in Rocky Mountains. Very similar *T. dubium* is smaller. Nonnative OLYM

See other *Trifolium*: white, page 97; red, page 333; blue, page 415; green/brown, page 466

Trifolium dubium FABACEAE
Small hop clover
Locally common, all summer, annual, 4–20
in. Coastal, disturbed, meadow

Erect to decumbent, slightly hairy. Leaves
held on short petioles along stems, divided
into 3 egg-shaped leaflets. Flower head
more or less spike-like. Flowers bright yellow, becoming brown and reflexing down-
ward. Weed in agricultural and disturbed soils, gardens, lawns,
at low elevations. Similar to *Medicago lupulina*, black medic,
which has a much denser flower head and spiral, black, kidney-shaped pods. See *T. campestre*, field clover, which is larger,
with a larger flower head. Nonnative OLYM, MORA, NOCA

Ulex europaeus FABACEAE
Gorse
Locally common, all spring and summer,
perennial, 2–6 ft. Coastal, disturbed

Upright shrub, dense, stiff, heavily armed.
Stems with dangerous thorns at ends, hairy
when young, hairs becoming barbs on older
wood. Leaves on young plants divided into 3
leaflets that become sharp thorns. Flowers
in clusters near tips of stems and singly
down stems, with pleasant smell of fruit. Grows in disturbed
places, logged forests, edges of fields, and roads near coast. Introduced from Europe, expanding over an ever-widening range.
Very flammable, invasive, noxious weed with seed viable for 30
years. Nonnative OLYM

Viola douglasii VIOLACEAE
Douglas's violet
Locally common, early spring, perennial,
3–9 in. Vernal-wet, meadow, shrub-steppe

Erect to reclining stems. Leaves divided into
narrowly oval, blunt-tipped leaflets. Golden
yellow petals have dark brown backs and
veins. The 2 side petals are bearded. Grows
in seasonally moist grasslands and rock flats
at low to mid elevations. Native

See other *Viola*: white, page 98; blue, page 416

Viola glabella VIOLACEAE
Smooth yellow violet, stream violet, pioneer violet
Common, midspring, perennial, 1–12 in.
Moist streambanks, meadow, west-side forest,
east-side forest, alpine, subalpine

Tall erect stems with a single flower. Leaves
heart-shaped, with sharp tips, entire or with
small teeth. Flower dark yellow with maroon
veins on 3 lower petals. The 2 side petals are bearded; lowest
petal is spurred. Streambanks, moist forests, from near coast to
high elevations. Native OLYM, MORA, NOCA, CRLA

Viola hallii VIOLACEAE
Hall's violet
Locally common, early spring, perennial, 2–9
in. Meadow, west-side forest

Clusters of short stems. Leaves divided into
sharp narrow leaflets. Upper 2 petals are
smaller than the others, burgundy. Lower 3
petals creamy yellow to white, with maroon
veins and yellow bases. Grows in rocky places,
including serpentine, from chaparral to grasslands, at low to mid elevations. Native

Viola lobata VIOLACEAE
Pine violet
Uncommon, late spring, perennial, 2–8 in.
West-side forest

Stems, leaves in erect cluster. Leaves basal and on stem near
tip. Plant may be without basal leaves. There are 2 forms.
Subsp. *integrifolia* has triangular leaves with
pointed tips, often toothed. Subsp. *lobata* has
deeply divided to lobed leaves that spread wide,
looking like an open hand. Flowers yellow with
maroon veins on lower 3 petals. Upper 2 petals
are maroon to brown on the back. The 2 side
petals are bearded. Grows in dry open pine
forests, woods, at low to high elevations. Native

211

Viola orbiculata VIOLACEAE
Roundleaf violet, dark woods violet
Common, early spring, perennial, 1–3 in.
Meadow, west-side forest, east-side forest,
alpine, subalpine

Clustered, without stolons. Basal leaves on
long stalks are thin, round, with scalloped
edges and rounded lobes at base of leaf
blade. Flower stalks reddish, with small
scale-like bracts on midstem. The 3 lower petals have maroon
veins. Grows in moist woods, subalpine meadows. Very similar
V. sempervirens has runners and bearded petals. Native
OLYM, MORA, NOCA

Viola praemorsa (*Viola nuttallii*, *Viola nuttallii* var.
praemorsa) VIOLACEAE
Prairie violet, yellow montane violet
Common, midspring, perennial, 3–6 in.
Meadow, west-side forest, east-side forest

Cluster of upright stems, leaves. Leaves narrowly oval to egg-shaped, edges wavy or
toothed, 1–3 in., often hairy. Flower bright
yellow, lower 3 petals with maroon veins.
The 2 side petals are bearded. The upper 2
petal backs mature to maroon. Grows in
moist to dry open woods, meadows, at mid to high elevations.
Subsp. *linguifolia* has stem leaves much longer than wide,
wavy-edged or sparsely toothed, with tapered bases. Subsp.
praemorsa has leaves almost as wide as they are long, regularly
toothed. The base of the leaf blade narrows suddenly. Native

Viola purpurea VIOLACEAE
**Goosefoot violet, purple-backed violet,
mountain violet**
Common, late spring, perennial, ½–4 in.
West-side forest, east-side forest, shrub-
steppe, alpine, subalpine

Flowers on green stalks arise from center of
basal rosette of leaves. Deep lemon yellow
flowers have maroon to brown network of
veins on the backs of the 2 upper petals. The
3 lower petals are maroon-veined. The 2 side petals are bearded.
Grows in dry soils at mid to high elevations. Leaf characteristics
vary among several subspecies: subsp. *purpurea* leaves are
tinged purple, toothed; subsp. *integrifolia* leaves are entire;
subsp. *quercetorum* leaves have very tiny hairs and a tapered
base on the blade. These 3 grow only in north to southwestern
Oregon. Subsp. *venosa* has dented to deeply toothed edges,
grows in deep shade above 4000 ft. Called goosefoot violet because its leaves resemble shape of goose print. Native MORA

Viola sempervirens VIOLACEAE
Evergreen violet, redwood violet
Uncommon, midspring, perennial, 3 in.
West-side forest

Rosette with reddish flower stalks. Mature plants produce new plants on aboveground runners. Shiny evergreen leaves thick, heart-shaped, with pointed tips, spotted purple underneath. Flowers pale yellow, the 3 lower petals maroon-veined and 2 side petals bearded. Grows in forests from coast inland to mid elevations. Very similar to *V. orbiculata*, which does not have stolons. Native

OLYM, MORA, NOCA

Viola sheltonii VIOLACEAE
Shelton violet, cut-leaf violet
Locally common, midspring, perennial, 1–8 in.
West-side forest, east-side forest

Forms small mats from spreading roots. Leaves horizontal to ground, nearly round, deeply divided into 3-lobed leaflets. Yellow flowers single on light brown stems have maroon veins on the 3 lower petals. The upper 2 petals have maroon backs. The 2 side petals are sparsely bearded. Grows in deep duff or sandy to gravelly soil in mixed woodlands at low to high elevations. Native NOCA

Hypericum anagalloides CLUSIACEAE
Tinker's penny, bog St. John's wort
Common, early summer, annual or perennial, 1–3 in.
Coastal, bog/fen/wetland, meadow

Small mats of numerous prostrate stems 1–3 in. long. Leaves small, with rounded tips, opposite, clasping stems. Flowers usually 1 but possibly to 15 atop short stalks, tiny, deep yellow to salmon, without spots, with many stamens. Grows in wet meadows and open, moist, sunny areas at 500–3000 ft. *Hypericum* derived from Greek *hyper* for "above" and *eikon* for "picture," because plants were traditionally placed above religious images to ward off evil spirits. Native

OLYM, MORA, NOCA, CRLA

Hypericum perforatum   CLUSIACEAE
Common St. John's wort, Klamathweed, goatweed
Common, all summer, perennial, 1–4 ft.
Coastal, disturbed, meadow

Stems erect from taproot. Shorter axillary stems without flowers 1–4 in. tall. Leaves opposite, ½–1 in., linear to oblong, with edges rolled under, with black dots especially on underside. Inflorescence consists of 25–75 flowers per stem. Flowers with 5 sepals, lance-shaped, sharply pointed with many black and green dots; petals 5, oblong, reflexed, yellow with many black dots, with many long stamens. Grows in disturbed places, roadsides, fields, pastures, below 5000 ft. Toxic to livestock. A noxious weed partially controlled by an introduced flea beetle. Traditionally thought to ward off evil spirits and often used during the feast of St. John during midsummer. Nonnative
OLYM, MORA, NOCA, CRLA

Hypericum scouleri subsp. nortoniae (Hypericum formosum var. nortoniae)   CLUSIACEAE
Western St. John's wort
Locally common, all summer, perennial, 6–24 in.
Moist streambanks, meadow, east-side forest

Erect, hairless. Stems few, usually unbranched from base. Leaves on stem opposite, sessile, egg-shaped to oval, ⅓–1 in., flat, with black dots along edges. Flowers in open clusters atop stem. Flower to 1 in. across. Sepals 5, with pointed tips, black dots. Petals 5, longer than sepals, bright yellow, with black dots on edges. Stamens showy, numerous in clusters. Grows in wet meadows, streambanks. Subsp. *scouleri* has rounded points on sepals. Native

Sedum divergens   CRASSULACEAE
Spreading stonecrop, Cascade stonecrop
Locally common, all summer, perennial, 2–5 in. Alpine, subalpine

Mat-forming perennial, succulent, hairless. Many sterile shoots ascending. Stems fleshy, to 5 in. long, with numerous green to bright red succulent leaves. Leaves oval to ball-shaped, with wrinkles or dimples. Leaves on flower stems oblong, convex. Flower clusters ⅓–2 in. across atop 2–5 in. stems. Flowers yellow; 5 lance-shaped petals with pointed tips curve out, star-like. Grows in gravelly areas or rocky slopes at mid elevations and in subalpine areas. Native OLYM, MORA, NOCA

See other *Sedum*: red, page 340

Sedum lanceolatum   CRASSULACEAE
Lanceleaf stonecrop
Common, all summer, perennial, 1–8 in.
Dry rocky sites

Rosettes of succulent leaves, flowering stems ascending. Basal leaves about ½ in. long, linear to lance-shaped, cylindrical with pointed tip. Flowering stems to 8 in. with many flat, lance-shaped, upward-pointing leaves, usually withered by flowering. Flower heads dense, ⅓–2 in. across, with 3–25 flowers. Flower petals 5, lance-shaped, with recurved pointed tips, yellow often with reddish central rib. Grows on basalt or sandstone outcrops and rocky soils at high elevations. Var. *nesioticum*, with stem leaves overlapping and flowers in loose cluster, is uncommon, grows on seashore rock cliffs. The word *Sedum* comes from the Latin *sedo*, "to sit," referring to the way many species grow. Native NOCA, **L&C**

Sedum obtusatum   CRASSULACEAE
Sierra sedum
Common, all summer, perennial, 1–9 in.
Dry rocky sites, west-side forest, alpine, subalpine

Mats of fleshy leaves in rosettes. Rosette leaves shiny or coated with white waxy powder, thick, widest below tip, tip slightly notched or rounded; stem leaves smaller, flat across tip end. Inflorescence often flat-topped, consisting of 6–65 yellow flowers aging to pink. Flower petals widely oval, with abruptly pointed tips; anthers light brown, yellow, or dark red-brown. Grows in crevices on rocky slopes at mid to highest mountain elevations. Native

Sedum oreganum   CRASSULACEAE
Oregon stonecrop
Locally common, all summer, perennial, 3–6 in.
Coastal, dry rocky sites, west-side forest, alpine, subalpine

Sprawling succulent with ascending flowering stems. Leaves in crowded rosette, egg- to spoon-shaped, widest above the middle, fleshy and somewhat flattened, green often turning bronze; stem leaves alternate. Inflorescence dense, with 3–16 flowers. Flowers united at base, then petals opening wide, lance-shaped, with long sharply pointed tips, yellow with red midvein and yellow to red-brown anthers. Grows in rocky ledges, gravelly places, talus slopes, from sea level to alpine. Native OLYM, MORA, NOCA

Sedum oregonense CRASSULACEAE
Creamy-flowered stonecrop
Uncommon, all summer, perennial, 3–6 in.
West-side forest, alpine, subalpine

Sprawling succulent with ascending flowering stems from basal rosette. Leaves covered in whitish powder, egg- to spoon-shaped, widest above middle, rounded, with slight notch. Leaves on stems smaller. Inflorescence dense, with 3–16 flowers. Flowers united more than halfway, with rounded or slightly pointed tips, pale yellow or cream, usually drying to salmon. Grows in rocky ledges, gravelly places, talus slopes, at mid elevations. Native CRLA

Sedum spathulifolium
CRASSULACEAE
Broadleaf stonecrop, Pacific sedum
Common, midsummer, perennial, 2–8 in.
Coastal, dry rocky sites, west-side forest,
alpine, subalpine

Succulent rosettes with outer leaves considerably larger than small leaves in center. Leaves hairless, gray to sage green, often some red, usually coated with blue waxy powder, widest near tip, thick and flattened. Inflorescence on ascending stem 1–3 in. across. Flower petals 5, separate, lance-shaped, with pointed tip, erect to open wide, yellow; anthers yellow to brown. Grows in rocky outcrops, often in shade, from coastal cliffs to alpine. Plants with many different leaf colors have been selected for gardens. Native OLYM

Sedum stenopetalum CRASSULACEAE
Wormleaf stonecrop, narrow-leaved sedum
Locally common, late spring–early summer,
perennial, 2–8 in. West-side forest, east-side
forest, shrub-steppe, alpine, subalpine

Clusters of leaves on lower stem, spreading to ascending flower stems. Frequently small bulblets instead of upper leaves or flowers. Leaves in small cluster on single short stalk attached near bottom of stem. Leaves lance-shaped, tapering to point, often curved, leaves on upper stem with ridge on outside, often falling before flowering. Flowers to 40 on short stalks atop stem. Flower petals 5, lance-shaped, yellow with red midrib; anthers yellow or light brown. Grows in open or shady well-drained slopes, woods, rocky cliffs, at mid to high elevations. Native OLYM, **L&C**

Menziesia ferruginea ERICACEAE
Fool's huckleberry, rusty menziesia, mock azalea
Uncommon, early summer, perennial, 3–9 ft.
West-side forest, alpine, subalpine

Spreading to erect, deciduous shrub. Stems with somewhat shredding bark. Leaves light green to blue-green, 1–2 in. long, thin, with pointed gland at tip, smelling musky when crushed, turning brilliant crimson-orange in autumn. Flower clusters hang from last year's growth. Bell-shaped flowers salmon pink to yellow-green. Seed capsules oval, standing upright when dry. Grows in deeply shaded, moist woods at low to high elevations. Looks much like huckleberry, thus the common name, but has brown seed capsules instead of tasty berries. Named for Archibald Menzies (1754–1842), physician and naturalist with George Vancouver's expedition of 1790–1795. Native
OLYM, MORA, NOCA

Monotropa hypopithys (*Hypopitys monotropa*) ERICACEAE
Pinesap
Uncommon, all summer, perennial, 2–10 in.
West-side forest, east-side forest

Erect, light yellowish to dull brown, clear yellow or red. Stems single or in clumps. Small scale-like leaves along stems. Waxy flowers 20–30, bell-shaped, nodding, atop stem. A saprophyte in old conifer forests in deep shade and deep humus, widespread around the world. *Monotropa* refers to the flowers all facing 1 way. Pinesap, like other plants with no chlorophyll, saps the roots of nearby plants for food. Native
OLYM, MORA, NOCA, CRLA

Phyllodoce glanduliflora ERICACEAE
Yellow mountain-heather
Uncommon, midsummer, perennial, 4–16 in.
Meadow, alpine, subalpine

Low-growing matted shrub with much-branched erect stems. Twigs hairy. Leaves to 1/3 in., needle-like, dark green, with edges rolled under. Flowers greenish yellow, solitary on hairy green stalks. Fused petals form a 1/3 in. long unopened bell, with 5 small spreading lobes. Flowers and stalks sticky with glands. Grows in subalpine and alpine on rocky sites in seeps and bogs. Also found in lower washes and at sea level in Prince William Sound. Native OLYM, MORA, NOCA, CRLA

See other *Monotropa*: white, page 111
See other *Phyllodoce*: red, page 343

Pterospora andromedea   ERICACEAE
Pine-drops
Common, midsummer, perennial, 1–3 ft.
West-side forest, east-side forest

Erect, reddish brown, densely sticky plant with small, narrow, scale-like leaves. Spikes of many flowers on arched stalks hang from top ½ of stem. Petals yellow, pink, or white, fused to form urn-shaped flowers to ⅓ in. long, nearly as wide. Rounded seed capsules persist on dried darkened stems through winter. Grows in humus in mixed forests at low to high elevations. A saprophyte living in association with conifer trees and manzanita. Native
OLYM, MORA, NOCA, CRLA

Aquilegia flavescens   RANUNCULACEAE
Golden columbine
Locally common, all summer, perennial, 12–30 in. West-side forest, east-side forest, alpine, subalpine

Ascending to erect. Leaves mostly basal, blue-green, shiny, divided palmately to 3 rounded segments, divided again and toothed. Flowers cream to yellow, sometimes tinted scarlet; 5 spurs shorter than petals, turning inward with a hook on the end. Grows in moist soils in meadows, mixed woods, at high elevations. Native
NOCA

Ranunculus alismifolius   RANUNCULACEAE
Water plantain buttercup
Locally common, late spring–early summer, perennial, 1–3 ft.
Vernal-wet, bog/fen/wetland, meadow

Cluster of stems erect to decumbent, branched from near base. Stems never root where touching soil. Stems and leaves hairless. Basal and lower stem leaves with 1–3 in. petioles, 1–5 in., oblong; upper leaves entire, linear, smaller. Flowers in loose cluster atop stems are large, bright yellow, with 5–10 widely oval petals about ½ in. long. Grows in wet edges of lakes, ditches, streams, meadows, or in damp forests, at mid to high elevations. Var. *alismellus* has egg-shaped basal leaves less than 1 in. long. Var. *alismifolius* has 2–5 in., lance-shaped to oblong, basal leaves. Native MORA

See other *Aquilegia*: red, page 355
See other *Ranunculus*: white, page 119

Ranunculus cymbalaria
RANUNCULACEAE
Shore buttercup
Common, late summer, perennial, 2–10 in.
Coastal, moist streambanks, subalpine

Clusters of leaves with strawberry-like stolons. Leaf egg- to heart-shaped, sharply scalloped on outer edge. Flower stems often branching, about same length as leaves. Flowers pale yellow, with 5–12 petals. Grows in mud along streams, marshes, ponds, with either salt or fresh water, from sea level to subalpine. Native OLYM

Ranunculus eschscholtzii RANUNCULACEAE
Snowpatch buttercup, Eschscholtz's buttercup
Locally common, midsummer, perennial,
4–10 in. Alpine, subalpine

Tuft with upright flower stem, hairless. Stem solid, erect. Leaves round to heart-shaped in basal cluster, divided 2 times into 3 segments with rounded lobes, the middle lobe entire to shallowly lobed. Flowers luminous yellow, 1–3, each about 1½ in. across top, on short stalks. Grows in rocky gravelly soils at edge of snowmelt or other wet cool places in subalpine and alpine. Very similar *R. suksdorfii*, often treated as a variety of *R. eschscholtzii*, has leaves with sharply pointed, deeply toothed lobes, the middle lobe of lower leaves usually deeply divided into 3–7 lobes; more common in same habitat in southern part of our region. Native OLYM, MORA, NOCA, CRLA

Ranunculus flammula RANUNCULACEAE
Creeping spearwort, creeping buttercup
Common, late spring–early summer, perennial,
1–10 in. Coastal, vernal-wet, lake/pond,
meadow

Amphibious. Stems prostrate, branched, growing outward for 18 in. or less, rooting like strawberry stolons. Basal and lower stem leaves with 1–3 in. petioles, linear to lance-shaped, entire; upper stem leaves smaller. Flowers small and yellow at stem tips, mostly with 5 petals. Grows in wet meadows, shallow water at edges of lakes, ditches, ponds, as water recedes in muddy soils, below 7500 ft. Native OLYM, NOCA

Ranunculus glaberrimus

RANUNCULACEAE

Sagebrush buttercup

Common, all spring, perennial

East-side forest, shrub-steppe

Decumbent to erect, hairless, usually in small clumps. Stem single, may be branched at top. Basal leaves narrow to spoon-shaped, 1½–2 in. long, entire to deeply 3-lobed and tapered at the base to a petiole at least as long as the leaf. Flowers yellow, often turning white with age, petals ½ in. long. Grows in sagebrush, juniper woods, conifer forests, at mid to high elevations. Var. *glaberrimus* has basal leaves egg-shaped to nearly round, scalloped with 1–3 bluntly rounded tips. Var. *ellipticus* has lance-shaped entire leaves; upper stem leaves may be deeply divided into 3 lobes. Native OLYM

Ranunculus occidentalis

RANUNCULACEAE

Western buttercup

Common, early to midspring, perennial, 6–30 in. Coastal, disturbed, meadow, west-side forest, east-side forest

Upright, usually branched, hollow stem with soft hairs. Basal leaves with 1–3 in. petioles, softly hairy, oval to heart-shaped, divided into 3, again divided deeply or shallowly; stem leaves alternate, more deeply divided. Flowers top plant, ½–1 in. wide, yellow, 5–6 petals each about ½ as wide as they are long. Grows in moist soils, meadows, coastal bluffs, forests, from sea level to high elevations. Similar *R. acris*, a European escapee, is usually shorter, with leaves divided into 3 lobes, usually found in waste places or fields at low elevations. Native OLYM, NOCA, CRLA

Ranunculus orthorhynchus

RANUNCULACEAE

Swamp buttercup, straight-beaked buttercup

Common, perennial, 6–36 in. Coastal, bog/fen/wetland, moist streambanks, meadow

Erect to prostrate, softly hairy to shiny. Stems to 36 in. long. Basal and lower stem leaves with petioles 2–8 in. long, divided into 3–5 coarsely toothed segments; upper leaves smaller, divided into 3 narrow lobes. Flower petals 5–8, about ½ as wide as they are long. Seeds clustered in ball have prominent straight beaks. Grows in wet areas, along streams, beaches and tidal marshes, forests, from sea level to high elevations. *Ortho* is Greek for "straight" and *rhynchus* "beak," in reference to the seeds. Native OLYM, NOCA

Ranunculus populago
RANUNCULACEAE
Blue Mountain buttercup
Locally common, early summer, perennial,
3–12 in. Bog/fen/wetland, moist streambanks,
meadow

Tuft. Stems erect, shiny, with few branches.
Lower leaves with 1–3 in. long petioles, widely
heart to egg-shaped, with tiny teeth or entire;
upper leaves smaller. Flowers yellow, petals to ¼ in. long.
Grows in wet meadows, along streams, at high elevations.
Native

Ranunculus repens   RANUNCULACEAE
Creeping buttercup
Common, all summer, perennial, 2–3 ft.
Coastal, bog/fen/wetland, disturbed, meadow

Prostrate. Stems creeping and rooting at lower
nodes, tips may point upward. Stems branching, hairless to rough hairy. Leaves on stems at
rooted nodes are erect. Leaf divided into 3
leaflets, dark green lightly spotted with white,
covered with short white hairs. Inflorescence
consists of several flowers at ends of long erect
stems. Flowers large, with 5 petals or possibly
doubled, deep yellow. An invasive European weed in wet soils,
waste areas, lawns, agricultural fields. Nonnative
OLYM, MORA, NOCA

Ranunculus sceleratus   RANUNCULACEAE
Celery-leaf buttercup, blister buttercup
Common, midsummer, annual or perennial,
6–20 in. Bog/fen/wetland, disturbed, meadow

Erect. Stem hairless or with few hairs, may be
branched. Leaves shiny green, celery-like, with
1–5 in. petioles, divided into 3 leaflets, lobed or
toothed. Flowers many, with 5 small petals,
large center that elongates as seed develops.
Found in waste areas, muddy places, edges of
lakes, ponds, along Columbia River. Native
across North America and in Europe. The juice
can cause blisters on skin. Native OLYM

221

Ranunculus triternatus (*Ranunculus reconditus*)   RANUNCULACEAE
The Dalles Mountain buttercup, obscure buttercup
Endemic, early spring, perennial, 2–5 in. Meadow

Tuft. Stems upright. Basal leaves with petioles, divided into many linear segments; few similar leaves along stems. Flowers with short stalks, bright yellow, large, 5 petals widely egg-shaped. Grows in spring-moist soils, slopes, open grasslands in high hills. Rare and endangered in Washington and Oregon. Similar to the common *R. glaberrimus*, with leaves only shallowly lobed. Native

Ranunculus uncinatus
RANUNCULACEAE
Small-flowered buttercup, woodland buttercup
Locally common, early summer, annual or perennial, 6–24 in. Coastal, moist streambanks, disturbed, meadow, west-side forest, east-side forest

Basal and lower stem leaves with 2–6 in. petioles, soft-haired, more or less round to heart-shaped, divided into 3 shallow lobes divided again, 3-toothed segments, hairs flat on surface; middle stem leaves smaller. Flowers single on stalks above large leafy bract. Flower tiny, 2–5 petals quickly falling, light to medium yellow. Seed with curved beak. Grows in moist soils, shaded woodlands, forests, beaches, disturbed places, at low to high elevations. Similar *R. macounii* has leaves divided into 3-lobed leaflets, seed with straight beaks. Native OLYM, MORA, NOCA

Thalictrum fendleri   RANUNCULACEAE
Fendler's meadowrue
Uncommon, late spring–early summer, perennial, 3–5 ft.
West-side forest, east-side forest

Erect plants with only male or female flowers. Stems often purplish, leafy. Basal and stem leaves egg-shaped, divided into 3 segments, divided again to narrow lobes; top surface smooth; underside glandular, rough-feeling. Flowers purplish or greenish white in stemmed clusters with small leaves at top; male flowers with 18–25 stamens. Seed tips pointing outward or upward when ripening. Grows in moist places in shady woodlands. Native

See other *Thalictrum*: red, page 356

Darlingtonia californica
SARRACENIACEAE
California pitcher-plant
Rare, late spring–early summer, perennial,
6–24 in. Coastal, bog/fen/wetland

Upright tubular leaves topped with large hood.
Leaves yellow-green to reddish, with translu-
cent patches, brown, green, or reddish dots,
veins on hood, fading downward. At front of
opening under hood are 2 large mustache-looking appendages.
Insects are trapped inside by stiff downward-pointing hairs,
drowned in fluids at bottom. Flower stalk above leaves with few
yellow bracts. Flower hangs down, with 5 overlapping sepals,
yellow-green, 1–2½ in. long, surrounding 5 dark red petals.
Grows in running water, on serpentine, at 100–7000 ft. It is
thought appendages and opening bear nec-
taries to attract insects. Native

Tribulus terrestris   ZYGOPHYLLACEAE
Puncture vine, caltrop
Locally common, all summer, annual, mat
Disturbed, shrub-steppe

Mat prostrate to 6 ft. across. Leaves divided,
leaflets oval, opposite, 6–12. Flowers small, yellow. Fruit splits into 5 nutlets, each nutlet with
2–4 hard sharp spines. Grows in dry disturbed soils. Mediterranean. This pernicious weed causes flat tires and injured feet,
and is named caltrop after a 4-spiked weapon used on the
ground to obstruct moving armies. Nonnative

Rhus glabra   ANACARDIACEAE
Smooth sumac, scarlet sumac, western sumac
Common, early summer, perennial, 3–18 ft.
Disturbed, meadow

Deciduous shrub or small tree with many
branches. Leaves 12–18 in. long, divided pinnately to 11–31 lance-shaped leaflets, each 1–4
in. long with sharply pointed tip, turning scarlet in autumn. Inflorescence dense, club-
shaped, to 8 in. long, upward-pointing. White
to green flowers each about ⅛ in. across. Fruit
is a pulpy, round, red berry covered with short red hairs; contains a single stone; usually persists through winter. Grows in
disturbed soils and grasslands near water in dry areas. Native

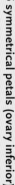

Toxicodendron diversilobum (*Rhus diversiloba*) ANACARDIACEAE
Poison-oak
Common, late spring–early summer, perennial, 1–8 ft. West-side forest, east-side forest

Vine or shrub, round stems reddish or gray. Leaves divided into 3 oblong shiny leaflets on twigs to 4 in. long. Edges can be smooth, wavy, or lobed. Dark green color becomes bright red in autumn. Oblong clusters of flowers on a separate stalk. Berries cream or brown. Grows at low to mid elevations in woodlands and on rocky slopes. Although resin in all parts of plant is toxic to life-threatening, most people only suffer from rashes or blisters after contact. *Toxico* is Latin for "poison" and *dendron* means "tree." Do not touch this plant or the similar *T. rydbergii*, poison-ivy. Native **OLYM**

Lomatium ambiguum APIACEAE
Swale desert parsley
Locally common, late spring–early summer, perennial, 2–16 in. Meadow, east-side forest

Upright, hairless, with leafy stems. Stems single or clustered, may have round thickened base with few alternating branches. Leaves all basal divided pinnately 2–3 times, linear leaflets to 2 in. long. Flowers in small clusters on stems of uneven length form umbels, are yellow, turning purplish with age. Grows on open slopes, flat lowlands, at mid elevations. Native **NOCA, L&C**

Lomatium cous APIACEAE
Cous lomatium, cous biscuit root
Locally common, early spring, perennial, 4–8 in. Shrub-steppe

Low spreading plant with small leaves. Leaves divided 3 times into small oval divisions that are widest near the rounded tips, withering as flowering finishes. Inflorescence consists of separated flower clusters on stalks of various lengths. Yellow to purple flowers are supported by oval, separated bractlets. Grows in rocky places, ridges, at low to high elevations. Native **L&C**

See other *Lomatium*: white, page 123; red, page 356; green/brown, page 467

Lomatium grayi APIACEAE
Gray's desert parsley, pungent desert parsley
Common, early spring, perennial, 6–14 in.
East-side forest, shrub-steppe

Tuft of upright to spreading stems in cluster.
Plant gives off strong, unpleasant odor. Leaf
smooth to slightly rough, divided pinnately
into several hundred crowded, narrow, fleshy
segments held in different planes that give an
illusion of thickness. Inflorescence is a flat umbel held on
leafless stems above foliage. Flowers bright yellow, clustered
in small tight groups. Grows in dry rocky slopes and flats in
foothills and to mid elevations in mountains. Native

Lomatium hallii APIACEAE
Hall's desert parsley
Locally common, midspring–midsummer,
perennial, 6–20 in. Meadow, west-side forest

Tuft with several unbranched stems. Leaf with
1–3 in. stalk and conspicuous appendage surrounding base; blade shiny green, 2–6 in., dissected pinnately 3 times, leaflets linear to oblong, with pointed tips. Flower stalk 5–12 in.
tall. Flowers yellow, at different levels within
the umbel. Grows on bluffs and slopes, scree,
river valleys. Native

Lomatium laevigatum APIACEAE
Smooth desert parsley
Locally common, midspring, perennial, 6–24 in.
Shrub-steppe

Tuft of basal leaves, erect flower stems. Leaves
hairless, shiny, divided 3 or 4 times into many
distinct linear segments to 1 in. long, tips
pointed. Stems hold umbels above leaves.
Flower stalks within the umbel unequal, ascending with bractless clusters of yellow
flowers. Grows on basalt bluffs and ridges
along Columbia River. Native

Lomatium martindalei APIACEAE

Martindale's desert parsley, few-fruited lomatium

Locally common, early summer, perennial, 4–14 in. Coastal, meadow, west-side forest, east-side forest, shrub-steppe, alpine

Prostrate from thick protruding root, 4–14 in. wide. Leaves primarily basal, shiny green to blue-green, pinnately divided. Leaflets crowded, oblong, toothed, round-tipped; few along stem similar. Umbels of small flowers, white, cream, or purplish, occur in stalked bundles. Grows in dry meadows, conifer forests, coastal bluffs, alpine rocky outcrops. Native OLYM, MORA, NOCA

Lomatium nudicaule APIACEAE

Barestem desert parsley, pestle lomatium

Common, early spring, perennial, 10–30 in. Coastal, meadow, east-side forest, shrub-steppe

Erect, glaucous blue throughout. Leaves mostly basal, pinnately divided, petiole 1½–10 in. long, sheathed to middle. Leaflets large, egg-shaped, untoothed or coarsely toothed. Flower stalk has no leaf or bract but is swollen at top. Flowers, which branch outward unequally in tight clusters, are tiny, cream-yellow or rarely purple, spicy-smelling. Grows in open areas with dry rocky clay or sandy soils from near coastline to mid elevations. *Nudicaule*, meaning "naked stem," refers to the leafless flower stalk. Native OLYM, NOCA, **L&C**

Lomatium suksdorfii APIACEAE

Suksdorf's desert parsley

Uncommon, late spring–early summer, perennial, 3–6 ft. Meadow, shrub-steppe

Erect, stout. Stems tall, hairless, from clustered old leaf sheaths. Leaves with long petioles, pinnately divided twice to linear sections 1½ in. long with pointed tips. Flowers small, yellow, in 15 or more bracted clusters in flat, wide umbel. Grows in gravelly or rocky soils, open grasslands, at low to mid elevations. *Lomatium dissectum* is similar but its leaves are covered with tiny hairs and divided into smaller, finer leaflets with red-brown or yellow flowers. Native

Lomatium triternatum APIACEAE
Nine-leaf lomatium, Lewis's lomatium
Common, midspring, perennial, 6–30 in.
Vernal-wet, meadow, west-side forest, east-side
forest, shrub-steppe, alpine, subalpine

Upright. Stems prominent, hairless. Stems
and leaves green to gray. Basal leaves with petioles 3–8 in. long, pinnately dissected 1–3
times, forming long, linear to lance-shaped,
toothless leaflets covered with fine hairs. Flower stems long,
mostly leafless, 1–4 in. stalks unequal, spreading to erect,
topped with thread-like bractlets sustaining compact bundles of
yellow flowers in loose flat umbels. Grows on open or sagebrush slopes, ridges, pine woodlands in vernal-wet spots, often
in serpentine areas. Native OLYM, MORA, **L&C**

Lomatium utriculatum APIACEAE
**Fine-leaf desert parsley, spring gold, foothill
lomatium**
Common, all spring, perennial, 6–24 in.
Coastal, meadow, west-side forest

Upright clump. Stems leafy, hairless or sparsely hairy. Leaves mostly basal, a few on lower
stem, petioles widely sheathing to first branch;
blade dissected pinnately into very narrow, lin-
ear, fern-like leaflets. Inflorescence small, with compact clusters in open umbels. Flowers small, bright yellow, sustained by
egg-shaped, overlapping bractlets. Grows in meadows, woodlands, open and often rocky places, from near coastline to mid
elevations. One of the longest-blooming flowers, starting as
early as January and found as late as July. Native OLYM

Osmorhiza occidentalis APIACEAE
Western sweet cicely
Locally common, late spring–early summer,
perennial, 1–4 ft. Vernal-wet, meadow, west-
side forest, east-side forest

Stems clustered, erect, 1 to few, shiny to
sparsely hairy. Leaf blade 4–8 in. long, divided
1–3 times. Leaflets lance- to egg-shaped, irregularly lobed, saw-toothed. Flower stalks leaf-
less, 2–8 in. tall, supporting loose groups of small yellowish
flowers. Seed needle-shaped, smooth, not tailed or barbed.
Grows in conifer forests, streamsides, seeps, moist places, at
mid and high elevations. Plant has strong odor of licorice.
Native OLYM, MORA, NOCA, CRLA

See other *Osmorhiza*: white, page 125

Oxypolis occidentalis APIACEAE
Western oxypolis
Uncommon, late summer, perennial, 2–4 ft.
Bog/fen/wetland, meadow, west-side forest

Upright. Stems hollow, branched, hairless.
Leaf petiole 4–20 in. circled with sheath at
base. Leaves pinnately divided into 5–13
egg-shaped leaflets toothed or irregularly
lobed, smaller on upper stem. Umbel
rounded with clusters of yellow, white, or purple flowers with
conspicuous calyx. Grows in wet meadows, bogs, along
streams, often near conifer forests, at low to high elevations.
Was recently discovered on the Queen Charlotte Islands on
midcoast of British Columbia. Native

Pteryxia terebinthina var.
terebinthina (*Cymopterus*
terebinthinus var. *terebinthinus*)
APIACEAE
Turpentine wavewing
Uncommon, late spring–early summer,
perennial, 4–20 in.
East-side forest, shrub-steppe

Erect stout stems. Leaves shiny yellow-
green, egg-shaped, 1–7 in. long, finely di-
vided, smallest section tiny, linear, with pointed tip. Inflorescences top leaves with open umbels of clustered flowers on
unequal stalks. Flower clusters contain linear bractlets about
equal in size to yellow flowers, occasionally white or purple.
Grows in dry sandy or gravelly soil. Plant has strong odor of
turpentine. Native

Sanicula arctopoides APIACEAE
**Footsteps of spring, yellow mats, bear's foot
sanicle**
Uncommon, early spring, perennial,
1–12 in. Coastal

Prostrate or ascending. Stems 1–12 in.,
branched, somewhat succulent. Leaves in
basal rosette, divided, 3 lobes, toothed, with
long needle-like tips. Juvenile leaves are
green, those on flowering plants are yellow-green. Flowers
small, bright yellow, in rounded umbels, surrounded by long
leaf-like bracts. Grows on coastal bluffs, dunes, to 600 ft. A
standout in early spring with its fresh, bright yellow leaves and
flowers in tight mats. Native OLYM

228

See other *Sanicula*: red, page 357

Sanicula crassicaulis APIACEAE
Pacific sanicle
Common, midspring, perennial, 1–4 ft.
Coastal, meadow, west-side forest, east-side
forest

Erect. Stem thick. Leaves alternate, divided into 3 or possibly 5 lobes, very sharply toothed; lower leaves with long petioles; upper leaves sessile. Flowers yellow, sometimes tinted purple, in 3–12 in. umbels at stem top; bracts at base of umbel are large, leaf-like. Grows on open slopes, woodlands, ravines near coastline and low elevations. *Crassicaulis* means "thickened stem." A variable and widespread plant. Native OLYM

Sanicula graveolens APIACEAE
Sierra sanicle
Locally common, midspring, perennial, 2–15
in. Coastal, west-side forest, east-side forest

Erect taprooted perennial, low and widely spreading. Stem narrow, smooth. Leaves closest to ground attached to main stem underground by long petioles. Leaf blades pinnately divided into sets of 3 lobes; few upper leaflets sessile, smaller, longer. Leaves smell like caraway when crushed. Flowers yellow, 10–15 in conspicuous umbel; bracts leafy, to 3 in. long, divided similar to leaves. Grows in dry open forests, rocky slopes, sometimes on serpentine, at low to mid elevations. *Graveolens* means "strong-smelling." Native OLYM, MORA, NOCA, CRLA

Mentzelia albicaulis (*Acrolasia albicaulis*)
LOASACEAE
White-stemmed stick-leaf
Locally common, midspring, annual, 4–24 in.
Dry rocky sites, shrub-steppe

Erect, with branches often in pairs. Stems shining white with short hairs. Leaves sessile, 1–4 in. long, oblong, with pointed tips; edges deeply lobed or comb-like or toothed to smooth. Flowers yellow, 1–3 in clusters at stem tops; petals 5–10, less than ½ in. long; stamens 15–25, shorter than petals. Grows in dry, often sandy to rocky soils, shrublands, woodlands, at low to high elevations. Native

Mentzelia laevicaulis LOASACEAE
Blazing star
Locally common, all summer, biennial or
perennial, 9–40 in. Dry rocky sites, shrub-
steppe

Erect whitish stem, widely branching.
Stems and leaves coated with stiff barbed
hairs. Leaves lobed. Basal leaves 7–10 in.;
stem leaves 1–4 in. Flowers at stem tips with
1 green bract per bright yellow flower, 5 sepals shorter and narrower than the five l in. long petals, many stamens at different
lengths. Grows in sandy, gravelly, or rocky slopes in washes or
roadsides below 9000 ft. Native NOCA

Argentina anserina (*Potentilla anserina, Potentilla argentina*) ROSACEAE
Common silverweed
Locally common, late summer, perennial,
3–10 in. Coastal, moist streambanks,
meadow

Mats of flat rosettes with runners. Basal
leaves 4–8 in., pinnately divided, many
larger leaflets interspersed with smaller
ones. Petioles with long spreading hairs.
Larger leaflets ½–1½ in. long, oblong or
lance-shaped, with rounded tips, sharply toothed, with white
silky hairs on upper and lower surfaces. Flowers yellow, solitary, with leafless stalks. Grows in mudflats, back waters, meadows, edges of ponds. Native

Argentina egedii subsp. *egedii* (*Potentilla anserina* subsp. *pacifica, Potentilla pacifica*) ROSACEAE
Pacific silverweed
Locally common, all spring and summer,
perennial, to 15 in. Coastal, vernal-wet,
bog/fen/wetland, moist streambanks

Upright, spreading by runners. Leaves to 15
in. long, with nearly hairless petioles, upright to spreading, divided pinnately into
many pairs of small and large leaflets with
woolly hairs on underside, toothed. Flower single, small, with
leafless stem; petals yellow, oval. Grows in wet marshy places,
along streams, beaches, coastal dunes, sand flats, estuaries
along coast or near coastline. Native OLYM, **L&C**

Dasiphora floribunda (*Potentilla fruticosa,* *Pentaphylloides floribunda*) ROSACEAE
Shrubby cinquefoil
Common, all summer, perennial, 2–4 ft.
Meadows, alpine, subalpine

Woody shrub with many crowded upright stems. Leaves divided; leaflets 3–7, oval, with inrolled edges, pointed at tip, less than 1 in. long, entire, lightly covered with silky hairs. Flowers 1 to few at ends of twigs, with 5 yellow petals, many stamens. Grows in meadows, moist rocky slopes, at high elevations. Circumboreal. Often cultivated, where many attractive garden varieties have been produced. Native
OLYM, MORA, NOCA, **L&C**

Geum macrophyllum ROSACEAE
Large-leaved avens
Common, all spring and summer, perennial, 1–3 ft. Moist streambanks, meadow, west-side forest, east-side forest

Erect, hairy. Basal leaves with long erect petioles, a more or less heart-shaped terminal leaflet many times larger than the variously sized small leaflets below; stem leaves usually sessile, deeply lobed to 3 lobes. Flowers 3–10 at top, with 5 nearly round yellow petals, many stamens. Grows in streambanks, edges of woods, moist meadows, usually at low elevations, but can grow to subalpine. Var. *macrophyllum* with the terminal leaflet of basal leaves shallowly lobed, all leaves finely toothed. Var. *perincisum* grows east of Cascades, has terminal leaflet of basal leaf more deeply lobed. Native
OLYM, MORA, NOCA, CRLA

Ivesia gordonii ROSACEAE
Gordon's ivesia, alpine ivesia
Uncommon, all summer, perennial, 2–8 in.
East-side forest, alpine, subalpine

Tufted perennial with blackened leaf bases. Stems ascending. Basal leaves bright green with glands, more than 20 pairs of overlapping lobes partly wrapped on stem; stem leaf single. Flower stems hold a 2–8 in. rounded cluster of 10–20 flowers at top. Flower petals small, yellow, oval, with 5 stamens and 2–4 pistils. Grows in dry rocky ridges, talus slopes, floodplains, at high elevations. In northern California, found on Mount Eddy. Native

See other *Geum*: red, page 357
See other *Ivesia*: white, page 131

Potentilla arguta ROSACEAE
Sharp-toothed cinquefoil, tall cinquefoil
Locally common, all summer, perennial,
14–40 in. Meadow, east-side forest, alpine,
subalpine

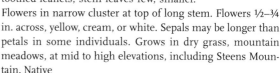

Tall, narrow, hairy. Top of plant with gland-tipped hairs. Basal leaves erect, 4–10 in. long, divided into 7–9 hairy, oval, sharp-toothed leaflets; stem leaves few, smaller. Flowers in narrow cluster at top of long stem. Flowers ½–¾ in. across, yellow, cream, or white. Sepals may be longer than petals in some individuals. Grows in dry grass, mountain meadows, at mid to high elevations, including Steens Mountain. Native

Potentilla brevifolia ROSACEAE
Short-leaved cinquefoil
Uncommon, midsummer, perennial, to 4 in.
Alpine, subalpine

Small mats hairy, yellow-green. Leaves deeply cut, usually with 3–7 nearly round crinkly leaflets crowded on stems 2–6 in. long. Smaller leaves on 2–4 in. flower stems. Flowers small in gland-sticky calyx; petals yellow, nearly round. Grows on exposed slopes near melting snow banks at high elevations in eastern Oregon. Found in Wallowa Mountains and Steens Mountain. Native

Potentilla diversifolia ROSACEAE
Mountain meadow cinquefoil, varileaf cinquefoil
Locally common, midsummer, perennial,
4–15 in. Alpine, subalpine

Tuft of greenish to grayish leaves with ascending flower stems. Stems clustered, hairy above, hairless at base. Basal leaves palmately divided to 3–5(–7) lobes, toothed on outer end, central leaflet ½–1½ in. long. Flowers to 20 with yellow oval petals and 20 stamens. Grows mostly in moist meadows and rocky areas in subalpine and alpine. Native OLYM, MORA, NOCA

Potentilla drummondii subsp. *breweri*

(*Potentilla breweri*)   ROSACEAE
Brewer's cinquefoil
Locally common, all summer, perennial,
4–24 in. Meadow, alpine, subalpine

Stems ascending, hairless or coated with gray, straight, stiff hairs. Basal and lower stem leaves pinnately divided, 3–7 leaflets per side, overlapping and lobed, petiole usually heavily coated with silky gray hairs. Flowers about 20. Grows in meadows and rocky places at high and alpine elevations. Subsp. *drummondii* petiole is less hairy, with 5–9 uncrowded leaflets. Similar *P. biennis* is annual or biennial, coated with glands, with leaves divided into oval, deeply toothed leaflets. Native

Potentilla flabellifolia   ROSACEAE
Fan-leaf cinquefoil
Locally common, all summer, perennial,
6–12 in. Alpine, subalpine

Cluster of upright stems and basal leaves. Leaves fan-shaped, roundish in outline, palmately divided to 3 hairless leaflets, each usually with 7 uneven teeth, looking much like a strawberry. Flower stems with few smaller leaves, topped with several flowers. Flower in hairy, glandular cup, bright yellow petals to ½ in. long, stamens about 20. Grows in moist meadows, scree, at high to alpine elevations. Somewhat similar but hairier *P. villosa* has leathery leaflets white-woolly below, hairless above, coarsely toothed on outer ½; only 1–2 flowers atop flower stalks; grows from sea level to alpine. Native OLYM, MORA, NOCA, CRLA

Potentilla glandulosa   ROSACEAE
Sticky cinquefoil
Common, all summer, perennial, 1–3 ft.
Meadows, west-side forest, east-side forest,
alpine, subalpine

Upright, with hairs ending in sticky glands. Basal leaves pinnately divided into 5–9 widely oval leaflets, the end leaflet the largest, teeth cutting ¼–½ of the way to midvein. Flowers in loose cluster with leafy bracts. Petals oval, yellow to cream, varying in length from shorter to longer than sepals. Grows below 10,000 ft. Subsp. *ashlandica* is less than 8 in. tall, petals yellow, with or without glands, more than 10 teeth on leaflets; grows from California to southern Oregon. Subsp. *pseudorupestris*, 2–7 in., has fewer than 10 teeth on leaflet, glands on upper plant, with cream to pale yellow petals. Subsp. *glandulosa* is densely glandular, cream to pale yellow, with leafy bracts. Native OLYM, MORA, NOCA, CRLA

233

Potentilla gracilis   ROSACEAE
Fivefinger cinquefoil, slender cinquefoil
Common, late spring–early summer,
perennial, 1–2 ft. Meadows, west-side
forest, east-side forest, shrub-steppe

Tuft. Stem ascending, with spreading hairs.
Leaves green, oval, divided palmately into
5–9 leaflets. Largest leaflet at center, with
sharply cut teeth or lobes, hairs on top
mostly at leaf base, more densely white-hairy on underside.
Flowers few to many in loose cluster of ascending stalks.
Flower petals wide, 1/8–2/3 in. long. Grows in meadows, open
forests, roadsides, at low to alpine elevations. Our most variable cinquefoil, with many varieties found over much of western North America. Telling them apart requires a technical key.
Native OLYM, MORA, NOCA

Potentilla millefolia   ROSACEAE
Cut-leaf cinquefoil, Klamath cinquefoil
Uncommon, late spring–early summer,
perennial, 1–6 in. Vernal-wet, meadow

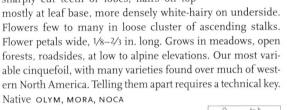

Rosette prostrate to ascending from central
taproot. Stems and leaf petioles with appressed hairs. Basal leaves nearly as long as
petioles, 6–10 pairs of overlapping leaflets
each divided into linear pointed lobes. Flowers in small clusters
at stem tips in slightly hairy cups. Stalks recurve with mature
seedpods. Grows in moist alkaline flats, vernal-wet meadows,
at low to mid elevations. Var. *klamathensis* (pictured), Klamath
cinquefoil, has spreading hairs; reported only from Siskiyou
County, California. Native

Potentilla recta   ROSACEAE
**Sulphur cinquefoil, rough-fruited cinquefoil,
erect cinquefoil**
Common, all spring and summer, perennial,
8–24 in. Disturbed, meadow

Tuft of upright stems sparsely coated with
long and short hairs or glands. Leaves
palmately divided into 5–7 oval leaflets.
Basal leaves usually withered by bloom;
stem leaves 3–6 in. long, toothed halfway to midvein. Flowers
many, in flat terminal cluster; petals pale yellow, about 1/4–1/3 in.
across. Seed brown, rough, with many deep ridges. Grows in
disturbed soils at low to mid elevations. On Oregon, Washington, and California noxious weed lists, widespread across North
America. Can be confused with *P. gracilis*, a native species.
Otherwise similar *P. norvegica*, another Eurasian import, has
only 3 leaflets. Nonnative NOCA

Potentilla rivalis ROSACEAE
Riverbank cinquefoil, brook cinquefoil
Locally common, late summer, annual or
biennial, 4–20 in. Bog/fen/wetland, moist
streambanks, disturbed, meadow

Ascending. Stems leafy, lightly coated with
short, spreading to ascending hairs without
glands. Leaves on stem divided into 3–5 oblong
leaflets, ¾–1½ in. long, hairy, toothed, lowest
leaves dropped by bloom time. Flowers numerous among
leaves at stem tops. Flower petals tiny, obscure, pale yellow;
calyx coated with long, shaggy, soft hairs. Grows in moist soils,
often on disturbed sites, along creeks and rivers, at low to mid
elevations. Native MORA

Purshia tridentata ROSACEAE
Bitterbrush, antelope-brush
Common, late spring, perennial, 3–10 ft.
East-side forest, shrub-steppe, alpine,
subalpine

Shrub with rigid stems. Leaves mostly deciduous, bright green to olive-green, wedge-
shaped, with 3-lobed tips, edges rolled under.
Flowers many, borne singly along stems.
Flower petals to ⅓ in. long, oval, cream to
bright yellow. Grows in relatively moist habitats, ponderosa
pine and western juniper communities, sagebrush-steppe,
rocky slopes, conifer forests, at mid to high elevations. Resembles big sagebrush in overall appearance and is an important
food for browsers. *Tridentata* means "3 teeth." First collected
July 6, 1806, by Meriwether Lewis along Blackfoot River. Native
NOCA, CRLA, **L&C**

Sibbaldia procumbens (*Potentilla sib-*
baldii, Potentilla procumbens) ROSACEAE
Creeping sibbaldia
Locally common, late spring–early summer,
perennial, mat. Alpine, subalpine

Creeping mat. Stems woody. Leaves with long
petioles, compound with 3 leaflets. Leaflets
wedge-shaped, with 3–5 teeth at wide tip end.
Flowers on 2–6 in. stems in hairy clusters, ¼ in. across, yellow
with 4–10 stamens. Seeds small, smooth, brown, in dried
flower. Grows in moist rocky areas at mid to high elevations.
Formerly classified in genus *Potentilla*. Members of *Sibbaldia*
have 10 or fewer stamens; cinquefoils (*Potentilla*) have more
than 10 stamens. Native OLYM, MORA, NOCA

Elmera racemosa SAXIFRAGACEAE
Yellow coralbells, elmera
Locally common, midsummer, perennial,
4–10 in. Alpine, subalpine

Tuft with upright flower stems. Leaves with long petioles, round blades, 1–2 in. across, palmately lobed, with fine-stemmed glands. Flower spike of 10–35 flowers atop 4–10 in. stalk. Flower with greenish white calyx; pale yellow petals divided into 5–10 lobes; 5 stamens. Grows on ledges, crevices, and talus. Native OLYM, MORA, NOCA

Heuchera cylindrica SAXIFRAGACEAE
Roundleaf alumroot, poker heuchera
Locally common, late spring–early summer, perennial, 5–34 in. West-side forest, east-side forest, alpine, subalpine

Tuft with erect stem. Basal leaves broadly oval, longer than wide, shallowly lobed, toothed, petiole glandular to hairy or shiny. Flower spike tops 5–35 in. leafless stem. Flowers usually without petals; calyx bell-shaped, pale yellow, green, cream, or pink; stamens not exerted. Grows in rocky slopes, cliffs, at mid to high elevations. Var. *alpina* has glands on leaves and base of stem. Var. *glabella* is hairless and glandless. Var. *cylindrica*, the most common, has hairs and glands on petioles and stem base, large bracts where stem attaches, thick leaves. This is a highly variable species and intermediate forms are common. *Heuchera grossulariifolia* is similar but with leaves always shorter than wide, shorter flower stem, and white petals on the flowers. Native NOCA

Mitella breweri SAXIFRAGACEAE
Brewer's mitrewort, Brewer's bishop's cap
Common, midsummer, perennial, 6–16 in. Moist streambanks, west-side forest, alpine, subalpine

Basal rosette with upright flower stem. Leaves round, about 1–3 in. across, divided into 7–11 indistinct lobes with shallow round teeth. Flowers small in narrow, 1-sided spike; shallow cup holds yellow-green petals that are long, thin, divided into 5–9 linear opposite lobes. Grows in moist woods, along streams, at high elevations. The smooth ripe seeds of mitellas are held in shallow cups and may be dispersed by raindrops hitting the cup and ejecting the seeds. Native OLYM, MORA, NOCA, CRLA

See other *Heuchera*: white, page 138
See other *Mitella*: white, page 139; green/brown, page 468

Saxifraga apetala (*Saxifraga integrifolia* var. *apetala*) SAXIFRAGACEAE
Petalless saxifrage
Rare, all spring, perennial, 4–12 in. Vernal-wet, meadow, subalpine

Erect stem, basal leaf rosette. Leaves egg-shaped, less than 1½ in. long, tapering into short petioles, entire or slightly toothed. Flower stalk stout, covered with glands, leafless, flowers at top in 1 or more tight balls. Flowers usually without petals; if present, petals yellow or green; sepals triangular; anthers short, yellow. Grows in grassy slopes and spring-moist meadows at mid to high elevations. Native

Utricularia macrorhiza (*Utricularia vulgaris*)
LENTIBULARIACEAE
Common bladderwort
Locally common, all spring and summer, perennial, floating. Lake/pond

Floating aquatic. Leaves divided many times into dense thread-like bristles. Small bladders along leaf margins trap small organisms when entrance hairs are triggered. Flowers 5–20, held on 1–12 in. stalks above water, yellow; 2 lips more or less equal in size, upper lip not lobed, lower lip with 3 shallow lobes; spur curved, shorter than lower lip. Grows in quiet waters. Forms ball-like, bristly winter buds. Circumboreal. Similar introduced *U. inflata* has a spoke-like float to support flower stalk. Native OLYM

Castilleja ambigua subsp. *ambigua* (*Orthocarpus castillejoides*)
SCROPHULARIACEAE
Johnny nip, paintbrush owl's clover
Locally common, all year long, annual, 4–12 in. Coastal

Ascending. Stems branched. Lower leaves lance-shaped, long, pointed; upper leaves wider, divided into 3–7 lobes with brightly colored or white tips. Inflorescence consists of a dense spike of bracts surrounding flowers. Flowers yellow with purple or red tips, or purple with lower tip yellow; beak straight. Grows in coastal salt marshes. Native OLYM

See other *Saxifraga*: white, page 140
See other *Castilleja*: white, page 146; red, page 365

5 symmetrical petals (ovary inferior)

5 irregular petals forming a tube

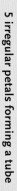

Castilleja arachnoidea

SCROPHULARIACEAE
Cobwebby paintbrush
Uncommon, midsummer, perennial,
3–12 in. Alpine, subalpine

Erect, covered with white-woolly hairs.
Leaves ¾–2¼ in. long, entire or divided, 1
or 2 pairs of somewhat dished lobes. Bracts
¼–¾ in. long, deeply divided; 3–5 rounded,
dull yellow to rusty red lobes. Flowers pale green or purple-red.
Grows on open dry rocks or summits of mountains at mid and
high elevations. Native CRLA

Castilleja campestris subsp. campestris (*Orthocarpus campestris*) SCROPHULARIACEAE
Vernal-pool paintbrush
Locally common, late spring, annual, 4–6 in.
Vernal-wet, shrub-steppe

Erect, hairless, unbranched to branched.
Leaves narrow, linear, ½–1½ in. long. Flowers in dense spike, bracts like leaves,
shorter, green. Flower calyx divided unevenly, hairy; flower pale yellow to orange,
with straight beak, stigma extending upward. Grows in spring-wet pools, moist
places, at low elevations to treeline. Native

Castilleja chrysantha SCROPHULARIACEAE
Wallowa paintbrush, yellow paintbrush
Locally common, midsummer, perennial, 4–12 in.
Alpine, subalpine

Clustered. Stems erect, unbranched, hairy.
Leaves pointed, not lobed except near stem
top. Flower head narrow, elongating with
maturity. Flower bracts green, pale yellow,
or occasionally pale purplish, rounded and
somewhat broader than leaves; upper bracts
divided with a pair of lobes on the sides that
point upward. Flowers yellow, longer than
bracts. Grows in moist alpine to subalpine
meadows and slopes, often near edges of
lakes, at high elevations. Native

Castilleja cusickii   SCROPHULARIACEAE
Cusick's paintbrush
Uncommon, early summer, perennial, 8–20 in.
Bog/fen/wetland, meadow, alpine, subalpine

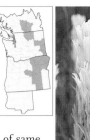

Clump, all parts covered with very small hairs.
Stems many, unbranched. Leaves numerous,
upward-pointing, lance-shaped, with 3–7 slender lobes. Yellow or occasionally pale violet
bracts and calyces, lobes rounded. Flower with
whitish lobes about 1–1½ in. long hidden in calyx of same
length. Grows in moist granitic meadows at mid and high elevations. Native

Castilleja glandulifera   SCROPHULARIACEAE
Sticky paintbrush, glandular paintbrush
Locally common, all summer, perennial,
4–15 in. Alpine, subalpine

Cluster from woody base, upper plant covered
with sticky glands. Stems erect, lower section
hairy. Leaves ½–2 in. long, lance-shaped,
whole or divided with 2 lobes. Flower bracts
and calyces are lobed, yellow or soft red. Flower
to 1 in. long, with narrow yellow or purplish
edges, lower lip dark green. Grows in sandy
granite soils at 6500–10,000 ft. Similar *C. vis-
cidula* is smaller; bracts and calyces usually yellowish green,
can be pink, orange, or reddish; flower lower lip reduced to
small pouch, with 3 teeth turned inward. Native

Castilleja lacera (*Orthocarpus lacera*)   SCROPHULARIACEAE
Cut-leaf paintbrush
Uncommon, early summer, annual, 6–12 in.
Vernal-wet, meadow

Upright stem with glandular-spreading hairs.
Leaves ⅓–2 in. long, linear to lance-shaped,
may be divided into 5 lobes. Flower spike 2–6
in., egg-shaped, green bracts with linear to
lance-shaped lobes. Flower calyx divided unevenly, hairs stiff, some glands, flower deep
yellow, straight beak, lower lip generally pur-
ple-dotted at base, stigma extended. Grows in
grassy places at low to high elevations in the Klamath Mountains. Native

Castilleja levisecta

SCROPHULARIACEAE

Golden paintbrush

Endemic, late spring, perennial, 10–14 in.
Meadow

Clump covered with very fine hairs and few tiny glands. Stems many, upright, usually unbranched. Leaves oblong, with 5–7 short lobes. Bract and calyx lobes pointed, yellow or occasionally orange-yellow. Greenish flowers shorter than bracts. Grows in low-elevation meadows, including Puget Sound. Federally listed as threatened in United States. Only 2 sites left in Canada with about 2000 plants; rare and endangered in Washington; reported extirpated from its historical range in Willamette Valley, Oregon. The pressures of an increasing human population have resulted in *C. levisecta* being among Washington's most endangered species. Consider yourself very lucky if you find this plant, and take special precautions to protect it and its habitat. Native OLYM

Castilleja lutescens (Castilleja pallida)

SCROPHULARIACEAE

Stiff yellow paintbrush, yellowish paintbrush

Rare, all summer, perennial, 1–2 ft.
Meadows, east-side forest

Erect stout stems, often many in a cluster, branched in upper section, glandless, hairy. Leaves linear to lance-shaped, upper leaves may have pair of short lobes. Bracts and calyces pale or dull yellow, bracts with 1–2 pairs of lobes. Calyx 2/3–3/4 in. long, flower slightly longer. Grows on open grassy slopes, open conifer forests. Native

Castilleja oresbia SCROPHULARIACEAE

Pale Wallowa paintbrush

Uncommon, late spring–early summer, perennial, 6–12 in. Alpine, subalpine

Stems erect or clustered on ground, very hairy, sometimes branched. Leaves linear, 3/4–1 1/4 in. long, pointed; leaves on upper stem divided into 3 lobes. Flower bracts pale yellow, shorter than leaves, divided into narrow lobes. Flowers pale pink, with short narrow beak, almost hidden among the more obvious bracts. Wallowa Mountains. Grows on open ridges at 7000–8000 ft. Native

Castilleja parviflora var. *albida*

SCROPHULARIACEAE
White small-flowered paintbrush
Locally common, midsummer, perennial,
4–12 in. Alpine, subalpine

Upright, sticky below flower head, entire plant
turning black as it dies. Stems clustered, glistening with glands. Leaves oval to lance-shaped, divided into 3–5 lobes; leaves from
midstem up to ⅛ in. wide. Flowers very small, yellowish green
to green with purple edges, hidden by dull yellow to whitish 3-
to 5-lobed bracts. Grows in alpine meadows and rocky slopes.
Native NOCA

Castilleja pilosa   SCROPHULARIACEAE

Hairy yellow paintbrush
Uncommon, midsummer, perennial, 6–14 in.
Shrub-steppe, alpine, subalpine

Upright or often spreading on ground before
stem rises upward. Stems hairy. Leaves linear
to lance-shaped, entire or 3-lobed. Flower head
1–8 in. long; bracts green to purplish, wide-spreading, with white margins, divided with
3–5 lobes. Flower pale yellow-green or pinkish.
Grows on rocky slopes with sagebrush, barren
alpine slopes, at mid to high elevations. Var. *pilosa* has curly
hairs. Var. *longispica*, with clusters of purplish stems, grows in
Wallowa Mountains at high elevations. *Pilosa* means "covered
with short, weak, thin hairs." Native

Castilleja pilosa var. *steenensis*   SCROPHULARIACEAE

Steens Mountain paintbrush
Endemic, midsummer, perennial
Alpine, subalpine

Upright. Stems with coarse reflexed or spreading hairs. Leaves linear to lance-shaped, entire
to 3-lobed with pointed tips. Flower head
greenish with bracts becoming yellowish or
dried on the edges. Flowers yellowish, not
much longer than bracts. Grows on dry rocky
slopes and ridges above 6500 ft. on Steens
Mountain, where it is endemic and fairly common in its habitat. Native

241

Castilleja thompsonii
SCROPHULARIACEAE
Thompson's paintbrush
Locally common, late spring–early summer, perennial, 8–12 in. Shrub-steppe

Upright cluster, greenish yellow, hairy. Stems simple or branched. Leaves narrow or divided into narrow segments covered with short hairs. Flower bracts divided; 5 lobes with center widest, tips slightly rounded. Grows on thin rocky soils and lava flows, with the host plant *Artemisia rigida*, stiff sagebrush, throughout steppe regions, at mid elevations to above timberline on Mount Adams. Endemic to the Columbia Basin, where it is commonly encountered. Native

Linaria dalmatica (*Linaria genistifolia*
subsp. *dalmatica*) SCROPHULARIACEAE
Dalmatian toadflax
Locally common, late spring, perennial, 2–4 ft. Disturbed, meadow

Clumps upright. Stems stout and branched, numerous. Leaves alternate, blue-green, egg-shaped, with pointed tip, clasping lower part of stem. Inflorescence consists of a crowded spike on upper stems. Flowers bright yellow, 1–2 in. long, 5-lobed with orange or white fuzzy beard on lower 2 lobes, and with ⅓–¾ in. long, straight, downward-pointed spur at back. Grows in disturbed soils, along roads, at low elevations. A garden escapee originating from the Mediterranean, this is the tallest toadflax in our region. Listed as a noxious and invasive weed. Nonnative MORA, NOCA

Linaria vulgaris SCROPHULARIACEAE
Common toadflax, butter and eggs
Common, midspring, perennial, 12–35 in. Disturbed, meadow

Stems erect, branched or unbranched, solitary or small clumps. Leaves linear, green to gray-green, opposite, crowded along stem, sessile. Flowers in dense cluster, more or less glandular atop stems. Flower yellow with orange hairy beard on lower lip, straight spur pointing downward. Grows in damp areas along roads and other disturbed places at low elevations, where it is a noxious weed. Nonnative OLYM, MORA, NOCA

Mimulus alsinoides SCROPHULARIACEAE
Chickweed monkeyflower
Locally common, late spring, annual, to 6 in.
Coastal, vernal-wet, meadow, west-side forest

Tiny plant with erect stem. Leaf oval to round.
Flower on short stalk; calyx with 2 lower lobes
widely rounded, 3 upper lobes smaller, with
pointed tips, finely hairy. Flower bright yellow
with large red spot on center lower lobe,
smaller dots going into throat. Grows in shady places in mosses
and moist banks at low to mid elevations. Native
OLYM, MORA, NOCA, CRLA

Mimulus dentatus SCROPHULARIACEAE
Tooth-leaved monkeyflower
Locally common, all summer, perennial,
6–15 in. Coastal, west-side forest

Ascending, hairy. Leaves bright green, 1–2½
in. long, strongly toothed. Flowers yellow,
about 1 in. across, noticeably 2-lipped, expanding out from rotund funnel-shaped tube.
Grows along coastal streams, wet shady places,
from coastline to 1300 ft. Native OLYM

Mimulus floribundus
SCROPHULARIACEAE
Purple-stemmed monkeyflower
Uncommon, all summer, annual, 1–20 in.
Moist streambanks, east-side forest, alpine,
subalpine

Creeping or climbing, hairy, often slimy. Stems purplish.
Leaves oval, rounded at base, toothed. Flower
together with its long stalk is longer than
leaves, yellow with red spots in throat. Grows
in wet seeps, crevices, especially on granite,
along streams, at mid elevations, higher in the
south. Native NOCA

See other *Mimulus*: orange, page 300; red, page 370

243

Mimulus guttatus

SCROPHULARIACEAE

Seep-spring monkeyflower, common western monkeyflower, seep monkeyflower
Common, all summer, annual or perennial, 3–36 in. Vernal-wet, bog/fen/wetland, west-side forest

Spreading to upright. Stems fleshy. Leaves oval to round, irregularly toothed, with pointed tip; upper leaves sessile, more or less clasping stem. Flower stalks ¼–3 in. long, usually 5 or more yellow flowers near top of flower stem. Flower lower lobes have large to small red dots in throat area; upper lobes plain, smaller. Grows in all types of wet places from near coastline to mid elevations in mountains. Native OLYM, MORA, NOCA, **L&C**

Mimulus moschatus

SCROPHULARIACEAE
Musk monkeyflower
Locally common, all summer, perennial, 3–12 in. Coastal, vernal-wet, disturbed, subalpine

Musky-scented, shiny to hairy, usually slimy. Stems prostrate to ascending. Leaves oblong, entire. Flower stalks with flowers are longer than leaves. Flowers have 5 equal lobes, deep grooves in the narrow tube floor, and red dots or lines in throat. Grows in wet places, along streams, usually in part shade, at low to subalpine elevations. Native OLYM, MORA, NOCA, CRLA

Mimulus primuloides

SCROPHULARIACEAE
Primrose monkeyflower
Uncommon, midsummer, perennial, to 5 in. Bog/fen/wetland, moist streambanks, meadow

Dense mats of leaves bearing erect thin stems. Leaves shiny or covered with slimy white hairs. Subsp. *linearifolius* has long, thin, erect leaves, flowering stems to 5 in. Subsp. *primuloides* has oval to round leaves in rosettes, short flower stems. Both subspecies have rigid leafless stems, single erect flowers. Flowers yellow, lobes widely spreading, tips notched, 3 lower lobes each with red dot at throat. Grows in wet seeps, edges of streams, at mid to high elevations. Native OLYM, NOCA

Mimulus tilingii
SCROPHULARIACEAE
Mountain monkeyflower, Tiling's monkeyflower
Uncommon, all summer, perennial, 2–8 in.
Alpine, subalpine

Small mat, not spreading by stolons, hairless. Leaves opposite, oval to round, stalkless but not clasping stem, shorter than flower stems. Flowers on single stems in leaf axils at top, about 1 in. long with unequal, deeply divided lobes, throat spotted with red. Grows in seeps, wet meadows, at mid to high elevations in mountains. Easily confused with *M. guttatus*, which has stolons, usually more obvious red dots on throat, and grows only to mid elevations. In areas where they come together they sometimes hybridize. Native OLYM, MORA, NOCA

Mimulus washingtonensis
SCROPHULARIACEAE
Washington monkeyflower
Uncommon, early summer, annual, 2–6 in.
East-side forest, shrub-steppe

Erect stem with many branches, coated with finely stemmed glands. Leaves egg-shaped, shallowly toothed, with petioles as long as blades. Flower stalks ascending about 1 in. Calyx with ridges; flower widely bell-shaped, with fine hairs in throat, yellow with few brown-red spots but no central blotch; lobes all rounded, with lower lobes longer. Grows in moist sandy soil in valleys, occasionally ranging higher. Native

Orthocarpus luteus   SCROPHULARIACEAE
Yellow owl's clover
Locally common, midsummer, annual, 4–16 in.
Meadow, east-side forest, shrub-steppe

Stem straight, erect, seldom branched, yellow-green, sometimes tinted purple and covered with small glands, with long, coarse, stiff hairs. Leaves dark green, long, thin, with pointed tip, drying to blackish; upper leaves deeply lobed. Flower spike narrow; bracts divided into 3 pointed lobes, with central lobe largest. Flowers golden yellow, extending beyond bracts. Grows in moist meadows, sagebrush openings, at high elevations. Native

See other *Orthocarpus*: red, page 372   **245**

Parentucellia viscosa

SCROPHULARIACEAE

Yellow parentucellia

Locally common, late spring, annual, 12–25 in. Coastal, vernal-wet, disturbed, meadow

Erect, hairy. Stems unbranched. Leaves opposite, stemless, with lance-shaped blade, heavily veined, toothed. Flower spike narrow, at top. Flower tube about same length as calyx. Flower yellow, 1 in. long, sticky-hairy; 2 lips, upper lip short, lower lip longer with 3 distinct lobes leading to 2 ridges on tube floor. A Mediterranean weed found in moist pastures, grassy sites, along coast and Columbia River. Nonnative OLYM

Pedicularis bracteosa

SCROPHULARIACEAE

Towering lousewort, wood betony

Common, midsummer, perennial, 1–4 ft. Meadows, west-side forest, east-side forest, alpine, subalpine

Stem erect, no basal leaves. Leaves alternate, widely oval blade 1–6 in., finely divided to center, double-toothed, fern-like. Inflorescence is a 2–7 in. long, densely hairy spike. Bracts sharply pointed, nearly as long as or longer than flowers. Flowers greenish yellow tinted purple or red (especially in northern Washington), larger upper lobe more or less straight, hooded, beakless or with short straight beak at tip. Grows in damp forests, meadows, at mid and high elevations. The tallest *Pedicularis* in the Northwest. Native OLYM, MORA, NOCA

Pedicularis rainierensis

SCROPHULARIACEAE

Mount Rainier lousewort

Endemic, early summer, perennial, 6–16 in. Alpine, subalpine

Cluster of erect hairless stems with basal leaves. Leaves lance-shaped, cut to many toothed segments, stem leaves few, smaller. Inflorescence dense with leaf-like bracts shorter than flowers. Flowers yellow to cream, upper lip of flower gently curving, tip beakless or with short straight beak, lower lobes small, flower throat large. Grows only in a few locations within Mount Rainier National Park on moist, north-facing, subalpine and alpine slopes, often near streams. Native MORA

See other *Pedicularis*: white, page 147; red, page 373

Penstemon confertus

SCROPHULARIACEAE
Yellow penstemon
Locally common, late spring, all summer,
perennial, 8–20 in. Moist streambanks,
meadow, east-side forest

Mats small with upright stems. Leaves lance-shaped, light green, entire. Dense whorls of flowers atop stems. Flowers small, light yellow to cream, purple markings or spots on inside, staminode bearded. Grows in moist meadows, forest openings, at mid elevations. *Confertus* means "dense" or "crowded," referring to the whorls of flowers. Native MORA, NOCA

Rhinanthus minor subsp. *minor* (*Rhinanthus crista-galli*)

SCROPHULARIACEAE
Yellow rattle, little rattlebox
Locally common, early summer, annual,
10–30 in. Meadow

Stems erect, leafy, sometimes branched. Plant slightly hairy. Leaves opposite, sessile, 1–3 in. long, lance-shaped, with pointed tip, deeply toothed. Flowers among leaves. Flower calyx inflated like a green balloon with a small yellow flower emerging; upper lip hood-like over 3 lobes below. Seeds inside enlarged calyx rattle when dry. Grows in moist fields, meadows, at low elevations. Circumboreal. Native MORA

Triphysaria eriantha subsp. *eriantha* (*Orthocarpus erianthus*)

SCROPHULARIACEAE
Butter and eggs
Common, all spring, annual, 4–12 in.
Meadow, shrub-steppe

Erect, purplish or reddish, with fine hairs and glistening glands. Leaves green, divided into 3–5 lobes; upper leaves, bracts tipped red. Inflorescence is a dense head of deep yellow club-shaped flowers; lower lip consists of 3 deep pouches. Grows in large masses in grasslands and foothills. Native

See other *Penstemon*: white, page 147; red, page 375; blue, page 427
See other *Triphysaria*: red, page 376

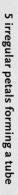

Verbascum blattaria
SCROPHULARIACEAE
Moth mullein
Common, all summer, biennial, 1–4 ft.
Coastal, disturbed, meadow, west-side
forest, east-side forest

Erect, sometimes branched stem from rosette of leaves. Basal leaves bright green, lance-shaped, to 10 in. long, toothed, with rounded tips, on short petioles; few small stem leaves sessile. Long spike of stalked flowers atop stems. Flowers yellow or white, flat, about 1 in. across, stamen filaments densely coated with purple hairs. Grows in fields, along roads, disturbed places, at low and mid elevations. Nonnative OLYM, NOCA

Verbascum thapsus
SCROPHULARIACEAE
Woolly mullein
Common, all summer, biennial, 4–6 ft.
Disturbed, meadow

Erect, sturdy, unbranched flowering stem grows out of first year's basal rosette, all parts covered with white-woolly hairs. Leaves thick, 4–15 in. long, oblong, entire, carried on very short, winged stalks. Inflorescence is a long spike, very dense, with just a few flowers in bloom at a time. Grows in disturbed areas at low to mid elevations. Sometimes distorted when sprayed with chemicals, especially along roads. Nonnative OLYM, MORA, NOCA

Lithospermum californicum BORAGINACEAE
California puccoon
Uncommon, late spring, perennial, 5–18 in.
West-side forest, east-side forest, shrub-
steppe

Many robust stems spreading, then ascending upward. Plant covered with coarse, sharp-pointed, spreading hairs. Leaves widely linear to oval, smaller near bottom of stem than those in middle. Flowers scattered in leaf axils on upper stem, most in small loose cluster at top. Flower small, long golden yellow tube, petals widely spreading. Grows on open slopes, sparsely treed woods in Siskiyou Mountains in Oregon and California. Native

Lithospermum ruderale
BORAGINACEAE
Columbia puccoon, western gromwell
Locally common, late spring–early summer,
perennial, 8–20 in. Disturbed, west-side forest,
east-side forest, shrub-steppe

Erect or spreading stems from large root base.
Stems robust, not branched in lower section.
Stems and leaves covered with coarse, rough,
spreading hairs. Leaves 1–3 in. long, linear to narrowly lance-shaped, crowded especially on upper part of stems. Inflorescence consists of many dense clusters of numerous pale yellow to greenish yellow flowers held in upper leaves. Grows in dry hillsides, open areas, open forests, at low and mid elevations. Native NOCA

Oxalis corniculata   OXALIDACEAE
Creeping wood sorrel, creeping yellow oxalis
Common, all year long, annual or perennial,
½–1 in. Disturbed, meadow

Prostrate creeping perennial. Plant maroon to
green, with deep fleshy taproot, will resprout
if broken in soil. Stems lie on soil and root at
nodes. Leaves along stem on petioles, divided
into 3 nearly round leaflets. Cluster of 2–7
flowers, deep yellow petals up to ¼ in. A pernicious, abundant weed in lawns and gardens, naturalized at all elevations except alpine. Nonnative OLYM, NOCA

Oxalis suksdorfii   OXALIDACEAE
Western yellow oxalis, Suksdorf's wood sorrel
Locally common, late spring–midsummer,
perennial, 4–12 in. West-side forest, east-side
forest

Trailing but not rooting at nodes or erect, more
or less hairy. Leaves on stem with petiole less
than 2 in., divided into 3 leaflets, each less than
¾ in. Flower single or 2–3 loosely clustered.
Petals ½–¾ in. long, bright yellow. Grows in
dry woods and shrubby areas at low elevations.
Rare in Washington. Native OLYM

See other *Oxalis*: white, page 158

Navarretia breweri POLEMONIACEAE
Yellow-flowered navarretia
Locally common, early summer, annual, 1–3
in. Meadow, alpine, subalpine

Mat of densely branched stems. Stems coated with tiny fine hairs. Leaves gray-green, alternate, deeply lobed to needle-like segments. Flower heads surrounded with leaf-like bracts, lobes all equal in size, prickly tips. Flower composed of long yellow tube, 4–5 lobes; stamens exserted, held in calyx with prickly-tipped lobes. Grows in open wet meadows, along streams, at mid to high elevations. Native

Polemonium carneum POLEMONIACEAE
**Salmon polemonium, royal polemonium,
great Jacob's ladder**
Locally common, early summer, perennial,
to 36 in. Meadow, west-side forest

Clumps more or less erect. Plant covered with tiny hairs. Stems leafy. Leaves opposite along stems becoming small upward, divided into lance-shaped leaflets, the uppermost leaflets fused to 2 just below. Flowers 3–7 in open bell-shaped cluster, petals and tube about same length, usually peach, sometimes lavender or white. Grows in openings of moist to dry woods, forests, from sea level to mid elevations. Native OLYM

Lonicera involucrata CAPRIFOLIACEAE
Black twinberry, bearberry honeysuckle, bush honeysuckle
Locally common, early summer, perennial,
3–9 ft. Bog/fen/wetland, meadow, west-side
forest, east-side forest

Spreading to erect shrub. Young stems square. Stem and leaves with glands, few hairs. Leaves opposite, egg-shaped, with pointed tip, 1–5 in. long, short petioles. Flowers in pairs, yellow, trumpet-shaped, with 5 lobes, surrounded by 2 pairs of large green to purple bracts. Berries 2, shiny black, in enlarged bright purplish or red bracts. Grows in moist forests, along streams, swamps, at all elevations except alpine. Var. *involucrata* is a 3–6 ft. widespread shrub with anthers exerted or equal the lobes. Var. *ledebourii* is a shrub to 12 ft. with anthers inside the tube; grows in Coast Range. Native OLYM, MORA, NOCA, CRLA, **L&C**

See other *Navarretia*: white, page 160
See other *Polemonium*: blue, page 444
See other *Lonicera*: orange, page 301; red, page 387

Lonicera utahensis CAPRIFOLIACEAE
Utah honeysuckle
Locally common, early summer, perennial, 3–6
ft. Bog/fen/wetland, west-side forest, east-side
forest, subalpine

Shrub with spreading branches. Leaves oblong
to lance-shaped, with rounded tip, few hairs
only on underside. Flowers in pairs on single
slender stalk to ½ in. long, bracts very small.
Flowers white or pale yellow fading to salmon yellow, trumpet-
shaped. Berries small, red, round, slightly fused. Grows in
bogs, along streams, moist places, at mid to subalpine elevations. Native

OLYM, NOCA, **L&C**

Ribes aureum GROSSULARIACEAE
Golden currant
Locally common, all spring, perennial, 3–9 ft.
Moist streambanks, east-side forest, shrub-
steppe

Upright woody shrub without spines on young
branches. Leaves 1–2 in. across, nearly round,
entire or toothed, with glands when young.
Flowers clustered, 5–15, spreading to hanging,
often spicy-fragrant. Sepal lobes more or less
¼ in. long. Petals small in flower center, turning orange or red
with pollination. Berries bitter, shiny red, orange, or black.
Grows in moist woods, along streams. Native **L&C**

Artemisia absinthium ASTERACEAE (anthemis tribe)
Wormwood, absinthium
Locally common, all summer, perennial, 1–4 ft.
Disturbed, meadow, east-side forest, shrub-
steppe

Stems in erect clusters, branched. Leaves gray
with silky hairs, pungent-smelling, lacy in appearance, widely oval, pinnately divided to
midvein into wide lobes, divided again or
toothed. Inflorescence consists of a large pyramid of leaves and stalks holding many nodding
flower heads, each dull yellow-green head with
30–50 small disk flowers. Grows in open dry places. Foliage
scent repels insects. Nonnative OLYM, NOCA

See other *Ribes*: white, page 165; orange, page 302; red, page 388

Artemisia dracunculus

ASTERACEAE (anthemis tribe)

Tarragon, dragon sagewort

Common, all summer, perennial, 2–4 ft.
Disturbed, meadow

Stiff, erect, nearly odorless to strongly tarra-
gon-aromatic. Stems brown. Leaves bright
green, on upper and lower stem, ½–3 in.,
linear to oblong, entire or occasionally di-
vided, hairless. Inflorescence 6–18 in. long, with many leaves at
base of several upright branches. Panicle consists of numerous, small, nodding, yellowish white, button-shaped flowers.
Grows in meadows, disturbed soils. Similar *A. campestris* is
shorter, 4–15 in., always odorless, with basal leaf rosette. Native
NOCA, **L&C**

Artemisia lindleyana

ASTERACEAE (anthemis tribe)

**Riverbank wormwood, Columbia River
wormwood**

Locally common, late summer, perennial,
8–30 in. Moist streambanks

Erect stems rising from woody base, with
few clusters of small leaves. Leaves lance-
shaped to linear, 1–2 in. long, may be lobed
and toothed or entire, covered with white hairs beneath, hairless above. Flower heads on branches form narrow spike; small
bell-shaped cups lightly coated with matted hairs hold ray and
disk florets. Grows along shores of rivers, streams, below high
water mark in Columbia River Gorge and elsewhere. Native

Artemisia ludoviciana

ASTERACEAE (anthemis tribe)

**Gray sagewort, silver wormwood, western
mugwort**

Common, all summer, perennial, 12–40 in.
Meadow, shrub-steppe

Erect, aromatic. Stems many, unbranched,
gray to white with matted hairs. Leaves linear to elliptical, ½–4 in. long, covered with
white matted hairs, entire to deeply divided.
Flower panicle to 12 in. with short branches holding generally
nodding flower heads. Flower heads include small cups
densely covered with small hairs, bearing tiny flowers. Grows
in dry rocky or sandy soil below 6000 ft. Var. *ludoviciana* has entire or shallowly lobed leaves. Var. *latiloba* has deeply divided
leaves with narrow lobes. Native OLYM, MORA, NOCA, CRLA, **L&C**

Artemisia michauxiana

ASTERACEAE (anthemis tribe)
Michaux' mugwort, lemon sagwort
Uncommon, all summer, perennial, 8–16 in.
Alpine, subalpine

Erect, lemon-scented. Stems green, many, unbranched. Leaves about 1 in. long, narrow, divided twice, often with small teeth, matted white hairs on the underside; top side hairless, green, dotted with yellow glands. Flower spikes narrow, 3–6 in. tall with nodding flower heads. Flower cup purplish, dotted with yellow glands, hairless. Grows in subalpine to alpine areas, rocky places, talus, scree, drainages, to 12,000 ft. *Artemisia tilesii*, mountain wormwood, does not smell of lemon, has leaves 2–6 in. long. Native NOCA

Artemisia rigida

ASTERACEAE (anthemis tribe)
Stiff sagebrush, scabland sagebrush
Locally common, late summer–autumn,
perennial, to 24 in. Shrub-steppe

Low mounding shrub, strongly scented. Stems woody, yellowish, hairy when young, becoming gray and shredding with age. Leaves deciduous, silver with dense short white hairs, ½–1½ in. long, wider at tip, divided into 3–5 narrow lobes, or entire, long and thin. Inflorescence with leaves and bracts of bell-shaped, gray-haired cup surrounding and extending well beyond the flowers. Grows in dry rocky steppe lands, where it becomes dominant species. Native

Artemisia suksdorfii

ASTERACEAE (anthemis tribe)
Suksdorf's sagewort, coastal mugwort
Uncommon, all summer, perennial, 2–4 ft.
Coastal, moist streambanks

Stems many, stiffly erect, brown. Leaves sessile, elliptic to lance-shaped, 2–4 in. long, coarsely lobed; dark green and hairless above; gray with short, intermingled matted hairs beneath. Flower panicle erect, 7–12 in. long, with upright branches, dense with many flower heads, usually leafless. Flowers small in upright narrow cups. Grows in coastal drainages, along roads, ditches and other wet places, at low elevations. Mugwort, *A. douglasiana*, is similar in size and color but with leaves lobed only near the tips. Native OLYM

Artemisia tridentata

ASTERACEAE (anthemis tribe)

Big sagebrush

Common, late summer–autumn, perennial, 3–6½ ft. East-side forest, shrub-steppe

Mounding shrub. Stems from thick woody trunk, hairless. Leaves are small, wedge-shaped, with 3 teeth on the wide tip, gray-green, hairs dense; most remain attached throughout year. Flower spikes erect or drooping, densely hairy, small leaves at base. Flower heads small, yellow, with hairy bracts, sometimes surrounded by leaves. Grows in fertile, dry to moist, mildly basic soils at all elevations. State flower of Nevada. The common large sagebrush east of Cascades throughout our region. Subsp. *vaseyana*, mountain sagebrush, with erect branches to 3½ ft., grows at mid to alpine elevations. Subsp. *tridentata*, also called big sagebrush, grows to 6½ ft., with spreading branches, grows in valleys at low and mid elevations. Similar *A. arbuscula* has lobed stem leaves. Native NOCA, CRLA, **L&C**

Cotula coronopifolia

ASTERACEAE (anthemis tribe)

Brass buttons

Common, all year long, perennial, 5–15 in. Coastal

Mat sprawling, prostrate, rooting at nodes, strong-smelling. Leaves fleshy, sessile, clasping all the way around stem to form a sheath; lower leaves divided into few linear lobes; upper leaves undivided, sometimes toothed. Flower heads consisting of ¼–¾ in. hard buttons of disk flowers. Introduced from South Africa. Common along beaches, in salt- and freshwater marshes, the length of our region. Compare to native *Jaumea carnosa*, which grows in same tidal flat habitat. Nonnative OLYM

Hymenopappus filifolius

ASTERACEAE (anthemis tribe)

Columbia cut leaf

Uncommon, late spring, perennial, 1–2 ft. Shrub-steppe

Tuft, densely hairy to hairless. Stems erect. Leaves oblong, divided into linear or thread-like leaflets, stiff hairs and sticky glands on upper sides. Basal leaves in rosette; stem leaves few, alternate. Flower heads few to many at top, often several per stem. Disk flowers 10–70, yellow or white, cup with sticky glands. Grows in dry places, sometimes on limestone. Flowers stay open in sunny or cloudy weather. Native

Matricaria discoidea (*Matricaria matricariodes, Chamomilla suaveolens*)
ASTERACEAE (anthemis tribe)
Pineapple weed
Common, all spring and summer, annual,
2–10 in. Disturbed, meadow

Erect, multibranched, hairless annual. When crushed has strong pineapple scent. Leaves to 2 in. long, deeply pinnately divided into many linear segments. Flower heads 1 or many on 1–2 in. stalks. Heads with very short or no ray flowers, cone of disk flowers yellow-green. Grows in moist waste places, cultivated soils, riverbanks. A common North American and European weed but a Pacific Northwest native. Native OLYM, MORA, NOCA

Tanacetum camphoratum
ASTERACEAE (anthemis tribe)
Dune tansy
Uncommon, all summer, perennial, 4–10 in.
Coastal

Stout, prostrate. Stems round, not ribbed, tips growing upward, covered with white-woolly hairs. Leaves 4–10 in. long, clasping, thick, oval, dissected 2 or 3 times to many leaflets with edges curled under and covered with glands. Flat-topped clusters contain 3–15 rayless, yellow, button-like flower heads. Grows on coastal dunes. Native OLYM

Tanacetum vulgare (*Chrysanthemum uliginosum, Chrysanthemun vulgare*) ASTERACEAE (anthemis tribe)
Common tansy
Locally common, late summer–autumn,
perennial, 24–40 in.
Coastal, disturbed, meadow

Erect, from rhizomes forming dense colonies. Stems ridged, branched, leafy, with pungent odor. Leaves 1–2 in. wide, dotted with glands but hairless. Leaves pinnately divided into pairs of leaflets that divide into sharply toothed lobes. Flower heads 20–200, held in dense flat-topped clusters, small disk flower buttons, no ray flowers. Grows in fields, along roads and other urban areas, at low elevations. Can cause skin irritation. Nonnative OLYM, MORA, NOCA

Columbiadoria hallii (*Haplopappus hallii*) ASTERACEAE (aster tribe)
Hall's goldenweed
Uncommon, late summer–autumn, perennial, 1–2 ft. Meadows, east-side forest, shrub-steppe

Shrub that smells like pine sap and is very sticky. Stalks branched, with woody base and erect annual stems. Leaves 1–2 in. long, oval, entire, stiff, rough. Lowest leaves with short petioles; upper leaves sessile. Flower heads numerous, on short stalks, held in narrow, hard, very sticky cups. Ray flowers 5–8, narrow, horizontal or slightly recurved, surrounding 15–25 disk flowers. Grows in rocky sites. Native

Ericameria bloomeri (*Haplopappus bloomeri*) ASTERACEAE (aster tribe)
Rabbitbush goldenweed
Locally common, late summer, perennial, 8–24 in. East-side forest, subalpine

Shrubby, with erect new growth, hairless to slightly woolly or with glands. Leaves thread-like, to 1–3 in., with pointed tip. Flower heads crowded at stem tips. Flower head has 1–5 ray flowers to ½ in. long, 4–13 disk flowers. Grows in open gravelly or rocky places in conifer forests at mid to high elevations. Native

Ericameria discoidea ASTERACEAE (aster tribe)
Discoid goldenweed
Locally common, midsummer, perennial, 4–15 in. Alpine, subalpine

Upright shrub. Stems, twigs white-woolly. Leaves oblong, 1/3–1½ in. long, sessile, coated with gland-tipped hairs. Flower heads in clusters at stem tops, bell-shaped cup created by 2–3 rows of bracts covered with gland-tipped hairs. Flowers composed of 10–26 yellow disk flowers, no ray flowers. Grows on dry rocky slopes, outcrops, at high elevations. *Discoid* refers to the head being composed entirely of disk flowers. *Ericameria humilis* is similar, with leafy stems, leafy-looking cup not sticky, 2–4¼ in. pale yellow ray flowers. Native

See other *Ericameria*: white, page 170

Ericameria nauseosa (*Chrysothamnus nauseosus*) ASTERACEAE (aster tribe)
Gray rabbitbrush, rubber rabbitbush
Common, late summer–autumn, perennial,
1–6 ft. East-side forest, shrub-steppe

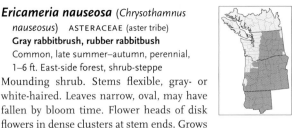

Mounding shrub. Stems flexible, gray- or white-haired. Leaves narrow, oval, may have fallen by bloom time. Flower heads of disk flowers in dense clusters at stem ends. Grows in dry soils in many habitats below 10,500 ft. Subsp. *nauseosa* var. *hololeuca* grows with sagebrush below 1700 ft.; leaves retain white, dense, woolly hairs. Subsp. *consimilis* var. *oreophila* grows on poorly drained alkaline soils; leaves lose all hairs by maturity. Subsp. *nauseosa* var. *speciosa* common at all elevations with twigs hairless or with few short, never tangled hairs. In autumn plants are showy; large stands on plains or hills glow with color. *Nauseosus* means "strong-smelling." Plant identifiable by strong odor. Native **L&C**

Ericameria viscidiflora (*Chrysothamnus viscidiflorus*) ASTERACEAE (aster tribe)
Laceleaf green rabbitbrush
Common, late summer, perennial, to 5 ft.
East-side forest, shrub-steppe

Shrub with some hairs on stems and leaves. Stems upright and brittle, white below, green above. Leaves pale green, very narrow to slightly oblong, flat or twisted. Disk flowers 3–13, bright yellow, in tight sticky heads extending well above leaves. Grows in dry rocky soils of much of the west above 3000 ft. Subsp. *lanceolata*, with bristly hairs under flower head, has lance-shaped leaves rough-haired on underside. Native **L&C**

Erigeron aphanactis
ASTERACEAE (aster tribe)
Rayless shaggy fleabane, basin rayless daisy
Locally common, late spring–early summer,
biennial or perennial, 3–10 in. Shrub-steppe

Densely matted. Stems covered in spreading, stiff hairs. Basal leaves 2–3 in., with varied petiole lengths, toothed, with stiff hairs; few stem leaves decreasing in size, sessile at top. Flower heads are large, rayless, bright yellow disks. Grows in dry hot places among sagebrush or juniper scrub at 4000–8500 ft. Native

See other *Erigeron*: white, page 171; red, page 391; blue, page 453   **257**

Erigeron aureus
ASTERACEAE (aster tribe)
Alpine gold daisy, golden fleabane
Uncommon, midsummer, perennial, 2–6 in.
Alpine, subalpine

Tuft of basal leaves, erect stem holding large flower. Leaves oblong to round. Basal leaves to ½ in. long with some soft hairs, varied petiole lengths; stem leaves few, much smaller, sessile. Single flower head to 1 in., golden yellow, with 25–70 rays ¼–⅝ in. long, yellow disk, green in center. Pink to purple hairs on bracts just under flower heads. Grows in rocky ridges, pumice slopes, in alpine and subalpine. Native
MORA, NOCA

Erigeron bloomeri
ASTERACEAE (aster tribe)
Scabland fleabane, Bloomer's daisy
Uncommon, all summer, perennial, 2–6 in.
Shrub-steppe

Stems erect, with dense, white, appressed hairs. Leaves in basal cluster, long and narrow, hairless or with fine white hairs. Flower heads solitary, ¼–¾ in., with hairy bracts under disk flowers; no ray flowers. Grows in exposed stony soils at mid to higher elevations, sometimes on serpentine. Var. *nudatus*, from Waldo in southwestern Oregon, has very fine hairs on cup at base of flower heads; leaves, both hairless and with stiff, straight, sharp hairs, arise from same roots in some plants. Native

Erigeron chrysopsidis
ASTERACEAE (aster tribe)
Dwarf golden daisy
Uncommon, midsummer, perennial, 2–6 in.
Meadow, east-side forest, shrub-steppe, subalpine

Tuft of basal leaves, naked stems. Leaves 1–3 in. long, very narrow, covered with hairs either spreading or pressed against leaf surface. Flowers held singly above leaves, 1 in. across, 20–50 ray flowers, each about ½ in. long. Grows in dry open areas with sagebrush and up into subalpine zone to 6000 ft. Smaller, compact var. *brevifolius*, found in Wallowa Mountains, is endemic to eastern Oregon and Washington in a small area along the state border extending up to 9500 ft. Smaller, rayless var. *austiniae* is found from central Oregon to the south and east. Native

Erigeron linearis
ASTERACEAE (aster tribe)
Desert yellow daisy, lineleaf fleabane
Locally common, all summer, perennial,
2–12 in. Meadow, shrub-steppe

Tuft of stems and very narrow leaves. Stem
bases sometimes tinted yellow or purple.
Leaves gray, with stiff white hairs pressed to
surface. Basal leaves 1–4 in., linear; few stem
leaves are similar, smaller, sessile. Flower heads ⅓ in. across,
held individually at stem top above leaves, 25–45 yellow ray
flowers, yellow disk. Grows in grasslands, sagebrush, on open
rocky slopes, at mid to high elevations. Native

Euthamia occidentalis (*Solidago occidentalis*)
ASTERACEAE (aster tribe)
Western goldenrod
Common, late summer, perennial, 3–6 ft.
Bog/fen/wetland, meadow, west-side forest,
east-side forest

Erect, with single or few stems branched near
top. Leaves alternate, narrow and grass-like,
largest at midstem, sessile. Leaf edges are dotted with resin, making them feel rough. Flower
heads in large clusters of panicles, at top of ascending branches, deep yellow, slightly sticky with resin. Each
flower head is about ¼ in. across, with 15–25 ray flowers.
Grows in ditches, damp meadows, along streams, below 7500
ft. Native

Grindelia columbiana ASTERACEAE (aster tribe)
Columbia River gumweed
Locally common, all summer, biennial,
12–30 in. Vernal-wet, moist streambanks

Erect, shiny, usually branching stems. Leaves
to 4 in. long, narrow, wider toward rounded tip,
entire or with few small teeth; upper leaves
clasping stem. Flower heads about 1 in. across,
disk flowers with no rays. Slightly gummy
bracts at base are recurved. Grows in vernal
ponds, along streams, in sandy soils, along
river shores. Native

Grindelia integrifolia

ASTERACEAE (aster tribe)

Willamette valley gumweed, Puget Sound gumplant

Locally common, all summer, perennial, 12–30 in. Coastal, meadow

Erect to decumbent. Stems stout, several, somewhat hairy. Leaves in basal tuft and on stem, to 14 in. long, entire or slightly toothed, with long pointed tips, heart-shaped at base; stem leaves alternate, clasping. Flower heads single to several on leafy stalks. Sticky cup bracts have long, thin, spreading tips that recurve. Flower heads 1–2 in. across, with 10–35 yellow ray flowers, yellow disk flowers. Grows in salt marshes, wet meadows. Native OLYM

Grindelia nana ASTERACEAE (aster tribe)

Idaho gumweed, low gumweed

Locally common, all summer, perennial, 12–35 in. East-side forest, shrub-steppe

Erect stems branching from base, copper-red or yellowish but not varnished-looking. Leaves on stem, narrowly oblong, 1–3½ in. long, finely toothed or entire; upper leaves sessile. Flower heads in wide, sticky, bell-shaped cups created of bracts with tips rolled back into circle; 11–28 ray flowers surrounding disk of 20–50 flowers. Grows on dry sandy hills, along roads or dry fields, at low to mid elevations. Native

Gutierrezia sarothrae ASTERACEAE (aster tribe)

Match brush, snakeweed

Common, autumn, perennial, 8–18 in. Meadow, shrub-steppe

Erect small shrub. Stems sprawling to upright, branching, brown at base and green above, gummy. Leaves alternate on stem, narrow to thread-like, sometimes in clusters. Inflorescence single or in small clusters of flower heads, each head with 6–14 flowers. Ray flowers 2–8, disk flowers 2–9. Grows in grasslands, deserts, mountains, in all elevations. Native L&C

Heterotheca villosa (*Chrysopsis villosa*)
ASTERACEAE (aster tribe)
Hairy goldaster, hairy goldenaster
Locally common, all summer–autumn,
perennial, 6–30 in. Shrub-steppe

Spreading to erect. Stems sparsely covered in
bristly hairs. Leaves oblong, basal, alternate on
stem, generally widest at tip end, rough with
glands on upper side, flat-edged, not wavy.
Flower heads 1 to many per stem, 7–30 yellow ray flowers ½ in.
long, many disk flowers. Grows in dry, gravelly or sandy soils,
crevices or lava flows, at low to high elevations. Variable plant
with many local forms. Most common var. *villosa* is without
glands except on inflorescence foliage. Native NOCA

Pyrrocoma carthamoides (*Haplopappus*
carthamoides)   ASTERACEAE (aster tribe)
Narrowhead goldenweed
Locally common, midsummer, perennial,
1–2 ft. Shrub-steppe

Erect stems stout. Leaves few, less than 2 in.
wide, in basal rosette, lance-shaped, with
pointed tip; stem leaves sessile. Inflorescence
at stem top, often single large flower, sometimes several. Flower consists of a cup of few
leafy bracts, lance-shaped and with papery edges; bristly hairs
fill center; yellow florets at edge are inconspicuous among
hairs. Grows in open prairies, hillsides. Var. *cusickii* is smaller,
3–16 in., with stems often decumbent, flower bracts of cup long
and narrow, with pointed tips and not overlapping; grows above
6000 ft. on barren rocky soils. Native

Pyrrocoma uniflora var. *uniflora*
(*Haplopappus uniflorus* var. *howellii*)
ASTERACEAE (aster tribe)
**One-flowered goldenweed, Howell's
goldenweed**
Locally common, all summer as water recedes,
perennial, 3–15 in. Bog/fen/wetland, meadow,
alpine, subalpine

Decumbent to ascending. Stems usually
tinged red. Leaves lance-shaped, coated with woolly hairs. Basal
leaves 1–5 in. long; few stem leaves shorter, clasping. Flower
heads usually single or to 4, cup bracts in 2 rows, leaf-like,
coated with fine to woolly hairs. Ray flowers yellow, 25–50, disk
flowers 60. Grows in alkaline meadows, marshes, mudflats,
near springs, at high elevations. Native

Solidago canadensis

ASTERACEAE (aster tribe)

Canada goldenrod, meadow goldenrod

Common, late summer–autumn, perennial, 2–5 ft. Coastal, meadow, west-side forest, east-side forest

Erect, tall, undivided stems from creeping root. Many stem leaves, middle ones largest. Leaves 2–5 in., lance-shaped, with fine even teeth. Lower leaves drop before bloom time. Inflorescence is large club-shaped cluster holding yellow flower heads. Flower heads in cups with sticky bracts, 10–13 short ray flowers around few disk flowers. Grows in meadows, thickets, at low to subalpine elevations. Prefers undisturbed places. Nonnative var. *salebrosa* grows on disturbed soils, has stem leaves all about same size, entire or slightly toothed, with flowers in dense pyramid-shaped cluster. Native OLYM, MORA, NOCA, CRLA

Solidago gigantea

ASTERACEAE (aster tribe)

Smooth goldenrod, late goldenrod

Rare, autumn, perennial, 2–5 ft. Moist streambanks, east-side forest

Erect, waxy, smooth stems hold smooth to slightly hairy leaves. Lance-shaped stem leaves are toothed. Largest leaves are 2–6 in. at midstem. Dense cluster of very waxy horizontal stalks at stem top, with many yellow flower heads held atop stalks. Ray flowers short, 8–15, about same number of disk flowers. Grows in streamsides, lakeshores, in moist soils. Much like the less shiny *S. canadensis* but less common. Native

Solidago missouriensis

ASTERACEAE (aster tribe)

Missouri goldenrod

Common, all summer, perennial, 8–20 in. Meadow, shrub-steppe

Erect stems in groups or tight clusters. Stems hairless below, sparsely hairy above. Basal leaves many, oblong, 2–8 in. long, entire or with few teeth, tapering into petioles edged with narrow wings; upper leaves short, linear, entire, sessile. Oblong inflorescence consists of erect to spreading branches with flowers arranged on 1 side. Flowers bear 8 petals, longer than cup. Grows in dry places in foothills, valleys. Native

Solidago multiradiata

ASTERACEAE (aster tribe)

Northern goldenrod, alpine goldenrod

Uncommon, all summer, perennial, 2–20 in.

Alpine, subalpine

Clump of leafy stems. Lower leaves 2–5 in., linear to spoon-shaped, with long straight hairs on shallow-toothed edges, short hairy petioles. Upper leaves much smaller, clasping. Leaf tips often point upward. Flower cluster at top dense, with 1 or 2 flower heads lower on stem. Flower heads have about 13 short ray flowers, 13–26 disk flowers. Grows in subalpine meadows, alpine. Native OLYM, MORA, NOCA

Stenotus acaulis (*Haplopappus acaulis*)

ASTERACEAE (aster tribe)

Stemless goldenweed

Locally common, all summer, perennial, 2–5 in.

Shrub-steppe, alpine, subalpine

Mat from short woody stems with persistent leaves. Leaves mostly at stem tips, oval, 1–4 in. long, with pointed tips, hairless or with short stiff hairs, sometimes sticky. Inflorescence consists of 2 or 3 rows of bracts creating a cup ⅓ in. across, 6–15 ray flowers to ½ in. long, 20 or more disk flowers. Grows in dry, rocky, open places in shrublands at high elevations. Native

Stenotus lanuginosus var. *lanuginosus* (*Haplopappus lanuginosus* var. *lanuginosus*) ASTERACEAE (aster tribe)

Woolly goldenweed, woolly stenotus

Uncommon, all summer, perennial, 1–6 in.

Meadow, east-side forest, subalpine

Small, often mat-forming, leaves crowded at branch tips. Linear leaves 1–4 in. long, entire, persisting for few years. Leaf densely to sparsely covered with short interwoven hairs, seldom glandular. Flower heads yellow, held individually, showy, with 7–20 ray flowers ⅓–½ in. long, center of 25–50 disk flowers. Grows in dry rocky soils, exposed places, from plains to subalpine. Native

Stenotus stenophyllus (*Haplopappus stenophyllus*)   ASTERACEAE (aster tribe)
Narrowleaf goldenweed
Uncommon, all summer, perennial, less than 6 in. Shrub-steppe

Mat to 16 in. across with perennial tiny leaves. Stems densely leafy. Leaves linear, less than ½ in. long, rough to touch with short glandular hairs. Flower heads held individually, 8–12 small ray flowers surrounding center of hairy disk flowers. Grows in rocky places, sagebrush scrub. Native

Tonestus lyallii (*Haplopappus lyallii*)
ASTERACEAE (aster tribe)
Lyall's goldenweed
Locally common, midsummer, perennial, 3–8 in. Alpine, subalpine

Upright stems from branched roots, plant coated with glands. Leaves spoon-shaped, ½–2 in. long, entire. Flowers in solitary head 1–2 in. across. Cup of lance-shaped, glandular, green or often purplish bracts. Ray and disk flowers yellow, numerous. Grows in alpine ridges, talus slopes, sandy places in subalpine. Native MORA, NOCA

Agoseris apargioides   ASTERACEAE (chicory tribe)
Seaside dandelion
Locally common, all summer, perennial, 4–10 in. Coastal

Basal tuft of leaves with erect stems, milky sap. Leaves pinnately lobed with narrow segments, lobe tips often rounded. Flowers yellow, single head with overlapping rows of square-tipped, toothed petals rising from wide cup of overlapping papery bracts 3–4 rows deep. Grows along coastline to 1500 ft. Although a native, resembles nonnative dandelion of gardens, lawns. Native OLYM

See other *Agoseris*: orange, page 302

Agoseris glauca   ASTERACEAE (chicory tribe)
Pale agoseris
Common, late summer, perennial, 8–20 in.
Meadow, west-side forest, east-side forest,
shrub-steppe, alpine, subalpine

Prostrate to erect. Basal tuft of erect leaves,
hairless or with soft white hairs. Leaves narrow,
lance-shaped, entire or slightly toothed or
lobed. Flower stem leafless, holds single head.
Ray flowers bright yellow. Grows in sagebrush scrub, conifer
forests, alpine slopes, at mid to high elevations. Torn leaf tis-
sues exude milky sap which when dried becomes rubber-like
and can be chewed as a bitter-tasting gum. Var. *glauca* leaves
are linear to widely oval, long, tapered, entire, hairless. Var.
laciniata has pinnately lobed leaves, the lobes pointing back to
center, rays lance-shaped and marked with red,
and grows in alpine areas. Var. *dasycephala* is
the only variety in subalpine and alpine areas
of northern Washington and British Columbia.
Native OLYM, MORA, NOCA

Agoseris grandiflora
ASTERACEAE (chicory tribe)
Large-flowered agoseris
Common, late spring–early summer, perennial,
10–35 in. Meadow, west-side forest

Dandelion-like, more than 10 in. tall, with soft white hairs
when young, hairless with age. Milky sap. Leaves linear to oblong, tips sharply pointed, entire to deeply lobed. Leaf lobes
point outward or toward tip. Single flower head on long bare
stalk, cup of overlapping papery bracts often reddish on exterior, many yellow petals, closing by noon on
sunny days, often drying to pinkish color.
Grows in meadows, woodlands, at low and mid
elevations. Easily confused with *Microseris borealis*, *M. bigelovii*, and *A. glauca* var. *laciniata*.
Native OLYM, MORA, NOCA

Agoseris heterophylla var. *heterophylla*
ASTERACEAE (chicory tribe)
Annual agoseris, woodland agoseris
Common, late spring–early summer, annual, 4–8 in. Coastal,
meadow, west-side forest

Slender, erect. Leaves in basal rosette, egg-shaped, widest at
top, covered with tiny, soft to rough, white hairs. Leaves vary
from entire to toothed or lobed; some leaves occur above basal
rosette. Inflorescence is a large calyx of 2 rows of bracts, with 5
to many yellow rays. Flowers open early morning, close in afternoon, often turning pink as they dry. Grows in many habitats
at low and mid elevations. Native OLYM, MORA, NOCA

Agoseris retrorsa

ASTERACEAE (chicory tribe)
Spearleaf agoseris
Uncommon, all summer, perennial, 4–20 in.
East-side forest, shrub-steppe

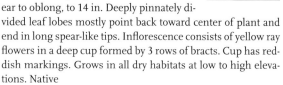

Erect plant, stout stems with soft white hairs especially on leaves and base of flower head. Exudes a milky sap. Leaves numerous, linear to oblong, to 14 in. Deeply pinnately divided leaf lobes mostly point back toward center of plant and end in long spear-like tips. Inflorescence consists of yellow ray flowers in a deep cup formed by 3 rows of bracts. Cup has reddish markings. Grows in all dry habitats at low to high elevations. Native
NOCA, CRLA

Crepis acuminata

ASTERACEAE (chicory tribe)
Longleaf hawksbeard, tapertip hawksbeard
Locally common, midspring, perennial,
8–28 in. Shrub-steppe

Stems erect, with milky sap. Basal leaves ascending, gray with interwoven matted hairs, 5–16 in. long, elliptic, divided into narrow, sharply pointed, triangular lobes, with long tapering tip. Flower heads 20–100 or more, small at top of branched stems; flower head with 5–10 ray flowers, cup narrow, hairless or with sparse hairs. Grows in gravelly to sandy soils throughout dry areas of our region. Similar *C. intermedia*, intermediate hawksbeard, with 7–12 flowers in a flower head and usually 10–60 heads on a full-grown plant, is unable to reproduce by seed. Usually considered a hybrid swarm. *Crepis pleurocarpa*, shorter with 5–8 flowers in a head, grows on dry open slopes or lightly wooded areas, often in serpentine, at low to mid elevations in the Klamath Mountains. Native

Crepis atribarba

ASTERACEAE (chicory tribe)
Slender hawksbeard
Common, late spring–early summer, perennial,
8–28 in. East-side forest, shrub-steppe

Stems 1–2 erect from base with narrow leaves. Stem gray, upper branches with few matted hairs, becoming less hairy with age. Basal leaves narrowing to winged petiole, 4–14 in. long. Leaf blade divided to center, with very slender untoothed lobes tapering to pointed tips. Stem leaves similar but sessile. Flower heads have about 65 yellow ray flowers. Grows in dry, grassy, open areas, pine forests in steppe. Native NOCA

Crepis capillaris ASTERACEAE (chicory tribe)
Smooth hawksbeard
Common, all summer, annual or biennial,
1–3 ft. Disturbed, meadow

Erect. Stem single, produces milky sap, branched usually only in upper ½, hairy near base. Basal leaves lance-shaped, to 12 in. long, dark shiny green, toothed or divided; upper leaves reduced in size, clasping stem. Flower heads in open cluster, with yellow flowers. Grows in waste places, meadows, roadsides, even lawns, at low to mid elevations. Nonnative OLYM, MORA, NOCA

Crepis modocensis ASTERACEAE (chicory tribe)
Modoc hawksbeard, low hawksbeard
Uncommon, late spring–early summer,
perennial, 4–15 in. Shrub-steppe

Low tuft with large basal leaves. Stems with few branches carry stiff straight hairs. Leaves 3–10 in. long, lightly covered with gray hairs and sparse yellow to black bristles, lobed into wide-toothed segments. Flower heads large, held singly or in small clusters at ends of short stems. Each head composed of 10–60 petals held in bristly cups. Grows in sagebrush on open dry slopes at mid to high elevations. Native

Crepis occidentalis ASTERACEAE (chicory tribe)
Western hawksbeard
Common, early summer, annual or perennial,
4–15 in. Meadow, shrub-steppe

Erect, densely gray with felt-like hairs. Leaves lobed and toothed much the same as the common dandelion. Basal leaves 12 in. long; stem leaves smaller, sessile. Stems branch into cymes with 12–30 flower heads; cups have short hairs with small glands at the ends, flowers 9–40. Grows in dry, rocky, open places, mostly in foothills and plains. Native
OLYM, NOCA

Crepis runcinata

ASTERACEAE (chicory tribe)

Meadow hawksbeard, dandelion hawksbeard

Locally common, late spring–early summer, perennial, 10–32 in. Vernal-wet, meadow

Erect. Stems branched, leafless. Basal leaves oval to lance-shaped, lobed, the lobes pointing back toward stem and sometimes with tiny teeth; stem leaves much smaller. Cymes of 10–30 flower heads. Flowers 20–50 in bell-shaped cup. Grows in moist soils, along streams, in low places. Often but not always found on alkaline soils. Native

Hieracium cynoglossoides

ASTERACEAE (chicory tribe)

Hound's-tongue hawkweed

Common, all summer, perennial, 1–4 ft. West-side forest, east-side forest

Upright with no stolons. Stems hairy. Basal leaves oblong, 3–10 in. long, entire, covered with soft to bristly hairs; stem leaves few, sessile, decreasing on upper stem. Flower heads 10–20 in open, branching cyme, each flower occurring on short stalk. Cup bracts short, blackish, with gland-tipped stiff hairs, 15–20 yellow, ray-like disk flowers. Grows in dry forests. Leaves similar to those of grand hound's tongue, *Cynoglossum grande*, thus the Latin and common names. Native MORA, NOCA

Hieracium gracile

ASTERACEAE (chicory tribe)

Alpine hawkweed, slender hawkweed

Locally common, late summer, perennial, 3–12 in. Alpine, subalpine

Slender. Stems unbranched, hairless. Leaves oblong, 1–3 in. long, entire or small-toothed, no or few hairs on surface. Basal leaves in rosettes; stem leaves sparse or none. Flower heads few, loosely clustered at top. Disk flowers 20–35, yellow, ray-like, held in a cup covered with black glandular hairs. Common in subalpine and alpine, on moist rocky soils at high elevations. Native OLYM, MORA, NOCA, CRLA

See other *Hieracium*: white, page 174; orange, page 302

Hieracium scouleri
ASTERACEAE (chicory tribe)
Scouler's hawkweed, woolly weed
Common, all summer, perennial, 1–3 ft.
Meadows, west-side forest, east-side forest

Erect stems with basal and stem leaves. Stems bristly or hairless. Basal and lower stem leaves 4–8 in. long, lance-shaped, entire, with long hairs. Inflorescence contains many flower heads in glandular cups, each yellow head composed of 15–50 ray-like disk flowers. Grows in open shrubby or wooded places in all elevations. Native OLYM, MORA, NOCA, CRLA

Hypochaeris radicata   ASTERACEAE (chicory tribe)
Rough cat's-ear, hairy cat's-ear
Common, all spring and summer, perennial, 6–24 in. Coastal, disturbed, meadow, west-side forest

Stems erect, with milky sap, leafless and branched near top. Leaves in basal rosette oblong, toothed or lobed, 1–4 in. Flower heads several per stem; numerous ray-like disk flowers showy. Cup hairless or bristled. Flowers entirely yellow, staying open in sunny or cloudy weather. An abundant weed found in lawns, roadsides, disturbed places, from near coast to open woods, at low elevations. Sometimes confused with common dandelion, *Taraxacum officinale*, when growing as a lawn weed, especially when not in bloom. Nonnative OLYM, MORA, NOCA

Lactuca serriola   ASTERACEAE (chicory tribe)
Prickly lettuce
Common, all spring and summer, annual or biennial, 2–5 ft.
Disturbed, meadow

Tall, erect, with milky sap. Stems prickly, bristled. Leaves oval, lobed or entire and prickly toothed, clasping stem. Lower leaves with spined midvein. Flower heads small, on widely spreading branches, containing 14–20 pale yellow ray-like flowers that quickly wither. Common weed in fields, along roads, other waste places, below 6500 ft. *Lac* means "milk," referring to the sap characteristic of this genus. The lettuce-like leaves are very bitter. Nonnative OLYM, MORA, NOCA

Lapsana communis

ASTERACEAE (chicory tribe)

Nipplewort

Locally common, midsummer, annual, 1–3 ft. Coastal, disturbed, meadow, west-side forest

Single erect stem to 3 ft. or more, milky sap. Leaves thin, 1–2 in. long, alternate on stem, sessile or short-stalked, oval, toothed or lobed. Flower heads in open clusters on short slender stalks based by scale-like leaves. Ray flowers 6–15, yellow, withering quickly. Grows in shady places in open woods, forests, at low and mid elevations. A pernicious weed of flowerbeds and gardens. Nonnative OLYM, MORA, NOCA

Microseris laciniata

ASTERACEAE (chicory tribe)

Cut-leaf microseris, cut-leaved scorzonella

Locally common, late spring–early summer, perennial, 1–2 ft. Meadows, west-side forest

Upright branched stems, each with single flower head, milky sap. Leaves mostly at base, 4–20 in., egg-shaped, pinnately divided into opposite lobes, with long pointed tip. Cup holding flower head narrow, with triangular phyllaries. Flowers yellow, with 13–100 petals; central bristles white or brownish, may be barbed. Grows in open grasslands, rocky soils, edges of forest, at low and mid elevations. In var. *siskiyouensis,* found near Siskiyou Pass on Oregon-California state line, outer side of phyllaries are mealy and may have some black hairs. Native OLYM

Microseris nutans

ASTERACEAE (chicory tribe)

Nodding microseris, nodding scorzonella

Locally common, late spring–early summer, perennial, 4–25 in. Meadow, west-side forest, east-side forest, shrub-steppe

Erect short-lived perennial, milky sap. Stems branched and leafy on lower parts. Leaves usually linear, pinnately divided into narrow segments, or entire. Flower head cup is mealy, covered with hair that is usually black. Flower opens only in mornings; flat head of 13–50 yellow, extended, ray-like disk flowers. Young buds nod, becoming erect before opening. Grows throughout our region in moist forests, meadows, sagebrush, at mid to high elevations. Native NOCA, CRLA

Mycelis muralis (*Lactuca muralis*)

ASTERACEAE (chicory tribe)
Wall lettuce
Common, all summer, annual, 2–4 ft.
Disturbed, meadow, west-side forest

Erect, slender plant with widely branched stems; contains milky sap. Leaves clasping; lower leaves unusually pinnately divided into usually 5 large, angular, toothed segments; few upper leaves smaller. Inflorescence consists of open clusters of many flower heads, each with 5 yellow, extended, ray-like disk flowers. Many flower heads open only for morning; flying seeds with long white bristles more noticeable in afternoon. Native of Europe, now found in large numbers along roads even in logged areas. Nonnative OLYM, MORA, NOCA

Nothocalais alpestris (*Microseris alpestris,*

Agoseris alpestris) ASTERACEAE (chicory tribe)
Alpine lake agoseris, smooth mountain dandelion
Uncommon, midsummer, perennial, 2–10 in.
Alpine, subalpine

Tuft of lobed leaves, erect flower stem containing milky sap. Stem is hairless below flower head. Basal leaves 2–10 in. long, narrow to widely oval, coarsely toothed to deeply lobed, usually hairless. Single flower head of cup with green bracts is evenly covered with purple dots, 13 to many rays, withering soon after opening. Grows on rocky slopes in subalpine. Native
MORA, NOCA, CRLA

Nothocalais troximoides (*Microseris*

troximoides, Scorzonella troximoides)
ASTERACEAE (chicory tribe)
False agoseris
Locally common, midspring, perennial, 2–15 in. Meadow, east-side forest, shrub-steppe

Erect, 1 or few flower stems, milky sap. Foliage covered with dense matted hairs. Leaves long, narrow, wavy-edged, sometimes toothed. A leafless 2–14 in. stem carries a single erect yellow flower head. Thirteen or more extended ray-like disk flowers open early morning, close about midday. Grows in dry, sandy or open rocky soils at mid elevations. Native NOCA

Sonchus arvensis
ASTERACEAE (chicory tribe)
Perennial sow thistle, corn sow thistle
Locally common, all summer, perennial,
15–60 in. Coastal, disturbed, meadow

Erect, with both flowering and nonflowering stems. Milky sap. Leaves entire to pinnately lobed; lower leaves 3–6 in., with short
petioles. Upper leaf edges with thorny teeth,
clasping stems; lowest lobes extend beyond stem and curl.
Flower stalks much divided, leafless. Flower heads 1–2 in.
across, containing yellow ray-like disk flowers. Grows in wet to
damp soils. Noxious weed. Common sow thistle, *S. oleraceus*,
has pointed tips on the basal, clasping lobes that are not curled
or coiled. Prickly sow thistle, *S. asper*, has coarse teeth on the
sometimes lobed, clasping leaves with the
basal lobes curled tight to stem. Nonnative
OLYM, NOCA

Taraxacum officinale
ASTERACEAE (chicory tribe)
Common dandelion
Common, all year long, perennial, 2–8 in.
Disturbed, meadow

Leaf rosette with erect stem. Stem leafless,
hollow, with milky sap. Leaves bright green, pinnately divided
into large lobes with lobe tips reflexed back toward stem,
toothed. Flower head single, 1 in. Ray flowers 70 or more, cup
formed of many bracts with outer bracts reflexed. Seeds olive-
tan. Many plants have a flower structure resembling dandelion.
Very similar to *T. laevigatum*, which has reddish brown seeds.
Nonnative OLYM, MORA, NOCA

Tragopogon dubius (*Tragopogon major*)
ASTERACEAE (chicory tribe)
Yellow salsify, goat's beard
Common, all summer, annual or biennial,
12–30 in. Disturbed, meadow, shrub-steppe

Tall, erect. Stems few, branched. Produces
very sticky, juicy, white latex sap. Leaves
grass-like, narrow, 5–6 in. long, clasping
stems. Leaves covered with soft hairs when young, becoming
smooth and coated with white waxy powder with age. Bracts
are longer than pale yellow ray flowers. Flowers close in cloudy
weather and at noon and night; they face the sun morning and
evening. Grows in dry grassy areas, along roads and other
urban places, at low elevations. Nonnative OLYM, MORA, NOCA

See other *Tragopogon*: blue, page 456

Uropappus lindleyi (*Microseris lindleyi*)
ASTERACEAE (chicory tribe)
Linearleaf microseris, silver puffs
Locally common, late spring, annual, 6–15 in.
Meadow, east-side forest, shrub-steppe

Flower stem erect from basal rosette of leaves.
Milky sap. Leaves 2–12 in. long, linear tapering to pointed tip, entire or with narrow lobes,
soft hairs. Flower head single, erect, phyllaries
lance-shaped, inside long, outer shorter. Flowers 5 to many, yellow, often reddish on underside, opening in morning and fading in afternoon. Grows in loose soils in meadows, woods,
steppe or deserts, at low and mid elevations. Native **L&C**

Arnica amplexicaulis ASTERACEAE (senecio tribe)
Streambank arnica, clasping arnica
Locally common, midsummer, perennial,
12–30 in. West-side forest, east-side forest,
moist streambanks

Erect, single, tall stem with gland-tipped hairs
on upper portion. Leaves lance-shaped to oval,
1½–4 in. long, toothed, clasping stem in opposite pairs. Smaller lower leaves often drop
before flowering. Flower heads pale yellow
throughout; 8–14 petal-like ray flowers toothed
at tips. Grows in moist open woods, along streambanks, at low
to high elevations. Native OLYM, MORA, NOCA, CRLA

Arnica cernua ASTERACEAE (senecio tribe)
Serpentine arnica
Endemic, late spring, perennial, 4–12 in.
West-side forest

Erect, shiny, hairless. Stems unbranched.
Leaves thick, lance-shaped, shallowly lobed or
toothed, in pairs along stem. Lower leaves on
petioles, upper sessile. Flower head single;
7–10 yellow ray flowers around tight center of
disk flowers. Stem, stalks, leaf veins all tinted
reddish. Grows on serpentine between 1200
and 5000 ft. Endemic to Klamath Mountains,
common within its range. Native

Arnica chamissonis

ASTERACEAE (senecio tribe)

Silver arnica, meadow arnica

Locally common, all summer, perennial,
1–3 ft. Meadow, subalpine

Erect. Single stem, branching at inflorescence. Leaves in 5–10 pairs, lance-shaped,
entire or slightly toothed, sessile or on short
stalks. Flower heads usually have 13 ray
flowers about ½ in. long. Flowers held in a cup composed of 2
rows of rounded bracts with long white hairs inside pointed
tips. Grows in high meadows, damp places, at high elevations.
Tallest arnica in our region. Native

Arnica cordifolia

ASTERACEAE (senecio tribe)

Heartleaf arnica

Common, all summer, perennial, 6–24 in.
Meadow, west-side forest, east-side forest,
alpine, subalpine

Erect, glandular, hairy. Stems 1 or few, usually unbranched. Leaves 2–4 pairs, heart-
shaped; lower leaves shallowly toothed.
Flower heads of 10–15 ray flowers with
pointed tips surrounding disk with long soft
hairs. Grows in light shade cast by trees or rocks at mid to high
elevations in mountains. Native OLYM, MORA, NOCA, CRLA

Arnica diversifolia   ASTERACEAE (senecio tribe)

Sticky arnica

Uncommon, all summer, perennial, 6–24 in.
Meadow, west-side forest, east-side forest,
alpine, subalpine

Erect. Stems 1 to several, unbranched, with
sticky gland-bearing hairs. Leaves triangular, irregularly toothed; 3–4 pairs along
stem, with largest pair 1–3 in. long and in
the middle. Lower leaves on petioles; upper
leaves sessile. Flower heads 1–5 in cluster,
8–13 ray flowers less than 1 in. long in head.
Found in grassy or wet sites, on rocks, in
conifer forests in high mountains. Native

OLYM, MORA, NOCA, CRLA

Arnica latifolia

ASTERACEAE (senecio tribe)

Broad-leaved arnica, mountain arnica

Common, all summer, perennial, 1–2 ft.

Bog/fen/wetland, meadow, west-side forest,
east-side forest, subalpine

Erect. Stems unbranched, either solitary or
with a few in a cluster. Leaves round to lance-
shaped, toothed; basal leaves on long stalks,
2–4 pairs sessile along stem, middle pair often larger than those
below. Inflorescence consists of 1–5 flower stalks at stem top,
each holding 1 or few flower heads. Flower heads have 8–13
ray flowers, ½–1 in. long, surrounding a slightly hairy central
disk. Grows in moist woods, meadows, along mountain
streams, mostly at lower elevations but can be found in high
mountains. Highly variable species, generally
more leafy than *A. cordifolia*. Native

OLYM, MORA, NOCA

Arnica longifolia

ASTERACEAE (senecio tribe)

Seep-spring arnica, longleaf arnica

Common, late summer, perennial, 1–2 ft.

Meadows, east-side forest, alpine, subalpine

Stems erect in large patches, tall blooming
stems sticky in upper part. Shorter leafy side shoots. Leaves
mostly on stem in 5–12 pairs; lance-shaped, long, narrow, entire, sessile, with lowest pair fused to stem. Flower heads 8–13,
with ½ in. ray flowers surrounding disk; bell-shaped cup
formed by bracts with sharply pointed, long-haired tips. Grows
in seeps, wet meadows, high in mountains. Native

MORA, NOCA, CRLA

Arnica mollis

ASTERACEAE (senecio tribe)

Hairy arnica, soft arnica

Common, all summer, perennial, 8–24 in.

Meadow, alpine, subalpine

Erect, covered with short to long hairs and
glands. Stems numerous, seldom branched.
Leaves on stem, 2–4 pairs, mostly sessile, elliptical, to 8 in. long, entire or uneven and shallowly toothed;
lowest leaf generally longest. Flower heads have 12–18 ray
flowers ⅓–1⅓ in. long. Grows in moist meadows, streambanks, in subalpine and alpine in higher mountains. Native

OLYM, MORA, NOCA, CRLA

Arnica nevadensis
ASTERACEAE (senecio tribe)
Sierra arnica, Nevada arnica
Locally common, midsummer, perennial,
4–12 in. Meadow, west-side forest, alpine,
subalpine

Erect, hairy, glandular. Stems 1 to several,
unbranched. Leaves 2–3 pairs, entire, widely oval to round, with short petioles; leaf
blade forming wings continues down both sides of petiole.
Flowers heads with 6–11 ray flowers surrounding glandular
disk. Grows in forests, meadows, at high elevations. Native
OLYM, NOCA

Arnica parryi   ASTERACEAE (senecio tribe)
Nodding arnica
Uncommon, late summer, perennial, 12–20
in. Meadow, west-side forest, east-side
forest, alpine, subalpine

Erect, usually single, unbranched stem,
somewhat hairy at base. Basal leaves oval,
sessile. Stem leaves lance- to egg-shaped, in
3–4 pairs; lower leaves 2–8 in. long with
short stalks; upper leaf pairs sessile, smaller.
Flower heads 3–10, nodding while in bud,
later becoming erect on long glandular stalks; yellow disk
flowers in a bell-shaped cup formed by green bracts. Usually no
ray flowers, but 1/3 in. long if present. Grows in dry woods, open
meadows, conifer forests, at mid to high elevations. *Arnica dis-
coidea*, another rayless species, is glandular, with soft-hairy disk
flowers; grows in chaparral and low woodlands in southern
part of our region. Native
OLYM, MORA, NOCA, CRLA

Arnica sororia
ASTERACEAE (senecio tribe)
Twin arnica, bunch arnica
Rare, early summer, perennial, 8–24 in.
Meadow, east-side forest, shrub-steppe

Erect, 1 to several 8–20 in. stems, sometimes branched, glands and hairs on upper
stems, white hairs in axils. Leaves in 2–6 pairs, 1–16 in., lance-
shaped to oblong, mostly sessile, spaced far apart along stem.
Flower heads single to few atop stem, each with 8–23 ray
flowers, 1/2–1 in. long. Grows in damp meadows, dry rocky soils
in sagebrush communities, at mid elevations. Similar *A. rydbergii* is 1/2 as tall, grows in dry meadows, mostly high in mountains. Native NOCA

Cacaliopsis nardosmia (*Luina nardosmia*)
ASTERACEAE (senecio tribe)
Tall silvercrown
Uncommon, late spring, perennial, 18–40 in.
East-side forest

Erect stems with alternate leaves decreasing in size up stem. Lower leaves on long petioles, almost round, 3–14 in. across, maple-like, palmately divided twice into sharply pointed lobes or toothed; upper leaves narrower. Flower heads in cyme on short stalks extending upward. Bell-shaped cup holds ¾–1⅝ in. wide bristly yellow disks, no ray flowers. Grows in open woodlands and meadows, sometimes on serpentine, at low to mid elevations. Native NOCA

Crocidium multicaule
ASTERACEAE (senecio tribe)
Gold stars, gold fields
Common, early spring, annual, 2–8 in.
Coastal, meadow, shrub-steppe

Tuft. One to few very delicate unbranched stems. Leaves alternate, linear to oval, slightly fleshy, entire or sparsely toothed. Small tuft of hair in leaf axils. Flower head single on long stem, with usually 8 ray flowers ¼–½ in. long, many disk flowers. Grows in sandy soils, open grasslands, at low and mid elevations. Often seen in dense populations covering large areas in early spring. *Crocidium* is Greek for "tufts," referring to the hair in the leaf axils. Native OLYM

Luina hypoleuca
ASTERACEAE (senecio tribe)
Silverback luina, littleleaf luina
Locally common, midsummer, perennial, 6–25 in. Dry rocky sites, subalpine

Clump of many erect stems. Stems white with woolly hairs. Leaves sessile, alternate on stem, egg-shaped, entire or toothed, about 1–2½ in. long, white-woolly on underside, less so or hairless on top. Flower heads 4–12, in flat-topped cluster, on stalks 1–2 in. long, atop stems. Disk flowers 11–15, creamy yellow, with erect lobes. No ray flowers. Grows in rocky open sites, on talus or sometimes serpentine, at low to subalpine elevations. Native
OLYM, MORA, NOCA

Packera cana (*Senecio canus*)

ASTERACEAE (senecio tribe)
Woolly groundsel
Common, all summer, perennial, 6–18 in.
Shrub-steppe, alpine, subalpine

Erect, with single or few stems. Basal leaves
on long petioles, 1–2 in. long, oval, widening toward tip, entire, gray, covered in felt-
like matted hairs; leaves along woolly stems
are smaller, toothed or lobed. Flower heads 6–12, on stalks, atop
stems, with 8 or possibly 13 ray flowers surrounding many disk
flowers. Found in rocky soils at mid to high elevations. Native
NOCA

Packera cymbalarioides (*Senecio cymbalarioides*)

ASTERACEAE (senecio tribe)
Alpine meadow groundsel
Common, all summer, perennial, 4–20 in.
Meadow, alpine, subalpine

Erect. Stems hairless when mature. Basal
leaves on petioles, blades thick and firm,
widely spoon-shaped, wavy- to round-
toothed or entire; stem leaves sessile, often
deeply lobed, becoming smaller upward.
Single flower head per stalk. Flower cup cre-
ated of hairless green bracts, often with red-tinged tips, about
13 rays around 40 disk flowers. Grows in damp alpine meadows at mid to high elevations. Native MORA

Packera flettii (*Senecio flettii*) ASTERACEAE (senecio tribe)

Flett's groundsel, Flett's butterweed
Uncommon, midsummer, perennial, 2–8 in.
West-side forest, alpine, subalpine

Tuft with erect flower stem, hairless. Leaves
mostly basal, 4 in. long including petiole, divided pinnately with largest leaflet at tip of
leaf. Leaflets wide, toothed. Stem leaves few,
smaller. Flower heads in cluster atop stem;
disk flowers yellow to orange; ray flowers
more or less 6, yellow. Grows in rocky open
places, talus slopes from foothills to tops of
mountains. Native OLYM, MORA

Packera macounii (*Senecio macounii*)
ASTERACEAE (senecio tribe)
Macoun's groundsel, Puget groundsel
Rare, mid to late summer, perennial, 12–20 in.
Disturbed, meadow, west-side forest, east-side
forest

Tuft of basal leaves, erect flower stems. Leaves
upright to spreading, lance-shaped, 1–3 in.
long, entire or with few teeth, edges often
rolled under. Flower heads in loose clusters at stem tops. Cups
with 13 or more green-tipped bracts. Ray flowers 8, disk flowers
less than 50. Grows in disturbed rocky places, streambanks,
roadsides, clearings, at low elevations. Native OLYM, NOCA

Packera streptanthifolia (*Senecio streptanthifolius*)
ASTERACEAE (senecio tribe)
Rocky Mountain butterweed
Locally common, all summer, perennial, 4–25
in. West-side forest, east-side forest, alpine,
subalpine

Erect stems from multileaved rosette. Leaves
thick, almost succulent, oval to round. Lower
leaves 1–2 in. long, on slightly longer petioles,
entire or slightly toothed. Upper leaves lobed,
sessile. Flower heads 4–20 on long stalks, with
8 or possibly 13 ray flowers, more than 40 disk flowers. Grows
in dry woodlands, rocky places, at low to alpine elevations.
Native MORA, NOCA

Raillardella argentea
ASTERACEAE (senecio tribe)
Silvery raillardella, silky raillardella
Uncommon, midsummer, perennial, 1–6 in.
Alpine, subalpine

Tuft of basal leaves, erect flower stem. Leaves
oblong, entire, coated with silky hairs, sometimes with glands. Single flower head at top of
stalk covered with sticky glands, without ray
flowers. Flower contains 7–26 yellow disk flowers. Grows in dry open sites at high elevations,
mostly in California, rare in Oregon. Native
CRLA

279

Rainiera stricta (*Luina stricta*)
ASTERACEAE (senecio tribe)
Rainiera, tongue-leaved luina
Uncommon, midsummer, perennial,
20–40 in. Alpine, subalpine

Erect stem from base of large leaves. Basal
and lower leaves carried by short petiole,
broadly oval, with pointed tip, 6–14 in. long;
middle and upper leaves becoming smaller
and sessile. Inflorescence consists of spike 4–15 in. long atop
stem. Each flower head bears about 5 flowers in elongated cup
created by 5–6 bracts. Grows in meadows, open areas, at high
elevations. Native MORA

Senecio crassulus
ASTERACEAE (senecio tribe)
**Thick-leaved groundsel, mountain meadow
butterweed**
Locally common, late summer, perennial,
8–26 in. Meadow, east-side forest, alpine,
subalpine

Several erect stems on hairless plant. Leaves
thick, succulent, toothed. Lower leaves 2–5
in. long, oval, with petioles; upper leaves
clasping stem. Inflorescence branched, with
few to several stalks, yellow flower heads. Flower heads hold 8
ray flowers surrounding ¼–½ in. center of disk flowers. Grows
in moist meadows, open forests, rocky places, in subalpine and
alpine. Native

Senecio fremontii
ASTERACEAE (senecio tribe)
Dwarf mountain groundsel
Uncommon, late summer, perennial, 2–6 in.
Alpine, subalpine

Prostrate to erect perennial. Stem with numerous branches growing outward, then
upward, to 6 in. Leaves thick, lance- to
spoon-shaped, widening at tip end, coarsely
toothed. Leaves on full length of the stem,
with largest approximately in the middle.
Flower heads numerous on individual stalks at top, with 8 ray
flowers, many disk flowers. Grows in rocky soils, talus, in
alpine. Native OLYM, MORA, NOCA

Senecio hydrophiloides (*Senecio foetidus*)
ASTERACEAE (senecio tribe)
Sweet marsh butterweed, stout meadow groundsel
Uncommon, late spring–early summer, biennial or perennial, 12–40 in.
Bog/fen/wetland, meadow, alpine, subalpine

Erect stems clustered in clump of basal leaves. Stems hairless. Leaves fleshy, not coated with white film, sharply toothed. Basal leaves on petiole, widely oval, 2–10 in. long, 1–3 in. wide; few stem leaves narrow and sessile near stem top. Inflorescence consists of 8 or more crowded heads; black-tipped bracts create deep cup containing few ray flowers, 40 or fewer disk flowers. Grows in damp meadows, hillsides, at mid to high elevations. Native

Senecio hydrophilus
ASTERACEAE (senecio tribe)
Alkali marsh butterweed, water groundsel
Uncommon, midsummer, biennial or perennial, 18–36 in. Coastal, bog/fen/wetland

Clump of large green leaves with upright flower stems. Stems hollow. Leaves fleshy, oblong to nearly round, 2–8 in. long, entire or shallowly toothed. Sessile stem leaves smaller. Flower heads clustered at stem top, some with 5 short rays, others rayless; bracts of cup often have black tips. Grows in muddy places along Columbia River, standing salt water, swamps, into high elevations. Native

Senecio integerrimus
ASTERACEAE (senecio tribe)
Western groundsel, white western groundsel
Common, late spring–early summer, biennial or perennial, 8–30 in. Meadow, west-side forest, east-side forest, alpine, subalpine

Single, stout, erect stem, thick basal leaves on petioles. Leaves lance-shaped to almost round, with matted hair when young, becoming smooth with age, entire or occasionally with shallow irregular teeth. Upper leaves alternate on stem, sessile. Flower heads numerous, tightly clustered on short hairy stalks atop stems. Eight ray flowers vary from yellow to almost white; disk flowers yellow. Grows in moist to dry soils in sagebrush-steppe, forests, alpine ridges. Var. *ochroleucus* has white ray flowers, cream disk, may have slightly blackened bract tips on cups. Var. *exaltatus* has no ray flowers, creamy disk, grows in forests. Native NOCA, CRLA

Senecio jacobaea

ASTERACEAE (senecio tribe)

Tansy ragwort, tansy butterweed

Common, all summer, perennial, 2–4 ft.
Coastal, disturbed, meadow, west-side
forest

Stems erect, unbranched, solitary to few, alternate. Lower leaves 8–10 in., deeply pinnately divided; lower leaves falling by bloom
time. Flower heads numerous, closely clustered on short stalks,
atop stem. Flower head with 13 ray flowers, ⅓ in. central disk.
Grows on roadsides, disturbed soils, at low and mid elevations.
Originally from Eurasia. Invasive in pastures and fields, very
toxic to cattle and horses. Nonnative OLYM, MORA, NOCA

Senecio neowebsteri

ASTERACEAE (senecio tribe)

Olympic Mountain groundsel

Endemic, midsummer, perennial, 2–8 in.
Alpine

Stems ascending from basal tuft. Stems and
leaves covered with cobweb-like hairs and
some glands when young, becoming shiny.
Basal leaves broadly oblong to 2½ in. long,
toothed; stem leaves smaller. Somewhat
nodding, usually solitary flower head with a cup of pale hairy-
tipped bracts and ⅓–⅔ in. yellow rays. Grows on talus slopes
in alpine. Native OLYM

Senecio serra ASTERACEAE (senecio tribe)

Butterweed groundsel, tall butterweed

Locally common, midsummer, perennial,
2–6 ft. Meadows, east-side forest, alpine,
subalpine

Erect. Stems clustered, leafy. Leaves all
about the same size, 3–6 in. long, linear to
lance-shaped, with pointed tips, entire to
sharply toothed; lower leaves with petioles,
dropping before flowering; upper leaves
sessile. Flower heads numerous, consisting
of ¼ in. high cup formed by about 13 bracts
tipped black holding 8 yellow ray flowers around yellow disk.
Grows in moist meadows, conifer forests, along streams, open
places, at high elevations. Native

Senecio triangularis

ASTERACEAE (senecio tribe)

Arrowleaf groundsel, bog groundsel

Locally common, all summer, perennial, 1–5 ft. Bog/fen/wetland, moist streambanks, meadow, west-side forest, east-side forest, alpine, subalpine

Cluster of very tall stems with evenly spaced leaves, same size to top. Arrow-shaped leaves 2–8 in. long, on short petioles or sessile, deeply toothed. Few to numerous yellow flower heads in small cluster at top. Head includes 8 ray flowers toothed at tips, 40 disk flowers in center. Grows in wet meadows, conifer forests, streambanks, at mid to alpine elevations. Native OLYM, MORA, NOCA, CRLA

Senecio vulgaris ASTERACEAE (senecio tribe)

Common groundsel, old man in the spring

Common, all year long, annual or biennial, 4–20 in. Coastal, disturbed, meadow

Winter-growing upright annual, hairless throughout, single stem arched near the top. Leaves oval, 1–4 in., pinnately lobed, teeth unevenly placed along edges. Leaves alternate on stem and stalks. Flower heads numerous, cups with black-tipped bracts. Disk flowers yellow, about 40 with white pappus, no ray flowers. Abundant Old World weed found in gardens, fields, all disturbed places throughout temperate zones of the world. More common west of Cascades in our region. Note the black bracts that distinguish this from any other groundsel. Nonnative

OLYM, MORA, NOCA

Balsamorhiza careyana

ASTERACEAE (sunflower tribe)

Carey's balsamroot

Locally common, late spring, perennial, 8–24 in. East-side forest, shrub-steppe

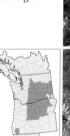

Clump of upward-pointing leaves from woody base. Stalks of equal lengths. Leaves shiny green, 6–20 in. long, heart-shaped, entire, with obvious white central vein and vein network most noticeable on underside. Flower stems 1 to many, upright, about as long as the leaves, each holding a single flower head. Ray flowers 8–13, yellow, about 1 in. long, held after initial flowering, becoming papery. Grows mostly in steppe. Native

Balsamorhiza deltoidea
ASTERACEAE (sunflower tribe)
Puget balsamroot, deltoid balsamroot
Common, late spring, perennial, 8–36 in.
Meadow, shrub-steppe

Clump of basal leaves and erect flower stems. Leaves with long petioles, widely spear-shaped, 8–24 in. long, entire to toothed, rough to thinly hairy. Flower stems carry few, small, entire leaves and 1 or 2 flower heads. Ray flowers 13–21, showy, 1–2 in. long, surrounding large center of short disk flowers above bracts that are only slightly woolly. Grows in open sites, grassy areas, at low to high elevations. Native

Balsamorhiza hookeri ASTERACEAE (sunflower tribe)
Hairy balsamroot
Locally common, late spring, perennial, 4–12 in. Shrub-steppe

Cluster of gray silky-haired leaves rises from a thick root. Leaves 4–12 in. long, divided into linear-oblong segments. Flower head single on leafless stem; ray flowers about 1 in. long. Grows along eastern Columbia River Gorge and throughout steppe. Differs noticeably from *B. incana*, hoary balsamroot, which is larger and very hairy. Native

Balsamorhiza incana ASTERACEAE (sunflower tribe)
Hoary balsamroot
Uncommon, late spring, perennial, 8–36 in.
Meadow

Cluster of basal leaves. Leaves 4–17 in. long, lance-shaped to oblong, pinnately divided to central vein, with toothed leaflets. Leaves gray with long woolly hairs. Pair of small deeply divided leaves occurs just under flower head, otherwise stem is leafless. Flower head with 13 or more ray flowers 1–2 in. long. Grows in wetter areas than other balsamroots. Sometimes confused with smaller *B. hookeri*, hairy balsamroot, which also has silky hairs pressed to leaf surface. Native

Balsamorhiza rosea
ASTERACEAE (sunflower tribe)
Rosy balsamroot
Rare, midspring, perennial, to 12 in.
Dry rocky sites, shrub-steppe

Prostrate plant from coarse woody root. Leaves 2–8 in. long, divided nearly to the reddish midrib, often expanding outward near ground. Leaf longer than stalk. Flower head on leafless stem or with 2 small leaves near base. Cup densely covered with white hairs. Ray flowers overlapping, deep yellow, becoming rosy red with age. A rare plant, found on rocky soils. Sometimes hybridizes with Carey's balsamroot, *B. careyana*. Native

Balsamorhiza sagittata   ASTERACEAE (sunflower tribe)
Arrowleaf balsamroot
Common, all summer, perennial, 8–36 in.
East-side forest, shrub-steppe

Clump of upright leaves, erect stems. Leaves widely triangular, with heart-shaped base, 8–24 in., entire, pale olive-green, velvety on both sides. Soon after bloom time, leaves become hairless, twisted, papery. Flower stem 1–3 ft. tall, leafless, holds single 4 in. flower above usually woolly bracts. Ray flowers 1–2 in. long. Grows in deep rich soils in ponderosa pine and sagebrush habitats, often in huge patches, at mid elevations. The most widespread *Balsamorhiza*. Native NOCA, **L&C**

Balsamorhiza sericea   ASTERACEAE (sunflower tribe)
Silky balsamroot
Endemic, late spring–early summer, perennial, 6–12 in. Meadow

Tuft with upright flower stem. Leaves form rosette at base, 2–3 at base of stem, 4–12 in. long, pinnately divided into rounded lobes, densely coated with fine silver hairs, becoming hairless late in season. Flower head single atop stem; ray flowers ¾–1½ in. long, wide at base, narrower tips rounded to pointed; disk flowers about ⅓ in. long. Grows in dry areas in rocky serpentine, endemic to Siskiyou Mountains of southwestern Oregon and northwestern California. Flower often with distinctive chocolate fragrance. Native

Balsamorhiza serrata

ASTERACEAE (sunflower tribe)

Serrate balsamroot, toothed balsamroot

Rare, late spring, perennial, 4–12 in.

East-side forest, shrub-steppe

Stem erect. Two leaves from base, green, glandular, soft-hairy, 3–8 in. long, narrow to widely oval, pinnately lobed into wide lobes with sharp teeth pointing toward leaf tip. Flower stem with basal leaves only; single flower head with ray flowers less than 1 in. long. Grows in dry rocky soils in open sagebrush, forests. Often hybridizes with *B. hookeri* in Steens Mountain area. Native

Bidens cernua   ASTERACEAE (sunflower tribe)

Nodding beggarticks, bur marigold

Locally common, all summer, annual, 4–40 in. Vernal-wet, bog/fen/wetland

Erect, hairless to sparsely hairy. Leaves opposite, stalkless, wrapping around stem, lance-shaped, 2–8 in. long, smooth to sawtoothed. Flower head single, with few green, lance-shaped, leafy bracts at base, nodding as they mature. Ray and disk flowers yellow; 6–8 ray flowers or none. Tan, wedge-shaped seed head has 3–4 barbed tips that attach to clothing if you walk among drying plants. Grows in freshwater wetlands at low elevations. Similar *B. amplissima* grows in same habitats but is rare, found in a few sites only in Puget Sound, on southern Vancouver Island, and in lower Fraser Valley; a robust plant, it grows to 4 ft., with many branches, simple or 3-lobed leaves, few but large heads with large ray petals. Native OLYM, NOCA

Bidens vulgata

ASTERACEAE (sunflower tribe)

Tall beggarticks, western sticktight

Locally common, all summer, annual, 25–44 in. Bog/fen/wetland

Slender, erect, branched stem. Leaves opposite, pinnately divided into 3–5 leaflets on short stalks. Flower heads at stem top, without noticeable petals, to 1 in. across in seed; 10–16 densely hairy phyllaries to 2 in. long surround the shorter yellow or olive-brown disk. Grows in moist places. Native

Coreopsis tinctoria var. *atkinsoniana*
ASTERACEAE (sunflower tribe)
Columbia coreopsis
Locally common, all spring and summer,
annual or biennial or perennial, 8–40 in.
Bog/fen/wetland, disturbed, meadow

Single erect stem multibranched in upper ½.
Leaves 1–5 in. long, opposite, with petioles
about 1 in. long. Lower leaves divided into nar-
row linear lobes; upper leaves linear, not divided. Flower heads
numerous in open clusters; usually 8 yellow ray flowers, wedge-
shaped on tip end. Disk flowers purple-brown. Grows at low
elevations in disturbed soils and along rivers, as inferred by the
common name. Native **L&C**

Eriophyllum lanatum
ASTERACEAE (sunflower tribe)
Oregon sunshine, woolly yellow daisy
Common, all spring and summer, annual or
perennial, 4–40 in. Coastal, meadow, shrub-
steppe

Subshrub densely covered with woolly hairs,
grows low with long stems reaching upward.
Stems numerous, bare. Leaves ½–3 in. long,
linear to oval, pinnately divided or entire.
Flower heads single on stalks, with 8–13 yellow ray flowers or
occasionally rayless, many yellow disk flowers. Grows in many
habitats, most often in dry lands with sandy or rocky soils,
sometimes along coastal bluffs from near coastline to mid elevations. Var. *achillaeoides* has leaves divided like yarrow, while
var. *integrifolium*, the typical Oregon sunshine, has fewer ray
flowers, leaves entire or with lobes only at tip
end. Native OLYM, MORA, NOCA, CRLA, **L&C**

Gaillardia aristata
ASTERACEAE (sunflower tribe)
Blanket flower
Common, all spring and summer, perennial,
1–3 ft. Meadows, shrub-steppe

Clump of erect stems. Plant rough-haired
throughout. Leaves on stem alternate, oblong,
entire to pinnately lobed; lower leaves 2–6 in. long, decreasing
in size upward. Single flower head tops stem. Ray flowers 6–16,
1 in. long, 3-lobed at tip, yellow, usually purple at base, creating
ring around purplish-woolly central dome of many red or
brownish disk flowers. Grows in roadside ditches, meadows,
grasslands, below 6500 ft. Commonly used garden plant with
many developed color forms. Native NOCA, **L&C**

Helenium autumnale
ASTERACEAE (sunflower tribe)
Large-flowered sneezeweed, common sneezeweed
Locally common, late summer, perennial, 1–4 ft. Vernal-wet, meadow

Tall, erect. Stems with few branches. Leaves mostly on stems, oblong-toothed; lower leaves have short petioles with wings continuing down stem; upper leaves sessile. Flower heads several, each on 1–4 in. stalk. Flower head has 10–20 reflexed yellow ray flowers with 3-lobed tips and rounded center with many 5-lobed disk flowers. Grows in wet soils below 7000 ft. A beautiful plant often used in gardens for its late summer bloom. Native OLYM

Helenium bigelovii
ASTERACEAE (sunflower tribe)
Tall sneezeweed, Bigelow's sneezeweed
Uncommon, all summer, perennial,12–40 in. Bog/fen/wetland, meadow

Erect. Stems few, often reddish at base. Leaves few, lance-shaped to linear, hairless, entire, thick, leathery. Basal and lower stem leaves have short, winged petioles; upper leaves clasp stem, with narrow wings continuing down stem. Flower head usually single at stem top. Ray flowers 14–20, yellow; ball-shaped disk has yellow tubular flowers with 5 yellow, brown, red, or purple lobes. Grows in wet meadows, streambanks, sometimes in serpentine fens. Native

Helenium bolanderi
ASTERACEAE (sunflower tribe)
Coast sneezeweed
Locally common, all summer, perennial, 1–5 ft. Coastal, bog/fen/wetland

Erect. Stems with few long hairs. Leaves alternate, lance-shaped, 2–4 in. long, hairless, with petioles very short or absent. Flower heads 1 to few, each with 12–21 yellow ray flowers, central yellow disk about 1 in. across. Grows in wet soils at low elevations. Native

Helianthella uniflora
ASTERACEAE (sunflower tribe)
Douglas's helianthella, false sunflower
Uncommon, all summer, perennial, 2–4 ft.
Shrub-steppe

Several erect stems in cluster. Stems have flattened hairs and a few stiff straight hairs. Oblong leaves with largest midstem on short petioles; lower and upper leaves sessile. Single flower head at stem top is held upright with leaf-like bracts underneath. Ray flowers 11–20, each about 1 in. long, surrounding yellow disk. Grows on dry hillsides, in brush, at mid to high elevations. Native

Helianthus annuus
ASTERACEAE (sunflower tribe)
Common sunflower
Common, all spring and summer, annual, 3–10 ft. Meadows, shrub-steppe

Erect annual. Stems rough-haired. Leaves broad, heart-shaped at base, usually with pointed tips, saw-toothed. Flower heads few to many, often 8 in. across in the wild, larger in cultivated plants. Yellow ray flowers 15 or more, surrounding center of yellow, red, or purple disk flowers. Grows in many habitats at low elevations. Sunflowers are thought to originate in southwestern and prairie states. They are cultivated over much of North America for their valuable seeds and to attract wildlife. Native

Helianthus cusickii
ASTERACEAE (sunflower tribe)
Cusick's sunflower, turniproot sunflower
Uncommon, late spring–early summer, perennial, 1–3 ft. East-side forest, shrub-steppe

Erect. Stems with few long hairs. Leaves alternate, lance-shaped, 2–4 in. long, hairless, with petioles very short or absent. Flower heads 1 to few, each with 12–21 yellow ray flowers, central yellow disk about 1 in. across. Grows on dry open slopes at mid elevations. Native

289

Hulsea algida

ASTERACEAE (sunflower tribe)
Alpine hulsea, fleshy hulsea
Uncommon, late summer, perennial, 4–16
in. Alpine, subalpine

Somewhat hairy throughout. Stem single,
erect. Leaves in rosette, soft, hairy, 6 in. long,
coarsely toothed, linear, with outside edges
folded upward. Few smaller leaves on lower
stems; upper stems bare. Flower head single, deep yellow, atop
stem. Ray flowers 25–60; disk flowers many. Grows in talus,
scree, or gravel among rocks in subalpine and alpine. *Algida*
means "cold," reflecting the plant's occurrence in cold places,
usually mountaintops. Native

Hulsea nana

ASTERACEAE (sunflower tribe)
Dwarf hulsea
Locally common, midsummer, perennial,
2–6 in. Alpine

Small plant covered with glands and long
hairs. Stems numerous and erect. Leaves in
basal rosette many, spoon-shaped, 1–2 in.
long, divided, with rounded lobes. Flower
heads single on leafless stem, with 12–30
ray flowers, many disk flowers. Grows in volcanic talus, sometimes in abundant colonies, in Cascades, Wallowas, subalpine,
alpine. Note that *H. algida* in same environment has only 1
stem to a plant and about twice as many ray flowers. Native
MORA, NOCA, CRLA

Jaumea carnosa

ASTERACEAE (sunflower tribe)
Fleshy jaumea, marsh jaumea
Locally common, all spring and summer,
perennial, 6–10 in. Coastal

Succulent-like, prostrate. Stems weak, often
almost flat on the ground. Leaves linear to
narrowly oblong, with rounded tips, fused
to stems. Flower heads small, with both ray
and disk flowers held in cups of fleshy, usu-
ally purple bracts. Found on tidal flats, in salt marshes, at base
of cliffs along coast. Compare to *Cotula coronopifolia*. Native
OLYM

Lagophylla ramosissima
ASTERACEAE (sunflower tribe)
Slender hareleaf, common rabbitleaf
Locally common, all spring and summer,
annual, 4–20 in. Shrub-steppe

Stems stiff, erect, branched, softly hairy in spring, becoming hairless. Leaves at base oblong, 1–5 in., drying before bloom time. Leaves on center stem entire; upper leaves bract-like, densely coated with silver hairs. Inflorescence glandular, consisting of clusters of few flower heads with pale yellow rays, purple veins in rays. Grows in numerous dry habitats at low and mid elevations. Flowers open in evening and close the next morning. Can be confused with *Madia citriodora*. Native

Lasthenia californica *(Lasthenia*
chrysostoma) ASTERACEAE (sunflower tribe)
Slender goldfields
Common, early spring, annual, 2–12 in.
Coastal, meadow, west-side forest

Erect. Stems branched or simple. Leaves linear to slightly oblong, entire, to 1/3 in. long, short-haired on upper side. Flower heads yellow; 6–13 ray flowers may be darker yellow toward center. Many yellow disk flowers; if magnified, the triangular style tips are seen. Abundant in many habitats. Often seen in vast fields, thus the common name. Plants in coastal habitats are somewhat fleshy. Native

Madia citriodora ASTERACEAE (sunflower tribe)
Lemon-scented tarweed, lemon tarweed
Locally common, late spring–early summer,
annual, 6–16 in. Meadow, west-side forest, east-side forest, shrub-steppe

Erect stem, lemon-scented. Bristles or soft hairs on lower part of stem. Upper stem has hairs tipped with glands. Leaves on stalks, hairy with black glands on upper surface. Flower heads openly clustered with 5–12 greenish yellow ray flowers surrounding black-anthered yellow disk flowers. Grows in scattered areas on dry soils. Can be confused with *Lagophylla ramosissima*. Native

Madia elegans
ASTERACEAE (sunflower tribe)
Common madia, autumn showy tarweed
Common, all summer–autumn, annual,
3–36 in. Meadow, west-side forest, east-side
forest

Upright, strongly fragrant. Stem simple or
branched, very leafy, with hairs on lower section, yellow or black glands on stalks. Leaves
1–8 in. long, alternating along stem, lance-shaped, entire or
sharp-toothed, hairy to bristly. Many flower heads atop stem.
Flowers in rounded cup more or less bristly on outside, petals
all yellow or red at base, anthers black or yellow, lobes of disk
flowers in center obvious. Flowers open late in day, remain
open until middle of next morning. Grows in grasslands. Native

Madia glomerata
ASTERACEAE (sunflower tribe)
Clustered tarweed, stinking tarweed
Common, midsummer, annual, 1–2 ft.
Meadows, shrub-steppe

Erect, strong-smelling. Stems with stiff upright branches, soft hairy to stiff bristles on
lower stem, stalked glands above. Leaves
upright, numerous on stems and in side
clusters, hairs stiff, sharp, and pressed to surface, some stalked
glands. Inflorescence consists of dense flower clusters at stem
tops. Flowers small, yellow or yellow-green stained purplish,
nearly sessile. Ray flowers none or 3, with square-cut tips and
1(–12) disk flowers in head surrounded by 3 hairy, glandular,
green bracts. Grows in open areas of forests at mid to high elevations. Native OLYM, NOCA

Madia gracilis
ASTERACEAE (sunflower tribe)
Slender tarweed
Common, all spring and summer, annual,
4–40 in. Meadow, west-side forest, east-side
forest, shrub-steppe

Upright, fragrant, dark green. Stem slender,
may be branched from middle upward, bris-
tles below, glands on upper section. Leaves linear, to 4 in. long,
covered with soft hair. Flower heads sessile or clustered on long
stalks. Cup holding flowers is covered with glands on hair-like
stalks. Flower heads consist of 3–9 lemon yellow ray flowers
with lobed tips, 2–12 black-anthered disk flowers. Grows in
grasslands, open woods, along roads, below 7500 ft. Native
OLYM, MORA, NOCA, CRLA

Madia minima

ASTERACEAE (sunflower tribe)

Small-headed tarweed, least tarweed

Locally common, all spring and summer, annual, 1–6 in. Meadow, west-side forest, east-side forest, shrub-steppe

Small, very slender, widely branched stems. Stems with soft hairs below, glands on upper sections. Leaves few, linear, to 1 in. long, sometimes toothed, clustered at joints. One or few flower heads tightly clustered. Flowers consist of 3–5 inconspicuous pale yellow ray flowers, 1–2 yellow-anthered disk flowers. Grows in open forests, shrublands, at mid to high elevations. Easy to miss unless many plants are growing together. Native

NOCA, CRLA

Madia sativa

ASTERACEAE (sunflower tribe)

Coast tarweed, Chilean tarweed

Common, all summer–autumn, annual, 8–40 in. Coastal, meadow

Erect, ill-smelling, covered with hairs and very sticky, stalked, yellow to black glands. Stems often in clusters, branched, leafy. Leaves on lower stem linear to oblong, 1–6 in., entire or toothed, upper stem leaves smaller. Flower heads sessile or short-stalked, in dense clusters; bracts green, hairy, glandular, with long flat tips. Ray flowers usually 8, greenish yellow or tinted red. Disk flowers 10–14, black-anthered. A coastal plant usually found in grassy places at low elevations. Native

OLYM, NOCA

Rudbeckia glaucescens

ASTERACEAE (sunflower tribe)

Waxy coneflower, California coneflower

Uncommon, late summer, perennial, 2–4 ft. Bog/fen/wetland

Erect, stout. Stem smooth, unbranched, with single flower head at top. Basal leaves 4–10 in. long, 2–3 in. wide, with few teeth or entire, hairless and coated with white or bluish waxy powder when young. Flower head has 8–21 often reflexed ray flowers 1–2½ in. long surrounding narrow cone about 1 in. high of green to yellow disk flowers. Grows on serpentine in seeps, along streams. Similar *R. californica* has green leaves without powder, sometimes lobed, with hairy lower surface; grows in seeps but not on serpentine. Native

See other *Rudbeckia*: green/brown, page 470

Wyethia amplexicaulis
ASTERACEAE (sunflower tribe)
Northern mule's ears, smooth dwarf sunflower
Locally common, late spring–early summer, perennial, 12–30 in. Meadow, shrub-steppe

Prostrate perennial. Leaves hairless, shiny, bright green, entire, to 20 in., pointed at tip; upper leaves clasp stem. Flower head deep yellow; large central flower head with small side flower heads tops stem. Ray flowers 8–18, rays 1–2 in. long, 2–3 teeth on tip, central disk of many flowers. Grows in dry meadows, open places. Native

Wyethia angustifolia ASTERACEAE (sunflower tribe)
Narrowleaf wyethia, narrowleaf mule's ears
Common, late spring–early summer, perennial, 18–24 in. Meadow

Clump of leaves, erect flower-bearing stems. Basal leaves lance-shaped, 4–20 in. long, tapering to point, lightly coated with rough hairs; stem leaves few, much smaller. Flower head, deep yellow sunflower-like, usually 1 per stem. Bracts 20–30, soft-haired, about 1 in. long, toothed, forming a cup containing 8–21 rays, each ½–1¾ in. long, and large central disk. Grows in grasslands below 6500 ft. Native

Xanthium strumarium ASTERACEAE (sunflower tribe)
Cocklebur
Uncommon, late summer–autumn, annual, 1–5 ft. Vernal-wet, disturbed

Erect annual. Stems thick and fleshy, spineless, green spotted red or black. Leaves alternate, 6 in. long, triangular with long petiole, a few glands on surface, coarsely toothed or lobed. Flowers very small, insignificant. Seeds held in tight clusters of round to oblong burrs at axils of leaf stalks and stems. Found in disturbed soils throughout the world. In Pacific Northwest found at low elevations. *Xanthium* is Greek for "yellow," the color of dye extracted from the fleshy stems. Native

See other *Wyethia*: white, page 181

Centaurea solstitialis
ASTERACEAE (thistle tribe)
Yellow starthistle, St. Barnaby's thistle
Common, all summer, annual, 8–32 in.
Disturbed, meadow

Spreading clump lightly coated with cobweb-like hairs. Stems upright and winged under leaves, stiff, much divided. Lower leaves linear, lobed; upper leaves becoming smaller until scale-like. Flower heads single, develop in shallow cup of brown bracts. Bracts tipped with very long, stiff, yellow spines surrounded by 2–4 short spines. Disk flowers elongated to create petal-like, fluffy flower head. Grows in disturbed soils, fields, along roads. Common at low and mid elevations. Highly aggressive noxious weed. Nonnative

Opuntia fragilis
CACTACEAE
Brittle prickly pear cactus
Locally common, late spring–early summer, perennial, 2–8 in. Coastal, meadow, shrub-steppe

Prostrate to sprawling. Stem segments somewhat flat or round and cylinder-like, easily coming apart. Spines 3–7, round, rigid, straight, gray with brown tips in cluster with whitish wool and small yellowish bristles. Flower yellow, sometimes reddish at base; filaments white or red; style white; stigma green. Grows in juniper woodland, dry open sandy or gravelly soils, from sea level to 3000 ft. Native OLYM, NOCA, **L&C**

Opuntia polyacantha
CACTACEAE
Plains prickly pear cactus, starvation cholla
Common, late spring–early summer, perennial, 4–12 in. Shrub-steppe

Mats of spreading, flattened, widely oval, pad-like stems. Pads round to oval, 1–4 in. long, light green. Spines stout, straight, dark brown or gray, ¼–2 in. long, clustered at circular areole, with gray-woolly hairs and numerous yellow to reddish, small, sharp prickles. Flowers with numerous light yellow petals 1–2 in. long. Grows in dry plains, hills in open or sparsely wooded areas, common on sand. Native **L&C**

See other *Centaurea*: white, page 181; red, page 394; blue, page 456

Nuphar polysepala (*Nuphar lutea*

subsp. *polysepala*) NYMPHAEACEAE
Yellow pond lily, spatterdock, cow-lily
Common, midsummer, perennial
Lake/pond

Leaves rise directly from underwater root system and float or rise above water. Leaves 4–18 in. long, heart-shaped. Cup-shaped flowers float or rise above water, are about 4 in. across, yellow, often tinted green or red. Flower center includes large, bright yellow, disk-like stigma surrounded by yellow or red-tinged stamens. Found in shallow ponds and slow streams usually 2–10 ft. deep at elevations below treeline. Native OLYM, MORA, NOCA, CRLA

Lysichiton americanus ARACEAE
Skunk cabbage, yellow skunk cabbage, swamp lantern
Locally common, early spring, perennial, 1–3 ft. Coastal, vernal-wet, bog/fen/wetland

Foul-smelling. Leaves appearing at flowering, egg-shaped, deep green, elongate to 1–2 ft. long and ½ as wide, overtaking the flower stalk, thick petiole graduating into thick midvein. Flowers yellow-green, numerous on stout spike partly surrounded by very large yellow bract. Grows in tree-shaded freshwater swamps, marshes, wet edges of streams, from coast to low elevations. Native

OLYM, MORA, NOCA

Lilium columbianum   LILIACEAE
Columbia lily, small-flowered tiger lily
Locally common, early summer, perennial,
1–4(–6) ft. Coastal, meadow, west-side
forest, alpine

Stem erect, unbranched. Leaves in 2–9
whorls, 2–4 in. long, lance-shaped, bright
shiny green. Flowers numerous at top on
separate bent stalks, light to dark orange
with brown spots, facing downward. Flower 1–2½ in. across,
widely bell-shaped, with petals flared or often recurved, long
stamens extending well beyond petals in tight cluster. Grows in
drier coastal meadows, forests, roadsides, subalpine meadows
in northern part of range. May hybridize with *L. pardalinum*
subsp. *vollmeri*, *L. pardalinum* subsp. *wigginsii*, or *L. occidentale*,
where ranges overlap, making identification
difficult. Native   OLYM, MORA, NOCA

Lilium pardalinum subsp. *vollmeri*
LILIACEAE
Leopard lily, Vollmer's tiger lily
Uncommon, midsummer, perennial, 30–40
in. Coastal, bog/fen/wetland, moist stream-
banks, west-side forest

Stems erect, unbranched, often in small
clumps. Leaves entire, in 3–4 whorls or scattered on upper
stem; lower leaves linear, longer than wide. Flowers to 35, hanging or facing outward from stem top. Flower widely bell-
shaped, with petals recurved back or rolled so point is toward
back of petal; inner flower yellow-orange to orange; outer
flower darker, spotted with magenta near tips. Stamens flare
out, forming a bell-shaped profile. Pollen
yellow to red-brown. Grows in streambanks,
moist places, fens, often with *Darlingtonia
californica*, California pitcher-plant. Native

Lilium pardalinum subsp. *wigginsii*
LILIACEAE
Wiggins' lily
Uncommon, midsummer, perennial, 30–48
in. Bog/fen/wetland, moist streambanks, meadow

Stems erect, single to many, nodding flowers at top. Leaves on
large plants in 3–4 whorls midstem, 2–5 in. long, linear, entire;
scattered leaves on smaller plants. Flowers 2–35, nodding;
petals uniformly yellow-orange or orange but not 2-toned, spotted magenta or brown, 1–3 in. long, recurved; pollen pale yellow to pale orange. Grows in drainages, edges of streams, other
moist places in sun or shade, at mid to high elevations. Native

See other *Lilium*: white, page 65; red, page 313

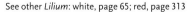

Eschscholzia californica PAPAVERACEAE
California poppy
Common, all spring and summer, annual or
perennial, 6–16 in. Coastal, meadow

Tuft upright from single root. Plant hairless.
Leaves mostly basal with petioles, much divided, segments linear, shiny green to bluish.
Flowers usually solitary, atop long stalks; buds
erect from base with wide round rim, pointed
at tip; 4 petals, in shades of orange to yellow, 1–2 in. wide, many
stamens. Grows in grassy or open areas from sea level to high
elevations. State flower of California. Native OLYM, NOCA

Sphaeralcea munroana MALVACEAE
Orange globe mallow
Locally common, late summer, perennial, 2–3
ft. Shrub-steppe

Erect, densely covered with grayish white star-
shaped hairs. Leaves 2 in., palmately lobed
with 5 bluntly rounded, coarsely toothed lobes.
Racemes of clustered flowers along upper
stems, which are leafless at top. Flowers consist of 5 bright orange to salmon pink ½ in.
petals forming bowl with many shorter yellow
stamens. Grows in dry rocky or sandy soils in
shrub-steppe habitat at mid to low elevations. Similar *S. grossulariifolia,* gooseberry leaf mallow, has deeply divided leaves, the
3 lobes often divided again; it grows at lower elevations and is
more common in volcanic soils. Native

Lewisia tweedyi (*Cistanthe tweedyi*) PORTULACACEAE
Tweedy's lewisia, mountain rose
Endemic, early summer, perennial, 4–8 in.
East-side forest, shrub-steppe

Large crowded rosette of spoon-shaped fleshy
leaves, large salmon flowers. Leaves 3–6 in.
long, with petioles the same length, egg-shaped
to oval, entire, shiny. Spreading flower stems
4–8 in., with 1–3 flowers. Flowers apricot, pink,
or white, sometimes with fine pink pencil
markings. Petals 10–12, about 1 in. long,
pointed or slightly notched; stamens about 15. Grows in rocky
slopes or cliffs, especially with snow cover and little precipitation, at low and mid elevations only in the Wenatchee Mountains in Washington and adjacent British Columbia. This rare
plant is named for its discoverer, Frank Tweedy, a government
railway surveyor working in the Wenatchee Range near Mount
Stuart in 1882. Native

See other *Lewisia*: white, page 114; red, page 352

Mimulus aurantiacus (*Diplacus auranti-acus* subsp. *aurantiacus*)
SCROPHULARIACEAE
Orange bush monkeyflower
Locally common, midspring, perennial,
4–60 in. Coastal

Hairy to hairless shrub. Stems with small clusters of leaves in larger leaf axils. Leaves 1–3 in. long, linear to widely oval, with edges rolled under, upper surface often sticky. Calyx ¾–1½ in., not swollen at base, with uneven lobes, white to pale tan. Flower orange, red, buff, or white, tube 1–2½ in. long with 5 wide lobes uneven on outer edges. Grows on rocky hillsides, cliffs, edges of chaparral and open forests from coast to mid elevations (farther south and inland). At northern extent of its range in northern California and southern Oregon, it is found only along coast. Native

Amsinckia lycopsoides BORAGINACEAE
Bugloss fiddleneck
Common, midspring, annual, 6–30 in.
Coastal, disturbed, meadow, shrub-steppe

Erect stem with long coarse and shorter softer hairs. Leaves linear, with stinging hairs often clustered at base of plant. Flower stalk does not get longer with age, unlike most other members of the family. Flower orange-yellow, less than ½ in. long, with 5 bumps of bristly hairs that fill the top of flower tube. Grows in disturbed or poor soils at low elevations. Native

Amsinckia menziesii BORAGINACEAE
Menzies' fiddleneck, small-flowered fiddleneck
Common, all spring, annual, 4–15 in.
Meadow, west-side forest, shrub-steppe

Erect. Stems, leaves green with bristles. As stem unrolls, flowers bloom from bottom upward. Flowers have calyx with 5 lobes; tube yellow with wide unrestricted throat with or without red dots. Pale yellow-flowered forms usually do not have red dots in throat. Anthers appressed to stigma in throat. Abundant over a wide range in open ground from coastline to mid elevations. Self-pollinating var. *menziesii* (pictured) has no red dots in throat; found throughout the range, including Steens Mountain. Var. *intermedia* is yellow-orange with red-orange dots in throat; grows throughout the range. Native
NOCA

See other *Mimulus*: yellow, page 243; red, page 370

Collomia grandiflora POLEMONIACEAE
Large-flowered collomia
Common, midsummer, annual, 4–36 in.
Meadow, west-side forest

Erect, sometimes branched stems. Basal leaves lance-shaped, toothed; stem leaves lance-shaped to linear, without teeth. Flowers in compact head at stem tip. Flower with long tube flared at top to 5 oval lobes, usually salmon but sometimes white or yellow; pollen deep blue. Grows in dry soils in lightly wooded areas from sea level to mid elevations. Native OLYM, NOCA, CRLA

Impatiens capensis BALSAMINACEAE
Cape jewelweed
Locally common, all summer, annual, 12–40 in.
Bog/fen/wetland, moist streambanks, meadow

Upright. Stems stout, little- or much-branched, enlarged at axils, hairless. Leaves alternate, to 4 in. long, widely oval, toothed. Flowers 1 to few from upper leaf axils, each on a long thread-like stalk. Flowers include a swollen yellow tube with curled spur and 4 orange petal lobes at opening. Grows in moist to wet soils in partly shady places along rivers and creeks. Native OLYM

Lonicera ciliosa CAPRIFOLIACEAE
Orange honeysuckle
Uncommon, late spring–early summer, perennial, 6–18 ft. West-side forest

Trailing to climbing vine with hollow stems. Stems, leaves hairless or with straight hairs on edges. Leaves deciduous, opposite, green above, whitish below, egg-shaped to oval, 1–4 in. long, upper pair fused around stem. Flowers held in short, dense, whorled spike beyond fused leaves at ends of stems. Flowers orange, trumpet-shaped, with 5 lobes, stamens and stigma protruding. Many small orange-red berries. Grows in forests, thickets, from sea level to 5500 ft. Native OLYM, MORA, NOCA, **L&C**

See other *Collomia*: red, page 379 ; blue, page 443
See other *Lonicera*: yellow, page 250; red, page 387

5 symmetrical petals forming a tube

5 petals joined into a bell

Ribes erythrocarpum
Crater Lake currant GROSSULARIACEAE
Locally common, midsummer, perennial,
1–20 in. West-side forest, alpine, subalpine

Shrub with prostrate branches rooting at
nodes throwing upright stems to 20 in.
Plant covered with fine hairs, glands. Leaves
nearly round, to 2 in. across, deeply cut, 3–5
rounded lobes. Flower stalks erect, flowers
copper to salmon, petals about ½ as long as sepals. Abundant
at conifer forest edges, often with mountain hemlock, from
Crater Lake to Mount Jefferson in the Cascade Mountains of
Oregon at 6000–8000 ft. Listed as a noxious weed where introduced in favorable climates. Similar *R. laxiflorum,* trailing black
currant, has stalked glands on lower side of leaf, purplish green
flowers with red petals. Native CRLA

Agoseris aurantiaca
ASTERACEAE (chicory tribe)
Orange agoseris
Common, all summer, perennial, 4–24 in.
Meadow, west-side forest, east-side forest,
alpine, subalpine

Clumps of basal, hairless, lance- to egg-
shaped leaves with or without lobes, sharply
pointed on tip. Flower stalk naked, about same length as leaves.
Flower head single, dense with many deep orange ray petals
squared on outer edge. Petals dry to dark pink or purplish.
Grows in meadows, among shrubs, along streams, at mid to
high elevations. Native OLYM, MORA, NOCA, CRLA

Hieracium aurantiacum   ASTERACEAE (chicory tribe)
Orange hawkweed
Common, all summer, perennial, 1–3 ft.
Meadows, west-side forest

Stems erect, with many stolons. Leaves entire or slightly lobed, coarsely hairy, 2–8 in.
long, oblong, with long petioles. Five to 25
flower heads on stem, each on a short stalk.
Ray-like disk flowers burnt orange, sometimes fading to purple or pink. Grows in
mountain meadows, other open areas. Considered a noxious
weed in some places since it spreads by runners as well as by
seed. Soon becomes common weed of urban lawns where
grown in flower gardens. Nonnative OLYM, MORA, NOCA

See other *Ribes:* white, page 165; yellow, page 251; red, page 388
See other *Agoseris:* yellow, page 264
See other *Hieracium:* white, page 174; yellow, page 268

Hymenoxys hoopesii (*Dugaldia hoopesii,*
Helenium hoopesii)
ASTERACEAE (sunflower tribe)
Orange sneezeweed, tall mountain helenium
Locally common, all summer, perennial, 1–3 ft.
Meadow

Erect stems. Basal and lower stem leaves oblong, entire, with short, winged petioles; leaves
become lance-shaped, sessile toward top.
Flower stalks white-woolly below heads. Flower heads large in
shallow bowl formed of 2 rows of bracts; ray flowers 14–26,
deep yellow to orange, surrounding slightly raised large flat
disk. Grows in meadows on high mountains, including Steens
Mountain. Native

Cuscuta salina   CUSCUTACEAE
Salt marsh dodder
Locally common, all summer, perennial,
tangled mass. Coastal

Twining parasite in salt marshes. Most often
orange, can be pink or white. Tangle of hair-
like stems attaches to many plants with knobby
projections invading stems of host plant.
These sucking parts are all along twisting
stems. Flowers (not pictured) small, white,
later becoming round berry-like capsules with 4 seeds that fall
to start process again. Grows in salt marshes, edges of ponds,
along coast. Other dodders look about the same and live on
herbs, grains, and shrubs. Native OLYM

303

Olsynium douglasii (*Sisyrinchium douglasii*) IRIDACEAE
Grass widows, satin flower
Locally common, early spring, perennial, 6–12 in. Coastal, vernal-wet, meadow, shrub-steppe

Erect clumps of grass-like leaves and round flower stems. Leaves round but not winged, basal to 12 in. Two leaf-like bracts at base of flower, 1 longer than flower extended well above it, the other shorter. Flowers bright purple-red, occasionally white, usually 2 atop stem. Grows at mid elevations in rocky vernal-wet places that dry hard later in spring. Var. *inflatum* has exaggerated points on tips of flower petals, and joined base of filaments in center is obviously enlarged. Colors range from magenta to white and all shades of pink. Native OLYM

Allium acuminatum (*Allium acuminatum* var. *cuspidatum*) LILIACEAE
Tapertip onion
Common, early summer, perennial, 4–14 in. Dry rocky sites, shrub-steppe

Erect stem with few basal leaves. Leaves long, with narrow tapering tips, withering before flowering. Flowers 10–40 held in cluster on 12 in. stem. Deep rose or white petals, tips reflexed, inner 3 petals shorter than outer 3; 2 small leaf-like bracts under the cluster. Grows in open, usually rocky places below 6000 ft. When looking for clues, check for the distinctive odor usually found in this family. Native OLYM, NOCA

Allium campanulatum LILIACEAE
Sierra onion
Uncommon, early summer, perennial, 4–20 in. East-side forest, shrub-steppe

Erect stem, 2–3 flat leaves. Leaves withering at flowering. Flowers at stem top in loose ball of 10–50 blossoms on individual stalks to ½ in., 2 bracts beneath the cluster. Flowers rose to lavender-blue, with dark curved mark at base of pointed petal, 6 low triangular appendages on ovary at center. Grows in forest openings, brushlands, at 1700–8500 ft. Similar *A. bisceptrum* grows in aspen groves and has leaves still green at flowering, flowers pale to dark pink. Also found on Mount Ashland. Native

See other *Allium*: white, page 59

Allium cernuum   LILIACEAE
Nodding onion
Locally common, midsummer, perennial, 20 in.
Coastal, meadow, alpine, subalpine

Erect leafless flower stem with hanging head, many basal leaves, just shorter than flowering stem. Grass-like leaves remain green through flowering. Flowers in numerous nodding clusters with bracts at base, pink to white, bell-shaped. Grows in moist rocky soils from coast to subalpine.
Native OLYM, MORA, NOCA

Allium crenulatum   LILIACEAE
Olympic onion
Uncommon, midsummer, perennial, 3–8 in.
Coastal, alpine, subalpine

Erect leafless flower stem with hanging head, many basal leaves, just shorter than flowering stem. Grass-like leaves remain green through flowering. Flowers in numerous nodding clusters with bracts at base, pink to white, bell-shaped. Grows in moist rocky soils at low to high elevations. Native OLYM, NOCA

Allium douglasii   LILIACEAE
Douglas's onion
Locally common, late spring, perennial, 6–16 in.
Vernal-wet, shrub-steppe

Erect to upright flowering stem, 2 grooved leaves. Plant particularly strong-smelling. Leaves shorter than flower stem, staying green through flowering. Flowers numerous, tiny, star-shaped, in upright, tightly clustered flower head. Often abundant populations of deep pink to white grow in spring-moist areas in steppe. Native

Allium falcifolium LILIACEAE
Coast flatstem onion
Locally common, late spring, perennial, 1–5 in. Dry rocky sites, west-side forest

Erect flat stem, 2 sickle-shaped leaves. Leaves flat, 2–3 times longer than stem, bending to 1 side. Flowers 10–30 in clustered head, deep rosy pink, occasionally pale pink or dirty white, petals pointed, 3 low appendages attached to ovary. Grows on heavy, rocky serpentine, low to high elevations. Native

Allium parvum LILIACEAE
Dwarf onion
Common, midspring, perennial, 1–5 in. East-side forest, shrub-steppe

Stem upright, round to slightly flattened, but no flattened edges. Leaves 2, flat and strongly curved, sickle-shaped, 2–3 times longer than stem. Flower heads round, with 5–10(–30) white to deep pink flowers. Flower petals contain dark pink midveins, stamens deep inside throat. Grows in rocky clay soils, talus, at mid to high elevations. Native

Allium platycaule LILIACEAE
Pink star onion
Locally common, midsummer, perennial, 4–10 in. Dry rocky sites, shrub-steppe

Stem erect, short. Leaves 2, flat-winged, flat sickle-shaped, twice as long as flowering stem, curving to 1 side. Flowers deep pink, 30–90, opening widely, with lance-shaped petals ending in pointed lighter-colored tips that flare or curl back. Stamens extend beyond petals. In seed a narrow constriction is just above ovary. Grows in rocky soils at mid to high elevations. Very similar are the coast flatstem onion, *A. falcifolium*, and Siskiyou onion, *A. siskiyouense*. Native

Allium robinsonii LILIACEAE
Robinson's onion
Endemic, late spring, perennial, 2 in.
Shrub-steppe

Stem erect, about 2 in. tall. Leaves approximately 3 in. long, round, staying green through flowering. Flower head tops purple bracts fused into ring. Flowers pale lavender-pink to white, containing conspicuous red-black pollen. Grows in pure sand, usually under bushes and between basalt outcrops just above high water mark in Columbia River Gorge. Native

Allium siskiyouense (*Allium falcifolium* var. *demissum*)
LILIACEAE
Siskiyou onion
Rare, late spring, perennial, 1–3 in.
Dry rocky sites, shrub-steppe

Erect, narrow, flat, 1–3 in. stem. Pink bulbs near or at surface of soil. Leaves 2, flat sickle-shaped, 2 or more times the length of flowering stem, curving to 1 side. Flower head atop 2 bracts. Flowers 10–35, rose to bright pink; erect petals often with darker midvein and pointed tips; stamens ½ as long as petals. Grows in open, usually serpentine, rocky soils, mid to high elevations. Sometimes makes large, dense displays. See similar species *A. platycaule*. Native

Allium tolmiei LILIACEAE
Tolmie's onion
Locally common, early summer, perennial, 2–6 in. East-side forest, shrub-steppe

Stem erect, flat, winged. Leaves 2, flat sickle-shaped, more or less twice the length of stem, often withering before flowering. Flowers 10–40, petals pink or white with darker pink midvein, pointed tips, edges rolled inward. Grows in clay soils on flats and slopes at mid to high elevations. Native **L&C**

Allium validum LILIACEAE
Tall swamp onion
Common, early summer, perennial, 20–40 in. Bog/fen/wetland, meadow

Stem erect, tall. Leaves flat, 3–6, more or less length of stem. Flowers rose-red to white, 15–40 atop stem in flat cluster; petals lance-shaped, pointed; stamens extending well above petals; pollen yellowish or purple. Grows in swampy meadows. Native MORA, CRLA

Calochortus macrocarpus LILIACEAE
Green-banded mariposa lily
Locally common, perennial, 8–23 in.
East-side forest, shrub-steppe

Erect sturdy stem. Single leaf withering by bloom time, much shorter than stem, edges rolled in, tip curled. Flowers 1–5, large, showy, held erect, purple, with green stripe down center of each petal often more evident on outside. Inside flower marked by purple band and fringe of hairs above triangular gland area at base of petals. Pointed sepals are longer than petals. Seedpod upright, lance-shaped, with sharp angles. Grows in sagebrush, pine forests, at mid to high elevations. Native

Calochortus tolmiei (*Calochortus coeruleus* var. *maweanus*)
LILIACEAE
Tolmie's pussy ears, Tolmie's mariposa lily
Common, early spring, perennial, 4–12 in.
Coastal, meadow, west-side forest

Stem upright, branching. Leaf basal, about same length as stem, persisting through flowering; 1 smaller leaf on stem. Flowers on branching stems single to several, white or lavender, with deeper lavender staining near base, inside covered with hairs, including tips, with straight hairs on edges. Seedpods nodding. Grows from near sea level to mid elevations. Native

See other *Calochortus*: white, page 61; blue, page 402

Calochortus uniflorus LILIACEAE
Pink star tulip

Uncommon, midspring, perennial, 3 in.

Coastal, vernal-wet, bog/fen/wetland, meadow

Stem upright, less than 4 in. tall. Leaf on stem, persisting through flowering. Single stem holds a single or few upward-facing flowers. Bowl-shaped flowers lavender, pink, or white, inside without a band or with a darker purple band, hairless except for a few yellow hairs inside near base of petal. Grows in moist to wet meadows, edges of bogs, fens, at low elevations. The similar lavender-flowered Shasta star tulip, *C. nudus*, found in same habitats, is taller, 5–10 in., and grows at high elevations. Native

Clintonia andrewsiana LILIACEAE
Andrews' clintonia, red bead lily

Uncommon, late spring–early summer, perennial, 1–2 ft. Coastal, west-side forest

Stem erect. Five or 6 leaves 6–12 in. long, 2–5 in. wide, egg-shaped, with pointed tip, some-what hairy. Flowers in terminal cluster, 20 or more, often 2 smaller clusters lower on stem. Flowers deep pink to red-purple, bell-shaped. Seeds contained in bright turquoise-blue

berries. Grows in shaded deep soils in coastal redwood forests. The genus is named for avid naturalist DeWitt Clinton, governor of New York (1817–1822, 1825–1828) and campaigner for the Erie Canal. Native

Dichelostemma ida-maia LILIACEAE
Firecracker flower

Uncommon, late spring–early summer, perennial, 12–40 in. Coastal, meadow, west-side forest

Stem upright but often bent by wind or grow-ing through shrubs. Roots spreading, produc-ing new corms. Leaves 3–5, with shiny blue wax, throughout length of back side, withered by flowering. Flower cluster dense, 6–20 flowers each nodding with ½–2 in. stalks, long cylinder-shaped tubes, bright red, with green tips turned back, green petal lobes and 3 stamens slightly projected. Grows in edges of forests and grassy areas near coast into high eleva-tions. Native

See other *Clintonia*: white, page 63
See other *Dichelostemma*: blue, page 403

Erythronium hendersonii   LILIACEAE
Henderson's fawn lily
Locally common, midspring, perennial,
5–12 in. Meadow, west-side forest

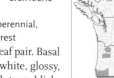

Erect flower stem centered in leaf pair. Basal leaves mottled with brown or white, glossy, 4–10 in. long. Stem pale pink to reddish, leafless. Flowers 1 to many in raceme, nodding. Flower petals pinkish lavender fading to white near center with deep purple markings at base, 3 small sac-like folds at base, stigma slightly shorter than brown to purple stamens. Grows in mixed woods, meadows, fields, at low to mid elevations. Native

Erythronium revolutum   LILIACEAE
Pink fawn lily
Locally common, midspring, perennial,
6–20 in. Coastal, moist streambanks,
meadow, west-side forest

Flower stem erect from pair of mottled basal leaves. Leaves 4–10 in., with smooth to wavy edges, mottled with white or brown. Stem carries raceme of 1–3 flowers. Flowers nodding, rose-pink with band of yellow in center, 4 sac-like appendages at base of the 3 true petals, filament section of stamens flattened. Grows in open to dense woods, along rivers, in meadows, from coast to low elevations. Native OLYM

Fritillaria recurva   LILIACEAE
Red bells
Locally common, midspring, perennial,
1–3½ ft. West-side forest

Stems erect, unbranched. Stems bare on bottom, with midstem whorls of 3–5 leaves, single leaves alternating at top with flower stalks from leaf axils. Leaves narrow, thinly coated with bluish powder. Flowers on short stalks, nodding, bell-shaped, with tips recurved, scarlet with yellow mottling. Grows in dry woods, shrubs, on hillsides in shade, at low to mid elevations. Rare and endangered *F. gentneri* is similar and grows in same range; flower tips are straight or slightly flared; plant is deeper, more maroon shade of red. Native

See other *Erythronium*: white, page 64; yellow, page 188
See other *Fritillaria*: yellow, page 188; green/brown, page 459

Lilium bolanderi LILIACEAE
Bolander's lily
Rare, early summer, perennial, 2–4 ft.
West-side forest

Stems erect, unbranched. Leaves in 2–6 whorls, egg-shaped, to 3 in. long, wavy-edged, covered with white or blue waxy powder. Flowers 1–9 atop stem with separate stalks, nodding to outward-facing, narrowly bell-shaped, dark wine red to pink with yellowish centers, darker spots on inner surface, dark red anthers, magenta or brownish red pollen. Grows in rocky serpentine in shrubby areas, conifer forests, at low to mid elevations. Native

Lilium occidentale LILIACEAE
Western tiger lily
Endemic, early summer, perennial, 1–4 ft.
Coastal, bog/fen/wetland

Stem erect, unbranched. Leaves light green, 1–3 whorls on central stem, scattered above and below; leaf lance-shaped to linear, entire, with pointed tips. Few to many odorless, pendent flowers at top. Petals recurve back; outer part of petal is bright scarlet fading to green center with dark red spots, often a connecting band of orange or yellow between red and green. Stamen filaments nearly straight, lying close to style. Grows in wet places along coast, where it is threatened with extinction. Note the different profile from *L. pardalinum*, with stamens flared into a bell shape. Native

Streptopus lanceolatus var. curvipes
(*Streptopus roseus*) LILIACEAE
Rosy twisted stalk
Locally common, early summer, perennial, 6–12 in. West-side forest

Stem erect, usually unbranched but not noticeably twisted. Leaves 2–4 in., oval, with sharply pointed tips, alternate on stem but not clasping it. Flowers hang singly from under leaf nodes on curved, not zigzag, stalks. Flowers ½ in., bell-shaped, pink to rosy purple, with white tips that slightly curl back. Berries oval, bright red. Grows in moist shade in forests, along streams, from coast to subalpine. Similar *S. streptopoides*, small twisted stalk, is less than 8 in., with hanging flowers saucer-shaped, greenish with purple tint, petals spreading out and back, leaves not clasping stem. Native
OLYM, MORA, NOCA, CRLA

See other *Lilium*: white, page 65; orange, page 298
See other *Streptopus*: yellow, page 189

Trillium kurabayashii LILIACEAE
Giant purple wakerobin
Rare, early spring, perennial, 8–28 in.
Coastal

Stem erect, with large sessile leaves at top. Leaves to 6 in. long, 5 in. wide, mottled with dark brown. Flowers sessile above leaves; sepals lance-shaped, green, often marked with purple, 2–3 in. long, held horizontally. Petals erect to spreading, oblong, widest near middle, 2–4½ in. long, dark liver red, often becoming twisted with age. Grows in rich moist soils with deep humus, near coast. Can form large colonies. Native

Trillium petiolatum LILIACEAE
Roundleaf trillium
Locally common, early spring, perennial,
4–27 in. Moist streambanks, east-side forest

Prostrate or with short erect stem. Leaves on long horizontal petioles near soil level, bright green, rounded, easily mistaken for plantain. Flower in center is sessile or on stalk to 6 in.; petals linear, 1–2½ in. long, with pointed tips, dark purplish red or greenish to yellow. Grows in rocky soils above edges of streams, river flats, openings in forests, in spring-wet and swampy soils. Native **L&C**

Lythrum salicaria LYTHRACEAE
Purple loosestrife
Common, all summer, perennial, 2–6 ft.
Coastal, bog/fen/wetland, meadow

Erect, often in large expanding clumps. Stems branched or not, covered with gray hair. Leaves opposite, whorled or alternate above, sessile, lance-shaped, with pointed tip, 2–6 in. long, hairy. Inflorescence consists of a spike at top with egg-shaped bracts, sessile flowers. Flowers wrinkled, purple or red-purple; petals 5–7, about ½ in. long; stamens more or less 12; styles 3 distinct lengths. Grows worldwide in ditches, margins of streams and ponds, marshy places, at low elevations. Among the most noxious aquatic weeds in North America, it takes over wetlands and displaces native plants. Nonnative **OLYM**

See other *Trillium*: white, page 67

Calypso bulbosa ORCHIDACEAE
Fairyslipper, deer's-head orchid
Uncommon, early summer, perennial, 3–7 in.
Coastal, west-side forest, east-side forest

Stem single, erect, with 1 widely oval basal leaf on short petiole. Leaf 1–2½ in. across at widest point, with parallel veins, emerging in autumn, persisting through winter, withering in summer. Flower consists of 3 showy, usually rosy pink, pointed sepals and 2 pink petals above large, hanging, white or lighter pink slipper with rose-madder spotting. Bracts wrapping stem 2–4, top bract erect above flower. Albinos are not rare. Grows in deep forests in mountains around the world, here below 5500 ft. The genus is named for the beautiful sea nymph in Homer's *Odyssey*. Picking will break the roots and kill the plant. Native

OLYM, MORA, NOCA, CRLA, **L&C**

Corallorrhiza maculata ORCHIDACEAE
Spotted coralroot
Locally common, early summer, perennial,
7–22 in. West-side forest, east-side forest

Stem erect, red to yellow-brown. Leaves bract-like wrapped on stem. Flowers on upper stem. Five upper flower petals similar color to stem; lower petal much larger, white, with 4–8 large red to purple spots. Inside flower is a curved column with pollen and nectar beneath. Lacking spur under base of lower petal. Grows in deep forest duff below timberline. Weight of an insect on lower petal exposes pollen and sticky stigma surface to receive pollen from other flowers. In same but damper habitat, closer to small streams, is *C. trifida*, northern coralroot, with yellowish stem and white to yellowish flowers.

Native OLYM, MORA, NOCA, CRLA

Corallorrhiza mertensiana
ORCHIDACEAE
Western coralroot, Mertens' coralroot
Uncommon, early summer, perennial, 6–18 in.
West-side forest, east-side forest

Stem slender, erect, red to brownish purple. Upper petals pink to reddish pink, with yellow to dark red veins; lower petal wider, deep pink to red, with 3 deep red veins; spur prominent, under base of lower petal. Grows in shady conifer forests at low to mid elevations. Similar to *C. maculata*, spotted coralroot, which lacks spur. Native

OLYM, MORA, NOCA, CRLA

Corallorrhiza striata ORCHIDACEAE
Striped coralroot
Uncommon, early summer, perennial,
12–20 in. West-side forest

Stem erect, red-brown to yellow, with bract-like leaves wrapping around lower stem. Flowers drooping from upper stem with petals spreading over lip. Flowers pale pinkish yellow or brown, with longitudinal stripes of deeper red to purple; lip wider, slightly cupped, almost solid deeper red. Lacks spur at base of lower petal. Grows in deep shade in decomposing duff or along streams. Similar to *C. maculata*, spotted coralroot, but is the largest-flowered coralroot. Native OLYM, MORA, NOCA, CRLA

Eriogonum niveum POLYGONACEAE
Snow eriogonum
Locally common, all summer, perennial,
6–18 in. Dry rocky sites, east-side forest,
shrub-steppe

Dense subshrub with erect leaves. Numerous stems with few branches. Leaves oblong to egg-shaped, with petioles 2–3 times as long, very white with thick matted hairs on both sides. Flower stalks, freely branched with leafy bracts at each fork, are covered with white matted hairs, as are bases of flower heads. Flowers pinkish, white, or occasionally pale yellow, scattered along stalks. Grows in dry, open, rocky or sandy places, sometimes in large masses. Native

Eriogonum thymoides POLYGONACEAE
Thyme buckwheat, thyme desert buckwheat
Locally common, midspring, perennial,
6–10 in. Dry rocky sites, shrub-steppe

Mat or low cushion, leaves at ends of branches. Stems with shredded bark. Leaves linear, less than ½ in. long, ash-gray to green and hairless above. Flower stem 1–3 in., with whorl of leafy bracts about midway. Flowers in dense roundish cluster in a single cup, bracts erect, yellow or white to rose-red. Grows in dry or rocky soils in sagebrush, on rocky ridges. Native

See other *Eriogonum*: white, page 75; yellow, page 191

Eriogonum vimineum POLYGONACEAE
Wire-stem buckwheat, broom buckwheat
Common, early spring–autumn, annual, 2–12
in. Dry rocky sites, shrub-steppe

Erect. Stem widely branched in top section.
Basal leaves to 1⅓ in., oval to round, coated
with matted hairs, thicker on underside. Small
cylinder-like base hugs stem holding small
cluster of rose to white or pale yellow flowers.
Common plant found in volcanic or granite sand or gravel at
low to high elevations, including Steens Mountain and Siskiyou Mountains. Native

Oxyria digyna (*Rumex digyna*) POLYGONACEAE
Mountain sorrel, alpine sorrel
Locally common, midsummer, perennial, less
than 20 in. Alpine, subalpine

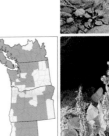

Erect stems, basal leaves. Plant hairless late in
the season. Leaves round to heart-shaped, with
long petioles, fleshy, sour-tasting. Flower stems
numerous, upper section crowded with many
red and green flowers on short stalks. Seed in
center of flat round disk. Grows in rocky open
sites, alpine rock crevices, talus, at high elevations. Circumboreal. *Oxyria* means "sour" and
refers to the very acid-tasting leaves, which can be used in sal-
ads. Native OLYM, MORA, NOCA, CRLA

Polygonum amphibium POLYGONACEAE
Water smartweed
Common, all spring and summer, perennial, 6–12 in.
Bog/fen/wetland, lake/pond

Aquatic or amphibious. Leaves along stems,
oblong to lance-shaped, often tinted brown,
shiny, with noticeable veins. Flowers numerous, bright pink, held on stalks from upper
part of stem. Floats in shallow water or grows
in wet soils at edges of water, at all elevations
below subalpine. Soils may dry in autumn. Var.
emersum (pictured, also known as *P. coccineum*)
has upright stems with lance-shaped leaves
and flower spike to 2 in. Var. *stipulaceum* floats, with oblong
leaf, and 1 in. flower spike. Native OLYM, NOCA

See other *Polygonum*: white, page 77; yellow, page 193

Polygonum aviculare POLYGONACEAE
Common knotweed, yard knotweed, doorweed
Common, all year long, annual or perennial, prostrate. Disturbed

Prostrate, round stems to 2 ft. long, branching from central stem. Plant hairless. Leaves bluish green, lance-shaped. Clusters of 1–5 flowers arise from leaf axils. Flower petals greenish with red or pink edges, united into tube halfway, then spreading. Grows in gardens, dry gravel, edges of concrete, roadsides, disturbed soils. Tolerant of compaction. Very similar *P. arenastrum* has larger green flowers with white or pink edges and linear leaves. Nonnative OLYM, MORA, NOCA

Polygonum persicaria
POLYGONACEAE
Lady's-thumb knotweed, heartweed
Common, all summer, annual or perennial, 8–36 in. Bog/fen/wetland, disturbed, meadow

Erect, shiny, smooth. Stem branching from base, sometimes swollen above joints. Bracts on stems at leaf joints papery and fringed. Leaves lance-shaped, pointed at tips, usually with a dark spot in the middle, dots on underside. Flowers atop shiny stalks in dense uninterrupted spikes, pink or rarely white. A weedy species most often found on moist places and disturbed soils at low to mid elevations. Nonnative OLYM, NOCA

Polygonum polygaloides POLYGONACEAE
White-margined knotweed
Locally common, midsummer, annual, 2–8 in. Vernal-wet, meadow, shrub-steppe, alpine, subalpine

Stems erect, more or less zigzag. Leaves narrow, with pointed tip, sessile with obvious appendage at joint. Flower stalks branched. Inflorescence to 3 in. long, clustered at stem tips, with white- or greenish-margined bracts. Flowers pink, red, or white with green or red midvein, may or may not open. Grows in vernal-moist places, often with ponderosa pine, to 10,000 ft. Subsp. *confertiflorum* has bracts in flower spike, pointing upward or outward with wide white edges becoming smaller near top. Subsp. *kelloggii* has narrow soft bracts with green edges, stem stout and compressed; often found in vernal-moist areas in shrub-steppe. Native CRLA

Rumex acetosella POLYGONACEAE
Sheep sorrel, red sorrel, sour dock
Common, all summer, perennial, less than 18
in. Coastal, disturbed, meadow, west-side
forest, east-side forest

Erect. Stems slender, usually in small colonies.
Leaves mostly basal, arrow-shaped, with a lobe
on each side. Plants with male or female
flowers or rarely both on top sections of
branches. Flowers red or yellow, male with long stamens that
hang. Grows in disturbed soils, fields, along beaches, at low to
high elevations. Both *Rumex* and *sorrel* mean "sour." The leaves
are full of vitamin C but also contain oxalic acid, which causes
medical problems if too much is eaten. Flavor is somewhat like
rhubarb, which also contains oxalic acid. Nonnative
OLYM, MORA, NOCA, CRLA

Rumex occidentalis (*Rumex aquaticus* var.
fenestratus) POLYGONACEAE
Western dock
Uncommon, early summer, perennial, 3–5 ft.
Coastal, vernal-wet, bog/fen/wetland

Erect. Stem single, stout, often tinted red, unbranched below inflorescence. Basal leaves numerous, leathery, heart- to lance-shaped, with
heart-shaped or square base, edge more or less curled; smaller
leaves along stem from base into bottom of inflorescence. Flowers pink or green held in dense clusters on upper, branched
stems. Grows throughout North America in wet or vernal-wet
ponds, salty wet places, at low to mid elevations. Native
OLYM, MORA

Rumex venosus POLYGONACEAE
Winged dock, wild begonia
Locally common, all summer, perennial, 6–18
in. Shrub-steppe

Stem upright or lying down with upturned
tips, few flexible side branches. Plants spread
by thick woody rootstalks, often forming a
dense mass. Leaves on stems, 1–4 in., oval,
with pointed tip, leathery, with obvious veins.
Flowers very large, bright red to pink, on upright spikes. Grows
in dry sandy places, even sand dunes, at low to mid elevations.
If buried in sand, plants send up new shoots. Native

See other *Rumex*: green/brown, page 463

Arabis aculeolata BRASSICACEAE
Waldo rockcress
Endemic, all spring, perennial, 8–15 in.
Rocky serpentine

Erect stems with spreading hairs on lower part. Leaves in basal rosette, ½–1 in., entire, surface densely coated with coarse, straight, branched hairs; stem leaves small, sometimes toothed. Flowers in terminal cluster, petals spoon-shaped, bright pink to rose-red, calyx rose-red. Seedpods straight, erect, to 2½ in. long, narrow. Listed as rare in California and Oregon, where it is endemic to the Siskiyou Mountains. Native

Arabis hirsuta BRASSICACEAE
Hairy rockcress
Locally common, late spring, annual or biennial or perennial, 8–25 in. Coastal, disturbed

Erect, covered with coarse hairs. Basal leaves with short petioles, oblong to egg-shaped, 1–3 in. long, entire to sharply toothed, tips rounded; stem leaves linear, alternately spaced more or less evenly, clasping. Flowers pinkish, cream, or white on single or branched stems in terminal cluster. Seedpods long and flat, hairless, erect to spreading. Grows in sandy to gravelly soils, disturbed places, from beach to high elevations. Var. *glabrata* has hairless leaves, is sparsely hairy on stem. Similar *A. glabra* has oblong to spoon-shaped, toothed or lobed leaves, and grows in meadows. Native OLYM, MORA, NOCA

Arabis lyallii BRASSICACEAE
Lyall's rockcress
Uncommon, early summer, perennial, 4–10 in. Alpine

Stems slender, upright. Leaves at base sessile or with short petiole, oblong, ⅓–1 in., with few smaller leaves on stem. Flowers 3–15 on stem top, rose to purple. Seedpods erect to spreading outward, straight, hairless, to 2⅓ in. long. Grows in rock crevices, on slopes, ridges, at high elevations. Native OLYM, MORA, NOCA

See other *Arabis*: white, page 80

Arabis sparsiflora BRASSICACEAE
Sicklepod rockcress
Locally common, midspring, biennial or
perennial, 6–24 in. Dry rocky sites

Clump with mostly basal leaves, 1 to few
stems. Stems straight or branched near top.
Leaves 1–4 in., lance-shaped, with sharply
pointed tip, entire or toothed, hairy; many stem
leaves similar with lobed base, clasping stem.
Flower petals spoon-shaped, pink or purple. Seedpods 2–5 in.,
recurved, held outward from stem, hairless. Grows in rocky
places at all elevations. Native NOCA

Cakile edentula BRASSICACEAE
American searocket, oval searocket
Common, all summer–autumn, annual or
biennial or perennial, 6–18 in. Coastal

Erect to prostrate, branched. Leaves fleshy, egg-
to spoon-shaped, with petioles wide or sessile,
edges wavy to toothed or entire. Flowers in
elongating cluster at stem tops; petals pale purplish pink or lavender to white, or sometimes
without petals. Seedpods in 2 segments, the
lower segment without lobes or horns. Grows
on sandy edges of ocean beaches. Young leaves
are edible, tangy and tasty. Native OLYM

Cakile maritima BRASSICACEAE
European searocket
Locally common, all spring and summer, annual
or perennial, to 20 in. Coastal

Prostrate to erect, fleshy, hairless. Stems
branch outward from base, often on ground,
sometimes forming upright mounds. Leaves
2–3 in. long, egg- to spoon-shaped, with short
petioles, deeply pinnately divided. Flowers
clustered at stem tops, 4 petals pale to deep
rose, rarely white, stems elongate to 8–14 in.
in fruit. Seedpods fleshy, green drying to tan,
with joint across center; upper section cone-
shaped, with sharp point; lower section 2 horn-
like projections; 1 seed in each section. Grows in coastal beach
sand. Nonnative OLYM

Cardamine californica var. integrifolia (Dentaria californica var. integrifolia, Cardamine integrifolia)

BRASSICACEAE

Coast toothwort, milkmaids

Locally common, midspring, perennial, 6–14 in. Coastal, meadow, west-side forest

Single or many upright stems from rhizome. Stem stout, hairless. Leaves thick, fleshy, green or tinted purple. Basal leaves 1–3 in. long, egg-shaped to almost round, usually divided into 3 leaflets; upper stem leaves divided, 3–5 linear to lance-shaped leaflets, entire, few teeth, or 1 at tip. Flower petals 4, white to pale pink, to ½ in. Grows in shady, moist woods, fields near coastline. Native

Cardamine nuttallii var. nuttallii

(*Cardamine pulcherrima*) BRASSICACEAE

Oaks toothwort, beautiful bittercress

Locally common, early spring, perennial, 4–8 in. West-side forest

Upright, hairless. Stem slender, undivided. Leaf at base single, entire to shallowly lobed; 2 upper stem leaves with short petioles are divided into 3–5 oblong sessile leaflets ½–2 in. with sharply pointed tips. Flowers in showy cluster; petals 4, pale pink to purple or rarely white. Seedpods ¾–2 in. long, narrow, ascending. Grows in deep humus soils in moist sites, forests, at low to mid elevations. Native OLYM, NOCA, **L&C**

Phoenicaulis cheiranthoides BRASSICACEAE

Dagger pod

Common, midspring, perennial, 4–10 in. Dry rocky sites, shrub-steppe, alpine, subalpine

Basal clump of many gray leaves from thick base. Leaves egg-shaped to narrowly oval, densely to lightly covered with white or gray forked hairs, 4–10 in. long, including petiole. Flowers in dense leafless clusters on horizontal stems. Petals pink to lavender or purple, spoon-shaped. Seedpods on elongating stems spread outward on short stalks, lance-shaped, flat, ½–3 in. long, hairless. Grows in basalt outcrops, rocky soils, in Great Basin, at mid to high elevations. Native CRLA

See other *Cardamine*: white, page 81

Streptanthus cordatus BRASSICACEAE
Heart-leaved jewel flower, twistflower
Uncommon, late spring–early summer,
biennial or perennial, 1–3 ft. East-side forest,
shrub-steppe, alpine, subalpine

Stem erect, small basal rosette. Foliage yellow-green. Basal leaves heart-shaped, toothed above middle, with petioles as long as leaf; stem leaves usually toothless, clasping. Flowers on extending stem. Calyx of 4 bristle-tipped sepals, yellow-green in bud, becoming purple in flower; 4 yellow or red-purple petals extend upward. Seedpods straight, 2–4 in., pointing upward. Grows in rocky or sandy scrub, pine forests, at high elevations. *Streptanthus tortuosus*, in rocky serpentine or volcanic soils, is shrub-like, its 1 to several stems with few branches. Inflorescence bracts pale greenish yellow, sepals purple or greenish yellow, petals tipped white and veined purple. Native

Corydalis scouleri FUMARIACEAE
Scouler's corydalis
Locally common, late spring, perennial, 20–50
in. Moist streambanks, west-side forest

Erect, sturdy, hairless, with a slight covering of bluish waxy powder. Stems hollow. Leaves usually 3 from upper part of stem, large, divided into oblong leaflets with rounded or pointed tips. Flowers pink, rose, or bicolored, about 1 in. long, held in neat rows on long narrow spike, long spurs pointing upward or outward. Grows in moist woodlands, along shaded streambanks, shaded moist roadsides. Native OLYM, MORA

Dicentra formosa FUMARIACEAE
Pacific bleeding heart
Locally common, all spring, perennial, 6–20 in.
Coastal, meadow, west-side forest

Upright. Leaves and long succulent flower stems from rhizomes. Leaves numerous, divided 3 times into fern-like segments, often with a bluish waxy coating. Flowers hang in clusters above foliage. Flowers heart-shaped, with flared tips. Grows in damp shaded places or near large rocks. Subsp. *formosa* has flowers pink to rose-red; does not grow on serpentine. Native OLYM, MORA, NOCA, CRLA

See other *Corydalis*: white, page 87; yellow, page 201
See other *Dicentra*: white, page 88

Dicentra uniflora FUMARIACEAE
Steer's head, longhorn steershead
Rare, all spring, perennial, 2–4 in.
West-side forest, east-side forest, alpine, subalpine

Prostrate to upright. Leaf single, basal, 2–3½ in. long including stem, deeply dissected, with whitish waxy powder on underside. Flower stem slightly longer than leaf, holds single flower. Flower white to brownish, peach, or pink, more or less nodding, 2 outer petals almost flat, curved up and inward to form horns. Grows in gravelly soils, sometimes with serpentine rock, at low to high elevations. Similar *D. pauciflora*, shorthorn steershead, has leaves with numerous finely cut lobes, flowers with 2 short sepals appearing as short horns. Native MORA, CRLA

Centaurium erythraea (*Centaurium umbellatum*) GENTIANACEAE
Common centaury, European centaury
Locally common, all summer, annual or biennial, 4–20 in. Disturbed, meadow, west-side forest

Erect, hairless. Leaves in basal rosette, bright green at flowering, 1–2 in., oblong, with rounded tips; few stem leaves opposite, narrow, with pointed tips. Inflorescence dense in flat-topped clusters, sessile with 2 bracts at base. Flowers bright reddish pink, funnel-shaped, with 5 lobes. Grows in fields, roadsides, meadows, disturbed places, more often west of Cascade Mountains, at low elevations. Nonnative OLYM, NOCA

Centaurium muehlenbergii
GENTIANACEAE
Monterey centaury
Common, all summer, annual or biennial, 1–12 in. Vernal-wet, meadow, east-side forest, shrub-steppe

Erect, slender. Basal leaves none or few, egg-shaped, ¼–¾ in. long; stem leaves sessile, smaller. Flowers few at stem top, each sessile or on short stalk with 2 bracts. Flowers funnel-shaped, with 5 lobes, pink to white, stigma at top of pistil oblong. Grows in moist open places in forests at low elevations. A common native often confused with *C. erythraea*, which has a more conspicuous basal rosette of leaves and many flowers in crowded clusters. Native

Gentianella amarella (*Gentiana amarella*)
GENTIANACEAE
Northern gentian
Locally common, mid to late summer, annual
or biennial, 2–16 in. Coastal, bog/fen/wetland,
meadow, subalpine

Erect. Stem often with long branches becoming shorter upward. Leaves 5–8 pairs, egg-shaped at base, becoming lance-shaped on upper stem. Flowers in crowded clusters at tips of stem and branches, blue, rosy lavender, or creamy white, with lance-shaped bracts at base of clusters. Flower lobes 4 or 5, without appendages between lobes, fringe of hairs on inner surface of each lobe nearly as long as lobe. Grows in open woods, thickets, wet meadows, along roads and moist areas, at low to high elevations. Native OLYM, NOCA

Abronia umbellata (*Abronia umbellata*
subsp. *acutalata*) NYCTAGINACEAE
Pink sand verbena
Rare, all year long, perennial, prostrate. Coastal
Prostrate mat. Stems often reddish, becoming
more than 3 ft. long, hairless or covered with
gland-tipped hairs. Leaves fleshy, oval to more
or less diamond-shaped, with ½–2½ in. long

petiole. Flower head with 1–6 in. stalk, contains 8–27 fragrant flowers. Flowers pink to magenta with yellowish white center. Grows in coastal sand on beaches, dunes, scrub, below 300 ft. Only 20 populations in California and Oregon. Historically in Washington but now apparently extirpated. Very rare in British Columbia. Native

Chamerion angustifolium (*Epilobium*
angustifolium) ONAGRACEAE
Fireweed
Common, all summer, perennial, 2–5 ft.
Disturbed, meadow, west-side forest, east-side
forest

Stems erect, unbranched, usually reddish, with short stiff hairs on upper part. Leaves numerous, alternate, lance-shaped, 2–8 in. long; petioles short. Inflorescence is a dense spike with small leaf-like bracts. Flowers face outward around stem; petals deep pink to magenta, ¾–1 in. long, with rounded tip; sepals between petals same color, ½ as long; pollen noticeably gray. Grows in open or disturbed sites, especially recent burns, from sea level to subalpine. Subsp. *circumvagum* is less than 12 in. tall, with distinctive leaf veins. Native OLYM, MORA, NOCA

See other *Abronia*: white, page 88; yellow, page 201

Chamerion latifolium (*Epilobium latifolium*) ONAGRACEAE
Red willowherb, broad-leaved willowherb
Uncommon, all summer, perennial, 2–15 in.
Bog/fen/wetland, moist streambanks,
meadow, alpine, subalpine

Sprawling to upright plant up to 20 in. tall.
Leaves 1–2½ in. long, widely oval, alternate
along stem, including among the flowers.
Flowers rose, pink, or rarely white in short spike at top, 1–1½
in. across. Petals 4, oval, narrow to pointed at tip; sepals 4, linear, same length as petals. Found in mountains on wet slopes, along streams, rivers. Native OLYM, MORA, NOCA

Clarkia amoena ONAGRACEAE
Farewell-to-spring
Common, late spring–early summer, annual,
6–24 in. Coastal, vernal-wet, meadow

Stem erect to decumbent, branched or unbranched. Leaves alternate, linear, 1–3 in.
long, entire. Buds held erect. Flowers cup-
shaped, pale pink to deep wine red, petals

round to fan-shaped, often with red spot in
center. Grows in seaside bluffs, open drying
soils, at low to mid elevations. *Amoena*
means "charming," an apt name for this plant. Native
OLYM, NOCA

Clarkia gracilis ONAGRACEAE
Slender clarkia
Common, midsummer, annual, 6–18 in.
Meadow, east-side forest, shrub-steppe
Stem erect, hairless to densely hairy. Leaves
1–2½ in., linear. Flower buds hang down;
open flowers pink or pinkish lavender, often
lighter toward base; petals fan-shaped, without any spots or veins. Grows in open dry
areas at low to mid elevations. Native

Clarkia pulchella ONAGRACEAE
Ragged robin, Elkhorns clarkia
Uncommon, early summer, annual, 6–18 in.
East-side forest, shrub-steppe

Erect, unbranched to widely branched, hairy stem, many leaves. Leaves linear to spoon-shaped, with pointed tips, entire or slightly toothed, 1–3 in. long; upper leaves about same size as below. Flowers dense in short spike with nodding buds. Petals pink to rose, with lighter veins, divided into 3 lobes, the central lobe wider, base of petal long and narrow. Grows in rocky sandy places at mid to high elevations. Blooms in abundance with plentiful rainfall. The shape of the petal reflects the common name. *Pulchella* is Latin and means "beautiful." Native **L&C**

Clarkia purpurea subsp. *quadrivulnera* (*Godetia quadrivulnera, Clarkia quadrivulnera*) ONAGRACEAE
Small-flowered godetia
Uncommon, early summer, annual, 6–20 in.
Meadow, west-side forest, east-side forest

Stem erect, variable in leaf and flower. Leaves long, narrow, hairless to densely covered with hairs. Flower buds erect. Flowers small, widely spaced, pink, lavender, purple, or wine red, sometimes with darker spot on upper part of petal; petals fan-shaped, with a slight uneven upper edge. Grows in grassy or shrubby places at low elevations. Often hybridizes in southern part of range with subsp. *purpurea*, with long, widely lance-shaped leaves, flowers in dense head. Native OLYM

Clarkia rhomboidea ONAGRACEAE
Common clarkia
Locally common, early summer, annual, 8–22 in. Disturbed, west-side forest, east-side forest, shrub-steppe

Stem decumbent to erect, with bent tip. Leaf lance- to egg-shaped, ½–1½ in. long. Flower buds hang down. Flowers lavender-pink with darker marks or stains; petals diamond-shaped, with 2 rounded protrusions near base; pollen blue-gray. Grows in pine forests, dry woodlands, open areas, at low to high elevations. Native NOCA

Epilobium anagallidifolium (*Epilobium alpinum*) ONAGRACEAE
Alpine willowherb
Uncommon, midsummer, perennial, 2–12 in. Bog/fen/wetland, meadow, moist streambanks, alpine, subalpine

Mats of reddish stems lie on ground with tips turned upward. Plant hairless, spreading by short rhizomes. Leaves usually opposite, spoon-shaped to oblong, pointed tips, entire or wavy-edged, to 2 in. long. Flowers pink to rose or white, petals notched. Grows in subalpine and alpine wet sites, at high elevations, including moist rocks and talus. Similar *E. oregonense*, *E. clavatum*, *E. lactiflorum*, and *E. hornemannii* are very difficult to distinguish and considered by some to be phases of the same species. Native OLYM, MORA, NOCA

Epilobium brachycarpum (*Epilobium paniculatum*) ONAGRACEAE
Autumn willowherb, parched fireweed, tall annual willowherb
Common, late spring–midsummer, annual, 1–6 ft. Disturbed, meadow, shrub-steppe

Stem erect, branched. Lower stem smooth, with outer layer peeling, some rigid hairs on upper stem. Leaves lance-shaped, mostly alternate, folded at midvein, to 2 in. long, deciduous at bloom time. Flowers pinkish purple to white, held on upper branches, variable in size. Grows in dry soils at all elevations. Extremely variable species, particularly in terms of flower size. Native OLYM, MORA

Epilobium canum subsp. *latifolium*
(*Zauschneria californica* subsp. *latifolia*, *Zauschneria latifolium*) ONAGRACEAE
Hummingbird trumpet, California trumpet
Locally common, late summer–autumn, perennial, 4–35 in. West-side forest, east-side forest, alpine, subalpine

Matted or upright, densely hairy, grayish to green, usually with glands. Stems may be woody at base. Leaves to 2 in. long, sessile, mostly opposite, lance-shaped to oval, usually entire, can be deeply toothed. Flowers bright red-orange, in clusters at stem tips, held horizontally. Four sepals and 4 petals form a 1–1½ in. long funnel-shaped tube with petals 2-lobed at the end. The 8 stamens and single pistil project beyond petals. Grows in rocky places, talus, open dry slopes, at high elevations from southern Oregon south. Native

See other *Epilobium*: white, page 89; yellow, page 203

Epilobium densiflorum (*Boisduvalia densiflora*) ONAGRACEAE
Dense-flowered willowherb, dense-flowered boisduvalia
Locally common, midsummer, annual, 6–40 in.
Vernal-wet, moist streambanks, meadow,
disturbed, shrub-steppe

Stem erect, sometimes branched in inflorescence. Leaves opposite, narrow, lance-shaped, ½–2 in. long; upper leaves hairy, sessile, becoming shorter, wider, alternate. Inflorescence with many leaves and spikes of many flowers, sometimes sticky with glands. Flower petals pink to rose-purple, deeply lobed, less than ½ in. long. Seed has no dandelion like fluff. Grows at all elevations in dry soils that were moist in spring. Similar *E. torreyi*, brook spike-primrose, with sharply pointed seedpods and also without dandelion fluff attached to the seed, grows in the Columbia River Gorge and on Steens Mountain. Native MORA

Epilobium glaberrimum ONAGRACEAE
Glaucous willowherb, smoothstem fireweed
Common, all summer, perennial, 1–3 ft. Moist
streambanks, meadow, west-side forest, east-
side forest, alpine, subalpine

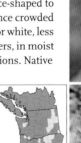

Erect clump with short stolons. Stems smooth, shiny or covered lightly with whitish waxy powder. Leaves lance-shaped to oval, with rounded tips, clasping stem. Inflorescence crowded with leaves and flowers. Flowers tiny, pink to rose or white, less than ½ in. long. Grows in gravelly places along rivers, in moist scree and other moist places, at mid to high elevations. Native
OLYM, MORA, NOCA

Epilobium minutum ONAGRACEAE
Threadstem fireweed
Common, all spring and summer, annual, 1–4
in. Vernal-wet, disturbed, east-side forest,
shrub-steppe

Upright stem, usually branched, with soft hairs. Flat leaves, sometimes clustered, usually opposite, narrowly oval to spoon-shaped. Flowers consist of 4 sepals with pointed tips and 4 rounded, pink or white petals. Grows in dry open areas, often after fire, drying vernal pools, at low to mid elevations. Native
OLYM, MORA, NOCA

Epilobium obcordatum ONAGRACEAE
Rock willowherb, rose willowherb
Rare, midsummer, perennial, 2–6 in.
Dry rocky sites, alpine, subalpine

Mats with stems seldom exceeding 6 in. Leaves many, alternate on stem, widely oval to nearly round, with widely rounded tip, ¼–¾ in. long with short petiole, shiny or lightly covered with white or blue powdery wax. Flowers pink to deep rose-purple, petals to 1 in. long, deeply lobed. Grows in rocky places, usually in colonies among rocks, at high elevations. Similar *E. siskiyouense* has sessile leaves with tip pointed; grows on rocky serpentine, scree in Siskiyou Mountains at high elevations. Native

Epilobium rigidum ONAGRACEAE
Siskiyou Mountains willowherb, rigid willowherb
Rare, late summer, perennial, 5–15 in.
Vernal-wet, moist streambanks, west-side forest

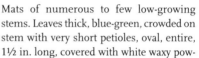

Mats of numerous to few low-growing stems. Leaves thick, blue-green, crowded on stem with very short petioles, oval, entire, 1½ in. long, covered with white waxy powder. Flowers with short stalks clustered at stem tip; calyx deep rose; petals pink to rose, to 1 in. long, with deeply cleft tips. Bloom continues on extending stalk through autumn. Grows on rocky serpentine in moist to dry places, often along creeks, and in hot dry streambeds in Siskiyou Mountains, at low to mid elevations. Native

Dalea ornata FABACEAE
Blue Mountain prairie-clover, ornate dalea
Uncommon, all summer, perennial, 12–20 in. Shrub-steppe

Cluster of erect stems. Plant hairless. Leaves pinnately divided into 5–7 leaflets. Leaflets egg-shaped, ⅓–¾ in. long, dotted with glands. Flower head is a crowded cylinder-shaped spike; calyx with long silky hairs; flowers rose to lavender. Seedpod enclosed by calyx, has single seed. Grows in dry, rocky or sandy soils at low to mid elevations. Native

Hedysarum occidentale FABACEAE
Western sweetvetch
Uncommon, all summer, perennial, 18–35 in.
West-side forest, alpine, subalpine

Stems erect from base. Leaves with 3–6 in. midvein, holding 9–21 evenly spaced, oval, hairless leaflets. Spikes above leaves have 20–75 reddish purple flowers with prominent blunt keels. Flowers hang downward. Grows on dry slopes near timberline. Northern sweetbroom, *H. boreale*, has similar flowers but 7–15 oval leaflets with gray hairs on underside; grows on gravel bars, along streams, in dry woods among shrubs on clay soils, at mid to high elevations. Seedpods of genus *Hedysarum* have joints that break apart into 1-seed sections when ripe. Native OLYM, NOCA

Lathyrus japonicus (*Lathyrus maritimus*)
FABACEAE
Beach pea
Locally common, all spring and summer, perennial, 1–5 ft. Coastal, bog/fen/wetland

Trailing or clambering over other plants. Stems round or angled, not winged. Leaves pinnately compound, ending with curly, straight, or branched tendrils; stipules at base same size as leaflet; even number of leaflets, 1–2 in. long, fleshy. Flowers 3–8 on upper flower stalk, upper petals reddish to purple-blue, wing petals white. Seedpods become hairless and to 3 in. long at maturity. Grows on dunes, sandy coastal beaches, wet areas inland. Native OLYM

Lathyrus latifolius FABACEAE
Everlasting pea, perennial sweetpea
Common, all spring and summer, perennial, 2–8 ft. Disturbed

Sprawling from single root. Stems have 2 opposite wings along sides. Leaves short, with wide wings, holding pair of lance-shaped to oval, pointed leaflets; branched tendril coiled at end of leaf midvein. Flowers clustered at top of long flower stalk, 4–15 reddish purple or occasionally white sweetpea flowers. Grows in moist soils along roads, ditches, homesteads, at low to mid elevations. Locally abundant plant throughout Pacific Northwest. Nonnative
OLYM, MORA, NOCA

See other *Lathyrus*: white, page 95; blue, page 408

Lathyrus nevadensis FABACEAE
Purple peavine, Sierra pea
Common, late spring–early summer,
perennial, 2–4 ft. West-side forest, east-side
forest

Stems erect to sprawling, angled but not
winged. Leaves with 4–8 opposite, oval to
widely oval, ½–1½ in. leaflets; vein can be
unbranched or branched, tendril can be
straight or coiled. Flowers 2–4, clustered, pink, red-purple, or
white, ½–1 in. long; calyx tube longer than lobes. Grows in
mixed forests, clearings, at 1400–7000 ft. Subsp. *nevadensis*
flowers are pinkish to reddish purple, tendril not branched;
grows west of Cascade Mountain Range. Subsp. *cusickii* flowers
are white with pink veins, tendril not branched; grows east of
Cascade Mountain Range. Native
OLYM, MORA, NOCA

Lotus crassifolius FABACEAE
Big deervetch
Common, all summer, perennial, 1–4 ft.
Disturbed, west-side forest, east-side forest

Erect or sprawling. Sturdy stems, thick blue-
green leaves with 9–15 oval leaflets. Flowers
in a round head, 10–20, yellowish or white,
blotched with dull reddish purple or pink. Grows in disturbed
soils, moist mixed forests, at 1000–7000 ft. Var. *crassifolius* is
greenish yellow, often spotted with deep purple. Var. *subglaber*
is whitish with red or purplish tints; grows west of Cascade
Mountain Range. Native OLYM, NOCA, CRLA

Onobrychis viciifolia FABACEAE
Sainfoin
Uncommon, late spring–early summer,
perennial, to 30 in. Disturbed, meadow,
east-side forest

Upright stems. Leaves pinnately divided,
with odd-numbered leaflets 15–21, oval,
½–1 in. long, upper surface finely red-dot-
ted. Flowers in dense short spike on leafless
stalk. Pink or red pea flower more or less ½
in., 2 side petals very small, with larger keel and banner. Keel
with blunt end. Grows in disturbed places at mid elevations.
Native of Eurasia. Nonnative

See other *Lotus*: white, page 96; yellow, page 206

Trifolium arvense   FABACEAE
Rabbit-foot clover
Uncommon, all summer, annual, 6–18 in.
Disturbed, meadow

Stem erect, silky-haired, with many branches.
Leaves on stems with short petioles, 3 leaflets 1
in. long, narrowly oblong. Flower spike to 1 in.,
dull green or gray, with many flowers. Flowers
pale pink or white, shorter than hairy calyx,
with lobes longer than tube. Grows in waste places, fields, usually in sandy soils, at low elevations. Native to Europe. Nonnative NOCA

Trifolium ciliolatum   FABACEAE
Foothill clover
Locally common, late spring, annual, 6–18 in.
Meadow, west-side forest

Stems erect, often branched. Stems carry most
of the leaves, with few or no basal leaves. Leaf
divided into 3 egg-shaped, toothed leaflets;
bristle-tipped stipules at base of petioles. Flowers in oval head reflex shortly after opening,
making head mop-like. Flowers white or pink
surrounded by a longer pink to purple calyx
with ragged sharp-pointed bristles. Grows in
grasslands, scrub, at low to mid elevations. Found in Columbia
River Gorge and Siskiyou Mountains. Native

Trifolium depauperatum   FABACEAE
Poverty clover
Common, all spring, annual, 4–10 in. Coastal,
vernal-wet, disturbed, meadow, west-side forest

Stems erect to decumbent. Plant very small,
hairless. Stem leaves divided palmately, 3
leaflets oblong to egg-shaped, entire to toothed,
tips blunt or lobed. Flower head small, with 3
to many flowers. Flowers pink to magenta,
often tipped with a darker zone and a white tip.
Remarkably, with age they expand and inflate
like tiny balloons. Grows in alkaline soils, salt
marshes, coastal meadows, vernal-wet areas, at
low elevations. Native OLYM

See other *Trifolium*: white, page 97; yellow, page 209; blue, page 415;
green/brown, page 466

Trifolium macrocephalum FABACEAE
Giant-head clover
Common, late spring, perennial, 3–8 in.
East-side forest, shrub-steppe, alpine,
subalpine

Stem ascending from rhizome. Plant hairy.
Leaves thick, basal and on stem, divided
palmately to 7–9 egg-shaped leaflets. Flower
head widely egg-shaped, 1–2½ in. long, ex-
panding with age to 3–4 in. or more. Flowers pale pink to purple or 2-colored. Grows in rocky soils with shrubs or juniper,
ridges at mid to high elevations. *Macrocephalum* is Latin for
"large head." Native **L&C**

Trifolium microcephalum FABACEAE
Small-head clover
Common, late spring–early summer, annual,
3–12 in. Bog/fen/wetland, moist streambanks, disturbed, meadow

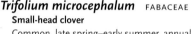

Decumbent to erect annual with soft wavy
hairs. Leaves on stems, divided palmately, 3
leaflets to ¾ in. long, with notched tip.
Flower head roundish, less than ½ in.
across, surrounded by hairy bowl-shaped
bract with entire pointed lobes. Flowers 7 or
more, pale pink to lavender. Grows in streambanks in moist,
disturbed soils, sometimes serpentine, at low to high elevations. *Microcephalum* is Latin for "small flower head." Native
OLYM, **L&C**

Trifolium oliganthum FABACEAE
Few-flowered clover
Locally common, late spring–early summer,
annual, 4–15 in. West-side forest, meadow

Tuft erect, hairless. Stem leaves sparse. Leaf
with toothed stipules, 3 leaflets about ½ in.
long. Flower head contains 5–15 flowers,
each in calyx divided almost to base, lobes
sharply pointed. Flower petals only slightly
longer than calyx lobes, usually tricolored:
pink, dark magenta, and white. Grows in
open woods, along roads, at low elevations. Native OLYM

Trifolium pratense FABACEAE
Red clover
Common, midspring–late summer, perennial,
6–24 in. Vernal-wet, disturbed, meadow

Hairy plant, ascending stems. Leaves on stems
divided palmately; 3 leaflets ½–1½ in., egg-
shaped, with lighter central patch. Flower head
at top, bright deep red, uppermost leaf with
bract-like stipules surrounding flower head.

Grows in disturbed soils at low to mid elevations. Important
forage crop originally from Europe, often planted in fields,
along roadsides; makes large displays in spring. Recently
thought to be toxic to horses. Nonnative OLYM, MORA, NOCA

Trifolium productum FABACEAE
Shasta clover
Uncommon, all summer, perennial, 4–16 in.
Vernal-wet, bog/fen/wetland, meadow

Upright hairless perennial with slender stems.
Leaves are on stalks ⅓–2 in., divided palmately; 3 leaflets oval to egg-shaped, with sharp tips,
saw-toothed. Flower heads dense, ⅓–1 in.
across, with projecting stem forked at top.
Flowers downward-pointing, white, with rose
to purple tips. Found in moist soils in rocky
places, including forests, to subalpine. Native

Trifolium variegatum FABACEAE
White-top clover
Common, early summer, annual, 4–14 in. Meadow
Prostrate to erect, tiny to robust, generally hairless. Leaves on
stems divided palmately to 3 oblong leaflets,
coarsely toothed. Stipules at leaf axil sharply
toothed. Flower head base has many long needle-like spines supporting upward-pointing
flowers. Flowers deep purple or pink, changing to pale pink or white near tip. Grows in wet
to vernal-wet soils in meadows, open ground.
Native OLYM

Trifolium willdenowii (*Trifolium tridentatum*) FABACEAE
Tomcat clover
Locally common, early spring–midsummer, annual, 4–8 in. Vernal-wet, meadow

Prostrate or erect annual. Leaves on stems, stipules at base with bristles on upper edge. Leaflets ½–2 in., linear to egg-shaped. Flower head tiny to 1 in. wide, with many flowers except on smallest plants, supported by partly fused bracts with sharp tips. Flower pink-purple or deep red with white tip. Grows on soils heavy and wet in spring, sometimes with serpentine rock, below 5000 ft. Native

Trifolium wormskioldii FABACEAE
Cow's clover, springbank clover
Common, early summer, annual, 4–12 in.
Coastal, meadow, alpine, subalpine

Decumbent to ascending stems. Leaves mostly basal, few alternate on stem, palmately divided, three 1 in. long leaflets, oval, finely toothed. Flower head about 1 in. wide with many flowers, supported by base of flat, fused, sharp-tipped bracts. Flowers pale to dark purple with white tips. Grows in moist to marshy places, beaches to mountain meadows. Form found at higher altitudes has much smaller flowers. Native
OLYM

Vicia nigricans subsp. *gigantea* (*Vicia gigantea*) FABACEAE
Giant vetch
Locally common, all spring and summer, perennial, vine, 2–6 ft. Coastal, west-side forest

Sprawling or climbing, with very little or no hair. Leaf divided pinnately, with 16–24 leaflets pointed or rounded at tip and descending in size upward; main leaf vein ends in a tendril. Flowers on stalk, not as long as leaves, with 2–16 flowers clustered at tip. Flowers purple-red or variegated yellowish white. Seedpods black, hairless. Found along streambanks, coastal bluffs, at edges of forests near coast. Native OLYM, NOCA

See other *Vicia*: blue, page 415

Vicia sativa FABACEAE
Common vetch
Locally common, late spring–early summer,
annual, vine, 1–2 ft. Disturbed, meadow

Stems sprawling. Leaves divided pinnately,
main vein ending in tendril. Leaflets 8–16, oval
to linear, ½–1 in. long, with pointed or notched
tip often with 1 tooth. Flowers usually paired
in leaf axils without stalk, pink-purple or
whitish. Seedpods 1–2 in. long, hairy when young, soon becoming hairless. Grows in disturbed soils, fields, at low to mid
elevations. Formerly used in hay fields and as a cover crop.
Nonnative NOCA

Polygala californica POLYGALACEAE
California milkwort
Uncommon, all spring, perennial, 2–12 in.
West-side forest

Mound, numerous upright and decumbent
stems from woody base. Leaves 1–2 in. long,
oval, dark green. Inflorescence thornless, a
small cluster of ½ in. flowers at stem tip, pink
or rarely white. Flower with 2 wing-like side
sepals larger than same-colored petals; upper
petal ridged to resemble 2 connected petals,
and notched or contorted; lowest petal folded or contorted, enclosing 8 stamens and pistil. Self-fertile flowers clustered near
base of stems. Seedpod flattened, oval, containing 1 seed. Grows
among shrubs, on exposed slopes, at low elevations. Native

Dianthus armeria CARYOPHYLLACEAE
Deptford pink, grass pink
Common, all summer, annual or biennial, 6–16
in. Disturbed, meadow

Basal rosette of leaves, erect flower stem.
Leaves opposite, narrowly oblong, with rounded tips. Inflorescence consists of dense heads
of few to many small flowers with linear bracts
extending beyond flowers. Flower petals pink
with small white dots, toothed; calyx ½–1 in.,
hairy. A garden escapee that grows in disturbed
soils at low to mid elevations. Often confused with *Centaurium
erythraea* in the gentian family, which is about the same size
and shade of pink but without dots on petals. Nonnative
OLYM, MORA, NOCA

337

Saponaria officinalis
CARYOPHYLLACEAE
Bouncing bet, soapwort
Locally common, early summer, perennial,
1–3 ft. Coastal, disturbed

Erect, hairless. Stems unbranched on lower section, branched inflorescence. Leaves egg-shaped, 1–4 in. long, with short petioles or sessile. Flowers on erect stalks in dense clusters of 20–40, topping stems. Flowers have 5 fused sepals; petals 5, pale to bright pink, 1–2 in. long, egg-shaped, notched at tip. Grows in edges of streams, roads, disturbed areas, below 3000 ft. Native of Europe. *Saponaria* is Latin for "soap," referring to the sap, which lathers with water. Native OLYM, NOCA

Silene acaulis CARYOPHYLLACEAE
Moss campion, moss catchfly
Locally common, all summer, perennial, 1–2 in. Alpine

Cushion. Stems branch from woody base into dense mound. Leaves mostly basal, crowded, persisting for many years, linear, with stiff sharp point at tip, with few hairs along edges or hairless, sessile. Flowers showy, 1 per stem; petals 5, pink, rose, pale lavender, or white, slightly toothed on rounded tip. Grows in rocky exposed sites, cliffs, rock crevices. Found in alpine areas of most mountains in the Pacific Northwest. Occasionally found on gravel bars, along shady streams, at lower elevations in the same mountains. Native OLYM, MORA, NOCA

Silene californica CARYOPHYLLACEAE
California Indian-pink
Locally common, all spring and summer, perennial, 8–20 in. West-side forest

Sprawling or clambering in bushes. Stems from woody base, weak, sparsely hairy. Leaves opposite on stem, widely lance- to egg-shaped; lower leaves withering by flowering; middle leaves 1–3 in. long, reducing in size upward. Flowers in loose clusters at top, 5 bright red petals each divided into 4 lobes with rounded or toothed tips, calyx ½–1 in. long with sticky glands. Grows in open woods at low to mid elevations. Native

See other *Silene*: white, page 105

Silene hookeri CARYOPHYLLACEAE
Hooker's Indian-pink
Locally common, midspring, perennial, 2–8 in.
Meadow, west-side forest

Decumbent to upright from much-branched
thickened root. Stems and leaves glandular or
lightly covered with short soft hairs. Leaves
egg-shaped, 1–3 in. long, green to gray, entire.
Flower clusters atop stems. Calyx densely
hairy, petals 5, pink, red, salmon, or white, each divided into 4
lobes, inner lobes somewhat wider, tips rounded. At center, 2
small appendages divided into 2 lobes, often a contrasting
color, top each petal. Grows in open woods, among shrubs and
conifers, at 1200–4000 ft. Subsp. *bolanderi*, with larger, deeply
divided, white flowers, grows in northern California. Plants in
Oregon are pink to red, occasionally white,
with smaller, less deeply divided petals. Native

Spergularia macrotheca
CARYOPHYLLACEAE
Sticky sand spurry, beach sand spurry
Common, all year long, perennial, 4 in. Coastal

Stems stout, sprawling. Stems and leaves covered with long, gray, glandular hairs. Stems
branched, to 20 in. long, leafy. Leaves fleshy,
crowded on stems, linear, ½–2 in., with pointed tip. Flowers
several to many in each leaf axil, pink to rose, small, calyx lobes
longer than petals, 9–10 stamens. Grows on beaches, in salt
marshes, fields, mudflats, coastal bluffs. Also in salt marshes is
S. marina, with 2–5 stamens, only 2 leaves at node. Native
OLYM

Spergularia rubra CARYOPHYLLACEAE
Red sand spurry, ruby sand spurry
Common, all year long, annual or perennial,
4–12 in. Disturbed, meadow, west-side forest

Mound. Stem with many branches. Leaves
dark green, not very fleshy, linear in pairs on
stems with 2–4 in axillary clusters held by conspicuous, shiny, silvery scales. Flowers at stem
tips consist of 5 partially fused sepals, 5 pink
petals, 6–10 stamens. Grows in meadows, open forests, disturbed sites and gardens, below 7500 ft. Similar *S. canadensis*,
with fleshy leaves, does not have axillary leaf clusters and is entirely coastal. Nonnative OLYM, MORA, NOCA

Rhodiola integrifolia subsp. *integrifolia* (*Sedum rosea* subsp. *integrifolium*)
CRASSULACEAE
Pacific roseroot, kingscrown
Uncommon, all summer, perennial, 4–10 in.
Alpine, subalpine

Erect sturdy stems with terminal, wide, flat clusters of dark wine-colored flowers. Stems with many leaves, green to rosy pink, covered with white waxy powder. Leaves flat, oval to spoon-shaped, to 1½ in. long, becoming smaller on lower stem. Flowers with 4 or possibly 5 petals and sepals, on erect stalks somewhat fleshy, dark reddish, occasionally yellow or pink. Grows in gravelly moist soils or among rocks at high elevations. Native OLYM, MORA, NOCA

Sedum laxum CRASSULACEAE
Rosy Siskiyou sedum
Uncommon, all summer, perennial, 3–16 in.
Dry rocky sites

Rosettes of basal leaves, sometimes bluish with waxy powder. Leaves ⅓–2 in. long, thick, usually widest just below tip; tip rounded or barely notched. Stem leaves flat, ⅕–¾ in. long. Inflorescence of 12–80 or more flowers atop stem. Rounded petals ⅓–⅔ longer than pointed sepals; anthers reddish brown to purple-black. Grows on outcrops at 200–6500 ft. Subsp. *flavidum* has pale yellow flowers, sessile stem leaves with ear-like base. Subsp. *heckneri* (pictured) has pink or white flowers, stem leaves wide, base clasping and wrapping partway around stem. Subsp. *laxum* has stem leaves sessile, slightly wider base than point of attachment, leaves pointing upward, flowers white or light pink. Native

Drosera rotundifolia DROSERACEAE
Roundleaf sundew
Uncommon, all summer, perennial, 2–10 in.
Bog/fen/wetland

Leaves spreading out from rosette, as wide as they are long, with long petioles. Upper-surface leaf hairs hold glands that secrete a sticky fluid to trap insects. Leaf folds around prey to digest it with enzymes and bacteria. Flower stems hold 1 to several flowers each (not pictured). Flowers in parts of 5. Calyx fused at base, petals white or pink. Seedpods long, narrow, light brown. Grows in freshwater bogs, seeps, usually on sphagnum moss, sometimes on partly submerged moss-covered logs, from coastline to mid elevations. Native OLYM, MORA, NOCA, CRLA

     See other *Sedum*: yellow, page 214

Andromeda polifolia ERICACEAE
Bog rosemary
Locally common, all spring, perennial, 1–2 ft.
Bog/fen/wetland

Dense stands of erect stems from creeping roots. Leaves 1–2 in. long, narrow, dull green, with edges deeply rolled under, white on underside. Flowers hanging in 2–6 in. loose clusters, bell-shaped, wider at open end, in shades of pink or white. Grows in acid bogs. Circumpolar; southern British Columbia is southern limit of its range in the Northwest, although it grows farther south in eastern North America and in cultivation. Native

Arctostaphylos patula ERICACEAE
Green manzanita
Common, late spring, perennial, 3–7 ft.
West-side forest, alpine, subalpine

Upright to spreading 3–7 ft. shrub. Branches, stems with bright reddish brown shredding bark. Twigs, leaf petioles with glistening yellow glands. Leaves 1–2½ in. long, shiny green, leathery, erect, widely oval, with rounded tips. Flowers pink, urn-shaped, with mostly scale-like bracts at base of each dense cluster. Berries dark reddish brown to black when mature. Abundant in open areas of conifer forests at low to high elevations. Often forms large, dense, rounded thickets of clones from spreading roots. Native CRLA

Arctostaphylos uva-ursi ERICACEAE
Kinnickinnick, bearberry
Common, all spring, perennial, trailing
West-side forest, east-side forest, alpine, subalpine

Low creeping shrub, seldom more than 8 in. high. Stems reddish brown, older bark rough, new growth shredding, covered with matted hairs. Leaves spreading outward to upward, 1 in. long or less, oval, wider near rounded tips, with light green shiny undersides, darker green upper surfaces. Flowers pinkish white, bell-shaped, in small dense clusters. Berries are flattened globes, shiny bright red. Grows in dry rocky soils, outcrops, from coast to alpine. Circumboreal. Often cultivated. Native
OLYM, MORA, NOCA, **L&C**

See other *Arctostaphylos*: white, page 108

Arctostaphylos viscida   ERICACEAE
Sticky whiteleaf manzanita
Locally common, midspring, perennial,
3–15 ft. West-side forest

Shrub without burl. Bark smooth, dark red-brown. Stems hairless, young twigs pale green coated with white waxy powder and glands. Leaves erect, ¾–1¾ in., egg-shaped to nearly round, with rounded base, entire or toothed. Leaf surfaces alike, in spring coated with sticky white glands, becoming smooth later. Flowers sticky, pink to white, nearly conical. Berries reddish brown, sticky. Grows on rocky slopes at low to mid elevations. Native

Chimaphila umbellata   ERICACEAE
Western prince's pine, pipsissewa
Common, all summer, perennial, 6–14 in.
West-side forest, east-side forest

Short stout evergreen shrub, upright flower stem. Leaves 1–3 in., lance-shaped, in whorls on lower stem and midstem, bright shiny green, leathery, teeth most pronounced near tip. Veins do not have white borders. Flowers hang from stem tip in small cluster. Petals pinkish to red, waxy, cupped, spread. Sepals remain after bloom. Grows in leaf mold at low to high elevations. *Chimaphila* comes from the Greek *cheima* ("winter") and *philos* ("loving"), in reference to the evergreen habit. Native OLYM, MORA, NOCA

Gaultheria ovatifolia   ERICACEAE
**Oregon wintergreen, slender teaberry,
western teaberry**
Common, midsummer, perennial, 1–3 in.
Bog/fen/wetland, west-side forest, alpine,
subalpine

Short, spreading, evergreen shrub. Stems to 8 in. long, coated with brownish hairs, sometimes tipped with glands. Leaves leathery, shiny, egg-shaped, 1–1½ in. long, with tiny teeth. Flowers in leaf axils, tiny pink bells held by cups covered by gland-tipped hairs. Berries edible, bright red. Grows in moist forests, bogs, with heaths, at mid to high elevations. Similar *G. humifusa*, usually found in moist subalpine to alpine environments, is without glands and usually without hairs, leaves toothless or with few teeth near tip, white flowers held in hairless cups with lobes about as long as petals. Native OLYM, MORA, NOCA, CRLA

See other *Chimaphila*: white, page 109
See other *Gaultheria*: white, page 110

Kalmia microphylla (*Kalmia polifolia*)
ERICACEAE
Western bog laurel, alpine laurel
Locally common, all summer, perennial, 6–18
in. Bog/fen/wetland, meadow, alpine, subalpine

Stems stand upright or lie prostrate on ground.
Leaves leathery, evergreen, 1–2 in. long, usually rolled under on edges; upper surface dark
glossy green; lower surface white with dense
fine hairs. Pink flowers in loose cluster atop stem. Five petals
are partially fused into an open cup, each petal with small
pocket that holds tip of the stamens under tension. When
touched by an insect, stamen pops out and covers insect with
pollen. Grows in peat soils, bogs, wet meadows, rock crevices,
at low to high elevations. Lower-elevation plants tend to be taller
with larger leaves. Native OLYM, MORA, NOCA, CRLA

Kalmiopsis leachiana ERICACEAE
Kalmiopsis
Rare, late spring–early summer, perennial,
10–20 in. Coastal, west-side forest

Upright shrub with numerous spreading
branches. Leaves oval, dark green, thick, ½ in.
long, dotted with glands. Flowers clustered on
upper ends of stems on stalks to 1 in. long.
Deep red calyx supports 5 light pink to deep rose ½ in. petals.
Pistil bright red, stamens formed by white filaments and purple
anthers, about length of petals. Grows on rocky well-drained
soils, cliffs, in areas of high rainfall. Discovered by Lilla Leach of
Portland in the Siskiyou Mountains in 1930, in what is now part
of the Kalmiopsis Wilderness in southwestern Oregon. Native

Phyllodoce empetriformis ERICACEAE
Pink mountain-heather
Common, all summer, perennial, 4–15 in.
Meadows, alpine, subalpine

Matted shrub with erect stems. Twigs much-
branched and hairy when young. Evergreen
leaves needle-like, alternate, with edges rolled
under; undersides whitish; upper surface a
deep shiny green. Flowers on reddish hairy
stalks above leaves. Pink to rose petals fused into a ⅓ in. long
cup with 5 rolled-back lobes. Style protrudes while 10 stamens
are within the cup. Grows in acid soils in moist meadows and
seeps. The genus is named for a sea nymph. Carl Linnaeus
(1707–1778), father of the binary naming system for plants, also
started the custom of naming members of the heath family
after nymphs and goddesses. Native OLYM, MORA, NOCA, CRLA

See other *Phyllodoce*: yellow, page 217

Pyrola asarifolia ERICACEAE
Heart-leaved pyrola, bog wintergreen, pink wintergreen
Common, all summer, perennial, 6–18 in.
Bog/fen/wetland, alpine, subalpine

Tall, erect, reddish stem from basal cluster of leathery evergreen leaves. Leaves oval to round, with tapered bases on long petioles, shiny dark green with underside often purple. Flowers on spreading stalks on top ½ of stem. Petals form cup, pink to dark red, with protruding downward-curving style. Grows in bogs to dry evergreen or deciduous forests, meadows, from near coast to subalpine. Subsp. *asarifolia* is common, with round leaves and short bracts; grows in swamps, along streambanks. Subsp. *bracteata* is uncommon, with bracts as long as flower stalks; grows in dry to moist forest.
Native OLYM, MORA, NOCA, CRLA

Rhododendron macrophyllum
ERICACEAE
Pacific rhododendron
Locally common, late spring–early summer, perennial, 3–15 ft. Coastal, west-side forest

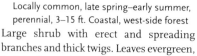

Large shrub with erect and spreading branches and thick twigs. Leaves evergreen, 3–8 in. long, oblong, leathery, entire, with sunken midvein, upper side dark green. Flowers pink to rose-purple, 1–1½ in.; 5 petals fused at base form a wide shallow bell with tips spreading wide. Grows in moist to dry coniferous forests from coast to high elevations. State flower of Washington. Native OLYM, **L&C**

Rhododendron occidentale
ERICACEAE
Western azalea
Locally common, late spring–early summer, perennial, 4–15 ft. Coastal, vernal-wet, bog/fen/wetland, west-side forest

Erect, deciduous, densely branched bush. Slender twigs reddish. Leaves thin, 2–4 in., upper surface green with small hairs on edges and no sunken midvein. Flowers very fragrant, showy, in terminal clusters. Buds usually deeply colored on outside, pink, salmon, or yellow. Open flowers white tinted with pink, salmon, or yellow, with large yellow spot at base of upper petal and protruding curved stamens. Grows in seeps, edges of streams, fens and wet places in coniferous forests. Native

See other *Pyrola*: white, page 112; green/brown, page 467
See other *Rhododendron*: white, page 112

Sarcodes sanguinea ERICACEAE
Snow plant
Uncommon, late spring–early summer,
perennial, 6–18 in. West-side forest, east-side
forest

Stout, fleshy, bright red spike emerging directly from saprophytic, brittle, hairy roots.
Leaves are scale-like. Flowers are closed bells
with 5 curved-back pointed tips and 5 sepals
persisting after seeding. Grows in coniferous, mixed forests, at
mid to high elevations, blooming as snow recedes. Native

Vaccinium alaskense ERICACEAE
Alaska huckleberry
Locally common, late spring–early summer, perennial,
to 6 ft. West-side forest, alpine, subalpine

Erect to spreading shrub with older gray bark
and new yellowish green twigs with angled
edges. Leaves deciduous, 1–2 in. long, oval to
egg-shaped, dark green on upper side, lighter
below. Single flowers hang from base of leaves,
appearing when leaves are nearly full size.
Pinkish to bronze flowers are widely rounded
urns with protruding style. Edible blue or purplish black berries about ⅓ in. diameter with
no powdery coating. Grows in moist forest openings from sea
level to subalpine. Very similar *V. ovalifolium* has pink flowers
longer than broad, powdery coated berries. Native
OLYM, MORA, NOCA, CRLA

Vaccinium deliciosum ERICACEAE
Cascades blueberry, blue-leaf huckleberry
Locally common, late spring, perennial, 4–15
in. Meadow, west-side forest, alpine, subalpine

Dwarf mat-forming shrub with smooth stems
rooting as they run. Leaves deciduous, thin, oblong to egg-shaped, with tapered bases, often
toothed on upper ⅔ of blade only and with a
waxy powdery coating underneath. Flowers
solitary, widely rounded, pinkish, hanging on
short stalks from bases of leaves. Berries ⅓ in.,
blue, coated with white waxy powder, usually abundant. Grows
in subalpine meadows, damp coniferous forests, from near
coast to alpine meadows. Similar *V. caespitosum*, dwarf blueberry, grows in wet places in alpine, with leaves green on both
sides and smaller berries. Both are favorite foods of bears and
humans. *Deliciosum* means "delicious," and these berries truly
are. Native OLYM, MORA, NOCA

Vaccinium membranaceum
ERICACEAE
Black huckleberry, thinleaf huckleberry
Locally common, late spring, perennial, 2–6 ft. Vernal-wet, meadow, west-side forest

Robust shrub, erect, with smooth stems, not rooting at the nodes, and yellowish green twigs. Older branches with grayish shredding bark. Very thin leaves are yellowish green, oval, with pointed tip. Solitary flowers are pinkish, widely urn-shaped, maturing into purple or reddish black berries. Grows in wet meadows, forests, at mid to high elevations. Berries edible, delicious. Native
OLYM, MORA, NOCA, CRLA, **L&C**

Vaccinium ovatum ERICACEAE
Evergreen huckleberry, California huckleberry
Locally common, midspring, perennial, 1–9 ft. Coastal, west-side forest

Tall evergreen shrub with thick branches and round twigs. Hairy stems do not root when touching soil. Leaves leathery, lance-shaped, 1–2 in. long, finely toothed, dark green on top, pale green underneath with few dark glandular hairs. Flowers 2–12 in dense clusters, pale pink, urn-shaped, with 5 lobes. Berries small, shiny, dark bluish black. Found from edges of beaches to conifer forests at low elevations. Berries are tasty in autumn and early winter, becoming even better after light frost. Native OLYM, MORA, **L&C**

Vaccinium oxycoccos ERICACEAE
Bog cranberry, wild cranberry
Locally common, all summer, perennial, 2–4 in. Coastal, bog/fen/wetland

Low creeping shrub. Stems slender, vine-like. Leaves evergreen, small, scattered along stems, oval, with sharp tips and edges rolled under, dark green above, with gray waxy coating below. Flowers at stem tips, solitary to few, nodding. Flower buds deep pink, becoming lighter as petals open and curve upward. Darker stamens hang below. Berries small, dark red to pink, juicy. Grows in sphagnum bogs. Native OLYM

Vaccinium parvifolium ERICACEAE
Red huckleberry
Locally common, midspring, perennial, 3–12 ft.
West-side forest

Erect shrub with green strongly angled twigs.
Stems do not root if touching soil. Thin leaves
nearly deciduous, oval, with tiny hairs underneath and sharp tips that fall off. Flowers pinkish, hanging singly from base of leaves, urn-
shaped, with 5 lobes. Berries bright red, ¼–½ in., edible but
somewhat tart. Grows in coniferous forests, in humus, from
coastline to mid elevations. Often seen growing out of old rotting stumps. Blooms more prolifically and sets more fruit in
forest openings that get a little more light. Native
OLYM, MORA, NOCA

Vaccinium scoparium ERICACEAE
Grouseberry, littleleaf huckleberry
Locally common, midspring, perennial, 6–20
in. West-side forest, east-side forest

Short shrub with many branches, rooting
when touching soil and often forming dense
stands. Older stems have smooth bark. Green
twigs are strongly angled. Leaves deciduous,
oval, ½–¾ in., finely toothed. Solitary pink
flowers are urn-shaped, hanging from bases of lowest leaves
on young shoots. Red berries about ¼ in. diameter are edible,
but more often eaten by birds and other animals. Grows in
high-elevation forests. Rare in California, but locally common
farther north. Native MORA, NOCA, CRLA

Erodium cicutarium GERANIACEAE
Redstem storksbill, red-stemmed filaree
Common, all spring, annual or biennial, 1–12
in. Disturbed, meadow

Tuft or rosette of 1–15 in. stems. Leaves upright or lying flat on ground, fern-like, divided
into leaflets with pointed tips, slightly hairy.
Flowers ⅓–⅔ in. across in clusters on long
stalks from leaf axils. Flower with 5 red-laven-
der petals. Seed capsules divide from beak at
bottom, twisting as they dry. Found throughout the western
states in fields, roadsides, other open disturbed places, at low
elevations. Nonnative OLYM, MORA, NOCA

Geranium dissectum GERANIACEAE
Cut-leaved geranium
Common, all spring and summer, annual or
biennial, 1–2 ft. Disturbed, meadow, west-
side forest

Upright to erect stems coated with rough
hairs. Lower leaves are about as long as they
are wide, deeply divided, 5–7 linear to oblong lobed segments with sharply pointed
tips. Flowers in loose clusters, pink to purplish. Flower with
4–7 sharply pointed sepals, notched petals about same length.
Seed capsule hairy, with purple-tipped beaks extending upward. Grows in open, disturbed places. Similar *G. carolinianum*
has leaves lobed only halfway to center with lobe tips rounded
and flowers congested at stem tops. Also similar, *G. bicknellii*
has leaves deeply divided into 5 lobes. Nonnative OLYM

Geranium molle GERANIACEAE
Dove's foot geranium
Common, all spring and summer, annual or
biennial or perennial, 3–16 in. Coastal,
disturbed, meadow

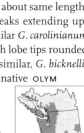

Upright to prostrate, with stem tips pointing upward. Plant covered with soft hairs.
Leaves nearly round, 1–2 in., palmately di-
vided into 5–7 evenly round-toothed lobes. Pairs of pink flowers
carried on stalks to 1 in. long. Flowers with 5 petals divided into
2 lobes. Grows in open or shaded sites on disturbed soils, including lawns and gardens, at low elevations. European native.
Very similar *G. pusillum* has fruits covered with fine hairs. *Geranium lucidum*, another similar European native so far found
only in western Oregon, has 5 shiny leaf
segments divided into 3 rounded lobes.
Nonnative OLYM, MORA, NOCA

Geranium oreganum GERANIACEAE
Oregon geranium
Uncommon, late spring–midsummer,
perennial, 18–30 in.
Meadow, west-side forest

Upright. Stem hairless to soft-hairy, glands
on upper section. Leaves 2½–5½ in. wide, nearly round, deeply
divided into 5–7 segments, the top ¾ of segments lobed. Flowers on 1–2 in. stalks; 5 petals ⅔–1 in. long, nearly round, red-
purple. Grows in open prairies, oak woodlands west of Cascade
Mountains from near sea level and upward in northern Oregon, and in more moist shaded conditions at higher elevations
in southern Oregon and California. Native

348   See other *Geranium*: white, page 112

Geranium robertianum GERANIACEAE
Herb Robert, stinky Bob
Locally common, all summer, annual or
biennial, 4–20 in. Disturbed, west-side forest

Prostrate to upright, unpleasant-smelling.
Stems hairy. Leaves triangular, lower leaves
1–2 in. wide, palmately divided into 3 leaflets
that are pinnately lobed. Flower stalks carry 2
flowers with rounded petals 1/3–1/2 in. long,
reddish or pink with white veins. Grows in moist open to shady
sites up to 4000 ft. A noxious weed originally introduced as a
garden plant; suppresses native species in west-side forests and
is spreading rapidly. Three other small geraniums, *G. carolinianum, G. dissectum,* and *G. bicknellii,* also have deeply dissected
leaves. Nonnative OLYM, MORA, NOCA

Geranium viscosissimum GERANIACEAE
Sticky geranium
Locally common, late spring–early summer,
perennial, 1–3 ft. Meadows, east-side forest,
shrub-steppe

Erect to ascending, covered with sticky glands
noticeable to the touch. Leaves nearly round,
1–4 in. wide, palmately divided, with 5–7 diamond-shaped leaflets that are variously lobed
again. Flower petals 1/2–3/4 in. long, with soft hairs near center,
deep pink to rose-purple, with red to purple veins. Grows in
meadows, near edges of sagebrush-steppe in coniferous forests
and aspen groves, at mid to high elevations. Var. *incisum* is
without sticky glands on lower stems and petioles. Native

Iliamna rivularis MALVACEAE
Streambank globe mallow
Locally common, all summer, perennial, 3–6 ft.
Moist streambanks, east-side forest

Stems erect, branched. Leaves sparsely coated
with star-like hairs, 4–8 in. long, maple-like,
deeply palmately lobed, 3–7 coarsely toothed
rounded segments. Flower clusters in loose
arrangement on spike-like raceme. Flowers
rose or white, with 5 egg-shaped overlapping
petals, each about 1 in. long. Grows in streambanks at mid elevations. Native NOCA

Malva neglecta MALVACEAE
Cheeseweed, buttonweed
Common, all summer, annual or biennial or
perennial, 6–24 in. Disturbed

Stems prostrate, with tips growing upward,
densely hairy. Leaves circular to kidney-
shaped, with shallow lobes. Flowers 1–6 in
cluster at base of leaves, petals pale lilac or
white with darker penciling and hairy base,
each about ½ in. across. Called cheeseweed because the fruits
are round and flat like a wheel of cheese. Common weed at low
to mid elevations. Nonnative OLYM, MORA, NOCA

Sidalcea campestris MALVACEAE
Meadow checker mallow
Uncommon, late spring–early summer,
perennial, 2–6 ft. Meadow

Clump of stout, erect, hairy, branched
stems. Hairy petioles 4–8 in. long with dark
green blades. Leaves round, divided palmately to narrow, toothed segments with
sharply pointed tips. Pink or white flowers
contained in densely hairy calyxes in a terminal raceme. Flower petals about ¾ in.
long. Both female and bisexual plants, fe-
male flowers smaller and lack anthers. Grows in fields, grassy
hillsides, along roadsides. Similar west-side species with red,
lavender, or purple flowers: *S. nelsoniana*, with petals of bisexual flowers ⅓ to just more than ½ in., calyx ⅕ in. long; *S. cusickii*, with petals of bisexual flowers ½–¾ in., calyx with
prominent veins, lobes widened above base; *S. virgata*, with bisexual flower petals ⅔–1 in., calyx not no-
ticeably veined. Native

Sidalcea hendersonii MALVACEAE
Henderson's checker mallow
Rare, all summer, perennial, 1–5 ft.
Coastal, bog/fen/wetland

Stems erect, hollow, usually tinted purplish,
hairless. Basal leaves with long petioles,
heart-shaped, round-toothed; stem leaves alternate, palmately divided into 5 oblong lobes. Flowers numerous in branched racemes atop stems. Plants both female and bisexual. Bisexual flowers larger, pale. Female flowers ½ in.,
darker pink, lacking anthers. Sometimes confused with *Lythrum
salicaria*, purple loosestrife, with red-purple flowers arranged in
a spike-like raceme, which is invasive in same habitat. Grows
along coast in tidal marshes and meadows. Extremely rare in
Oregon, uncommon in Washington and rare in British Columbia. Native OLYM

Sidalcea neomexicana MALVACEAE
New Mexico sidalcea, prairie mallow
Uncommon, late spring–early summer,
perennial, 6–36 in. Meadow, shrub-steppe

Stems clustered, upright. Leaves nearly round,
dark green, fleshy, to 6 in. across. Upper leaves
divided into 5–9 linear lobes; basal leaves shallowly lobed. Flowers numerous on short stalks
in loose spike above leaves. Flower consists of
¼ in. calyx coated with tiny star-like and longer hairs, ¼–¾ in.
petals. This species may also have both bisexual and female
plants. Found in alkaline seeps and seasonally wet meadows
mostly at low to mid elevations. Native

Sidalcea oregana MALVACEAE
Oregon checker mallow, marsh hollyhock
Locally common, late spring–early summer,
perennial, 2–4 ft. Meadows, east-side forest,
shrub-steppe

Upright from a woody taproot. Stem with
coarse, bristly, or star-shaped hairs on lower
section, smooth upper section. Leaves on lowest section of stem lobed. Inflorescence stems
and branches leafy, leaves usually deeply lobed
and sharply toothed. Flowers in loose spike-
like raceme with pink to deep rose, oval, ½–¾ in. long petals.
This species may have bisexual plants and female plants with
smaller-petaled flowers lacking anthers. Grows in meadows,
stream margins, wet places, also in ponderosa pine forests and
sagebrush, at low to high elevations. Native

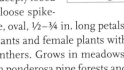

Paeonia brownii PAEONIACEAE
Western peony, Brown's peony
Locally common, late spring–early summer,
perennial, 8–20 in. West-side forest, east-side
forest, shrub-steppe

Stems erect, 1 to several in cluster. Leaves 5–8
per stem, divided 2 or 3 times, leaflets oval,
with rounded tips. Leaves fleshy and coated
with white to blue waxy powder. Flowers 1 or
more, clustered at stem top. Flowers with 5
leathery, greenish to purplish sepals persisting until winter; 5
smaller, deep red to brownish, round petals with edges yellow
to greenish; many stamens and 2–5 thick pistils, surrounded by
fleshy disk at base. Grows in open meadows, sagebrush deserts, edges and openings in dry forests, at mid to high elevations. Native NOCA

Calandrinia ciliata PORTULACACEAE
Red maids

Locally common, late spring, annual, ½–7 in. Coastal, vernal-wet, disturbed, meadow, west-side forest

Upright to spreading mat. Stems single or branched, with alternate linear to oblong leaves with rounded tips, flat, thick to fleshy. Flowers single in leaf axils. Petals 5, brilliant rose-red or rarely white, may have hairs around edges, stamens 3–15. Grows in vernal-wet, loamy, sandy soils, coastal turf, disturbed and cultivated places, at low to mid elevations. *Cilia* are the hairs on the edges of the pointed leaves and on the sepals. Native OLYM

Claytonia lanceolata PORTULACACEAE
Western spring beauty, spring beauty, Indian potato

Common, midspring, perennial, to 8 in. Coastal, vernal-wet, west-side forest, east-side forest, alpine, subalpine

Erect. Basal leaves sometimes absent; stem leaves a single pair clasping the stem partway from ground. Leaves wedge-shaped tapering to sharp tips. Flowers 3–15 with short stalks or sessile above leaves in loose, sometimes 1-sided cluster. Flower petals white or pink with pink veins or occasionally yellow or orange. Found in moist meadows, slopes, woodlands, at mid to alpine elevations. Grows from corms that taste like potato when cooked. Native

OLYM, MORA, NOCA, CRLA, **L&C**

Lewisia columbiana
PORTULACACEAE
Columbia lewisia

Locally common, early summer, perennial, 4–10 in. East-side forest, alpine, subalpine

Crowded basal rosette of leaves. Leaves 1–3 in. long, fleshy, linear and entire with rounded tip, tapering to base. Flower stems numerous, with large loose clusters of flowers with bracts. Petals 7–10, rose, pink, or white, with fine pink to red pencil markings, notched at the tip. Grows on rocky slopes, cliffs, at mid to high elevations. Native

OLYM, MORA, NOCA

See other *Claytonia*: white, page 113
See other *Lewisia*: white, page 114; orange, page 299

Lewisia cotyledon PORTULACACEAE
Siskiyou lewisia
Uncommon, early summer, perennial, 6–20 in.
West-side forest, subalpine

Crowded rosette of flat leaves from carrot-like root. Leaves many, egg- to spoon-shaped, fleshy. Flower stems 4–12 in., with loose flower clusters. Flowers on 1 in. stalks, each flower about 1 in. across, petals typically pink or orange with white stripes but may be a solid color, including white. Grows in well-drained sandy slopes and rocky sites, including serpentine, at low to mid elevations. Three varieties easily recognized by leaf margins: var. *cotyledon* leaves are entire, often wide at tip end; var. *heckneri* leaves are sharp-toothed; var. *howellii* (pictured) leaves are wavy-edged. Native

Lewisia leana PORTULACACEAE
Quill-leaved lewisia
Rare, early summer, perennial, 3–10 in.
West-side forest, alpine, subalpine

Dense rosette of basal leaves and stems. Leaves many, ½–2 in. long, linear, flat, somewhat fleshy or cylindrical, rounded at tip. Flower stems 1 to several, with many branches, each branch bearing 2 to many flowers; flower stalks with small bracts at base. Flower petals 6–8, purple, pink, or white, with rounded tips, supported by 2 oval sepals tipped with dark gland. Grows in sandy, rocky places in open pine forests at mid to high elevations. Hybridizes with *L. cotyledon* where the 2 come into contact. First collected in 1876 by L. W. Lee, a member of U.S. Geological Survey in Josephine County, Oregon (location in which photo was taken). Native

Lewisia pygmaea PORTULACACEAE
Dwarf lewisia
Uncommon, early summer, perennial, ½–3 in.
Vernal-wet, alpine, subalpine

Tight rosette to 6 in. across. Leaves narrowly linear to lance-shaped, 1–3 in. long, fleshy, entire, with blunt tip. Stems each with single flower (rarely 2) about same length as leaves. Flower is pink or white with many petals, a little jagged or toothed at tips. Grows in streambanks, in wet gravel or sand, rocky slopes or moist meadows in high mountains, where it often blooms immediately after snow melts and before soil dries. Hybridizes with *L. nevadensis* where the 2 come together. Native OLYM, MORA, NOCA

Lewisia rediviva PORTULACACEAE
Bitterroot
Locally common, all spring, perennial, 1–3
in. East-side forest, shrub-steppe, alpine,
subalpine

Rosette of small leaves arising from thick
carrot-like root. Root often shows above
ground. Leaves fleshy, 1–3 in., pencil-
shaped. Flowers deep rose, pink, or white,
with satin-like sheen. Petals to 1 in. long, stamens 40–50, stigmas 6–8. Plants shrivel after flowering, remaining dormant
through summer. Grows in rocky soils in open places from just
above sea level to alpine. The genus *Lewisia* is named for Meriwether Lewis, who collected the first herbarium specimens of
L. rediviva in the Bitterroot Mountains of Montana. The name
rediviva ("restored to life") was given when a
specimen grew some 2 years after the original collection. Native **L&C**

Montia parvifolia PORTULACACEAE
Littleleaf montia
Common, all summer, perennial, 6–12 in.
Coastal, vernal-wet, west-side forest, east-
side forest

Many small rosettes of basal leaves. Stolons
present, often reddish. Basal leaves many, oval, fleshy, ½ in.
long; stem leaves smaller, alternate, often replaced with fleshy
bulblets. Flowering stems unbranched, topped with clusters of
5-petaled white or pink flowers with deeper pink veins. Grows
in wet mosses along streams, in wet rocks from beach to alpine
areas, sometimes in large patches. Native
OLYM, MORA, NOCA, CRLA

Talinum spinescens (*Phemeranthus*
spinescens) PORTULACACEAE
Spiny talinum
Uncommon, early summer, perennial, 4–12
in. Dry rocky sites, shrub-steppe

Woody-based stems crowded with leaves.
Leaves succulent, green, ½–1 in. long,
round at tip. Overwintering hardened mid-
ribs are spine-like. Flowers 6–12 in loose clusters open in the
afternoon on leafless stems to 10 in. long. Flower with 5 magenta petals, 20–30 stamens. Grows in rocky places, outcrops in
shrub-steppe, deserts. Rare and endangered in Oregon, where
it is endemic to Wasco and Jefferson counties, but somewhat
more widespread in central Washington. Native

See other *Montia*: white, page 115

Anemone multifida RANUNCULACEAE
Cut-leaf anemone
Uncommon, midsummer, perennial, 6–20 in.
West-side forest, east-side forest, alpine,
subalpine

Erect. Stems 1 to several. Basal leaves with 1–4
in. hairy petioles, dissected to many long,
lance-shaped, lobed segments; stem leaves
without petioles. Inflorescence consists of 1–3
flowers with 5–8 petal-like sepals, pink, cream, reddish, or purplish, underside often purplish or reddish, with soft hairs.
Seeds, with woolly or silky tails less than 1 in., form tight globe-
shaped heads. Grows in open rocky places at low elevations to
subalpine and alpine zones, where it is most likely to be encountered. Similar but smaller *A. drummondii*, with white or
bluish flowers and linear leaves, is more commonly found in same subalpine and alpine
habitat, never at low elevations. Native
OLYM, MORA, NOCA

Aquilegia formosa RANUNCULACEAE
Red columbine, Sitka columbine
Common, all spring and summer, perennial,
8–48 in. Coastal, meadow, west-side forest,
east-side forest, alpine, subalpine

Upright plant with spreading branches. Basal and lower stem
leaves on petioles 1–12 in., divided 2 or 3 times; upper leaves
sessile or nearly so. Flowers nodding, bright red, with some
yellow; 5 straight to inward-curved spurs with rounded tips.
Grows in moist, open to partly shaded areas from coastline to
subalpine meadows. Very attractive to hummingbirds and but-
terflies. Closely resembles the eastern red columbine, *A. canadensis*. Native
OLYM, MORA, NOCA, CRLA, **L&C**

Clematis hirsutissima RANUNCULACEAE
Sugar bowls, leather-flower
Uncommon, late spring–early summer,
perennial, 6–24 in. East-side forest

Cluster. Stems erect, not vine-like. Leaves in
pairs on stem; upper leaves pinnately divided 2
or 3 times, segments linear; lower leaves smaller, entire. Flowers urn-shaped, with long stalks. Flower nodding, leathery, rose
on inside with purple on outside, long hairs on tube exterior,
tips curved back. Seed with dense plumes to 2 in. long. Found
in woods, often under pine, to about 6500 ft. Native **L&C**

See other *Anemone*: white, page 116; blue, page 419
See other *Aquilegia*: yellow, page 218
See other *Clematis*: white, page 118

355

Delphinium nudicaule
RANUNCULACEAE
Cañon delphinium, red larkspur
Locally common, late spring–early summer, perennial, 1–4 ft. Coastal, vernal-wet, west-side forest

Erect stems branched in upper section. Leaves on lower part of stem, shiny, nearly round, divided into 3–10 lobes. Flowers on ½–3 in. stalks, scarlet to orange-red, occasionally dull yellow, facing outward; spur straight, ½–1 in. long. Grows in lightly shaded woods, moist rocky slopes, from coast to high elevations. Native

Thalictrum occidentale   RANUNCULACEAE
Western meadowrue
Locally common, late spring–early summer, perennial, 12–40 in. Coastal, meadow, west-side forest

Erect, with male and female flowers on separate plants. Mostly stem leaves, few basal. Leaves blue-green, shiny, or with fine hairs with glands, divided 3 times; leaflets 3–4 pairs, very delicate, oval, lobed with coarse teeth. Flowers in loose clusters at top, greenish white or purplish red; male flowers with 15–30 stamens hanging down. Seed points down. Grows in openings in forests, woodlands, along streams, wet places, at low elevations. (Inset photo: female flowers.) Native OLYM, MORA, NOCA

Lomatium columbianum   APIACEAE
Columbia desert parsley
Uncommon, mid May, perennial, 12–30 in. Shrub-steppe

Large upright clump of dense silver-gray foliage. Leaves with reddish or light brown petioles carry pinnately divided leaves. Leaflets linear to ¾ in. long. Flowers wine red. Grows on dry rocky slopes along Columbia River. The only parsley family plant in the Pacific Northwest with this color combination. Native

See other *Delphinium*: blue, page 420
See other *Thalictrum*: yellow, page 222
See other *Lomatium*: white, page 123; yellow, page 224; green/brown, page 467

Sanicula bipinnatifida APIACEAE
Purple sanicle
Locally common, late spring, perennial, 6–36
in. Coastal, meadow, west-side forest
Erect or spreading stems. Leaves green, purple, or grayish, double pinnately divided, leaflets toothed; flat, sharply pointed wings along
sides of main vein. Flowers in round balls, usually purplish red, rarely yellow, with pistils and
stamens exceeding petals. Grows in open grasslands, open oak
and pine woods, often on rocky serpentine, at low elevations.
Native OLYM

Comarum palustre (Potentilla palustris) ROSACEAE
Marsh cinquefoil
Locally common, all summer, perennial, 8–20
in. Vernal-wet, bog/fen/wetland, lake/pond,
moist streambanks, meadow
Amphibious, mat or often floating. Stems to 3
ft. long, prostrate or ascending, reddish. Leaves
mostly on flower stalks; lower leaves pinnately
divided. Leaflets 5–7, oblong, coarsely toothed,
hairy. Inflorescence usually consists of fewer
than 10 flowers. Flower dark red, ¾–1½ in.
across, with 5 petals much shorter than sepals,
many stamens. Grows in bogs, marshes, banks of streams and
lakes, at low to high elevations. Circumboreal. Native
OLYM, MORA, NOCA

Geum triflorum ROSACEAE
Prairie smoke, old man's whiskers
Common, midsummer, perennial, 8–20 in.
Meadow, shrub-steppe
Clumps of basal leaves, erect stems. Plant gray-
green with long hairs. Leaves fern-like with
largest 3-lobed segment at top, few deeply cut
teeth. Flower stem has 1 leaf pair near center.
Flowers usually 3 on nodding stems, sepals
fused to form a cup with tips curved outward,
petals red, cream, or yellow. Seed heads more
than 2 in. long of feathery tails, often glowing
purplish in the sun. Grows in dry meadows, sagebrush scrub,
pine forests, at mid to high elevations. Native OLYM, NOCA, **L&C**

See other *Sanicula*: yellow, page 228
See other *Geum*: yellow, page 231

Rosa canina ROSACEAE
Dog rose
Common, late spring–early summer,
perennial, 3–9 ft. Disturbed, meadow

Shrub or upright thicket. Stems olive-green, stout thorns flattened and curved. Leaves shiny, pinnately divided to 5–7 toothed leaflets, the teeth often gland-tipped. Leaf surfaces sparsely coated with glands, terminal leaflet broadly oval, ½–1½ in. long, with pointed tip. Flower calyx glandless, with toothed lobes, petals pale pink or white, ¾–1¼ in. long. Hips ¾ in. long, bright red, without hairs, old fruits persistent and turning black. Eurasian native. Grows in dry open areas at low elevations. Thorns on our introduced roses, *R. canina* and *R. eglanteria*, are generally curved, while those on our native roses are more or less straight. Nonnative

Rosa eglanteria ROSACEAE
Sweetbrier rose
Locally common, late spring–early summer,
perennial, 3–10 ft. Disturbed, meadow

Rounded shrub with olive-green arching stems, often evenly spaced. Stems with many compressed and curved thorns. Leaves with 5–7 leaflets, small glands that exude a sweet fragrance when crushed. Leaflets widely oval, with rounded tips, double-toothed. Inflorescence consists of 1–8 flowers in loose cluster with shiny stalks. Flower petals about ½–¾ in. long, 5 prominent sepals at base of flower have long expanded tips and stalked glands. Sepals usually fall off when hips mature. Often exhibits mossy rose galls. European native naturalized on dry, open, disturbed sites at low elevations. Nonnative OLYM

Rosa gymnocarpa ROSACEAE
Baldhip rose, wood rose
Locally common, all summer, perennial, 1–5
ft. West-side forest, east-side forest

Slender, weak-stemmed shrub. Stems grayish brown, prickles few to many, slender, more or less straight. Leaves deciduous, with odd number of hairless leaflets. Leaflets with rounded tips, double-toothed glandular edges. Inflorescence is loose cluster of 1–3 small flowers with stalked glands. Flowers pink, each petal about ⅓ in. Five green sepals at base have glands, smooth edges, tips equal length of flower. Sepals fall off, leaving the scarlet hip bare when ripe. Grows in forests, shrublands, from near sea level to high elevations. May hybridize with *R. nutkana*. Native
OLYM, MORA, NOCA, CRLA

Rosa nutkana ROSACEAE
Nootka rose
Locally common, late spring–early summer,
perennial, 3–6 ft. Coastal, meadow

Shrub forming loose thickets. Stems often really black, 2 broad straight thorns at leaf bases.
Leaves divided, 3–7 leaflets with rounded tips,
sparsely hairy, glandular. Flowers solitary, to 3
in. across, pink, petal tips broadly notched. Sepals green, as
long as petals, tips toothed. Purplish red hips have withering
sepals at base. Grows in moist flats at low to mid elevations.
Var. *nutkana*, chiefly west of Cascades, has leaflets double-
toothed with glands on tooth tips, thorns becoming very wide
and flat toward stem base. Var. *hispida*, chiefly east of Cascades,
has leaflets single-toothed, not glandular, thorns not enlarged
or flat. Varieties intergrade in the north and
may hybridize with *R. woodsii* and *R. gymno-
carpa.* Native OLYM, MORA, NOCA, **L&C**

Rosa pisocarpa ROSACEAE
Clustered wild rose, peahip rose
Locally common, late spring–early summer,
perennial, 3–6 ft. Coastal, meadow

Erect shrub, may form thickets. Stem with few
prickles. Prickles straight, with thick base, pair of thorns just at
base of leaf. Leaves pinnately compound, with 5–9 hairless,
glandless, toothed leaflets. Inflorescence consists of 2–10
flowers in clusters on hairless, glandless stalks. Sepals narrowly
oval, coated with glands, smooth-edged tips nearly as long as
petals. Pink flowers ½–¾ in. across. Grows in moist or shady
places from near sea level to near treeline. Native

OLYM, MORA, NOCA, **L&C**

Rosa woodsii var. ultramontana
ROSACEAE
Pearhip rose, Wood's rose, interior rose
Locally common, all summer, perennial, 3–6 ft.
Moist streambanks, meadow

Loose shrub to dense thicket. Stems straight,
gray or red-brown, with few to many slender,
round, straight thorns. Leaves have 5–9 leaflets
without glands. Leaflets widest in middle, round at tips, single-toothed. Flowers small, 1–5 in cluster. Petals 5, ¾–1 in.
long, deep pink to rose, 5 sepals without glands or teeth nearly
equal in length to petals. Hips pear-shaped, about ⅓ in. long.
Grows in moist places in otherwise dry habitats at low to mid elevations, higher in the southern part of our region. Native
CRLA, **L&C**

Rubus spectabilis ROSACEAE
Salmonberry
Locally common, early to midspring, perennial, 3–15 ft. Coastal, moist stream-banks, west-side forest, east-side forest

Erect shrub often growing in thickets, strongly bristly below, with few to many weak thorns above. Stems round, yellowish or brownish, bark shredding. Leaves divided into 3 or sometimes 5 distinct, sharply toothed leaflets. Flowers 1–1½ in. across, 5 petals pink to magenta. Fruit yellow, salmon, or reddish, mushy in texture, edible but not flavorful. Grows along coast and streams, in deep moist woods, burns and clearings, banks of Columbia River, to 5000 ft. First collected by Meriwether Lewis on the banks of the Columbia on March 27, 1806. Native OLYM, MORA, NOCA, **L&C**

Spiraea douglasii ROSACEAE
Hardhack, Douglas's spiraea
Common, all summer, perennial, 2–6 ft. Bog/fen/wetland, moist streambanks, meadow, west-side forest, east-side forest

Erect, thicket-forming shrub with many shoots and branches. Leaves deciduous, alternating along branches, with short petioles, oval to oblong, dark green on top. Flowers many, pink to rose in pointed, erect cluster, much longer than broad. Grows in moist areas in forest, bogs, fens, streambanks, at low to mid elevations. Var. *douglasii* has finely matted gray hairs on underside of leaves. Var. *menziesii* is without hairs on underside of leaves. Native OLYM, MORA, NOCA, CRLA

Spiraea splendens (*Spiraea densiflora*)
ROSACEAE
Rosy spiraea, mountain meadow-sweet
Uncommon, all summer, perennial, 1–2 ft. West-side forest, east-side forest, alpine, subalpine

Small upright shrub. Leaves egg-shaped, with rounded tips, toothed near tip, hairless to lightly hairy. Flowers pink to rose in flat-topped cluster wider than tall, tops stem. Grows in moist rocky areas such as serpentine, conifer forests, at mid to high elevations. Hybridizes in Oregon Cascades with *S. douglasii*, which has tall, narrow, pointed flower clusters. Native
OLYM, MORA, NOCA, CRLA

See other *Rubus*: white, page 133
See other *Spiraea*: white, page 137

Darmera peltata SAXIFRAGACEAE
Umbrella plant, Indian rhubarb
Uncommon, late spring–early summer,
perennial, 1–4 ft. Moist streambanks

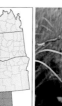

Flower stems erect, 2 ft. or more, without
leaves. Roots fleshy rhizomes crawling among
and over rocks. Leaves emerging after flowering, 1–2 ft. across, with petioles attached in
middle like umbrellas, round deep lobes, irregular teeth. Flowers many in rounded cluster, petals deep to
light pink. Grows on rocky islands, edges of mountain streams,
at mid to high elevations. Native

Leptarrhena pyrolifolia SAXIFRAGACEAE
Leatherleaf saxifrage
Locally common, midsummer, perennial, 8–16
in. Alpine, subalpine

Erect, unbranched flowering stems, basal
rosette. Leaves 1–4 in. long, oblong, round-
toothed, leathery, evergreen, deep green above,
lighter green beneath. Flower stems reddish,
8–16 in., topped with clusters of white flowers
in red calyxes, aging to bright red seed heads
(most often seen this way, as pictured). Grows
in streambanks, mossy seeps, meadows, in
subalpine and alpine. Native OLYM, MORA, NOCA

Lithophragma glabrum (*Lithophragma glabra,*
Lithophragma bulbifera) SAXIFRAGACEAE
Bulbiferous woodland star, rocket star
Locally common, early spring, perennial, 4–8 in.
Meadow, east-side forest, shrub-steppe

Erect, sticky, hairy, red-purple stems with few
flowers. Basal leaves hairless, deeply divided,
leaflets may be divided again, sharp-tipped.
Flowers white or pale pink, with 4 or 5 petals so
deeply divided into 3–5 parts that they look like
long thin petals with very sharp points. Red
bulblets, which produce new plantlets, often in
leaf axils on upper stem. Grows in grasslands,
sagebrush plains, ponderosa or Douglas-fir
forests, dry gravelly places, at low to mid elevations. Native
OLYM, NOCA

See other *Lithophragma*: white, page 139   **361**

Lithophragma parviflorum (*Litho-phragma parviflora*) SAXIFRAGACEAE
Prairie star
Common, early spring, perennial, 4–12 in.
Coastal, meadow, west-side forest, east-side
forest, shrub-steppe

Tuft with upright, sticky, hairy, purplish
stems. Leaves in basal cluster deeply divided
into 3–5 leaflets, divided again and sharp-
toothed, with 2–3 smaller leaves alternate on stem, no bulblets.
Flowers 5–11 in raceme that lengthens as flowers open, 5 pink
or white petals each divided into 3 lobes at tips. Grows in grasslands, sagebrush plains, dry open areas, at low to high elevations. Var. *parviflorum* with pink flowers is fragrant. This species has larger flowers than *L. glabrum*, bulbiferous woodland
star, even though the name means "small-
flowered." Native OLYM, NOCA

Suksdorfia violacea SAXIFRAGACEAE
Violet suksdorfia
Uncommon, late spring, perennial, 4–16 in.
Vernal-wet, east-side forest

Tuft. Stems and leaves covered with glistening glands. Leaves mostly basal with long
petioles, blades round, with 3–5 rounded
lobes; stem leaves smaller but with enlarged stipules. Flowers
¾ in. across in loose cluster, petals violet, rarely white, slightly
spreading at tips. Grows in rocky crevices, mossy banks, cliffs,
sandy shaded areas, usually where wet. Rare in Oregon. Similar, white-flowered *S. ranunculifolia* is intermittently distributed over a wider range, from British Columbia to northern
California. Named for Wilhelm Suksdorf
(1850–1932) of Bingen, Washington, among
the foremost collectors and students of
Northwest flora during his time. Native
NOCA

Lamium amplexicaule LAMIACEAE
Henbit, clasping henbit
Common, all spring and summer, annual or
biennial, 4–15 in. Disturbed, meadow

Upright to spreading stems from single root. Leaves opposite,
middle and upper ones clasping stem, ½–1 in., widely oval to
round, edges toothed to lobed. Flowers from leaf axils along
upper stem. Flower consists of a red-purple tube, hairless inside, upper lip hood-like, about same length as lower lip. Grows
in disturbed soils at low elevations. Nonnative
OLYM, MORA, NOCA

Lamium purpureum LAMIACEAE
Purple dead-nettle, red henbit
Locally common, all spring and summer,
  annual, 4–12 in. Coastal, disturbed, meadow

Decumbent to erect, hairy to smooth. Square
stems are branched from base. Leaves opposite, middle and upper with short petioles,
round to egg-shaped, with heart-shaped base,
toothed. Flowers under leaves, upper lip hood-
shaped, lower lip with 3 small lobes. Pink to purple, often with
spots. Grows in disturbed soils, meadows, gardens, at low elevations. Nonnative OLYM, MORA, NOCA

Monardella odoratissima LAMIACEAE
Western mountain balm, coyote mint
Common, all summer, perennial, 6–24 in.
  West-side forest, east-side forest, shrub-steppe

Stems erect, green or reddish. Leaves lance- to
widely egg-shaped, entire, densely to sparsely
hairy, green to gray, often tinted reddish.
Flower heads flat, in a shallow cup of upright
bracts, the outer bracts reflexed or spreading.
Flowers pink, purple, lavender, or soft white,
with woolly hairs on lobes of calyx. Grows in
sagebrush and mountain forests at mid to high
elevations. Native MORA

Stachys chamisonis var. cooleyae LAMIACEAE
Great hedge-nettle
Locally common, late summer, perennial, 25–60 in.
  Coastal, bog/fen/wetland, meadow, west-side forest

Erect from spreading roots. Stems square,
mostly unbranched, with stiff hairs on edges.
Leaves opposite, triangular, 2–6 in. long,
toothed, with rounded tip, hairy on both sides.
Flowers deep red to purple, 1–2 in. long, hairy,
sessile, with 2 lips: upper lip without lobes,
lower lip larger and 3-lobed. Grows in moist
open areas, roadsides, at low elevations. Native
OLYM, MORA, NOCA

See other *Monardella*: blue, page 424

Stachys mexicana LAMIACEAE
Mexican hedge nettle
Locally common, early summer, perennial,
12–40 in. Coastal, bog/fen/wetland,
meadow, west-side forest

Erect stems from spreading roots. Stems
square, with spreading hairs on edges.
Leaves lance-shaped, opposite, with short
petioles, 1–5 in. long, slightly hairy on both
sides, toothed. Flowers atop stems and in leaf axils, light pink to
lavender-pink, airy, stalkless, ½–¾ in. long, with 2 lips open
wide, the lower lip longer and wider than the upper. Grows in
moist woods, edges of clearings, mostly near coast. Native
OLYM

Orobanche fasciculata
OROBANCHACEAE
Clustered broomrape
Locally common, late spring–early summer,
annual, 2–8 in. Shrub-steppe, meadow

Erect plant without chlorophyll, hairless or
with soft colorless hairs. Stems more than
2 in. tall, often branched, or cluster of flower
stalks each with single flower. Flowers generally 4–10, calyx lobes less than or equal to
tube, tubular flower curved, 5 lobes, purplish or sometimes yellow. Grows in dry open places attached to shrubs such as erio-
gonums and artemisias. Easily confused with naked broomrape, *O. uniflora*, which has single flower on stalk with violet
hairs. Similar *O. corymbosa* is less than 1½ in. tall, with few,
densely hairy, purplish to pink flowers, and is parasitic on
Artemisia tridentata, big sagebrush. Native
OLYM, NOCA

Besseya rubra (*Synthyris rubra*)
SCROPHULARIACEAE
Red besseya
Uncommon, late spring, perennial, 8–24 in.
Meadow, east-side forest

Tuft of erect leaves, stems hairy when
young, later hairless. Basal leaves with long
petiole, blade widely oval, 1–5 in. long, toothed. Inflorescence
tops stem, dense spike of flowers to 8 in. long. Flower calyx 3–4
often unequal lobes, petals absent, 2 stamens with dark red
filaments. Grows in open woodlands, rocky meadows, at low
to mid elevations. Native

See other *Orobanche*: blue, page 425; green/brown, page 469

Castilleja affinis subsp. *litoralis*
(*Castilleja litoralis*) SCROPHULARIACEAE
Seashore paintbrush
Locally common, early summer, perennial,
6–24 in. Coastal

Purplish erect stems, hairless or with fine
short hairs, glandless, with few branches.
Leaves lance-shaped, 1–3 in. long, entire or
lobed, tips rounded. Inflorescence includes
green bracts with 3–5 long red lobes, narrow red calyx lobes,
hairy flower with yellow or red on edges of beak, green to dark
violet lower lip. Grows in dry places along bluffs, chaparral near
coast. Similar *C. mendocinensis* grows on California coast
among shrubs, on dunes and bluffs below 300 ft., rarely in
Curry County, Oregon. Leaves somewhat fleshy, inflorescence

¼–¾ in. long, with bright red to orange-red,
widely wedge-shaped bracts, entire or 3-lobed,
the central lobe widest with sharply pointed
tips. Calyx shaggy-haired, with some glands,
flower tiny, with shaggy hairs on back, edges
reddish, lower lip green. Native

Castilleja applegatei subsp.
pinetorum SCROPHULARIACEAE
Wavy-leaved paintbrush
Common, late spring–early summer, perennial, 12–25 in.
West-side forest, east-side forest, shrub-steppe

Erect, with very sticky foliage and inflorescence. Green leaves
are wavy along edges, undivided below, divided into 3 lobes on
upper section of plant. Inflorescence most often red-orange but
can be yellowish. Flower hood extends well beyond bracts.
Grows in sagebrush, open conifer woods.
Native

Castilleja chromosa SCROPHULARIACEAE
Desert paintbrush
Locally common, midsummer, perennial,
12–35 in. Shrub-steppe

Clustered, erect, without glands. Stems stiff,
brittle, often branched, finely haired. Leaves
with fine short and long hairs. Basal leaves lin-
ear, entire; upper leaves deeply divided, 3–7 linear lobes. Bracts
and calyx similar, upper ½ usually bright red to red-orange to
yellow, never purple. Flower tube twice as long as calyx, with
upper tip slender and pointed. Grows in Great Basin, sagebrush-steppe, deserts. Often confused with closely related *C.
angustifolia*. Native

See other *Castilleja*: white, page 146; yellow, page 237

Castilleja elmeri SCROPHULARIACEAE
Wenatchee paintbrush
Locally common, midsummer, perennial, 10–20 in. Alpine, subalpine

Ascending to erect. Stems slender, unbranched. Leaves linear, entire. Fine hairs on stems and bracts in the inflorescence. Bracts and calyx red except innermost section. Upper bracts broad, rounded with pair of small lobes. Flower exceeds bracts with age, lower lip green. Grows in mountains of central Washington. Native NOCA

Castilleja hispida SCROPHULARIACEAE
Harsh paintbrush
Locally common, early summer, perennial, 8–24 in. Coastal, meadow, west-side forest, east-side forest

Cluster from woody base, with many bristly hairs. Stems erect to ascending, usually unbranched. Leaves lance-shaped to linear; upper stem leaves may be divided into 3 or more shallow lobes. Inflorescence short, elongating later. Bracts bright scarlet, sometimes yellow, broad, deeply lobed, 3–5 lobes, partly covering greenish flowers. Grows in dry openings in forests, meadows, from coast to high elevations. Native OLYM, MORA, NOCA

Castilleja hispida subsp. *brevilobata* (*Castilleja brevilobata*) SCROPHULARIACEAE
Shortlobe paintbrush
Rare, late spring–early summer, perennial, 4–8 in. Meadow

Upright, short, green or yellowish plant, glistens but is not sticky, with hairy glands and few long hairs. Leaves lance-shaped to oval, ½–2 in. long, with 2 or sometimes more rounded shallow lobes. Flowers densely arranged along upper stem, just above bracts, which are similar to the leaves. Outer part of both bract and flower bright red or yellow. Rare. Found on rocky serpentine in Siskiyou Mountains. Native

Castilleja linariifolia SCROPHULARIACEAE
Wyoming paintbrush, linear-leaved paintbrush
Locally common, midsummer, perennial,
12–40 in. Dry rocky sites, east-side forest,
shrub-steppe

Erect, gray-green becoming purplish, hairless
or slightly hairy. Stems with few branches.
Leaves linear, edges rolled upward, entire or
rarely with upper leaves 3-lobed. Flower bracts ⅓–1 in., generally divided into 3 narrow lobes, bright red, orange, or yellow;
calyx unevenly divided, more deeply cut in front, red, more noticeable than bracts. Flower yellow-green with red edges. Grows
in dry rocky sites, plains, sagebrush, juniper forests, at mid to
high elevations. State flower of Wyoming. Native

Castilleja miniata SCROPHULARIACEAE
Slender paintbrush, giant red paintbrush
Common, midsummer, perennial, 12–30 in.
Coastal, moist streambanks, meadow, west-
side forest, east-side forest

Tall, erect, slightly sticky, with few branches.
Leaves flat, lance-shaped, deep green, without
lobes. Flower heads deep bluish red to pinkish
or bright yellow-orange. Flowers mostly concealed by brightly colored, sharply toothed and
pointed, hairy bracts, the green beak of flower extending out
with age. Grows in moist meadows, forest openings, from coast
to mountains. Most common species of *Castilleja* in the Northwest. Subsp. *elata*, Siskiyou paintbrush, has bluish red to yellow-orange flowers; found in bogs, near serpentine, below 4500
ft. Subsp. *miniata* is bright red to orange-red, with stout stems;
grows in wet meadows, along streambanks, at
low to mid elevations in mountains. Native
OLYM, MORA, NOCA

Castilleja parviflora SCROPHULARIACEAE
Small-flowered paintbrush, magenta paintbrush
Uncommon, midsummer, perennial, 6–15 in.
Alpine, subalpine

Stems upright, short, hairy, turning black as
they die. Leaves oval to lance-shaped, divided
into 3–5 lobes, hairy. Flowers green to yellowish green, with
purple edges hidden among bright magenta-red to rose, pink,
or whitish 3- to 5-lobed bracts. Grows in alpine meadows, often
with heathers, at mid to high elevations. Var. *oreopola*, found
on Mount Rainier, has rose-purple bracts, flowers about ¾ in.
long. Very similar var. *olympica* has flowers less than ¾ in. and
is endemic to upper Olympic Mountains. Native OLYM, MORA

Castilleja pruinosa

SCROPHULARIACEAE

Frosted paintbrush

Locally common, midsummer, perennial, 12–30 in. West-side forest

Upright, may have few branches. Stems and lower leaves densely covered with hairs, the most highly branched giving the plant a frosted appearance. Flower head 1–8 in. long, with tricolored bracts with bright orange-red tips, narrow yellow stripe, green at base; calyx with orange-red sharp tips, green base; flower green with red margins. Grows in dry, open, rocky serpentine areas or edges of forest at mid to high elevations. For an interesting view of branched hairs, which among members of *Castilleja* are unique to this species, use a hand lens. Native

Castilleja rhexifolia

SCROPHULARIACEAE

Rosy paintbrush, alpine paintbrush, rhexia-leaved paintbrush

Locally common, midsummer, perennial, 5–12 in. Bog/fen/wetland, meadow, alpine, subalpine

Small upright clusters. Plant with few hairs, or more often hairless. Stems unbranched, purplish red or scarlet. Leaves broadly lance-shaped without lobes or with few lobes in upper part of plant. Flower bracts 1- to 3-lobed, center lobe very wide and often somewhat rounded, all with round tips. Grows in subalpine meadows, bogs, alpine talus slopes. This species is the common high-altitude paintbrush in eastern Washington and northeastern Oregon. Similar to and known to hybridize with *C. miniata*, which generally grows at lower elevations. Native NOCA

Castilleja rupicola SCROPHULARIACEAE

Cliff paintbrush

Locally common, late spring, perennial, 6–10 in. Alpine, subalpine

Cluster of short ascending stems with unbranched fine hairs. Leaves linear to lance-shaped, upper ones divided into 3–7 sharply cut lobes. Bracts, calyces scarlet on outer portion. Flower about twice as long as calyx, narrow, with thin red margins, lower lip dark green. Grows in subalpine meadows, basalt cliffs, alpine ledges, talus of the western Columbia River Gorge, at high elevations. Native MORA, NOCA

Castilleja schizotricha
SCROPHULARIACEAE
Splithair paintbrush
Endemic, midsummer, perennial, 3–6 in.
Alpine, subalpine

Erect stems in small cluster from woody base, white with woolly branched hairs. Leaves to ¾ in. long, linear to lance-shaped, entire or 3-lobed. Flower spike 1–3 in. tall. Bracts pinkish or reddish purple, with 3 rounded lobes. Calyx deeply divided, upper ½ of flower deep red, with pistil extended outward. Rare. Grows on decomposed granite, marble, at high elevations in Siskiyou Mountains. Native

Castilleja suksdorfii   SCROPHULARIACEAE
Suksdorf's paintbrush
Rare, early summer, perennial, 12–25 in.
Meadow, alpine, subalpine

Upright, smooth, nearly hairless. Upper leaves divided into 3–5 lobes; lower leaves linear, entire. Flower bracts and calyx bright red at top, pale green on lower section often separated by a narrow yellow band, narrowly lobed, mostly 5 lobes with sharply pointed tips. Grows in wet meadows in upper montane to subalpine areas. Native

Cordylanthus capitatus   SCROPHULARIACEAE
Yakima bird's beak, clustered bird's beak
Uncommon, late summer, annual, 8–20 in.
East-side forest, shrub-steppe

Erect, shiny green to gray-purple, densely hairy, glandular. Erect stem, many spreading branches. Leaves narrow, ¾–1½ in. long, often divided into 3 parts. Inflorescence consists of 2–5 flowers in head. Flower red or maroon with yellow tips, calyx gray-purple, ⅓ in. long, with tips curved back. Grows in open conifer or juniper forests or other dry open places at low to mid elevations. Closely related to paintbrush, *Castilleja* species, which also lives partially off the living roots of other plants. Native

Digitalis purpurea
SCROPHULARIACEAE
Foxglove
Common, late spring, biennial, to 6 ft.
Coastal, disturbed, meadow, west-side
forest

Erect stem to 6 ft. Basal and lower stem leaves oval, 4–12 in. long, covered with soft hairs. Flowers held on 3 sides of elongating upper stem. Flowers nodding, bell-shaped, 1–3 in. long, pink, lavender, or white, with deep pink to purple spots inside. Grows in moist fields, grasslands, edges of forests, from coast to mid elevations. A garden escapee originally from eastern Europe and Turkey. The heart medicine known as digitalis is derived from this plant. However, it can be highly poisonous when ingested by humans and livestock. Nonnative
OLYM, MORA, NOCA

Mimulus breweri   SCROPHULARIACEAE
Brewer's monkeyflower
Locally common, midsummer, annual, 1–6
in. Meadow, alpine, subalpine

Stems upright, hairy. Leaves sessile, linear, more or less hairy. Flowers small on short stalks, pale pink to rose or lavender, all lobes about equal length, throat yellow. Grows on rocky outcrops, in meadows, scree near seepages, mountains, at mid to high elevations. Often seen in large masses. Native
OLYM, MORA, NOCA, CRLA

Mimulus cusickii   SCROPHULARIACEAE
Cusick's monkeyflower
Locally common, early summer, annual,
1–10 in. Shrub-steppe

Densely hairy. Stems upright. Leaves opposite, linear to oblong, tips sharply pointed, covered with sticky glands. Flowers on short stalks, with 5 more or less equal lobes, medium pink to rich magenta, with yellow bands in throat margined by slightly deeper pink but no darker colors. Grows in moist to drying sandy or gravelly places in desert steppe. Often creates extensive shows in early summer. Native

See other *Mimulus*: yellow, page 243; orange, page 300

Mimulus lewisii SCROPHULARIACEAE
Lewis's monkeyflower, great purple monkeyflower
Locally common, all summer, perennial, 1–4 ft.
Moist streambanks, west-side forest, east-side forest, alpine, subalpine

Clustered, hairy to sticky-hairy. Stems spreading to upright, with clasping leaves. Leaves 1–3 in. long, oblong, with pointed tip, entire or slightly toothed. Flowers pink to bright rose, 1 in. or longer, with yellow markings in throat. Grows in wet areas, streambanks, moist meadows, at mid to high elevations in mountains. Often forms large showy clumps. Native
OLYM, MORA, NOCA, CRLA, **L&C**

Mimulus nanus SCROPHULARIACEAE
Dwarf monkeyflower
Uncommon, all summer, annual, ½–4 in.
East-side forest, shrub-steppe, subalpine

Tiny tuft, slightly hairy. Stems are upright, branched in larger plants. Leaves oval, more or less purple underneath, with rounded tips. Flowers with 2 upper lobes larger than 3 lower lobes; tube floor with 2 yellow stripes, surrounded with purple-rose dots and lines. Grows on sandy or bare soils at mid to high elevations. Native
MORA, NOCA, CRLA

Nothochelone nemorosa (*Penstemon nemorosus*)
SCROPHULARIACEAE
Turtlehead, woodland penstemon, beardtongue
Locally common, midsummer, perennial, 12–40 in. West-side forest, east-side forest

Erect but sometimes bending over. Stems clustered. Leaves opposite, on short petioles, blades to 5 in. long, lance-shaped to widely oval, with rounded base, saw-toothed, with pointed tips. Flowers several on long stalks along upper stem. Flowers distinctly 2-lipped with lower lip longer, pinkish purple, often lighter on underside and inside, glandular-hairy on outside, anthers woolly. Grows in moist woods, on rocky places in mixed forests, at mid to high elevations. Separated from but similar to *Penstemon*. Native OLYM, MORA, NOCA

Orthocarpus bracteosus
SCROPHULARIACEAE
Rosy owl's clover
Locally common, all summer, annual, 4–15 in. Vernal-wet, meadow

Erect, tinted purple, with minute glands. Stems slender, with linear leaves. Lower leaves entire, upper divided into 3 lobes. Inflorescence finely haired, 1–8 in. long, includes 3-lobed bracts that merge into upper leaves. Flowers sac-like, rose or rarely white, protruding beyond bracts and showing the hooked, downward-pointing peak. Grows in moist meadows at low to high elevations. Native

Orthocarpus cuspidatus subsp. *copelandii*
(*Orthocarpus copelandii*)
SCROPHULARIACEAE
Copeland's owl's clover
Locally common, all summer, annual, 4–8 in. Meadow, shrub-steppe, alpine, subalpine

Erect spike, rounded head wider than stem. Lower stem leaves ½–2 in., narrow, with pointed tips. Bracts in flower head are green, with pink tips, wide, top bracts with narrow side lobes. Flowers usually less than ½ in. long, pink to purple. Grows in open grassy or rocky slopes at mid to high elevations. Known to hybridize with subsp. *cuspidatus*, Siskiyou Mountains owl's clover, which is stout-stemmed, larger-flowered, ½–1 in. long, grows at mid to high elevations. Subsp. *cryptanthus*, cryptantha owl's clover, has shorter flowers hidden by bright pink tips of bracts, grows at mid to high elevations in central and eastern areas. Native

Orthocarpus imbricatus
SCROPHULARIACEAE
Mountain owl's clover
Uncommon, midsummer, annual, 4–14 in. Meadows, alpine, subalpine

Single stem, straight or branched near top. Leaves narrow, pointed, slightly hairy. Flower head dense, with broad rounded bracts lobed on each side, green with showy purplish pink tips. Flowers hairy, white or yellow below, purplish pink near tip, beak with noticeable round hooked tip. Grows in dry meadows, rocky slopes or outcrops, at high elevations. Native OLYM, NOCA, CRLA

See other *Orthocarpus*: yellow, page 245

Orthocarpus tenuifolius
SCROPHULARIACEAE
Thin-leaved owl's clover
Locally common, midsummer, annual, 4–12 in.
Meadow, east-side forest, shrub-steppe

Erect. Slender stem holds very narrow leaves; lower leaves entire; upper leaves divided into 2–4 narrow lobes. Dense flower spike at top has wide deep purple-pink bracts almost concealing the yellow flowers. Flowers may be tinted purple-pink on tips. Grows in meadows, open woods, at low to high elevations. Native **L&C**

Pedicularis attollens SCROPHULARIACEAE
Baby elephant's head, little elephant's head
Locally common, midsummer, perennial, 6–16 in. Bog/fen/wetland, meadow, alpine, subalpine

Erect stem topped with dense flower spike. Leaves mostly basal, more or less linear, divided to center into 12 or more pairs of toothed segments; alternate stem leaves same, smaller. Inflorescence 1–12 in. long, very hairy, flowers between shorter bracts. Flowers lavender to pink with purple markings; short upper lip curving upward; 3 lower lobes spreading fan-like give the look of an elephant's head. Found along streams and in wet meadows at high elevations, including Steens Mountain. Similar to *P. groenlandica*, which does not have dense hairs in the inflorescence. Native

Pedicularis densiflora
SCROPHULARIACEAE
Indian warrior
Locally common, midspring, perennial, 6–24 in. West-side forest

Erect leafy stem with large flower head, flowers covered with brown hairs. Leaves mostly basal, becoming smaller up the stem, oblong to lance-shaped, 2–12 in., divided, toothed segments, lobed with pointed tips. Flower head club-shaped, 2–5 in. long, containing leafy bracts longer than flowers, which are flaming to wine red or occasionally yellow. Flower has sturdy straight upper lip covering small lower lip. Grows in dense dry oak and pine forests at low to mid elevations. Widely distributed in California; northern limit of its range is southern Oregon. Native

See other *Pedicularis*: white, page 147; yellow, page 246

Pedicularis groenlandica

SCROPHULARIACEAE
Elephant's head lousewort, bull elephant's head
Locally common, midsummer, perennial, 8–32 in. Bog/fen/wetland, moist streambanks, meadow, alpine, subalpine
Single or cluster of erect stems, hairless. Basal leaves 1–10 in. long, lance-shaped, divided, with more than 25 linear toothed segments, smallest along stem. Inflorescence consists of a long spike; lower leafy bracts equal in length to flowers. Flowers light pink to darkish purple, without markings, upper hood curved down and swinging outward, looks much like elephant trunk, lower lip with spreading ear-like lobes. Grows in wet meadows, seeps, streambanks, at low to high elevations. Similar to *P. attollens*, which has dense hairs in the inflorescence and slightly smaller flowers with "trunk" pointing upward, not down and out. Native

OLYM, MORA, NOCA, CRLA, **L&C**

Pedicularis ornithorhyncha

SCROPHULARIACEAE
Bird's-beak lousewort
Uncommon, late summer, perennial, 4–8 in.
Meadow, alpine, subalpine
Clump of erect stems from basal leaves. Leaves mostly basal, with petioles, divided into short toothed lobes; few stem leaves smaller. Flowers rose to purple, clustered with shorter leafy bracts in short hairy head atop stem. Flower upper lip bent at right angle, with beak pointing outward like a baby bird; shorter lower lip 3-lobed, spreading. Grows in moist subalpine and alpine meadows. Native OLYM, MORA, NOCA

Pedicularis racemosa

SCROPHULARIACEAE
Sickletop lousewort, parrot's beak
Common, midsummer, perennial, 8–20 in.
West-side forest, east-side forest
Cluster of leafy, decumbent or spreading, branched, hairless stems. Leaf blade lance-shaped, undivided, saw-toothed. Flowers on upper stem with leaf-like bracts. Flowers pale pink, purplish, or white, upper lip pointing downward with long, narrow, crescent-shaped tip to 1 side resting on 3 larger lobes of lower lip. Grows in conifer forests, dry woods, slopes, at low to mid elevations. Native OLYM, MORA, NOCA

Penstemon barrettiae
SCROPHULARIACEAE
Barrett's penstemon
Endemic, late spring, perennial, 9–15 in.
Dry rocky sites

Ascending stems often in large clumps, hairless. Leaves wide, to 3 in. long, tapering to pointed tip, succulent-like, coated with blue waxy powder. Inflorescence is 2–6 in. long, atop stem. Showy flowers rosy to lilac, 1–1½ in. long. Grows in shady dry places, hanging in cliffs or on talus slopes, only in Columbia River Gorge in transition zone between Columbia Basin, eastern Cascades, and western Cascades. Native

Penstemon newberryi SCROPHULARIACEAE
Mountain pride, Berry's penstemon
Locally common, midsummer, perennial, 6–12 in. West-side forest, alpine, subalpine

Shrubby plant, as wide as it is tall, with woody base, ascending flower stems to 12 in. Leaves mostly basal, lance-shaped, evergreen, thick, saw-toothed. Inflorescence consists of a loose cluster of flowers at stem top, covered with small glistening glands. Flowers narrow, 1–1½ in., tubular, bright deep rose-red to red-violet, with white-woolly hairs inside, staminode with pale yellow hairs and stamens extending outward. Grows in rocky outcrops, talus, at mid to high elevations at the northern edge of its range in southern Oregon. Native

Penstemon richardsonii SCROPHULARIACEAE
Richardson's penstemon
Locally common, late summer, perennial, 12–34 in. Dry rocky sites, shrub-steppe

Large plant with many upright hairless stems, sticky inflorescence. Leaves opposite, hairless, lance-shaped, deeply saw-toothed, sometimes lobed to narrow 1–3 in. segments. Inflorescence consists of many spreading stalks holding bright pink, pinkish red, or bluish flowers. Flower tube long, with spreading lobes; throat lined with white beelines; staminode extending outward, usually coated with yellow hairs. Grows in cliff crevices, talus and other dry places, at lower elevations. Native NOCA

See other *Penstemon*: white, page 147; yellow, page 247; blue, page 427   **375**

Penstemon rupicola

SCROPHULARIACEAE

Rock penstemon

Locally common, May–August, perennial, 2–6 in. Dry rocky sites, alpine, subalpine

Mats of evergreen leaves, flower stems less than 4 in. tall. Leaves widely oval to round, ¼–¾ in. long, finely toothed, deep blue-green, with a blue-white waxy surface. Flowers deep rose to pink, lavender-pink, or violet, rarely white, ¾–1½ in. long, staminode hairless or bearing golden-woolly hairs. Grows on rocky outcrops at mid to high elevations. Where they come in contact, hybridizes with *P. davidsonii* or *P. newberryi*. Native MORA, NOCA

Scrophularia lanceolata

SCROPHULARIACEAE

Lance-leaved figwort

Locally common, early summer, perennial, 20–40 in. Coastal, vernal-wet, meadow

Clustered, erect, 4-sided, sticky stems. Leaves egg- to lance-shaped, 4–5 in. long, tapering to pointed tip, saw-toothed. Inflorescence consists of a long narrow cluster of stemmed flowers with soft hairs and glands. Flowers small, bicolored, yellowish green or brownish green tinted light maroon on upper side; 2 lobes of upper lip pointing out; 3 lobes of lower lip small, with center lobe folded outward; staminode fan-shaped, wider than long. Grows in moist meadows, streambanks, at low to mid elevations. *Scrophularia californica* has longer leaf petioles, upper lip of flowers with 2 dark maroon projecting lobes, staminode purple to brown, baseball bat–like to egg-shaped, longer than wide.

Native OLYM, NOCA, CRLA

Triphysaria pusilla (*Orthocarpus pusillus*) SCROPHULARIACEAE

Dwarf owl's clover

Locally common, midspring, annual, 1–6 in. Meadow

Stem slender, branched, prostrate, with growing tips turned upward. Leaves tiny, lobed many times, often coated with fine purplish or yellow-brown hairs. Tiny flowers hidden among bracts, reddish purple or sometimes yellow, include 3 shallow pouches below hooked beak. Grows in grasslands at low elevations. Native OLYM

See other *Triphysaria*: yellow, page 247

Apocynum androsaemifolium

APOCYNACEAE

Spreading dogbane, mountain dogbane
Locally common, all summer, perennial, 6–16 in. Disturbed, west-side forest, east-side forest, shrub-steppe

Erect stem with many branches spreading from ground. Milky sap oozes when stem is cut. Leaves opposite on stems, 1½–2½ in. long, with petioles shorter than blade. Leaf blade widely oval, with rounded tip, somewhat drooping to horizontal, dark green above, lighter below. Flowers in terminal clusters, small, bell-shaped, pink, rose, or white with pink stripes; lobes spreading or curved backward. Grows in rocky places, dry open areas in conifer forests and adjacent shrub-steppe and prairies, at low to subalpine elevations. Native

OLYM, MORA, NOCA, CRLA

Asclepias fascicularis ASCLEPIADACEAE

Narrow-leaved milkweed
Common, all summer, perennial, 2–4 ft.
Moist streambanks, meadow, shrub-steppe

Erect stem. Leaves linear, in whorls of 3–6 with short petioles, often with smaller side shoots. Inflorescence consists of umbels with leafless stalks. Flowers greenish white or tinted purplish pink, corolla lobes reflexed back, 5 hood-like appendages folded inward, each containing a small horn extending outward. Seedpods erect. Grows in dry to moist soil near streams in valleys, foothills, from sea level to mid elevations. Native

Asclepias speciosa ASCLEPIADACEAE

Showy milkweed
Common, all summer, perennial, 18–50 in.
Coastal, moist streambanks, disturbed, meadow, shrub-steppe

Erect stem. Leaves opposite with short petioles or clasping, narrow to widely oblong, white with soft fine hairs. Large rounded umbel of rose-purple flowers tops stem. Flower with 5 corolla lobes reflexed back, 5 hood-like appendages folded inward, each containing a small, exserted horn with sharp tip. Seedpods point upward. Grows in fields, roadsides, railroad margins, near streams, from sea level to mid elevations. Native

See other *Apocynum*: white, page 148

Cynoglossum officinale
BORAGINACEAE
Burgundy hound's tongue
Uncommon, early spring, biennial, 1–3 ft.
Disturbed, meadow, east-side forest, shrub-steppe

Erect, with single hairy stem and numerous leaves. Leaves egg-shaped, soft hairy on both sides. Basal leaves 3–8 in. long with petioles 2–4 in.; stem leaves many, smaller, sessile. Flower clusters in upper leaves. Flowers burgundy, the 5 nubs in center same color. Seeds are 4 large, tongue-like, distinctive nutlets with raised margins and numerous small prickles. Nutlets are spread by passing animals. Grows in disturbed places at low to mid elevations. Toxic to cattle. Nonnative

Calystegia soldanella
CONVOLVULACEAE
Beach morning glory
Locally common, all spring and summer, perennial, prostrate. Coastal

Creeps on sand but does not twine. Stems 8–20 in. Leaves smooth, wider than long, heart-shaped, with rounded tip. Bractlets egg-shaped to round, attached just below calyx and concealing it. Flowers on 1–3 in. stalks, wide, funnel-shaped, 1–2 in. across, pink to rose with a white throat. Found on coastal beaches. Grows worldwide. Native OLYM

Convolvulus arvensis   CONVOLVULACEAE
Field bindweed, orchard morning glory
Common, all spring and summer, perennial, trailing, to 80 in. Coastal, disturbed, meadow, shrub-steppe

Trailing vine making large carpets or climbing. Very persistent, with deep root. Leaves 1–2 in. long, usually arrow-shaped, with rounded points. Flowers 1 or several in cluster on twining 1–2 in. stalks. Flower 1 in. or less across, with 5 petals united into open funnel shape with folds, white or pink, usually purple on outside at folds. Rampant weed in all types of disturbed soils and agriculture at low to mid elevations. Nonnative OLYM, NOCA

See other *Cynoglossum*: blue, page 438
See other *Calystegia*: white, page 153

Armeria maritima PLUMBAGINACEAE
Sea thrift, sea pink
Common, all spring and summer, perennial,
4–16 in. Coastal

Mounding to flat perennial from single root.
Leaves 2–5 in. long, narrow, flat, hairless, with
linear veins. Flower petals and calyx pink, possibly white, in tight round head on hairless,
leafless, unbranched stalks less than 16 in.
high. Flower petals 5, calyx with 10 ribs, few hairs along ribs, 5
lobes with sharp tips. Grows in bluffs, grasslands, coastal
sands, from sea level to 600 ft. Native OLYM

Collomia heterophylla POLEMONIACEAE
Varied-leaf collomia, variable-leaf collomia
Common, early summer, annual, 6–16 in.
West-side forest, east-side forest

Erect stem with many spreading branches.
Leaves hairy, slightly glandular; lower leaves
lobed; upper leaves less lobed or entire. Flowers small, pink, white, or lavender, in clusters
on branches and at tips. Grows on sandy or
gravelly soils at low to mid elevations. Native
OLYM, MORA, NOCA

Collomia linearis POLEMONIACEAE
Narrow-leaved collomia, tiny trumpet
Common, midsummer, annual, to 15 in.
Meadow, shrub-steppe

Erect, unbranched except occasionally near top. Basal leaves
lance-shaped, toothed; stem leaves all about the same size, narrow, entire. Flowers clustered at top, stalkless,
white or pink; pollen white. Grows in dry open
ground in all elevations. Native
OLYM, MORA, NOCA, **L&C**

See other *Collomia*: orange, page 301; blue, page 443

Collomia tinctoria POLEMONIACEAE
Yellow-staining collomia
Locally common, midsummer, annual, 1–3
in. East-side forest, shrub-steppe

Upright, branches widely spreading. Leaves lance-shaped, entire, coated with glands. Flowers 2–3 at leaf axil. Flower tube slender, maroon to violet; lobes pink to white, tapered to a bristly point; stigma and anthers with blue pollen extend outward from tube. Grows in gravelly or rocky soils in open places at low to high elevations, including Steens Mountain. Similar *C. tracyi* grows in northern California, with stigma not extended beyond tube throat. (Note: Whitish powder on leaves pictured is powdery mildew.) Native

Gilia capillaris POLEMONIACEAE
Miniature gilia, smooth-leaved gilia
Common, early summer, annual, 1–8 in.
Vernal-wet, meadow, alpine, subalpine

Erect stem, ascending branches. Stem and branches fine-haired with glands at tips. Leaves on stem pointing upward, narrow, entire. Flowers tiny, 1–3 atop each branch. Flower with yellow tube opening to pink, blue, or white lobes. Grows in masses in open sandy places, streambanks, meadows or snow pockets, at mid to high elevations. Native MORA, NOCA

Gilia sinistra POLEMONIACEAE
Alva Day's gilia
Locally common, early summer, annual, 2–34 in.
West-side forest, alpine, subalpine

Erect stem, spreading branches. Stems with many leaves dense with sticky black or yellow glands. Leaves linear to narrowly lance-shaped, entire or with 3–5 lobes, the middle lobe longer. Inflorescence consists of 2–3 flowers on long branch, each above a leaf, the thin flower stalks unequal. Flower in gland-coated calyx with pointed tips, red edges. Flower narrowly funnel-shaped; tube and throat yellow, with red stripes; lobes bright pink, round-tipped; stamens extending outward; pollen blue. Grows in open shrublands, forests, on serpentine or volcanic rocky soils, at all elevations. Subsp. *sinistra* style and stamens, except longest, do not extend beyond flower tube. Native

See other *Gilia*: blue, page 443

Ipomopsis aggregata (*Gilia aggregata*)
POLEMONIACEAE
Scarlet gilia, skyrocket
Common, midsummer, biennial or perennial,
1–4 ft. West-side forest, east-side forest, shrub-
steppe, alpine, subalpine

Stem erect, sticky with glands or hairy. Plant
dies after flowering. Basal leaves much divided; stem leaves reducing in size up the
stem. Inflorescence tops stem, loose flower clusters with short
stalks. Flowers brilliant orange-red spotted or mottled with yellow; can be pink, yellow, or white. Flower tubes ¾–1½ in.,
topped with pointed lobes, stamens extending outward. Grows
in dry soils, in openings of woodlands, meadows, in all elevations. Subsp. *aggregata* has orange-red flowers speckled white,
tube gradually flaring to the lobes. Subsp. *for-
mosissima* has white or yellow pollen, stem
leaves sharply lobed. Native NOCA, CRLA, **L&C**

Linanthus bicolor POLEMONIACEAE
Babystars, bicolored flaxflower
Common, late spring, annual, 2–6 in.
Vernal-wet, west-side forest

Stem erect, unbranched, a whorl of leaves at
stem top. Leaves divided into many narrow
segments, stiff hairs on upper surface, shiny below. Few
flowers open at a time from within the leaves. Flowers with
erect, long, slender, reddish tubes have 5 pink lobes at top;
throat of tube yellow, with yellow ring under lobes, or colors
sometimes reversed; stamens extending outward. Grows in
spring-damp to fairly dry places at low to mid elevations. Native
OLYM, NOCA

Phlox adsurgens POLEMONIACEAE
Woodland phlox
Locally common, late spring, perennial, 4–12
in. West-side forest

Mat-forming, creeping, hairless evergreen.
Stems near or along soil, flowering branches
upright. Leaves opposite, oval, ½–1 in., shiny.
Flower branches erect. Flowers pink with vari-
ety of white and darker pink markings in center. Petals narrow
to wide, overlapping. Grows in open woods, partly shaded
conifer forests, at low to mid elevations. Native

See other *Ipomopsis*: white, page 159
See other *Linanthus*: white, page 160
See other *Phlox*: white, page 161

Phlox diffusa POLEMONIACEAE
Spreading phlox
Locally common, midspring, perennial, 2–8 in. West-side forest, alpine, subalpine

Mat or open mound with woody base and branches, hairless or covered with thin white hairs, not glandular. Leaves very narrow, sharp on tips, hairy at base. Flowers solitary on leafy branch tips, stemless, lavender, purple, white, pink, or darker rose; petals narrow to round, overlapping, often with dark area near center forming ring. Grows in gravelly soils in dry open areas at all elevations. Native OLYM, MORA, NOCA, CRLA

Phlox gracilis (Microsteris gracilis) POLEMONIACEAE
Midget phlox, annual phlox, pretty little phlox
Common, all summer, annual, 2–8 in. Vernal-wet, disturbed

Short stems spreading to erect, branching, glandular-hairy near top. Leaves lance-shaped, opposite on lower stems, alternate near top. Flowers on separate stalks in clusters at stem ends; tube yellowish, with bright pink or lavender notched lobes. Grows in moist or dry soils at all elevations. Subsp. *humilis* is as broad as it is high, numerously branched, with shining white hairs and glands; flower has white tube, purple lobes. Native MORA, NOCA

Phlox longifolia POLEMONIACEAE
Longleaf phlox
Locally common, early summer, perennial, 4–20 in. Meadow, east-side forest, shrub-steppe, alpine, subalpine

Stems upright from woody base, sometimes shrub-like. Leaves narrow, to 3 in. long, with pointed but not sharp tips, hairless or with few hairs. Flowers few to many on thin stalks covered with glands. Flower to 1¼ in. across, white, lavender, or deep pink, outer edges of petals notched or irregular, inner eye white. Grows on dry hillsides among sagebrush at low to high elevations. Native NOCA

Phlox speciosa POLEMONIACEAE
Showy phlox
Locally common, midspring, perennial, 6–16 in.
Meadow, east-side forest, shrub-steppe

Erect branched stems. Leaves opposite, linear, with pointed tip, few hairs and glands on top surface, smooth below. Flower head at top, loose, flowers solitary, with ½–2 in. stalks. Flowers pink or sometimes white, with lighter or darker central rings; tube about twice as long as deeply notched heart-shaped petals. Grows in open rocky soils, shrub-steppe, grasslands, lightly wooded areas, at low to mid elevations. Native NOCA, **L&C**

Phlox viscida POLEMONIACEAE
Sticky phlox
Uncommon, midspring, perennial, 4–8 in.
Meadow, shrub-steppe

Erect, with woody base. Stems, leaves densely to sparsely coated with sticky glands. Leaves linear to lance-shaped, 1–2 in. long, with fine hairs, some tipped with glands. Flowers 3–15 in tight cluster at stem top, with many glands on stalks ½–2½ in. long. Flowers purple, pink, or white, some with pale eye and darker streaks. Grows in thin open woods, rocky or gravelly slopes, at mid to high elevations. There are nonglandular forms with interwoven hairs in Hells Canyon. Similar *P. caespitosa* is not sticky with glands, has blue-green broadly linear leaves with 3 raised veins, stiff with sharp points and inrolled hairy edges; grows on rocky soils and ridges and in open dry forests at low to mid elevations. Native

Dodecatheon alpinum PRIMULACEAE
Alpine shooting star
Locally common, midsummer, perennial, 4–20 in. Bog/fen/wetland, meadow, east-side forest, alpine, subalpine

Basal upright leaves, erect stem. Plant hairless. Leaves 4 or more, linear to lance-shaped, 8 in. or less in length. Stem leafless, shiny, topped with 1–10 downward-turned flowers. Flower with 4 of each part; petals magenta, outer part changing to white with deep magenta or black band at wrinkled base; stamens black. Grows in boggy meadows, along streams in high mountains. Flowers of different species of shooting star sometimes have 4 parts, sometimes 5, sometimes both. Native CRLA

See other *Dodecatheon*: white, page 161   **383**

Dodecatheon conjugens

PRIMULACEAE

Bonneville shooting star

Uncommon, midspring, perennial, 3–11 in.

Meadow, east-side forest, shrub-steppe

Basal leaves spreading, stem erect. Leaves spreading outward to upward, 1–6 in. long, narrow to egg-shaped, usually tapering into petiole. Flowers to 7 at top of hairless stem have 5 of each part. Flower petals less often pink or white, usually magenta turning to white then yellow near base, base maroon or black, wrinkled. Grows in moist meadows, along banks, shady places with sagebrush, at low to mid elevations. Native

Dodecatheon hendersonii

PRIMULACEAE

Henderson's shooting star, broad-leaved shooting star

Locally common, early spring, perennial, 5–16 in. Vernal-wet, meadow, west-side forest

Basal rosette, erect stem. Plant hairless. Leaves broadly egg-shaped to nearly round, plump, 1–2 in. long, prostrate to spreading upward. Flowers few to many in cluster atop stem. Flower can have 4 or 5 parts even on same plant. Petals short, round-tipped, magenta with yellow and dark purple-black bands at white-edged base; tube purple-black, pointed at tip. Plant becomes dormant by early summer. Grows in open woods, grassy or shady sites, in moist to dry areas, below 6500 ft. Native

OLYM

Dodecatheon jeffreyi   PRIMULACEAE

Tall mountain shooting star, Jeffrey's shooting star

Uncommon, midsummer, perennial, 6–24 in. Coastal, vernal-wet, bog/fen/wetland, moist streambanks, meadow, alpine, subalpine

Erect stem, leaves to 20 in. Plant hairless or stem covered with gland-tipped hairs. Leaves oval to lance-shaped, with shallow rounded teeth or entire. Stem topped with 3 to many flowers. Flower with all parts in 4 or 5, lavender to magenta, occasionally white petals, lower part cream or yellow, red band at base. Grows in very wet places that are usually drier in summer, boggy areas and shorelines, from coastal to high elevations. Native   OLYM, MORA, NOCA

Dodecatheon poeticum PRIMULACEAE
Poet's shooting star
Locally common, early spring, perennial, 5–8
in. Vernal-wet, meadow, shrub-steppe

Erect stem and leaves. Plant covered with
rough, gland-tipped hairs. Leaves 2–5 in. long,
narrow to widely oval, with fine teeth; petioles
about same length or shorter. Flowers 1–10
atop stalks. Flowers in parts of 5, petals rose-
pink, yellow, black at base, tube black-purple sometimes tinged
with yellow. Grows in vernal-wet open places or in light woodlands, streambanks. Native **L&C**

Dodecatheon pulchellum (*Dodecatheon cusickii,*
Dodecatheon pauciflorum) PRIMULACEAE
Few-flowered shooting star, pretty shooting star
Common, midspring, perennial, 6–20 in.
Coastal, vernal-wet, bog/fen/wetland, meadow,
alpine, subalpine

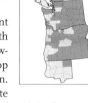

Erect stem, upright spreading leaves. Plant
hairless. Leaves oval to egg-shaped, often with
some fine teeth, 2–10 in. long, entire, narrowing gradually to petiole. Flowers 2–15 atop
stem. Flower with 5 of all parts; petals ¼–½ in.
long, magenta to lavender with large white

spot near base, dark ring at base; tube yellow where joined, purple-black near tip. Grows along streambanks, waterfalls, wet
meadows, seeps, sometimes in salt water near coast, at low to
high elevations. Subsp. *pulchellum* is hairless throughout.
Subsp. *cusickii* has fine, slightly sticky glands on surfaces of
stems and leaves. Native NOCA

Douglasia laevigata PRIMULACEAE
Smooth douglasia
Rare, late spring–early summer, perennial, 2–6
in. Coastal, alpine, subalpine

Mat with ascending stems. Leaves oblong, less
than 1 in. long, hairless or with small straight
hairs along edge, entire or with few teeth,
crowded in pairs below and rosette at stem top.
Flowers 2–10 in tight clusters on branched

leafless stalks above foliage; 5 round petals open out flat from
funnel-shaped tube, deep pink or rose fading to lighter. Blooms
soon after snowmelt at higher elevations. Grows in moist rocky
bluffs, talus slopes and ledges, from coast to alpine. The genus
is named for David Douglas, Scottish botanist who explored
the Northwest extensively in the early 1800s. Native
OLYM, MORA, NOCA

Trientalis borealis subsp. *latifolia*

(*Trientalis latifolia*, *Trientalis europaea* var. *latifolia*) PRIMULACEAE

Pacific starflower, western starflower, oval-leaved starflower

Locally common, late spring–early summer, perennial, 4–8 in. Coastal, west-side forest

Single, erect, unbranched stem with brown glands bearing whorl of 4–7 leaves at top, each 1–3 in. long, broadly oval, with pointed tip, brown glands on upper side. Flower stem from center of leaves shorter than the leaves, with single star-shaped pink flower with 5 pointed petals. Grows in shady moist woods. Similar but smaller *T. europaea* var. *arctica*, northern starflower, has white flowers and leaves scattered on stem below whorl at stem top. Native OLYM, MORA, NOCA, CRLA

Triodanis perfoliata

CAMPANULACEAE

Cupped Venus looking glass

Locally common, midspring–midsummer, annual, 4–12 in. Disturbed, west-side forest

Erect. Stem stiff, branched or unbranched, with bristle-like hairs. Leaves to 1 in. long, widely egg-shaped to nearly round, sessile below, clasping on upper stem. Flowers 1–3, sessile, nestled above each leaf, open, 5-petaled, deep purple to pale lavender. Lower flowers self-pollinating, upper flowers with 5 calyx lobes. Grows in dry woods, rocky soils, disturbed places, below 3000 ft. *Triodanis* is Greek and means "3 teeth" in reference to the teeth on the calyx. Native OLYM

Linnaea borealis CAPRIFOLIACEAE

Twinflower

Common, all summer, perennial, 2–6 in. West-side forest, east-side forest

Creeping evergreen vine, often forming large mats. Stems with short-petioled leaves. Leaves opposite, oval, shiny, with few shallow teeth on upper edges. Flowers in pair at top of leafless, 2 in., erect stalk. Flowers are fragrant, pale pink, trumpet-shaped, nodding bells. Seed, when dry, has sticky hairs that attach to passing creatures for dispersal. Grows in moist shady woods, forests, from near coastline to timberline. Circumboreal. The genus is named for Carl Linnaeus (1707–1778), father of modern botanical nomenclature. Native OLYM, MORA, NOCA, CRLA

Lonicera conjugialis CAPRIFOLIACEAE
Purple-flowered honeysuckle
Locally common, late spring–early summer,
perennial, 2–7 ft. West-side forest, alpine,
subalpine

Erect shrub. Stems and leaves with fine hairs.
Leaves 1–3 in. oval to round, base tapering to
short petiole, tips round or sharply pointed.
Flowers in pairs, without bracts, dark red, hair-
less or sparsely hairy, strongly 2-lipped, upper lip erect, with 4
shallow lobes, lower lip reflexed downward, 3 anthers pressed
to upper lip. Berries 2, partially joined, bright red. Grows in
moist places in forests, open rocky places, talus, streambanks,
at high elevations. Native CRLA

Lonicera hispidula CAPRIFOLIACEAE
Hairy honeysuckle
Common, midsummer, perennial, 3–10 ft.
West-side forest

Vine, usually climbing, with many branches.
Covered with hairs and glands to hairless.
Leaves oval, with pointed tips, opposite, connected and wrapped around stem below the
inflorescence. Inflorescence hairy with glands.
Flower is a 1 in. tube with 2 flaring lobes, the
upper lobe with 4 rounded teeth; interior yellow; exterior purplish red or pink, hairy with glands; stamens and style extending outward. Berries bright red. Grows on dry sites in open
mixed woods, sometimes lying on ground in clearings, at low
to mid elevations. Native OLYM, NOCA

Symphoricarpos albus CAPRIFOLIACEAE
Common snowberry
Common, late spring–early summer, perennial,
2–6 ft. Coastal, west-side forest, east-side forest

Slender shrub. Stems erect, with stiff branches.
Leaves opposite, deciduous, oval to round, 1–2
in. long, entire. Flowers 6–18, clustered at stem
tips. Flowers pink or white, bell-shaped, divided ½ the length of bell into 5 lobes, densely
hairy inside. Fruit is white, berry-like, each with
2 seeds; hangs through winter after leaves fall; inedible and considered poisonous by some. Grows in moist to dry forests,
shady to open slopes, at low to mid elevations. Var. *laevigatus*
differs, its flower swollen and covered with glands on lower
side. Similar *S. occidentalis* has style extended beyond flower
lobes; grows on moist low ground in shrub-steppe. Native
OLYM, MORA, NOCA, **L&C**

See other *Lonicera*: yellow, page 250; orange, page 301

Symphoricarpos hesperius

(*Symphoricarpos mollis, Symphoricarpos mollis* var. *hesperius*) CAPRIFOLIACEAE
Creeping snowberry, trailing snowberry
Common, late spring–early summer, perennial, spreading, to 16 in. Coastal, west-side forest

Vine-like shrub, creeping or trailing, hairless or soft-hairy. Arching branches on ground often root where touching. Deciduous leaves very small, entire to lobed. Flowers few in cluster near stem tip; 2 bracts fused together bear short flower stalk. Flowers pink, often red outside, bell-shaped, with 5 lobes, hairs inside. Grows in dry forests and openings in woods at all elevations. Native
OLYM, MORA, NOCA

Symphoricarpos oreophilus

(*Symphoricarpos rotundifolius*)
CAPRIFOLIACEAE
Mountain snowberry
Locally common, early summer, perennial, 2–4 ft. East-side forest, meadow, subalpine

Shrub with stiff stems, very fine hairs. Deciduous, opposite, green leaves ¼–1 in. long, with pale underside, prominently veined. Flowers 1–2, hanging with leaves from axils. Flowers pink or white, bell-shaped, with wide tube and erect lobes, hairy inside and on middle section outside. Seed is small, round, white berries. Grows in open places on ridges, forests, at mid to high elevations. Native

Ribes acerifolium (*Ribes howellii*)

GROSSULARIACEAE
Maple-leaved currant
Locally common, midsummer, perennial, 3 ft. West-side forest, subalpine

Shrub with spreading branches but no bristles. Leaves maple-like, 1–3 in. across, with 5–7 rounded, finely toothed lobes. Hanging stem of 8–12 greenish flowers, each less than 1⁄3 in. across with tiny red petals and stamen filaments broad at base. Berry black, coated with bluish powder. Grows from mid elevations to treeline in Cascade and Olympic mountains. Native OLYM, MORA, NOCA

     See other *Ribes*: white, page 165; yellow, page 251; orange, page 302

Ribes lacustre GROSSULARIACEAE
Black swamp gooseberry, prickly currant
Locally common, early summer, perennial, 2–4
ft. Coastal, bog/fen/wetland, moist streambanks, west-side forest

Upright to spreading shrub, bark on older part
of plant reddish brown. All branches and
stems covered with small, sharp, yellow spines.
Leaves 1–2 in. across, almost round, palmately
divided into 3–7 lobes, toothed, hairless, upper side dark green,
lower side lighter. Flowers 5–15 on hanging stalks, green or
purple sepals, petals pinkish, ½–⅔ the length of the sepals.
Fruit shiny black with black hairs. Grows on slopes and in
swamps, seeps, along creeks, from coastline to mid elevations.
Native OLYM, MORA, NOCA, CRLA

Ribes lobbii GROSSULARIACEAE
**Fuschia-flowered gooseberry, gummy
gooseberry**
Uncommon, early summer, perennial, 18–36
in. Meadows, west-side forest, east-side forest,
subalpine

Erect to spreading shrub. Stems with 3 spines
at nodes. Leaves ½–1 in. wide, nearly round,
shallowly lobed, upper surface shiny, lower
surface with some hair, glandular-sticky to the touch. Petioles
and flower stalks glandular-sticky. Flowers 1–3, hanging in
cluster, with red sepals about ½ in. long folded back; white
petals shorter than sepals, pointing downward and curling inward, sometimes nearly touching. Anthers extend well beyond
petals. Berries oblong, red, densely covered with bristles.
Found from lowland into subalpine. Flower
looks like a red and white fuchsia. Native
OLYM, MORA, CRLA

Ribes montigenum GROSSULARIACEAE
Mountain gooseberry
Locally common, midsummer, perennial, 8–40
in. Alpine, subalpine

Low, spreading, branched shrub. Stems and
branches coated with gland-tipped hairs and
spines. Leaves to 1 in. across, deeply 5-lobed, lobes toothed,
hairy, glandular. Cluster of 4–7 small flowers. Flower in whitish
green to pinkish cup of reflexed sepals, petals red, pink, or purplish, stamens about equal in length to petals. Berries orange-
red, covered with gland-tipped bristles. Grows in many habitats at high elevations. Native

Ribes sanguineum GROSSULARIACEAE
Red-flowering currant
Locally common, late spring, perennial, 3–9 ft. West-side forest

Erect to spreading shrub, without spines on stems. Leaves nearly round, 1–3 in. across, palmately divided, 3–5 shallow lobes irregularly toothed, upper side slightly hairy, underside sparsely hairy to covered with white hair. Flowers in terminal cluster, 10–20 usually bright blood red, sometimes pink or white. Berries blue-black, tasteless. Grows in many habitats in open woods, forests, rocky slopes, near sea level to 7000 ft. *Sanguineum*, meaning "blood red," refers to the flowers. Plants with white-woolly hairs matted on lower surface of leaf are var. *sanguineum*. Var. *glutinosum*, with leaf blade sparsely hairy on lower surface, and with pink to white sepals, grows along southern Oregon and California coastline. Native OLYM, MORA, NOCA, CRLA, **L&C**

Plectritis ciliosa VALERIANACEAE
Long-spurred plectritis
Locally common, late spring, annual, 6–18 in. Meadow, west-side forest

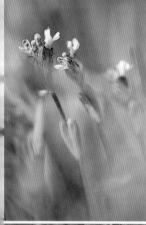

Upright stems with clasping opposite leaves. Leaves narrow, entire, hairless. Inflorescence consists of a few-flowered clustered head at stem top. Flowers pink to dark pink with 5 unequal lobes; upper lobe largest; lower middle lobe with 2 red spots, 1 on each side; long spur at back slender, usually slight curved, with pointed tip facing downward. Grows in open moist places at low to mid elevations. Native

Plectritis congesta VALERIANACEAE
Sea blush, short-spurred plectritis
Locally common, late spring, annual, 4–22 in. Coastal, vernal-wet

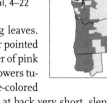

Erect slender stems with clasping leaves. Leaves widely oval, with rounded or pointed tips. Inflorescence is a round cluster of pink to dark pink flowers at stem top. Flowers tubular, divided at opening to 5 same-colored unequal lobes with no spots, spur at back very short, slender with wider rounded tip, turned to inside of cluster. Grows in coastal bluffs or partly shaded spring-wet slopes from coastline to mid elevations. Often forms large showy patches. Native OLYM, NOCA

390   See other *Plectritis*: white, page 167

Valeriana scouleri VALERIANACEAE
Scouler's valerian
Locally common, early summer, perennial,
6–20 in. Coastal, bog/fen/wetland, meadow,
west-side forest, subalpine

Erect stem with mostly basal pairs of leaves.
Leaves divided into 3–7 nearly round, entire or
finely toothed leaflets. Inflorescence consists
of tight heads of pink or white flowers atop
stem. Flower tube opens to 5 lobes, more or less equal, 3 stamens and long pistil extending outward. Grows in moist woods, streamsides, from near sea level to subalpine. Distinguished from *V. sitchensis*, which has mostly smooth leaf margins, fewer stem leaves, flowers more often white than pink.
Native OLYM, MORA, NOCA

Erigeron aliceae ASTERACEAE (aster tribe)
Alice Eastwood daisy, Alice fleabane
Uncommon, all summer, perennial, 4–28 in.
West-side forest, alpine, subalpine

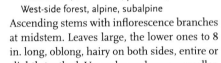

Ascending stems with inflorescence branches
at midstem. Leaves large, the lower ones to 8
in. long, oblong, hairy on both sides, entire or
slightly toothed. Upper leaves become smaller,
sessile. Flower heads on long stalks, with
45–80 ray flowers ⅓–½ in. long, white, drying to lavender pink, slightly coiling around yellow disks. Grows in shady to open, moist to dry places. Easily confused with wandering daisy, *E. peregrinus*, which has spoon-shaped, hairless leaves. Discovered in Siskiyou Mountains in 1900 by Thomas Howell, the most prolific plant hunter of Oregon. Named for Alice Eastwood, then curator at the California Academy of Sciences. Native OLYM

Erigeron foliosus ASTERACEAE (aster tribe)
Leafy fleabane
Locally common, all summer, perennial, 4–40
in. Alpine, subalpine, dry rocky sites

Variable, usually erect. Stems divided or undivided from base. Leaves on stems narrow to
very narrow, ½–2½ in. long, evenly spaced, all
the same size, may be hairy or smooth. Flower heads single to numerous, ¼–¾ in. across, 15–65 ray flowers pink, white, or blue with yellow disk flowers. Grows in dry, often rocky soils over wide range at all elevations. Native CRLA

See other *Valeriana*: white, page 167
See other *Erigeron*: white, page 171; yellow, page 257; blue, page 453

Erigeron glaucus

ASTERACEAE (aster tribe)

Beach fleabane, seaside daisy

Locally common, all spring and summer, perennial, 2–12 in. Coastal

Small, compact. Stems thick, spreading outward then turning upward. Leaves oval to spoon-shaped, somewhat thick or succulent, shiny or coated with white waxy powder or densely hairy. Basal leaves to 2 in. wide, 4 in. long, widest near rounded tip; upper leaves sometimes clasping stem. Flower heads single, ½–1½ in. across; ray flowers 80–160, reddish purple or white; disk yellow; cup sticky. Grows on coastal bluffs, sandy beaches. Native

Erigeron poliospermus var. poliospermus ASTERACEAE (aster tribe)

Cushion fleabane, hairy-seeded daisy

Uncommon, late spring, perennial, 3–6 in. Meadow, shrub-steppe

Cushion plant, very low. Stems hairy and glandular. Leaves mostly basal, to 3 in. long, narrowly oblong, with some hairs; stem leaves smaller. Flower heads large, with 15–45 pink to dark purple ray flowers ¼–½ in. long; yellow disk ¾ in. across. Grows in dry rocky places, foothills, among sagebrush, below 5000 ft. Steens Mountain in southeastern Oregon is the southern limit for this uncommon daisy. Native

Townsendia florifera ASTERACEAE (aster tribe)

Showy townsendia

Locally common, late spring–early summer, annual, 2–8 in. Shrub-steppe

Rosette winter-hardy, with erect, spreading stems. Leaves ash gray, oval, entire, widest at tip end, ½–1½ in. including long petiole. Stems leafy, often branched, topped with flower heads. Flower heads with 18–30 pink, pale lavender, or white ray flowers, each ray ¼–½ in. long; many yellow disk flowers with projecting tufts of hair. Grows in gravelly and sandy places in sagebrush-steppe. Very similar *T. parryi* has flowers and basal leaves about ½ as big. Native

See other *Townsendia*: blue, page 455

Stephanomeria minor var. minor
(*Stephanomeria tenuifolia* var. *tenuifolia*)
ASTERACEAE (chicory tribe)
Narrowleaf stephanomeria, bush wirelettuce
Locally common, late summer, perennial, 8–24
in. East-side forest, shrub-steppe

Mound of many multibranched, flexible, slender stems. Stems do not end in thorns. Milky sap. Flexible thread-like leaves present at flowering. Flower head at stem tip is solitary, contains 5 pale pink flowers. Grows in scrub, dry slopes, at mid to high elevations. Similar *S. paniculata* grows in the same habitats, its leaves fallen by bloom time and flowers tinted light blue. Native NOCA

Antennaria rosea (*Antennaria microphylla*)
ASTERACEAE (everlasting tribe)
Rosy pussytoes, rosy everlasting
Locally common, all summer, perennial, 3–16
in. Meadow, shrub-steppe, subalpine

Mat with many stolons. Basal leaves spoon-shaped, white-woolly on both sides, ½–1½ in. long. Flower stalks 3–16 in. with leaves, topped with many flowers in cluster. Cup at base of flower head has pale to very bright pink bracts that are woolly at the base. White flowers. Grows in dry meadows, rocky barrens. Subsp. *confinis* has decumbent stolons ½–2 in. long; bracts at flower base often have brown tips. In subsp. *rosea* the bracts are not brown but white, yellow, or pink. Native OLYM, MORA, NOCA, CRLA

Acroptilon repens (*Centaurea repens*)
ASTERACEAE (thistle tribe)
Russian knapweed
Locally common, all summer, perennial, 12–40
in. Disturbed, meadow, shrub-steppe

Erect stems from black, mealy, creeping roots, have matted hairs pointing upward. Lower leaves oblong, lobed; upper leaves linear, entire or toothed. Flowers small, dark maroon, blue, or white in papery tan cups with several rows of bracts. Grows in cultivated soils, roadsides, in wet and dry areas to subalpine. Noxious weed, toxic to horses. All parts taste extremely bitter. Nonnative

See other *Antennaria*: white, page 175

Arctium minus ASTERACEAE (thistle tribe)
Common burdock

Locally common, late summer–autumn, biennial, 2–4 ft. Disturbed, meadow, shrub-steppe

Erect, with stiff stems branching near top. Leaves green, widely egg-shaped, largest 16 in. or more; upper side soft-haired, hairless with age; underside gray with matted hairs. Flowers purple, protruding from a round burr of hooked bracts clustered along reddish stalks at axils with large leaves. Grows in disturbed places at low elevations. Similar *A. lappa*, great burdock, with purple or pink long-stalked heads 2–4 in. across, also grows in disturbed soils. Bats can become tangled in the burrs of common burdock and die. Nonnative

OLYM, MORA, NOCA

Centaurea biebersteinii (*Centaurea maculosa, Centaurea stoebe*)
ASTERACEAE (thistle tribe)
Spotted knapweed

Common, all summer, biennial or perennial, 2–4 ft. Disturbed, meadow, shrub-steppe

Erect stems branching at midheight. Stems gray or green, ridged and covered with cobwebby hairs. Leaves 4–6 in., dotted with resin, deeply lobed into narrow, sharply pointed segments, widely spaced, entire at top. Flower head with a brown deep cup fringed at top, with pink or occasionally white disk flowers. Grows along roads, in light soils with some summer rain, below 6000 ft. Common invasive weed. Similar but shorter, diffuse knapweed, *C. diffusa,* has smaller, white to very pale pink flowers and fringed bracts with sharp points that turn outward. Nonnative

OLYM, MORA, CRLA

Cirsium arvense ASTERACEAE (thistle tribe)
Canada thistle, creeping thistle

Common, all summer, perennial, 20–40 in. Coastal, disturbed, meadow

Stems erect, in dense colonies. Leaves sessile, green on both sides, lance-shaped, lobed, with short spines. Flower heads small, red to pink or lavender. Cup ¾ in. high. Male and female flower heads on separate plants. Grows in fields, open areas, disturbed soils, at low to mid elevations. A noxious weed sometimes found in great abundance. Nonnative OLYM, MORA, NOCA

See other *Centaurea*: white, page 181; yellow, page 295; blue, page 456
See other *Cirsium*: white, page 181

Cirsium brevistylum
ASTERACEAE (thistle tribe)
Short-styled thistle, cluster thistle
Common, all summer, annual or biennial or
perennial, 1–7 ft. Coastal, meadow, west-side
forest

Erect plant, usually 1 stem branched above
middle. Stem cobweb-hairy especially just
under flower head. Leaves shallowly lobed,
slightly hairy above, with denser short gray hair below. Lower
leaves are 6–10 in. long, tapering to winged, spiny stalks. Upper
leaves small with slender spines, clasping main stem. Flower
heads round, clustered at stem ends, sessile, with bract-like
spiny leaves at base of each head. Cup about 1 in. high, with
cobwebby hairs. Flowers pink to red-purple. Grows in moist
soils at low elevations. Native NOCA

Cirsium edule ASTERACEAE (thistle tribe)
Indian thistle, edible thistle
Locally common, all summer, biennial or
perennial, 20–80 in. Coastal, meadow, west-
side forest, alpine, subalpine

Stems erect, hairy, succulent and stout in lower
portion, becoming thin above. Leaves lance-
shaped, lobed or coarsely toothed, with spiny
tips. Leaves covered with woolly hair when young, becoming
less hairy with age, but midrib hairs persist on underside. Basal
leaves of the flowering season are 15 in. long. Flower heads of
pink disk flowers held singly or clustered at branch ends;
flower heads hang when young. Bowl-shaped cups about 1 in.,
covered with webbed hairs; short spines at bract tips. Grows in
moist deep soils of meadows, forests, or along
ridges. Stems are edible when peeled. Native

OLYM, MORA, NOCA, **L&C**

Cirsium occidentale
ASTERACEAE (thistle tribe)
Snowy thistle
Uncommon, late spring–early summer,
biennial or perennial, 3–4 ft. West-side forest

Erect single-stemmed plant, basal leaves deciduous, densely white with matted woolly hairs. Leaves oblong, pinnately lobed halfway to midrib; lobes triangular,
toothed or divided. Lower leaves with bristly petioles winged
so that they appear 4-sided. Flower heads held singly or tightly
clustered. Flowers usually bright red, occasionally pink or
white, held in egg-shaped cup ½–2 in. deep, covered with white
cobwebby hairs. Grows on serpentine and other rocky soils
below 6000 ft, in Cascade-Siskiyou National Monument and
elsewhere in Klamath Mountains. Native

395

Cirsium peckii ASTERACEAE (thistle tribe)
Steens Mountain thistle, Peck's thistle
Endemic, all summer, perennial, 2–4 ft.
Disturbed, alpine, subalpine

Erect stem single, unbranched, with long straight hairs. Leaves hairless or with few hairs on midrib, lance-shaped, deeply divided, with yellow spines on lobe points. Lowest leaves 6–8 in. long. Flower heads clustered at leaf base along upper stem and at top. Bowl-shaped cup is 1–2 in. high, loosely haired, bract tips tapering to long yellow spines. Flowers light lavender. Grows in streambanks, disturbed soils. Endemic to Steens Mountain, where it is common along the loop road above 6000 ft., and in Pueblo Mountains in southeastern Oregon. Native

Cirsium undulatum
ASTERACEAE (thistle tribe)
Wavyleaf thistle
Locally common, midsummer, biennial or perennial, 2–5 ft. Meadows, shrub-steppe

Clump. Stems few, erect, branched only in upper parts, matted white-hairy. Leaves oblong, divided into wavy shallow lobes ending in short yellow spines, longer on upper leaves. Leaves with matted hairs, gray on top, white below. Lower leaves with 6–12 in. spiny petioles. Flower heads on short, profusely leafy stalks. Flower head with bell-shaped, slightly hairy cup has spines spreading outward or downward and holds pink and white disk flowers. Grows in open dry areas at low to mid elevations. Native

Onoopordum acanthium
ASTERACEAE (thistle tribe)
Scotch cottonthistle, Scotch thistle
Common, midsummer, biennial, 2–4 ft.
Disturbed, meadow

Erect. Stem usually single, widely branched above, lightly covered with scratchy hairs and spines. Leaves widely attached with wide spiny wings running down stems, toothed or shallowly lobed with 8–10 pairs of widely triangular lobes, very spiny. Purplish rose or white flower heads are single or clustered, cobwebby, spined. Found in disturbed soils at low to mid elevations. Noxious weed introduced from Eurasia. Similar bull thistle, *Cirsium vulgare*, has narrow leaves shallow to deeply lobed and toothed with harsh spines on leaf surface. *Onopordum* (or *onopordon*) refers to the ability of plants from this genus to cause flatulence in donkeys. Nonnative

Ageratina occidentalis (*Eupatorium occidentale*) ASTERACEAE (thoroughwort tribe)
Western snakeroot, western boneset, western eupatorium
Common, late summer, perennial, 5–25 in.
Bog/fen/wetland, alpine, subalpine

Stems erect, numerous from woody base, rough with small hairs. Leaves ½–2 in. long, triangular, toothed, alternate, with pointed tips. Inflorescence consists of many clusters of 8–12 flower heads at stem top. Flowers pink, white, blue, or purple, 8–12 in. Grows in streambanks among rocks at mid to high elevations. Native

Pediocactus simpsonii CACTACEAE
Hedgehog cactus
Uncommon, late spring–early summer, perennial, 3–8 in. Shrub-steppe, dry rocky sites

Single or clumps of small round to oblong stems 3–5 in. across. Strong vertical ridges carry warts with clusters of 8–12 stout, upright, white spines with reddish brown to nearly black tips and smaller yellow or white spreading spines. Flowers rose to bright magenta, 1–1½ in., crowded at top center, surrounded by woolly hairs. Grows in dry mountain valleys, rocky ridges. Var. *robustior* (pictured) is a clustered plant from Pacific Northwest with vivid flowers, rose fragrance. Native

Paxistima myrsinites (*Pachystima myrsinites*) CELASTRACEAE
Oregon boxwood, myrtle boxwood
Common, early summer, perennial, 1–2 ft.
West-side forest, east-side forest

Ascending to spreading shrub. Stems stiff, reddish brown to brown, 4-angled with corky ridges, densely branched. Leaves dark green, opposite, evergreen, leathery, oval to egg-shaped, serrate, ¼–1½ in. long. Flowers tiny, 1–3 held in clusters on upper stem, 4 red-brown petals. Grows in shaded woods, openings, at edges of meadows, at all mid elevations. Native OLYM, MORA, NOCA, CRLA, **L&C**

Grayia spinosa CHENOPODIACEAE
Spiny hopsage
Locally common, late spring, perennial,
12–40 in. Shrub-steppe

Erect much-branched shrub. Male, female flowers on separate plants. Stems straw-colored, becoming gray with age, stiff, with spiny tips. Leaves alternate, fleshy, oblong, to 1 in., entire, sessile. Flowers green in dense spikes at stem tips. Male flower in 4-lobed calyx; female flower without calyx, in seed bracts that become reddish. Seedpods round, shiny, showy. Grows in sandy rocky soils in shrublands or juniper woods at all elevations. Named for eminent botanist Asa Gray. Native

Empetrum nigrum EMPETRACEAE
Crowberry
Locally common, early spring, perennial,
mat. Coastal, alpine

Evergreen mat. Stems reddish, crowded with needle-like leaves. Leaf hairless, with edge noticeably rolled under, back of leaf grooved. Flowers very small, 3 petals, dark purplish red. Berries in small clusters, red when young, turning black as they ripen (as pictured). Grows in wet to dry areas with members of the heath family along coast and in alpine, but not in between. Circumboreal in cold-temperate areas. Foliage easily confused with that of mountain-heathers when out of season. Native
OLYM, MORA, NOCA

Iris douglasiana   IRIDACEAE
Douglas's iris
Common, late spring, perennial, 6–36 in.
Coastal, meadow

Large, upright, aggressive clumps. Stems
sometimes branched. Leaves evergreen, dull
dark green with red base, to 1 in. wide. Cluster of 1–9 flowers per branched stem. Flowers consist of ¾–1 in. perianth tube, nipple-
like projection at top of ovary, petals deep purple to lavender,
blue, or cream with purple, blue, or gold veins. Dried withered
flower persists on top of seed capsule. Grows in pastures,
grassy slopes, coastal cliffs, usually less than 300 ft. above sea
level. Never found more than 2 miles from coast. Hybridizes
with other irises; all color combinations are found. Native

Iris missouriensis   IRIDACEAE
Rocky Mountain iris, western blue iris
Common, early summer, perennial, 8–24 in.
Bog/fen/wetland, moist streambanks,
meadow, shrub-steppe

Stem erect, with few, short, grass-like leaves.
Rhizomes stout, covered with old leaf bases.
Leaves narrow, sometimes stained purple,
shorter than flower stem. Flower light to
dark lavender-blue; yellow-orange patch on the 3 lower petals,
surrounded by white; dark blue pencil lines over all. Flower sits
on top of widened ovary without a perianth tube. Grows in
moist areas along rivers, meadows, at mid elevations. Native
OLYM, **L&C**

Iris tenax   IRIDACEAE
Toughleaf iris
Uncommon, late spring, perennial, 8–14 in.
Meadow, west-side forest

Erect flower stems shorter than grass-like
leaves. Leaves bright green, with red to pink
base, deciduous, to 14 in. tall, in tight cluster. Flowers usually blue to deep purple,
sometimes white to cream. Flowers 1 or occasionally 2 per stem, perianth tube from
flower to ovary only ¼ in., 1 or 2 clasping leaves protect the
buds. The tough leaf fiber has been used for nets, snares, and
ropes. Native OLYM

See other *Iris*: white, page 59; yellow, page 187

Sisyrinchium idahoense (Sisyrinchium angustifolium) IRIDACEAE
Idaho blue-eyed grass
Locally common, midsummer, perennial, 4–16
in. Meadow, east-side forest, subalpine

Clump of narrow, flattened leaves, much
shorter than the unbranched flower-bearing
stem. Flowers are a blue to violet cluster at top
of flattened, leafless stem. Flower petals
rounded to notched, with long sharp point at tip. Grows in
moist meadows, edges of wetlands, at mid to high elevations,
mostly in mountains. Var. *idahoense* has a few teeth on upper
margin of stem, while var. *occidentale* has no teeth on stem.
Similar blue-flowered *S. bellum*, with branched stems, leaves
and flower stems roughly equal in length, and smaller point
on petal tips, is found in moist meadows and
woodlands at low to mid elevations. Native
OLYM, NOCA, CRLA

Brodiaea coronaria LILIACEAE
Harvest brodiaea
Common, early summer, perennial, 3–10 in.
Coastal, meadow

Stem erect. Leaves 1–3 from base, grass-like,
withering before bloom time. Flower clusters
open on uneven stalks. Flowers lavender-blue, violet, or rose,
vase-shaped, consisting of 6 petals, 3 fertile stamens, and 3 sterile staminodes that are flat, wider at base, with margins tightly
inrolled and leaning inward toward stamens. Grows in grasslands, volcanic mesas, often in large populations, at low to mid
elevations. *Brodiaea* and closely related *Bloomeria, Dichelostemma,* and *Triteleia* are best separated by
small characteristics in reproduction parts.
Use of a small hand lens is most helpful. Native OLYM, MORA, NOCA

Brodiaea elegans LILIACEAE
Elegant brodiaea
Locally common, early summer, perennial,
4–20 in. Meadow, west-side forest

Stem erect. Leaves 1–3 from base, withering
before bloom time. Flowers lavender-blue to deep purple; petals
ascending, with recurved tips; concave to flat staminodes are
erect, do not lean inward. Grows in grasslands, on thin soils in
meadows, open woodlands, below 7000 ft. Native

See other *Sisyrinchium*: yellow, page 188

Calochortus lyallii LILIACEAE
Lyall's star tulip, Lyall's mariposa
Locally common, late spring–early summer, perennial, 4–10 in. Meadow, east-side forest, shrub-steppe

Stem erect but flexible. Leaf single from base, pair of clasping bracts at junction with flower stalks. Flowers to 9, star-shaped. Petals 3, with long narrow base, widest at center, with pointed tip, white or tinted lavender, with obvious purple crescent just above green gland area, similar spot on sepals. Petal tips hairless, lower edges bordered with long hairs, also with scattered hairs on top surface. Sepals shorter than petals, hairless. Grows in sagebrush prairies, conifer forests, at mid to high elevations. Native

Camassia cusickii LILIACEAE
Cusick's camas
Uncommon, midspring, perennial, 16–32 in. Meadow, east-side forest

Flower stems erect in large clumps, each crowded with many flowers. Leaves numerous, linear, 1–2 in. wide, shorter than flower stalks. Flower stalks stout, crowded at top with pale blue flowers. Flowers consist of 6 petals, each ½–1 in. long, bottom petal somewhat separated from others. Petals wither separately. Grows on steep moist hillsides and meadows near Snake River. Native

Camassia leichtlinii LILIACEAE
Great camas
Locally common, midspring, perennial, to 48 in. Bog/fen/wetland, meadow, west-side forest

Stem erect, sturdy. Basal leaves linear, shorter than stem. Flowers many, in spike at stem top, a few opening at same time but not opening out flat. Flower pale blue, purple, or white; pollen dull yellow to violet; petals twist as they dry to cover seeds as they mature. Grows in wet, soggy, deep soils at mid elevations. Subsp. *suksdorfii* is blue or purple and sometimes dwarf. Subsp. *leichtlinii* (pictured, inset) is creamy white and grows only in Umpqua Valley, Oregon. Native CRLA

See other *Calochortus*: red, page 310; white, page 61

Camassia quamash LILIACEAE
Common camas
Common, midspring, perennial, 6–26 in.
Vernal-wet, meadow

Stem erect. Leaves slender, long, hairless. Flower spike with many flowers, which open all at the same time. Flowers blue to purple, occasionally white, star-shaped, opening wide; pollen bright yellow or dull yellow to violet. Grows in moist meadows that dry by summer at low to high elevations. Plant varies in size and color over its very large range. Subsp. *quamash* is slender, flowers somewhat sparse on stem, anthers dull yellow to violet. Subsp. *breviflora* is stout, flowers dense, anthers bright yellow. Lewis and Clark reported that this plant occurred in such huge quantities that the meadows resembled lakes of clear water. Native

OLYM, MORA, NOCA, **L&C**

Dichelostemma capitatum (*Dichelostemma pulchellum*) LILIACEAE
Blue dicks
Common, early summer, perennial, 6–27 in.
Meadow, west-side forest, shrub-steppe

Erect straight stem, dense head of blue flowers. Stem and leaves about the same length. Leaves 2 or 3, grass-like. Stem topped with tight head of bell-shaped flowers held by 2–4 papery white to dark purple bracts. Flowers have 6 stamens, 3 longer and 3 shorter, covered by 3 deeply notched projections, white, sometimes pink at base, angled toward center. Often grows in large numbers in grasslands, deserts, dry woods, below 7000 ft. Native

Dichelostemma congestum (*Brodiaea congesta*) LILIACEAE
Forktooth ookow
Common, midsummer, perennial, 8–40 in.
Meadow, west-side forest, shrub-steppe

Stem erect. Leaves 3–4, 2–4 in., with deep channel down center. Flower cluster round and dense, fewer than 20 flowers above 4 purple to white bracts. Flowers light to very dark blue or purple, bell-shaped, with 3 fertile stamens, 3 lavender-blue, erect, forked, sharp, tooth-like projections. Blooms later than similar *D. capitatum*, blue dicks, in open woodlands, grasslands. Native OLYM, CRLA

See other *Dichelostemma*: red, page 311

Dichelostemma multiflorum

LILIACEAE

Roundtooth ookow

Uncommon, early summer, perennial, 1–3
ft. Meadows, west-side forest

Stem erect. Leaves flat, shiny, about same
length as stem. Flower cluster is a round
dense ball atop stem. Flowers 10–35, blue-
purple or sometimes pink, above oval bracts
streaked with purple. Flower constricted above the ovary, lobes
spread out or backward, 3 white to pale purple, tooth-like projections at base have rounded tips, edges roll inward. Grows in
the foothills in clay or heavy soils, grass to scrubland, below
6000 ft. Native

Triteleia grandiflora var. *grandiflora*

(*Brodiaea douglasii*)   LILIACEAE

Large-flowered brodiaea

Uncommon, late spring–early summer,
perennial, 12–20 in. Meadow, shrub-steppe

Stem erect, with flowers at top. Leaves 1–2
from base, linear, less than ½ in. wide,
12–20 in. long. Flower stem topped with
6–20 large, pale to deep blue flowers with
deeper blue-purple midvein, on stalks about

1 in. long in an open umbel. Flowers have funnel-shaped tube
with 6 flared segments, outer lobes ruffled, 2 sets of stamens
very unequal with pale blue tips. Grows in meadows, on open
hillsides, in sandy or heavy soils. Native **L&C**

Triteleia laxa (*Brodiaea laxa*)   LILIACEAE

Wally basket

Common, late spring, perennial, 1–4 ft.
Meadows, west-side forest

Stem erect. Leaves 8–15 in., narrow, with rib
down back. Flowers in wide loose head on
stalks ⅓–3 in. long, blue, purple-blue, or
white, long funnel-shaped tube with ovary,
style hidden inside, anthers attached at 2
levels, blue or white pollen. Grows in clay
soils in open woods, grassy areas, from

coast to fairly high elevations. Often planted in gardens. Native

See other *Triteleia*: white, page 68; yellow, page 190

Chorispora tenella BRASSICACEAE
Blue mustard
Locally common, late spring–early summer,
annual, 4–14 in. Disturbed, meadow

Erect. Stem branched from near ground. Leaves oblong to widely lance-shaped; lower leaves with short petioles, 1–3 in. long, wavy-edged to pinnately lobed; upper leaves scattered on stem, sessile. Flowers, sepals form a tube around purple petals. Seedpods on ascending stalks, 1⅓–1¾ in. long, narrowly lance-shaped, usually curved and covered with prominent stalked glands. Grows in fields, roadsides, waste places. Widespread at low to mid elevations. Common weed in eastern Washington. Nonnative

Lunaria annua BRASSICACEAE
Honesty, moonwort, moneywort
Locally common, all spring, annual or biennial,
18–36 in. Disturbed, west-side forest

Stems erect, branched, few straight hairs. Leaves oval, with rounded base, 2–4 in. long, toothed. Lower leaves with petioles; upper leaves clasp stem. Flowers in spreading to erect cluster at top, purple to lilac, petals spoon-shaped, with long thin base. Seedpods on long spreading stalk, round or widely oval, 1–2 in., with beaks ¼ in. long, flat, semitransparent, with 2–5 round deep brown seeds on each side. Two outer husks fall, revealing shiny white inner wall. Grows in disturbed soils, along roads, urban areas. Escapee from gardens. *Lunaria* means "moon," a reference to the shiny inner wall of the seedpod. Nonnative OLYM, NOCA

Frasera albicaulis (*Swertia albicaulis*)
GENTIANACEAE
Whitestem frasera
Locally common, late spring–midsummer,
perennial, 12–30 in. Meadow, dry rocky sites,
east-side forest, shrub-steppe

Erect stem from basal rosette. Stems with few opposite leaves at base up to 10 in. long. Leaves narrow, with very narrow white stripe down each edge, densely hairy to hairless. Flower cluster dense, near stem top. Flowers on short stalks, greenish white with pale blue tint; sometimes darker spots at petal tips or flower dark blue; 4 petals, center of each petal with oblong fringed gland. Grows in dry, open, often rocky places at low to high elevations. Var. *columbiana* is pale to dark blue with darker spotting. Native

See other *Frasera*: green/brown, page 464

Gentiana affinis GENTIANACEAE
Trapper's gentian, marsh gentian
Locally common, mid to late summer, perennial, 2–26 in. Bog/fen/wetland, meadow, east-side forest, alpine, subalpine

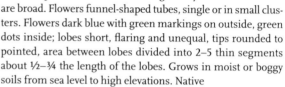

Prostrate to spreading plant with few to many stems from central root. Stems hug ground, tips turned upward. Leaves oval to lance-shaped, at least 3 times as long as they are broad. Flowers funnel-shaped tubes, single or in small clusters. Flowers dark blue with green markings on outside, green dots inside; lobes short, flaring and unequal, tips rounded to pointed, area between lobes divided into 2–5 thin segments about ½–¾ the length of the lobes. Grows in moist or boggy soils from sea level to high elevations. Native

Gentiana calycosa GENTIANACEAE
Explorer's gentian, mountain bog gentian
Locally common, late summer–autumn, perennial, 8–20 in. Bog/fen/wetland, moist streambanks, meadow, alpine, subalpine

Clumps of prostrate to upright stems. Leaves sessile, egg-shaped to round. Flowers in top set of leaves 1–3, sessile, facing upward, deep blue, often with yellow spots, petals forming open bell, 5 lobes pointed at tips. Between petals, appendages are divided into 2 triangular sections that abruptly become long and pointed only at tip. Calyx lobe margins finely toothed. Grows in wet mountain meadows at mid to high elevations. *Gentiana* is named for King Gentius of Illyria, who lived around 500 BC. It is alleged he discovered medicinal uses for *G. lutea*, from which a tonic of bitters is still made. Native OLYM, MORA, NOCA

Gentiana sceptrum GENTIANACEAE
King's scepter gentian, staff gentian
Uncommon, late summer, perennial, 1–2 ft. Coastal, bog/fen/wetland, moist streambanks, meadow

Erect. Stems single or many in cluster. Leaves opposite, 10–15 pair on stem, largest at top ½–1½ in. long, spreading outward. Lowest leaves smallest, becoming larger up stalk. Flowers 1 to several with bracts at base, lower flowers may be without bracts. Calyx of 5 sepals fused into a short tube with wide pointed tips. Flower blue with green streaks or spots, 1–2 in. rounded tube with 5 wide ascending lobes, the sinus between lobes pleated, flat across and without appendages. Grows in wet meadows, bogs, edges of lakes, at low elevations. Native OLYM

Gentiana setigera GENTIANACEAE
Mendocino gentian
Rare, mid to late summer, perennial, 8–18 in.
Bog/fen/wetland, meadow

Rosette with spreading stems turned upward.
Basal leaves 1–3 in., spoon-shaped, with
rounded tips. Stem leaves in pairs with base
wrapped around stem; lower leaves crowded
and wider than long; upper leaves less
crowded. Flowers funnel-shaped, usually single at stem top.
Flower 1½ in. long, white throat spotted green, green outside,
lobes blue. Sinus appendages divide only into 1–3 short thread-
like parts. Grows with *Darlingtonia californica* in serpentine
fens. Rare in Oregon, California. The name *G. bisetaea* has been
wrongly applied in southern Oregon. Native

Gentianopsis simplex (*Gentiana simplex*,
Gentianella simplex) GENTIANACEAE
One-flowered gentian, hiker's gentian
Uncommon, late summer, annual, 4–8 in.
Bog/fen/wetland, moist streambanks, meadow,
alpine, subalpine

Erect. Basal and lower stem leaves less than 1
in. long, spoon-shaped, often withered by
blooming; upper stem leaves 3–6 pairs, lance-
shaped. Flower single on undivided stem without bracts at
base, calyx tube with 4 lance-shaped pointed lobes. Flower is a
deep blue funnel-shaped tube ¾–1½ in., divided nearly ½ its
length into 4 lance-shaped pointed lobes, with toothed tips.
There are no appendages between lobes. Ovary distinctly
stalked. Grows in boggy meadows, springs, near streams, at
mid to high elevations. Native CRLA

Astragalus purshii FABACEAE
**Woolly-pod milkvetch, Pursh's woolly pod,
woolly-pod locoweed**
Locally common, all spring, perennial, to 5 in.
Shrub-steppe

Tuft from woody base. Stem to 6 in. tall. Stems
and leaves covered with very fine, wavy, entan-
gled silver or gray hair, leaves divided. Leaflets
3–17, oval to almost round, tips rounded or notched. Flower
stalks erect to prostrate among leaves, with 1 to many flowers.
Flowers purple, pink to lavender, or cream. Seedpods straight
or curved, covered with thick white hairs and looking like balls
of cotton. Grows in dry plains or slopes with juniper or sagebrush at mid to high elevations. Four varieties occur in Oregon
and Washington. Native

See other *Astragalus*: white, page 92; yellow, page 205

Lathyrus littoralis FABACEAE
Silky beach pea, silvery beach peavine
Common, late spring–early summer,
perennial, 6–24 in. Coastal

Stems prostrate to ascending, angled but
not winged. Entire plant gray-hairy. Leaf divided into 4–8 widely oval to almost round
leaflets, ½–¾ in. long, opposite, with bristle-like tendril. Leaf-like stipules as large as or
larger than leaflets. Dense flower head consists of 4–8 flowers.
Flowers bicolored, white and pinkish purple. Grows on coastal
sand dunes. Native OLYM

Lathyrus pauciflorus FABACEAE
Steppe sweetpea, few-flowered pea
Locally common, midspring, perennial, 1–2
ft. Meadows, east-side forest, shrub-steppe

Sprawling to climbing. Leaves pinnately divided, 2–10 leaflets with small wing-shaped
stipules, ½ as long as leaflets. Leaflets
mostly more than 1 in. long, thick, with
sharply pointed tips, tendrils at leaf tip well
developed, usually divided. Flower stem
long, holding flower above leaves; flowers
3–7, pink, lavender, or violet. Found in grass-lands, dry woods, sagebrush slopes. Native NOCA

Lathyrus polyphyllus FABACEAE
Leafy peavine, Oregon pea
Common, late spring–early summer, perennial, 1–4 ft. Coastal,
disturbed, meadow, west-side forest, east-side forest

Vine with tangled stems, many leaves. Plant
hairless. Stem angled but not winged.
Leaves with stipules at the base as big as
leaflets, tendril at end of leaf branched,
coiled or very short. Leaflets 10–16, oval,
1–2½ in. long. Inflorescence on leafy stalk,
more or less 1-sided with 6–12 flowers.
Flowers purple, fading to blue. Grows in
and at edges of forests at low to mid elevations. Native OLYM, MORA, NOCA

See other *Lathyrus*: white, page 95; red, page 331

Lupinus albifrons FABACEAE
Whiteleaf lupine
Uncommon, late spring, perennial, 1–2 ft.
Coastal, meadow, west-side forest
Upright to ascending from woody base. Plant
covered with silver hairs. Multiple stems can
reach 2 ft. Stems rather flimsy, can be either
decumbent or erect. Leaves mostly at base of
plant, palmately divided, 8–10 leaflets. Inflorescence is 4–12 in. Flowers purple or lavender with yellow or
white patch. Seedpods hairy. Found in open or rocky places at
low to mid elevations. Native

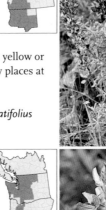

Lupinus arcticus subsp. subalpinus (Lupinus latifolius
var. subalpinus) FABACEAE
Subalpine lupine
Common, midsummer, perennial, 8–15 in.
Meadow, alpine, subalpine
Stems ascending, with few leaves. Petioles
4–12 in. long, with green leaf blades palmately
divided, 6–9 leaflets. Largest leaflets 2–3 in.
long, spoon-shaped, with rounded tips. Inflorescence 6–12 in. long, bearing many blue to
blue-violet flowers with upper petals turned
back. Grows on open slopes and forest openings, meadows, at high to alpine elevations. Native
OLYM, MORA, NOCA

Lupinus argenteus FABACEAE
Silvery lupine
Locally common, late spring–early summer, perennial,
4–16 in. East-side forest, shrub-steppe
Erect stems. Plant green, often silvery with
dense short and longer silver hairs. Basal and
stem leaves with ½–6 in. long petioles, palmately divided, with 5–9 leaflets, each ½–2 in.
long. Flower spike to 16 in. tall. Flowers on 1–4
in. stalk with blue, violet, or rarely white petals
with white to yellow patch. Grows in forests,
shrublands, at mid to high elevations. Native
L&C

See other *Lupinus*: white, page 96; yellow, page 207   **409**

Lupinus bicolor FABACEAE
Miniature lupine, two-colored lupine
Common, midspring, annual, to 16 in.
Vernal-wet, disturbed, meadow

Stem single, erect, hairy, often branched. Leaf petiole ½–2½ in., leaf palmately divided into 5–7 narrow leaflets, hairless or covered with tiny hairs on upper surface. Flower heads to 3 in. long, with flowers held in tight whorls along stalk. Flowers blue with white banner spot that becomes deep magenta after fertilization; keel often whitish with pointed tip. Grows in thin or disturbed soils below 4500 ft. Abundant, often making large waves of blue across open areas in early spring. Very similar *L. polycarpus* has very brown hairs along stems. Native OLYM

Lupinus bingenensis var. *subsaccatus* (*Lupinus sulphureus* var. *subsaccatus*) FABACEAE
Bingen lupine
Locally common, all summer, perennial, 15–40 in. Shrub-steppe

Stem erect, leafy. Plant covered with silky hairs. Leaves with petioles 2–8 in. long, both sides greenish, with more hairs on upper side, divided, 9–15 leaflets with pointed tips. Flowers in 4–8 in. long racemes. Flower on short stalk, petals blue, upper petal somewhat hairy on back. Grows on dry slopes. Native

Lupinus caudatus FABACEAE
Tailcup lupine
Common, mid to late summer, perennial, 8–20 in. East-side forest, shrub-steppe

Widely spreading, with upright flower stalks. Stems and leaves coated with silvery hairs. Lower leaves with long stalks, often withered by blooming; stem leaves with 5–7 narrowly oval leaflets 1–2 in. long. Flower stems with 3–6 in. spike. Flower spur behind silky-haired banner, flower violet-blue, upper petal arching upright, wings hairless. Grows in open hillsides, pine forests, sagebrush-steppe, at mid to high elevations. Native NOCA

Lupinus latifolius FABACEAE
Broadleaf lupine, arctic lupine
Common, late spring–midsummer, perennial,
2–4 ft. Meadow, west-side forest, east-side
forest

Stems numerous, erect. Leaves green, attached
to lower section of stem, petioles 1–8 in. long,
palmately divided, 5–11 leaflets broadest near
tips, hairy below, hairy or smooth above. Flowers in tiered whorls up the stalk. Flower blue or purple with white or yellowish patch that later turns magenta. Flower ages brown. Grows in moist, open to shady woods and meadows. Var. *latifolius* flowers are 1/3–1/2 in., and unlike other varieties, its keel is not covered by wings; grows below alpine elevations. Var. *thompsonianus*, of Columbia River Gorge, has long soft hairs on calyx, stems, and leaves. Native
OLYM, MORA, CRLA, NOCA

Lupinus lepidus var. *aridus* FABACEAE
Dry-ground lupine, desert lupine
Locally common, all summer, perennial, 4–8 in.
East-side forest, shrub-steppe

Erect short flower stalks, not woody at base.
Leaves on upright or spreading stalks, crowded
with silky-haired leaves. Leaves palmately divided, 6–8 oblong leaflets ¾ in. long. Flower stalks 1–4 in. long, with flowers among foliage. Flowers in short, wide, dense, cone-shaped spike, violet or rarely pure white, center white or pale yellow. Grows in dry barren soil, gravel. Native

Lupinus lepidus var. *ashlandensis* FABACEAE
Ashland lupine
Endemic, early summer, perennial, 3–5 in.
Alpine, subalpine

Clumps of silver-edged leaves, sturdy upright
to spreading flower stalks. Plant covered with
dense woolly hairs except on flowers. Leaves
ascending, divided palmately, 5–7 leaflets, each
about ¾ in. long. Flower stalks bear large
dense spike 1½–3 in. long of numerous purple flowers with reddish banner and white keel. Grows in granitic soil above 6500 ft. Endemic on Mount Ashland in Siskiyou Mountains. Native

Lupinus lepidus var. *lepidus*
FABACEAE
Elegant lupine
Locally common, early summer, perennial,
2–18 in. Meadow, dry rocky sites

Mat to erect, silky or hairy, gray or sometimes rusty-colored. Basal leaves on 1–4 in.
petiole. Leaflets 5–9, less than 1½ in. long.
Inflorescence dense, among or just beyond
leaves. Flowers deep or pale blue to violet, with lighter or darker
standard, banner patch yellow or white sometimes fading to
red or brown. Found in rocky places on prairies and foothills.
There are many named varieties of this elegant lupine throughout the western states. With variable distinctions between most
populations, the taxonomy is still under discussion. Only a few
varieties are listed. Native OLYM

Lupinus lepidus var. *lobbii*   FABACEAE
Dwarf lupine
Locally common, late spring–early summer,
perennial, 4–6 in. Alpine

Woody-based low plant covered with silvery
silky hairs. Leaves with long petioles
crowded at base, palmately divided into 5–7
leaflets, each about ⅓ in. long. Flower
stalks spreading to upright, topped with crowded flower clusters, 1 in. long, usually ½ as wide. Flowers ⅓ in., blue or purplish, with white patch on upper petal. Seedpods covered with
silky hairs. Grows on mountain sides in talus or pumice at high
elevations. Native MORA, NOCA, OLYM

Lupinus littoralis   FABACEAE
Seashore lupine
Locally common, late spring–early summer,
perennial, mat, 1–2 ft. wide. Coastal

Trailing or mat-forming perennial, can
spread out for 2 sq. ft. Plant more or less silver with long shaggy hairs, especially at
nodes. Leaves many, along stems on 1–3 in.
petioles, divided palmately to 5–9 leaflets,
each ⅓–1½ in. long. Flower spike 5–6 in.
long, on 1–3 in. stalk. Flowers well spaced in whorls, pale purple or blue, with white patch that fades to brown. Grows in
coastal sands. Native OLYM, **L&C**

Lupinus polyphyllus var. *burkei*

FABACEAE

Large-leaved lupine

Locally common, late spring–early summer, perennial, 1–2 ft. Meadow, east-side forest

Erect stout stem. Leaves basal and along stem, petioles 3–8 in. with blades palmately divided; 5–11 leaflets 2–3 in. long, bright green, hairless or with sparse hairs and lighter-colored on underside. Flowers blue, lavender, pink, or white, with white or yellow patch that often turns reddish with age. Grows in moist places at high elevations, including Wallowa Mountains. Subsp. *polyphyllus* has stiff sharp hairs pressed to surface of stems; grows in eastern Oregon and Washington. The species name refers to the many leaflets: *poly* means "many," and *phyllus* means "leaf." Native OLYM, CRLA

Lupinus rivularis FABACEAE

Streambank lupine

Locally common, midspring, perennial, 18–42 in. Coastal, moist streambanks, meadow

Erect perennial, rarely woody at base, green, without hairs. Stems red to brown, hollow. Leaves only on stem, at well-spaced intervals, with short petioles, oval, divided palmately, 5–9 leaflets each 1–2 in. long. Flower heads 6–20 in. long. Flowers held loosely on stem, violet or blue, often 2 shades of color. Grows in sand or gravel near marshes, streams, and other wet places, at low elevations. Native OLYM

Lupinus saxosus FABACEAE

Stony-ground lupine

Locally common, early spring, perennial, 6–10 in. Shrub-steppe

Erect, bright green. Leaves mostly basal, palmately divided, 6–12 leaflets, each ½–1½ in. long, long stiff hairs on underside, hairless on top. Inflorescence 2–8 in. long, dense with blue flowers. Flower calyx hairy; upper petal without hairs on back, with yellow patch, turning violet with age. Seedpods 1–2 in., with shaggy hairs. Grows in sagebrush or open areas at mid to high elevations. Native

Lupinus sericeus   FABACEAE
Silky lupine
Locally common, all summer, perennial, 8–24 in. Meadow, east-side forest, shrub-steppe

Upright leafy stems with silky spreading hairs. Leaves at base of stem lacking by bloom time or, if present, with long petioles. Leaflets 7–9, silky on both sides, oblong, with pointed tips, each 1–2½ in. long. Flower spike 5–6 in. long, rarely dense. Flowers purple, blue, rose, cream, or white, with banner longer than it is wide, deeply reflexed and silky hairy on back. Grows on dry hills, valleys. Native NOCA, **L&C**

Medicago sativa   FABACEAE
Alfalfa
Common, all spring and summer, annual or perennial, 8–35 in. Disturbed, meadow

Erect, hairless or with very fine hairs. Leaves with ½ in. long narrow lance-shaped leaflets. Flower spike with 8–25 purple, violet-green, or yellow flowers. Seedpods coiled 2–3 times, without prickles. Grows in disturbed soils, along roads mostly in agricultural areas, below 5000 ft. A common hay crop throughout our region. Subsp. *falcata* has yellow flowers, pods that do not twist. Nonnative OLYM, MORA, NOCA

Psoralidium lanceolatum   FABACEAE
Lemon scurfpea, lanceleaf scurfpea
Locally common, all summer, perennial, to 30 in. Moist streambanks, shrub-steppe

Erect from rhizomes, without thorns. Stem green, sometimes yellow at base. Leaves palmately compound with petioles to 1 in. long. Leaflets 3, lance-shaped. Flowers few, purple or white, in clusters on short stalks from main stem. Seedpod more or less round. Grows in floodplains, sandy soils, savannas. Native **L&C**

See other *Medicago*: yellow, page 208

Trifolium douglasii FABACEAE
Douglas's clover
Rare, early summer, perennial, 15–34 in.
Meadow, east-side forest

Stems several, erect, unbranched. Plant without hairs. Leaves with petioles mostly covered by appendage with fine teeth, divided, 3 leaflets, each 1½–4 in. long. Flower heads bottlebrush-like, held atop long erect stalks. Heads without bracts, oval, about 1¼ in. thick and about twice as long, crowded with 50–200 reddish purple to purple flowers. Flowers ½–¾ in., erect to spreading, each held in hairless toothed calyx. Seedpod usually bears 1 seed. Grows in wet meadows, streambanks, moist forests, at about 4000 ft. Native

Vicia americana FABACEAE
American vetch
Common, late spring, perennial, vine, to 40 in.
West-side forest, east-side forest, shrub-steppe

Decumbent or upright when small. Stems tangled or sprawling, sometimes climbing, to 3 ft. long. Leaves pinnately divided, long curling tendril possibly branched at end of petiole. Leaflets 8–18, widely oval, with small spine at tip. Flowers 3–9 in widely spaced spikes, blue, blue-lavender, or purple. Grows in forests, meadows, at low to high elevations. Native
OLYM, MORA, NOCA, CRLA

Vicia villosa FABACEAE
Woolly vetch, hairy vetch
Locally common, late spring–early summer, annual or biennial or perennial, vine, 1–3 ft.
Disturbed, meadow

Stems sprawling or climbing to 3 ft. Leaves ending in tendrils, pinnately divided, 12–18 leaflets, narrowly oblong, rounded on tip. Inflorescence shorter than leaves, with 9 or more violet, purple, lavender, or white flowers in crowded, often 1-sided spike. Seedpods widely oblong, ½–1½ in. long, hairless. Formerly planted as a cover crop, also found along roads, usually in urban areas, at low to mid elevations. Nonnative OLYM, NOCA

See other *Trifolium*: white, page 97; yellow, page 209; red, page 333; green/brown, page 466
See other *Vicia*: red, page 336

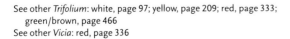

Viola adunca VIOLACEAE
Early blue violet, western dog violet, hooked violet
Common, midspring, perennial, stemless, to 4 in. Coastal, moist streambanks, meadow, alpine, subalpine

Branched stem from hairy rhizomes. Round to oval leaves to 2 in. long. Pale to deep violet flowers with a white patch, purple veins at the base of lower 3 petals. Veins are visible to bees in the ultraviolet as nectar guides. The 2 side petals have white beards at the base and hooked spurs at the tips. Seeds are explosively thrown some distance when pods burst open. Grows in damp streambanks, meadows near trees, at all elevations. *Adunca* means "hooked." Native OLYM, MORA, NOCA

Viola beckwithii VIOLACEAE
Beckwith's violet, Great Basin violet
Uncommon, early spring, perennial, 2–20 in. Dry rocky sites, shrub-steppe

Stems erect, clustered, with finely divided leaves. Leaves basal on long stalks and on stems fleshy, nearly round, divided into many narrow leaflets. Flowers variable in color. Generally, upper pair of petals deep maroon; lower 3 petals light bluish white to lavender with yellow centers and maroon veins. Lowest petal is short-spurred. Grows in very dry rocky places, baked clay soils, at mid to high elevations. Native

Viola cuneata VIOLACEAE
Wedge-leaved violet
Locally common, late spring, perennial, 3–10 in. West-side forest

Stems smooth, prostrate to erect. Leaf blade widely triangular, pointed at tips, tapering toward base. Flowers at stem top are white with yellow base and spur, petals purple-veined on the face and streaked with purple on back. The 2 side petals have dark purple spot near sparse beard at base. The lower 3 petals have dark purple veins. Often found on rocky serpentine in damp open woods at mid elevations. Native

See other *Viola*: white, page 98; yellow, page 210

Viola flettii VIOLACEAE
Olympic violet, Flett's violet
Endemic, early summer, perennial, 1–6 in.
Alpine

Tiny, upright. Dark green leaves round to kidney-shaped, succulent, purple-veined, with coarsely dented edges. Flowers lavender to rose-violet, lightening toward the yellow base. The 2 side petals are yellow-bearded. The 3 lower petals are veined darker violet. Found only in rock crevices on basalt outcrops and alpine talus of Olympic Mountains. Native OLYM

Viola howellii VIOLACEAE
Howell's violet
Common, all spring and summer, perennial,
3–8 in. Meadow, west-side forest

Tuft with leaning stems. Leaves with rounded edges, widely triangular, with a deep basal cleft, toothed, with few hairs on veins. Flowers often entirely light blue to lavender, sometimes with white bases and deeper bluish purple backs, never yellow. Lower petal lighter toward base with dark purple veins and spur as wide as it is long. The 2 side petals have a small tuft of hair at base. Grows in moist ground on prairies, in woods. Plants found east of Klamath Lakes may be white. Native OLYM, NOCA

Viola langsdorfii VIOLACEAE
Alaska violet, Aleutian violet
Uncommon, early summer, perennial, to 6 in. Coastal,
bog/fen/wetland, meadow, alpine, subalpine

Basal cluster of heart-shaped leaves below leafless, upright, white to light green flower stem bearing a single lavender flower. The upper 2 petals are shorter than the 2 white-bearded side petals. The lower petal has a small yellow patch at the base. The 3 lowest petals have purple veins. Spur has a short upturned pouch. Grows in moist places, bogs, talus, scree, at low to high elevations. Native
OLYM, MORA, NOCA

417

Viola palustris   VIOLACEAE
Marsh violet, blue-runner violet
Uncommon, midspring, perennial, 2–8 in.
Coastal, bog/fen/wetland, meadow
Clustered upright leaves and flower stems
from running underground stolons. Leaf
elongated, heart-shaped, entire, on 2–4 in.
petioles. Flowers lavender to pale blue, 3
lower petals with darker veins. Lower petal
larger, with pointed nectar spur. Grows in swampy places from
coastline to subalpine. Native OLYM, MORA, NOCA

Viola trinervata   VIOLACEAE
Sagebrush violet, three-vein violet
Locally common, all spring, perennial, 2–3 in.
Shrub-steppe
Clustered. Leaves fleshy to leathery, hairless. Leaves divided into oval leaflets with
sharply pointed tips, each with 3 prominent
veins. Brownish green flower stalks are
longer than leaves. The upper 2 petals are
darker violet, the 3 lower petals lighter to
pale lavender with a yellow and purple patch
at base and dark purple veins. Grows in seasonally moist sagebrush flats, rocky hillsides. Goes dormant with summer heat. Native

Linum lewisii (Linum perenne var. lewisii)   LINACEAE
Western blue flax
Locally common, late spring–early summer, perennial,
6–36 in. Meadow, east-side forest, shrub-steppe, subalpine
Upright. Stems in tight clump, slender, flexible, hairless. Leaves alternate on stem, linear, less than 1 in., hairless. Flowers with 5
thin blue or occasionally white petals, yellow at base, usually fall within a day of opening. Grows on ridges, open slopes, mountain meadows, shrub-steppe, grasslands, at
1300–8000 ft. Plants in this family are cultivated for their fibrous stems, which are
used to make cords. Also a source of linen.
Native L&C

Aconitum columbianum

RANUNCULACEAE
Monkshood
Locally common, late summer, perennial, 3–7
ft. Meadows, west-side forest, subalpine

Erect, occasionally twining or reclining. Stem
not branched, may have bulblets in axils with
leaves. Leaves 1–7 in. long, 2–6 in. wide,
maple-like, divided into 3–7 lobes, toothed or
lobed again. Flowers on upper 12–25 in. of stems, dark purple
to blue, white, or yellow-green, with top petal-like sepal folded
down to make a hood that conceals center of flower, which includes 2 petals and many stamens. Grows in moist to wet areas
along streams, in seeps, meadows, often among bushes, at mid
to high elevations. Toxic and can cause death if eaten. Native
MORA, NOCA, CRLA

Anemone lyallii (*Anemone quinquefolia* var.

lyallii) RANUNCULACEAE
Western wood anemone, Lyall's anemone
Uncommon, late spring–early summer,
perennial, 4–6 in. Coastal, west-side forest,
subalpine

Stem erect, with 3 leaves whorled at midstem.
Leaf with long petiole, divided into 3 leaflets
with rounded coarse teeth. Flowers small, petal-like sepals less
than ½ in. long, pale blue, white, or pink, with fewer than 35
stamens. Grows in wet openings, moist forests, from coast to
subalpine. Can be confused with *A. oregana*, which has more
than 35 stamens and is usually larger. Native
MORA, NOCA, CRLA

Anemone oregana RANUNCULACEAE

Oregon anemone
Uncommon, midspring, perennial, 3–10 in.
Coastal, west-side forest, east-side forest

Erect single stem. Single basal leaf divided into
3 lobes that may be divided again, has some
teeth, may wither before flowering; stem leaves
divided into 3 lobes with teeth. Flower usually
single with 5 petal-like sepals, blue, reddish,
purple, or white, more than 35 stamens. Grows in moist
shaded conifer forests among moss or other plants from beach
to 5000 ft. Similar to *A. lyallii*. Native OLYM, NOCA, CRLA

See other *Anemone*: white, page 116; red, page 355

Delphinium burkei RANUNCULACEAE
Tall meadow larkspur
Uncommon, late spring–early summer, perennial, 16–40 in. Meadow, east-side forest, shrub-steppe

Tall erect stems, spike of flowers. Basal leaves have long petioles, wither by bloom time; stem leaves have short petioles. Leaves linear, divided or overlapping narrow segments covered with fine hairs. Flowers dense in spike atop stem or on few branches. Flower stalks ascending, short, about same length as spurs, spur tip pointing slightly downward. Showy sepals, pale to deep blue, are cupped forward around white petals. Grows in moist meadows, open spots in sagebrush, ponderosa pine, at mid to high elevations. Native NOCA

Delphinium decorum
RANUNCULACEAE
Yellow-tinge larkspur, coast delphinium
Locally common, all spring, perennial, 4–12 in. Coastal, meadow

Erect stems easily broken away from roots. Lower stem hairy. Basal leaves divided, 3–15 lobes with rounded tips, hairless above, fine hairs on underside and edges; stem leaves few. Spike contains 2–20 flowers, each on a ½–2½ in. finely haired stalk. Oblong, dark blue-purple flower sepals not reflexed; spur ½–¾ in. long. Found in grasslands, open bushy places, primarily along coast. Native

Delphinium depauperatum RANUNCULACEAE
Dwarf larkspur, meadow larkspur
Locally common, early summer, perennial, less than 16 in. Shrub-steppe, alpine, subalpine

Small, slender. Stem single, weak, sometimes branched. Leaves mostly basal, 1–2 in. across, divided palmately into 5-toothed lobes, smaller leaves on stem. Flowers small, 2–8 mostly on 1 side of stem, held upright on ascending stalks; sepals bright to dark blue; upper petals bluish with white along edges, notched; spur slender, curved at tip, about ½ in. long. Grows in poor soil in valleys or on hillsides in meadows that dry up by midsummer, at mid to high elevations. Native CRLA

See other *Delphinium*: red, page 356

Delphinium glareosum

RANUNCULACEAE

Rockslide larkspur, Olympic delphinium

Uncommon, midsummer, perennial, 5–12 in.

Alpine, subalpine

Tuft with erect stems. Stems hairy with glands on upper section. Basal leaves fleshy and round to about 2 in. across, divided fan-like 2 times into narrow lobes. Inflorescence is upper ½ of plant. Flowers a distinctive bright blue. Grows on alpine and subalpine ridges, talus slopes. Native OLYM, MORA

Delphinium glaucum RANUNCULACEAE

Tower delphinium, tall larkspur, mountain larkspur

Uncommon, midsummer, perennial, 3–6 ft.

Vernal-wet, moist streambanks, meadow,

alpine, subalpine

Ascending stems clustered, stout, hollow, easily broken from root. Leaves hairless, with sharply pointed, deeply cut lobes. Inflorescence often divided, with many tightly clustered flowers. Flower purple-blue, with sharply pointed sepals pointing forward or flaring outward, and a short spur. Grows in wet streambanks, meadows, seeps, at high elevations. Native OLYM, MORA, CRLA

Delphinium menziesii RANUNCULACEAE

Menzies' larkspur, coastal larkspur

Common, late spring, perennial, 8–20 in.

Coastal, meadow

Cluster. Stems spreading, unbranched. Leaves with long petioles, few basal, most on stem, 1–2 in. across, divided palmately, 5 segments each with 3 fine-haired lobes. Flowers 3–10, deep purple-blue with some pale blue or white, in cluster at stem top. Flower spur ½–¾ in. long, straight. Grows on coastal bluffs, spring-wet grasslands, meadows, lower mountain slopes. Can be confused with *D. nuttallianum*, which is more widespread east of Cascades. Native OLYM, NOCA, **L&C**

Delphinium multiplex

RANUNCULACEAE

Kittitas larkspur

Endemic, early summer, perennial, 18–36 in.
Vernal-wet, shrub-steppe

Erect, usually a cluster of stems from single root. Stems do not break easily from root, coated with stemmed glands. Leaves yellow-green, basal and on stems, with largest on stem near base. Basal leaves on wide spreading petioles, round, with wide lobes; stem leaves upright, narrower, with more lobes. Flowers deep blue-purple, dense or open on stem, with spurs often crossing stem. Grows in rocky areas along streams, roadside ditches. Endemic to central Washington. Native

Delphinium nuttallianum

RANUNCULACEAE

Upland larkspur, common larkspur

Common, early summer, perennial, 4–20 in.
Meadow, west-side forest, east-side forest, shrub-steppe

Slender, very erect stem, breaks easily from root at ground level, occasionally branched. Leaves mostly on lowest part of stem, divided, 6–25 narrow lobes, hairless. Fewer than 14 flowers on ascending hairless stalks, bright blue with whitish or sometimes yellowish or purple petals in center. Sepals reflexed, spur slender, straight, about ½ in. long. Grows in open meadows, near streams, ponderosa pine woodlands, sagebrush, at low to high elevations. Often hybridizes with other larkspurs when growing together. Can be confused with *D. menziesii*, which is more widespread west of Cascades. Native NOCA, CRLA

Delphinium nuttallii RANUNCULACEAE

Nuttall's larkspur

Locally common, early summer, perennial,
1–2 ft. Meadows, east-side forest

Erect, with undivided stem covered with fine upward-curved hairs. Leaves erect, 2–3 in. long, divided nearly to center; 3 lobes, each divided into shorter lobes. Inflorescence somewhat sticky, with many single flowers in a spike with ascending stalks 1 in. or shorter. Flower composed of 5 light to deep blue oval sepals, long slender light blue spur, 2 upper pale blue notched petals, 2 bright blue petals to the sides. Grows on low moist ground, gravelly outwashes, basalt cliffs. Common in south Puget Sound prairies. Do not confuse this with the much shorter upland larkspur, *D. nuttallianum*; both are named after Thomas Nuttall (1786–1859), botanist and plant explorer. Native OLYM

Delphinium trolliifolium
RANUNCULACEAE
Cow poison, poison delphinium
Locally common, late spring–early summer,
perennial, 2–6 ft. Meadow, west-side forest

Erect. Stems hollow, easily broken from root.
Leaves with petioles to 10 in., shiny, hairless,
divided into many wide-tipped lobes with irregular sharp teeth. Flower spike narrow. Flow-
ers dark blue, with white upper petals in center, spur straight,
may have yellow hairs on stalk. Flower is 4 times as long as it is
wide and curved back. Grows in moist shady places in oak
woods or chaparral at low to mid elevations. Delphinine, a poison in this species and many members of this family, can cause
death. Native

Agastache urticifolia LAMIACEAE
Nettleleaf horsemint
Common, all summer, perennial, 3–6 ft.
Meadows, shrub-steppe

Erect cluster of stems, strong odor. Stems
branched or not, more or less square, with 4
edges. Leaves broadly lance-shaped, 1–3 in.
long, with sharp teeth, lighter green on underside. Flowers in dense spike 1–6 in. long, leaf-
like bract at base. Flowers are open tubes, upper 2 lobes shorter
than 3 lower lobes, violet to rose or white. Grows at low to high
elevations. Plants near the coast are hairier than those inland.
Agastache occidentalis has similar deep rose-violet flowers in
spike above leaves, but usually unbranched stems, leaves with
hairs and no sharp teeth; common in Yakima River and other
rocky canyons east of Cascades. Native

Glecoma hederacea LAMIACEAE
**Ground-ivy, Gill-over-the-ground, creeping
Charlie**
Locally common, all spring, perennial, 1–6 in.
Disturbed, meadow

Prostrate to decumbent, with upright stalks.
Stems creeping, rooting at nodes, stalks
square, with 4 sharp edges, somewhat hairy.
Leaves with short petioles or sessile, hairy, nearly round, with
coarse round teeth. Flowers lavender, on short stalks, in clusters at upper leaf axils. Flowers in 5-lobed calyx; pouch near
base of funnel-shaped tube flared to 2 lips; upper lip divided
into 2 shorter lobes, lower into 3 unequal longer lobes, darker
spots near center. Grows in moist shaded places in disturbed
soils at low elevations. Common weed in lawns and gardens.
Nonnative OLYM, MORA, NOCA

Monardella purpurea LAMIACEAE
Siskiyou monardella
Uncommon, all summer, perennial, to 6 in.
West-side forest, dry rocky sites

Clump, does not smell like mint. Stems dark purple, branched. Leaves deep green or purplish, broadly oval, 1 in. long, shiny on top, with small hairs underneath, edges rolled under. Flowers numerous in tight cluster, surrounded by purplish leaf-like bracts coated with fine hairs. Flower deep rose-purple, extending well above hairy calyx with long pointed lobes. Grows in open forests, on rocky serpentine, at low to mid elevations. Native

Prunella vulgaris LAMIACEAE
Self-heal, heal-all
Common, late spring–early summer,
perennial, 4–16 in. Disturbed, meadow
Clumps or single stem, upright to prostrate, hairy, unbranched. Leaves lance- to egg-shaped, entire or slightly toothed, opposite; lower leaves with petioles; upper leaves sessile. Flowers with short stalks in stout round head above 2 spreading, pointed bracts at stem top. Flower purple, pink, or white; upper lip hood-like; lower lip 3-lobed with middle lobe fringed. Grows in disturbed soils, moist places at edges of forests. Circumboreal. Native OLYM, MORA, NOCA

Salvia dorrii LAMIACEAE
Purple sage
Locally common, late spring–early summer,
perennial, 12–34 in. Shrub-steppe, subalpine

Shrub with upright divided stems. Strongly scented of mint, densely white-scaly. Leaves less than 1 in., linear to spoon-shaped, entire. Flowers atop stems in series of clusters, each above thick often purplish bracts about as long as flowers. Flowers blue or purple to rose or rarely white; upper lip 2-lobed; lower lip longer and divided into 3 parts; stamens and style extending well beyond lips. Grows in dry rocky places, talus slopes, outcrops, often in sagebrush, at low to high elevations. Native

See other *Monardella*: red, page 363

Scutellaria angustifolia LAMIACEAE
Narrowleaf skullcap
Locally common, late spring–early summer,
perennial, 4–12 in. Meadow, shrub-steppe

Stems erect from underground running roots.
Stems single or branched near bottom. Stems
and leaves coated with small curved hairs, no
glands. Leaves gray-green, ½–2 in., linear to
oblong, entire, with rounded tips. Flowers on
upper stem in leaf axils. Flowers blue, with upper lip notched,
about same size as lower lip, throat open, tube about 1 in. long,
bent above calyx. Grows in moist, often rocky places. Similar *S.
antirrhinoides* has smaller flowers, with long, white, gland-
tipped hairs inside nearly closed throat. Shorter *S. nana* has
mats of crowded leaves covered with downward-pointing glandular hairs; flowers solitary in leaf axils, white
to yellow; lower lip light yellow with purple
spots; upper lip darker yellow; grows on open,
dry volcanic soils or basalt. Native **L&C**

Pinguicula vulgaris LENTIBULARIACEAE
Common butterwort
Locally common, late spring–early summer,
perennial, 1–4 in. Coastal, alpine, subalpine

Rosette of fleshy entire leaves. Leaves green to
pale yellow-green, oval to egg-shaped, with inrolled edges.
Upper leaf surface covered with sticky stalked glands that cap-
ture small insects; other stalkless glands then digest the insects.
Stems thin, leafless, supporting single flower. Flowers deep violet-blue, rarely white, 1 in. across, 2-lipped, the upper lip with
2 lobes, lower lip longer with 3 lobes, throat hairy. Grows in wet
serpentine banks, edges of streams, bogs,
mossy seeps, from near coast to subalpine.
Similar *P. macroceras* grows in moist rocky serpentine, has yellow-green leaves and spur.
Native OLYM, MORA, NOCA

Orobanche uniflora OROBANCHACEAE
Naked broomrape
Locally common, all spring, annual, ½–3 in.
Meadow, moist streambanks

Erect, less than 3 in., without chlorophyll. Stem covered with violet to yellow hairs and glands. Flower stalks 1–3, bractless.
One flower per stalk; calyx lobes narrow, pointed, longer than
tube. Flower held more or less horizontal to ground, purple to
yellow. Grows in moist to dry places, parasitic on sedums, saxifrages, and species of the aster family, at low to mid elevations.
Native OLYM, MORA, NOCA

See other *Orobanche*: red, page 364; green/brown, page 469

Collinsia grandiflora

SCROPHULARIACEAE

Giant blue-eyed Mary, large-flowered blue-eyed Mary
Common, late spring, annual, 4–16 in.
Vernal-wet, meadow, west-side forest, east-side forest

Stems upright, sturdy. Leaves opposite and round below, narrow and often in whorls above. Flowers ½–¾ in. on short stalks from axils with upper leaves, calyx 5 unequal lobes, flower tube bent, flower standing at about 45° angle from calyx. Flower petals larger, the upper 2 white or pale lavender-blue, the lower 3 deeper lavender-blue; small, folded, lower petal between others holds stamens. Grows in open, moist or dry, grassy, rocky places, edges of conifer forests, at low to mid elevations. Native
NOCA, **L&C**

Collinsia parviflora

SCROPHULARIACEAE

Small-flowered blue-eyed Mary
Common, early spring, annual, 2–15 in.
Vernal-wet, meadow, west-side forest, east-side forest

Stems upright or sprawling, occasionally branched. Leaves numerous, long, with rounded points, edges slightly rolled under. Flowers small from leaf axils on hairy stalks, slightly angled; 2 upper lobes purplish blue to white; 3 lower lobes deep purplish blue. Grows in many moist places at all elevations. Native OLYM, MORA, NOCA, CRLA

Collinsia rattanii SCROPHULARIACEAE

Sticky blue-eyed Mary, Rattan's collinsia
Common, late spring, annual, 3–15 in.
Meadow, west-side forest, east-side forest

Erect, covered with hairy glands, sticky. Single stem. Leaves gray-green to purplish, edges rolled under. Flower held on long stalks spreading outward from stem, throat slightly bent from tube. Calyx lobes pointed. Flower upper 2 lobes white to pale lavender, lower 3 lobes darker lavender. Grows in open woods, spring-wet areas, at low to mid elevations. Native

Collinsia sparsiflora SCROPHULARIACEAE
Spinster's blue-eyed Mary, few-flowered blue-eyed Mary
Locally common, midspring, annual, 2–12 in.
Vernal-wet, meadow, east-side forest

Upright plant with only a few flowers. Leaves linear to oblong, entire. Inflorescence smooth or finely haired, on 1–3 long flower stalks from axils. Flowers generally shades of lavender and purple, occasionally white. Lower middle lobe hairy, throat somewhat bent in calyx, calyx lobes pointed, edges finely toothed, longer than flower. Grows in spring-moist open areas at low elevations. Native

Nuttallanthus canadensis (*Linaria canadensis*)
SCROPHULARIACEAE
Blue toadflax
Locally common, all spring and summer, annual or biennial, 6–24 in. Coastal, meadow

Basal rosette of leaves. Stems slender, erect to prostrate. Leaves shiny, narrowly linear, becoming fewer near top. Inflorescence tall, sticky, small-flowered. Flowers pale blue to violet, about 1/3 in. long, consisting of 2 erect upper lobes and 3 larger lower lobes with 2 rounded lighter-colored humps in flower center, round-tipped spur. Grows in gravel or moist sandy soils in open areas at low to mid elevations. Native NOCA

Penstemon acuminatus SCROPHULARIACEAE
Sand-dune penstemon, sharp-leaved penstemon
Locally common, late spring, perennial, 1–2 ft.
Shrub-steppe

Basal clump of wide leaves, single or clump of stout erect stems bearing clasping leathery leaves. Stems and leaves coated with sticky glands. Leaves deep green, with long sharp tips, stem leaves widely oval, shiny or covered with blue waxy powder. Flowers less than 1 in. long, bright to pale blue or purple, in whorls along upper stem, usually with golden hair on tip of staminodes. Grows in sandy soils in steppe. Native

See other *Penstemon*: white, page 147; yellow, page 247; red, page 375

Penstemon attenuatus

SCROPHULARIACEAE

Taper-leaved penstemon

Locally common, all summer, perennial, 1–2
ft. Meadows, shrub-steppe

Clumps to 2 ft. across. Stems erect. Leaves
in basal rosette deep green, 2–4 in. long,
oval to lance-shaped, entire, tips pointed,
stem leaves reduced in size. Flowers in
whorled clusters blue or purple to pale yellow or white, no
guidelines, few white hairs on floor of the throat. Grows on
open slopes and in meadows and wooded areas. Subsp. *palustris* with very short, deep blue flowers grows in marshes in Blue
Mountains. Similar *P. spatulatus* is only 4–10 in. tall, has darker
blue guidelines inside flower, and is found only at higher elevations of Wallowa Mountains. Native
NOCA

Penstemon azureus

SCROPHULARIACEAE

Azure penstemon

Locally common, midsummer, perennial,
8–30 in. West-side forest, alpine, subalpine

Ascending stems with leaves from woody
base. Stems and leaves hairless, not sticky.
Leaves blue with waxy coating, oval, widest at base, clasping
stem, pointed tip. Flower bright lavender-blue, opens from a
yellow bud, staminode hairless. Grows on dry open slopes in
hills and mountains at low to high elevations. Native

Penstemon cardwellii   SCROPHULARIACEAE

Cardwell's penstemon

Uncommon, early summer, perennial, 12 in.
West-side forest

Large cushions with upright hairless stems
that root along the ground. Evergreen leaves
oval, ¾–1½ in. long, ½ as wide, tips
rounded, entire or toothed. Flower cluster
at stem top. Flowers 1 in. or more in length,
bright purple to blue-purple. Grows on rock
slopes, including Mount St. Helens, in
openings in forests, at mid elevations. Native

Penstemon davidsonii SCROPHULARIACEAE
Davidson's penstemon
Common, midsummer, perennial, 2–5 in.
Alpine, subalpine

Dense mat with creeping woody stems, ever-green. Leaves small, oval, dark green, leathery, hairless. Leaves on flowering stems smaller, bract-like. Flowers ¾–1½ in. long, blue-laven-der to purple, wide tubes usually flattened on the sides, white-woolly hairs on bottom of throat, staminode densely hairy. Var. *davidsonii*, the only form in California and most of Oregon, has more rounded leaves, large flowers about 1–1½ in. long. Var. *menziesii* is generally smaller, with leaves broadest at the base, toothed, with short petioles, flowers 1 in. long, blue-violet. Var. *praeteritus*, endemic on Steens Mountain, is larger, with 1–2 in. flowers, leaves with sharply pointed tips. All prefer rocky, well-drained soils, some shade, at high elevations. Native OLYM, MORA, NOCA

Penstemon euglaucus SCROPHULARIACEAE
Glaucous penstemon
Locally common, mid to late summer, perennial, 6–24 in. Meadow, east-side forest

Clump of upright stems. Leaves form well-developed rosette at base. Leaves firm, oval, with pointed tip and short petioles, coated with whitish waxy powder; stem leaves lance-shaped. Flowers in 1–5 whorls, each dense with flowers. Flowers more or less ½ in. long, deep blue with pale yellow beard; staminode covered with short golden hairs. Grows in volcanic soils in forest openings. *Euglaucus* refers to the glaucous surface of the foliage. Native

Penstemon fruticosus SCROPHULARIACEAE
Shrubby penstemon
Locally common, all summer, perennial, 12 in.
East-side forest, shrub-steppe, alpine

Sprawling mat to 36 in. across, hairless, lower stems woody. Leaves lance-shaped, saw-toothed, with pointed tips. Flowers lavender or blue-purple, to 2 in. long, lower lip with 2 deep folds, golden hairs on inner parts near mouth. Grows in well-drained places at low to alpine elevations. Var. *scouleri* is smaller, with very narrow, slightly toothed leaves; grows in northeastern Washington and adjacent British Columbia. Var. *serratus* is the smallest form, with almost round, prominently serrate leaves; found near Snake River. Var. *fruticosus* leaves are wider, up to 2½ in. long, ½ in. wide. All varieties are generally larger and have longer flower stems than *P. davidsonii*, with which they can be confused. Native MORA, NOCA, **L&C**

429

Penstemon gairdneri

SCROPHULARIACEAE
Gairdner's penstemon
Locally common, late spring, perennial, to
12 in. Dry rocky sites, shrub-steppe

Mounding from woody base. Stems upright, numerous, with deciduous leaves. Looks like dead sticks in winter with no overwintering rosette. Leaves on stems many, narrow, entire with rounded or pointed tips, bluish with fine gray hairs. Flowers ½–¾ in., lavender-pink to purple, white on inside of tube, hairy beard at mouth of tube. Face of flower, with 5 equal lobes, is more or less flat. Grows on thin, dry, rocky soils, sometimes with sagebrush, to mid elevations. Native

Penstemon glandulosus

SCROPHULARIACEAE
Sticky-stem penstemon
Uncommon, late spring, perennial, to 40 in.
Meadow, east-side forest, shrub-steppe

Upright leafy stems from basal clump of leaves, woody at base, sticky throughout, including flowers. Leaves egg-shaped, with sharply pointed tip, toothed. Basal leaves with long petioles; stem leaves clasping. Flowers 1–1½ in. long in various shades of purple with beeline markings inside. Staminode not hairy. Grows in light woods or open areas at mid elevations, sometimes in rocky soils. Native

Penstemon globosus SCROPHULARIACEAE

Globe penstemon
Locally common, late spring–late summer,
perennial, 8–24 in. Vernal-wet, meadow,
subalpine

Rosettes of bright green leaves with erect flower stems. Basal and stem leaves oval, with pointed tip; smaller leaves clasp stem. Flowers to ¾ in. long, bright blue to purple-blue, in small clusters or more often in 1 large globe at stem top. Inside flower tube the floor has white-haired beard, staminode hairy. Grows in moist or vernal-wet sites at high elevations to timberline. Native

Penstemon humilis SCROPHULARIACEAE
Lowly penstemon
Locally common, midsummer, perennial, 4–10
in. East-side forest, shrub-steppe, subalpine

Tuft formed of basal rosettes with erect flower
stems, sometimes covered with ash-colored
hairs. Leaves spoon-shaped, ½–3 in. long, entire. Basal leaves with petioles; stem leaves
smaller, clasping. Inflorescence in whorls
along stem, covered with small glands. Flowers narrow, funnel-shaped, bright blue to purple, inside light lavender to white
with dark beelines, with dense orange to yellow hairs on staminode. Grows in open sagebrush scrub, juniper woodlands,
rocky ridges, into high elevations. Height, leaf size, and number of hairs are variable. Native

Penstemon ovatus SCROPHULARIACEAE
Broad-leaved penstemon
Locally common, late spring–early summer,
perennial, 2–4 ft. West-side forest

Large, upright. Leaves broadly egg-shaped,
with wide base, strongly saw-toothed, lower on
short petioles, stalkless on upper stem. Inflorescence gland-covered, loose to tight whorls
of many flowers. Flowers deep blue to purple,
¾ in. long, hairy staminode extending slightly outward. Grows
at low to mid elevations in shady places on mossy rocks and
outcrops. Native OLYM, MORA, NOCA

Penstemon payettensis SCROPHULARIACEAE
Payette penstemon
Uncommon, all summer, perennial, 6–24 in.
Dry rocky sites, subalpine

Compact clump with woody base, few to many
stems. Leaves thick, bright green, widely oval,
entire, hairless; lower leaves with long petioles;
upper leaves clasping flower stem. Flowers in
small clusters along upper stem. Flower about
1 in. long, bright purple-blue, hairless or with
few hairs just inside widely open throat; staminode hairless. Grows on sandy or rocky soils
at low to moderately high elevations in mountains. Named for
Payette National Forest, Idaho, where it was first found. Native

Penstemon pennellianus

SCROPHULARIACEAE

Blue Mountain penstemon, Pennell's penstemon

Uncommon, late spring–early summer, perennial, 10–18 in. Dry rocky sites, subalpine

Clumps of basal leaves with erect stout stems. Basal leaves thick, narrow, oblong, entire, 3–10 in. long, with long petioles; stem leaves clasping, largest leaves midstem, widely oval, with pointed tips. Flowers in well-spaced cluster, becoming tighter above. Flowers bulging on 1 side, 1–1½ in. long, with short-haired staminode at throat, sparsely hairy anthers just inside. Grows in rocky soils in mountains. Native

Penstemon procerus   SCROPHULARIACEAE

Small-flowered penstemon, pincushion penstemon, tall alpine beardtongue

Locally common, midsummer, perennial, 2–12 in. Shrub-steppe, alpine, subalpine

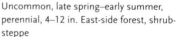

Tuft from woody creeping stems. Leaves thin, oval, entire. Basal leaves on petioles; stem leaves opposite, clasping, with tips pointing upward. Inflorescence a series of dense whorls of small downward-facing flowers, to ¾ in. long, tube floor white, lobes spreading, few yellow hairs on staminode. Grows on rocky slopes at mid to high elevations. Var. *procerus* is up to 24 in. tall, with more than 1 flower cluster per stem, few basal leaves; found at mid elevations. Var. *formosus*, with well-developed basal rosette, is usually less than 6 in. tall, with single flower cluster; grows in subalpine, alpine. Var. *tolmiei* is 2–6 in. tall, with blue or yellowish flowers, usually one flower cluster; common in high Cascades and Olympics. Native OLYM, MORA, NOCA

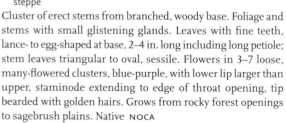

Penstemon pruinosus

SCROPHULARIACEAE

Chilean beardtongue

Uncommon, late spring–early summer, perennial, 4–12 in. East-side forest, shrub-steppe

Cluster of erect stems from branched, woody base. Foliage and stems with small glistening glands. Leaves with fine teeth, lance- to egg-shaped at base, 2–4 in. long including long petiole; stem leaves triangular to oval, sessile. Flowers in 3–7 loose, many-flowered clusters, blue-purple, with lower lip larger than upper, staminode extending to edge of throat opening, tip bearded with golden hairs. Grows from rocky forest openings to sagebrush plains. Native NOCA

Penstemon roezlii SCROPHULARIACEAE
Purple penstemon
Locally common, late spring–midsummer, perennial, 6–24 in. East-side forest, shrub-steppe

Ascending from woody base, stems carrying short flowers. Leaves on stems ½–2½ in. long, linear, folded lengthwise to show back of leaf. Inflorescence sticky. Flowers sky blue to purplish blue, ½–¾ in. long; tube hairless inside; staminode hairless. Grows in dry scrub at mid to high elevations. Similar *P. speciosus* has flowers mostly on 1 side of stem. Closely related *P. laetus*, which prefers lightly shaded shrubby areas within conifer forests, has leaves 1–3 in., narrow, entire, hairless; flowers ¾–1¼ in., violet-blue to red-purple, hairless on outside, inner edges long-haired; staminode hairless. Native

Penstemon rydbergii SCROPHULARIACEAE
Rydberg's penstemon
Locally common, midsummer, perennial, 8–25 in. Vernal-wet, meadow, east-side forest, subalpine

Basal rosette of bright green leaves from woody base. Leaves to 2 in. long, widely oval to spoon-shaped, entire, hairless; lower stem leaves well developed; upper stem leaves lance-shaped, sessile. Inflorescence dense with well-separated whorls of flowers standing straight out or upward from stem, not hanging. Flowers small, bright blue or purple, with few white or pale yellow hairs on inside floor of tube, staminode densely covered with golden hairs. Grows in wet rocky soils. Similar to but taller than *P. procerus*, which often occurs in similar habitats and which has flowers facing downward. Native CRLA

Penstemon serrulatus
SCROPHULARIACEAE
Cascades penstemon, coast penstemon
Common, midsummer, perennial, 8–30 in. Coastal, vernal-wet, meadow, subalpine

Tall, upright, unbranched stems from woody base. Leaves oval to lance-shaped, 1½–3 in. long, sharp-toothed, hairless; upper stem leaves clasping; lower leaves on short petioles. Inflorescence is a single flower cluster at stem top. Flowers bright blue to purple-blue, to ¾ in. long, hairless inside and out, staminode bearded. Grows in moist meadows, along streams, rocky areas, from near coast to subalpine. Native
OLYM, MORA, NOCA

433

Penstemon speciosus

SCROPHULARIACEAE

Showy penstemon, royal penstemon

Common, early summer, perennial, 6–30 in.
Dry rocky sites, shrub-steppe, subalpine

Sturdy stems tend to spread out sideways, bearing clasping, long, oval leaves. Leaves often folded lengthwise, entire, with little hair or hairless. Inflorescence usually hairless, rarely covered with glands, with flowers on short stalks, usually all on 1 side of elongating stem. Flowers vivid blue, with white throat; widest part of flower tube is a noticeable pouch on underside; staminode sometimes hairy. Grows in sagebrush, rocky places, at mid to high elevations. Can be confused with *P. roezlii*, with sticky glandular inflorescence. Native NOCA, CRLA

Penstemon subserratus

SCROPHULARIACEAE

Fine-tooth penstemon

Locally common, late spring, perennial,
12–30 in. Dry rocky sites, west-side forest,
east-side forest

Upright, 1 or few hairless stems. Leaves oval, fine-toothed or entire, upper clasping stem, basal with short petioles. Inflorescence consists of few to 10 clusters of flowers on branching stalks near stem top. Flowers with deep blue outer lobes, purple throat sometimes white inside, staminode with golden-yellow hairs. Grows in rocky soils at low to mid elevations. Native

Penstemon venustus SCROPHULARIACEAE

Elegant penstemon

Locally common, midsummer, perennial,
1–3 ft. Dry rocky sites, east-side forest,
shrub-steppe

Large spreading shrub, no basal leaves. Leaves widest at middle section, stiff, sharply saw-toothed or rarely entire, sessile. Inflorescence hairless, 1 in. long, flowers upward-facing, attached along main stems with upright stalks. Flowers bright blue to lavender-blue, white hairs sometimes on floor of tube, white hairs on staminode just inside open flower. Grows in dry rocky slopes at high elevations. Sometimes naturalized from gardens in parts of our region. (Note: Pictured with many buds as plant is just coming into bloom.) Native

Synthyris missurica subsp. *missurica*
SCROPHULARIACEAE
Mountain kittentails
Uncommon, early summer, perennial, 4–20 in.
East-side forest, alpine, subalpine

Clump of nearly round basal leaves, erect flower stem. Leaves shiny, hairless, with long petioles, smooth, 1–3 in. across, cut to somewhat rounded lobes or teeth, tips pointed.

Inflorescence more or less hairy, with many mid to deep blue flowers in 2–7 in. erect spike above leaves. Flowers small, upper lobe slightly larger than other 3, bluish stamens exserted beyond the petals. Grows in moist to dry shade, among rocks, in openings in forests, at mid to high elevations. Similar subsp. *stellata* with larger flowers also has brown hairs on short flower stalks. Native **L&C**

Synthyris missurica subsp. *stellata*
SCROPHULARIACEAE
Columbia kittentails
Endemic, early spring, perennial, 5–12 in.
West-side forest

Clump of basal leaves, erect flower stem. Leaves with hairless petioles, thick, shiny, round, 1–2½ in. wide, deeply cupped toward

middle, edges deeply toothed and toothed again with sharp tips. Dense inflorescence 3–6 in. atop smooth stem, flowers on short brown-haired stalks, lavender to purple, few long soft hairs. Flower bell-shaped, 4 lobes about ¼ in. long, blue stamens extending outward, pistil longer than stamens. Grows on shaded cliffs, banks in the Columbia Gorge from Crown Point to The Dalles. Subsp. *missurica*, more widespread, has smaller flowers on hairless stalks. Native

Synthyris pinnatifida subsp. *lanuginosa* SCROPHULARIACEAE
Olympic cut-leaf synthyris
Endemic, late spring–early summer, perennial, 3–7 in. Alpine

Erect stem with spikes of deep blue flowers. Plant coated with soft white hairs. Leaves pinnately divided, 9–15 segments cut again into lance-shaped to linear, toothed lobes. Flower stem leafless, longer than leaves, dense spike of flowers ½–2 in. long. Flowers are short slightly bent tubes with 4 lobes, upper lobes somewhat hood-shaped, 2 stamens extending outward. Grows in gravelly alpine summits in Olympic Mountains, where it is at risk from mountain goats. Native OLYM

Synthyris reniformis

SCROPHULARIACEAE
Snow queen, deer flower
Common, early spring, perennial, 2–6 in.
West-side forest

Basal leaves, weak stems, prostrate to ascending flower stalks. Plant lightly covered with soft to shaggy hair. Leaves heart-shaped shallow lobes with toothed margins. Flowers in clusters at stem ends, bell-shaped purple to blue-violet or rarely white. Grows in open conifer forests, at forest edges, grassy places, at low to mid elevations. Native OLYM

Tonella tenella   SCROPHULARIACEAE

Small-flowered tonella
Locally common, early spring, annual, 4–8
in. West-side forest

Upright weak stem, smooth, straight, sometimes branched. Leaves ⅓–½ in. long, lowest leaves on petioles and broad, middle leaves divided into 3 lobes; upper leaves often entire and sessile. Flowers small, 1 or sometimes 2, on short stalk arising from pair of leaf-like bracts. Flowers white in center with broken dark markings, violet on outer edges; lower petal lobe is larger and wider than other 4. Grows in moist rocky soils, often shaded by scrub oaks, at low to mid elevations. Native OLYM

Veronica americana   SCROPHULARIACEAE

American speedwell
Common, all summer, perennial, 4–40 in.
Vernal-wet, bog/fen/wetland, meadow

Ascending stems from creeping rhizomes, rooting at the joints. Leaves opposite, on short petioles, lance-shaped, to 2 in. long, saw-toothed to entire. Flowers violet-blue with dark lines, in long upright sprays at stem ends. Each flower to ⅓ in. across. Grows in wetlands, edges of streams, ditches, at all elevations below alpine. Native OLYM, MORA, NOCA

See other *Veronica*: white, page 147

Veronica anagallis-aquatica

SCROPHULARIACEAE

Water speedwell

Common, all summer, biennial or perennial, 8–40 in. Vernal-wet, bog/fen/wetland, meadow

Prostrate stems with upright tips. Plant hairless. Stems often branched many times, rooting at nodes. Leaves 1–3 in. long, oval, with pointed tips, entire, clasping stem. Flowers pale lavender, in short spikes from leaf axil. Grows in wet meadows and along streams. Introduced from Europe. Nonnative

Veronica cusickii SCROPHULARIACEAE

Cusick's speedwell

Locally common, midsummer, perennial, 2–8 in. Meadow, west-side forest, east-side forest, alpine, subalpine

Ascending unbranched stems form loose clump. Plant finely hairy or hairless. Dark green leaves oval, to 1 in. long, sessile, entire. Inflorescence is a loose cluster atop stem. Flowers up to ½ in. wide, deep blue, with styles and stamens noticeably longer. Grows in forest openings, moist meadows, at high elevations. Native OLYM, MORA, NOCA

Veronica scutellata SCROPHULARIACEAE

Marsh speedwell

Common, all summer, perennial, 4–24 in. Vernal-wet, bog/fen/wetland, disturbed, meadow

Creeping, prostrate to upright, hairless. Leaves sessile, linear, ¾–1½ in., often tinted purple. Alternating long stalks from axils of upper leaves bear flowers. Flower pale blue, lavender, or white with purple lines. Grows in wet meadows, ditches, drying ponds, lawns, at low elevations. Native OLYM, MORA, NOCA

Veronica wormskjoldii *(Veronica alpina)* SCROPHULARIACEAE
Alpine speedwell, alpine brooklime
Uncommon, all summer, perennial, 2–12 in.
Vernal-wet, bog/fen/wetland, disturbed,
alpine, subalpine

Erect hairy stems, inflorescence sticky with glands. Stems root at nodes. Leaves lance-shaped, with pointed or rounded tips, entire or shallowly scalloped, sessile. Flowers blue or violet in spike at tip of stem. Grows in moist alpine meadows, along streams and lake edges, in disturbed soils, at high elevations. Native
OLYM, MORA, NOCA, CRLA

Cynoglossum grande BORAGINACEAE
Grand hound's tongue, blue buttons
Locally common, early spring, perennial,
2–3 ft. Coastal, west-side forest

Erect, often single, hairless stem. Leaves lance- to heart-shaped, smooth above, hairy below. Basal leaves 3–6 in. long, 1–4 in. wide, abruptly narrowing to petioles 3–6 in. long; few smaller leaves on lower stems. Flowers blue in panicle atop bare stem. Flowers have 5 conspicuous white raised nubs in a central ring. Grows in lightly shaded, open mixed woods, at low to mid elevations. Native NOCA

Hackelia micrantha *(Hackelia jessicae)* BORAGINACEAE
Blue stickseed, Jessica stickseed, meadow forget-me-not
Locally common, all summer, perennial, 12–40 in.
Meadow, shrub-steppe, subalpine

Erect. Stems hairless or with hairs sparse and spreading. Leaves lance-shaped, with pointed tips. Few basal leaves 3–6 in. long with winged petioles; upper leaves smaller, sessile. Blue flowers with yellow or white eye, on widely spreading branches of upper stem. Flowers can be ⅓ in. across but are often smaller. Seed nutlets have winged margin with numerous prickles. Grows in moist meadows with aspen, moist slopes, streambanks in mountains, at high elevations. *Hackelia floribunda* is similar but has a denser inflorescence, coarse hairs on stems, few or no prickles on seeds. Native NOCA, CRLA

See other *Cynoglossum*: red, page 378
See other *Hackelia*: white, page 151

Mertensia ciliata BORAGINACEAE
Fringed lungwort, broadleaf bluebells
Locally common, late spring–early summer,
perennial, 16–45 in. Bog/fen/wetland, meadow

Erect cluster of stems. Stems and leaves shiny
green, sometimes with white waxy sheen on
hairless surface. Leaves elliptic or lance-
shaped, numerous on upper stems, with conspicuous veins, sessile; lower leaves with short
petioles. Flowers dark blue, held on 1 side of stem, each on its
own stalk. Hanging flowers have a fringe of hairs on inside.
This bluebell is taller than others (except *M. paniculata*) and
often forms dense stands adjacent to small streams and seeps
at mid to high elevations, including Steens and Wallowa mountains. Native

Mertensia longiflora BORAGINACEAE
Trumpet lungwort, leafy bluebells
Uncommon, early spring, perennial, 2–8 in.
Vernal-wet, east-side forest, shrub-steppe

Erect, 1–2 succulent stems. Basal leaves usually missing; stem leaves sessile, few, broadly
egg-shaped, 1–4 times as long as they are
broad, hairless or with few hairs, with obscure
side veins. Flowers in tight nodding cluster at

top. Flower to 1 in., tubular, with open end spreading. Stems
and flowers easily detach from plant when touched. Grows in
open places that are spring-wet and summer-dry, often with
sagebrush and ponderosa pine, at low to mid elevations. Native
NOCA

Mertensia oblongifolia BORAGINACEAE
**Prairie mertensia, Toiyabe bluebells, sagebrush
bluebells**
Common, late spring–early summer, annual or
perennial, 4–12 in. Meadow, shrub-steppe,
alpine, subalpine

Erect, with many firmly attached stems, hairless to slightly hairy. Basal leaves with short
petioles, seldom on flowering plants; stem
leaves sessile, oblong, usually 2–7 times longer

than wide. Flowers hanging in dense cluster, each flower less
than ½ in. long. Grows with sagebrush or on open slopes at
low to high elevations, including Steens and Wallowa mountains. *Mertensia* is named for German botanist Franz Carl
Mertens (1764–1831). Native NOCA

Mertensia paniculata BORAGINACEAE
Tall bluebells, tall lungwort
Locally common, early summer, perennial, 2–5 ft. Meadows, west-side forest, east-side forest

Ascending to trailing stems few to many. Leaves with hairless upper surface, underside hairy. Basal leaves 2–8 in. long, about ½ as wide, with long petioles, egg- to heart-shaped; stem leaves thin, easily bruised, with obvious veins and short, winged petioles. Flowers blue, occasionally pink, in loose cluster among top leaves. Flower is a short tube flaring into longer bell shape with 5 lobes, hairy. Grows in moist meadows and woods in mountains to 8000 ft. Native
OLYM, MORA, NOCA, CRLA

Myosotis laxa BORAGINACEAE
Small-flowered forget-me-not
Common, all spring and summer, annual or biennial or perennial, 2–12 in. Lake/pond, meadow, moist streambanks

Upright or prostrate. Stems weak and often curved, may be branched, with straight stiff hairs. Leaves alternate. Basal leaves egg-shaped; stem leaves oval or lance-shaped. Inflorescence consists of numerous flowers in coil that extends as plant matures. Flowers on short stalks, very small, only slightly exceeding the calyx, with few straight hairs, tubes with 5 flat lobes. Grows in moist open places, shallow fresh water, from sea level to mid elevations. Circumboreal. Native
OLYM, NOCA

Myosotis scorpioides BORAGINACEAE
Marsh forget-me-not
Uncommon, late spring–early summer, perennial, 8–24 in. Bog/fen/wetland, disturbed

Upright from creeping stems and stolons. Stems unbranched, leafy, covered with sharp rigid hairs pressed against surface. Leaves oblong to elliptic, covered with rigid hairs; lower leaves narrow to winged petioles; upper leaves sessile. Many flowers spread out on leafless stem top that uncoils and lengthens with blooming. Flowers small, blue with a conspicuous yellow eye, 5 rounded lobes. Grows in shallow standing water, stream edges, at low to mid elevations. Native to Europe, as is the similar *M. sylvatica*, which has light blue flowers to ⅓ in. across, a garden escapee growing in moist shady places in urban areas and mountains but not in standing water or streams. Nonnative OLYM, NOCA

Eriodictyon californicum
HYDROPHYLLACEAE
Yerba santa
Locally common, early summer, perennial,
3–9 ft. Meadows, west-side forest

Erect shrub with shredding bark. Twigs hairless, sticky. Leaves leathery, 2–6 in., lance-shaped to oblong, with short stalk, toothed or entire, shiny to sticky with hair between veins on underside, edges rolled under. Flowers in open clusters at ends of twigs. Flower ⅓–⅔ in. long, funnel-shaped, with 5 lobes, white to lavender or purple, sparsely hairy. Grows in sunny, dry to moist places, roadsides, fields, woodlands, chaparral, at low to mid elevations. *Eriodictyon* is Greek for "woolly net," referring to the pattern of the hairs on underside of leaf. Native

Hydrophyllum capitatum var. *capitatum*   HYDROPHYLLACEAE
Ballhead waterleaf, wool breeches
Locally common, early spring, perennial,
4–18 in. East-side forest, shrub-steppe

Erect stem with spreading leaves. Stem very short. Leaves 2–5 in. long, with 1–6 in. petioles, divided pinnately, with 5–7 rounded leaflets. Flowers near ground under leaves; petals 5, white to purple; calyx bell-shaped, hairy; stamens and style exserted beyond petals. Grows in moist slopes, woodlands, sagebrush-steppe, at mid to high elevations. Var. *alpinum* is smaller, flowers also just above ground, with stems mostly underground and stalks becoming recurved; found in Great Basin, central Oregon. Native NOCA

Hydrophyllum capitatum var. *thompsonii*   HYDROPHYLLACEAE
Ballhead waterleaf
Uncommon, all spring, perennial, 4–16 in.
East-side forest

Erect stem with spreading leaves. Leaves 2–5 in. long, with 1–6 in. petioles, divided pinnately, with 5–7 rounded leaflets. Flowers on stalks equal to or surpassing the leaves; petals 5, purple to white; calyx bell-shaped, hairy; stamens, style exserted beyond petals. Grows in moist slopes, woodlands, sagebrush-steppe, including Columbia River Gorge, at low to higher elevations. *Hydrophyllum occidentale* also has flowers in a ball above leaves, but leaflets have 2–4 teeth per side and foliage is hairier; found from Coast Range to Cascades, central Oregon to California. Native

See other *Hydrophyllum*: white, page 155

441

Nemophila menziesii
HYDROPHYLLACEAE
Baby blue-eyes
Locally common, all spring, annual, 4–12 in.
Coastal, vernal-wet, meadow

Sprawling to erect. Stems delicate, succulent, with fine hairs. Leaves opposite, pinnately divided into odd number of lobes, fine hairs. Flowers on long stalks beyond leaves, wide open large bowls of 5 petals, sky blue with white center or with darker blue veins or black-spotted center. Grows in spring-moist flats, or slopes, at low elevations in southern Oregon and California. *Nemophila menziesii* var. *atomaria* (pictured, inset), with white flowers and black dots almost to edges of petal, is the form in the north. Native

Phacelia bolanderi HYDROPHYLLACEAE
Bolander's phacelia
Locally common, late spring–early summer,
perennial, 1–2 ft. Coastal

Stems erect to decumbent, covered with gland-tipped hairs. Alternate leaves on petioles are widely oblong, coarsely toothed. Bluish to purple flowers occur in 1-sided loose coil. Flower face is flat with 5 equal lobes, falling soon after opening. Grows on bluffs, slopes, canyons near coast. Native

Phacelia linearis HYDROPHYLLACEAE
Threadleaf phacelia
Locally common, all spring, annual, 3–20 in.
Disturbed, east-side forest, shrub-steppe

Erect stem may be branched near top, covered with hair. Leaves narrowly linear to lance-shaped, usually entire; sometimes lower leaves have linear lobes. Flower stalk short. Flower wide, bowl-shaped, to 1/3 in. across; calyx with short stiff hairs; petal with white to pale blue center, purple outer edges; stamens about same length as petal. May form dense colonies in sandy soils, shrublands, woodlands, forests, at mid elevations. Plants larger and flowers more deeply colored during damp springs. Native
OLYM, NOCA, **L&C**

See other *Nemophila*: white, page 155
See other *Phacelia*: white, page 156

Phacelia sericea var. *sericea*
HYDROPHYLLACEAE
Silky phacelia, alpine phacelia
Rare, all summer, biennial or perennial,
6–16 in. Alpine, subalpine

Erect perennial with a dense covering of silky silver hairs. Stems from woody base often branched. Leaves lance-shaped to narrowly oblong, pinnately divided, often divided again, lobes rounded. Flower clusters at stem top form showy bottlebrush head. Flowers dark blue to purple, bell-shaped, with hairy calyx and conspicuous yellow or orange stamens extending out beyond petals. Drying petals persist in seed. Grows on ridges, in talus, near or above tree line. *Sericea* means "silky." Var. *ciliosa* has several clusters of numerous flowers held in long loose cyme. Native OLYM, MORA, NOCA

Collomia debilis (*Collomia larsenii*)
POLEMONIACEAE
Alpine collomia, talus collomia
Rare, midsummer, perennial, 2–6 in.
Alpine, subalpine

Prostrate plant with sprawling stems in talus. Stems and leaves hairless or coated with fine hairs, sometimes including glands. Stem branched, often turned upward, leaves crowded toward tips. Leaves oval, with wide tip, can be shallowly to deeply divided or entire. Flowers in cluster at end of short stems just beyond leaves. Flower bell-shaped, with 5 lobes, often lavender, blue, pink, sometimes yellowish white, with 5 stamens. Grows in rocky slopes at high elevations. Native OLYM, MORA, NOCA

Gilia capitata   POLEMONIACEAE
Blue-headed gilia, globe gilia
Common, early summer, annual or perennial,
6–36 in. Meadow

Stem erect, branched near top, leafy below flowers. Leaves at base and on stem, divided once or twice to narrow lobes, central lobe widest; stem leaves reducing in size, with upper leaves undivided. Flowers numerous in tight balls at stem tips. Flower tube and lobes light blue, stamens and style exserted beyond lobes. Grows in open, sandy or rocky soils, grassy hillsides, below 7000 ft. Subsp. *capitata*, with a colorless calyx, grows on rocky slopes and hillsides. Subsp. *pacifica* has a blue-violet calyx and grows on coastal slopes and bluffs. Native OLYM, MORA, NOCA

See other *Collomia*: orange, page 301; red, page 379
See other *Gilia*: red, page 380

Gilia millefoliata POLEMONIACEAE
Yarrowleaf gilia
Locally common, all spring and summer,
annual, ¼–1½ in. Coastal

Basal rosette of leaves, short stem with long branches. Entire plant densely coated with glands, skunky-smelling. Leaves somewhat fleshy, pinnately lobed. Flowers 2–6, clustered on stalk. Flower about ⅓ in. long; throat containing pair of purple spots is partly inside calyx and topped by 5 lobes; stamens with white pollen and style in top of throat. Grows on stable sand dunes. Native

Gilia sinuata POLEMONIACEAE
Shy gilia
Uncommon, midspring, annual, 4–12 in.
Shrub-steppe

Spreading stems, 1 to many from basal leaf rosette. Stems hairless, covered with bluish wax below middle. Basal leaves lobed or toothed, more or less covered with a white cobweb of hairs; stem leaves few, with pointed tips, clasping. Inflorescence covered with glands, consists of flower clusters atop long stalks. Flower tube purple, veined white, lobes lavender, pink, or white, stamens and style slightly extended, noticeable white pollen. Grows among sagebrush in sandy soils, open places, at 500–6200 ft. Native

Polemonium californicum POLEMONIACEAE
Showy Jacob's ladder
Uncommon, midsummer, perennial, to
12 in. West-side forest, east-side forest,
subalpine

Prostrate, with tips curved upward. Stems soft with gland-tipped hairs. Leaves hairless, lance-shaped to oval, pinnately divided into 11–19 leaflets, with end leaflet fused to 2 just below. Inflorescence is an open head on 4 in. stem from upper leaves. Flower stalks less than ½ in., tube shorter than lobes, white with blue or yellow throat, bell-shaped, lobes blue to violet, stamens and style extending outward. Grows in open and shaded places in mixed woods at mid to high elevations. Can hybridize with *P. pulcherrimum* where ranges overlap. Native
OLYM, MORA, CRLA

See other *Polemonium*: yellow, page 250

Polemonium occidentale

POLEMONIACEAE

Western Jacob's ladder, western polemonium

Uncommon, all summer, perennial, 8–40 in.

Bog/fen/wetland, meadow, east-side forest

Erect, often solitary stems. Stems slightly glandular-sticky. Leaves with long bare stalk, divided pinnately. Leaflets 9–17, lance-shaped, upper surface green to yellow-green, lower surface with waxy blue powder. Flowers in open clusters. Flower bell-shaped, blue with yellow throat, lobes flat and overlapping, twice as long as tubes, extending stamens and style. Grows in wet meadows, lakeshores, along streams, marshes, woodlands, at mid elevations. Native NOCA, CRLA

Polemonium pulcherrimum

POLEMONIACEAE

Showy polemonium, short Jacob's ladder, skunk-leaved polemonium

Uncommon, midsummer, perennial

East-side forest, alpine, subalpine

Tuft, erect to decumbent, distinctive skunky-smelling. Plant with soft hairs. Basal and stem leaves, the latter becoming abruptly smaller upward. Leaves pinnately divided into 9–21 widely oval to round leaflets. Inflorescence is a crowded cluster or head-like. Flower tube and lobes about same length, tube white, throat usually yellow, lobes blue to white. Grows in talus in subalpine and alpine zones, further north in dry rocky places, at mid to high elevations. Uncommon var. *pilosum* has hairy stems and leaves, white flowers with yellow throat. Var. *pulcherrimum* has glands and few hairs on stems and leaves, blue to purple flowers, white to yellow throat. Native

OLYM, MORA, NOCA, CRLA, **L&C**

Polemonium viscosum (Polemonium confertum) POLEMONIACEAE

Sky pilot

Rare, all summer, perennial, 4–20 in. Alpine

Flower stem erect from mostly basal leaves. Plant skunky-smelling. Leaf pinnately divided; leaflets 3–5, divided; lobes less than ½ in. long. Inflorescence is a tight cluster of blue or white flowers. Flowers with short stalks, rounded lobes ⅓ the length of tube, stamens only slightly extending outward. This alpine plant grows on cliffs, ledges, and rocky places at high elevations. Native NOCA

445

Ceanothus prostratus RHAMNACEAE
Prostrate ceanothus, mahala mat
Locally common, late spring–early summer,
perennial, mat. West-side forest, east-side
forest

Prostrate plant less than 8 ft. wide. Stems
round, red-brown, may root when touching
ground. Leaves opposite, evergreen, oblong
to widely oval, usually about 1 in. long,
leathery, with 3–9 teeth; upper surface smooth, green, hairless;
lower surface lighter-colored, with hairs on veins. Flowers in
small clusters, shades of blue, lavender, white. Seedpods often
bright red, round, with 3 sections, wrinkled on top. Grows in
open areas of conifer forests at mid to high elevations. Plants
with larger or smaller leaves are often found. Native

Ceanothus pumilus RHAMNACEAE
Siskiyou mat, dwarf ceanothus
Endemic, late spring–early summer,
perennial, mat. Meadows, dry rocky sites

Prostrate evergreen shrub usually less than
8 ft. wide. Stems red-brown and angled
when young. Leaves evergreen, opposite,
less than ¾ in. long, with short petiole.
Leaves widely oval, with few very small teeth
near tip, dark green on top, lighter underneath. Flowers in
small clusters, blue, lavender, or white. Seedpods rounded on
top, not wrinkled, bright red. Grows in dry rocky serpentine at
100–6000 ft. Native

Ceanothus thyrsiflorus RHAMNACEAE
Blueblossom ceanothus
Common, midspring, perennial, 2–18 ft.
Coastal, west-side forest

Erect to prostrate shrub. Stem green when
young, hairless, twigs growing at an angle
from stem. Leaves alternate, evergreen, oblong to egg-shaped, with 3 veins raised on
light-colored slightly hairy lower surface,
upper surface dark shiny green, edges with
glands on teeth. Flowers light to deep blue
in dense clusters to 3 in. across. Seedpod sticky. Grows in low-
elevation woods and coastal bluffs. Prostrate plants found only
on north coast of California. If you rub the blossoms briskly
between your hands with some water, you'll make soapsuds.
Native

See other *Ceanothus*: white, page 162

Solanum dulcamara SOLANACEAE
Bittersweet nightshade
Common, late spring–early summer, perennial,
3–9 ft. Bog/fen/wetland, disturbed, meadow,
west-side forest

Climbing or sprawling woody stems. Plant
foul-smelling. Leaves egg-shaped, entire or
with 1 lobe to each side, 1–3 in. long, short-
haired or hairless, alternate. Inflorescence is a
loose cluster on a leafless stalk. Flowers violet-blue; 5 petals
fused halfway form tube, petal tips reflexed backward; 5 stamens joined form bright yellow central cone with pistil extended. Berries bright red. Often found in shrubby thickets at
edges of wetlands or ponds, also in forest openings, orchards,
gardens, roadsides, at low elevations. Leaves and berries poisonous if eaten. Nonnative OLYM, NOCA

Campanula piperi CAMPANULACEAE
Olympic harebell
Endemic, midsummer, perennial, 1–4 in.
Alpine, subalpine

Clusters of stems, with leaves to stem top.
Stems and leaves hairless. Leaves spoon-
shaped, sharply toothed, about same size from
top to bottom, with wide petioles to 1 in. long.
Flowers 1 or few atop stem. Calyx with few bristles; petals forming open bell-shaped flowers, pale to medium blue or white,
about 1/3 in. long. Grows on open rocky slopes, crevices in cliffs,
in subalpine and alpine. Native OLYM

Campanula rotundifolia CAMPANULACEAE
Scotch bluebell, common harebell
Common, all summer, perennial, 4–20 in.
Meadow, west-side forest, subalpine

Upright, branched stems with few round
leaves at base. Plant hairless. Stems thin, single or in clusters. Basal leaves withering before
flowering; stem leaves sessile, to 3 in. long,
narrow, entire or saw-toothed. Flowers bell-
shaped, with tips only slightly flared, blue or
white, hanging on thin stalks from tops of
stems. Grows on moist slopes and in meadows. Circumboreal.
Native OLYM, MORA, NOCA

See other *Solanum*: white, page 164

5 symmetrical petals forming a tube

5 petals joined into a bell

5 petals joined into a bell

Campanula scouleri CAMPANULACEAE
Scouler's bluebell
Uncommon, mid to late summer, perennial,
4–12 in. West-side forest

Erect or spreading. Stem slender. Leaves
½–2½ in., lance-shaped to round, coarsely
toothed; lower leaves with petioles. Flowers
on upper stem with curved stalks. Calyx
lobes spreading outward, sometimes curling back. Flower widely bell-shaped, pale blue to white, petals reflexed back. Style same color as flower, extended well beyond petals. Grows in shaded woods, edges of streams, at low to mid elevations. Native OLYM, MORA

Downingia elegans CAMPANULACEAE
Elegant downingia
Locally common, late spring–early summer,
annual, 2–12 in. Vernal-wet

Stem decumbent or erect, many pairs of
flowers. Usually grows in masses. Leaves on
stems, small, sessile, entire, often withered
before flowering. Flowers held by long ovary
tube looking like swollen stem. At top of
tube are 5 narrow green bracts under flower
corolla; lower lip of corolla with central large
white spot (no yellow); 3 purple to blue sharply pointed lobes.
Upper 2 lobes are same color, narrow, pointed. Long hooked
stamen column extends from center. Grows in vernal-wet areas
below 6500 ft. Very similar *D. bacigalupii* has rounded lower
lobes, 2 oblong yellow spots in large white patch. Native

Downingia yina CAMPANULACEAE
Cascade downingia, Willamette downingia
Locally common, late spring–early summer,
annual, 1–4 in. Vernal-wet, lake/pond

Erect to decumbent, grows in masses. Stem
branching. Leaves small, sessile, linear to
lance-shaped, with pointed tip, often withered by flowering time. Flowers with long
ovary tube sustain 5-bracted calyx topped by
corolla. Flower corolla blue, about ⅓ in.
across, with 2 lips; lower 2 yellow spots surrounded by white
and 3 rounded blue lobes with small tooth at tip. Upper lip
blue, with 2 short lobes. Stamen column does not extend above
corolla. Found in lakes, ponds, vernal-wet areas, below 5400 ft.
Native OLYM

Dipsacus fullonum (*Dipsacus sylvestris*)
DIPSACACEAE
Fuller's teasel, common teasel
Locally common, all summer, biennial, 3–6 ft.
Vernal-wet, disturbed, meadow

Erect stem topped by cone-shaped spiny flower head. Stem hollow, stout, with few branches, covered with some rough hairs. Leaves lance-shaped, in pairs clasping around stem, may be shallowly toothed; underside of midrib spiny. Flowers lilac to pink, held by everlasting spiny bracts forming 2–4 in. stiff cone-shaped head. Long leaf-like bracts with spiny edges, 4–5 at base of flower head. Flowers open in ring around head starting at bottom. Grows in moist to wet places, disturbed soils, at low to mid elevations. Flower heads of this species are used in the wool industry to raise the nap on cloth. Non-native

Valerianella locusta   VALERIANACEAE
European corn-salad, lamb's lettuce
Locally common, all spring, annual, 4–15 in.
Vernal-wet, disturbed

Erect stem, repeating equally forked branches. Stem with sparse hairs pointing downward. Leaves opposite; lower leaves on short petioles; upper leaves sessile; blades oval to oblong, entire or slightly toothed near tip. Inflorescence at stem top, usually 2 dense clusters with ring of bracts at base, flowers on short stalks. Flower without calyx, a white funnel-shaped tube with 5 bluish or pink, unequal, rounded lobes. Grows in moist shaded places. Escapee from cultivation, grown for edible leaves. Nonnative
OLYM

Aster alpigenus subsp. *haydenii*
(*Oreostemma alpigenum* var. *haydenii*)
ASTERACEAE (aster tribe)
Hayden's aster
Locally common, all summer, perennial, 4–15 in. Meadow, alpine, subalpine

Erect to decumbent flower stalks from rosette of many leaves. Narrow leaves 1–10 in. long in rosette, hairless; stem leaves are shorter, if present. Single flower head with many lavender to deep purple rays. Grows in meadows, moist gravelly slopes, in subalpine and alpine of Blue, Wallowa, and Steens mountains. Native MORA

See other *Aster*: white, page 168

5 petals joined into a bell

Composite flowers

Aster alpigenus var. alpigenus

(*Oreostemma alpigenum* var. *alpigenum*)
ASTERACEAE (aster tribe)
Alpine aster
Locally common, midsummer, perennial,
4–12 in. Meadow, alpine, subalpine

Stems erect to decumbent from single taproot. Leaves in basal rosette, linear to lance-shaped, 1–6 in. long, without petioles, woolly when young, becoming shiny with age; stem leaves small, sparse. Flower stem to 12 in. with solitary 1 in. flower head. Flower head with cup, bracts lance-shaped, green often tinted purple, 10–40 blue-purple to pink ray flowers surrounding yellow disk. Grows in damp meadows at mid to high elevations in Olympic, Cascade, and Wallowa mountains. Native
OLYM, MORA, NOCA

Aster ascendens (*Symphyotrichum*

ascendens) ASTERACEAE (aster tribe)
Long-leaved aster
Common, all summer, perennial, 8–25 in.
Meadow

Slender, sprawling to upright. Stems with some short stiff hairs on upper part. Basal leaves 2–6 in. long, lance-shaped, with petioles, withering as plant blooms; stem leaves linear to elliptical, very short, sessile. No small leafy shoots in leaf axils. Inflorescence consists of numerous branches with small flower heads. Flowers violet. Grows in meadows, open areas, at low to mid elevations. Native

Aster chilensis (*Symphyotrichum*

chilense) ASTERACEAE (aster tribe)
Common California aster, Pacific aster
Locally common, all summer–autumn,
perennial, 20–40 in. Coastal, meadow

Sprawling to upright. Stems slender, somewhat hairy on upper parts. Basal leaves 3–8 in. long, lance-shaped, with petioles, withering as the plant blooms; stem leaves linear to elliptical, very short, sessile, entire, slightly hairy. Inflorescence consists of cymes with numerous small flower heads; oblong to egg-shaped, large, green bracts form cup; violet, lavender, or white ray flowers. Grows in meadows, open areas. Native OLYM

Aster foliaceus (*Symphyotrichum foliaceum*)
ASTERACEAE (aster tribe)
Leafybract aster
Common, late summer, perennial, 6–24 in.
Meadow, west-side forest, east-side forest,
alpine, subalpine

Erect, highly variable in height. Stems often
reddish, hairy to hairless. Basal leaves 2–5 in.
long, egg-shaped, on short petioles; stem leaves
sessile. Flower heads single or few in open cyme with leaf-like,
oblong to egg-shaped bracts. Ray flowers violet, purple, blue,
or rose; disk yellow. Grows in open woods, subalpine meadows, along streams, at high elevations. Var. *apricus* is less than
9 in. tall, with decumbent or ascending stems; grows in alpine
to subalpine. Var. *parryi*, more than 9 in. tall, has upper leaves
smooth, moderately clasping; bracts under
flowers small; grows along streams and wet
places in mountains. *Aster cusickii*, of Wallowa
Mountains, is more than 9 in. tall, with middle
and upper leaves hairy, strongly clasping; not
in alpine zone. Native OLYM, MORA, NOCA, CRLA

Aster integrifolius (*Eurybia integrifolia*)
ASTERACEAE (aster tribe)
Thick-stem aster, entire-leaf aster, sticky aster
Common, midsummer, perennial, 8–28 in.
Meadow, alpine, subalpine

Erect stems in clusters, sticky glands on top section. Basal and
lower stem leaves green through flowering, 2–9 in. long, entire, egg-shaped, with short petioles; upper stem leaves smaller,
lance-shaped, sessile to clasping. Flower clusters atop stems.
Flower cup glandular, green, bract tips tinted purple, 10–20 ray
flowers lavender to purple surrounding yellow
to purplish disk. Grows in dry meadows at
high elevations. Native

Aster ledophyllus (*Eucephalus ledophyllus*)
ASTERACEAE (aster tribe)
Cascade aster, tea-leaved aster
Locally common, late summer, perennial, 1–2
ft. Meadows, west-side forest, subalpine

Erect clump of hairy stems rise from woody base. Leaves elliptical to almost round, tips pointed to round, entire, sessile,
upper surface shiny, underside pale green with matted hairs.
Lower leaves scale-like, middle and upper leaves equal in
length. Inflorescence is a cyme. Flowers have few to 21 ray
flowers, dark purple, blue, or pink, to 1 in. long, in cup of oblong green bracts with sometimes purple reflexed tips. Grows
in meadows, open woods, mostly in subalpine. Native
MORA, NOCA

Aster modestus (Canadanthus modestus)
ASTERACEAE (aster tribe)
Great northern aster, few-flowered aster
Locally common, late summer, perennial,
1–4 ft. West-side forest, east-side forest,
moist streambanks

Single tall stem, often branched at top. Stem
glandular or hairy near flower heads. Basal
leaves slightly smaller than the rest, wither-
ing by bloom time; stem leaves lance-shaped, clasping, 2–6 in.
long, entire or with few sharp teeth. One to many flower heads
atop stems. Flowers with 21–45 very narrow purple ray flowers,
yellow disk; cup green, glandular, narrowly linear, with spreading tips. Grows in moist shady woods, along streams, at low to
mid elevations. Native OLYM, MORA, NOCA, CRLA

Aster occidentalis (Symphyotrichum
spathulatum var. spathulatum)
ASTERACEAE (aster tribe)
Western aster, western mountain aster
Uncommon, late summer, perennial, 1–2 ft.
Vernal-wet, meadow

Erect stems shiny to hairy. Leaves linear,
hairless, entire, with pointed tips. Basal
leaves 2–6 in. long, ½ as wide; stem leaves
smaller. Flower heads held in open cyme, each with many
lavender to violet ray flowers, many yellow disk flowers. Grows
in damp meadows and other vernal-damp places at mid to high
elevations. Native

Aster subspicatus (Symphyotrichum subspicatum)
ASTERACEAE (aster tribe)
Douglas's aster
Locally common, all summer, perennial, 1–4
ft. Coastal, moist streambanks, disturbed,
west-side forest

Cluster of erect leafy stems from spreading
roots. Stems with many hairy leaves. Leaves
toothed; lower leaves lance-shaped, with
short petiole; midstem leaves usually without petiole but do not clasp stem. Flowers
few to many, held in cyme. Flower cup of overlapping bracts,
the outer bracts with paper-like margins and light yellow to reddish brown base; ray flowers purple or blue, about ½–1 in.
long. Grows on beaches, along streams, disturbed areas, other
open moist sites, at low elevations. Native OLYM, MORA, NOCA

Erigeron breweri ASTERACEAE (aster tribe)
Brewer's daisy, Klamath daisy
Locally common, late spring–early summer,
perennial, 4–12 in. Subalpine, dry rocky sites

Stems upright, arising from underground
crown, branched near base, occasionally above.
Stems and leaves rather densely covered with
straight stiff hairs, rough to the touch, but
without glands. Leaves numerous on stems,
linear to oblong, to 1/3 in. long, about the same size from bottom to top. Flower heads several, with glands sometimes sticky; cup bracts green throughout with brown midrib; rayless or with 1–45 pink or white rays. Grows in open, dry, rocky areas in foothills and mountains, at low to mid elevations. Native

Erigeron corymbosus
ASTERACEAE (aster tribe)
Foothill daisy, longleaf fleabane
Locally common, midsummer, perennial,
10–20 in. Shrub-steppe

Erect stems with some leaves. Leaves and
stems covered with short spreading hairs.
Basal leaves to 10 in. long, narrow, with
pointed tip; stem leaves reduced in size. Three
veins run lengthwise on larger leaves. Flower
heads 1–16 on each stem; rays 35–65, deep blue, possibly pink; disk yellow. Grows in open dry soils among sagebrush. Native

Erigeron elegantulus ASTERACEAE (aster tribe)
Blue dwarf fleabane
Uncommon, midsummer, perennial, 2–6 in.
Shrub-steppe, alpine, subalpine

Erect, with many unbranched stems from root.
Stem with sparse, tiny, white hairs. Leaves on
lower stem 1/2–2 in., linear to lance-shaped,
with wide whitish base, sessile, partly surrounding stem. Flower head above leaves single atop leafless stalk, 1/4–1/2 in. across. Ray
flowers 15–25, blue or pink. Disk flowers yellow. Grows in open areas in sagebrush, juniper
woodlands, dry pumice slopes, at mid to high
elevations. Native CRLA

See other *Erigeron*: white, page 171; yellow, page 257; red, page 391

Erigeron pumilus

ASTERACEAE (aster tribe)
Shaggy daisy
Uncommon, late spring–early summer,
perennial, 8–20 in. Shrub-steppe

Cluster of stems, somewhat thick at base,
divided top with 1 to several flower heads,
stiff dense hairs covering entire plant. Basal
leaves many, erect, lance-shaped, to about 3
in. long; stem leaves few, gradually decreasing in size. Flower
heads with 50–100 blue, pink, or white reflexed ray flowers and
¼ in. center of yellow disk flowers. Grows in open places in
foothills, valleys, and often among sagebrush. The common
name refers to the dense, stiff hairs that give a disheveled appearance. Native

Erigeron speciosus

ASTERACEAE (aster tribe)
Showy fleabane, showy daisy
Locally common, all summer, perennial,
6–30 in. Meadow, west-side forest, east-side
forest

Clustered erect stems bear many leaves.
Leaves oblong to lance-shaped, hairless except straight hairs along leaf edges; lowest
leaves with petiole, dropping early; upper leaves sessile. Flower
heads 1–3 with many purple to blue, or rarely white, narrow
ray flowers, surrounding yellow disk. Grows in moist places,
in open woods, meadows, at low to mid elevations. Native
OLYM, MORA, NOCA

Erigeron subtrinervis

ASTERACEAE (aster tribe)
Three-nerved daisy
Locally common, midsummer, perennial,
1–2 ft. Meadows, west-side forest, east-side
forest

Erect cluster of stems bearing many leaves.
Leaves and stems with long spreading hairs;
hairs on leaves sometimes only on edges
and veins. Lower leaves oval, petioles with
extensions on sides; upper leaves wider, with 3 obvious veins,
sessile. One to several flower heads held in a cup covered with
glands and long spreading hairs; more than 100 purple to blue
ray flowers. Grows in meadows, open woods in dry soils, at low
to mid elevations. Very similar to *E. speciosus*, showy daisy.
Native OLYM, MORA

Machaeranthera canescens (*Dieteria*
canescens, Aster canescens)
ASTERACEAE (aster tribe)
Hoary aster
Common, late summer, annual or biennial or
perennial, 1–4 ft. Disturbed, meadow, shrub-
steppe

Spreading to erect. Stems, leaves with dense,
fine, grayish white hairs, glands. Stems several
from base, branched, bushy. Leaves narrow, linear, slightly or
finely toothed, upper leaves sometimes clasping. Flower head
has cups of 2–3 rows of sharply pointed bracts, blue or purple
ray flowers, many yellow disk flowers. Common in many habitats at low to mid elevations. Subsp. *canescens* var. *shastensis*, in
mountains of southern Oregon, northern California, has no ray
flowers. Subsp. *canescens* var. *canescens*, in dry
shrublands of eastern Oregon, has mostly entire leaves. Subsp. *canescens* var. *incana* is less
than 24 in., usually with single, stiff, erect stem
and many branches; found in much of eastern
Pacific Northwest in dry soils and along
streams. Native NOCA, **L&C**

Townsendia parryi ASTERACEAE (aster tribe)
Parry's townsendia
Uncommon, all summer, biennial or perennial, 2–12 in.
Shrub-steppe, alpine, subalpine

Basal leaf rosette. Stem stout, unbranched. Basal leaves gray-
haired, ⅓–2 in. long, widest at tip end; stem leaves few, smaller.
Flower head single with more than 40 ray flowers, blue or violet, ½–1 in. long, large yellow disk. Grows on rocky ridges in
high steppe, subalpine, alpine. Native

Cichorium intybus
ASTERACEAE (chicory tribe)
Chicory, wild succory
Common, late summer, biennial or perennial,
1–4 ft. Disturbed, meadow

Erect, with branching stems and milky juice.
Leaf blades, the lowest tapering into stalks with
winged sides, are lance-shaped, lobed to
toothed. Upper leaves smaller, entire, stalkless. Flower heads
have ray flowers only and are 1–2 in. across, sessile, sky blue,
with evenly toothed square tips. Grows in fields, roadsides, at
low to mid elevations throughout North America. An invading
weed brought from Europe so roots could substitute for coffee.
Nonnative OLYM, MORA, NOCA, CRLA

See other *Townsendia*: red, page 392

Tragopogon porrifolius

ASTERACEAE (chicory tribe)

Purple salsify, oyster plant

Locally common, all spring and summer, biennial, 16–40 in. Coastal, vernal-wet, bog/fen/wetland, meadow

Erect biennial. Stems branched, wider near flower buds, producing sticky white sap. Leaves 8–15 in. long, narrow, waxy blue at maturity, clasping stem. Flowers held in long triangle of 1–2 in. green bracts; when open, bracts are longer than the purple ray flowers. This European native has spread throughout Pacific states in moist habitats. Not as common as yellow salsify, *T. dubius*, and grows in damper places. Native OLYM, MORA, NOCA

Centaurea cyanus

ASTERACEAE (thistle tribe)

Bachelor's button, cornflower

Common, all summer, annual, 1–3 ft. Disturbed, meadow

Stems erect, slightly hairy, loosely branching. Leaves linear, 1–4 in., lightly coated with gray hairs, entire or slightly lobed. Flower heads bright blue, pink, purple, or white; cup ¼–½ in. high, bell-shaped, with green phyllaries, not spiny. Outer disk flowers are enlarged to form a petal-like fringe. Grows in grasslands, open woods, below 7000 ft. Native to southern Europe, sometimes used in wildflower mixes along roads or in parks, spreading by seed and considered a noxious weed. Nonnative OLYM

Saussurea americana

ASTERACEAE (thistle tribe)

American sawwort

Uncommon, midsummer, perennial, 12–50 in. Bog/fen/wetland, meadow, subalpine

Stems erect, leafy, with fine hairs and glands. Leaves thin, basal and on stems, largest 2–6 in. long, lance-shaped to triangular, toothed; upper leaves smaller. Inflorescence in upper leaf axils, consists of single or cluster of flower heads. Flower head with a cup of many green bracts with few long hairs, tips often blackish purple or brown; flowers 10–20, violet to dark purple or rarely white. Brownish bristles in center attach to seed. Grows in bogs, wet meadows, creeksides or wet rocky places, at high elevations. Native OLYM, MORA, NOCA

See other *Tragopogon*: yellow, page 272
See other *Centaurea*: white, page 181; yellow, page 295; red, page 394

Asarum caudatum ARISTOLOCHIACEAE
Long-tailed ginger
Locally common, late spring–early summer,
perennial, 4–6 in. Coastal, west-side forest,
east-side forest

Spreading evergreen, often in large mats.
Brittle, horizontal, root-like rhizome just
under soil. Leaves uniformly green, heart-
shaped, in pairs with long petioles. Flowers
at tip end of rhizomes, dark maroon or rarely green, 3 calyx tips
tapering into long tails, inner surface of tube white with 1 red
horizontal stripe. Grows in moist places on forest floors from
coastline to high elevations. All asarums have the scent of ginger when touched or broken. Native
OLYM, MORA, NOCA, CRLA, **L&C**

Asarum hartwegii ARISTOLOCHIACEAE
Hartweg's wild ginger
Uncommon, late spring–early summer,
perennial, 4–8 in. West-side forest

Tight clumps of evergreen leaves. Leaf dark
green, heart-shaped, with white marbling
along veins, hairs along edges curling toward tip. Flowers face upward but are under
leaves; dark brownish red tube is white in-
side with red stripes, covered with bands of white hairs. Tips of
flower tube end in a point but not an extended tail. Grows on
rocky places in dry open woods at low to subalpine elevations.
Native

Asarum marmoratum ARISTOLOCHIACEAE
Marbled wild ginger
Rare, late spring–early summer, perennial,
4–8 in. West-side forest

Clump. Leaves leathery, heart-shaped, dark
green marbled silver along veins, rarely
plain green; petioles sparsely coated with
coarse wavy hairs. Flowers pale reddish
brown, red on the inner surface with some
dark hairs; tube with 3 more or less upright
olive-brown lobes with very long extended
tails. Grows in moist woods and forests, on rocky outcrops,
other rocky places. This beautiful uncommon plant is found
only in Siskiyou and Klamath mountains. Native

Fritillaria affinis (*Fritillaria lanceolata*)
LILIACEAE
Mission bells, checker lily
Locally common, midspring, perennial, 1–3 ft.
Coastal, meadow, west-side forest, east-side
forest

Stem erect, unbranched, with nodding flowers
at top. Leaves on stem only, narrow, may be
whorled below, alternate and erect above.
Upper leaf axis with flower stalk bends to hold hanging, bowl-
shaped, sometimes squared, top flower. Flower yellow to greenish yellow at base, checkered more or less with brown, red, or
purple, petals lance-shaped, with pointed tips. Grows among
shrubs or trees, where cool and moist, from coast to mid elevations. *Fritillaria* in Latin refers to the checkered mottling on
the flowers. *Affinis* means "related to" or "sim-
ilar to" and refers to this being the species that
best represents the genus. Native
OLYM, MORA, NOCA, **L&C**

Fritillaria atropurpurea   LILIACEAE
Spotted mountain bells
Uncommon, late spring–early summer,
perennial, 5–25 in. East-side forest, shrub-
steppe, alpine, subalpine

Stem erect, unbranched. Leaves on stems only, all about the
same size, long, narrow; lower leaves in 2 whorls; upper leaves
1–3 per node. Flowers 1–3 per stalk from leaf axis, hanging or
facing outward, opening wide, brown or greenish brown with
yellow, red, or white markings and often with a noticeable yellow edge. Grows in sheltered edges of forests, near shrubs, at
mid to high elevations. Native NOCA, CRLA

Fritillaria camschatcensis   LILIACEAE
Kamchatka fritillary, chocolate lily
Locally common, early summer, perennial, 1–2
ft. Coastal
Stem erect, unbranched. Leaves entirely along
stem; 1–3 whorls of 3–10 lance-shaped leaves
to 3 in. long. Flowers 1 to several from upper
leaf axil on short stalks. Flowers often with pu-
trid odor, bronze, chocolate, or liver-colored, widely bell-shaped,
with petals slightly turned back, small parallel ridges on inside.
Grows in wet soils that never dry in coastal areas and rain forest. The odor attracts pollinators, usually flies. Native

See other *Fritillaria*: yellow, page 188; red, page 312   **459**

Scoliopus hallii   LILIACEAE
Oregon fetid adder's tongue
Uncommon, early spring, perennial, 2–5 in.
Coastal, west-side forest

Leaves 2, opposite, with or without mottling, from underground stem, oval, with pointed tip, 3–6 in. long, green, with many ribbed veins. Flowers smell like dead meat, on slender stalks to 8 in.; 3 broad spreading sepals mottled with yellow and purple; 3 petals very narrow, held upright; 3 stamens. Grows in damp shaded woods. Larger *S. bigelovii*, California fetid adder's tongue, has distinctly mottled leaves 4–8 in. long; flowers with 3 slightly recurved green with red-purple sepals, 3 narrow upward- or inward-pointing petals; found in moist woods, redwoods, only in Curry County, Oregon, and Humboldt County, California.
Native

Stenanthium occidentale   LILIACEAE
Mountainbells, bronze bells
Uncommon, midsummer, perennial, 1–2 ft.
Bog/fen/wetland, moist streambanks, west-side forest, subalpine

Stem weakly upright, slender. Basal leaves 2–4, grass-like, 4–12 in. long. Flowers hang along top part of nodding stem, bronzy yellow to green bells spotted with purple, tips of petals curling back, fragrant. Grows in moist meadows, banks of shady streams, at low to subalpine elevations. Native   OLYM, MORA, NOCA

Veratrum viride (*Veratrum eschscholtzii*)   LILIACEAE
Green corn lily, green false hellebore
Locally common, late summer, perennial, to 80 in. Meadow, alpine, subalpine

Large erect plant with drooping flower stems. Leaves 4–10 in. long, widely egg-shaped, short hairs along upper side of veins. Inflorescence 12–35 in. tall, main stem erect, woolly, lower side branches drooping. Flowers well spaced, green to yellowish green, with 6 widely spread, oblong, hairy lobes that are irregularly toothed; stamens about ½ the length of lobes. Grows in bogs and wet meadows, most abundant in high-elevation subalpine as snow melts. Native
OLYM, MORA, NOCA, CRLA

See other *Veratrum*: white, page 69

Cypripedium fasciculatum
ORCHIDACEAE
Clustered lady's-slipper, Brownie lady's-slipper
Rare, mid to late spring, perennial, 5–10 in.
West-side forest, east-side forest

Stem erect, hairy, bent above leaves. Leaf pair nearly opposite, sessile, oblong, usually 1–3 in. long. Flowers 1–6, clustered above leaves, each on curved stem, with bracts as long as the densely fine-hairy ovary. Slipper large, all flower parts greenish brown or greenish purple with dark brown or purple veins and splotches. Dependent on mycorrhizal fungi in forest duff. Grows in moist to dry, shaded, mixed evergreen woods through mid elevations. Plants become very old in areas not disturbed, and any disturbance, including picking, can kill the plants. Native

Epipactis gigantea   ORCHIDACEAE
Stream orchid, giant helleborine, chatterbox
Common, midsummer, perennial, 12–35 in.
Bog/fen/wetland, moist streambanks, meadow

Stem erect, leaves and flowers at top. Leaves oval, clasping stem, smaller upward. Flowers from upper leaf axils, opening a few at a time, on 1 side of stem. Flower yellowish green with red-purple veins; top 3 sepals and 2 petals flat; lower, extended, pouch-like petal green to yellow outside, tinted and lined with purple inside, deeply concave. Grows in wet places below treeline. From Europe, *E. helleborine* grows in dry places along roads, on slopes; flowers are smaller, white or green tinted pink-purple, pouch-like petal white or tinted pinkish outside, purple to brown on inside. Native OLYM, NOCA

Listera caurina   ORCHIDACEAE
Northwestern twayblade
Uncommon, midsummer, perennial, 4–12 in.
Coastal, moist streambanks, west-side forest, east-side forest

Stem erect, pair of opposite leaves clasping at midstem. Leaves nearly round, 1–3 in. long. Flowers small, few to 40, greenish yellow on upper 2–3 in. of stem. Flower has 3 sepals; 2 petals at top about ¼ in. long; lower petal longer, broadly rounded at tip end, tapering toward center point, with a tiny thread-like tooth on each side near flower center. Grows in shady moist conifer forests, at mid elevations. Similar *L. convallarioides*, broad-leaved twayblade, has no teeth at top edge of lower petal, which is narrow at base and wide at tip end, but notched with rounded lobes. Native OLYM, MORA, NOCA, CRLA

See other *Cypripedium*: white, page 71

Listera cordata ORCHIDACEAE
Heartleaf twayblade
Uncommon, late spring–early summer, perennial, 3–8 in. Bog/fen/wetland, moist streambanks, west-side forest, east-side forest

Stem erect, with 2 leaves at midstem. Leaves to 1½ in. long, heart-shaped. Flowers 5–15 in short spike at stem top. Flower yellow-green to brownish, with 2 petals and 3 sepals at top all the same, egg-shaped, lower petal much longer, deeply forked, with lance-shaped pointed lobes. Grows in shady damp conifer forests, along streams, in bogs, at low to mid elevations. Native OLYM, MORA, NOCA, CRLA

Piperia unalascensis (Platanthera
unalascensis, Habenaria unalascensis)
ORCHIDACEAE
Short-spurred rein orchid, Alaska habenaria
Uncommon, early summer, perennial, less than 15 in. West-side forest, east-side forest

Stem erect, with small flowers. Basal leaves oval, 3–4 in. long. Stem with small flowers, widely spaced or denser at top. Flowers scentless or musky, green; upper sepal pointing up or forward; lower petal wider than the others, hanging down but with tip pointing upward; short spur extending backward toward stem but not crossing it. Grows in dry places in mixed forests at low to mid elevations. The species is named for Unalaska, an island in the Aleutian chain. Native OLYM, MORA, NOCA, CRLA

Platanthera hyperborea (Habenaria
hyperborea) ORCHIDACEAE
Northern green bog orchid
Uncommon, midsummer, perennial, 6–40 in. Bog/fen/wetland, west-side forest, subalpine

Erect stem with green flowers. Leaves only on stem, lance-shaped, 2–5 in. long. Inflorescence includes flowers, leaves in loose to dense spike with flowers attached at leaf axils. Flowers green to yellowish green; 2 upper petals and sepal nod together, covering rest of flower; lower petal tapers smoothly to sharp point; round spur noticeably curved, with rounded point. Grows in wet conifer forests from coast to subalpine. Found above Arctic Circle. *Hyperborea* means "beyond the north." Native OLYM, NOCA

See other *Piperia*: white, page 72
See other *Platanthera*: white, page 72

Plantago lanceolata PLANTAGINACEAE
English plantain, lanceleaf plantain
Common, all year long, annual or biennial or
perennial, 6–25 in. Disturbed, meadow
Tuft of basal leaves, upright brown spike.
Leaves lance-shaped, 2–6 in. long, with many
noticeable veins, sometimes hairy at base.
Flowers in 1–3 in. dense rounded spike atop
6–25 in. stalk. Flowers green, with numerous
pale yellow stamens extending out as they bloom from bottom
to top, flowers turning brown and persisting as spike matures
and elongates. Grows in waste places, gardens, lawns, at low
to mid elevations. Nonnative OLYM, MORA, NOCA, CRLA

Plantago major PLANTAGINACEAE
Broadleaf plantain
Common, all year long, perennial, 2–16 in.
Disturbed, meadow
Tuft with basal rosette of wide leaves, long
flower spike. Leaves widely oval, 2–7 in. long,
abruptly narrowing to petiole, with numerous
parallel veins. Flowers in 1–8 in. spike atop
stalk to 20 in. Flowers small, white, soon fading to brown as seedpods develop. Found in all
disturbed places, including lawns and gardens,
at low to mid elevations. Nonnative OLYM, MORA, NOCA, CRLA

Plantago maritima var. *juncoides* PLANTAGINACEAE
Seaside plantain
Locally common, all year long, perennial, 2–10 in.
Coastal
Tuft of long, narrow, spreading to upright
leaves, erect stalk. Plant without hairs except
flower stalk. Leaf 1–6 in. long, fleshy, tapering
to base but not stalked. Flowers numerous in
dense spike 1–4 in. long atop stalk just longer
than leaves. Flowers, green stamens not
exserted. Grows on rocky shorelines, salt
marshes, bluffs, river edges near coast. Native
OLYM

Plantago patagonica
PLANTAGINACEAE
Woolly plantain, Indian-wheat
Locally common, all spring and summer,
annual, 2–8 in. Shrub-steppe

Erect tuft of densely hairy leaves and flower
stems. Linear leaves 1–4 in. long, entire.
Few to many flower stems carry nearly
cylindrical woolly spikes well above leaves.
Linear bract about 2 times as long as calyx, oval white petals
with pointed tips are widely spreading. Grows in grassy, sandy,
or rocky places. Two other plantains with upright hairy leaves:
P. erecta, often with a few teeth on 1–5 in. linear leaves, 1½ in.
hairy flower spike, growing on dry grassy clay or sandy soils,
often on serpentine rock, at low elevations; *P. coronopus*, with
pinnately divided leaves, tips pointed, dense
flower spikes nodding in bud and becoming erect, found on coastal bluffs, marshes,
grassy areas at low elevations. Native NOCA

Amorpha fruticosa (Amorpha dewin-
keleri, Amorpha occidentalis) FABACEAE
Western false indigo, desert false indigo
Locally common, late spring, perennial,
6–10 ft. Bog/fen/wetland, moist streambanks

Upright shrub with spike of brownish purple flowers. Main
stems without prickles. Leaves divided pinnately to odd number of leaflets, each usually ending in short bristle. Flower
spikes usually clustered. Flower consists of 1 petal and 10 stamens extending beyond. Introduced for erosion control. Grows
along major rivers in mudflats. Note that *A. fruticosa* is native in
the eastern ⅔ of the United States but not
in the west. Lewis and Clark collected it in
South Dakota. Nonnative **L&C**

Trifolium cyathiferum FABACEAE
Bowl clover
Common, early summer, annual, 4–14 in.
Vernal-wet, disturbed, meadow

Small plant with stems ascending to erect.
Leaves divided palmately, 3 leaflets ⅓–1 in.
long. Flower heads upright surrounded by united, finely
toothed bracts. Calyx tips very long, divided bristles that surround individual flowers. Flowers pale green, sometimes with
pink blush at tip, before quickly aging to brown. Grows in vernal-damp valleys, ditches, shrublands, forests, at low to mid elevations. Native OLYM, NOCA

See other *Trifolium*: white, page 97; yellow, page 209; red, page 333;
blue, page 415

Cardionema ramosissimum
CARYOPHYLLACEAE
Sandmat cardionema
Locally common, all spring and summer,
perennial, mat. Coastal

Mats woolly. Stems prostrate, numerous, concealed by silver-white leaf bracts. Leaves fine needle-like spines. Flowers in small clusters scattered on stem, 5 tiny, densely woolly sepals enclosed with stout spiny calyx. Grows on dunes and sandy beaches along coast. Native OLYM

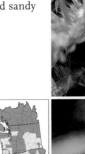

Pyrola chlorantha (*Pyrola virens*)   ERICACEAE
Green wintergreen
Uncommon, all summer, perennial, 4–8 in.
Bog/fen/wetland, west-side forest, east-side forest

Erect stem from basal rosette of leathery oval leaves. Leaves less than 2 in. long, pale green above, darker on underside, veins not bordered with white. Flowers few, petals greenish white to cream, with protruding style curved downward. Grows in conifer and mixed forests in humus or boggy places, mostly at high elevations. Circumboreal. Presumed extirpated from California but historically present. Native
OLYM, MORA, NOCA

Lomatium dissectum   APIACEAE
Fernleaf lomatium, chocolate tips
Locally common, early summer, perennial, 18 in.–5 ft.
Meadow, east-side forest, shrub-steppe

Large, upright, robust, shiny green. Stems hollow. Leaf petioles on lower stem 1–12 in. with blades 6–12 in. wide, finely divided into very narrow segments to ½ in. long, usually coated with fine hairs. Umbel borne on stems above foliage. Flowers chocolate red (rarely yellow), dense in small short-stalked clusters above very narrow bracts. Seeds short, to ¾ in. long, oval. Grows in wooded or brushy slopes, talus and steep rocky slopes, at low to high elevations. Similar *L. suksdorfii* is hairless and always has yellow flowers. Native OLYM, MORA, NOCA, **L&C**

See other *Pyrola*: white, page 112; red, page 344
See other *Lomatium*: white, page 123; yellow, page 224; red, page 356

Mitella caulescens SAXIFRAGACEAE
Leafy mitrewort
Locally common, midspring–midsummer, perennial, 6–12 in. West-side forest

Tuft of 1–2½ in. nearly maple-shaped leaves with 3–7 sharp-toothed lobes. The only mitrewort with a few leaves along flower stems. Flower stem 2–12 in. tall, flowers on short stalks, blooming from top to bottom. Flowers greenish, stamens alternating with petals. Petals linear, with 5–7 feathery lobes. Style unlobed. Grows in swampy soils to deep woods from coast to mid elevations. Native
OLYM, MORA, NOCA, CRLA

Mitella pentandra SAXIFRAGACEAE
Alpine mitrewort, five-point bishop's cap
Locally common, early summer–midsummer, perennial, 8–16 in. Bog/fen/wetland, moist streambanks, meadow, west-side forest, alpine, subalpine

Tuft of oval leaves, erect stems. Leaves about ½–3 in. wide, with 5–9 lobes, sharp teeth. Flower spike 1-sided, blooming from bottom to top. Flowers in shallow saucer, 5 green petals, cut into 5 or more opposite linear lobes, stamens opposite petals. Grows in moist subalpine meadows, bogs, along streams, at mid to high elevations. All other mitellas have stamens and petals alternating. *Mitella caulescens* is distinguished by a tuft of maple-shaped leaves, a few small stem leaves, and flowers that start blooming at the top of the stem. Native OLYM, MORA, NOCA, CRLA

Tolmiea menziesii SAXIFRAGACEAE
Piggy-back plant, youth-on-age, bristle flower
Common, late spring–early summer, perennial, 12–30 in. West-side forest

Trailing plant with tall stem. Plant more or less hairy. Basal and stem leaves widely oblong, shallow lobes with pointed tips, sharp teeth, short bristles on top surface. Small plantlets often grow on top of leaf. Flowers in spike, 4 petals thread-like purplish or brown. Grows in moist woods at low to mid elevations. Often grown as a houseplant. *Tolmiea* is named for William Fraser Tolmie (1812–1886), surgeon for the Hudson's Bay Company at Fort Vancouver. Native
OLYM, MORA, NOCA

468

See other *Mitella*: white, page 139; yellow, page 236

Boschniakia strobilacea

OROBANCHACEAE

California ground-cone

Locally common, late spring–early summer, perennial, 4–12 in. West-side forest

Cone erect to 12 in. tall. Reddish brown to dark purplish, lowest bracts ½–¾ in. across, widely oval, overlapping, edges pale and tips rounded. Flowers 2-lipped with 4 lobes; lower 3 lobes similar, upper lobe wider and somewhat hood-like, all are pale purple on edges, deeper toward center. Grows in open wooded areas, parasitic on *Arctostaphylos* or *Arbutus*, at low elevations to treeline. Similar *B. hookeri*, Vancouver ground-cone, is smaller, up to 5 in. tall, grows on roots of *Gaultheria shallon* along or near coast, more widespread in Washington and British Columbia but rare in California. Named for Russian botanist Boschniaki. Native

Orobanche pinorum   OROBANCHACEAE

Pine broomrape

Uncommon, midsummer, annual, 4–12 in. Dry rocky sites, west-side forest, east-side forest

Erect, with fine-stemmed glands. Stem slender, with many overlapping bracts, base larger. Flowers in dense inflorescence elongating and becoming less dense with age, tinted pale purple. Calyx tube and lobes are about the same length. Flowers pale yellowish or yellowish brown with hairs at base of stamens, lobes all erect and tinted pale purple. Roots attach to *Holodiscus*, ocean spray, but not known on conifers. Uncommon in rocky soils, open forests, below 7000 ft. Native OLYM, NOCA

Ambrosia chamissonis (*Franseria chamissonis*)   ASTERACEAE (sunflower tribe)

Silver burweed, cut-leaf beach bur

Locally common, all summer, perennial, 6–40 in. Coastal

Sprawling clumps. Decumbent stems much branched, gray- to brown-haired. Leaves thick, pinnately lobed or toothed, upper and lower surfaces with gray sticky hairs. Flowers rayless, greenish; male flowers held in dense 3 in. spikes above larger female flowers crowded at spike base in spiny bracts. Bracts later form seed-bearing silver burrs with 2–4 rows of sharp thorns. Grows on sand dunes and in gravelly places along coast. Plant smells sweet. In ancient times people thought eating sweet-smelling plants rendered long life, as *Ambrosia*, food of the gods, rendered immortal life. Native OLYM

See other *Orobanche*: red, page 364; blue, page 425

5 irregular petals forming a tube

Composite flowers

Rudbeckia occidentalis

ASTERACEAE (sunflower tribe)

Western coneflower, western chocolate cone

Locally common, late summer, perennial, 24–80 in. Vernal-wet, bog/fen/wetland, meadow

Stems tall, erect, branchless or with few branches. Leaves 4–12 in. long, widely oval, with short rough hairs on both sides or just the underside. Leafless stalks hold 1 or more dark purple-brown disk cones about 1 in. high, no ray flowers. The cones become twice as tall and black when in seed. A noticeable plant growing in wet meadows, seeps, along streams, at pond edges, at mid elevations. Native CRLA

Salicornia virginica CHENOPODIACEAE

American glasswort, slender pickleweed

Locally common, all summer, perennial, 8–35 in. Coastal

Perennial or small shrub. Stems creeping, root at nodes. Branches look like pickles, round, fleshy, erect, prostrate to upright, jointed. Usually 3 tiny flowers are attached into the joint rings along with rounded bracts. Grows in saltwater marshes, alkaline flats, from sea level to 3500 ft. Native OLYM

Salsola kali (*Salsola tragus*) CHENOPODIACEAE

Russian thistle, Russian tumbleweed

Common, late summer, annual, 1–4 ft. Disturbed

Spreading stems numerous from single root, much-branched. Stems and leaves green to red or purple, supple when young, aging to hard, round, prickly tumbleweeds. Alternate leaves numerous, linear to thread-like, thick. Flowers tiny, single in upper leaf axils, same color in center as stems, white on outside, bracts spine-like. Seed capsules pink to orange. Grows in steppe and coastal regions along roads, fencerows, in pastures. Noxious weed, invasive on disturbed ground. *Salsola*

is Latin for "salty," referring to the habitats of this genus. Non-native

See other *Rudbeckia*: yellow, page 293

Euphorbia crenulata EUPHORBIACEAE
Chinese caps, beetle spurge
Locally common, late spring, annual or
biennial, 1–3 ft. Moist streambanks, west-side
forest

One to several upright stems, milky sap. Stem
branching in upper section. Leaves egg-shaped,
usually with short petioles. Leaves near flowers
sessile, wide at base to 1 in. long. Flowers with
central cluster of stamens and 4 glands each with pair of points
shaped like thick horns, 3-lobed ovary hanging to 1 side. Grows
in shady sites in foothills. Native

Euphorbia esula EUPHORBIACEAE
Leafy spurge
Common, all spring and summer, perennial,
12–30 in. Disturbed, meadow

Stems erect, many sterile densely leafy
branches. Leaves 1–2½ in. long, linear to oblong, with pointed tip, entire, hairless. Umbel
with 1–3 in. stalks topped by pair of yellowish
green bracts. Flower composed of 2–3 stalks
above leafy bracts holding second set of bracts
with bell-shaped tiny male or female flowers.

Grows in disturbed soils, fields, road edges,
under 5000 ft. European native considered a noxious weed.
Milky juice may burn skin or damage eyes. Nonnative

Euphorbia peplus EUPHORBIACEAE
Petty spurge
Common, all spring and summer, annual, 4–12 in.
Disturbed

Erect, hairless, yellow-green plant with milky
sap. Stem hairless, 4–14 in. tall. Leaves with
short petioles, smaller at top, opposite, widely
oval, entire, with rounded to notched tip. Flowers in upper leaf axils, tiny, 4 green glands each
with 2 slender horns. Grows in moist soils in
gardens, disturbed places, below 1500 ft. Nonnative OLYM, NOCA

471

Typha latifolia TYPHACEAE
Broadleaf cattail, common cattail
Common, late spring–early summer, perennial, 3–8 ft. Bog/fen/wetland, lake/pond

Erect, stout, undivided stems. Leaves upright, long, narrow, ½–1½ in. wide, attached along stem, reaching about same height as flower spike. Inflorescence is a round thick spike; lower section thicker, holds female flowers; male flowers in thinner tail portion above. Female flowers green when fresh, aging dark brown. Male and female portions meet without space between. Grows in ponds, along lakes, all shallow waters, at low to mid elevations. *Typha angustifolia*, narrowleaf cattail, ages to pale brown, has space on stem between male flower portion above and female portion below. Native OLYM, MORA, NOCA

Urtica dioica URTICACEAE
Stinging nettle
Common, all spring and summer, perennial, 3–9 ft. Coastal, moist streambanks, disturbed, meadow, west-side forest, east-side forest, shrub-steppe

Clustered, erect, leafy stems with spreading roots and stinging hairs. Leaves opposite, lance- to heart-shaped, 2–6 in. long, coarsely toothed. Inflorescence consists of drooping catkin-like stalks from leaf axils holding dense clusters of small greenish flowers. Female flowers in separate clusters near top. Grows in moist deep soils in meadows, forests, shrubby places, sometimes in thick patches in disturbed places. Can cause painful rash if touched. Subsp. *gracilis* is green, with nonstinging hairs only on stem and lower leaf surface. Subsp. *holosericea* has gray-green stems, dense nonstinging hairs only on lower stem and lower leaf surface. Stinging hairs cover other surfaces on both varieties. Native

OLYM, MORA, NOCA, CRLA, **L&C**

About the Photographs

The photographs in this field guide meld art and science into images that are both graceful and functional, pleasing the eye while conveying enough information to help identify the plants. They were made over a period of more than a dozen years, with a large proportion created in two marathon field seasons. Mark drove more than 40,000 miles and hiked uncounted additional miles in search of flowers in peak bloom.

Wildflowers don't fly away or duck behind a tree when a photographer approaches, yet they present their own challenges. Mother Nature can be a very messy housekeeper, so it's necessary to find ways to separate the flowers from their surroundings. The light was often far from ideal, especially after spending the morning hours hiking through trees only to reach a subalpine meadow at noon. Wind was a frequent challenge, particularly in the Columbia Gorge and on mountain ridges. Moreover, Mark needed enough botanical knowledge to identify each subject and decide which characteristics to emphasize.

Mark used a combination of professional 35 mm film and digital SLR (single-lens reflex) cameras to create the photos in this book, employing several lenses, from wide-angle to telephoto. The great majority of the photos were made with a 100 mm macro lens. Almost every image was made with the camera on a tripod, both to control camera shake and to facilitate careful control over composition and framing. The sun provided the light for most photos but was usually controlled and modified with a combination of handheld diffusers and reflectors. Occasionally Mark used a small flash to fill shadows or illuminate a plant in a dark woodland setting. All told, his camera bag usually weighed between 25 and 30 pounds.

In the field, Mark looked for flowers that were in prime condition and appeared to be representative of the population of plants at that location. He photographed several variations of most plants and, when photography was complete, had more than 30,000 frames from which to select the 1220 that appear in this book. About 30% of those selected originated on film; the other 70% came from digital originals. Each image was optimized in Adobe Photoshop, essentially a digital darkroom, to improve density, color balance, and contrast. Editing, scanning, and optimizing the photos required hundreds of hours of work.

Additional Photography

All photographs in *Wildflowers of the Pacific Northwest* are by Mark Turner with the
exception of the following:

ED ALVERSON
Geranium oreganum, page 348
Piperia elegans, page 72
Prenanthes alata, page 174

WILBUR BLUHM
Agoseris retrorsa, page 266
Calystegia atriplicifolia subsp. *atriplicifolia*,
    page 153
Campanula scouleri, page 448
Fritillaria camschatcensis, page 459
Gentianella amarella, page 325
Nephrophyllidium crista-galli (main and
    inset), page 158
Oxalis suksdorfii, page 249
Viburnum edule, page 165

PAULA BROOKS
Cerastium fontanum subsp. *vulgare*, page
    102
Corydalis aurea, page 201
Lilium occidentale, page 313
Listera caurina, page 461
Orobanche pinorum, page 469
Sium suave, page 126
Triodanis perfoliata, page 386

MARK EGGER
Castilleja affinis subsp. *litoralis*, page 365
Castilleja campestris subsp. *campestris*,
    page 238
Castilleja elmeri, page 366

Castilleja lacera, page 239
Castilleja lutescens, page 240
Castilleja oresbia, page 240
Castilleja pilosa, page 241
Cordylanthus capitatus, page 369
Mimulus floribundus, page 243
Penstemon pruinosus, page 432
Platanthera orbiculata, page 73
Pyrola chlorantha, page 467
Vicia nigricans subsp. *gigantea*, page 336

GLENN & BARBARA HALLIDAY
Opuntia fragilis, page 295

BETH HORN
Gentiana sceptrum, page 406
Gentianopsis simplex, page 407
Honckenya peploides, page 103
Sisyrinchium californicum, page 188

DON JACOBSON
Centaurium erythraea, page 324

PENN MARTIN
Ageratina occidentalis, page 397
Lonicera conjugialis, page 387
Oxypolis occidentalis, page 228
Platanthera sparsiflora (inset), page 463
Viola macloskeyi, page 99

JOSHUA McCULLOUGH
Platanthera sparsiflora (main), page 463

Bibliography

Abrams, LeRoy, and Roxana Stinchfield Ferris. *Illustrated Flora of the Pacific States.* 4 vols. Palo Alto, California: Stanford University Press, 1923–1960.

Aiken, Marti, and Catherine Gray Parks. *Guide to the Common Potentilla Species of the Blue Mountains Ecoregion.* Portland, Oregon: USDA Forest Service, 2004.

Bailey, Robert G. *Description of the Ecoregions of the United States.* Fort Collins, Colorado: USDA Forest Service, 1995. http://www.fs.fed.us/land/ecosysmgmt/ecoreg1_home.html. Accessed 17 November 2004.

Begnoche, Don. *Siskiyou Sundays: A Tour of Southwestern Oregon.* Ashland, Oregon: Don Begnoche, 1999.

Biek, David. *Flora of Mount Rainier National Park.* Corvallis, Oregon: Oregon State University Press, 2000.

British Columbia Conservation Data Centre. *Red and Blue Listed Vascular Plants of Selected Forest Regions of British Columbia.* Database. Victoria, British Columbia: Resource Information Branch, Ministry of Sustainable Resource Management, 2004.

British Columbia Ministry of Forests. *Provincial Digital Biogeoclimatic Subzone/Variant Mapping.* http://www.for.gov.bc.ca/hre/becweb/subsite-map/provdigital-01.htm. Accessed 16 November 2004.

Bryce, Sandra A., and Alan J. Woods. *Level III and IV Ecoregion Descriptions for Oregon.* Draft 8. Corvallis, Oregon: Oregon Natural Heritage Program, 2000. http://www.gis.state.or.us/data/metadata/k250/ecoregion.pdf. Accessed 14 November 2004.

Buckingham, Nelsa M., Edward G. Schreiner, Thomas N. Kaye, Janis E. Burger, and Edward L. Tisch. *Flora of the Olympic Peninsula.* Seattle, Washington: Northwest Interpretive Association, Washington Native Plant Society, 1995.

Burke Museum of Natural History and Culture. *University of Washington Herbarium (WTU) Database.* Seattle, Washington: University of Washington. http://www.washington.edu/burkemuseum/collections/herbarium/index.php. Accessed 2 October 2005.

Calflora Database. Berkeley, California: Calflora, 2000. http://www.calflora.org/. Accessed 2 October 2005.

CalPhotos Digital Library Project. Berkeley, California: University of California. http://elib.cs.berkeley.edu/photos/. Accessed 2 October 2005.

Case, Fredrick W., Jr., and Roberta B. Case. *Trilliums.* Portland, Oregon: Timber Press, 1997.

Clark, Lewis J. *Wild Flowers of the Pacific Northwest.* Madeira Park, British Columbia: Harbour, 1998.

Cohen, Victor A. *A Guide to the Pacific Coast Irises.* Watford, Hertfordshire, United Kingdom: British Iris Society, 1967.

Davidson, B. LeRoy. *Lewisias*. Portland, Oregon: Timber Press, 2000.

Demarchi, Dennis A. *An Introduction to the Ecoregions of British Columbia*. Victoria, British Columbia: Wildlife Branch, Ministry of Environment, Lands and Parks, 1996. http://srmwww.gov.bc.ca/ecology/ecoregions/index.html. Accessed 14 January 2005.

Douglas, George W., Gerald B. Straley, Del V. Meidinger, and Jim Pojar, eds. *Illustrated Flora of British Columbia*. 8 vols. Victoria, British Columbia: Ministry of Environment, Lands and Parks, Ministry of Forests, 1998–2002.

Flora ID Northwest. *Plants of Pacific Northwest: Interactive Keys and Color Photos*. CD-ROM. Pendleton, Oregon: Flora ID Northwest, 2001.

Franklin, Jerry F., and C. T. Dyrness. *Natural Vegetation of Oregon and Washington*. Corvallis, Oregon: Oregon State University Press, 1988.

Grimshaw, John. *The Gardener's Atlas*. Buffalo, New York: Firefly Books, 1998.

Halda, Josef J. *The Genus* Gentiana. Dobré, Czech Republic: SEN, 1996.

Hickman, James C., ed. *The Jepson Manual: Higher Plants of California*. Berkeley, California: University of California Press, 1993.

Hitchcock, C. Leo, and Arthur Cronquist. *Flora of the Pacific Northwest*. Seattle, Washington: University of Washington Press, 1973.

Hitchcock, C. Leo, Arthur Cronquist, Marion Ownbey, and J. W. Thompson. *Vascular Plants of the Pacific Northwest*. 5 vols. Seattle, Washington: University of Washington Press, 1955–1969.

Horn, Elizabeth L. *Coastal Wildflowers of the Pacific Northwest*. Missoula, Montana: Mountain Press, 1993.

Huxley, Anthony, and Mark Griffiths. *The New Royal Horticulture Society Dictionary of Gardening*. New York: Stockton Press, 1992.

Ingwersen, Will. *Manual of Alpine Plants*. Portland, Oregon: Timber Press, 1986.

Jolley, Russ. *Wildflowers of the Columbia Gorge*. Portland, Oregon: Oregon Historical Society Press, 1988.

Kirkpatrick, Golda, Charlene Holzwarth, and Linda Mullens. *The Botanist and Her Muleskinner*. Portland, Oregon: Leach Garden Friends and Siskiyou National Forest, 1994.

Klinkenberg, Brian, ed. *E-Flora BC: Atlas of the Plants of British Columbia*. A partnership project of the Native Plant Society of British Columbia; the Spatial Data Lab, Department of Geography, University of British Columbia; and the UBC Herbarium, Department of Botany. Vancouver, British Columbia: UBC, 2004. http://www.eflora.bc.ca/. Accessed 2 October 2005.

Kruckeberg, Art. *Geology and Plant Life: The Effects of Landforms and Rock Types on Plants*. Seattle, Washington: University of Washington Press, 2002.

Kruckeberg, Art, Karen Sykes, and Craig Romano. *Best Wildflower Hikes: Washington*. Seattle, Washington: The Mountaineers Books, 2004.

Lyons, Chess, and Bill Merilees. *Trees, Shrubs and Flowers to Know in British Columbia and Washington*. Redmond, Washington: Lone Pine, 1995.

Mansfield, Donald H. *Flora of Steens Mountain*. Corvallis, Oregon: Oregon State University Press, 2000.

Marshall, Ian B., and Peter H. Schut. *A National Ecological Framework for*

Canada. Ottawa, Ontario: Ecosystems Science Directorate, Environment Canada and Research Branch, Agriculture and Agri-Food Canada, 1999. http:// sis.agr.gc.ca/cansis/nsdb/ecostrat/intro.html. Accessed 14 January 2005.

Mason, Georgia. *Guide to the Plants of the Wallowa Mountains of Northeastern Oregon.* Eugene, Oregon: University of Oregon Press, 2001.

Mathews, Daniel. *Cascade-Olympic Natural History: A Trailside Reference.* Portland, Oregon: Raven Editions, 1999.

McGary, Jane, ed. *Bulbs of North America.* Portland, Oregon: Timber Press, 2001

Native Seed Network. *United States Ecoregions.* Corvallis, Oregon: Native Seed Network, 2004. http://www.nativeseednetwork.org/resources/ecoregion_map.php. Accessed 16 November 2004.

Niehaus, Theodore F., and Charles L. Ripper. *Pacific State Wildflowers.* Boston: Houghton Mifflin, 1976.

Nold, Robert. *Penstemons.* Portland, Oregon: Timber Press, 1999.

North Cascades National Park. *NOCA Vascular Plants—Present or Probably Present (1410)—Local List.* Unpublished database. Marblemount, Washington: North Cascades National Park, 2003.

Omernik, James M. Perspectives on the nature and definition of ecological regions. *Environmental Management.* 2004.

Oregon Flora Project. *Oregon Vascular Plant Atlas.* Corvallis, Oregon: Oregon State University. http://www.oregonflora.org/oregonplantatlas.html. Accessed 2 October 2005.

Oregon Natural Heritage Information Center. *Rare, Threatened and Endangered Species of Oregon.* Portland, Oregon: Institute for Natural Resources, Oregon State University, 2004. http://oregonstate.edu/ornhic/2004_t&e_book.pdf. Accessed 2 October 2005.

Peck, Morton E. *A Manual of the Higher Plants of Oregon.* Portland, Oregon: Binfords & Mort, 1941.

Piper, Charles V. *Flora of the State of Washington.* Washington, D.C.: Government Printing Office, 1906.

Pojar, Jim, and Andy MacKinnon, eds. *Plants of the Pacific Northwest Coast: Washington, Oregon, British Columbia and Alaska.* Redmond, Washington: Lone Pine, 1994.

Rickett, Harold William. *Wild Flowers of the United States.* 5 vols. New York: McGraw-Hill, 1966–1973.

Ross, Robert A., and Henrietta L. Chambers. *Wildflowers of the Western Cascades.* Portland, Oregon: Timber Press, 1988.

Russell, George F., ed. *Lewis and Clark as Naturalists: The Collection.* Washington, D.C.: National Museum of Natural History, Smithsonian Institution. http://web4.si.edu/lewisandclark/index.html?loc=/lewisandclark/home.html. Accessed 13 November 2004.

Simpson, Charlene, John Koenig, Jennifer Lippert, Rhoda Love, Bruce Newhouse, Nick Otting, Scott Sundberg, David Wagner, and Phil Wagner. *Vascular Plants of Lane County, Oregon: An Annotated List.* Eugene, Oregon: Emerald Chapter, Native Plant Society of Oregon, 2002.

Stearn, William T. *Botanical Latin.* Newton Abbot, Devon, United Kingdom:

David & Charles, 1991.

Stearn, William T. *Stearn's Dictionary of Plant Names for Gardeners: A Handbook on the Origin and Meaning of the Botanical Names of Some Cultivated Plants.* London: Cassell, 1994.

Taylor, Ronald J. *Northwest Weeds: The Ugly and Beautiful Villains of Fields, Gardens, and Roadsides.* Missoula, Montana: Mountain Press, 1990.

Taylor, Ronald J. *Sagebrush Country: A Wildflower Sanctuary.* Missoula, Montana: Mountain Press, 1992.

Taylor, Ronald J., and George W. Douglas. *Mountain Plants of the Pacific Northwest.* Missoula, Montana: Mountain Press, 1995.

Thomas, John H. Botanical explorations in Washington, Oregon, California and adjacent regions. Preprint. In *Huntia*, vol. 3. Pittsburgh, Pennsylvania: Hunt Institute for Botanical Documentation, Carnegie Mellon University, 1979.

USDA Agricultural Research Service. *Common Weeds of the United States.* New York: Dover, 1971.

U.S. Department of the Interior Bureau of Land Management. *Wind Energy Development Draft Programmatic EIS, Appendix F: Ecoregions of the 11 Western States and Distribution by Ecoregion of Wind Energy Resources on BLM-Administered Lands within Each State.* http://windeis.anl.gov/documents/dpeis/appendices/Appendix_F.pdf. Accessed 14 November 2004.

U.S. Environmental Protection Agency. *Primary Distinguishing Characteristics of Level III Ecoregions of the Continental United States.* Draft. ftp://ftp.epa.gov/wed/ecoregions/us/useco_desc.doc. Accessed 14 November 2004.

U.S. Environmental Protection Agency. *Level III Ecoregions.* http://www.epa.gov/wed/pages/ecoregions/level_iii.htm. Accessed 17 November 2004.

Washington Natural Heritage Program and U.S. Department of the Interior Bureau of Land Management. *Field Guide to Selected Rare Vascular Plants of Washington.* http://www.dnr.wa.gov/nhp/refdesk/fguide/htm/fgmain.htm. Accessed 14 January 2005.

Washington State Department of Ecology. *Major Ecoregions of Washington State.* http://www.ecy.wa.gov/apps/watersheds/maps/state/level3_ecoregions.html. Accessed 16 November 2004.

Weber, William A. *Rocky Mountain Flora.* Boulder, Colorado: University Press of Colorado, 1976.

Wheeler, David L. *Guide to Common Forest Plants: Rogue River, Siskiyou, and Umpqua National Forests.* Seattle, Washington: Northwest Interpretive Association, 1990.

Wherry, Edgar T. *The Genus* Phlox. Philadelphia, Pennsylvania: Morris Arboretum Monographs, University of Pennsylvania, 1955.

Zika, Peter F. *A Crater Lake National Park Vascular Plant Checklist.* Crater Lake, Oregon: Crater Lake Natural History Association, 2003.

Glossary

alkaloids. Water-insoluble, nitrogen-containing compounds that often exhibit pharmacological action, such as nicotine

alpine. Found above timberline at high altitude

alternate. Arranged singly at different heights along the stem

annual. Plant that germinates, flowers, seeds, and dies in one year

anther. Pollen-producing segment of the stamen

appressed. Pressed flat against another organ, as hairs pressed against the surface of a leaf or stem

aquatic. Growing in or on water, floating or rooted to soil at the bottom with submerged stems or shoots

armed. Bearing prickles, thorns, or spines

ascending. Curving or angling upward from the base

axil. The upper angle between the leaf and the stem

axillary. Pertaining to the axil, or in the axil

banner. Upper and usually largest petal of many members of the pea family

basal. Found at or near the base of a plant or plant part

berry. Fleshy fruit with more than one seed within the soft tissue

biennial. Plant that completes its life cycle in two years

blade. The expanded part of the leaf

brackish. Somewhat salty

bract. 1. Small leaf-like structure associated with an inflorescence. 2. Small scale or leaf-like structure on a stem

bractlet. Small secondary bract

branch. Secondary stem, growing from the main stem

bristles. 1. Large, stiff, straight hairs. 2. In the aster family, fine hairs at the top of the flower arising from an inferior ovary

burl. Dome-shaped growth on the trunk of a tree

calyx (calyces). Whorl of sepals, the lowest or outermost part enclosing the rest of the flower. Often green or tan

capsule. Dry, many-seeded fruit

circumboreal. Around the world at northern latitudes

compound leaf. Leaf with blade dissected into separate leaflets, or divided into lobes, perhaps many times

corolla. Collective term for the petals and reproductive parts of a flower, often brightly colored

cup. Cup-like structure on which the parts of the flower are born

cyme. Branched inflorescence in which the central flower on the main stem opens before the side flowers

deciduous. Falling off at the end of the growing season or sooner. Also said of plants that are leafless part of the year

decumbent. Lying on the ground with the tips pointing upward

disk. In Asteraceae, the part of the head made up of disk flowers

disk flower. Ligule-free flower often in the center of the plant

egg-shaped leaves. Oval leaves that are wider at the base and narrower at the tip

emersed. Rising above or standing out of water

entire. Having a margin without any teething or division

erect. Upright from the ground

evergreen. Remaining green throughout the year

exserted. Projecting beyond another structure

extirpated. No longer existing in a particular region but still found in other areas of the world

filament. Stalk of the stamen that holds the anther

fleshy. Thick and juicy. Often said of plants in the stonecrop family

florets. Small individual flowers in the larger flower head, as occur in sunflowers

fluff. Light, feather-like particles

fruit. Any ripened ovary where seed is held

fused. United, as petals to a calyx or to each other, not free

gland. Small, round body that emits a sticky substance on the outer plant surface, sessile or on the end of the hair

glaucous. Covered with a fine powdery or waxy film, causing the surface to appear bluish or whitish

hair. Thin to thick thread-like growth on the outer surface

head. Dense collection of sessile or nearly sessile flowers making up the inflorescence. Often used to describe plants in the aster family

hybrid. Plant created when two different species interbreed

inferior ovary. Ovary attached below the sepals, petals, and stamens

inflorescence. Arrangement of the flowers, or cluster of flowers of a plant

ligule. In Asteraceae, a complete, fertile floret with a long, outer, petal-like portion that is typically five-toothed

linear. Narrow, with parallel sides

lip. Upper or lower section of an unequal corolla or calyx

lobe. Projecting segment of an organ. Free parts of a flower tube

margin. Edge

native. Growing in a place without the aid of people or because of human activities

nectary. Nectar-producing part of a flower

nut. Dry fruit containing a single seed

nutlet. Small fruit, usually one of several

oblong. Longer than wide, rounded

opposite. Arranged in pairs at the same level and on opposite sides. Often said of leaves on the stem

oval. Nearly round

ovary. Organ that develops into fruit after fertilization and contains the seeds. The wide portion of the pistil

parasite. Plant that receives part or all of its nutrition from another plant. Nongreen plants cannot live without this association

perennial. Plant that lives more than two years

persistent. Remaining attached, not falling off the plant for some time

petal. Flower part, often brightly colored

petiole. Stalk part of the leaf attached to the blade

phyllary. Bract on the cup of many members of the aster family

prickle. Sharp growth, thorn, or spine, usually restricted to smaller growths

raceme. Unbranched, elongated cluster of flowers with the oldest flowers at the base

radially. With all petals the same shape and size

ray flower. Flower in Asteraceae with the long outer portion, often with three lobes

reflexed. Bent or curved downward or backward

regular flower. Flower with parts similar in size and shape and arranged symmetrically. Can be divided in many ways to mirror-image halves

rhizome. Creeping underground stem

root. Underground structure from the base of the stem, anchors the plant and allows for absorption of nutrients and water

rosette. Cluster of leaves at ground level, usually in a circle

saprophyte. Plant that lives on dead organic matter

scalloped. Curved projections with sharp depressions between

scree. Steep mass of rock debris with scant soil

seed. Product of fertilization

sepal. Fused or free member of the calyx, usually green and leaf-like

serpentine. Rock and the soil associated with it, containing high concentrations of magnesium, iron, nickel, and toxic metals. Often has specialized flora

sessile. Without a stalk or petiole

sheath. Vertical coating surrounding the stem at the leaf base

shredding. Pulling apart in strings. Often said of bark

shrub. Woody plant, branched from the base

simple. Composed of one part, unbranched, undivided

sinus. Indentation or recess between adjacent lobes or segments of a margin

spadix. Small flowers crowded along a central spike

spathe. Large bract just below and enclosing a spadix

spike. Unbranched inflorescence with sessile flowers; used here to include a raceme with stalked flowers

spine. Sharp, pointed growth

spreading. Held outward from the point of attachment

spur. Hollow, usually rounded projection from a petal or sepal, containing nectar

stalk. Secondary stem, often referring to the structure supporting the flower

stamen. Male organ bearing pollen composed of a stalk (filament) and pollen sacs (anther)

staminode. Modified stamen that does not produce pollen

stem. Central support of a plant, bearing other organs such as leaves and flowers

stipule. Appendage at the base of a leaf petiole, generally paired, variable in form, often leaf-like, sometimes scale-like or a spine

stolon. Elongated stem lying along the ground (runner), forms new roots and stems

subalpine. Just below timberline

subtended. Occurring immediately below, as bracts just under a flower

superior ovary. Ovary attached above the sepals, petals, and stamens

talus. Mass of rock fragments at the base of a cliff

teeth. Alternating projections and indentations on the margin

tendril. Slender, twining or coiling structure by which a climbing plant grasps for support

throat. Expanded opening of flowers with fused sepals or petals

tube. Cylindrical structure formed by fused sepals or petals

tuft. Cluster of short-stemmed leaves and flowers growing from a common point

twig. In woody plants, the smallest segment, produced during the latest growing season

umbel. Inflorescence with three or more stalks radiating from a common point

vascular. Pertaining to plants with veins or to the veins in a plant structure

vein. Vessels by which water and nutrients are transported. Often easily seen in leaves

vernal. Pertaining to spring

vine. Trailing or climbing plant with long, flexible stem, often supported by tendrils

wings. 1. Thin, flat extensions of a surface or edge. 2. In many plants in the pea family, the two lateral petals

Index

Main species entries are in bold type. Species only mentioned in the descriptions are in roman type.

About the Authors

MARK TURNER is a freelance editorial photographer specializing in botanical subjects, especially Northwest wildflowers and gardens. He photographs extensively for books and magazines both in gardens and in a wide range of native plant environments. He is an avid member of the native plant societies of Washington and Oregon and has more than 25 years of experience exploring for native plants. He lives in Bellingham, Washington. Photo by Matt Brown

PHYLLIS GUSTAFSON ran a small seed-collection business specializing in Northwest natives and is well acquainted with the wide flora of the region. She also worked with native plants in the nursery trade for more than 20 years. She is an officer of the North American Rock Garden Society (NARGS) and writes frequently for their bulletin. For the last 35 years she has been active both in gardening and in exploring for native plants, mostly in Oregon but also in other climates around the world. She is often asked by plant societies around the country to lecture about the plants found on those quests. She lives in Central Point, Oregon. Photo by John Sloan

LEAF PARTS

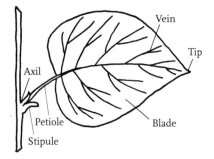

Vein

Tip

Axil

Petiole

Blade

Stipule

LEAF ARRANGEMENTS

Sessile   Petioled

Clasping   Whorled   Basal Rosette

LEAF EDGES

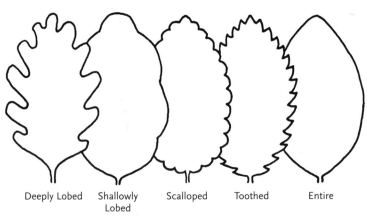

Deeply Lobed   Shallowly   Scalloped   Toothed   Entire
               Lobed